THE
OTHER GOD THAT
FAILED

JERRY Z. MULLER

The Other God That Failed

HANS FREYER AND THE

DERADICALIZATION OF GERMAN

CONSERVATISM

PRINCETON, NEW JERSEY

PRINCETON UNIVERSITY PRESS

1987

COPYRIGHT © 1987 BY PRINCETON UNIVERSITY PRESS
PUBLISHED BY PRINCETON UNIVERSITY PRESS, 41 WILLIAM STREET
PRINCETON, NEW JERSEY 08540
IN THE UNITED KINGDOM: PRINCETON UNIVERSITY
PRESS, GUILDFORD, SURREY

LIBRARY OF CONGRESS CATALOGING IN PUBLICATION
DATA WILL BE FOUND ON THE LAST PRINTED PAGE OF THIS
BOOK. PUBLICATION OF THIS BOOK HAS BEEN AIDED BY THE
WHITNEY DARROW FUND OF PRINCETON UNIVERSITY
PRESS. THIS BOOK HAS BEEN COMPOSED
IN LINOTRON BASKERVILLE

ISBN 0-691-05508-4
ISBN 0-691-00823-X (PBK.)

CLOTHBOUND EDITIONS OF
PRINCETON UNIVERSITY PRESS BOOKS
ARE PRINTED ON ACID-FREE PAPER, AND BINDING
MATERIALS ARE CHOSEN FOR STRENGTH AND
DURABILITY. PAPERBACKS, ALTHOUGH
SATISFACTORY FOR PERSONAL COL-
LECTIONS, ARE NOT USUALLY
SUITABLE FOR LIBRARY
REBINDING

PRINTED IN THE UNITED STATES OF
AMERICA BY PRINCETON UNIVERSITY PRESS
PRINCETON, NEW JERSEY

To
my mother and
my father

CONTENTS

PREFACE

This is a book about intellectuals and totalitarianism, about ideology and social science, and about the transformation of the German intellectual right. It initially grew out of my interest in the recurrent pattern among modern intellectuals of attraction to and disillusionment with totalitarian solutions to the problems of modernity. The emergence of a successful democratic political culture in Germany out of the ashes of a totalitarian regime was a second theme that interested me, as did the role of the National Socialist past in shaping the political identity of later generations of German intellectuals. Like Banquo's ghost, the specter of past misdeeds seems to haunt the German right when it celebrates its more recent contributions to the building of a thriving liberal democracy in West Germany. The case of Hans Freyer seemed a promising vehicle through which to examine these problems. My interest in the relationship between political ideology and social science, which became another major theme of this study, arose in the course of my research on Freyer.

This book uses the biography of Hans Freyer to explore these larger problems and patterns in modern European history.

Since acknowledgments are the currency in which we pay our intellectual debts, first books, like first homes, tend to come heavily mortgaged. This book exemplifies the general pattern.

The foundations of my historical concerns were laid during my undergraduate years at Brandeis University. I would particularly like to thank Gerald Izenberg, now of Washington University, who sowed the seeds of my ongoing interest in intellectual history, and Morton Keller, whose skepticism regarding the claims of intellectuals to superior wisdom has colored my approach to their history.

This book began at Columbia University, where it was my good fortune to pursue graduate studies. Robert Paxton introduced me to the comparative study of fascism during my first semester at Columbia and remained a valued adviser thereafter. From Robert Merton I learned to look for patterns and structural parallels in diverse historical contexts. My contact with him has taught me that there is value in sitting at the feet of giants as well as standing on their shoulders. From John Toews, now of the University of Washington, I learned a good deal about the temptations of totality. Laurence Dickey provided a thoughtful sounding board while the thesis took shape. I am most deeply indebted to Fritz Stern, my thesis supervisor, for his continuing confidence and good counsel at every stage in the development of this book.

Among the pleasures (and possible pitfalls) of writing contemporary history is the opportunity to draw upon living sources. I am grateful to many of Freyer's colleagues, students, family members, and antagonists who agreed to be interviewed for this study, as well as to those who answered my written inquiries. Their names are recorded at the end of the book. My attempt to empathetically reexperience the atmosphere of the German universities under a variety of regimes owes much to these discussions. I am particularly grateful to Ernest Manheim, one of Freyer's earliest students and latest friends, and Hans-Georg Gadamer, Freyer's colleague at Leipzig from 1938 through 1947, each of whom met with me twice, at various stages of my research. Hellmut Becker, who studied with Freyer briefly during the mid-1930s, was both an informed primary source and a fount of sound advice. Mrs. Käthe Freyer graciously submitted to my long lists of questions about her late husband and his associates and allowed me to copy a previously unknown work that he had written during the Third Reich. Mindful of the lapses and tricks of memory, however, I have relied upon interviews to supplement documentable evidence rather than as a source of hard facts.

For illuminating discussions of the history and politics of German sociology and of Freyer's role within it I am grateful to Lars Clausen, René König, Wolf Lepenies, M. Rainer Lepsius, Friedrich Tenbruck, and the late Helmut Schelsky, who also invited me to a conference at Aachen that brought together some of Freyer's former students and colleagues. Ralf Dahrendorf read parts of the manuscript and made some useful suggestions for revision.

At a very early stage of my research, Elfriede Üner kindly sent me a copy of her *Diplomarbeit* on Freyer. Sven Papcke was a helpful academic host during my stay in Münster. While there I met Carsten Klingemann, now of the University of Osnabrück, who had begun his important research on the role of sociology in the Third Reich and who generously shared with me his hypotheses as well as information on archival and printed sources. After my return to the United States he continued to serve as my link to recent German scholarship. For his continuing friendship and cooperation I am thankful.

A conversation with Daniel Bell that occurred before I began my research on the German right alerted me to the possibility of recurrent patterns of intellectual disillusionment with totalitarian movements. At various stages of my research I have also had the benefit of advice from David Bankier, Michael

Kater, Otto Dov Kulka, David Landes, George Mosse, Fritz Ringer, and Kurt H. Wolff. Walter Struve and Wolf Lepenies read the manuscript for Princeton University Press and made thoughtful suggestions for revision. Malachi Hacohen, Jeff Herf, and Scott McConnell have been a source of intellectual companionship and numerous discussions regarding intellectuals, social theory, and totalitarianism. Another friend, Ferenc Katona of the Voice of America, read and corrected the portions of the manuscript dealing with Hungary. The final manuscript profited greatly from the keen editorial eye of Steve Whitfield. Noam Zion, my brother-in-law and sometime study partner, has been a stimulating interlocutor for many years.

My colleagues at the Catholic University of America have provided a congenial atmosphere in which to work and granted me a leave of absence to complete this study. My research was aided by fellowships from the Social Sciences and Humanities Research Council of Canada, the Social Science Research Council, the Whiting Foundation, and the American Council of Learned Societies. Though the "cash value" of a study of intellectuals and totalitarianism is not readily calculated, I hope that the taxpayers who made their indirect and not entirely voluntary contributions to this study will regard it as a good investment.

My parents, Bella and Henry Muller, have long provided direct and voluntary support of both a moral and a material nature. To them this book of ten chapters is dedicated, though repaying my full debt to them would surely put me into chapter 11. My grandparents (who in the spring of 1939 already knew more than they wanted to about National Socialism) took time out during a trip to Budapest to help me obtain information about Freyer's teaching there.

Like most historians, I have depended upon the assistance of librarians and archivists. I would like especially to thank Eileen McIlvaine of the Butler Library of Columbia University, Frau I. Kießling of the Universitätsbibliothek Münster, Dr. Maria Keipert of the Politisches Archiv of the Auswärtiges Amt in Bonn, Dr. G. Schwendler and Prof. Renate Drucker of the Universitätsarchiv Leipzig, Dr. Jürgen Zander of the Schleswig-Holsteinischen Landesbibliothek in Kiel, and the reference librarians in the Jefferson Reading Room of the Library of Congress.

I am grateful to the Eugen Diederichs Verlag for permission to use their archives and to M. Rainer Lepsius and the Deutsche Gesellschaft für Soziologie for permission to consult the papers of that organization.

I am blessed to have lived under the same roof for over a decade with a historian, librarian, archivist, editor, and goad—my wife, Sharon Muller. Without

ABBREVIATIONS AND CITATIONS

BAK   Bundesarchiv Koblenz
BDC   Berlin Document Center
IIS   Institut Internationale de Sociologie
DGS   Deutsche Gesellschaft für Soziologie
KZfSS   *Kölner Zeitschrift für Soziologie und Sozialpsychologie*
NF   Nachlaß Freyer, Universitätsbibliothek Münster
NP   Nachlaß Plenge, Universitätsbibliothek Bielefeld
NT   Nachlaß Tönnies, Schleswig-Holsteinischen Landesbibliothek, Kiel
PA   Personalakte
PA-AA   Politisches Archiv—Auswärtiges Amt, Bonn
UAL   Universitätsarchiv der Karl-Marx-Universität Leipzig

Several of Hans Freyer's major works are abbreviated in the footnotes as follows:

ES   *Einleitung in die Soziologie.* Leipzig, 1931.
SdZ   *Schwelle der Zeiten: Beiträge zur Soziologie der Kultur.* Stuttgart, 1965.
SW   *Soziologie als Wirklichkeitswissenschaft: Logische Grundlegung des Systems der Soziologie.* Leipzig, 1930.
TGZ   *Theorie des gegenwärtigen Zeitalters.* Stuttgart, 1955.
WE   *Weltgeschichte Europas*, 1st ed., 2 vols. Wiesbaden, 1948.

Works are cited by author and title in the first footnote in which they appear, with the date of publication included when significant. Thereafter, works are cited by the author's last name and a short title. The bibliography contains full citations for all works cited.

THE

OTHER GOD THAT

FAILED

INTRODUCTION

Hans Freyer? The name has little resonance among contemporary English-speaking social theorists or historians, and among the younger generation of Germans he is almost forgotten. Yet he was perhaps the most articulate and historically self-conscious thinker associated with the movement for a "conservative revolution" in the 1920s, one of the most prestigious intellectuals to lend his support to National Socialism in the years immediately before and after Hitler's accession to power, and one of the more respected voices of German conservatism during the first decade and a half of the Federal Republic. In the years after the First World War his status as a social theorist was acknowledged by intellectuals as diverse as Georg Simmel, Karl Mannheim, Herbert Marcuse, and Talcott Parsons. The title of his book of 1931, *Revolution von rechts* (Revolution from the Right) passed into the political discourse of the Weimar Republic. After Hitler's rise to power he became president of the German Sociological Association and head of one of the most eminent institutes of historical research in Europe. The history of Europe that he published in 1948 was admired by Arnold Toynbee and regarded by Werner Conze, a father of the new social history, as "a high point of postwar historical consciousness in Germany." Freyer's widely read *Theorie des gegenwärtigen Zeitalters* (Theory of the Current Age) of 1955 contributed to the reformulation of conservative thought in West Germany. Not a few of the most influential West German sociologists and historians of the 1950s and 1960s were Freyer's former students. The name of Hans Freyer has not always lacked recognition. The eclipse of his reputation is itself a part of our story.

This book is intended neither to restore Freyer's name nor to rehabilitate his reputation. It is a study in "intellectual history" in two senses: a history of intellectuals and their role in society and a history of the ideas that they hold. Not a comprehensive biography of Hans Freyer, it uses his biography to explore more general patterns that Freyer shared with other German intellectuals who were attracted to totalitarian solutions to the problems of modernity and who were ultimately disabused of the totalitarian temptation by their experience of National Socialism. Though much of Freyer's work in the fields of social analysis and intellectual history can still be read with profit, his greatest significance was not as an innovator of ideas. Our interest in him is in his representative rather than in his creative function in history.[1]

[1] This formulation is borrowed from Leonard Krieger, *The Politics of Discretion*, 3.

On Representative Biography

The reconciliation of the particular and the general is the task of every historian who aspires to be more than an antiquarian or a retrospective gossip. The working premise of this study is that it is possible to use biography to exemplify shared patterns of experience. In this sense it is "representative biography": the story of an individual whose interest for us lies not primarily in what was unique about him, examined in such a way as to highlight those formative contexts and experiences which he shared with others who followed some common pattern. In order to contribute to methodically obtained generalizations that go beyond the particular case of Freyer, the study focuses not on the peculiarities of Freyer's psyche, family, or personality but rather on those social and cultural contexts which he shared with those who followed a similar intellectual and political trajectory. The development and shift of their ideas are explained by recapturing the collective movements and institutions of which Freyer was a part, and the interpretation of historical events dominant in the groups and institutions in which he most directly participated. The narrative will therefore shuttle back and forth between texts and contexts.

In keeping with the broad theme of the relationship of intellectuals to totalitarianism, the representative experiences of Freyer's biography may be divided into three periods. Chapters 1 through 6—spanning the years from Freyer's birth in 1887 to Hitler's assumption of power in 1933—explore the totalitarian temptation, the attraction to the ideal of a society fully integrated into a shared collective purpose through the state.

Among the most formative influences on the intellectuals of the Weimar Republic was the "youth movement," which flowered in the decade before the First World War. For Freyer, the prewar youth movement was the cultural context in which he spent his college years. It owed its existence to a widely shared sense that the educated middle class was incapable of providing its offspring with a sense of shared purpose and higher meaning. Faith in Protestant Christianity, which had once provided this sense of purpose, lost its intellectual plausibility for many of Freyer's generation, and the philosophical doctrines that had contributed to the demise of Christian faith seemed incapable of providing a secular substitute. The longing within the youth movement for spiritual renewal served as a goad to university professors to develop sweeping systems that would provide a spiritual compass for the younger generation. Students from the youth movement were in turn attracted to those professors who echoed their discontents and who promised to provide a new social science that would lead beyond bourgeois society. Hans Freyer's relationship to his academic mentors at the University of Leipzig and at the University of Berlin in the decade before the First World War illustrates these shared patterns, which are explored in the first chapter.

The coming of the war was interpreted by the academic intellectuals admired by the youth movement as a break with the individualistic and egoistic era that had preceded it and the beginning of a new sense of national community (*Volksgemeinschaft*). For some members of the youth movement, such as Hans Freyer, who served as a junior officer at the front, the war experience itself provided intimations of a solution to the problem of collective purpose. Their mood was captured in a book written by Freyer in the trenches, which was hailed in the youth movement and by its academic supporters as a "fanfare of the younger generation." This experience of the war and its institutionalization in the immediate postwar years are the subject of chapter 2.

During the early years of the Weimar Republic, Hans Freyer became a professor of philosophy and wrote a series of works that established his reputation as a leading proponent of neo-Hegelian philosophy and as a radical conservative social theorist. Chapter 3 provides an exposition of Freyer's radical conservative social thought and shows how Hegel's thought was reinterpreted in a totalitarian direction by Freyer and other neo-Hegelians of the right.

In 1924 Freyer was appointed to one of first chairs of sociology in Germany, at the University of Leipzig. In the years that followed he straddled the roles of social scientist and radical conservative ideologist. His writings drew upon the more pessimistic assessments of capitalist society in the work of Karl Marx, Ferdinand Tönnies, Max Weber, and Georg Simmel, in an attempt to develop the new discipline of sociology in an antiliberal direction. Freyer spelled out the logic of a radical brand of sociology that appealed to politically engaged academic intellectuals on both the left and the right. Chapters 4 and 5 focus on the tension between the roles of ideologist and academic social scientist within a pluralist liberal democracy.

Throughout the 1920s Freyer attempted to stoke the smoldering dissatisfaction with capitalist, liberal democracy among the educated German middle class. For Freyer and other radical conservative intellectuals, the National Socialist electoral breakthrough of September 1930 offered the hope of an end to their political impotence. Freyer published a booklet, *Revolution from the Right*, which interpreted the rise of National Socialism as evidence of a deep-seated revolt against "bourgeois society" and the Weimar polity, and which appealed to his readers of the educated middle class to add their weight to the movement. Chapter 6, a study of the movement of ideas up and down the cultural ladder, explores the background, significance, and influence of *Revolution from the Right*.

The second period of Freyer's relationship to totalitarianism began with Hitler's assumption of power in January 1933. The twelve years that followed—the years of Freyer's encounter with the reality of a totalitarian revolution from the right—are the subject of chapters 7 and 8.

At the dawn of the Third Reich, radical conservatives had high hopes of creating a sense of shared collective purpose through the use of political power, and they anticipated a major role for themselves in shaping the direction of the now-triumphant revolution of the right. During the process of *Gleichschaltung* (government "coordination") in 1933 and 1934, as we will see in chapter 7, Freyer and like-minded intellectuals rose to important posts in the academy, in cultural institutions, and in government. Their dual roles as respected academics and as known ideological sympathizers of the regime served to propel them into positions of prestige. This pattern is demonstrated by Freyer's experience at the University of Leipzig, where he became head of a renowned institute of historical research, and within the German Sociological Association, whose rump membership elected him as its president. Freyer and other fellow travelers of the regime responded to National Socialist attempts to enforce ideological orthodoxy by adapting their public language and actions, in a process of self-*Gleichschaltung*.

Freyer's disillusionment with totalitarian solutions to the problems of modernity is examined in chapter 8. A careful reconstruction of his relations with the cultural institutions and organs of ideological control in the years from 1934 to 1938 illuminates the sources of his disillusionment. His dual roles as academic social scientist and as ideologist now worked against him. In a regime that placed a premium on ideological orthodoxy, the charge of insufficient ideological commitment was used against him by professional rivals and party zealots. Surveillance of mail, the pervasive threat of denunciation, and the political persecution of Freyer's valued colleagues all contributed to the souring of his hopes. His personal experiences reinforced his perceptions that on the national level the National Socialists had by no means overcome the egoism he had attributed to bourgeois society and were incapable of prudent consolidation. The process of his disillusionment can be documented, since like other intellectual critics of the regime, he expressed his doubts publicly but not explicitly, through the use of allusion and analogy in his published works. They reveal not only his disenchantment with the regime but a principled rejection of the desirability of radical transformation through "the alchemy of politics." Yet, like many conservative Germans disabused of their hopes for the Third Reich—including those of Freyer's friends who participated in the assassination attempt on Hitler—Freyer continued to serve the regime. From 1938 through 1945 he lived in Budapest as visiting professor of German studies and as director of a German scientific institute; both positions were creations of the German foreign office, intended to boost the prestige of the regime abroad. Freyer's roles in Budapest illustrate the utilization of prestigious intellectuals by the Nazi regime.

The fate and fortunes of Freyer and like-minded intellectuals who had shared his political trajectory in the decades after the collapse of the Third Reich are the subject of chapters 9 and 10.

The years following Germany's defeat brought the fortunes of erstwhile intellectual supporters of the Third Reich like Freyer to a low ebb. As a resident of the Soviet zone of occupation from 1945 to 1948, Freyer experienced yet another (and more successful) attempt at totalitarian transformation. Chapter 9 begins by re-creating the political transformation of the University of Leipzig, which led not only to Freyer's dismissal but eventually to the sovietization of the university. Freyer moved to the western zone in 1948 but was unable to secure a university post, owing in part to the negative repute in which he was held in some quarters for his role in legitimating the rise of National Socialism. Freyer's fall in fortune, as well as the institutional and legal means through which he and other former radical conservative intellectuals recouped their respectability and prestige, is explored. Chastened by the experience of totalitarianism, Freyer formulated a brand of conservative social theory that remained skeptical of the claims of modern liberal democratic society but was reconciled to its inevitability, and sought to bolster what he termed "the forces of conservation," which lay largely outside the realms of politics and economic production. Freyer's *Theory of the Current Age* articulated the resigned reconciliation of German intellectual conservatives to pluralistic liberal democracy, a reconciliation that distinguished the political culture of the German right in the postwar era.

Freyer's new respectability did not go unchallenged. Beneath the facade of comity, the suspicion between former supporters and consistent opponents of National Socialism remained and continued to shape the intellectual life of the Federal Republic. The conflict among German sociologists in the 1950s provides a case study of such tensions. The failure of Freyer and other radical conservative intellectuals to publicly confront their past helped fuel the suspicion

that they had not really distanced themselves from their former radicalism and
hence represented an ongoing obstacle to the consolidation of liberal democracy in Germany. German conservatism proved to be of limited appeal to the
new generation of German intellectuals who came of age in the postwar years,
in part because of the lingering odium of National Socialism that clung to some
of its leading intellectual expositors. The recovery of traditionally conservative
themes by this generation of predominantly liberal intellectuals began in the
1970s, once Freyer and other erstwhile supporters of National Socialism had
passed from the scene.

Many of the central concerns and analytic perspectives of Freyer's social
thought were formulated by the mid-1920s and remained consistent through
the course of his long and active life. The problems that Freyer posed were
drawn from "the best that has been thought and said" in the world of modern
European social thought, and his intellectual talents were such that he articulated these problems with unusual clarity and historical self-consciousness.
Since they are questions shared by many other social thinkers of modern Europe and its cultural offshoots, the contemporary reader is likely to feel at
home in this world of discourse. Freyer's solutions to these problems, by contrast, changed radically in the course of his life, and the totalitarian nationalist
solutions he once espoused are likely to strike the reader as eminently implausible and morally repellent.

In any confrontation—scholarly or otherwise—with ideas or views that we
find distasteful or abhorrent, there is an all-too-human urge to ignore the substantive argument in question and focus instead on the motives—witting or
unwitting—of the arguer. If he is sincere but his views seem to us entirely un-
reasonable, we are apt to attribute them to some hidden motive of which the
author is unaware, to reduce his argument from a proposition to be analyzed
to a motive to be analyzed away by psychoanalysis or social psychology, or by
attribution to economic self-interest or to linguistic structure. When this reductive practice is widespread, it becomes impossible to take arguments seriously, since all intrinsic meaning is reduced to a symptom of some "deeper"
level, the structure of which can be revealed through the aid of one or another
explanatory theory. Since intellectual historians are by no means agreed on
which theory is appropriate to their enterprise, the recourse to a multiplicity of
reductive modes of explanation necessarily leads to mutual incomprehension
or the dissolution of shared scholarly discourse.[2]

---

[2] On the eroding effect upon the humanities
of recourse to mutually exclusive, reductivist
theories of explanation, see Frederick Crews,
"In the Big House of Theory." See also Hayden

In an age of general intellectual suspicion, one ought to think twice before resorting to reductive means of explanation. The historian must leave room for the reality of individual choice, even while demonstrating the way in which choice is constrained and structured. The individual chooses his course. But he does not do so at random; he chooses between alternatives structured by the collective experiences in which he participates—by his role in a variety of institutions, by the rewards and sanctions they offer, and by the shared understandings they provide.[3] Representative biography provides the possibility of exploring patterns and dilemmas generated by overlapping social contexts and by successive shared experiences. Our attempt is to weld the genre of biography to the historical sociology of knowledge and to explain shared choice while eschewing reductionism. Without ignoring Freyer's particularities or the choices he made, our attention is focused upon the patterns of shared experience that his biography exemplified. In an attempt to demonstrate the representative nature of Freyer's intellectual and political trajectory, an appendix following chapter 10 briefly traces the careers of several other radical conservative German intellectuals from a variety of fields.

The remainder of this introduction places the major themes of the succeeding chapters in historical and comparative perspective.

Intellectuals and Totalitarianism

The central concern of our study, the relationship of intellectuals to totalitarianism, is a twentieth-century variant of an older phenomenon, namely the political radicalization and deradicalization of modern European intellectuals and its effect upon European social thought. The phenomenon is at least as old as modern politics itself. For a whole generation of European intellectuals who came of age at the end of the eighteenth century the promise and disappointment of the French Revolution marked a turning point in their intellectual and political development. In the early years after the fall of the Bastille—and sometimes beyond—many intellectuals from across Europe thought they

White, "Method and Ideology in Intellectual History," 288–89. For an attempt to specify the conditions under which a psychobiographical explanation might be called for, see Gerald Izenberg, "Psychohistory and Intellectual History."

[3] The theoretical orientation on which this study draws most heavily is explicated in Robert K. Merton, *Social Theory and Social Structure*, 422–40 and passim; idem, "Sociological Ambivalence," in his *Sociological Ambivalence and Other Essays*; Arthur Stinchcombe, "Merton's Theory of Social Structure"; and Ralf Dahrendorf, "Homo Sociologicus: On the History, Significance, and Limits of the Category of Social Role."

saw in France the creation of a new polity that might restore a sense of collective meaning to a society divided by the characteristic processes of incipient modernity. It was this generation—of Hegel, Schleiermacher, and the *Frühro-mantiker* in Germany; of Coleridge, Wordsworth, and Southey in England; and of Saint-Simon in France—that began to formulate a critique of societies characterized by an advanced division of labor, market economies, and an attenuation of traditional religious and political authority, a critique that continues in recognizable form to the present day. It was in these years that the alternatives to such a society were also conjured up—visions that despite their diversity shared the hope of imposing some common goal to which all members of society could subordinate themselves. Then, in revulsion against the bloody excesses of the Jacobins or the imperialist policy of the new French Republic, the members of this generation turned away from revolutionary solutions to their dilemmas, in some cases to a less radical politics, in others to realms beyond the political.[4] The high hopes of many intellectuals for the French Revolution, followed by their shared disappointment, were the first of several successive waves of attraction to and disenchantment from radical political movements by modern European intellectuals.

In the twentieth century this pattern of attraction to and disillusionment with radical political movements repeated itself, not only with greater tragedy but with greater force. The critique that European intellectuals voiced in the interwar decades of the twentieth century was more comprehensive and more shrill than that of their nineteenth-century predecessors. The solution that many intellectuals proposed was correspondingly more radical, more all-encompassing, namely the prospect of a totally integrated society, a society in which all would subordinate their egoistic interests to some shared belief and goal, which would restore a sense of meaning to the individual and purpose to

[4] On the attraction exerted by the French Revolution upon European intellectuals and the effect of their disenchantment on their subsequent work, see M. H. Abrams, *Natural Supernaturalism*; John Edward Toews, *Hegelianism*, esp. chapters 2–3; Joachim Ritter, *Hegel and the French Revolution*; and Isaac Deutscher, "The Ex-Communist's Conscience."

It is tempting to emphasize the generational aspect of such waves, and one student of the process has attributed the recurrent waves of the political radicalization of intellectuals solely to "the unconscious defense of generational re-volt" (Lewis S. Feuer, *Ideology and the Ideologists*, 84). In fact, however, it is the shared response to a common extraordinary experience by small sections of a particular cohort that defines a historical "generation" of intellectuals. This was the thrust of Karl Mannheim's definition in his "The Problem of Generations." Despite Feuer's stress on the social-psychological dynamics of generational revolt, the intellectual generations that he cites as examples are almost invariably defined by a shared response to a common historical event.

society as a whole. This new faith was to be embodied first in a political movement and then enforced by the state. "A man's admiration of absolute government is proportionate to the contempt he feels for those around him," wrote
Tocqueville in his foreword to *The Old Regime and the French Revolution*. A principled contempt for the present combined with the hope of a totally integrated
society in the future often led twentieth-century intellectuals to support political movements that were totalitarian.

The characteristic world view of totalitarianism was delineated some three
decades ago by Jacob Talmon:

> It recognizes ultimately only one plane of existence, the political. It widens the scope of
> politics to embrace the whole of human existence. It treats all human thought and action
> as having social significance, and therefore as falling within the orbit of political action.
> . . . Politics is defined as the art of applying this philosophy to the organization of society,
> and the final purpose of politics is only achieved when this philosophy reigns supreme
> over all fields of life.[5]

Totalitarian movements, then, believed in total politicization in principle and,
when in power, acted on this belief to the limits of the feasible.[6] This working
definition focuses deliberately on the aims of such movements and is not
meant to imply that the resultant regimes achieved social integration, monolithic authority, or even an integrated apparatus of control. While Mussolini,
for example, explicitly declared his aim of a *stato totalitario*, few scholars would
regard the Fascist regime as effectively totalitarian.[7] Though most of those
scholars who accept the concept of totalitarianism as of heuristic value in historical studies agree that it is applicable to Germany under National Socialism,
they do so in the recognition of a continuing stuggle of competing authorities

[5] Jacob L. Talmon, *The Origins of Totalitarian Democracy*, 2. Among the advantages of Talmon's treatment of the intellectual origins of to-
talitarianism is that despite his recognition of the
commonalities of the "political messianism" of
the left and right, he treats them as separate historical traditions.

[6] The importance of the concept of "totalitarianism" as well as the difficulties of operational-
izing this ideal-typical construct for historical
research are explored in the transcript of a
symposium held at the Institut für Zeitgeschichte in 1978, published as *Totalitarismus
und Faschismus*. Also useful are Karl Dietrich
Bracher, "Der umstrittene Totalitarismus: Er-

fahrung und Aktualität" in his *Zeitgeschichtliche
Kontroversen*; Carl J. Friedrich, Michael Curtis,
and Benjamin R. Barber, *Totalitarianism in Perspective: Three Views*; the essays by Michael Walzer and Richard Lowenthal in Irving Howe, ed.,
1984 Revisited: Totalitarianism in Our Century;
Guy Hermet, Pierre Hassner, and Jacques Rupnik, eds., *Totalitarismes*; and the excellent review
essay by Eckard Jesse, "Renaissance der Totalitarismuskonzeption? Zur Kontroverse um einen
strittigen Begriff," *Neue Politische Literatur* 28,
no. 4 (1983): 459–92.

[7] See, e.g., the contribution by Wolfgang
Schieder in Institut für Zeitgeschichte, *Totalitarismus und Faschismus*.

in the Third Reich.[8] Similarly, those scholars who agree on the applicability of the term *totalitarian* to the Soviet Union before, during, or after Stalin's domination do not claim that total or monolithic control had been achieved.[9] Our concern is with the attraction of intellectuals to movements *promising* total integration through political power.

Totalitarian politics are often portrayed as having arisen without, or indeed in spite of, the efforts of intellectuals.[10] But before it became a historical reality, totalitarianism existed as an idea and ideal, spawned by men who defined and prided themselves on their mastery of ideas and commitment to ideals.[11] The ideal of a totally integrated society looked very compelling on paper. It attracted, as we shall see, not only cultural "hacks" or aspiring cultural bureaucrats but also men such as Hans Freyer, who were among "the best and the brightest" of Weimar intellectual life.[12] Yet, in the long run, few major intellectuals who had advocated totalitarian solutions to the problems of modernity were pleased by the behemoth they had helped to conjure up.

The disenchantment of European intellectuals with totalitarian solutions to the purported problems of modern life provided the ferment for much of Western European social thought in the two decades after the Second World War. The fruits of these reflections were themselves of political consequence: the roots of the political stability of Western Europe in the postwar era no doubt lie beyond the cultural realm, but the effect of the intellectuals' disillusionment with radical politics had a perceptible effect on political culture, on

[8] That the structure of domination in the Third Reich was less than monolithic was already recognized in studies of the early 1940s. Ernst Fraenkel in *The Dual State* (1941) focused upon the competing sources of authority in the state bureaucracy and the Nazi party, and Franz Neumann, *Behemoth*, 2d ed. (1944), added the elites of industry and the army as competing sources of power. Hannah Arendt's *Origins of Totalitarianism* (1951) noted that "what strikes the observer of the totalitarian state is certainly not its monolithic structure. . . . Many, moreover, have stressed the peculiar 'shapelessness' of the totalitarian government" (395). See also the useful discussion in Stephen J. Whitfield, *Into the Dark: Hannah Arendt and Totalitarianism*, 69ff. Recent detailed studies of aspects of the Third Reich have revealed that its institutional structure was even more "polycratic" and anarchic than these earlier observers had imagined.

See Helmut Heiber, *Walther Frank und sein Reichsinstitut für Geschichte des neuen Deutschlands*; Reinhard Bollmus, *Das Amt Rosenberg und sein Gegner: Zum Machtkampf im nationalsozialistischen Herrschaftssystem*; and Uwe Dietrich Adam, *Judenpolitik im Dritten Reich*, esp. 355–61. Nowhere was this institutional anarchy more evident than in Nazi cultural policy.

[9] See, for example, Leonard Schapiro, *Totalitarianism*; and Arendt, *Origins*.

[10] See, for example, Dennis Mack Smith, "The Great Benito?"; and Arendt, *Origins*.

[11] This aspect of the self-definition of intellectuals is explored in Talcott Parsons, "The Intellectual: A Social Role Category."

[12] For a brief overview of the attraction of Weimar intellectuals to a "total state," see Gerhard Schulz, "Der Begriff des Totalitarismus und des Nationalsozialismus," 452–56.

the public discourse about matters political. This generational experience with totalitarian movements of the left and right and the subsequent return of the intellectuals from the periphery to the center of their respective political cultures were stabilizing factors in postwar Western Europe.[13] Many historians have focused attention on the radicalization of modern intellectuals; the story of their deradicalization has often been neglected, though it has been no less significant for the development of modern European thought.[14] Indeed, it was the most striking feature of European (and American) intellectual life from at least the end of the Second World War until the rise of the New Left in the early 1960s.[15]

Most historians or contemporary observers who have recognized the importance of the attraction of intellectuals to totalitarianism and their subsequent disillusion have regarded it as a phenomenon of the political left.[16] It might be dubbed the "God that failed" paradigm, after the collaborative autobiographical volume by Arthur Koestler, Ignazio Silone, André Gide, Richard Wright, Stephen Spender, and Louis Fischer.[17] Communism was not the only god that failed, however. Many intellectuals placed their hopes for the radical reordering of political life in those movements of the right often subsumed under the generic term *fascist*.[18]

[13] The role of the disillusionment of intellectuals with totalitarian solutions as a stabilizing factor in postwar Western Europe is entirely ignored, for example, in Charles S. Maier, "The Two Postwar Eras and the Conditions for Stability in Twentieth-Century Western Europe," and in the critical responses that follow thereafter. A welcome recent exception among historians is found in Hans-Peter Schwarz, *Die Ära Adenauer: Gründerjahre der Republik, 1949–1957*, 431ff.

[14] Feuer, *Ideology*, 84–85, notes that "the process of deideologization has been far less studied than that of ideological conversion" despite the fact that many authors "did their most enduring work in their post-ideological phases." Among recent studies that have begun to make up the deficit, at least with regard to American intellectuals, are John P. Diggins, *Up from Communism: Conservative Odysseys in American Intellectual History*; Job Dittberner, *The End of Ideology and American Social Thought*; Richard H. Pells, *The Liberal Mind in a Conservative Age*; and Alexander Bloom, *Prodigal Sons: The New York Intellectuals and Their World*, which traces the intellectual development of some of most creative minds of the postwar era to their striving for upward social mobility and hence provides an excellent example of the fallacy of reductivism.

[15] The phenomenon was widely noted by contemporaries and was regarded with varying degrees of relief and dismay. Many of the pertinent contemporary observations on the phenomenon are collected in Chaim I. Waxman, ed., *The End of Ideology Debate*. See also Sidney Hook, "The Literature of Political Disillusionment" (1949), reprinted under the title "Communism and the Intellectual," in George B. de Huszar, ed., *The Intellectuals: A Controversial Portrait*.

[16] Raymond Aron, *The Opium of the Intellectuals*, Jean-François Revel, *The Totalitarian Temptation*, and Paul Hollander, *Political Pilgrims*, for example, deal with "the totalitarian temptation" only among left-wing intellectuals.

[17] Richard Crossman, ed., *The God That Failed* (1949).

[18] The only transnational treatments of this phenomenon are the broad but rather superfi-

The intellectuals who pinned their hopes on movements on the totalitarian left and those who looked to the totalitarian right often drew from common traditions and from one another in formulating their radical critique of liberal democratic capitalism. Hans Freyer and Georg Lukács, for example, both had their intellectual roots in neoromanticism and neo-Hegelianism, both were students of Georg Simmel, and in the 1920s both emphasized the cultural critique of modern capitalism propounded by the young Marx.[19] Carl Schmitt's radical conservative analysis of the Weimar state as the captive of particular social interests echoed Marx's critique of the Prussian state in his "Introduction to a Critique of Hegel's *Philosophy of Right*," and leftist Weimar intellectuals such as Walther Benjamin and Otto Kirchheimer were in turn deeply influenced by Schmitt's delegitimation of contemporary liberal democracy.

To note such affinities between intellectuals of the radical left and radical right is by no means to obscure the differences in the political solutions for which they hoped. As men of the left Lukács and Benjamin looked to the international proletariat as the "historical subject" that would overcome bourgeois society; men of the right such as Freyer and Schmitt believed it was the *Volk* who would provide such a historical subject.

The choice of the proletariat rather than the *Volk* or nation reflected a deeper divergence between intellectuals of the left and right, a divergence whose origin lay in the eighteenth century. It hinged upon differing answers to the question "What is the *source* of the purposes that men ought to hold in common, and of the institutions that embody those purposes?" Those who believed that the ultimate source of such purposes lay in "reason," which was capable in principle of providing answers for men and women in all times and places, arrayed themselves as the party of Enlightenment. Despite great internal divergences, it was the universalist, cosmopolitan thrust of its thought that united what Peter Gay has called "the party of humanity"—a designation that recaptures the self-understanding of the *philosophes*.[20] Though it may have

---

cial work of Alastair Hamilton, *The Appeal of Fascism: A Study of Intellectuals and Fascism, 1919–1945*, and the suggestive essay by George L. Mosse, "Fascism and the Intellectuals." The use of the term *fascism* to refer to anything other than the Fascist regime in Italy is also much disputed among historians. Both the leading historian of German National Socialism and that of Italian Fascism have cast doubt upon the generic use of the term. See Karl D. Bracher, "Kritische Betrachtungen zum Faschismusbegriff," in his

Zeitgeschichtliche Kontroversen; and Renzo de Felice, *Fascism: An Informal Introduction to Its Theory and Practice*.

[19] On the intellectual and political development of the young Georg Lukács, see Michael Löwy, *Georg Lukács—From Romanticism to Bolshevism*; Andrew Arato and Paul Breines, *The Young Lukács and the Origins of Western Marxism*; and Lee Congdon, *The Young Lukács*.

[20] Peter Gay, *The Party of Humanity: Essays in the French Enlightenment*.

shifted the locus of reason in the direction of the methods of natural science, the Enlightenment maintained the far older belief in a rational universe with a necessary harmony of values accessible to human reason.[21] The theory and practice of enlightened absolutism, revolutionary republicanism, and the application of the Code Napoleon to non-French nations within the Napoleonic empire all shared the premise that because men were fundamentally the same everywhere, there were universal goals and universalizable institutions for their pursuit. In its universalism—its commitment to a proletariat that was to know no fatherland and whose interests were held to be identical with those of humanity—Marxism and its totalitarian communist variant were intellectual descendants of the Enlightenment. Indeed, it was the premise and promise of universalism that made communism disproportionately attractive to intellectuals who sprang from ethnic and religious minorities.

The intellectuals who placed their hopes on totalitarian movements of the right usually descended from what Isaiah Berlin has termed the "Counter-Enlightenment." Its advocates formed no party; what they shared was a skepticism toward "the central dogma of the Enlightenment," the belief that the ultimate ends of all men at all times were identical and could be apprehended by universal reason.[22] The orientation of the thinkers of the Counter-Enlightenment was usually historicist and particularist. They regarded the attempt to discover universal standards of conduct as epistemologically flawed, and the attempt to impose such standards as a threat to the particular historical cultures from which individuals derived a sense of purpose and society a sense of cohesion. The thinkers of the Counter-Enlightenment regarded the *variety* of existing historical cultures as both inescapable and intrinsically valuable and suggested that the multiplicity of historical cultures embodied values that were incommensurable or equally valid. For thinkers of the German Counter-Enlightenment such as Johann Gottfried von Herder and Justus Möser, cosmopolitanism was the shedding of all that makes one most human, most oneself. Although by no means uniform in their politics, they all resisted the attempt at a rational reorganization of society based upon purportedly universal and rationalist ideals.[23]

In countering the claims of the Enlightenment, the most original thinkers of the Counter-Enlightenment enunciated claims that represented a major departure from the central stream of the Western tradition, which had held that problems of value were in principle soluble and soluble with finality.[24] The

[21] Isaiah Berlin, "The Counter-Enlightenment," in his *Against the Current: Essays in the History of Ideas*, 2–3.

[22] Ibid., 3–4.

[23] Ibid., 12–14.

[24] Isaiah Berlin, "Introduction" to his *Vico and*

Counter-Enlightenment, by contrast, maintained that the traditions which gave a group its identity and which were expressed in its culture were not themselves rationally grounded and could not always be rationally justified.[25] The value of a culture or institution was conceived of as deriving from its history, from its role in the development of a particular group. Proponents of the Counter-Enlightenment such as Möser or Burke revived the argument of the Sophists that moral order was a product of convention that varied from group to group. To this they added the perception (pioneered by David Hume) that emotional attachment to an institution—what Burke called "reverence"—was often a product of the institution's longevity. This social-psychological perception lay at the heart of the argument for the functional value of continuity, a theme that provided the basis for numerous variations among later generations of conservative thinkers.

The correlation between the Enlightenment and Counter-Enlightenment traditions and subsequent political ideologies is by no means tidy. If liberalism, cosmopolitanism, socialism, and communism owed more to the Enlightenment, and conservatism, nationalism, and fascism more to the Counter-Enlightenment, it was also possible to deploy arguments based upon the universalist rationalism of the Enlightenment tradition to coerce the recalcitrant at home and abroad, just as it was possible to draw upon the intellectual arsenal of the Counter-Enlightenment to promote tolerance based upon a respect for diversity. To claim that totalitarianism of the left descended from the rationalist, universalist legacy of the Enlightenment while totalitarianism of the right descended from the historicist, particularist legacy of the Counter-Enlightenment is not to argue that these twentieth-century phenomena were "caused" by their eighteenth-century antecedents, or that the wayward twentieth-century offspring of either tradition should be seen as discrediting their forebears.[26] Both traditions were susceptible to totalitarian reformulations by their twentieth-century legatees.

Prior allegiance to one or another of the two traditions was a factor not only in the choice of intellectuals to place their hopes in fascism or communism but also in the choices they made *after* their disillusionment. For radical intellec-

---

Herder: Two Studies in the History of Ideas, xxiii–iv.

[25] Maurice Mandelbaum, *History, Man, and Reason: A Study in Nineteenth-Century Thought*, 56.

[26] Among the more important trends in recent Anglo-American moral and political philosophy has been the rediscovery of the major arguments of the Counter-Enlightenment by thinkers bred in the Enlightenment tradition but increasingly aware of its limitations. See, for example, Hilary Putnam, *Reason, Truth and History*; Stuart Hampshire, *Morality and Conflict*; Michael Sandel, *Liberalism and the Limits of Justice*; and Michael Walzer, *Spheres of Justice: A Defense of Pluralism and Equality*.

tuals in interwar Europe the choice of whether to commit oneself to a totalitarian movement of the left rather than of the right often depended on whether one regarded oneself as a legatee of the Enlightenment or the Counter-Enlightenment. This allegiance also had its effects after the disenchantment with totalitarian movements of the right and left. Put schematically, those intellectuals who became disillusioned with communism more often maintained an attachment to the universalism and rationalism of the Enlightenment: they typically evolved into liberals or social democrats. Those who became disillusioned with fascism often continued to remain skeptical of the universalism and rationalism of the Enlightenment, even when, like Freyer, they came increasingly to accept liberal democracy. It was upon the particularist and historicist legacy of the Counter-Enlightenment that Hans Freyer and his intellectual circle drew.

German Intellectual Conservatives and National Socialism

Hans Freyer was part of a social circle of radical conservative intellectuals who were bound by friendship, by membership in common organizations, by readership of the same periodicals, and by common intellectual assumptions and political hopes.[27] Among the members of this circle, in addition to Freyer, were the political philosopher Carl Schmitt, the jurists Ernst Forsthoff and Ernst Rudolf Huber, the social theorist Arnold Gehlen, the philosopher Martin Heidegger, and the writer Ernst Jünger.[28] Those surprised at the suggestion that men of great intellectual stature may have been conservative—or indeed radical conservative—in their political orientation and sympathetic toward National Socialism should recall that in interwar Germany "the great majority of critical intellectuals as well as conformist academics, insofar as they had politi-

---

[27] As compared to more institutionalized forms of organization, such circles lack formal leadership and formal roles. Their members are not all personally acquainted but are related to one another by a chain of mutual acquaintances. On the concept of the "social circle" and its importance in the study of structures of intellectual influence, see Charles Kadushin, *The American Intellectual Elite*, 9–10; and Lewis Coser, Charles Kadushin, and Walter Powell, *Books: The Culture and Commerce of Publishing*, 72–73.

[28] Secondary works on the thought and political development of these men are—with the exception of Carl Schmitt, to whom a large second-

ary literature has already been devoted—few, but growing in number. Works dealing in depth with two or more of these men include Christian Graf von Krockow, *Die Entscheidung: Eine Untersuchung über Ernst Jünger, Carl Schmitt, Martin Heidegger*; Jeffrey Herf, *Reactionary Modernism: Technology, Culture, and Politics in Weimar and the Third Reich*; and the volume of radio lectures (of uneven quality) edited by Karl Corino, *Intellektuelle im Bann des Nationalsozialismus*, which includes an essay by Iring Fetscher, "Hans Freyer: Von der Soziologie als Kulturwissenschaft zum Angebot an den Faschismus."

cal convictions at all, were on the political right."[29] The identification of the majority of German intellectuals with "the left" is a phenomenon of the post–World War II era.[30] For many German intellectuals who came of age in the late 1940s and 1950s the link of former radical conservative intellectuals like Hans Freyer with National Socialism served to discredit German intellectual conservatism as such.

Like their counterparts on the left, the right-wing intellectuals were more often than not disappointed with the actual reality created by the radical movements they had once supported. The path to disillusionment was rarely a smooth one and often involved backtracking. Yet for Freyer and many like him, disillusionment with Nazism led to a reevaluation and moderation of their own earlier critical analysis of modern, liberal, pluralist societies. Freyer's journey from totalitarian conservatism to his more moderate, pluralist conservatism of the 1950s and 1960s was shared to varying degrees by other intellectuals for whom National Socialism had been the god that failed.[31]

The lives and influence of those who had served movements of the totalitarian right did not, of course, come to a sudden stop with the defeat of these regimes at the end of the Second World War. The extent of continuity among political, economic, and social elites from the interwar to the postwar era has been a topic of considerable interest to social scientists, but the careers of former radical conservative intellectuals have been little studied.[32] This study of the development of Hans Freyer's thought and career is intended to illuminate the continuities and discontinuities of German intellectual conservatism in the twentieth century.

Sociology and Radical Conservative Ideology

Freyer's social theory represents the confluence of two streams of European thought and culture rarely seen as part of the same intellectual landscape, namely radical conservatism and the tradition of sociological thought.

[29] Richard Löwenthal, *Der romantische Rückfall*, 12. On political opinion within the academy, see Fritz K. Ringer, *The Decline of the German Mandarins*, esp. chapter 4.

[30] On the monopolization of the term *intellectual* by the political left in the FRG, see Kurt Sontheimer, "Intellectuals and Politics in Western Germany," 30–31.

[31] To my knowledge, the first to use the phrase "the god that failed" in regard to those I have termed radical conservatives was Klemens von Klemperer, who did not, however, explore its implications. See Klemperer, *Germany's New Conservatism*, 218–19. A brief but insightful discussion of this phenomenon is in Schwarz, *Ära*, 431–50; see also Martin Greiffenhagen, *Das Dilemma des Konservatismus in Deutschland*.

[32] See, for example, Robert O. Paxton, *Vichy France: Old Guard and New Order, 1940–1944*, 330–52; and Schwarz, *Ära*, 405–30.

Although radical conservatism is a recurrent phenomenon in modernizing societies, both those who regard themselves as progressives and those who regard themselves as conservatives often find its existence difficult to acknowledge. To many a self-professing conservative, the predisposition toward continuity and prudence by which he defines conservatism makes the term *radical conservative* or *revolutionary conservative* a *contradictio in adjecto*. The use of the term *radical* or *revolutionary* in reference to the political right is sometimes viewed as a sacrilege by those of the political left.[33]

Since the analysis of radical conservatism—its characteristic concerns, its strategic ambiguities, and its relationship to traditional conservatism and National Socialism—will be among the principal concerns of the work that follows, we will make do provisionally with a tentative definition. Samuel Huntington has suggested that we do well to define conservatism neither as an inherent, substantive set of eternal values and institutions nor as merely the ideology of a particular and invariant social group but rather "positionally," as the ideology of those who in any situation of fundamental political disaccord defend the existing order. "Conservatism," Huntington writes, "is the intellectual rationale of the permanent institutional prerequisites of human existence. . . . When the foundations of society are threatened, the conservative ideology reminds men of the necessity of some institutions and the desirability of the existing ones."[34] This definition of traditional conservatism goes a long way toward describing radical conservatism as well. The last sentence, however, would have to be amended to read, "When the foundations of society and of existing institutions are perceived as decayed beyond restoration, the radical conservative ideology reminds men of the desirability of strong institutions and the necessity of new ones." The radical conservative shares many of the *concerns* of more conventional conservatism, such as the need for institutional authority and continuity with the past, but believes that the processes characteristic of modernity have destroyed the valuable legacy of the past for the present, and that a restoration of the virtues of the past therefore demands radical or revolutionary action. Hence the self-description of one radical conservative as "too conservative not to be radical," and the credo of another, "Conservative means creating things that are worth preserving."[35]

---

[33] See Eugen Weber, "Revolution? Counter-revolution? What Revolution?"; and K. D. Bracher, "Tradition und Revolution im Nationalsozialismus," in his *Kontroversen*, 62–78.

[34] Samuel Huntington, "Conservatism as an Ideology," 362.

[35] The self-description stems from Paul de Lagarde, *Deutsche Schriften*, 5, quoted in Rudolf Hermann, *Kulturkritik und konservative Revolution*, 241. The credo is from Arthur Moeller van den Bruck, *Das Dritte Reich*, 3d ed. (Hamburg, 1931), quoted in Greiffenhagen, *Dilemma*, 243.

Like the traditional conservative, the radical conservative has an acute appreciation for the role of authority, the "sacred," and continuity with the past in the life of the individual and of society. But while the traditional conservative seeks to shore up the authority of existing institutions, these institutions lack authority in the eyes of the radical conservative. For him existing institutions are incapable or unworthy of assent. Radical conservatism is a revolt against existing institutions in the name of authority.[36]

Radical conservatism unites several predilections that, in combination, make it a recognizably distinct and recurrent phenomenon. It shares with conservatism an emphasis on the role of institutions but seeks to create *new* institutions that will exert a far stronger hold on the individual than do existing ones, which because of their relative tolerance are perceived by radical conservatives as "decayed." Like other political radicals, radical conservatives look to *state power* to reach their goals. These aims typically include the *reassertion of collective particularity* (of the nation, the *Volk*, the race, or the community of the faithful) against a twofold threat. The internal threat arises from ideas and institutions identified by radical conservatives as both foreign and incapable of providing worthy goals for the collectivity and the individuals who comprise it. These threats usually include the market as the arbiter of expressed preferences, parliamentary democracy, and the pluralism of value systems that capitalism and liberal democracy are thought to promote. But the ideas and institutions perceived as threatening may also include those of internationalist socialism, which is similarly perceived as corrosive of collective particularity. The external threat arises from powerful foreign states that are perceived as using their power to spread ideas and institutions identified by radical conservatives as corrosive.

Yet together with its antipathy to such "modern" phenomena as liberalism, Marxism, capitalism, and parliamentary democracy, radical conservatism typically advocates *technological modernization*, in part because a successful challenge to the power of these external states demands the mastery of technology. The defense against the cultural and political effects of modernity on the body politic is thus thought to require a homeopathic absorption of the organizational and technological hallmarks of modernity.[37] What we have termed "rad-

---

[36] The term *conservative revolution* and the notion of a revolt for authority were first articulated in Hugo von Hofmannsthal's lecture of 1927, *Das Schrifttum als geistiger Raum der Nation*; see also Fritz Stern, *The Politics of Cultural*

Despair, 225 and passim.

[37] On the affirmation of technology by radical conservatives see Herf, *Reactionary Modernism*, esp. chapters 1 and 9.

ical conservatism" is among the most ubiquitous patterns in the development of political culture in the twentieth century. Yet its pervasiveness is rarely appreciated. A major conceptual barrier to recognizing radical conservatism as a distinct and recurrent phenomenon is the tendency to view modernization as a package deal, as a series of necessarily related processes of social, cultural, and political change. This view assumes (often tacitly) that the economic and technological processes required for increased productivity necessarily require an institutional structure of greater political participation and a world view increasingly tending toward liberty, equality, and the embrace of universal fraternity. Such a structure of assumptions makes it difficult to identify the characteristic features of intellectual and political movements that embrace technological and economic modernization, political activism, and state power yet do so in name of a particularist cultural ideal. "Radical conservatism" as we have defined it conveys the common sensibilities that Freyer and other intellectuals who advocated a "conservative revolution" shared with National Socialism. It is also a useful conceptual tool for comparative research, since it calls attention to the common denominator among a range of modern political movements that extend beyond Europe and beyond the interwar era. These include fascism, National Socialism, "Japanese fascism," African socialism, and Arab socialism.[38]

In its propensity to regard certain characteristic processes of modernity as disintegrative, and in its emphasis upon the socially and individually integrative roles of authority and the sacred, radical conservatism shares much intellectual terrain with the thinkers from Comte to Durkheim and from Hegel to Weber who together constitute the core of the sociological tradition. The debt of the major sociological theorists to conservative critiques of modernity has been demonstrated by Robert Nisbet and others.[39] Yet the early sociologists differed from their conservative forebears and contemporaries in a manner underemphasized by Nisbet but crucial for specifying the nature of the "con-

---

[38] I have explored the topic of the conceptual barriers to the recognition of National Socialism as "radical conservative" and its implications for historical research and interpretation in "Enttäuschung und Zweideutigkeit: Zur Geschichte rechter Sozialwissenschaftler im Dritten Reich."

Works that suggest the relevance of this pattern among intellectuals and political movements beyond interwar Europe include Walter Laqueur, "Fascism: The Second Coming"; V. S. Naipaul, *Among the Believers: An Islamic Journey*; Crawford Young, *Ideology and Development in Africa*, 97–103; Miles Fletcher, *The Search for a New Order: Intellectuals and Fascism in Prewar Japan*, esp. 155–62; and Ian Buruma, "Japanese Lib."

[39] Robert Nisbet, *The Sociological Tradition*; Robert Spaemann, *Der Ursprung der Soziologie aus dem Geist der Restauration: Studien über L.G.A. de Bonald*.

servatism" of the early sociological theorists. For while the conservative critics of the French and industrial revolutions sought to reassert the authority of Christianity and of existing institutions, the sociologists—critical of existing institutions and incapable of belief in the divine origins of Christianity—sought to forge new institutions that could command authority and a new faith that would serve as a functional substitute for Christianity.[40] In this they had a good deal in common with radical conservatism as described above.

It was Freyer's radical conservative sensibilities that led him to his interest in sociology as a tradition and as a profession. In the 1920s, as leading German sociologists attempted to professionalize and depoliticize their discipline, Freyer became a spokesman for those who sought to restore sociology to its radical, activist origins. At the same time he devoted himself to recapturing the legacy of Machiavelli, a thinker whom sociologists of the day usually ignored.

Freyer's interest in Machiavelli was not coincidental, for the Florentine was the common intellectual ancestor of both radical conservatism and the tradition of sociological thought. The disintegratory effects of the pursuit of self-interest, and the need to create social solidarity through active participation in new institutions of collective purpose—these Machiavellian concerns were shared by radical conservatives and by the central figures of the sociological canon.[41] Like earlier sociologists, Freyer sought to re-create a virtuous community under the conditions of modern society. Yet, as a legatee of the German historicist variant of the Counter-Enlightenment, Freyer believed that new integrative institutions would be successful only if they reasserted collective ethnic particularity. As a committed partisan of the conservative revolution of the 1920s and erstwhile supporter of the Third Reich versed in the history of modern social thought, Freyer was a participant-observer of the attempt to create a community of purpose devoted to the collective reassertion of particularity through the use of state power.

Freyer's intellectual and political biography represents a confluence of

---

[40] This was true not only of Saint-Simon (who as early as 1802 called for a new "religion of Newton" and later for a "New Christianity") and Comte (who founded a "Religion of Humanity") but for Durkheim, Pareto, and Weber as well. As Raymond Aron noted, "Durkheim, Pareto and Weber . . . albeit by different paths, discovered Comte's idea, namely that societies can maintain their coherence only through common beliefs. . . . As sociologists, they could see that traditional religion was being exhausted; as sociolo-

gists also, they were inclined to believe that society could retain structure and coherence only on condition that a common faith bind together the members of the collectivity" (Raymond Aron, *Main Currents in Sociological Thought*, 2:2).

[41] On Machiavelli's social thought and the subsequent recurrence of his concerns, see the very suggestive work by Jeff A. Weintraub, "Virtue, Community and the Sociology of Liberty: The Notion of Republican Virtue and Its Impact on Modern Western Social Thought."

historical movements and contexts that have been studied individually but rarely in their interrelation. It represents a meeting of the sociological tradition and radical conservatism, the former usually regarded as part of the "high road" of intellectual history—"the study of major ideas in their pristine form on the higher level" or "intellectually clear and significant statements"—and the latter as part of the low or middle levels of thought—"popular effusions in the nature of slogans" or "the activities and aspirations of ruling minorities and of the rival minorities striving to supplant them."[42] Freyer shared the critical analysis proffered by earlier sociologists of modernity as a process of spiritual disenchantment and the increasingly meaningless domination of men by their own creations. He embraced a political movement of the radical right out of a conviction that the movement embodied "popular effusions in the nature of slogans" that offered a plausible solution to the dilemmas bequeathed by the preceding generation of "high" social theorists. As such he combined the roles of analyst and advocate of what Peter Berger has termed "demodernization," a stage in which the liberating process of modernity becomes that from which liberation is sought.[43] This acute awareness of the costs and limits of modernity, as well as a consideration of how these costs might be minimized or modernity "overcome," was the central concern of Freyer's thought in both his radical conservative and his moderate conservative phases. In recent years these concerns have reemerged and are arguably the central themes in contemporary social thought.[44]

As an individual committed to both the advancement of sociology and the realization of radical conservative ideology, Hans Freyer straddled the roles of social scientist and ideologist. His writings were addressed to and read by both fellow academic social scientists and a larger public of politically concerned readers. His works served as a conduit for the movement of ideas between ide-

---

[42] H. Stuart Hughes, *Consciousness and Society.* This distinction between the high, middle, and popular levels of social thought is often implicitly maintained in the historical literature on radical conservatism, even when it remains unavowed. Ringer, for example, understates the degree to which the criticisms of modernity leveled by German professors were shared by their nonacademic counterparts. In *The Crisis of German Ideology*, George L. Mosse deals at length with the popular forms of *völkisch* thought, with hardly a reference to comparable notions in the academic world.

[43] Peter Berger, Brigitte Berger, and Hansfried Kellner, *The Homeless Mind: Modernization and Consciousness*, 195–96.

[44] These are key themes expressed in a variety of modulations by Daniel Bell, "Beyond Modernism, Beyond Self" and "The Return of the Sacred," in his *The Winding Passage*; Peter Berger, "Toward a Critique of Modernity," in his *Facing Up to Modernity*; Ralf Dahrendorf, "Life Chances: Dimensions of Liberty in Society," in his *Life Chances*; Jürgen Habermas, "Modernity versus Postmodernity"; and Philip Rieff, *Fellow Teachers.*

CHAPTER ONE

Science as a Vocation, 1887–1914

Why a bright boy from a pious Protestant family was led toward radical conservatism and a career as a social theorist is the subject of this chapter.

Had he not become disaffected from the major institutions of his society, Freyer might have become a conservative, but not a radical conservative. His estrangement was not an individual peculiarity but was widely shared and even institutionalized in the *Jugendbewegung* (youth movement), which attracted a high percentage of the generation of German intellectuals who came of age in the decade before the First World War. It helps explain why so many of them were drawn toward political radicalism of the left or right.

Like many other builders of systems of social theory, the young Freyer was destined for a theological career but found himself cut off from his theological moorings by forces within the institutions of secular culture, not least the Gymnasium and the university. Following an already established and oft-repeated pattern, he sought a more secular guise in which he might maintain his appointed destiny as a spiritual guide. When he and others caught up in the same experience looked to their academic teachers for a secular substitute for the faith they had lost, they found that these purported guides had themselves become seekers after a new key to the riddle of history. These cultural forces generated extremely broad expectations of theoretical adequacy among Freyer's teachers. For them and for many social theorists of Freyer's generation, "theories of the middle range" were insufficient.

Freyer emerged not just as a radical and as a social theorist but as a radical conservative social theorist, who built upon the historicist tradition of the Counter-Enlightenment. The dominant assumptions in his academic milieu, as we shall see, predisposed those who studied the humanities and social sciences toward that tradition.

The Secularization of the Religious Vocation

In the disabused aftermath of the Third Reich and of three years in Soviet-occupied Germany, Hans Freyer described the sort of intellectual most susceptible to the creation of totalitarian ideologies. He was likely to be a man whose structure of thought preserved a good deal of the theological orientation of his ancestors but who had himself become an apostate. "Thus," Freyer wrote, "his religious organs are highly developed but have lost their function."[1] Was this a bit of tacit autobiography? Such motives—witting or unwitting—cannot be known with certainty, but several facts are indubitable: Hans Freyer came from a deeply religious home, lost his faith in his youth, and spent a good deal of his subsequent life searching for a sociological equivalent of traditional religion.

Curt Johannes Freyer was born in Plagwitz, a suburb of Leipzig, in 1887. The family into which he was born was economically comfortable but not wealthy. His father, Ludwig Israel Freyer, was a middle-level bureaucrat in the German civil service and rose to the position of *Postdirektor* of the small town of Burgstadt—where Curt Johannes attended grammar school—before retiring to Dresden in 1901. The father's middle name is a mark of his own family's religiosity, for his ancestors had been Lutheran pastors for several generations. The religious roots of Ludwig Israel's wife, Helene Broesel, went even deeper, for she was of Herrenhut stock. The village of Herrenhut was peopled by the Saxon branch of the Moravian Brethren, a pietistic sect that had come to Saxony in the early eighteenth century. Curt Johannes was raised in a household permeated by Protestant religiosity. It was a faith he was expected to carry on, for it was his mother's wish that he become a theologian, and it was in the faculty of theology that he first enrolled as a university student.[2]

In so doing, Freyer was replicating one of the most significant patterns evident in the history of modern European intellectuals in general and of German intellectuals in particular. For over a century, the German literary and humanistic intelligentsia was drawn disproportionately from men of devout origins, who began their higher education with the intention of pursuing a pastoral vocation—and who were themselves often the sons of clergymen— only to lose their traditional belief and embark upon a secular, academic career. A good deal of attention has been devoted to "secularization" as a gradual historical trend stretching over generations and denoting a gradual decline of the influence of traditional religion in modern European intellectual life.[3]

[1] Hans Freyer, *Theorie des gegenwärtigen Zeitalters* (1955), 127.

[2] Hans Freyer, "Lebenslauf," 1945, UAL, PA Freyer, 202ff.; "Ein Gespräch mit Hans Freyer," 2; interview with Käthe Freyer, Münster, 23 February 1982.

[3] This approach is employed in differing forms by Owen Chadwick, *The Secularization of the European Mind in the Nineteenth Century*; and Karl Löwith, *Meaning in History*.

Alongside this ongoing collective process of secularization, a *recurrent* phenomenon has occurred that one might term the secularization of the religious vocation. Each generation has included those who traversed the path not only from traditional religious belief but from a prospective career as theologian or clergyman to the secular vocations of philosopher or—when much of the purview of traditional philosophy was parceled out among the social sciences—sociologist.

Secularization is not simply the attenuation of traditional religion but a process in which objects outside the sphere of traditional religion are endowed with the emotional significance previously accorded to the divine. For those raised with the expectation of pursuing a pastoral vocation, the experience of secularization has tended toward a recurrent pattern. The expectation of providing spiritual leadership is often transferred from the religious to the secular vocation by the person undergoing the process. To the extent that previous religious beliefs are perceived as antiquated but the need for that general orientation toward man and the cosmos which traditional religion provided remains undiminished, the new incumbent of the secularized vocation will take it upon himself to provide just such an orientation.[4] This may help to account for the penchant of such intellectuals to develop theories so all-encompassing as to depart from their avowed procedures of rational explanation.[5]

Freyer's observation thus suggests a good deal about the often unarticulated expectations that many modern intellectual innovators in the field of social and political thought have shared by virtue of a common social origin. But it may suggest too much, for not all modern thinkers who have undergone this personal process of secularization have become advocates of totalitarian solu-

---

[4] Though this pattern is most salient among German Protestants—Hegel, Hölderlin, Schelling, Nietzsche, and Dilthey are among its outstanding examples, not to mention such lesser lights as Paul de Lagarde—its application is much broader. Martin Heidegger, a German Catholic, began his higher education at a Jesuit college in Constance and studied theology at the University of Freiburg before turning entirely to philosophy. Hermann Cohen, a cantor's son, began his studies at the Jewish Theological Seminary in Breslau before embarking on a philosophical career. In France, Émile Durkheim, a rabbi's son, turned to philosophy and later sociology in an attempt to discover an integrative faith for the Third Republic. Isaac Deutscher,

the scion of a Hasidic court in Poland, became a leading Trotskyite theoretician. A remarkable number of British "new liberal" and socialist intellectuals, including Hobhouse and Hobson, were the offspring of Evangelical parents whose exposure to Darwin's thought had disabused them of their Protestantism. The New World's foremost sociological system builder, Talcott Parsons, was similarly a descendant of generations of Congregationalist ministers. On this theme see also Friedrich H. Tenbruck, *Die unbewältigten Sozialwissenschaften*.

[5] See Hans Blumenberg, *Säkularisierung und Selbstbehauptung*, 60–62. See also Helmuth Plessner, *Die verspätete Nation*, passim and esp. 104.

tions to the problems of the modern age. The outcome of the secularization of
the religious vocation—indeed, whether such a process occurs at all—depends
upon more varied factors, not least of which are the site and content of formal
education.

For most, the first major institution that competes with the family as a source
of influence is the school, and in Freyer's case the cultural norms that he encountered there must have been partly at odds with those prevailing in his
family household. The Royal Gymnasium of Dresden, where he received the
bulk of his high school education and from which he graduated first in his class
in 1907, was an institution devoted to providing historical knowledge and a
sense of political responsibility for a student body expected to become the elite
of the province of Saxony. The curriculum was guided by a conservative humanistic model of education that stressed exposure to the history and philosophy of classical Greece and Rome and to the German "classical" authors—
Kant, Goethe, Alexander von Humboldt—whose portraits graced the school's
auditorium.[6] This educational program was "conservative" compared to the
more "practical" courses of study that were beginning to gain acceptance, but
it was neither intended nor likely to "conserve" Freyer in the Christian world
view of his forefathers.

Since the age of Winckelmann, Goethe, and Schiller, German high culture
had been increasingly divorced from Christianity. In the course of the nineteenth century their orientation toward pagan Greece and Rome as models of
thought and action permeated the educated classes of Germany, where it existed uneasily alongside a residual Christianity.[7] This classical, pagan orientation marked Freyer deeply: his education had made the culture of ancient
Athens second nature to him, Freyer once wrote. The controlling metaphors
of several of his works were drawn from Greek mythology.[8]

Yet—perhaps because as a Gymnasium student living at home he was in continuing contact with his family and thus in an environment that reinforced his
traditional Protestant faith—Freyer enrolled in the theological faculty of the
University of Greifswald, intending to pursue a vocation as a Lutheran theologian. A semester later, in October 1907, he transferred to the University of

[6] Karl Buchheim, "Beziehungen des alten
Königlichen Gymnasiums in Dresden zur sächsischen Geschichte und Kulturgeschichte," unpublished manuscript quoted in Elfriede Üner,
"Hans Freyer in der deutschen Soziologie bis
1933."

[7] Franz Schnabel, *Deutsche Geschichte im neun-*

zehnten Jahrhundert, 4:561–75; Stern, *Politics*,
xxv–xxvi and passim.

[8] Hans Freyer, "Das Problem der Utopie"
(1920), 340. The titles of these works were *Antäus* (1918), *Prometheus* (1923), and *Pallas Athene*
(1935).

Leipzig, where he again enrolled in the theological faculty but began to take courses in philosophy, history, and literature.[9] At the end of the semester, he decided to abandon his theological studies, which led to a bitter confrontation with his mother.[10]

What led Freyer to alter the vocational plans set out for him? We cannot be sure, but the influence of his university experience would seem to be paramount. With its physical and spiritual distance from home and family, the university signified for Freyer—as for many others before and after—a new environment free from previous norms and expectations and from those who embodied them. More important, perhaps, was the substance of the intellectual currents to which Freyer was exposed in his studies. The courses that he attended in his last semester as a student of theology included—in addition to explications of Isaiah 1:39 and "Letter to the Galatians"—a course in the department of philosophy entitled "Explication of Nietzsche's *Thus Spoke Zarathustra*." The course was offered by a young *Privatdozent*, Raoul Richter, who was known for making his students question their existing beliefs and presuppositions and who insisted on a relentless critique of existing theological and philosophical positions.[11]

Richter seems to have made a powerful impression on the young Freyer. The next semester Freyer switched his major entirely to philosophy and took two more of Richter's courses (including "A Critical History of Ethics"), and the next semester yet another two (including "The Philosophy of Religion"). Freyer was honored with the annual prize of the faculty of philosophy for an essay that he wrote for Richter, "The Ethics of J. M. Guyau"—a French contemporary of Nietzsche, whose major works included *Esquisse d'une morale sans obligation ni sanction* (1885) and *L'irréligion de l'avenir* (1887). Ultimately Freyer remained unsatisfied by the stark choice between egoism and altruism in Guyau's work. Guyau's affirmation of altruism seemed to Freyer as superficial and limited as the British utilitarianism which they both opposed.[12]

Whether or not Freyer had heard the tidings that God was dead before he entered upon his higher education, it is clear from his subsequent writing that he took the news very much to heart. Another contention that Freyer accepted from Nietzsche—via Richter—was that all previous attempts to construe a uni-

---

[9] This and other references to courses in which Freyer enrolled at Leipzig are drawn from UAL, "Zeugnisprotokoll," rep. I.

[10] Interview with Käthe Freyer.

[11] Heinrich Hasse, "Die Philosophie Raoul Richters," in *Raoul Richter zum Gedächtnis (1871–1912)*, 94.

[12] Hans Freyer, "Lebenslauf," 1919, UAL, PA Freyer, 2. See Freyer's review of Guyau, *Erziehung und Vererbung*.

versally valid *content* of ethics had failed.[13] Ethical philosophy in itself, Freyer learned, was incapable of discovering universally valid concrete norms.[14]

Thus the initial impact of Freyer's experience at the University of Leipzig was one of cultural disinheritance—of alienation from the transcendent values and secular expectations of his parental home.[15] Like the protagonist of Shaw's *Too True to Be Good*, he might have said, "I am by nature and destiny a preacher. . . . But I have no Bible, no creed."

The Educated Bourgeoisie and the Search for Cultural Renewal

Given Freyer's sense of the inadequacy of the immediate culture to which he was heir, but also of his perceived obligation to provide cultural leadership, it is not surprising that his social life at the university centered upon a group with similar hopes and aspirations. From the time he was an undergraduate at Leipzig until its dissolution at the end of the First World War, Freyer was part of the Serakreis, a nexus of the varied movements of cultural renewal that were pulsating through the German educated bourgeoisie (*Bildungsbürgertum*) in the decades before the Great War. These overlapping and intersecting movements included the youth movement, the new nationalism, and a cluster of organizations of cultural renovation broadly known as the movement for cultural reform (*Reformbewegung*). Centered upon the publisher Eugen Diederichs, the Serakreis was a closely knit group composed mainly of university students, many of whom were also active in the youth movement, the "free student" movement (*freideutsche Studenten*), and the "free school" movement (*Freischulgemeinden*). It was in this cultural ambience that Hans Freyer's concerns were forged.

These movements of cultural renewal had a good deal in common. Like most modern cultural movements, all were a revolt of a part of the bourgeoisie against that which they characterized as bourgeois. But since the terms *bourgeoisie* and *bourgeois* are notoriously imprecise and since the social groups that they denote and the cultural characteristics that they connote vary across time and place, a more precise definition is required. The "bourgeoisie" from which most of the followers of these movements sprang was the *Bildungsbür-*

---

[13] Raoul Richter, *Friedrich Nietzsche*, 3d ed. (1917), 310. This book is based on Richter's class lectures in Leipzig. See also Hasse, "Philosophie," 115.

[14] Hans Freyer, review of *Hauptprobleme der Ethik*, by Paul Hensel, (1914), 79; see also Freyer's doctoral dissertation and *Antäus*, discussed below.

[15] The term *cultural disinheritance* is borrowed from Toews, *Hegelianism*, 13.

gertum, that sector of the middle and upper middle class which derived its income from occupations for which a humanistic education—usually a university degree, or at least graduation from a Gymnasium—was required. The *Bildungsbürger* as a whole—and the participants in the various reform movements—were for the most part of Protestant origin.

The anxiety caused among the educated bourgeoisie by the coming of technological society and the increasing political mobilization of the German working class through the Social Democratic party have often been regarded as the stimulus to the new search for cultural renewal. But the educated bourgeoisie had long defined itself in good part in contradistinction to the industrial and commercial bourgeoisie *(Besitzbürgertum).*[16] These new movements of cultural renewal of the last two prewar decades converged in their expressed disaffection with the perceived ascendancy of materialistic values and the greater prestige accorded to wealth in the culture of imperial Germany. The new movements of vegetarianism, of abstinence from tobacco and alcohol, the new fascination with folklore and with nature were all expressions of dissatisfaction with the urban, industrial, and technological transformations of the German *Reich.* In this sense it was a movement of the educated bourgeoisie against the values imputed to the propertied bourgeoisie.[17]

But the new movements of cultural renewal were also—and not least of all—a generational revolt *within* the educated bourgeoisie. As traditional Protestant faith was replaced among educated Germans first by idealist philosophy and later by a faith in science, their residual Protestant observance came to seem increasingly hollow and spiritually unsatisfying to their offspring—hence the quest for new or authentic forms of religiosity, one expression of which was the attempt to formulate a "Germanic faith."[18] The rote learning and stress on philology that dominated in the Gymnasia were condemned as inimical to true

[16] On the definition of the *Bildungsbürgertum,* its self-understanding, its relationship to other social groups, and its overrepresentation in the movements of cultural reform, see Rudolf Vierhaus, "Umrisse einer Sozialgeschichte der Gebildeten in Deutschland"; Klaus Vondung, "Probleme einer Sozialgeschichte der Ideen" and "Zur Lage der Gebildeten in der wilhelminischen Zeit," in his *Das wilhelminische Bildungsbürgertum,* as well as other essays therein; Konrad Jarausch, *Students, Society and Politics in Imperial Germany,* passim; Ringer, *German Mandarins,* chapters 1–2; Fritz Stern, "The Political

Consequences of the Unpolitical German," in his *The Failure of Illiberalism;* Walther Janzen, "Die soziologische Herkunft der Führungsschicht der deutschen Jugendbewegung, 1900–1933"; and the review of the literature in Dirk Käsler, *Die frühe deutsche Soziologie 1909 bis 1934 und ihre Entstehungs-Milieus,* 235ff.

[17] On the various *Reformbewegungen,* see Ulrich Linse, "Die Jugendkulturbewegung," and Janos Frecot, "Die Lebensreformbewegung," in Vondung, *Wilhelminische Bildungsbürgertum;* Mosse, *Crisis,* parts 1–2.

[18] On the quest for a Germanic faith, see

self-development (*Bildung*). Within the university, the temple of the educated bourgeoisie, the free student movement objected not so much to the content of instruction as to the anti-intellectual and hedonistic tone that the established German fraternities (*Corps, Korporationen, Burschenschaften*) imparted to university life.[19] Thus the new, varied movements of cultural reform chastised the "bourgeois nature" (*Bürgerlichkeit*) not only of the propertied but of the educated bourgeoisie as well.

The Serakreis arose on the initiative of Eugen Diederichs. Since 1896 the head of a publishing house that bore his name and from 1912 the publisher and later the editor of the journal *Die Tat*, Diederichs was a dedicated and skilled promoter of many of the trends that together constituted the movement for cultural renewal—Max Weber referred to one of the cultural conferences that Diederichs organized as a *"Warenhaus der Weltanschauungen"* (a department store of world views).[20] Though by no means the major intellectual influence on Hans Freyer in the years before the war, Diederichs was Freyer's extra-academic mentor, the publisher of two of his early books, and was responsible for Freyer's first contribution to a major periodical—a review of Oswald Spengler's *Decline of the West* that appeared in *Die Tat* in 1919. This put Freyer in very prestigious company indeed, for the Eugen Diederichs Verlag published not only distinguished German authors such as Ferdinand Avenarius, Eduard Bernstein, Lujo Brentano, Martin Buber, Hermann Hesse and Hugo Preuss but also German translations of Bergson, Chekhov, Gorky, Jaurès, Ruskin, and Sidney Webb—in short, a panorama of the political and cultural avant-garde. Diederichs was also concerned to develop younger authors who shared a broad dissatisfaction with "bourgeois" Germany; among those who contributed to *Die Tat* before 1920 were Alfred Kurella, Ernst Krieck, Karl Korsch, Georg Lukács, and Walther Benjamin.[21]

Although they were to follow very different political paths after World War I—Kurella, Korsch, Lukács, and Benjamin were members of, or close to, the communist movement, Krieck became a Nazi, Buber a Zionist with a vaguely socialist orientation—these men shared with Diederichs and the young Hans Freyer a yearning for an intense emotional commitment to some larger com-

---

Mosse, *Crisis*; Stern, *Politics*. For a succinct, contemporary expression of this quest for authentic religiosity, see Walter Benjamin, "Die religiöse Stellung der neuen Jugend," *Die Tat* (1914–15).

[19] The style of life of the fraternities and the activities of the *freideutsche Studenten* are explored in Jarausch, *Students*, chapters 5–6.

[20] Theodor Heuss, *Erinnerungen*.

[21] Gary Stark, *Entrepreneurs of Ideology: Neoconservative Publishers in Germany, 1890–1933*, chapter 4.

munity of purpose that they found lacking in contemporary Germany. The movements of cultural renewal with which Diederichs and the Serakreis were associated in Wilhelmine Germany included the reform movement, the youth movement, the free student movement, and those currents of thought which various observers have in retrospect termed "romantic anticapitalism," "the search for synthesis," or "the hunger for wholeness."[22] All stood in opposition to the social and cultural status quo, but they were not easily pigeonholed as progressive or reactionary, as right or left, or even as nationalistic or cosmopolitan.[23] Both Martin Heidegger and Rudolf Carnap were members of the Freideutsche Jugend (Carnap was a leading figure in the Serakreis); both went on to develop philosophies radically at odds with the dominant neo-Kantianism of Wilhelmine academic philosophy; Carnap became a communist for a brief period after the First World War, Heidegger a Nazi after 1933. On opposite poles both philosophically and politically, both men owed their radicalism in part to the same critical ambience in Wilhelmine Germany.

Diederichs' own critical predilections were rather aesthetic and vaguely *völkisch*. His major concerns were the lack of beauty and of a unified style in German cultural life and a rather inchoate religiosity.[24] He sought solutions to both problems in a restoration of premodern and non-Christian cultural forms some of which survived among the peasantry, the least "modernized" group in the population. The Serakreis originated out of Diederichs' attempts to revive the celebration of the *Sonnenwende* (the solstice), a rite with pagan "Germanic" connotations. On such occasions *Volk* dances were danced and *Volk* songs sung, peasant costumes donned, and garlands reminiscent of the ancient Greeks sported. The formal raison d'être of the Serakreis was the preparation for such events.

It soon developed into much more, however, as it attracted university students active in the Wandervogel and in the Freideutsche Jugend of the universities of Jena and Leipzig, lured less by Diederichs' vague ideas than by his open-mindedness, earnestness, and readiness to *épater le bourgeois*. Through

---

[22] The three labels are respectively from Löwy, *Lukács*; Ringer, *Decline*; and Peter Gay, *Weimar Culture*, chapter 4.

[23] The political ambiguity of the early *Jugendbewegung* is best developed in Thomas Nipperdey, "Jugend und Politik um 1900," in his *Gesellschaft, Kultur, Theorie*; see also Walther Laqueur, *Young Germany*, 4 and passim.

[24] The locus classicus of this brand of *Kultur-kritik* was Nietzsche's essay on D. F. Strauß in his *Unzeitgemässe Betrachtungen*, in which he contended that "Kultur ist vor allem Einheit des künstlerischen Stiles in allen Lebensäußerungen eines Volkes" (13). Diederichs' religious thought was much influenced by Paul de Lagarde. On Diederichs' cultural and religious views, see Stark, *Entrepreneurs*; and Mosse, *Crisis*, chapter 3.

frequent informal social evenings, common discussions of philosophical problems, recitations of current authors (Stefan George, Hofmannsthal, Rilke),
group singing, dancing, theater, and music making, a common life-style that
eschewed alcohol and tobacco and practiced equality of the sexes, and not least
of all through long hikes in the countryside, the Serakreis became what its
members described as a *Gemeinschaft*, a community. The community was
marked at first by a devotion to individual self-education, to the search for "authentic" culture, and to the emotional warmth generated by the common pursuits of like-minded young men and women. The Serakreis was a continuing
expression of its members' commitment to companionship (*Geselligkeit*) and to
rounded self-development (*die Einheitlichkeit des Lebens*).[25]

If a certain disaffection from the cultural tone of Wilhelmine Germany and
of the university first propelled Freyer and others into the Serakreis, the very
intensity of the collective life of the circle created its own dynamic. When compared with the immediacy and emotional intensity of their *Gemeinschaft* and its
relative freedom from social conventions, the bourgeois world outside came to
seem all the more artificial, constraining, and fragmented.[26]

Leipzig: Scholars in Search of a Philosophy of History

Estranged from his Christian faith and distanced from the cultural conventions of contemporary Germany by his academic studies and by the social milieu of the Serakreis, Freyer looked in good part to his professors to provide a
conceptual compass and a substitute for the faith he had lost. In addition to
philosophy Freyer studied history, economics, psychology, and literature in
his student years in Leipzig. While his disciplinary span was broad, the focus
of his studies was considerably narrower. Among philosophers he studied
Kant, Schopenhauer, and Nietzsche in depth; among writers Lessing, Hebbel,
and Goethe. With Karl Lamprecht he studied German cultural history from
the age of absolutism to the present. The disproportionate focus on *German*

[25] My portrait of the Serakreis is based on Eu-
gen Diederichs, "Skizze zu einer Selbstbiogra-
phie, 1920–21," Eugen Diederichs Verlag Ar-
chiv, Cologne, which was partially published as
Eugen Diederichs, *Aus meinem Leben* (1938); Karl
Brügmann, "Leipziger Gespräche" (1914), and
Wilhelm Flitner, "Freideutsche Studenten in
Jena, 1909–1914" (1963), both reprinted in *Die*

Wandervogelzeit, ed. Werner Kindt; and Wilhelm
Flitner, "Wilhelm Flitner," in *Pädagogik in Selbstdarstellungen*, vol. 2, ed. Ludwig Pongratz.

[26] The best analysis of this phenomenon in the
Jugendbewegung is found in the essay by Her-
mann Mau, "Die deutsche Jugendbewegung:
Rückblick und Ausblick."

history, philosophy, and literature in Freyer's course of studies was typical of the offerings at all German universities in his day. The intensive concern with modern history, society, and philosophy reflected his own interests.

Though Freyer studied with and was influenced by the older and stellar names on the faculty—including the historians Karl Lamprecht and Erich Brandenburg, the philosopher and psychologist Wilhelm Wundt, and the economist Karl Bücher—the greatest immediate impact upon him seems to have come from several younger members. It was Raoul Richter who introduced Freyer to Nietzsche, Guyau, and others on the cutting edge of the critique of Christianity and of existing moral systems. Through the lectures of a young lecturer, Johann Plenge, on the history of socialism Freyer became acquainted with the critique of capitalism offered by the utopian socialists and by Marx and with the intimate connection between Marx's critique and Hegelian philosophy.[27] Several of Freyer's future concerns were sparked by courses entitled "The Psychology and Ethics of Economic Life," "The Origins and Major Forms of Social Structure," and "The Philosophy of History" offered by another young scholar, Felix Krueger, who would later become Freyer's academic mentor. From all three young scholars Freyer imbibed a critical attitude toward contemporary culture and society, a stance reinforced and radicalized by his contacts in the youth movement. Freyer's initiation within the academy into the works of Hegel, Marx, and Nietzsche, of Tönnies, Sombart, and Max Weber, allowed him to formulate the rather inchoate discontents of his comrades in the youth movement in a more scientific fashion.

From contemporary observers of the academic scene, we know that Freyer's discontents and expectations were shared by many other German students of his day. In an address of 1910 to the Heidelberg Academy of Sciences, the distinguished philosopher Wilhelm Windelband spoke of the younger generation's "hunger for an integrated view of the world" (*Hunger nach Weltanschauung*) and "a yearning for a comprehensive meaning of reality" with religious overtones.[28] Three years later—at about the time when Freyer was studying with him in Berlin—the philosopher Georg Simmel noted that for some time there had been a strong yearning for a *Weltanschauung* among the young, a need that the university for the most part had not sought to satisfy.

---

[27] See Johann Plenge, *Marx und Hegel* (1911), which, as he notes in the foreword, is an expansion of ideas that he developed in his lectures on the history of socialism, a course that Freyer took.

[28] Wilhelm Windelband, *Die Erneuerung des Hegelianismus* (1910), 6–7.

Unless the universities met this challenge, he warned, the best of the young would turn elsewhere—to mysticism, to a misunderstood Nietzsche, to a skeptical materialism, or to social democracy.[29]

During the first half of the nineteenth century, German idealistic philosophy in general and Hegelianism in particular had provided the conceptual anchor for the ethos of self-cultivation (*Bildung*) that served as a secular substitute for religion for much of the Protestant *Bildungsbürgertum*. To the adept it explained where man had come from, where he was going, and what his duties were in between. Even the unadept knew that should such questions arise, there were learned men who were sure of the answers. This anchor no longer held after mid-century, when the *Bildungsbürger* prided himself on his new realism and the scholar on the substantive discoveries of his empirical research: *Hegelei* became a term of intellectual abuse. By the end of the century, however, and with ever greater force after 1900, the young searchers of the youth movement, participants in the other reform movements, and many academics evinced a need for some system of thought that would provide them with a sense of their place in history, for what Germans have since come to call an *Orientierungswissenschaft*.[30]

This dissatisfaction among senior scholars was much in evidence at the University of Leipzig. Two of Freyer's teachers, Karl Lamprecht and Wilhelm Wundt, turned from their earlier empirical, monographic research toward all-encompassing theories of history, to create what they considered inductive substitutes for the philosophy of history. After a lifetime devoted largely to the establishment of experimental psychology as a distinct academic discipline, Wundt sought after 1900 to provide a key to world history by using ethnographic and historical materials to determine the stages that each *Volk* necessarily traversed in the course of its development.[31] Similarly, Karl Lamprecht saw the task of history as the discovery of regularities in the psychic development of *Völker*. On the basis of his encyclopedic research in German history Lamprecht, like Wundt, sought to develop a theory of necessary historical stages.[32] Both men asserted that culture, economy, polity, and social structure

[29] Georg Simmel, "An Herrn Professor Karl Lamprecht," *Die Zukunft* (May 1913), 233.

[30] Jarausch, *Students*, 410; Ringer, *German Mandarins*, chapter 5; Plessner, *Verspätete*, chapter 12. Freyer's own brief description of the search for such an *Orientierungswissenschaft* in prewar Germany—a search that he shared—is found in his "Ferdinand Tönnies und seine

Stellung in der deutschen Soziologie" (1936), 3.

[31] Wilhelm Wundt, *Völkerpsychologie*, 10 vols. (1911–20); for a summary, see his *Elements of Folk Psychology*, esp. 522–23, in which he discusses his method as the basis of an empirical philosophy of history.

[32] Lamprecht's methodological writings are found in *Karl Lamprecht: Ausgewählte Schriften*,

were expressions of the *"Volksseele"* (roughly, "national psyche") at a particular stage of development and hence inextricably intertwined.

Another senior figure at Leipzig with whom Freyer studied, the economist Karl Bücher, also developed a theory of historical stages, in this case of the development of the economy of western Europe from the Greeks to his own day. While the span and scope of Wundt's and Lamprecht's works was widely admired, the arbitrariness of their periodization and of their explanatory devices led to a dismissal of their work by most serious scholars. Max Weber, a man given to verbal austerity, especially in his methodological writings, described Lamprecht's work as "appalling" and indicated that Wundt's was little more rigorous.[33] Of the three men it was Bücher, whose project was the most modest, whose theory exerted the most lasting influence on historical research.[34]

What is most conspicuous in historical retrospect is that so many of the leading figures around Freyer at Leipzig should have been so caught up in the quest for "synthesis," as if no explanation was worth anything that did not explain everything. This spiritual urgency in the search for a new *Weltanschauung* and a new *Orientierungswissenschaft* created an elective affinity between some of the more innovative scholars of the era and their students with ties to the youth and reform movements.

Karl Lamprecht, in an essay of 1906, noted that in contradistinction to the economic orientation of much intellectual and political activity in the first decades of the new *Reich*, recent years had seen the rise of what he called "an idealism of yearning" (*Sehnsuchtsidealismus*) that was still in search of new values and goals, including political ones.[35] He welcomed this trend and hoped for a "politicization of society," a greater degree of "moral-political activity" that, beginning from subpolitical associations (*Genossenschaften*), would eventually lead

---

ed. Herbert Schönebaum. For a good summary of his view of history, see Karl Weintraub, *Visions of Culture*, chapter 4. An analysis of Lamprecht's methodological statements is offered in Ernst Cassirer, *The Problem of Knowledge*, chapter 17. Cassirer's treatment is too systematic, however, and ignores the degree to which Lamprecht—who claimed that psychology provided the key to history—was eclectic in his use of psychological theories and changed his theory as he went along, a process explicated in Herbert Schönebaum, "Karl Lamprecht, Leben und Werk eines Kämpfers um die Geschichtswissen-

schaft, 1856–1913," 740ff. The best analysis of Lamprecht's methodology and its intellectual historical context is Susan D. Schultz, "History as a Moral Force against Individualism."

[33] Max Weber, "Knies and the Problem of Irrationality" (1906), in his *Roscher and Knies*, 111.

[34] On Bücher, see *International Encyclopedia of the Social Sciences* (1968), s.v. "Bücher, Karl," by Karl Polanyi; and Georg Jahn, "Die historische Schule der Nationalökonomie und ihr Ausklang."

[35] Karl Lamprecht, "Freiheit und Volkstum," reprinted in his *Ausgewählte Schriften*, 606–7.

to a new political ideal (*Staatsideal*).[36] As rector of the University of Leipzig in 1910–11, he encouraged the free German student movement and defended it from attack after it invited Eduard Bernstein to deliver a lecture on the Social Democratic party's Erfurt Program.[37] He regarded his own research as a basis for a new *Weltanschauung*[38] and the Institut für Kultur- und Universalgeschichte, which he founded at Leipzig, as a model for other interdisciplinary centers "which, despite increased division of labor, [will] provide the necessary synthesis of efforts without which further specialization threatens to undermine culture."[39] Scholarship for Lamprecht was, if not politically *engagé*, nevertheless "relevant." The last course that Freyer attended as a student at Leipzig in 1912 was Lamprecht's "Introduction to the Cultural Historical Understanding of the Present." It is easy to see why the "free students," who demanded of the university that it "become a school for life, which . . . enables the individual to comprehend present-day culture in its entirety,"[40] should have invited Karl Lamprecht to address their national rally at the Hohe Meißner in 1913.[41] Nor is it surprising that Lamprecht was in contact with Eugen Diederichs and planned to contribute a book on the development of culture in a series that Diederichs planned to edit.[42] Lamprecht was a link between the academy and the extra-academic reform movement.

Another contemporary movement in which the educated bourgeoisie in general and the German professoriate in particular was heavily overrepresented was the new nationalism and imperialism. The new imperialism embodied in organizations such as the Navy League drew much of their intellectual leadership from *Bildungsbürger* of National Liberal origins who by the end of the nineteenth century were frustrated and disappointed by the lack of cultural integration and the obvious social polarization that prevailed in the new *Reich*.[43] Karl Lamprecht was an active lecturer and publicist for the Navy

[36] Ibid., 613. On Lamprecht's political ideals and activity, see Luise Wiese-Schorn, "Karl Lamprecht: Kulturgeschichtsschreibung zwischen Wissenschaft und Politik," esp. 246–406.

[37] L. Langerbeck, "Die Universitätsreformpläne Karl Lamprechts," in *Karl-Marx-Universität Leipzig, 1409–1959: Beiträge zur Universitätsgeschichte*, ed. Ernst Engelberg, 2:42–43.

[38] Ringer, *German Mandarins*, 304.

[39] Quoted in Jarausch, *Students*, 50.

[40] Quoted in ibid., 51.

[41] Kindt, ed., *Deutsche Jugendbewegung*, 487.

[42] Eugen Diederichs to Karl Lamprecht, 11 July 1914, Nachlaß Lamprecht, Universitätsbibliothek Bonn.

[43] Peter Hampe, "Sozioökonomische und psychische Hintergründe der bildungsbürgerlichen Imperialbegeisterung," in Vondung, *Wilhelminische Bildungsbürgertum*. Geoff Eley, *Reshaping the German Right*, while attesting to the importance of the new nationalism as a system of belief that gave meaning to its adherents and alluding to the major role of professionals and civil servants in the nationalist associations (112, n. 2), more or less ignores the role of the *Bil-*

League and a member of the Pan-German League, though he came to reject the latter's anti-Semitism.[44] Time and again he urged the government to adopt an active cultural policy in foreign affairs, one that would expand the influence of German culture while respecting the cultural individuality of other national cultures.[45] The study of universal history, he explained in a lecture of 1912, would provide a knowledge of other cultures without which a German foreign cultural policy was impossible.[46] The new nationalism, then, was a salient ingredient of the new world view toward which Lamprecht and others were groping.

Lamprecht was by no means singular among the social scientists and philosophers of his day in seeking to formulate a new *Orientierungswissenschaft*, a discipline that would provide a sense of the relationship of the present to the past, of the meaning of the present age and the demands of the future. Though he insisted on the gap between ethical judgment and science, Max Weber—in a more sober and modest fashion—aimed at something similar in his studies of the connection between religious and economic life. Ferdinand Tönnies, Alfred Vierkandt, Werner Sombart, and others were engaged in a similar enterprise which they, like Weber, termed sociology. Karl Lamprecht, Wilhelm Wundt, and Felix Krueger were members of the German Sociological Association (Deutsche Gesellschaft für Soziologie) and dealt with sociological writings in their seminars.[47] In the Wilhelmine era a commitment to sociology rested less on a shared definition of the discrete subject matter or methodology of the discipline than on the common search of historians, economists, and philosophers for such an *Orientierungswissenschaft*.

There were therefore numerous links connecting the concerns of Freyer's major teachers with the youth movement, the reform movements, the new nationalism, and the emerging discipline of sociology. It was in this web of persons and organizations that Freyer spent his most formative years, and it was from this cultural matrix that both his conception of sociology and his radical conservatism emerged.

---

dungsbürgertum as a distinct social group. Thus, as one critic has noted, the book implicitly raises but does not answer the question of "the mediation of political ideology within society and the rise of new value-systems." See Wolfgang Mock, " 'Manipulation von oben' oder Selbstorganisation an der Basis?," 374.

[44] Schönebaum, "Lamprecht," 422–23; Wiese-Schorn, "Lamprecht," 394.

[45] Wiese-Schorn, "Lamprecht," 381–82. On the rise of professorial politicking after 1906 see Rüdiger vom Bruch, *Wissenschaft, Politik und öffentliche Meinung*.

[46] Wiese-Schorn, "Lamprecht," 388.

[47] See Dirk Käsler, "Die Streit um die Bestimmung der Soziologie auf den deutschen Soziologentagen, 1910–1930."

Freyer's Early Writings

The influence of the intellectual milieu in Leipzig upon Freyer is evident in the central concerns and presuppositions of his doctoral dissertation, which he began in Karl Lamprecht's seminar on German cultural history in 1910 and completed in 1911.[48] The dissertation was entitled *The History of the History of Philosophy in the Eighteenth Century*, and one is inclined to agree with the evaluation of one of his sponsors that he managed to do a good deal with a rather boring topic.[49] His success was due in part to his analytic skill, to his broad approach to the topic, and not least to the personal passion that he brought to bear upon the central issues of the work.

Freyer took pains to sketch the methodological presuppositions of his work, which were hermeneutic, holistic, and dialectical. To understand (*verstehen*) a particular historical idea, he wrote, means to determine the motive behind it, and this in turn involves recognizing its place within a philosophy as a whole.[50] The aim of the history of philosophy ought to be to understand each previous philosophical system as a unified whole (*Einheit* or *Ganzheit*),[51] based on a particular view of the world (*Weltanschauung*).[52] The task of the historian was to elucidate the particular structure of historical objects, but also to see them dialectically, as part of a historical series that contains its own contradictions and hence leads to its own dissolution.[53]

It is no coincidence that all this had a very Hegelian ring, for Lamprecht, Wundt, and Krueger had all been led by their quest for total and developmental historical explanations back to Hegel's work, though all three remained critical of its speculative nature. Krueger had studied in Berlin with Wilhelm Dilthey, the man most responsible for the renewed interest in Hegel, and was engaged in trying to develop a holistic and historicist psychology in keeping with Dilthey's methodological writings.[54] Freyer's own fascination with Hegel's thought was typical of the wider neo-Hegelian wave that began to sweep over German philosophy and social science in the decade before the First World War—part of the new search for synthesis and for an *Orientierungs-*

---

[48] In his official evaluation of the dissertation Lamprecht noted that it originated in his seminar (UAL, Promotionsakte Freyer). The official sponsor of the dissertation was Johannes Volkelt, the chaired professor of philosophy; Freyer took two courses from him but does not seem to have been much influenced by him.

[49] The comment is Volkelt's (UAL, Promotionsakte Freyer).

[50] Karl Lamprecht, gen. ed., *Beiträge zur Kultur- und Universalgeschichte* (1912), vol. 16: *Geschichte der Geschichte der Philosophie im achtzehnten Jahrhundert*, by Johannes Freyer, 8–13.

[51] Ibid., 86, 90.

[52] Ibid., 90–91.

[53] Ibid., 146.

[54] Felix Krueger, *Über Entwicklungspsychologie* (1915), 20–21.

wissenschaft—and reached its apogee at about the time when Freyer published his own *Theorie des objektiven Geistes* in 1923. Neo-Hegelianism, like most "neo-" movements, was far from accepting the thought of its namesake in its entirety, as will become apparent in our discussion of Freyer's work of the 1920s. Yet even Freyer's first major work, his doctoral dissertation, appeared under the sign of Hegel.[55]

The theme that Freyer set out to investigate in his dissertation was the very problem that most exercised the youth movement, namely the relationship of authority to history. For those who, like Freyer, felt themselves to have cast off the authority of their own past, this was more than a merely "academic" issue.

The Enlightenment, he wrote, counterposed to traditional authority derived from the past its own ideal of authority. This new authority was based upon the assumption of the Enlightenment that there existed universal reason, which in turn presupposed a universal human nature.[56] The goal of the Enlightenment was to mold the world according to universal norms derived from universal reason.[57]

Through his study of Enlightenment historiography Freyer sought to explore the problematic relationship created by the world view of the Enlightenment toward the comprehension and appreciation of the past. Given its assumption of a universal human nature, Freyer wrote, the Enlightenment was unable to explain the reality of change in history;[58] given its assumption of a universal reason, it could not explain the change in the answers which philosophers of the past had posed to their questions, and it could not comprehend that the very questions which philosophers asked changed over time and place.[59] Enlightenment attempts to write the history of philosophy as a history of more or less correct answers to the same set of questions forced earlier systems of thought into a procrustean bed that distorted them beyond recognition.[60] Freyer judged the Enlightenment to have violated the philosophical systems of the past by submitting them to the Enlightenment's own standards. Since it presumed that the questions which philosophy had addressed had always been the same, but that its own age had been the first to answer them correctly and to begin to realize them in the world, the Enlightenment viewed itself as an age of progress.[61] Within this "progressive" view of history as

[55] On the neo-Hegelianism of the late Wilhelmine and Weimar years, see Windelband, *Erneuerung*; Georg Lukács, *Die Zerstörung der Vernunft*, vol. 3, chapter 5; Heinrich Levy, *Die Hegel-Renaissance in der deutschen Philosophie*; and the discussion of Freyer's neo-Hegelianism in chapter 3.

[56] Johannes Freyer, *Geschichte*, 2–3.
[57] Ibid., 27.
[58] Ibid., 3.
[59] Ibid., 38.
[60] Ibid., 39, 86.
[61] Ibid., 55ff.

culminating in the present, the past became little more than a history of error.

Freyer's critique of the Enlightenment was an expression of his own romantic and historicist presuppositions, which are revealed not only in his explicit methodological strictures but in his obiter dicta as well. Freyer shared the respect for the particular and unique in history and that delight in the multiplicity, variety, and diversity of culture displayed by Herder and later by the romantics.[62] The Enlightenment's universalist, rationalist view of man and history, Freyer wrote, could not appreciate "the diversity of actual life"[63] because it proceeded without regard for the intrinsic value of that which was foreign to it.[64]

The belief in universal moral norms derivable from reason was one that Freyer did not share. "The [moral] certainty of the Enlightenment is hard to recapture," he wrote, "in an age like ours, for which relativism is an accepted principle, or which at least regards the relationship between norm and reality as a mediated one."[65] He made it clear that his own world view was historical, and that each philosophy could be properly understood and judged only by the values peculiar to its age.[66] Freyer's view was thus historicist, if we mean by historicism the belief that all human communities, values, and indeed human nature itself are products of history and hence in a continuous process of change.

The heritage of the German historical school of social science, with its affinities to romantic philosophy, was very much alive among Freyer's teachers at Leipzig. Both Lamprecht and Wundt consciously harked back to the contention of the historical school that the ultimate unit of history was the *Volk*, and that culture in the widest sense —including beliefs, institutions, and economic systems—must ultimately be understood as the expression of a collective spirit (*Volksgeist*) or soul (*Volksseele*).[67] Freyer's teacher of economics, Karl Bücher, was a representative of the historical school of economics. In contradistinction to the attempt of neoclassical political economy to derive universal laws of economic behavior from the assumptions of marginal utility theory, the historical school pursued empirical research out of the conviction that basic motives of economic life differed radically over time.[68]

---

[62] On the tradition of German historicism, see Friedrich Meinecke, *Die Enstehung des Historismus*; Hans-Georg Gadamer, *Truth and Method*, 153–203; and Georg C. Iggers, *The German Conception of History*, chapter 1 passim.

[63] Freyer, *Geschichte*, 150–51.

[64] Ibid., 42.

[65] Ibid., 3.

[66] Ibid., 26.

[67] Willy Hellpach, "Geschichte als Sozialpsychologie, zugleich eine Epikrise über Karl Lamprecht"; Wundt, *Elemente*, introduction. See also Schultz, "History," passim.

[68] See the works cited in n. 34 as well as Eric Roll, *History of Economic Thought*, 303–11.

Thus, as we might expect, Freyer concluded his dissertation with the observation that it was only in the writings of Herder, in those of the German historical school of the early nineteenth century, and ultimately in Hegel's history of philosophy that the universalist, rationalist perspective of the Enlightenment was overcome. It was only their work, Freyer wrote, that made possible a real appreciation for and understanding of the past.[69] The quote from Hegel that Freyer used as the motto of his dissertation summed up what in his view was the Enlightenment's essential error: "Nature reaches its goal by the most direct route, but the way of the spirit is through mediation, a circuitous route."[70]

Spurred on by a sense of alienation, Freyer and his comrades had rebelled against a spiritual climate that they perceived as stultifying. The naturalistic, positivistic spiritual climate of the late nineteenth century was clearly in decline, brought down in part by the dissatisfaction expressed in the *Jugendbewegung* and its allied movements. As yet, however, the claim of the youth movement to provide an alternative order was based merely on the emotional intensity that it embodied. Within the youth movement—indeed, within Freyer's own Serakreis—there was no consensus: *völkisch* and socialistic, ascetic and aesthetic, individualistic and collectivistic trends were juxtaposed, sometimes in the same individual. What was needed was a new science that would articulate the ethos of the new reform movement.

Freyer's academic teachers had taught him to regard the standard of universal reason as a chimera and as a threat to the intrinsic values of the cultural past. He also imbibed from them the desire to create a new social science that would help men orient themselves within history. It was to the development of a social science suspicious of the claims of universal reason that Freyer devoted most of the next two decades.

Science and the Quest for Community

Freyer sought to remain within the orbit of the youth movement, which he regarded as the catalyst of a new social order. After completing his doctorate in 1911 he became a teacher at the Freischulgemeinde Wickersdorf, one of the few institutionalized embodiments of the *Jugendbewegung*.[71] The "Free Community School" was founded in 1906 by Gustav Wynecken, a pedagogue and advocate of a new "youth culture" in which "youth" would be recognized as a

[69] Johannes Freyer, *Geschichte*, 150–52.

[70] "Die Natur kommt auf dem kürzesten Weg zu ihrem Ziel; aber der Weg des Geistes ist die Vermittlung, der Umweg."

[71] Freyer, "Lebenslauf," 1919. UAL, PA Freyer, 2.

distinct social group with its own needs and demands. There were close ties between the Freischulgemeinde and the Serakreis: Diederichs published the school's annual reports, and several members of the Serakreis became teachers at Wickersdorf.[72]

A boarding school located not far from Leipzig, the Freischulgemeinde was a model of progressive pedagogy. It was coeducational and stressed the active participation of the pupils in the government of the community. Through instruction in art and music, an active experimental approach to natural science, and a compulsory program of gynmastics and athletics it aimed at the development of all facets of the individual; but it objected in principle to "unfettered individualism" and sought to convey a sense of mutual responsibility to its students.[73] The school was too progressive for the provincial educational authorities, who objected to the unorthodox religious instruction at Wickersdorf, where a course on the history of religion had replaced dogmatic instruction. Wynecken departed under government pressure in 1910, and the school was led by his successor, Martin Luserke, when Freyer taught there in 1911–12.[74] Under Luserke's leadership the school acquired a more nationalist tone. It held a celebration to mark the two-hundredth anniversary of the birth of Friedrich the Great. Among the celebrants was Hans Freyer, who offered a character sketch of Friedrich, a figure who continued to interest him for several decades.[75] Impressed by Wickersdorf, Freyer became an "exterior member" of the school after completing his year of teaching in 1912.[76] The Freischulgemeinde provided him with another experience of life in a closed community of youth.

Freyer spent the most formative years of his late adolescence and early manhood within the Serakreis and the Freischulgemeinde, each of them self-contained communities of common purpose. But these groups and others like them were youth groups and thus inherently incapable of permanent perpetuation. Their members had eventually to return to a larger world from which they had come, but which had been increasingly delegitimated in their eyes. Participation in a communitarian subculture furthered inner estrangement from the dominant institutions of society. This dynamic, which was common to many groups in the youth movement, therefore raised the problem of the relationship of the members of the Serakreis to the larger society around them. It is a problem that informs much of Freyer's early work.

[72] On Wickersdorf, see Linse, "Jugendkulturbewegung."

[73] Martin Luserke, *Die Freie Schulgemeinde Wickersdorf*.

[74] Martin Luserke, *Vierter Jahresbericht der Freien Schulgemeinde Wickersdorf* (1912).

[75] Ibid., 34.

[76] 26. *Bericht an die auswärtigen Mitglieder und*

The internal dynamics of the youth movement also raised the questions of authenticity and commitment. In October 1913, at the initiative, among others, of Diederichs and the Serakreis, over one thousand members of the movement gathered at the Hohe Meißner near Kassel to commemorate the centennial of the Wars of Liberation, in a deliberate countercelebration to the official commemoration in Leipzig, which they deprecated as mere "Hurrah-Patriotismus."[77] Among those attending, as a member of the Serakreis, was Hans Freyer. The assembled youth perceived themselves as the avant-garde of a wider movement of spiritual renewal and the event as a possible turning point in German history.[78] But it was far from clear to them in what direction history ought to turn. The official speakers included representatives of the highly divergent currents within the reform movement: aesthetic reformers, heralds of a "youth culture," advocates of abstinence from alcohol and tobacco, *völkisch* nationalists, and socialist agitators.[79] The concluding resolution of the convocation, adopted after a talk by Martin Luserke of the Freischulgemeinde Wickersdorf,[80] was as decisive in tone as it was vague in content:

The Free German Youth intends to shape its life in keeping with its authentic mission, with authentic responsibility and inner veracity. For this inner freedom we stand united under all circumstances.[81]

But what did authenticity mean? Having asserted the freedom to choose authentically, how was one to decide *what* was authentically to be chosen? The movement prided itself on its preparedness to commit itself to some spiritual principle and to some larger whole. But to which principle and to what whole? These were the dilemmas facing the youth movement in general—and Hans Freyer in particular—in the wake of the Meißner rally. It was to the resolution of these problems that Freyer's prewar essays and his wartime work, *Antäus* were dedicated.

In the fall of 1913 Hans Freyer came to Berlin in order to further his education and begin work toward his habilitation.[82] It was probably the desire to study with the philosopher Georg Simmel that attracted him there. Freyer attended all of Simmel's lectures at the university and even visited several times at Simmel's home. Among Freyer's circle of friends in Berlin, several of them

Freunde der F.S.G. Wickersdorf, Dez. 1912.

[77] Flitner, "Wilhelm Flitner," 158–59; Kindt, ed., *Jugendbewegung*, 484–520.

[78] Jakob Müller, *Die Jugendbewegung als deutsche Hauptrichtung neukonservativer Reform*, 101–2.

[79] Ibid., 101–5.

[80] Kindt, ed., *Jugendbewegung*, 519.

[81] Ibid.

[82] Freyer, "Lebenslauf," 1919, UAL, PA Freyer, 3.

former members of the Serakreis, Simmel's philosophy of culture was a focus of attention.[83] Two essays that Freyer composed in Berlin in 1914 demonstrate the impact of Simmel on his thought—of Simmel's teaching, however, as filtered through the concerns of the *Jugendbewegung*.

Freyer's admiration for the work of Georg Simmel was shared by many others of his generation. Simmel's regular lectures at the University of Berlin drew several hundred listeners and filled his lecture halls to overflowing.[84] This was due in part to Simmel's sensitivity to the changing spiritual currents of his time. It was not that he pandered to his audience, but rather that his own development—from Spencerian positivism to neo-Kantianism and finally, in the past decade before his death in 1918, to a revival of certain romantic patterns of thought in his *Lebensphilosophie* (life philosophy)—paralleled the broader meanderings of the German *Zeitgeist*.[85] In describing the relationship between the protest of the youth movement against bourgeois culture and the recrudescence of the concepts of *Erlebnis* (experience) and *Leben* (life) in German thought, Hans-Georg Gadamer notes "the seismographical accuracy with which the philosophy of Georg Simmel reacted to these events."[86] Simmel's listeners even spoke of him as an embodiment of the new *Weltanschauung*.[87]

It was Simmel's philosophy of culture and the metaphysics of his *Lebensphilosophie* that attracted the young Freyer and left a permanent impression on the younger man's work.[88] What a teacher teaches and what a student learns are by no means the same thing, however. We will focus only on those aspects of Simmel's thought which particularly influenced Freyer and on the manner in which Freyer transformed the ideas he took from Simmel to meet his own, very different purposes.

The central theme of Simmel's philosophy of culture is the dialectic of dynamism and stasis in human existence.[89] Culture begins with the life of the individual, conceived as a bundle of prerational desires, as yet undifferentiated

---

[83] Hans Freyer to Michael Landmann, 22 February 1966, Nachlaß Landmann, Staatsbibliothek Preußischer Kulturbesitz, Berlin.

[84] See the memoirs collected in Kurt Gassen and Michael Landmann, eds., *Buch des Dankes an Georg Simmel*.

[85] On the stages of Simmel's development, see Max Frischeisen-Köhler, *Georg Simmel*; Hans Liebeschutz, *Von Georg Simmel zu Franz Rosenzweig*, 103ff.; and Michael Landmann, "Georg Simmel: Konturen seines Denkens."

[86] Gadamer, *Truth*, 57.

[87] Kurt Gassen, "Georg Simmel," in Gassen and Landmann, eds., *Buch*, 302.

[88] By the time Freyer came to study with him, Simmel had turned away decisively from his earlier sociological interests. Georg Simmel to Vorstand der Deutschen Gesellschaft für Soziologie, 11 October 1913, NT.

[89] The best work on Simmel's philosophy of culture is Rudolph H. Weingartner, *Experience and Culture: The Philosophy of Georg Simmel*. Simmel's major essays on the philosophy of culture are collected in his *Philosophische Kultur*, 3d ed.

and in constant flux. When some of man's needs or desires are frustrated, he creates instrumentalities—from tools, to concepts, to social institutions—to meet them. In time these instrumentalities become "objective culture": they acquire a fixity and a validity independent of their creator and of the circumstances of their creation.[90] It is this continuing process of objectification that makes culture possible. The objectification of subjective experience makes it possible to pass on experience over time and is therefore the basis of tradition.[91] The multiplication of cultural objects not only makes life richer, Simmel taught; it also makes human freedom possible. The multiplicity of cultural objects from which to choose makes possible that choice which is the prerequisite of freedom.[92]

The dynamic of subjective experience and objective culture was therefore a prerequisite of individual self-development. By adapting existing culture to his own inner needs—by internalizing the experience that had once been objectified—the individual became self-cultivated and developed more fully than would ever be possible in isolation. By virtue of objective culture, of traditions and institutions, each individual and each generation was spared the need to begin *de novo*.

Alongside Simmel's affirmative portrait of the relationship of culture to life was a more critical thrust. Already present in his *Philosophy of Money* (1900), this more pessimistic evaluation of the role of culture was to grow in emphasis in Simmel's work and was most succinctly expressed in his concept of the "tragedy of culture."[93] He meant the tendency of the objective, fixed forms that man had created out of his own needs to acquire a life and dynamism of their own, which would ultimately confound and frustrate man's subjective needs. Objective culture was of real value to the individual only insofar as he could assimilate it and make it his own. Unfortunately, Simmel felt, the increasing division of labor in society had upset the balance between objective culture and subjective culture in the modern era.[94] The division of labor and the increasing complexity of modern life meant that amid an explosion of objective cultural

---

[90] This dialectic of dynamic subjectivity and static objective creations was expressed by Simmel in a variety of terminologies in the course of his life: as the relationship of subjective to objective culture, of life to form, or of life to more-than-life. The underlying notion was the same in each case. Freyer too moved with ease and imprecision between these various terminologies.

[91] Georg Simmel, *The Philosophy of Money*

(1900), 453.

[92] Ibid., 505, 297, 469.

[93] The essay originally appeared as Georg Simmel, "Der Begriff und die Tragödie der Kultur," *Logos* 2 (1911–12); it was reprinted in Georg Simmel, *Das individuelle Gesetz: Philosophische Exkurse*, 116–47.

[94] Ibid., 145.

products the individual had to become more specialized and one-sided. This cultural overload led to a sense of frustration in the individual and to a cultural malaise. While devoting themselves to the accumulation and perfection of techniques, men had lost a sense of ultimate purpose. Modernity was thus characterized by the increasing domination of means over ends, by an ever-increasing number of possibilities, none of which seemed compelling.[95]

So it was that Simmel's philosophy of culture increasingly took on strains of cultural criticism.[96] Simmel was not alone in describing modernity as characterized by the growth of technical means and the eclipse of ultimate goals: the theme was already audible in the work of the German romantics and was expressed, with variations, in the "classic" works of Wilhelmine social thought, including Tönnies' *Community and Society*, Sombart's *Modern Capitalism*, and Max Weber's *Protestant Ethic*. It was Simmel, however, who developed the theme most explicitly. In so doing he articulated feelings and perceptions that were expressed less systematically and eloquently by the members of the youth movement.

Another key concept in Simmel's later work that was of particular interest to Hans Freyer was that of *Leben*. The term is, of course, remarkably vague and functions in Simmel's later thought (as in Dilthey's) as something of a deus ex machina.[97] Yet it had two connotations in Simmel's usage that were particularly significant.

On the one hand, it is a negative concept, meant to emphasize that man is constituted by more than just his rational capacities. Our comprehension of life, Simmel emphasized, is distorted when we try to analyze it into isolated, component parts; in fact, all aspects of the individual were inextricably intertwined.[98] In describing the individual's moral experience Simmel therefore sought to consider what he termed the whole life of the individual (*Gesamtleben des Individuums*), the totality of our being (*Totalität unseres Wesens*). This was the organicistic connotation of *Leben*.[99]

[95] Simmel, *Money*, 483. On this theme in the work of Simmel and of other sociologists of the Wilhelmine era, see Kurt Lenk, *Marx in der Wissenssoziologie*, chapter 1, "Das tragische Bewußtsein in der deutschen Soziologie"; Arthur Mitzman, *Sociology and Estrangement*, chapter 1.

[96] See Hans-Joachim Lieber, *Kulturkritik und Lebensphilosophie*, especially his essay "Kulturkritik und Gesellschaftstheorie im Denken Georg Simmels."

[97] At various times Simmel's use of the word seemed to connote unconscious drives, consciousness, creativity, and biological existence; it was used more or less synonymously with soul, psyche, or personality. On Dilthey's promiscuous use of the term, see Michael Ermarth, *Wilhelm Dilthey: The Critique of Historical Reason*, 349.

[98] Georg Simmel, "Das individuelle Gesetz: Ein Versuch über das Prinzip der Ethik," *Logos* 4 (1913). The essay is reprinted in Simmel, *Das individuelle Gesetz* (to which page references refer), 181.   [99] Ibid., 193.

A second connotation was vitalistic. In Simmel's late work the term *Leben* is often associated with the image of a stream or river: *Leben* was said to "flow." Life, Simmel taught, was in constant flux.[100] Objective culture, however—including systems of thought and social institutions—was fixed and static. Thus the dominant image in Simmel's *Lebensphilosophie* was of the unstoppable flow of the current of life, resisted by the congealed forms of its own past activity. The image fit perfectly with the self-image of the *Jugendbewegung* as a dynamic, youthful force restrained and straining against the ossified social and cultural institutions of Wilhelmine Germany.

Freyer may also have found Simmel's concept of *Leben* compelling because it so effectively captured the underlying metaphysic of German historicism once the latter had been cut off from its earlier moorings in Christianity. The major philosophers associated with *Lebensphilosophie*—Nietzsche, Dilthey, and Simmel—were all products of German historicist thought. With its stress on history as change and flux and on the uniqueness of individual *Leben* and its irreducibility to general rules, *Lebensphilosophie* represented the thinking through of historicism to its ultimate premises.[101] The upshot of this process was a moral relativism, as Dilthey, Simmel, Weber, and Troeltsch were ultimately to recognize.[102] The problem of moral relativism, of the arbitrariness of any particular ethical choice once it was realized that all ethical systems were passing products of history rather than permanently valid truths discovered by a universal reason, was one with which Freyer was to wrestle in his early writings.[103] It was a problem to which Simmel suggested a solution in an essay of 1913 entitled "The Individual Law."[104] The essay had an immediate impact on Freyer and influenced much of his work through the 1920s.

[100] Ibid., 205. Simmel's concept of *Leben* was influenced by the work of Henri Bergson, whom Simmel befriended and whose thought he helped disseminate in Germany.

[101] Lieber, 118–19.

[102] The problem was expressed with pith and pathos by Dilthey in 1903: "I undertook to investigate the nature and conditions of historical consciousness—a critique of historical reason. This task led me to the most general of problems: a seemingly insoluble contradiction arises if we pursue historical consciousness to its last consequences. The finitude of every historical phenomenon, whether it be a religion, an ideal, or a philosophic system, hence the relativity of every sort of human conception about the connectedness of things, is the last word of the historical world view. All flows in the process; nothing remains stable. On the other hand, there arises the need of thought and the striving of philosophy for universally valid cognition. The historical way of looking at things [*die geschichtliche Weltanschauung*] has liberated the human spirit from the last chains which natural science and philosophy have not yet torn asunder. But where are the means for overcoming the anarchy of convictions which threatens to break in on us?" (Quoted in Iggers, *German*, 143–44.)

[103] For a succinct discussion of the problem of historicism and relativism in late Wilhelmine social thought, see Guy Oakes, "Methodological Ambivalence: The Case of Max Weber," 594–98.

[104] First published in 1913 (see n. 99).

It was Simmel's dissatisfaction with Kantian ethics that led him to the notion of "the individual law." Ethics for Kant were universal by definition: it was precisely the universalizability of the categorical imperative—"to act so that I could also will that my maxim should become a universal law"—that made its authority incumbent upon rational men. This rational ideal, never the real, phenomenal world, was the *source* of ethics according to Kant. Simmel objected to Kant's definition of ethics and to his account of moral experience. Kant's view of man, Simmel contended, was analytic and based on the extension of models drawn from Newtonian mechanics into the human sphere: Kant assumed that we can divorce part of man—his reason—from the rest of him. In fact, however, *Leben* is organic and indivisible. It is not by virtue of their reason that men act ethically.[105]

An ethical law, Simmel claimed, must have some inner connection to the individual who is to fulfill it. The perception of a law as *necessary* is based upon its correspondence to some state of affairs in the real world.[106] In opposition to what he termed Kant's "rational moralism," Simmel insisted that the sense of duty arises ultimately from the individual's life as a whole, as it exists in a particular time and place.[107] Since only individuals have life and since each life is particular, moral norms could pertain only to a particular individual in a particular time and place.[108]

Simmel insisted, however, that this relativist ethics need not be subjectivist, that is, totally dependent upon the personal, emotional disposition of the individual. Each individual, he maintained, is confronted by some objective "ought" that arises from his life and makes demands on it. There are absolute demands, even if they pertain only to individuals at a particular time and place.[109] Thus there is an "ought," a norm, which is rooted in real (*wirklich*) life and not in abstract, universal ideals.[110] Such an "ought" exists *in principle* whether or not it is actually acknowledged by the individual. But, Simmel noted, there is no assurance that the individual, subjective will is correct in its evaluation of the "ought" appropriate to its historical situation.[111] Simmel thus offered the tantalizing suggestion that ethics might be relative without being arbitrary, that there might be some objective ethic appropriate to each time and place. But he gave no real indication of how such an ethic was to be ascertained.

[105] Simmel, "Gesetz," 174–82.
[106] Ibid., 183–84.
[107] Ibid., 201, 205, 212, 215–16.
[108] Ibid., 217.
[109] Ibid., 218.
[110] Ibid., 230.
[111] Ibid., 218.

It was Simmel's distinction between an atemporal and unworldly "moralism" and an ethic of the historically particular that formed the central theme of Freyer's essay of 1914, entitled "The Material of Duty: A Study of Fichte's Later Ethical Theory."[112] Freyer's choice of subject was by no means fortuitous, for Fichte was among the favorite philosophers of the youth movement. In this scholarly study of the transformation of Fichte's theory of ethics Freyer reflected on what he regarded as a turning point in ethical thought.

The key problem for the young Fichte, according to Freyer, was the preservation of the transcendental, pure will in the material world.[113] This conception of the moral will as transcendental—as part of an eternal, ideal realm—was an immediate legacy from Kant. But its broader antecedents were in Christianity and in the classical Protestant theory of duty.[114] Fichte's problem of the preservation of a transcendental, pure will in the historical, material world was therefore a phase of the conceptual and moral system of Christianity, in which the believer attempts to order his life according to the intervention of the transcendent into his soul.[115] Even when Protestantism was secularized, Freyer wrote (with a reference to Max Weber and to Nietzsche's *Genealogy of Morals*), the structure of its ethics remained the same. The result of this residual Christianity in Fichte's moral philosophy was, according to Freyer, a devaluation of "the real context of life" (*wirklicher Lebenszusammenhang*), of the actual historical communities in which individuals live and act.[116]

In Fichte's later thought (especially in his *Sittenlehre* of 1812), Freyer discovered a very different view of the nature of ethical action, one that he clearly favored. In Fichte's later writings the absolute was expressed in a multiplicity of forms *within* history, in the *Völker* (peoples), each of which constituted an ethical order (*sittliche Ordnung*).[117] This historicization and particularization of moral values was a transformation of cardinal import, for it overcame the problems inherent in "pure moralism," that is, in the Christian tradition and its secularized philosophical legacy.[118] To embrace such an ethic thus meant to break definitively with the heritage of Christianity.

It meant no less than to embrace the implications of Simmel's individual law. But by embracing Simmmel's historicist, individualist notion of ethics as it ap-

---

112 Hans Freyer, "Das Material der Pflicht: Eine Studie über Fichtes spätere Sittenlehre" (1920). This article and the article on utopia discussed below were both written by Freyer in Berlin in 1913–14 (Freyer, "Lebenslauf," 1919, UAL, PA Freyer). Their delayed publication was almost certainly due to the intervening war.

113 Freyer, "Material," 129.
114 Ibid., 129–30.
115 Ibid., 135.
116 Ibid., 129–35.
117 Ibid., 152.
118 Ibid., 145–53.

peared in Fichte's later thought, Freyer drew implications that had not been intended by Simmel himself, implications that were indeed at odds with the thrust of Simmel's concerns. Simmel's essay on the individual law was one expression of his broader attempt to defend the individual—the single human being—from those philosophical systems, social developments, and cultural trends which threatened his freedom to develop his unique, particular self in a balanced fashion. Simmel was ultimately a liberal, an advocate of cultural individualism, and a child of the classical German ideal of self-cultivation (*Bildung*). For Simmel, the ultimate repository of a *telos* in history was the individual.[119] The individual law for Simmel was an assertion of freedom.

Freyer's ultimate concern—and that of many of his comrades in the youth movement—was quite different. As children of the *Bürgertum*, they were not necessarily wealthy, but they were sufficiently well off to remain relatively unencumbered by economic constraints in their choice of career. Offspring of the *Bildungsbürgertum*, they found that the guardians of *Bildung*—the humanistic professoriate—were themselves in search of orientation. Having rejected the culture and often the religion of their ancestors, they found themselves faced by multiple cultural choices, none of which seemed to be compelling. The dominant intellectual tradition within the humanities and social sciences asserted that all human values and communities were changing products of history. But freed of the older premise that history itself was a product of divine providence, historicism seemed to result in relativism, in a situation in which all choices were arbitrary. Under these circumstances it was not the *absence* but the *surfeit* of freedom that seemed to threaten Freyer and his comrades.

In Fichte's historicist, particularist view of ethics, as Freyer pointed out at length, moral order was secured only within the historical community of the *Volk*. This *collective* subject was the bearer of historical purpose. Thus the ethical was no longer a matter of individual decision, no longer based on a merely "formal" freedom of choice. Rather, the truly ethical situation was one in which freedom of the will is replaced by historical necessity. Freyer's study of Fichte thus concluded that it was not freedom but necessity that constituted a truly ethical order.[120] It was this sense of historically dictated necessity that Freyer and his comrades lacked.

Another essay written during the first half of 1914 (but published only after

---

[119] See Liebeschutz, *Von Georg Simmel*.   [120] Freyer, "Material," 149–53.

the war), entitled "The Problem of Utopia," picked up where the essay on Fichte left off.[121] Once again Freyer adopted concepts from Simmel but put them to uses their author did not intend.

The central problem of the essay was the search of the individual for incontestable values within "the stream of history," for some permanence in the face of human life, "which so quickly passes and vanishes without a trace."[122] It was, in short, the problem of moral orientation in a world of change. Again Freyer rejected the answer offered by "pure moralism," that of the pure will which acts in accordance with eternal norms regardless of its actual impact in the historical world. On the contrary, he argued, our sense of purpose comes from participation in the great "objectifications of culture," from membership in a real historical group.[123] In opposition to the ethos of "pure moralism" based upon the "free autonomous self," Freyer proposed an objective ethic based on the participation of the individual in a particular moment of a historical culture.[124]

Such an ethic was by no means conservative in its implications, Freyer emphasized. On the contrary, it could at times be radical, for change was intrinsic to human *Geist* (used here as an equivalent of the term *Leben* in Simmel's essay), which eventually came into conflict with any given cultural order.[125] There were eras of human history in which the objective cultural order harnessed and successfully restrained the energy of human *Geist* by providing it with a unified direction. Such ages of repose were ages of "culture" in the highest sense of the word.[126] But the same dynamic, developing energy that makes such eras possible ensures that they will not last forever. When an existing society no longer fulfills the needs of *Geist*, when social and cultural forms have become hollow, an objective ethic demands their reform or the transformation of society by revolution.[127]

The notion that the tensions of the present would be resolved in a future era of stability, Freyer recognized, was hardly new. In fact, he wrote, it had a long history and was the essence of the Christian chiliastic ideal of the "the third kingdom" (*das dritte Reich*).[128] But the ideal of the third *Reich* lived on even when men stopped believing in God and when they acquired an activist view

[121] Hans Freyer, "Das Problem der Utopie" (1920). On dating the composition of this essay, see n. 112.

[122] Ibid., 321.

[123] Ibid., 323–25.

[124] Ibid., 324.

[125] Ibid., 325.

[126] Ibid.

[127] Ibid.

[128] Ibid., 326.

of their role in history. When man recognizes that the world can be transformed in keeping with his reason, chiliastic hope is transformed into political
intention.[129]

At this point, in what had been a rather scholarly essay, Freyer interpolated
a dialogue between two unidentified friends. The dialogue is steeped in the
sensibility of the youth movement. It probably contains fragments of conversations in which Freyer had been involved at the Meißner rally, or perhaps it
was the distillation of many an inner dialogue of his own:

> "You accuse our age of having enervated man and having sucked all chivalry out of
> him, body and soul."
>
> "I condemn it because I won't find any point to life until a healthy, daring, proud man
> has been re-created. I'll devote my powers to making him possible once again!"
>
> "Don't you see, my friend, that we must pay a price for the commodities which our
> culture provides? That we can't put heroes behind our machines? That the knight had
> to become a bureaucrat and the yeoman a docile bourgeois to make possible the artificial
> order in which we live?"
>
> "I'm determined to give up those commodities that common opinion values above all
> if they must be bought at the price of the only type of humanity that I truly value. I shall
> eliminate all the obstacles that stand between us and our ideal."
>
> "How can you repeal the last few centuries of history?"
>
> "The natural sciences teach me the conditions of physical health: psychology will show
> me the conditions required to create those qualities with which I would endow the soul."
>
> "I'm afraid you'll find your worst enemy in those men who have become accustomed
> to the flabby atmosphere of civilization."
>
> "I know the power of laws and the means to make them effective. I'll surround men
> with a world that will compel those virtues which I find missing today. In the form of art
> and in new myths I'll lay their ideals before their eyes. In new schools I'll train their
> senses, their conscience, their taste."
>
> "Hold on, my friend; you're writing a whole utopia!"[130]

Reverting to a more scholarly tone, Freyer constructed an ideal-typical utopia. Utopia, he wrote, was intended as both a cultural ideal and a cultural reality to be realized within history. In utopia, Freyer wrote, "the stream of history
is dammed up. . . . It is meant to arise in history but to endure."[131] In order to
endure it must have internal equilibrium, and this in turn can be achieved only

---

[129] Ibid., 327. This was the major theme in the
work of another student of Simmel's, Ernst
Bloch.

[130] Ibid., 327–28.
[131] Ibid., 328.

through institutions that create the virtues necessary to preserve the utopian order. Each historical utopia, Freyer showed—using More's *Utopia*, Campanella's *City of the Sun*, and Plato's *Republic* as examples—was based upon the premise of a science that would maintain this self-perpetuating system, thus creating an enduring order in the flux of history.[132]

The utopias of the past, from Plato to Cabet, all shared the same fatal flaw, according to Freyer. While their creators were convinced that their utopias were constructed on scientific principles, none of them had discovered a scientific path toward implementing their schemes. They all came to depend, ultimately, on either force or persuasion to bring about the transformation from the flawed present to the utopian future, and they usually looked to a powerful politician who could be persuaded to use the might at his disposal to realize the utopian scheme. Scientific in designing their ideal states, the utopians abandoned science when the problem of implementation arose.[133] Had they remained true to their scientific pretense, they would have had to turn to sociology, to conduct an inventory of the factors in the present that might lead in the direction of their utopian goals.[134]

The exception to this rule was the "scientific socialism" of Karl Marx, which claimed to have discovered the path from the present to the future through a scientific grasp of the causal laws of historical development. It was possible, Freyer acknowledged, to predict individual historical events using methods analogous to the natural sciences. But the direction of history as a whole could not be grasped by a science of general laws. The future could not be predicted through scientific means, for it ultimately depended on the free will of each member of the current generation.[135]

Yet despite the unscientific nature of utopias past, Freyer ended his essay with an affirmation of the role of utopian thought in human history. Utopianism, he concluded, remained valid as a creative form of practical reason.[136]

Radical conservatism as a political and cultural movement is generally identified with the Weimar Republic. Like so many of the innovative cultural movements of the Weimar era, radical conservatism was incubated in the Wilhelmine *Reich*. The same might be said for German sociology: while it achieved academic and intellectual legitimation in the 1920s, most of its "classic" works had already been written by the end of the First World War. Hans Freyer's ma-

---

[132] Ibid., 328ff.
[133] Ibid., 342–43.
[134] Ibid., 343–44.

[135] Ibid., 344–45.
[136] Ibid., 345.

jor works were all ahead of him when war broke out in the summer of 1914, but the lineaments of both his radical conservatism and his sociolological theory were already visible in his prewar writings.

The posture of the cultural circles with which Freyer identified toward much of the existing cultural, economic, and institutional order of Wilhelmine Germany was one of disdain, if not disgust. Through nascent counterinstitutions they sought to minimize contact with the fraternity student, the bourgeois, and the bureaucrat. While their critique of Wilhelmine Germany drew on diffuse sources, their own predicament became the ultimate warrant for their indictment. A cultural and political order that could not provide them with an "objective ethic," an ultimate purpose embodied in concrete institutions to which they might subordinate themselves, had by definition lost its authority. To Freyer the inability of the existing cultural forms to command his obedience—of "objective culture" to harness subjective *Leben*—was the ultimate proof of the hollowness of those forms, of the brittleness of existing institutions.

Yet the tone of Freyer's dissatisfaction with the culture and society of Wilhelmine Germany was not one of despair or even of pessimism. He and his comrades in the youth movement perceived themselves as a movement of total cultural renewal, as a future cultural order in embryo. In time Freyer came to see himself as the theoretician and spokesman of this movement.

It is characteristic of Freyer's radical conservative sensibility that he was obsessed by the reality of historical change, a reality that both attracted and repelled him. The social and intellectual sources of Freyer's awareness of the ubiquity of change are not difficult to discern. The growth of industrial capitalism in the Germany of his day was quite literally changing the landscape. In the last decades of imperial Germany, Saxony experienced a higher rate of population growth than any other major province. The population of Leipzig, less than 200,000 at the time of Freyer's birth in 1886, had swelled to over half a million in 1907, when Freyer began his university studies; and the sleepy town of Plagwitz in which he was born had become an industrial suburb and working-class stronghold.[137]

At least as important for Freyer's sense of change was the spiritual distance he had traversed from the pious Lutheranism of his home through the historicism of his college years to the explicitly post-Christian and often anti-Christian stance evident in his essays of 1914. Thus it is not surprising that he

[137] Karl Czok and Horst Thieme, eds., *Leipzig: Geschichte der Stadt in Wort und Bild*, 44–45.

fastened onto Simmel's notion of *Leben*, which stressed the inexorability of flux in the human world.

Freyer's desire to escape such contingency and insecurity is demonstrated in his essay on utopia. Utopia—the third *Reich*—was the social order in which "the stream of history is dammed up." The "problem of utopia" for Freyer was above all the problem of its realization. The science devoted to this purpose was sociology, whose task it would be to investigate those processes in the present which made possible an authoritative and hence stable order in the future. The development of such a science was to become his vocation.

CHAPTER TWO

War, Revolution, and Generational Mission, 1914–1920

Like so many of the intellectuals and aspiring intellectuals of his generation, Hans Freyer felt alienated from a society that seemed incapable of offering a sense of higher, collective purpose. It was the experience of the Great War that provided Freyer and part of his generation of the youth movement with an unanticipated solution to their dilemmas. How the war and its aftermath transformed their lives and reoriented their sense of generational mission is the subject of this chapter.

Interpreting the War

In keeping with the expectations and social privileges of the *Bildungsbürgertum*, Hans Freyer had fulfilled his military duty as a "one-year volunteer" after completing his doctorate. He served from 1912 to 1913 in the prestigious Royal Saxon Guard of Dresden before resuming his academic studies in Berlin. When the war broke out in 1914 he volunteered immediately and became a second lieutenant in his regiment. He spent most of the next four years on the western front.[1]

Freyer thrived as a junior officer and in later years looked back fondly on his years of command and camaraderie.[2] He displayed a great deal of military courage and by the end of the war had earned the Iron Cross First Class, the Iron Cross Second Class, and the *Heinrichsorden*, the Saxon equivalent of the *pour la mérite*. He was awarded the latter in April 1918 for conveying combat orders and field reports under fire to and from the frontmost lines of battle.[3] Freyer was seriously wounded twice. The symbolism of death and resurrection, so central to the iconography of World War I, was more than a symbolic

---

[1] On the privilege of one-year military service granted to university graduates in imperial Germany, see Ringer, *Decline*, 32. Hans Freyer, "Lebenslauf," UAL, PA Freyer, 3.

[2] Interview with Käthe Freyer, Münster, 23 February 1982.

[3] BAK, R21, Anhang Wissenschaftlerkartei, Hans Freyer. For Freyer's citation of merit see Georg Richter, ed., *Der Königlich Sächsische Militär–St. Heinrichs Orden*, 245.

experience in his case.[4] Shot through the stomach—a wound which was often fatal during the First World War—in 1915, he passed out believing he would die. When he awoke in a field hospital surrounded by nuns dressed in white, he thought he had gone to heaven. A head injury received on the Marne in July 1918 resulted in a partial loss of hearing and in the loss of a part of one earlobe—physical reminders of the war experience that accompanied him thereafter.[5]

These, then, are the "external" facts of Freyer's experience of the war, but they cannot explain what the war meant to him and for him. What the war signified for individuals can be understood only through the ideological filters through which they tried to make sense of it. In Freyer's case these filters were provided by his comrades in the youth movement and by the response of his academic mentors to the outbreak of the war.

Though the leading lights of German academic philosophy were regarded as part of the nation's elite, their prewar works conveyed a thinly veiled disgust with the dominant values of their society. With the outbreak of war, the sluice gates of self-restraint were opened, and from the humanistic professoriate poured a flood of criticism directed at Wilhelmine Germany. While the exhortative speeches by academic humanists struck a note of enthusiastic patriotism, their predominant theme was often that the war marked a turning point in the recent history of Germany, separating the decadent egoistic past from a more collectivistic and altruistic future.

Though the vocabulary and nuances varied from one academic author to another, their arguments had a common pattern.[6] The outbreak of war was attributed to British (and sometimes French and Russian) attempts to encircle Germany and prevent it from playing an independent role on the international stage; the war was thus legitimated as one of national self-defense.[7] Yet

[4] Freyer alludes to this experience in an autobiographical portion of his *Pallas Athene*, 66. On death and resurrection in the iconography of the First World War, see George L. Mosse, "National Cemeteries and National Revival: The Cult of the Fallen Soldiers in Germany," 4ff.

[5] Interview with Käthe Freyer; Hans Freyer to Felix Krueger, 24 August 1918, UAL, PA Krueger; Hans Freyer to Eugen Diederichs, 2 August 1918, Diederichs Archiv, Universitätsarchiv Jena.

[6] The most significant discussions of this academic war literature are Hermann Lübbe, *Poli-

tische Philosophie in Deutschland*, chapter 4; Klaus Schwabe, *Wissenschaft und Kriegsmoral*, chapter 2; Ringer, *Decline*, 180–99; and Klaus Vondung, "Deutsche Apokalypse 1914," in *Wilhelminische Bildungsbürgertum*. On the broader response of intellectuals to the war, see Roland Stromberg, *Redemption by War*; and Robert Wohl, *The Generation of 1914*.

[7] This was the opinion not only of Freyer's teacher Wilhelm Wundt, in his *Über den wahrhaften Krieg* (1914), but of the contributions to *Deutschland und der Weltkrieg*, ed. Otto Hintze et al. (1915), the most important collection of

the hardships that the war brought were discovered to be a blessing in disguise. The age before the war had been dominated by individual and group egoism: the war had now brought home to the individual the necessity of self-sacrifice on behalf of the nation, and a new spirit of national unity had resulted.[8] The professors hoped that this new sense of higher collective purpose would not be a temporary wartime mood but would be preserved in the postwar era, and they suggested that the leading role in preserving this new spirit of subordination to the concerns of the national collectivity would fall upon the young men now in uniform. To this end great efforts were made to publish these wartime lectures in huge editions, which were distributed to the troops.

Several of the themes conveyed by Freyer's academic teachers and mentors during the early years of the war were especially important for his subsequent intellectual and political development.

The first was a new stress on the legitimacy of national cultural particularity. Georg Simmel, one of the most cosmopolitan of thinkers, told an audience in September 1916 that while each nation had its own essence and inner potentialities, those of France and England had largely been played out, while Germany was only beginning to actualize its own potential.[9] Rivers of ink were spilled on this theme in the early years of the war. It was the subject, for example, of a widely read essay, "The Spirit of German Culture," by Ernst Troeltsch, who wrote that the "fateful moment" of the war had brought about "a revelation of the hidden or obscured cultural unity of the spirit. The inner connections are instinctively illuminated, and the spiritual unity flashes into view like lightning."[10]

Time and again it was asserted that German idealism, especially the thought of Fichte and Hegel, was not merely *a* philosophical current in German history but *the* characteristically German philosophy or *Weltanschauung*. The essence of German philosophy lay in its emphasis on the predominance of national culture, of *Gemeinschaft* and of the *Staat* over the desires of the individual.[11] Thus the wave of national unity experienced in the early war years was interpreted as the catalyst of a process that would transform the individualistic,

---

wartime writings by German academics.

[8] This view of events was exemplified by Emil Lederer's assertion that on the day of mobilization the existing *Gesellschaft* had been transformed into a *Gemeinschaft*; see Emil Lederer, "Zur Soziologie des Weltkriegs," 349.

[9] Georg Simmel, "Die Dialektik des deutschen Geistes" (September 1916), in his *Der Krieg und die geistigen Entscheidungen*, 35.

[10] Ernst Troeltsch, "Der Geist der deutschen Kultur," in *Deutschland und der Weltkrieg*, 69.

[11] Wilhelm Wundt, *Die Nationen und ihre Philosophie* (1915), 114–15; idem, *Die Weltkatastrophe und die deutsche Philosophie*, 5.

economistic ethos of the prewar *Reich* into a new, more collectivistic culture.[12]

The expansion of the economic role of the state during the war was welcomed by many German academics who had long harbored an antagonism toward capitalism. The most systematic herald of a new "national socialism" was Freyer's former instructor, Johann Plenge. Plenge coined the term "the ideas of 1914," which he contrasted with "the ideas of 1789." The nineteenth century had been "an essentially atomized, critical, disorganized century," dominated by the ideas of the French Revolution, which Plenge considered "an abstract idea of freedom of empty atomized individual wills." The twentieth century was to be dominated by "the ideas of 1914," "the ideas of German organization." "We are the twentieth century," he proclaimed, and he called for a state-organized economy in which the individual would subordinate his interests to those of the whole.[13] This neo-Hegelian emphasis upon the moral role of the state as a counterweight to the egoism engendered by a market economy was also present in the wartime writings of the philosophers Paul Natorp and Alois Riehl—both senior sympathizers with the youth movement—and the sociologist Werner Sombart. It was a theme that Freyer would push to an extreme in his political writings of the 1920s. Plenge's contrast between the spirit of the nineteenth century and that of the twentieth—a dichotomy that he adapted from Houston Stewart Chamberlain's *Myth of the Nineteenth Century*—was to become the *Leitmotiv* of Freyer's habilitation thesis, written shortly after the war.[14]

Georg Simmel was the philosopher to whom Freyer had felt most spiritually akin before the outbreak of the war, an affinity that was strengthened during the war itself. It was probably Simmel's wartime essays that most influenced Freyer during 1916 and 1917 when he was writing his second book, *Antäus*, and planning his third book, which he wrote in 1919.

Simmel's wartime writings shared many of the sentiments of his colleagues but added some novel interpretations of the war experience based on his philosophy of culture. The war, Simmel wrote in November 1914, marked a turning point, and while the future was difficult to predict he felt that "Germany

---

[12] Karl Lamprecht, *Krieg und Kultur: Drei vaterländische Vorträge* (1914), 53ff.; Wundt, *Die Weltkatastrophe*, 4.

[13] Johann Plenge, *1789 und 1914: Die symbolischen Jahre in der Geschichte des politischen Geistes* (1916), and *Der Krieg und die Volkswirtschaft* (1915), both quoted in Einhard Schrader, "Theorie und Praxis: Johann Plenges Pro-

gramm eines organisatorischen Sozialismus," 23.

[14] Plenge acknowledged Chamberlain as the source of his notion of the nineteenth century in a letter to Felix Krueger, 4 September 1934, Nachlaß Plenge, Universitätsbibliothek Bielefeld.

was pregnant with great possibilities." From the war, he hoped, would emerge the "new man" who had been much discussed in the prewar years. The introduction of rationing during the war and the relative poverty that would necessarily follow the physical destruction wrought by the war would, he hoped, lead to a turn away from the "Mammonism," the worship of money as an end in itself, that had dominated the previous decades.[15] More boldly, he offered what might be termed an existentialist explanation of the war experience and its cultural significance. In long eras of peace, Simmel observed, there is a tendency to confuse nonessential aspects of life with essential goals, since there is no need to distinguish the nonessential from the essential.[16] During the decades before the war "the disintegration and perversion of cultural life had reached an extreme" as the hypertrophication of cultural and technological means led to the eclipse of a sense of broader purpose. The war, however, presented an "absolute situation." It acted as a "unifying, simplifying and concentrating force," in which even individual self-preservation—the usual end of life—was clearly subordinated to the higher goal of national self-preservation.[17] The war had brought temporary respite from the emphasis on the nonessential, from the eclipse of ultimate goals by proximate means so characteristic of modern culture. It thus held out the possibility of surmounting "the rigidities and insularities that had turned our culture into a chaos of disjointed elements devoid of any common style."[18]

The war might also reverse the decline of a sense of community, Simmel suggested. In peacetime the means to which the individual devoted himself seemed to have no perceptible connection to the community as a whole. But in war the individual experiences the importance of his task for society as a whole, an experience most intense for the soldier on the field of battle.[19] Simmel suggested that this sense of reconciliation of individual pursuits and communal purposes might be carried over into a postwar era by those who had experienced it most intensely. This was the message that the philosopher whom many regarded as the embodiment of the *Zeitgeist* conveyed to his youthful admirers in the trenches.

For Freyer's generation of the youth movement, the war appeared as an unanticipated solution to their prewar dilemmas, including the vexing problem of the relationship of a movement of youth to adult society. Before the war the

[15] Georg Simmel, "Deutschlands innere Wandlung" (November 1914), and "Die Krisis der Kultur" (January 1916), both in his *Der Krieg*, 14–15, 56–57.

[16] Ibid., 59.
[17] Ibid., 64.
[18] Ibid., 59–62.
[19] Ibid., 11–12, 61.

notion of a separate "youth culture" had been proffered, but this solution was unacceptable to most of the ideologists of the movement and certainly to Freyer. Moreover, Freyer and his comrades of the Serakreis were of an age when even the most extended adolescence must give way to the prospect of adulthood. Suddenly the war forced them into the most adult of roles and soon into positions of responsibility as junior officers who daily confronted the task of keeping themselves and their subordinates alive. It bound Freyer's generation of the youth movement to adult concerns and the general society.

War and combat were not among the concerns of the prewar movement. Indeed, it is difficult to imagine less soldierly types than the members of the Serakreis with their philosophical, cultural, and folkloristic concerns. Among their prewar leaders—and among Freyer's friends—was Karl Brügmann, who had distinguished himself by gathering and publishing a collection of German folksongs and who carried on an extensive correspondence with Rainer Maria Rilke. Early in August 1914 he described to his comrades with a sense of foreboding the horrors and senselessness of the anticipated war.[20] Yet when the declaration of war came, Brügmann, his comrades in the Serakreis, and the ranks of the youth movement were among the first to volunteer. The call to sacrifice on behalf of the *Volk* was greeted almost with relief by those who had chided their society for failing to provide a higher sense of purpose in which the individual might partake. They came to the war not without fear but with a degree of enthusiasm that others—those with wives, children, or parents to support, for whom a sense of daily purpose had been unproblematic—were unlikely to match. The heroism of Langemarck, of German youth storming a fortress in Flanders and marching to their deaths singing the "Deutschlandlied," was a myth.[21] But like most myths it embellished a certain reality, a reality embodied in the members of the Serakreis in uniform. Brügmann led his fellow troops in the singing of folksongs as they marched off to battle—and died in an assault at the Plogsteedwald in Belgium in November 1914.[22] "The *Jugendbewegung*," one of Freyer's comrades later wrote, "interpreted the war as a sacred offering for the sake of the *Volksgemeinschaft*, as in mythical ages."[23]

In the widespread exhortation of the *Volksgemeinschaft* during the war years, the youth movement heard the echo of its own call for community. Now it

---

[20] Wilhelm Flitner, "Erinnerung an Karl Brügmann (1889–1914)," 95–101.

[21] Wohl, *Generation*, 48; Mosse, "National Cemeteries," 6.

[22] Flitner, "Erinnerung," 95–101; Hermann Nohl, "Vom deutschen Ideal der Geselligkeit: Zum Andenken Karl Brügmanns gewidmet," *Die Tat* (1915), 630–31.

[23] Wilhelm Flitner, "Der Krieg und die Jugend," 294.

seemed that—for a time at least—the experience of collective concern that had been confined to its small conventicles was transposed to the national level. This was true not only on the political scene, in which the *Burgfrieden* between the parties and the Kaiser's declaration "I no longer recognize parties; I recognize only Germans" seemed to eclipse the political and social conflicts of the immediate past. On a more intimate level the experience of active war service provided many of those in the youth movement with their first extended contact with members of the peasant and working classes. The experience of the *Schützengräbengemeinschaft*, of a community of the trenches, was certainly most intense for those who had long sought in vain for a larger community. That it was a temporary community constituted by a common threat was less likely to escape the common soldier, likely to be drawn from the lower classes, than his junior officer, who was more likely to be drawn from the bourgeoisie. For the common soldier, drawn from the peasantry or the working class, the war was a forced diversion from the pressing concerns of feeding and clothing one's family, and the end of war would mean a return to the civilian communities of village, church, and party. To his junior officer—especially if, like Freyer, he was the offspring of the educated bourgeoisie and a member of the youth movement—the collective threat provided by war might appear above all as the glue of a future national community.

Yet the war ultimately split the youth movement as it divided the German nation. The spirit of national unity that swept the country in the summer of 1914 was based on the almost universally held belief within Germany that the country was fighting a defensive war and a short one at that. It proved evanescent. As the war and its accompanying economic hardships dragged on for years and as radically divergent visions of the internal constitution and external boundaries of the postwar *Reich* came to the fore, the unbridgeable cleavages in the body politic reemerged.[24] The members of the youth movement regarded themselves as the heralds of a restored *Volksgemeinschaft*, but they too were divided as to the form and political expression that the new community was to take.

The split within the youth movement derived in part from the very different manner in which the war was experienced by those who had fought in it as front-line soldiers and those who had remained in, or returned to, civilian status.[25] Those who for reasons of age or physical constitution had remained in

---

[24] See Jürgen Kocka, *Facing Total War: German Society, 1914–1918.*

[25] Flitner, "Der Krieg," 297ff. Flitner's observations in this regard are particularly significant since he not only had been a member of the Serakreis but had studied together with Freyer

civilian life were struck as the war progressed by the senselessness of the conflict, a perception that was intensified by the reports of battle brought back by
their wounded comrades who returned from the front. "The social question"
had been among the concerns of the prewar movement. Now the awareness of
the futility of the war and of the unequal distribution of hardships on the
home front combined to propel these members of the movement toward the
socialist camp and opposition to the war.[26] After the armistice they found
themselves estranged from their former comrades who had spent the war at
the front. These veterans, who like Freyer had for years confronted death day
in and day out on behalf of their country and the *Volksgemeinschaft* of 1914,
viewed themselves as the regenerators of a Germany that by no means
conformed to the pacifist and internationalist visions of their erstwhile
comrades.[27]

Philosophy from the Trenches: Freyer's Antäus

Freyer's first nonacademic work was composed in the trenches of the western
front. It was written during 1916 and early 1917 as a series of letters to a fe-
male friend from the Serakreis who typed up the manuscript and presented it
to Eugen Diederichs, who published it in mid-1918.[28] Entitled *Antäus: Foundations of an Ethic of Conscious Life*, the book is difficult to classify according to
conventional genres. Though primarily a work of philosophical reflection, it
was by no means systematic or propositional. Its pages contained a loosely
linked series of prose poems and extended aphorisms, a hybrid of Rilke and
Nietzsche, though it hardly matched the former's imaginative genius or the
latter's psychological acuity. Its deliberate invocation of classical myths and its
mythopoeic style were evidence not only of the new respect accorded to mythic
forms of thought in the German academic scholarship of the period but also
of a turning away from rationalistic ethics typical of the youth movement and
the circles around Diederichs.

The work does, however, advance substantive philosophical propositions,
albeit in an often metaphorical form. This extensive use of imagery remained
a continuing feature of Freyer's literary style, though it was attenuated in his
more academic works. Among the benefits of this poetic style of theorizing was

---

in Berlin before the war. See also Jakob Müller,
*Die Jugendbewegung als deutsche Hauptrichtung
neokonservativer Reform*, 220.

[26] Flitner, "Der Krieg," 298ff. On the left wing

of the *Jugendbewegung*, see Linse, "Jugendkulturbewegung," 129ff.

[27] Flitner, "Der Krieg," 297ff.

[28] Käthe Freyer interview.

its accessibility and attractiveness to an educated but nonprofessional audience. Though apt to be perceived by the modern reader as precious and obscure, it was more than acceptable to educated German readers of the day,
even the more prosaic of whom were expected to write poetry as an avocation.
This style also had its costs. Not only did it favor evocation over precision, but
as one contemporary critic noted of the author of *Antäus*, "a great linguistic
talent leads here to pseudo-philosophical perception. . . . Freyer is so carried
away by images that the thoughts which they are originally intended to express
slip into vacuity."[29] Nor was this the last charge that Freyer's verbal facility
often outran his conceptual rigor.

Much of *Antäus* was in fact a restatement of themes that Freyer had explored
in his prewar essays, now altered by the experience of the war.

As its subtitle implied, *Antäus* sought to explore the ethical ramifications of
Lebensphilosophie. Freyer emphasized the seemingly inexorable onward flow of
time, the lability of *Leben*, and its nonrational basis.[30] The book expressed a voluntaristic sense of the intrinsic purposelessness and openness of human life
that later became a hallmark of existentialist philosophy.[31]

The emphasis on the undetermined future was combined with a strong generational bias. The future, Freyer wrote, would be a product of the decision of
the "current generation," or what he called *die lebendige Generation*, thereby rel-
egating its elders to a less than vital status.[32] "For a while all of life lies in our
hand. That which we grasp onto will live on; that which we allow to fall away
will die."[33] Given this absolute openness and undetermined nature of the future, the current generation longed to know how to end its feeling of "empty
infinity."[34] It sought direction and demands upon its life.[35] It hankered after a
new ethic. The problem to which *Antäus* was devoted was the construction of a
new ethical order. The inadequacy of the existing order was not demonstrated, it was assumed, for as we have seen this was the reigning assumption
among Freyer's peers and his academic mentors.

[29] Hellmuth Falkenfeld, review of *Antäus*, by
Hans Freyer, in *Kantstudien* (1920), 440–41.
Freyer shared this "rhetorical expressionism"
with many writers of his generation. "The rhetorical Expressionist spouts out a cataract of
highly charged emotional words and allows this
verbal cataract to carry him away to empty the-
atricality and pose and to unintended inaccura-
cies and absurdities" (Walter Sokel, *The Writer in
Extremis*, 111).

[30] Hans Freyer, *Antäus: Grundlegung einer*

Ethik des bewußten Lebens (1918), 26 and passim.
[31] Ibid., 28–29.
[32] Ibid., 48.
[33] Ibid., 30.
[34] Ibid., 41.
[35] For similar sentiments, see Thomas Mann,
Betrachtungen eines Unpolitischen (1918), 528–29,
who asked rhetorically, "Befreiung, immer noch
mehr Befreiung *wäre* das Wort und der Sinn
der Stunde—und nicht vielmehr etwas ganz
anderes, nämlich Bindung?"

The thrust of Freyer's argument was both radical and conservative. This twofold thrust was epitomized by one of the dominant metaphors of the book: "Man on earth," Freyer wrote, "is both Antäus the Giant and Hercules the Hero."[36]

The image of man as Hercules expressed the radical and voluntarist side of Freyer's thought. Through *action* (*Tat*) and *will*, he wrote, man could create "objective *Geist*" and bring into being a whole order.[37] This moral order would give stability and direction to the life of future generations. Eventually, like all things historical, it too would be superseded.[38]

Only if it was founded upon a sound basis, Freyer wrote, could a new ethical order be effective.[39] Much of *Antäus* was a rhetorical disparagement of the possibility of discovering a "deductivist ethics," a universal ethical system based upon rational foundations.[40] Such an ethical system was a chimera, he again insisted, for the real basis of an ethical order was the prerational, what he now termed "Leben" or the "Erde." Ethics was the rationalization and systematization of *Leben*. Since *Leben* was in a process of flow and flux, discovering real ethics meant becoming conscious of its demands.

Here the image of man as Antäus came into play. In Greek mythology Antäus was a giant who replenished his strength whenever he touched his mother, Gaea, the earth. Man was like Antäus, Freyer wrote, in that he derived his power from contact with the earth (*Erde*). The earth is covered with a multiplicity of traditions created by human collectivities over time, each of which is ethically valid. The rationalist ideal, Freyer wrote, is to uproot all of these particular, historical traditions and replace them with a single ethic based on rational foundations and valid for all men. This was a tragic error, he declared, since there is no "general humanity." A morality freed from the accidents of birth was bound to be bloodless, trivial, and unsatisfying. What appears to the rationalist as freedom is actually "a mad distrust of the basis of one's own being, an arbitrary confusion, an attempt to drain the color out of life, an uprooting of particular drives." The creation of a new appropriate ethic therefore required an affirmation of membership in a particular historical community and culture.[41]

Antäus thus offered an emotive and mythopoeic restatement of the German historicist critique of the ethical theory of the Enlightenment, a critique prominent in Freyer's prewar intellectual milieu and reemphasized by the academic

---

[36] Freyer, *Antäus*, 5.
[37] Ibid., 12, 16.
[38] Ibid., 20, 28.

[39] Ibid., 1.
[40] Ibid., 9off.
[41] Ibid., 80, 82.

humanists in their wartime appeals for the preservation of German cultural particularity.

By making the struggle of Hercules and Antäus—one of the favored subjects of ancient Greek sculpture—the metaphorical center of his book, Freyer revealed the ambivalent relationship to the past characteristic of his radical conservative sensibility. On the one hand he was exquisitely conscious of the role of tradition and continuity with the past in bestowing authority upon social norms. On the other hand, he was unsure as to the content and ultimate warrant of this authority. The book begins with the words:

He who would lay the foundation for a thing must necessarily begin beneath the thing itself. For nothing that is constructed rests upon itself: it must be grounded on natural soil [es muß auf gewachsenem Boden gegründet werden].[42]

The importance of "gewachsenem Boden" as the basis of culture was a recurring motif in Freyer's thought and reappears as late as his *Theorie des gegenwärtigen Zeitalters* of 1955. It was intended to express the need for the culture of the present to derive its authority from that of the past. In *Antäus* (and in later works of the 1920s and 1930s) Freyer played upon two connotations of the term *gewachsenem Boden*. In normal German usage it is the equivalent of "virgin soil," of ground untouched by human civilization. It thus connotes a natural, biological basis of identification with the past. Yet the root of the adjective *gewachsenem* is the verb *wachsen*, meaning growth. Freyer plays upon this second meaning to express the proposition that ethical authority must be rooted in history, in growth over time. The natural and historical bases of cultural authority are therefore combined into a single ambiguous image. The present-day reader unfamiliar with the cultural context in which *Antäus* was written might mistakenly regard this image as simply racist. In fact, the tendency to elide the biological and historical bases of collective particularity was widespread at the time, even among the most respected of social scientists and philosophers;[43] Freyer's image of founding authority "auf gewachsenem Boden" exalted the social *function* of tradition while remaining vague as to the *content* of tradition. In keeping with a recurrent pattern of conservative thought, Freyer's work recognized the psychological utility of the veneration of the past but failed to specify which aspects of the past merited veneration. In the absence of rational criteria, the pastness of tradition became its major justification. Freyer's alienation from Wilhelmine culture left him unprepared to rec-

---

[42] Ibid., 1.   [43] See, for example, Troeltsch, "Geist," 76.

WAR, REVOLUTION, AND MISSION 69

ommend to his comrades the preservation of the status quo. In the Herculean imagery of *Antäus* he insisted that there were "sublime moments" in history when existing moral laws and habits must give way to "the moral force of a new necessity," in which "the old laws are fulfilled in a new way, so to speak."[44] Having ruled out the possibility of ascertaining the moral demands of the hour through universal reason, Freyer sought them in surrendering to the demands of *Leben*, which he equated with the affirmation of collective historical fate.

The great formula of our life [Leben] is fated and set. We are given a being, destined for death, we encounter our wives and friends at a particular time, a war breaks out, the earth takes us into its rhythm in an ecstatic moment, and we are carried along. . . . the origin of will is within fate; in one stroke this sublime gift of the gods is transformed into a sphere of duties.[45]

The war as such is barely mentioned in *Antäus* but provides the background of the book's reflections. The war was "the sublime moment" that legitimated the break with the past. But more importantly it was a fate that Freyer affirmed. In his prewar essays Freyer had endorsed Simmel's contention that ethical demands arose not out of universal rational contemplation but out of an awareness of duty rooted in the totality of a particular life. But he and his comrades had felt no such sense of obligation in prewar Wilhelmine Germany. The experience of the war provided such a sensation of duty, of calling to a collective purpose, which Wilhelmine Germany had been unable to provide in peacetime.[46] For Freyer and his comrades in the youth movement the war appeared not as an intrusion but as rescue from the purposelessness of civilian life. *Antäus* proclaimed that those in whom this sense of duty and commitment to the preservation of Germany's cultural particularity had been awakened— the generation of the youth movement that had gone through the war—were the bearers of German cultural regeneration.

Antäus had great appeal to a relatively small audience. It combined some of the most avant-garde themes of prewar academic philosophy with the war experience (*Kriegserlebnis*) as interpreted by a spokesman of the youth movement. Senior professors were pleased to see their concerns embraced by a self-conscious spokesman of the younger generation, a generation whose prestige had been heightened by the burden that it carried during the war years. The members of the prewar youth movement found their ethos and their experi-

44 Freyer, *Antäus*, 83–86.   46 Müller, *Jungendbewegung*, 198–218.
45 Ibid., 99.

ence of the war expressed with verve and in a style that was erudite and emotive. The book was advertised by Diederichs Verlag as "the fanfare of the younger generation." It not only drew hefty praise from the more fashionable academic philosophers; it also sold well.

Early in 1917 Freyer sent a copy of the manuscript of *Antäus* to Georg Simmel. The senior philosopher was so impressed that he urged Freyer to habilitate after the war and invited him to his home in Strasbourg, which Freyer visited on a leave in July 1917.[47] Advertisements for the book carried Simmel's endorsement: "The author has marched though the door that Nietzsche pushed open." Another came from Karl Joel, professor of philosophy in Basel, who provided fulsome praise and concluded, "the book is an event."[48] Most impressive perhaps were the comments of Ernst Troeltsch, one of the foremost historicist philosophers of the day. To Diederichs Troeltsch wrote that while he found the style of the prose rather fanciful for his taste, he regarded the book as "truly significant and conceptually rich. . . . It is very close to my own philosophical tendencies, to such a degree in fact that I suspect we have common roots. . . . One will certainly have to keep an eye on this book and its author." In an influential book published after the war, Troeltsch cited Freyer's *Antäus* as an outstanding work of the younger generation that combined activism with a commitment to the past.[49]

The book was also reviewed in the daily press. Most reviewers were quite positive and regarded the book as a product of the *Zeitgeist* and its author as a spokesman for the younger generation.[50] Others were put off by the vagueness of its style: "Counterfeit Nietzsches are intolerable," was one such comment, and a reviewer for an academic philosophical journal noted that though the book claimed to lay the foundations for a conscious ethic "any other designation would be more appropriate than 'foundation.' "[51]

The most enthusiastic response came from the youth movement and the circle around Eugen Diederichs and *Die Tat.* In the closing stages of the war the movement split into right- and left-wing factions. The *völkisch* or nationalist faction regarded the *Volk* as the ultimate value and the war as a legitimate and

[47] Hans Freyer to Michael Landmann, 22 February 1966, Nachlaß Landmann; Käthe Freyer interview.

[48] Hans Freyer, *Prometheus: Ideen zur Philosophie der Kultur* (1923), publisher's advertisement bound in at the end of the volume.

[49] Ernst Troeltsch to Eugen Diederichs, 3 October 1918, Rezenzionsmappe *Antäus*, Universitätsarchiv Jena; Troeltsch, *Der Historismus und seine Probleme* (1922), 26n.

[50] See, for example, the reviews in *Der Tag* (Berlin), 1 November 1918; *Tägliche Rundschau* (Berlin), 5 November 1919.

[51] Wilhelm Börner, review of *Antäus*, by Hans Freyer, in *Archiv für Geschichte der Philosophie*.

ennobling act of collective self-defense. The left-wing faction was increasingly pacifistic and saw the war as evidence of the decadence of capitalist society. During the war it established connections to the socialist parties, and some of its members joined the Communist party at its founding late in 1918. Yet even this faction maintained a nationalist tone at least until November 1918.[52]

In May 1918 Diederichs had organized a cultural congress at Lauenstein made up largely of senior members of the youth movement to discuss the future role of the movement. The discussions at the gathering brought to light the lack of consensus within the movement as to its future goals, whereupon Diederichs told those assembled that he was about to publish a book of "Blut und Leben" that would provide them with an answer.[53] When the book in question, Freyer's Antäus, was published in the fall of 1918 it was greeted by representatives of both factions as an authentic and important expression of the ethos of the youth movement. Ernst Krieck, a pedagogue in Diederichs' circle who was later associated with Moeller van den Bruck's periodical Gewissen and who eventually became the leading educational theorist of the National Socialist regime, praised Antäus enthusiastically in the pages of the Deutsche Bücherzeitung.[54] Alfred Kurella, a leader of the leftist wing of the youth movement, reviewed the book for Die Tat and was adulatory. The book marked the consummation of the previous thought of the youth movement, he wrote. It had formulated the ethos of the movement into a new ethic and a new myth. Shortly thereafter Kurella joined the newly founded German Communist party. He rose within its ranks and ultimately became a member of the Politburo and a leading cultural functionary of the East German regime in the 1950s.[55]

Men as different in their orientations as Krieck and Kurella could so heartily endorse Antäus because it was essentially a nonpolitical—or better, an incipiently political—work, more striking for its radical tone and its proclamation of generational mission than for its programmatic content. By the standards of the Diederichs publishing house Antäus was a good seller, and by 1923 its first edition of three thousand copies had sold out, requiring a second printing. It continued to sell almost one hundred copies per year throughout the 1920s.[56] Although these figures are modest, the audience for the book was of qualita-

[52] Müller, Jugendbewegung, 205ff.

[53] Alfred Kurella, "Zur Ethik der neuen Jugend," Die Tat 10 (1918–19): 635.

[54] Ernst Krieck, review of Antäus, by Hans Freyer, in Deutsche Bücherzeitung, no. 1 (1919). On Krieck, see Gerhard Müller, Ernst Krieck und die nationalsozialistische Wissenschaftsreform.

[55] Kurella, "Zur Ethik," 634–37. On Kurella, see Müller, Jugendbewegung, passim.

[56] Sales figures for Antäus are taken from the archives of the Eugen Diederichs Verlag, Cologne.

tive importance, for it included many senior members of the youth movement
and its external supporters who moved into leading positions in German cultural and academic life during the 1920s. Thus even before his habilitation
Freyer's name had a certain cachet within academic circles as a spokesman for
the idealistic younger generation that had passed through the fires of the
front.

Revolution and the Institutionalization of the War Experience

Lieutenant Freyer was wounded in the summer of 1918 and spent the next
several months recuperating from his head injury. He reported for duty to his
unit's headquarters in Dresden in November 1918 only to discover that a revolution had broken out and officers were being demonstratively stripped of
their epaulets by the new soldiers' council in a symbolic display of the new egal-
itarianism.[57] It was on this dramatic and unanticipated note that the war ended
for Freyer.

Many German veterans of the First World War reacted to their demobiliza-
tion with disorientation and aimlessness; Freyer's reaction was quite the opposite. Now convinced of his pedagogic calling and, at age thirty-one, eager to
embark upon an academic career, Freyer returned to the University of Leipzig. Regarded by himself and others as something of a spokesman for the new
generation, and urged to habilitate by no less a figure than Georg Simmel,
Freyer appears to have thrown himself into the rapid completion of his *Habilitationsschrift*—a second dissertation required for habilitation and a professorial career. A fellowship at the Institut für Kultur- und Universalgeschichte
allowed him to devote himself fully to his research, and in November 1919
he submitted his work to the faculty.[58]

As we have seen, the significance of the war in *Antäus* was more a reflection
of the expectations of Freyer's academic mentors and his peers than of his actual experience of combat. This was even more true of Freyer's later writings,
in which the war took on a new significance when contrasted to the events of
the postwar period.

Political events in Leipzig and the response to them within the university in
the immediate postwar years help to explain the subsequent direction of Freyer's work. The radicalization of the working class in Leipzig resulted in class
conflict as raw as anywhere else in Germany and must have brought home to

[57] Käthe Freyer interview.

[58] Hans Freyer, *Die Bewertung der Wirtschaft im philosophischen Denken des 19. Jahrhunderts* (1921), i.

Freyer the depths of the cleft within German civil society. This disaccord was contrasted with the perceived unity of the nation during the early years of war. Within the professoriate and parts of the youth movement the war had brought about a renewed emphasis on the value and particularity of German culture. This interpretation of the war as a period of national unity and particularist self-assertion was expressed repeatedly in Freyer's milieu during the postwar years. Time and again the message was conveyed to the returning veterans that the burden of this regeneration rested largely upon their shoulders.

The conflict of classes took a particularly stark form in Leipzig. Shortly after the workers' and soldiers' councils seized power, a *Bürgerausschuß* (citizens' committee) headed by Prof. Walter Goetz was formed by the city's bourgeois residents. Goetz was Lamprecht's successor as head of the Institut für Kultur- und Universalgeschichte, politically a Naumannite liberal, and, together with Felix Krueger, the supervisor of Freyer's *Habilitationsschrift*. On 26 February, 1919 the German communists organized a workers' strike in Leipzig, hoping to gain control of the city through a demonstration of proletarian power. The next day the *Bürgerausschuß* called for a *Bürgerstreik*, which appears to have been very successful: it halted the distribution of foodstuffs, suspended medical care, froze bureaucratic activity, and in general paralyzed the city. The two strikes were ended only by the arrival in March of federal troops, which occupied the city and permanently dissolved the councils.[59] These events could not but impress upon Freyer the depth of the organized social antagonisms that faced the new Germany.

Hostility toward the revolution was rife among much of the student body and faculty of the University of Leipzig. The course of the revolution in Leipzig from November 1918 though March 1919 was dominated not by the social democrats but by the more radical independent socialists and communists. When the defeated troops returned to the city on 22 November 1918 the workers' and soldiers' council ordered that the red flag be flown from all public buildings to greet them—including those of the university. This led to indignation among professors and students. A group of students composed of returning veterans forcibly removed the red flag. They issued a manifesto that set the tone within the university for much of what followed, and that might have served as a preamble to Freyer's subsequent writings:

[59] Rudolf Kittel, *Die Universität Leipzig im Jahr der Revolution 1918–19: Rektoratserrinerungen,* 85ff.; Karl Czok and Horst Thieme, eds., *Leipzig: Geschichte der Stadt in Wort und Bild,* 65. On Walter Goetz, see his memoirs included in his *Historiker in meiner Zeit,* and Douglas Fred Tobler, "German Historians and the Weimar Republic."

We who have returned from the field view with deep shame and a heavy heart the way in which our *Volk* has lacked the power to proceed united, internally and externally, in this most sacred of hours. For what have we fought and suffered, for what have our dearest friends fallen? Why are there suddenly so many who have forgotten the sanctity of those August days of 1914? . . . The spirit of class must vanish and give way to an ethical socialism. But we must not relinquish our sense of the nation.[60]

This symbolic act led to physical confrontations between armed soldiers acting on behalf of the councils on the one hand, and students supported by their professors on the other. In January 1919, during the course of a workers' demonstration outside the gates of the university, a professor rumored to have fired a shot was pummeled by the crowd, and later the university was invaded by armed soldiers searching for weapons.[61] Far from accommodating to the new situation, the faculty senate sent a letter to the recently deposed King Friedrich August of Saxony, thanking him for his support of the university during the years of his reign.[62] Many older members of the faculty never ceased to long for the Bismarckian *Reich*, the founding of which they continued to celebrate annually on 18 January.

The official ceremony in honor of the soldiers now returning to their university studies took place in the auditorium of the university on 1 June 1919. The main speech was delivered by Felix Krueger. As a young lecturer Krueger had befriended Freyer, who later sent him a manuscript of *Antäus*. Though he was almost forty when war broke out in 1914, Krueger had immediately volunteered, and he saw action from 1914 to 1917, including the battle of Verdun. In the fall of 1917 he returned to Leipzig to succeed his teacher, Wilhelm Wundt, as professor of psychology. During the summer of 1918 Krueger worked for the Prussian War Ministry on plans for raising morale in the army (*geistige Versteifung der Front*) and lectured to Saxon troops in the Ukraine.[63] He therefore spoke to his audience as one veteran to another.

When they had left their slain comrades on the battlefield, Krueger said, they had done so in the belief that Germany would be saved by their holy sacrifice. Those soldiers who returned to Germany with their honor intact found themselves confronted by scolding criticism from the "shirkers" and "the most immature elements of the work force" in the war industries. They discovered

---

[60] Quoted in Kittel, *Universität Leipzig*, 17–18.
[61] Ibid., 76–81.
[62] Ibid., 112–15.
[63] Ibid., 138ff. Hans Freyer to Felix Krueger,

24 August 1918, UAL, PA Krueger; Kittel, 37. BAK, R21, Anhang Wissenschaftlerkartei, Felix Krueger.

that "a vanguard of unworldly ideologues had led a war of destruction against the state in its hour of need."

Krueger laid great stress on the role of ideas in his account of the war and of Germany's defeat. The ideals of the Allies represented "a sin against the spirit," a utilitarian morality based upon the conscious, consistent, calculating pursuit of material self-advantage. Yet Germany had also suffered from an economization of its life in recent years, which had finally led to the present anarchy. It was typical of the age to underestimate the role of ideas in national life, Krueger maintained. During the war the army command had paid inadequate attention to morale (*geistige Versorgung*), thereby leaving the population prone to the appeal of Wilson's ideas. The true aim of the victors, which these ideas only masked, had since been revealed at Versailles.

The salvation of Germany in this dark hour, Krueger asserted, lay in the hands of those who sat before him. With a reference to the role of Fichte in the Wars of Liberation, he again emphasized the historical power of ideas: "Our salvation today—as one hundred years ago—can only grow out of the ethically steadfast emotional commitment to things German, a commitment that stands ready for action."[64]

Three weeks later, at the summer solstice, the remnants of the Serakreis met on a mountaintop outside of Jena to commemorate the nineteen members of the circle who had fallen during the war. On the spot where the circle had met before the war they planted a linden tree in memory of Karl Brügmann, one of its fallen leaders. Beside it they placed a memorial stone, inscribed with a poem written by Hans Freyer for the occasion. It ended with the lines,

> Friends in the grave
> You are the surrogate for our deaths
> The surrogates of your power are we
> who have remained in the light.
>
> We will incorporate your will
> into the structures we build.[65]

The deaths of young men in battle may be difficult to justify, but never more so than when their army goes down to ultimate defeat and their deaths appear

---

[64] Felix Krueger, *Selbstbesinnung in deutscher Not: Rede an die aus dem Felde Zurückgekehrten der Universität Leipzig* (1919), 5–16.

[65] On the memorial solstice, see *Gedächtnisfeier zur Friedenssonnenwende* (1919), and the sources reprinted in Werner Kindt, ed., *Die Wandervogelzeit*, 469–83. Freyer's poem is on p. 483.

to have been in vain. Their survivors are then tempted to engage in retroactive theodicy, to show that their deaths had meaning by harnessing their memory to some present cause. Such was the response of Freyer's teachers, mentors, and peers. It fell upon the returning veterans to demonstrate that the deaths of their comrades had not been without purpose by bringing about a revival and renewal of the German nation. It was this widely shared interpretation of the war experience that Freyer's poem and his subsequent writings of the post-war years express.

This commitment to the invigoration of German culture and German particularity was institutionalized in several organizations that Krueger and his circle helped establish and to which Hans Freyer belonged. Among these were the German Philosophical Association (Deutsche Philosophische Gesellschaft, DPG) and the Fichte Society (Fichte-Gesellschaft).

Though it was not readily apparent from its innocuous name, the DPG owed its origin to the reassertion of German cultural particularism during and after the war. The DPG arose out of a factional split from the Kant-Gesellschaft, which despite its name was in fact the umbrella organization of German academic philosophers. Bruno Bauch, a philosopher in Jena and managing editor of the association's journal, *Kantstudien*, left the organization in the spring of 1917 because he was prevented from expressing his strongly nationalist and anti-Semitic views. Together with Max Wundt—the son of Wilhelm Wundt, but a far more rabid nationalist than his father—Bauch founded the Deutsche Philosophische Gesellschaft, devoted to "the preservation and development of German idealist philosophy and the defense of German cultural life from present dangers."[66] Krueger's circle was very prominent within the society, and by the early 1930s its journal, the *Blätter für deutsche Philosophie*, was edited from Leipzig by Gunther Ipsen and Hugo Fischer, two close associates of Freyer.

The Fichte-Gesellschaft began its existence in Leipzig at the end of 1918 when Krueger and some of his friends discovered that many of their countrymen were unsure about what it meant to be German. As Krueger explained in a pamphlet published by the society,

We younger people felt within us a core of certainty which a thousand immediate experiences had awoken within each of us, experiences of belonging to a precious *Volk*—not to the masses of the metropolis, not to any particular party, and not even to a narrow

---

[66] BAK, NS15, Amt Rosenberg, no. 292, citing *Reichls philosophischer Almanach, 1923,* 121–22.

stratum of educated humanists. Our faith in Germandom [das Deutschtum] seemed to us to be well grounded in historical, psychic, and ultimately national realities.[67]

During June 1919 Krueger and his friends, with the blessing of Wilhelm Wundt, founded the Gesellschaft für deutsche Volksbildung, designed to foster the spread of German values through education. It sponsored cultural evenings and a series of pamphlets devoted to the legacy of the great figures of German culture. Its principal undertaking was the Fichte-Hochschule, an institute for adult education staffed largely by younger scholars from Krueger's circle at the university. The Fichte-Hochschule competed with a municipally funded Volkshochschule, which had a decidedly Marxist orientation.[68] Freyer taught briefly at the Fichte-Hochschule in 1920. It was there, in his course on Fichte, that he met the woman he would later marry.[69]

In 1920 the Gesellschaft für deutsche Volksbildung became the Leipzig branch of the Fichte-Gesellschaft, a nationwide organization with a similar program, founded in Hamburg by Wilhelm Stapel. Felix Krueger became the vice-chairman of the national Fichte-Gesellschaft. The Fichte-Gesellschaft and Fichte-Hochschule were part of a network of overlapping organizations, journals, and personalities that together made up the communicative network of the new nationalist right of the Weimar Republic. Stapel, for example, was the editor of the *Deutsches Volkstum*, a radical conservative periodical launched during the war by the Deutschnationaler Handlungsgehilfen Verband (DHV), an association of German white-collar employees. Founded in 1893 on a program of extreme racial nationalism and opposition to Marxism and liberal capitalism, the DHV was the largest non-Marxist labor association during the Weimar Republic. It funded and operated a broad web of periodicals, book clubs, and publishing houses, including the Hanseatische Verlagsanstalt, one of the most prominent publishers of radical nationalist literature. The director of the Fichte-Hochschule was a salaried official of the DHV. Also overlapping in leadership and purpose with these organizations was the Jungdeutscher Bund, the most intellectually respectable offshoot of the right-wing, *völkisch* branch of the postwar youth movement.[70] It was with this broad extra-academic network that Krueger's academic circle was identified and identified

[67] Felix Krueger, *Deutscher Geist: Schriften der Fichte Gesellschaft*, appended to Felix Krueger, gen. ed., *Deutscher Geist* (1921), vol. 1: *Deutsche Kultur*, by Bruno Golz.

[68] Nelson Edmundson, "The Fichte Society: A Chapter in Germany's Conservative Revolution," 108–11.

[69] Käthe Freyer interview.

[70] Edmundson, "Fichte Society," 96, 111. Stark, *Entrepreneurs*, 22ff.

itself. It was no wonder that in the course of the Weimar period Krueger's
Institute of Psychology won a reputation as a "völkisch cell."[71]

Hans Freyer was by nature a nonjoiner and a remarkably open-minded
individual, and his association with Krueger, the Deutsche Philosophische
Gesellschaft, and the Fichte-Hochschule neither determined his thought nor
circumscribed his intellectual horizons. Indeed, as we will see, he drew many
of his friends, students, and ideas from the German left. Yet it was this broad
network of radical nationalist organizations—organizations created or radically reoriented by the war experience and the national collapse that followed—
that provided the atmosphere from which Freyer drew his ideological breath.

Freyer as Radical Intellectual Historian

In 1919, while working on his *Habilitationsschrift*, Freyer wrote a review of the
recently published first volume of Oswald Spengler's *The Decline of the West*,
which appeared in Diederichs' journal, *Die Tat*. Freyer was deeply impressed
by the book—as was almost every intellectual on the German right for the next
decade and a half.[72] Spengler displayed great insight into the psychic significance of cultural artifacts, Freyer wrote, and his book refuted the view of history as one of linear progress. The notion that each culture had some vital
center and was dominated by a particular kind of man struck Freyer as particularly important. Moreover, he agreed wholeheartedly with Spengler's belief
that the future called for "socialism"—but a "clear, hard, grand version" of
socialism beyond its contemporary utilitarian form.

Freyer's criticisms of Spengler were a reflection of the generational and vocational differences that separated them. Spengler displayed a strong animus
against the "guild historians" of the universities—the *réssentiment* of the *Real-
gymnasiumlehrer* against his academic betters. Freyer, who was at home in the
academy, noted that Spengler's organic view of culture as a product of some
essence that grew over time was not as novel as Spengler imagined. Hegel had
been of a similar view, as had Lamprecht in his theory of historical types and
Dilthey in his conceptualization of vital entities as governed by their own discernible laws. This scholarly ability to put fashionable contemporary ideas into

---

[71] Felix Krueger, "Otto Klemm und das Psychologische Institut der Universität Leipzig,"
*Zeitschrift für angewändete Psychologie und Charak-
terkunde* 56 (1939): 289, quoted in Edmundson,
"Fichte Society," 106.

[72] Ernest Manheim, "The Sociology of Hans
Freyer," 363. On Spengler's influence, see Golo
Mann, *The History of Germany since 1789*, 617–21.

a broader intellectual and historical context was characteristic of much of Freyer's work, including the *Habilitationsschrift* that he was engaged in writing.

For all his admiration of Spengler, Freyer was at odds with the determinism and fatalism of *The Decline of the West*. He warned his readers not to be ensnared by the powerful organic metaphors of the book, such as the *"Abend der Kultur"* or *"Greisenalter der Seele."* The demands of the present and of the future could not be "deduced" from insights into patterns of culture, Freyer asserted, but were ultimately based on "the wager of action" (*das Wagnis der Tat*). His review ended on the voluntaristic note of generational mission.[73]

Freyer's habilitation thesis, which he completed in November 1919 and later published as *The Evaluation of the Economy in Nineteenth-Century Philosophic Thought*, was a work of radical intellectual history. The substantive theme of the book stemmed from a suggestion by Felix Krueger, the primary sponsor of the *Habilitationsschrift*.[74] A former student of Dilthey increasingly attracted to the tradition of German historicism, Krueger had become dissatisfied with the attempts of psychologists to discover fixed and universal laws of higher mental functions. Instead he sought to heed Dilthey's call for a descriptive, historical psychology that would marshal historical evidence to reconstruct the development of the human spirit.[75] In practice this amounted to an attempt to replace psychology with a search for patterns in cultural history. Krueger had long been interested in the interaction of modern ethics and modern economic life. In 1909 he had offered a course entitled "The Psychology and Ethics of Economic Life," which Freyer had attended.[76] Krueger's course reflected the growing concern among German academics with the cultural history and moral implications of modern capitalism. It was this concern that before the war had motivated the scholarship of Ferdinand Tönnies, Max Weber, Werner Sombart, and Johann Plenge, whose works were cited in Freyer's book.

Freyer attempted to contribute to this wider effort by analyzing the interpretation of the capitalist economy in the work of a broad range of German, French, and British thinkers of the eighteenth and nineteenth centuries. He tried above all to analyze the role allotted to economic values within various nineteenth-century intellectual currents. In so doing he hoped to reveal the

---

[73] Hans Freyer, review of *Der Untergang des Abendlandes*, vol. 1, by Oswald Spengler, in *Die Tat* (1919–20), 304–8. Spengler himself soon moved away from the pessimistic determinism of his book. See Herf, *Reactionary Modernism*, 49ff.

[74] Freyer, *Bewertung*, i.

[75] Krueger, *Entwicklungspsychologie*, 20ff. Freyer's *Bewertung* was published in the same series.

[76] UAL, Zeugnisprotokoll, Rep. I.

distinctive presuppositions held by the various systems of nineteenth-century thought in regard to the economy and to demonstrate the significance of these presuppositions for the broader world views of which they were a part.[77]

Freyer's substantive enterprise was to apply Dilthey's method of intellectual history to the study of the role of the economy in nineteenth-century European thought. Seen from this perspective it was a scholarly tour de force. Freyer's purview reached from William Petty to Ruskin, from Turgot to Comte, and from the German idealists and romantics to Marx and Nietzsche. His evaluations of topics as varied as Marx's relationship to Hegel and John Stuart Mill's ambivalent attitude toward classical political economy were often insightful and subtle, and far from the nationalist prejudices characteristic of much German writing on such topics in the aftermath of the war. The book was—and despite the intervening decades remains—of scholarly value, regardless of its evaluative commitments. Like his earlier doctoral dissertation, Freyer's *Habilitationsschrift* combined scholarship and commitment, or more precisely, used historical scholarship to illuminate the origins of his own dilemmas. Alongside the substantive historical theme enunciated in the book's title lay a normative concern, manifest in Freyer's continuous evaluative commentary on the substantive topic of his research. As Freyer wrote in a preface added to the second edition of the book (published in 1939, when value neutrality was not a highly prized attribute of scholarship), "The book not only deals with value judgments, but in and between the lines it is chock full of the value judgments of the author. It therefore has nothing in common with the positivistic ideal of a value-free science and was never intended to."[78]

Its evaluative and programmatic aspects were very much in evidence, reflecting the ethos of the youth movement and of the intellectual anticapitalism that Freyer had imbibed from his academic mentors, especially Johann Plenge. In his book *Marx und Hegel* (1911) and especially in his wartime writings Plenge had suggested that the liberal "spirit of the nineteenth century" was about to give way to a new "spirit of the twentieth century."[79] This rhetorical dichotomy appealed to the young Freyer, who heard in it the youth movement's generational claim to cultural renewal; it remained one of his favorite rhetorical devices throughout the 1920s and 1930s.

---

[77] Freyer, *Bewertung*, 6–7.

[78] Hans Freyer, "Vorwort zur zweiten Auflage," in his *Die Bewertung der Wirtschaft im philosophischen Denken des 19. Jahrhunderts*, 2d ed.

(1939).

[79] Johann Plenge, *Marx und Hegel*; Schrader, "Theorie und Praxis."

Freyer's book was an effort to flesh out the notion of a "spirit of the nine-teenth century" and to suggest by contrast the spirit of the twentieth. In his introduction Freyer claimed that behind the various philosophical approaches to the role of the economy one could discover a "unified spirit [*Geist*] of the nineteenth century," which—in analogy to Burckhardt's depiction of a unified *Quattrocento*—he termed the *Ottocento*. His historical inquiry, Freyer wrote, was intended to contribute to "the task which we have inherited from the past," namely that of transcending the *Ottocentogeist*.[80]

In fact the range of attitudes within nineteenth-century philosophy regard-ing the relationship of the economy to the rest of culture was so broad that no common spirit could be distilled inductively. What Freyer actually did was to assume that a particular social philosophy—roughly equivalent to Manchester-ian liberalism—was the real spirit of the nineteenth century. Much of the book was an account of the origins and development of this doctrine and of com-peting positions advanced by its major nineteenth-century critics. These posi-tions were in turn evaluated by Freyer for their current utility. From a pro-grammatic perspective, then, the book might have been called "What Is Living and What Is Dead in Nineteenth-Century Anticapitalism."

Freyer's portrait of economic liberalism and of classical political economy was of a system of thought that had resulted in the reification of the economy. In utilitarianism, its philosophical adjunct, he saw the translation of all human values into economic ones. Drawing on the work of Weber, Troeltsch, and Dil-they, Freyer sketched the religious and philosophical origins of capitalism and of "modern vocational, economic man, who finds it natural that he exists for the sake of the enterprise, not that the enterprise exists for his sake."[81] He stressed the importance of the naturalistic world view of the Enlightenment as the basis of classical political economy but noted that the full implications of this naturalism were made plain only in nineteenth-century Manchesterian-ism, which jettisoned the reformist and interventionist elements of Smith's *Wealth of Nations*. When the providential, teleological overtones of Smithian political economy were dropped by Malthus, Ricardo, and their successors, the market economy came to be viewed as a natural phenomenon to whose iron laws men had best accommodate themselves.[82] In Bentham's utilitarianism Freyer saw the profit-maximizing criteria of political economy transferred to the domain of ethics.[83] It was the subordination of all realms of existence to the

[80] Freyer, *Bewertung*, 1st ed., 8.
[81] Ibid., 12.
[82] Ibid., 100–103.
[83] Ibid., 113.

demands of the market economy and the extension of the modes of thought characteristic of the market to the realm of ethics that Freyer regarded as the spirit of the nineteenth century.

Though Freyer traced the British and French origins of economic liberalism he also sketched the permeation of the doctrine into German thought and political practice, beginning with the German followers of Adam Smith in the eighteenth century, the partial adoption of liberal economic policies by Stein and Hardenberg, through to the laissez-faire liberalism of John Prince-Smith in the 1860s. Freyer saw the new German *Reich* of 1871 as the embodiment of the *Ottocentogeist*.

The spirit of the nineteenth century, then, was equated with economic liberalism—the belief that the laws of the market are immutable—which was perceived as the logical result of the acceptance of the naturalistic premises of Enlightenment social science. From Freyer's description of liberalism there was no reason to suppose that it represented anything other than the unbridled pursuit of economic self-interest, a priority that was anathema within the cultural circles in which Freyer traveled, not least in the German university.

The bulk of Freyer's book dealt with the nineteenth-century critics of classical political economy and the liberal economic creed. In addition to recapitulating their criticisms of the effects of the economic liberalism, Freyer attempted to analyze the philosophical basis of the various critiques and to offer some guidelines toward a future alternative to liberalism.

Freyer's treatment of the romantic critique of liberal political economy focused on Adam Müller's *Elemente der Staatskunst*. Müller's major contribution to the critique of classical political economy, Freyer wrote, was conceptual. Müller attacked the presuppositions of political economy as static, mechanistic, and overly analytic and insisted that the economy be viewed as part of a larger organic "whole" or "totality," which like any organism was in a process of continual development. The economy ought to be regarded and regulated according to the broader interests of a *Volk* as a whole, conceived as a developing historical entity linking past and future, and not in the interests of individual gain. The portrait of the Middle Ages offered by Müller, Novalis, and other romantics, Freyer wrote, was deliberately idealized and intended as an ideal model for a future organic national economy (*Volkswirtschaft*) in which spiritual and economic reality would no longer be at odds. It represented a conceptual foil to the liberal market economy of the age of capitalism, then in its infancy in Germany.

Freyer's critique of the economic theory of romanticism was aimed not at its goals but at its efficacy. Müller's romantic political economy was largely hortatory, Freyer wrote, and the vagueness of his terminology made it incapable of offering a clear description of the actual functioning of the economy. Moreover, Freyer continued, the organic analogies so beloved by the romantics, with their promise of collective harmony, were ill suited for an analysis of the conflict engendered by the new capitalist economy. Indeed, they were ill suited to the necessary demands of any highly technical economy, since they imputed harmony to the natural order of things, rather than making it a conscious task to be realized by social practice. Romanticism, according to Freyer, provided noble visions but little practical direction in overcoming the spirit of the nineteenth century.[84]

Freyer devoted his greatest attention to the changing evaluation of the economy in the thought of the German humanists and idealists and to their later nineteenth-century heirs, Marxism and the historical school of economics.

The works of the "classical" German humanists and idealists—of Goethe, Schiller, Pestalozzi, Fichte, and Hegel—at the turn of the nineteenth century focused much of their criticism of the Enlightenment on "the question of the ethical value of *Zivilisation*, of external goods, bourgeois labor, and the bourgeois social order." They regarded the new order based upon egoism and the increasing division of labor as leading to the ruin of culture, since it inhibited ethical strivings and threatened to destroy the individual as a well-rounded, multifaceted "totality." In their mature writings, however, Pestalozzi, Goethe, Fichte, and Hegel concurred in accepting the legitimacy of the new economy as expanding man's powers and completing his personality.[85] Hegel alone among the idealists, however, made a serious attempt to understand the new economy and explain its positive role in historical development. Yet, Freyer claimed, he did so largely by accepting the naturalistic, mechanistic explanation of economic life offered by the classical political economy of the Enlightenment. Hegel's view of the new economy, Freyer believed, was essentially undynamic and not in keeping with the dialectical perspective of his system as a whole. Not only was the economic basis of the three political estates in *The Philosophy of Right* backward-looking, but Hegel's analysis failed to consider new trends within ascendant capitalism, such as the greater scale of technology, the intensification of the market economy, and the new forms of organizing work.

[84] Ibid., 49–53. [85] Ibid., 23, 27–29, 35.

The greatest exponent of German idealism, according to Freyer, therefore failed to consider the dialectical implications of the ongoing transformation of the technical and economic basis of society.[86]

It was Karl Marx who, in Freyer's view, first succeeded in applying the dialectical principles of Hegelian idealism to the economic realm. In the concept of surplus value he discovered the principle of dynamic change for the capitalist economy just as Hegel had discovered it for previous stages of history. Yet in bringing German idealism down to earth by considering the material basis of historical development, Marx—and especially Engels—had, in Freyer's eyes, gone overboard and embraced a materialist philosophy of history that was as one-sided as the German idealism it sought to correct. By portraying the material basis of society as the source of society's ideals it ignored the cultural and social-psychological context in which economic life itself was embedded. Moreover, Freyer felt that Marx had failed to develop Hegel's "concrete and organizationally oriented ideal of freedom" in a more social direction and had instead embraced a "superficial, egalitarian" notion of freedom characteristic of the French utopian socialists. Thus, despite the advance over Hegel, Marx had also helped to set back the "realization of German socialism" to which Freyer himself was committed.[87]

Freyer charted a second road leading from Hegel through a more "realistic Hegelianism," one that he felt was more likely to lead to a German socialism. This road began with Lorenz von Stein and then branched out into a number of intellectual paths in the second half of the nineteenth century. The most significant of these paths, from Freyer's perspective, was that of the German historical school of economics. The historical school rejected the universal and naturalistic categories of classical political economy. It regarded the economy not as the effect of natural laws but as a historical product of the culture of a particular *Volk* and hence comprehensible only within the larger national culture. This methodological stress on the connection between culture and economic life had led to a normative concern with the proper role of the economy in realizing cultural goals. Many members of the historical school had been avid supporters of capitalism, but Freyer held that it was not the particular policies of its members but the critique of the premises of classical political economy that made the school particularly significant. On the whole the historical school had remained "bourgeois" and had failed to recognize that capitalism itself might be a historically passing phase, as Marx had made clear. Though

[86] Ibid., 54–59.　　　　　　　　　[87] Ibid., 92–98.

its premises did not necessarily lead to state-socialist conclusions, they made such conclusions possible, and such conclusions had been drawn by some nineteenth-century philosophers such as Lorenz von Stein, Friedrich List, and Johann Karl Rodbertus.[88] It was the historical, national, and social road from Hegel that emerged from Freyer's book as the harbinger of the new spirit of the twentieth century.

In the penultimate chapter of his book Freyer introduced a new theme that was to occupy a central place in his concerns for the next five decades, namely the relationship between technology (*Technik*) and culture. The development of capitalism in the nineteenth century had been accompanied by the rapid growth of technology. As this system of means had become ever more complicated and differentiated, it threatened, according to Freyer, to overshadow human ends and goals. Out of the broader discussion of the value of the economy during nineteenth-century thought, there arose the burning issue of the value of technology.[89]

Freyer's sympathies lay with those thinkers who combined the ethical critique of technology with a desire to maintain the material benefits that technology had brought, who sought a new culture that would preserve technological advance while integrating it into a larger moral purpose. The positivist legatees of eighteenth-century naturalism—Saint-Simon, Comte, Mill, and Spencer—had suggested such a program. The inadequacy of their solution, Freyer held, lay in their naturalistic conception of ethics, which remained formalistic, detached from historical particularity and unable to appeal to the human heart. Yet it was they who had correctly formulated what Freyer saw as the task of his generation, namely to create a "culture not *through* technology, but also not in opposition to technology, rather culture within technology through overcoming capitalist man."[90]

This was the problem to which the final chapter of the book was devoted. Among those who had suggested the need to transcend capitalist man were the nineteenth-century heirs of romanticism, Schopenhauer, Jakob Burckhardt, Richard Wagner, and Nietzsche. All of them, according to Freyer, had seen *Zivilisation* and technology as unnatural and in inexorable conflict with culture, the unfolding of man's creative essence. They railed against the economized "pseudoculture" of the nineteenth century and looked to the man of genius to create a culture that would transcend capitalist man.

---

[88] Ibid., 117, 128–31.

[89] Ibid., 134–35.

[90] Ibid., 146–48.

While Freyer sympathized with their low evaluation of the cultural worth of the spirit of the nineteenth century, he saw their solution as a cul-de-sac. For the message offered by these critics—whom he referred to collectively and somewhat deprecatingly as *die Kultivierten*—involved turning one's back entirely on the economic realm. Though they were unaware of it, Freyer wrote, the cultural criticism of the *Kultivierten* was based on the economic security provided them by the capitalist economy. It was intentionally detached from real life (*lebensfern*) and uninterested in solving the problems presented by the economy.[91] Freyer's stance toward the existing German tradition of cultural criticism was one of respectful dissatisfaction.

Freyer evinced the greatest admiration for those thinkers who had revolted against the ethical and cultural deficiencies of the nineteenth century, had been haunted by "the social question," and yet had sought to affirm the legitimacy of modern technology. They had realized that capitalist man could only be transcended by the creation of a "unified, concrete, total culture rich in its power to bind." They had recognized, Freyer wrote, that

What is necessary is the construction of a strongly structured spiritual unity that completely grasps and envelops the individual. Only a new religion which releases the deeper powers of man from their petrification and integrates them into a productive will beyond the petty interests of party and class; a system of ethical ideals that operate with the immediate power of self-understood truths; in short regaining or awakening common and certain constants of will and faith that are related to one another and to the center of our lives, will be able to lead us from the individualistic fragmentation and the overrefined materialism of the nineteenth century to a new culture.[92]

Freyer deemed this to be the task of his generation. The owl of Minerva, he wrote, did not fly only at dusk; philosophy could also provide the age with "the consciousness of its present and future tasks." The contemporary role of the human sciences (*Geisteswissenschaften*) was to aid in the creation of a new culture in which economic life was once again subordinated to broader cultural ends. This task required the formulation of a new social science of cultural development. It would share with the Enlightenment's conception of social science the aim of uncovering the lawful regularities of cultural life, but—like German historicism—it would pay attention to the "genetic context of cultural structures" and hence transcend rationalistic errors of the Enlightenment. This new *Geisteswissenschaft* was to be complemented by a new philosophical ethic

[91] Ibid., 153–54.   [92] Ibid., 159–60.

that would reconsider the value of *Zivilisation* and *Kultur* in human life.[93] It was to the formulation of a new philosophy which embodied these aspirations and a new social science which could aid in their realization that Freyer was to devote the next decade of his life.

[93] Ibid., 160–61.

CHAPTER THREE

Radical Conservatism as Social Theory,
1920–1925

Hans Freyer was a prolific writer, but he was never so productive as in the years between his habilitation and his return to Leipzig in 1925, during which he wrote and published three books. A sense of personal and generational mission, the extreme economic and political crises of the Weimar Republic, and a talent for synthesizing disparate intellectual currents resulted in an outpouring of prose. But his achievement was more than quantitative; all of the key themes of his radical conservative social theory are to be found in his works of this period, as is his totalitarian political solution to the problems of his age.

Academic Success and Young Adherents

The three years following the completion of his *Habilitationsschrift* were years of financial and professional uncertainty for Hans Freyer. In 1920 he began his career as a *Privatdozent*, remunerated by the fees that his students paid to hear his lectures. His pedagogy mirrored his broad interests. The introductory lecture (*Antrittsvorlesung*) on the occasion of his habilitation in 1920, entitled "The Individual Law in Ethics," reflected the continuing influence of Georg Simmel on his thought.[1] Freyer lectured during 1920 and 1921 on "The History of Sociology" and "The Philosophy of History" and led tutorials on "Nietzsche's Philosophy of Culture" and "The Developmental Psychology of Higher Economic Forms."[2] In addition he taught courses on German philosophy at the Fichte-Hochschule. Among his students there was Käthe Lübeck, a young woman active in the Leipzig Wandervogel, who would eventually become his wife.[3] Yet Freyer was without a dependable source of income and in no financial position to marry. His earnings from lectures at the university and the Fichte-Hochschule were insufficient, and he depended for financial

---

[1] Michael Landmann, "Einleitung der Herausgebers," in *Georg Simmel: Das individuelle Gesetz*, 24.

[2] Universität Leipzig, *Verzeichnis der Vorlesungen*, 1920; 1921.

[3] Interview with Käthe Freyer.

support on his brother, a businessman who had settled in New York before the war.[4]

During these years Freyer published his *Habilitationsschrift* in a series edited by Felix Krueger and his prewar essay on Fichte and duty in *Kantstudien*, one of the foremost journals of academic philosophy. He published his earlier essay on utopia in the *Deutsche Rundschau*, one of the leading magazines of the intellectual right. The first edition of his wartime *Antäus* had sold out its initial run of three thousand copies, and a second edition was published by Diederichs in 1922. In the same period Freyer completed and published two new books. The first, *Prometheus: Ideen zur Philosophie der Kultur*, written in the image-laden, aphoristic style characteristic of the youth movement and dedicated to Käthe Lübeck, was published by Eugen Diederichs. Freyer also planned to publish his third book, *Theorie des objektiven Geistes: Eine Einleitung in der Kulturphilosophie*, with Diederichs. The editors at Diederichs Verlag felt it was too "academic," however, a characterization that Freyer later disputed.[5] Each party had a point. The book was written in the formal, propositional style of academic philosophy, but its intentions were no more "academic" than those of Freyer's earlier works. The book was finally published by Teubner Verlag, a very academic publisher indeed, but because of financial constraints, no doubt connected with the great inflation, it appeared in a somewhat abbreviated form.[6]

Professional recognition and a measure of economic security came at the age of thirty-six, when, in October 1922, Freyer was called to a chair of philosophy at the small, provincial University of Kiel. Before assuming his new post early in 1923, he married his fiancée. Freyer's familial and vocational status was thereby consolidated, but the inflation left his economic status precarious: during the inflation he too was paid twice a week and was nearly bankrupt.[7] The years in Kiel were happy nevertheless. Freyer's manner was far from the aloofness usually associated with contemporary German professors, and he attracted a group of students, some of whom later followed him to Leipzig.[8]

Among those to whom Freyer was closest was a doctoral student nine years his junior. Wilhelm Ahlmann, the scion of a Kiel banking family, was one of

[4] Felix Krueger to philosophische Fakultät, 26 June 1922, UAL, PA Freyer, 19.

[5] Hans Freyer to Eugen Diederichs, 22 March 1926, Diederichs Archiv, Universitätsarchiv Jena.

[6] Philosophische Fakultät to Ministerium des Kultes und öffentlichen Unterrichts, 14 June 1923, UAL, PA Freyer, 46–52 (written by Krueger).

[7] Käthe Freyer interview.

[8] Interview with Ernest Manheim, Martha's Vineyard.

Freyer's friends of *großbürgerlich* origins. Like so many of Freyer's friends, Ahlmann had enlisted as a volunteer when the war broke out and rose to the rank of officer. Then in 1916 he blinded himself in an accident. He obtained a law degree in Berlin nevertheless, and he returned to Kiel to study psychology. There he was befriended by Freyer, who interested him in political thought. The young professor so impressed Ahlmann that he followed him in 1925 to Leipzig, where he remained until 1933, when he would depart for the Ministry of Education in Berlin.[9]

Another student whom Freyer affected deeply was Graf Karlfried von Dürckheim-Montmartin. The son of an army officer and estate owner, Dürckheim was twenty when the war broke out and spent most of it at the front. He returned from the war in November 1918 to find his native Bavaria under the control of the radical socialist government of Kurt Eisner and passed several weeks in prison for his armed resistance to the Spartacist movement there. Released from prison, he spent the first months of 1919 engaged in anticommunist pamphleteering. Convinced that the reconstruction of Germany required the creation of a "new man" who embodied a "new world view," Dürckheim decided to study philosophy and to become a pedagogue. After studying in Kiel he too followed Freyer back to Leipzig, where he became an *Assistent* in the institute of Freyer's mentor, Felix Krueger.[10]

The student to whom Freyer developed the closest academic relationship was Ernst (later Ernest) Manheim. Of Hungarian-Jewish origin, Manheim grew up in Budapest with a firm sense of Austro-Hungarian identity and had served in the First World War. Upon his return to Budapest after the war he joined the Red Army of Béla Kun and fought against Czech and Romanian forces to preserve Hungarian sovereignty in the disputed border areas of the new successor states. After the war he studied in Vienna and then in Kiel, where he met and befriended Hans Freyer and his wife. In 1925 he too followed Freyer to Leipzig.[11]

As the incumbent of a chair of philosophy, Freyer taught a number of survey courses, mostly on modern and contemporary German philosophy, and courses on the philosophy of culture and the philosophy of history. The topics of Freyer's seminars were usually reliable indices of his current interests. In his

---

[9] On Ahlmann, see *Tymbos für Wilhelm Ahlmann*, ix–xii; interviews with Käthe Freyer and Ernest Manheim.

[10] Graf Karlfried von Dürckheim-Montmartin, "Einige Daten aus meinem Lebenslauf" (n.p., n.d.), BDC.

[11] Interview with Ernest Manheim; "Einführung des Herausgebers," in Ernst Manheim, *Aufklärung und öffentliche Meinung*; Mathias Greffrath, "Der analytische Geist der deutschen Wissenschaft, nicht der spekulative, hat mich beeindruckt: Ein Gespräch mit Ernst Manheim."

last two semesters at Kiel, they dealt with "The Economic and Social Philosophy of the Romantics" (which included an examination of Adam Müller) and "The Contemporary Philosophy of History" (in which Spengler's work loomed large).[12] He also held an informal study group for advanced students of contemporary social theory which met on Sunday mornings in Ferdinand Tönnies' office, though the two men do not appear to have been personally close.[13]

In October 1924 Freyer was called back to Leipzig to assume the newly created chair of sociology. Before his return to Leipzig in the spring of 1925 he completed work on *Der Staat*, a book that combined the philosophy of history with social and political theory. It marked a culmination of his earlier endeavors and straddled the two earlier styles in which he had written, combining a systematic, dialectical presentation with an evocative and urgent style unburdened by footnotes.

Meaning and Delimitation

The three works that Freyer wrote between 1920 and 1925 cover the same intellectual ground but with differing conceptual emphases and in varying modulations appropriate to their disparate prospective audiences. *Prometheus: Ideen zur Philosophie der Kultur* was written in the aphoristic, metaphorical style of *Antäus*, a style much favored among the popular expositors of *Lebensphilosophie* and the older generation of the youth movement. Many of the same thoughts were presented in a more austere, systematic form in *Theorie des objektiven Geistes: Eine Einleitung in die Kulturphilosophie*, a book thrice reprinted (in 1928, 1934, and 1963) and of importance in the subsequent history of German philosophy and social science, as a transitional work in the transformation of hermeneutics from a methodology of the *Geisteswissenschaften* (in Dilthey) to a broader philosophy of existence (in the work of Hans-Georg Gadamer) and in the development of "philosophical anthropology."[14] Freyer's third work,

[12] Universität Kiel, *Verzeichnis der Vorlesungen*, 1924 and 1925.

[13] Rudolf Heberle, "Soziologische Lehr- und Wanderjahre," 199; Rudolf Heberle to author, 17 February 1981; Annemarie Hermberg to author, 7 March 1981.

[14] In an interview with the author (Boston, 12 December 1982) Gadamer acknowledged that he had read Freyer's *Theorie des objektiven Geistes* upon its publication in 1923 with great interest. There are striking similarities between Freyer's

theory of tradition as analyzed below and Gadamer's notion of the "fusion of horizons" in interpreting a tradition, summarized in David E. Linge, "Editor's Introduction," to Hans-Georg Gadamer, *Philosophical Hermeneutics*, xix.

Freyer's emphasis on the role of institutions created by men in providing meaning and orientation for the otherwise purposeless individual appears to have influenced both Helmuth Plessner and Arnold Gehlen, the two major theorists of "philosophical anthropology" in twen-

Der Staat, drew out the implications of his philosophy of culture and his critique of contemporary society for political philosophy and political action. Though written in differing voices and vocabularies, the three works complement one another where they do not actually overlap and hence will be treated collectively.

Freyer's views on the nature of culture, of politics, and of the contemporary human predicament were based upon a core conception of the nature of man, on what Germans have come to call a "philosophical anthropology."[15] Freyer often expressed this core conception of his social thought in metaphorical terms. The controlling metaphors were of boundedness and unboundedness or of openness and closedness. Freyer used these metaphors to express his central concern, that of possibility and limitation. For Freyer it was unbounded possibility that most threatened contemporary man. His political philosophy stressed the need for boundaries, and his political program was a quest for collective delimitation.

The image that underlay Freyer's social theory was of life as a constantly flowing stream. The image referred both to the life of the individual, which was characterized by spontaneous, vital energy, and to collective history, which was a dynamic process of change and flux.[16] As we have seen, Freyer adopted this Heraclitean perspective from Simmel and Dilthey, and he now attempted to develop an entire philosophy of culture on the basis of their *Philosophie des Lebens*.

In Freyer's *Antäus* he explored at length the anxiety attendant upon the perception that life lacks fixed purpose. Though less overt in his subsequent works, this anxiety—soon to become the stock in trade of Weimar existentialism—remained the dominant presentiment in his later books as well. Individ-

---

tieth-century Germany. Both Plessner and Gehlen drew attention to the biological basis of this human dependence on external institutions, a perspective that did not interest Freyer. See the positive reference to Freyer's "objectivism" in Plessner's early work, *Grenzen der Gemeinschaft* (1924), now in his *Gesammelte Schriften*, vol. 5. On Gehlen's theory of institutions, see his *Der Mensch* (1940 and later editions). Gehlen was a younger colleague of Freyer's at Leipzig and his friend from the early 1930s until Freyer's death in 1969. Gehlen's intellectual and political development are briefly recounted in the Appendix of this book. On "philosophical anthropology"

as an intellectual current, see Karl-Siegbert Rehberg, "Philosophische Anthropologie und die 'Soziologisierung' des Wissens vom Menschen."

[15] The reference here is to "philosophical anthropology" as systematic philosophizing about human nature, not to the specific movement discussed by Rehberg. On "philosophical anthropology" in this broader sense, see Jurgen Habermas, "Philosophische Anthropologie," in his *Kultur und Kritik*.

[16] Hans Freyer, *Theorie des objektiven Geistes: Eine Einleitung in die Kulturphilosophie* (1923), 58, 66; Hans Freyer, *Der Staat* (1925), 15–16.

ual life in its immediate, energic, vital flux was devoid of meaning. A feeling of individual purpose or meaning was therefore tied to the possibility of gaining a sense of fixedness, of boundaries. Only through a limiting relationship to something *more* than himself could the individual acquire a sense *of* himself.

The source of boundaries on the labile self and hence of meaning was culture, a term that Freyer (following Simmel) used in the broadest sense to indicate all the externalized creations of men. Culture was created whenever subjective actions resulted in the transformation of the material world such that they took on an objective existence of their own, independent of the process of their creation.[17] Echoing the Hegelian dictum that had served as the motto of his doctoral dissertation ("der Weg des Geistes ist die Vermittlung, der Umweg"), Freyer regarded culture as "the attempt of mankind to find a transcendent meaning for its life by the circuitous route through the objective."[18]

The individual could escape the limitless flux of subjective life only by internalizing the delimiting purposes provided by culture, a process that Freyer termed *Bildung* (cultivation, or formation).[19] It was only through his relations with others that the individual acquired such delimiting purposes. The solution to the problem of individual identity thus lay in the ability of social groups to convey a set of delimiting purposes to the individual, and this in turn depended upon the stability of the social groups of which the individual was a part. The overt emphasis of Freyer's social theory was on the problem of social integration; behind it lay his conviction that only through membership in stable, well-integrated social groups was the individual freed from the sense of limitlessness intrinsic in subjective life.

The thrust of Freyer's theory of social groups was voluntaristic or idealistic.[20] Men existed as a group primarily by virtue of sharing some common purpose, some collective end or goal. They ultimately cohered through the voluntary subordination of the individual to a collective purpose, and their degree of cohesion reflected the intensity of the commitment to such supraindividual ends.[21] The social groups upon which the individual depended for a sense of stability and delimitation were thus themselves dependent upon the

---

[17] Freyer, *Theorie*, 12.

[18] Ibid., 78.

[19] Ibid., 55. Freyer here follows Hegel's use of the term in the *Phenomenology*, in which the culture to be internalized is not only "high culture" but culture in the anthropological sense of the sum total of institutions and beliefs of a society.

On Hegel's usage, see Judith Shklar, *Freedom and Independence: A Study of the Political Ideas of Hegel's "Phenomenology of Mind,"* 144.

[20] The terms *voluntaristic* and *idealistic* are drawn from Talcott Parsons, *The Structure of Social Action*, 2 vols., passim and esp. 81–82.

[21] Freyer, *Theorie*, 52–54.

affirmation of some higher purpose, of some Aristotelian *telos*. This voluntaristic theory of society and the social origins of individual identity remained the premise of Freyer's social thought throughout his lifetime. In his radical conservative phase the source of individual purpose was presumed to lie in the tight integration of society as a whole.

Purpose and Particularity

Assuming, as Freyer did, that society required some ultimate purpose or collective aim, from where was this goal to come? This has of course been the core question for any voluntarist social theorist who aims, as Freyer did, to be not merely descriptive but normative—who intends not merely to describe the aims by which societies *might* be held together but to prescribe the aims by which a particular society *should* be integrated.

Could a society not agree on some ultimate purpose and a system of institutions and symbols through which to embody such a purpose? Could such a purpose not be freely and rationally chosen, based on universal, rational standards? Could man not create such a rational and universal culture *de novo*? This had in large part been the project of the political theory of the Enlightenment and of its liberal and socialist successors.[22] Freyer's response to all of these questions was negative. His skepticism was a product of the central premises of his radical conservative social theory, namely the connection between meaning, tradition, and particularity.

Freyer's theory of tradition is an outgrowth of his overriding concern for stability in the face of the natural flux of life. In his theory of objective culture this concern was expressed through metaphors of closedness and delimitation. In his theory of tradition the same concern is expressed in metaphors of weight and depth. The role of culture was to slow down the river of time, to provide stability amid flux. Were culture to change as quickly as life itself, it would fail to fulfill the stabilizing function that it occupied in Freyer's social thought. Life lived only in an awareness of the present, in a system of institutions, values, and symbols that reflected only the needs of contemporary life, lacked "depth," that is, the ability to slow down the river of life, the subjective

---

[22] This rationalist universalism had been most characteristic of the French Enlightenment. The universalist element was weaker in the German Enlightenment (see Peter Reill, *The German Enlightenment and the Rise of Historicism*), while the leading lights of the Scottish Enlightenment had been more attuned to the unanticipated consequences of purposive action as the motor force of history. See Friedrich Hayek, *The Constitution of Liberty*, chapter 4, and the rejoinder by Lionel Robbins, "Hayek on Liberty."

experience of time. Since the needs of life changed, cultural forms that expressed only present needs and sensibilities were "shallow," subject to constant replacement by new cultural forms.

How, then, did cultural forms acquire "depth," some degree of permanence amid the changing needs of men over historical time? The cultural products of the past had, after all, embodied the immediate needs and purposes of past life that brought them into being. "Life" had since changed. How could the objective culture of the past be relevant to the subjective life of the present? How could subjective life appropriate the objective culture of the past?

Freyer's answer was that the appropriation of the culture of the past was in part its misappropriation. Each objective cultural form embodies some meaning that it had for its creator, a meaning of which later men are to some degree aware. But in appropriating the cultural form for their own use later men give it a differing interpretation, one commensurate with the needs of their own lives. They "reinterpret" it by superimposing this new meaning upon the old object. Yet they also retain some awareness of the older meaning of the object. Thus a cultural object from the past, reinterpreted and reappropriated time and again by succeeding generations, acquires multiple meanings. This addition of meanings to cultural forms gives them a greater "weight" than forms created *de novo* by contemporary life. Stated less metaphorically, cultural forms acquire greater emotional resonance for the present by virtue of their multiple past associations and connotations. Through tradition—the reappropriation of past culture—contemporary life thus acquires some historical "weight," some continuity with the past that gives "depth" to the culture of the present and enhances social stability.[23]

This theory of tradition is distinct from "traditionalism," the belief that things ought always to be done as they have been in the past. "Traditionalism" is grounded in the assumption that the most essential aspects of existence remain the same over time. Freyer's theory of tradition is premised upon the opposite—and characteristically modern—historicist assumption that fundamental change predominates in human history.[24] Freyer's historicist, *lebensphilosophische* theory of tradition is dynamic, based on the need to actively reappropriate the culture of the past for present purposes, which inevitably involves its partial reinterpretation.

Freyer's critique of enlightened, rationalist universalism was two-pronged. The role of tradition, of grounding in the past as the source of cultural

[23] Freyer, *Theorie*, 94–98.
[24] Leo Strauss summarizes the presup- positions of historicism in the first chapter of his *Natural Right and History*.

"weight," was the first prong. His conception of the relationship between meaning and particularity formed the second prong. Since for Freyer personal meaning was linked to collective stability, collective integration was linked to collective purpose, and collective purpose was linked to the renewal of tradition, the question inevitably arose of *which* tradition ought to form the basis of collective purpose. Those aware of the great multiplicity of national and historical cultures were most apt to regard the choice of cultural traditions with which to identify as arbitrary. Were such a choice truly arbitrary—were there no overriding criteria for choosing one cultural tradition over another—the result would be indecision and inaction, accompanied by the sense of meaninglessness that Freyer's entire program was intended to obviate. In such a case, he wrote, "The melancholy of multiple possibilities lies upon us and paralyzes our action."[25] This was precisely the situation in which Freyer and other intellectual legatees of German historicism had found themselves.

In contradistinction to all philosophies that asserted the existence of some universal set of norms appropriate for all men on the basis of their common humanity and accessible to all through reason, revelation, or participation in some unified process of historical development, Freyer maintained that meaning exists in history *only* in multiplicity.[26] "History," he wrote, "thinks in plurals, and its teaching is that there is more than one solution for the human equation."[27] The "plurals" were the various distinct historical cultures, each of which was created and transmitted by a historical collectivity or *Volk*. This assumption, as Freyer often noted, was a legacy of the German historicist tradition, the axioms of which had been laid bare by Wilhelm Dilthey. Dilthey's primary concern had been scholarly, to lay the conceptual foundations for a social science based upon historicist assumptions. In the case of Hans Freyer, these historicist assumptions now became the basis of a normative social theory and a prescriptive plan of political action centered on the concept of the *Volk*.

No concept was more important for Freyer's political program of the 1920s and 1930s than that of the *Volksgeist*—and none is less given to precise definition. The pivotal role of the concept and its conceptual haziness were not unconnected.

Freyer's entire project of the creation of a cohesive society integrated by a common commitment to a particular cultural tradition depended upon the possibility of making a nonarbitrary choice of cultural traditions. It depended, that is to say, on the existence of some authoritative basis for choosing to com-

[25] Hans Freyer, *Prometheus: Ideen zur Philosophie der Kultur* (1923), 70.

[26] Freyer, *Der Staat*, 194.

[27] Freyer, *Prometheus*, 78.

mit oneself and one's society to the renewal of a particular tradition. Building upon the German historicist critique of the Enlightenment, he held that this basis of authority could not be rationalist. Nor could there be a scientific basis of selection, for the historicist methodology of the *Geisteswissenschaften* was premised upon the equal legitimacy of all cultures and could not provide the basis for normative choice from among historic or national cultures. Nor was a revival of the right-Hegelian principle that the real was the rational possible for Freyer; his system was an expression of disaffection from the existing cultural order. This left the frank affirmation of the nonrational as the only possible source of authority.

The *Volksgeist* (collective spirit or culture) of one's own *Volk* was to be affirmed not because of its superiority to other *Volksgeister* as judged by some universal, rational standard, but—since no such standard existed—because it was the historical basis of continuing particularity. Rationalist universalism, according to Freyer, dissolved all connection with a particular culture of the past that could add depth to the culture of the present, leaving no bounded collectivity toward which the individual could subordinate himself. During his radical conservative phase Freyer judged the affirmation of collective historical particularity in the form of the *Volk* to be the only alternative to the unbounded society and ephemeral culture of rationalist universalism. Since there could be no meaningful culture without historical particularity, Freyer asserted that the individual ought to embrace the *Volk* into which he was born. Thus birth into a particular *Volk* was to be elevated into a consciously affirmed fate.[28]

The premises of this affirmation of collective particularity in Freyer's social thought of the 1920s and 1930s was that there existed a homogeneous collectivity that could be identified as the *Volk* and a relatively homogeneous cultural tradition that was the product of the *Volksgeist*. Unfortunately, in the case of the Germans at least, neither condition could be demonstrably fulfilled.

Freyer was almost certainly aware at some level that these premises could not

[28] The anxiety attendant upon the recognition of the purposelessness of individual life and the resulting arbitrariness of a life of unbounded possibilities—the dominant presentiment underlying Freyer's social theory—was the central theme of Martin Heidegger's *Sein und Zeit* (1927). Like Freyer, Heidegger sought to resolve the dilemmas of individual purposelessness through a voluntaristic affirmation of the collective fate of one's *Volk* and generation; see *Sein und Zeit*, 382–87, and the discussion in Gerald Izenberg, *The Existentialist Critique of Freud*, 250–55. The parallels between Freyer's work of the 1920s and that of Martin Heidegger are significant not because of the former's influence upon the latter but because they underline the extent to which Freyer's broad concerns and political solutions were shared by other major intellectuals on the Weimar right.

survive systematic historical scrutiny. For in 1919, Walter Goetz—the co-sponsor of Freyer's *Habilitationsschrift*, one of Germany's most accomplished historians, and an active member of the German Democratic party—published a small book entitled *Das Wesen der deutschen Kultur*. Goetz set out to refute by historical evidence the belief that there existed some ongoing essence of the German *Volk*. The book was aimed against those "who dream of an enclosed state based on German culture."[29] Goetz pointed to major differences in the cultural traditions of the northern, southern, eastern, and western portions of Germany; chronicled the continuing role of foreign influence on German culture; and demonstrated historically that contemporary Germans were a mixture of many races. Goetz emphasized the multiplicity of German culture and the impossibility of achieving some unitary definition thereof and pointed out the conceptual difficulties of notions such as *Volkskultur, Volkstum,* or *Volksgeist*.[30]

Freyer's use of the concepts of *Volk* and *Volksgeist* as the plinths of his political program was thus based upon a selective forgetfulness, a tacit decision not to apply rational, critical scrutiny to these notions. It represented the embrace of a myth in the Sorelian sense, of a belief that is affirmed not because it is necessarily true but because it is functional in terms of some integrative, political cause.[31] The notion of a distinctive historical unit called the German *Volk* and of a distinctive homogeneous culture that was the product of its underlying *Volksgeist* played an essential function in Freyer's program of social integration. It was a notion with a long pedigree in German intellectual history and with broad contemporary political resonance.[32] If scientific scholarly research showed it to be faulty, so much the worse for science.

This is not to say that Freyer was consciously aware of the untenability of his usage of the concepts of *Volk* and *Volksgeist*. Yet he offered a variety of definitions of the *Volk*, indicating a tacit awareness of the problematic nature of the concept; he seemed in fact to be constantly in search of a conceptualization of the *Volk* that would make it plausible—not least to himself.

In his *Theorie des objektiven Geistes*, written for a professional, academic audience, Freyer referred to the concept of *Volksgeist* as a "mythology" through which German historians and philosophers of history since Herder had expressed insights into the social psychology of cultural creation. He derided the

[29] Walter Goetz, *Das Wesen der deutschen Kultur* (1919), 3.

[30] Ibid., passim, esp. 3–8, 42–45.

[31] Georges Sorel, *Reflections on Violence*, 125.

[32] On the centrality of the concept of the *Volk* in the work of Freyer's teachers, see Schultz, "History," passim. On the tradition of *völkisch* thought, see Mosse, *Crisis*.

notion of a collective mind or psyche and insisted that every social-psychological experience was ultimately reducible to individual consciousnesses.[33] In this scientific setting he described *Volk* in a manner similar to the notion of "national character," as common psychological predispositions shared by members of a particular nation. His definitions left open the question of whether such common predispositions are biological or cultural in origin.[34]

In the same book Freyer drew on Hegel, Dilthey, and Spengler in an attempt to reformulate the concept of *Volksgeist* in a systematic, scientific manner, but even this most systematic of his expositions remains little more than suggestive. Each historical culture, he wrote, is the expression of a basic group attitude, "which is thoroughly prerational, unformulated, and nonconscious." The entire culture of each group (which he equated with *Volk*) is the realization or development of this particular "primordial attitude toward the world."[35] Each culture therefore places a different accent on the characteristic features of human life.[36] Freyer provided few specific examples of the manner in which such collective particularities were expressed in culture. He regarded language as the most important expression of the *Volksgeist* and the major constitutive element of the *Volk*.

When writing for a nonscientific audience drawn from the youth movement and the intellectual right Freyer wrote of the organic origins of the *Volk* in race or blood.[37] Writing for the same audience he would elsewhere refer to *Volk* as the result of the historical interaction of a particular race with a particular landscape—as a product of *Blut* and *Heimat*.[38] Yet whenever Freyer sought to define these terms he did so not according to their literal *meaning* but to their social or psychological *function*. Thus blood was "that which comprises our essence, and from which we cannot separate ourselves without degenerating." *Heimat* was "that place from which we come and which we cannot abandon without becoming sick."[39] The key terms in Freyer's programmatic thought were thus tautological metaphors; to write of blood as the ultimate source of collective identity and then to *define* blood as the ultimate source of collective identity is to have added nothing to our knowledge of the actual origin of collective identity. What remains is the affirmation of an image of emotive power, an image that evoked the importance of collective particularity.

For ultimately it was this reassertion of collective particularity as a basis of

[33] Freyer, *Theorie*, 80–81.
[34] Ibid., 86–87.
[35] Ibid., 111–13.
[36] Ibid., 119.

[37] Freyer, *Prometheus*, 58, 89.
[38] Freyer, *Der Staat*, 151.
[39] Ibid.

social integration that concerned Freyer. He did indeed believe that each *Volk*
embodied some *telos*, some distinct meaning that it could express, and that the
expression of this particular meaning was the only sort of meaning in history
and hence the only source of higher purpose for the individual. But both the
origins and the substantive expressions of this particular collective attitude remained shrouded in mist in Freyer's work. A comparison of the various uses
of the term *Volk* in Freyer's work of the early 1920s shows it to have *denoted*
very little but to have *connoted* a good deal, namely the myth of common origin
and common cultural substance.

Freyer's use of the term *Volk* could remain so substantively vague in his
works of the 1920s because neither the academic nor the extra-academic audience to whom these works were addressed was likely to question the legitimacy of the term or demand a precise definition. We have seen that, even before World War I, Freyer's teachers at Leipzig had based much of their
scholarly work on the premise of the reality of the *Volk* as a unit of investigation. During the war the sensitivity toward national cultural differences was
heightened, and the notion of some unchanging collective essence became a
commonplace—among scholars no less than outside the academy. The frequent and blurry use of the term dated back at least as far as Herder, was
brought into greater currency by the *völkisch* movements of the Wilhelmine
era, and was reinvigorated by the nationalist outpourings of the war years. By
the Weimar period Freyer's extra-academic audience was so accustomed to in-
vocations of the *Volk* that it took the concept for granted. Especially to those
with memories of the war fresh in their minds, the concept of the *Volk* represented a plausible source of collective affirmation and individual meaning.

Culture, Technology, and the State

A society that lacked a common collective purpose, Freyer believed, left the
lives of its members bereft of meaning. It might leave them free to pursue their
individual interests and vocations, but without some larger collective goal the
pursuit of individual choices would be arbitrary. Only a society devoted to the
affirmation of its particularity could provide the individual with a sense of purpose. It was this perspective that lay at the heart of Freyer's critique of contemporary Germany in the 1920s. In *Prometheus* Freyer expressed his hate for
"chaotic ages without any limits."[40] "We have a bad conscience in regard to our

---

[40] Freyer, *Prometheus*, 57.

age," he wrote. "We feel ourselves to be unconfirmed, lacking in meaning, un-fulfilled, not even obligated."[41] For Freyer an open society was a meaningless society. His philosophy of history was primarily concerned with explaining how modern society had become so open, his political philosophy with how it could be closed again.

The philosophy of history was among Freyer's major concerns from his doc-toral dissertation through his last book, published in 1965. The philosophy of history was the most direct secular descendant of religion in offering a broad vision of the direction and meaning of history, and Freyer came to regard so-ciology as the legitimate heir of the philosophy of history. In an essay pub-lished in 1931, "Systems of Contemplating World History," he remarked that one's ordering of the past depended upon one's evaluation of the present and future, and therefore "in the deepest sense historical contemplation has always reflected the self-understanding of the present." The stages of history pre-sented by a philosopher of history therefore exemplify the philosopher's own values.[42] This was certainly true of Freyer's own writings on the philosophy of history; his changing periodization and evaluation of the past reflected his own changing attitude toward the present.

The close relationship between the evaluation of present and past is most explicit in Freyer's book *Der Staat*. The book combines a schematized philoso-phy of history with political philosophy and an explicit political program for the future. History is divided into three stages. In Hegelian fashion, each of the first two stages embodies certain positive traits and negative limitations. In the third stage the positive traits are preserved and combined, the negative limitations transcended. Within this historical scheme contemporary Euro-pean man found himself on the threshold of the third stage.

The earliest of these stages of social and cultural life Freyer termed "faith" (*Glaube*). It is the prealienated stage of collective life, the stage at which there is no conflict between human ends and human means. Above all it is a closed and self-enclosed society.

Man at the stage of *Glaube* is completely surrounded, encircled, and bound up in a culture that ties him closely to the other members of his society. His culture is composed of myth, cult, and language, all of which complement one another to create a "closed, all-inclusive, airtight realm of forms." The group's beliefs about the natural world are expressed in myth, which interprets the

---

[41] Ibid., 107.
[42] Hans Freyer, "Systeme der weltgeschichtlichen Betrachtung," 5–7.

world solely in terms of its immediate significance for man rather than as an object of intrinsic, disinterested investigation.[43] Man stands at the center of this world, and all of its happenings have meaning for him. By "cult" Freyer refers to customs that regulate man's relations with the world of nature. These customs are hallowed by time, taken for granted, and passed on from generation to generation. They are closely interwoven with myth and reflect the mythic understanding of the world. Nature is of concern insofar as adaptation to it and manipulation of it are required for collective self-sustenance.[44] In language the objects of the external world are named in such a way as to reflect the needs and concerns of the men who name them. Thus language forms a third bond between man and his external world.[45] Together with myth and cult, language creates a relationship between man and his world in which the world is understood in its direct relation to man's needs. In this sense, men at the stage of *Glaube* are unalienated. They live, wrote Freyer, in a "thou-world" (*Du-Welt*), an existence surrounded with meaning.

By virtue of their shared faith, men at this stage constitute a community (*Gemeinschaft*), which Freyer defined as "the most complete of human ties."[46] Through common faith men acquire a shared attitude toward the world. They share what Freyer termed a common "horizon," a horizon created by the all-encompassing interdependent culture in which they live. Through various metaphors—"shared horizon," "closed realm of forms," "realm of common fate" (*Schicksalsraum*)—Freyer emphasized the closed, delimited, unified culture and society characteristic of this primeval stage.

The closed world of *Gemeinschaft* or *Glaube* was based on consanguinity and common surroundings—on what Freyer elsewhere termed *Blut und Heimat*.[47] Freyer's portrait of this stage was not totally uncritical. Since men lived an unalienated existence in close reliance upon nature, there was no "higher" culture at this stage. Higher culture—science, art, law—was a product of the next stage of culture, the stage that Freyer referred to as "style" (*Stil*).

Given the rather idyllic account of *Glaube*, a society in such a stage would have no internal cause for change. Culture advanced beyond *Glaube* only when two such groups, each united by consanguinity, came into conflict with one another, and one group established its domination (*Herrschaft*) over the other by force.[48] Social relations at the stage of *Stil* are characterized by domination and

---

[43] Freyer, *Der Staat*, 50–51.

[44] Ibid., 52–53.

[45] Ibid., 55.

[46] Ibid., 61.

[47] Ibid., 107.

[48] Ibid., 85. This view of the origins of *Herrschaft* had found its way into German sociology through the work of Ludwig Gumplowicz

dependence. In an enduring *Herrschaft*, society is divided into estates (*Stände*), and social status is based upon ancestry and the belief that blood reflects a natural superiority. The ruling estate exploits the dominated class economically, but the continuing source of inequality lies in the ruling estate's will to dominate and its belief in its own superiority.[49] When this will and belief decline, economic motives replace the will to domination as the predominant ethos of society. The source of social status shifts from ancestry to wealth, and the society of estates is transformed into a class society. The stage that Freyer terms *Stil* is clearly meant to span what Marx and others called the feudal and capitalist stages of development.

It was neither the historic origins of *Stil* nor the structure of domination at this stage that most concerned Freyer, however, but its cultural implications. This is indicated by his rather aesthetic characterization of the era as one of "style." The latent conflict between social groups characteristic of this stage destroys the primeval harmony of *Gemeinschaft* and creates the tension (*Spannung*) that is a prerequisite of high culture. Culture now lost the self-enclosed unity it once possessed.

In the age of "style" the process that Simmel had called "the tragedy of culture" took hold. Each realm of culture takes on a life of its own: new cultural products are created in order to advance a particular realm of culture, rather than to satisfy human needs directly.[50] As each realm develops independently it loses its connection to a specific human group and to a specific historical culture; it thus has a universalistic impetus.[51] Science, for example, is based upon abstracting universal properties from particular instances and discovering the relationships between such properties. "It reaches its goal when the entire contents of the world have been transformed into a structure of relationships, freed from any living subject."[52]

Art becomes devoted to the creation of "absolute forms," works valued for their own sake rather than for their significance in a particular human context. Freyer maintained that in general each realm of culture tended to become an "absolute form," tended toward that self-reference and self-sufficiency characteristic of works of art.[53] In an advanced stage of *Stil*, the various realms of

---

(1838–1909); see, for example, his *Der Rassenkampf: Soziologische Untersuchungen*, 2d ed. (1909), 219ff. Harry Elmer Barnes, "The Social Philosophy of Ludwig Gumplowicz"; Gerald Mozetic, "Ein unzeitgemässer Soziologe: Ludwig Gumplowicz."

[49] Freyer, *Der Staat*, 85–88; Freyer, *Prometheus*, 11–17.

[50] Freyer, *Der Staat*, 66–68.

[51] Ibid., 68, 76.

[52] Ibid., 76.

[53] Ibid., 79–80.

objective culture become independent of one another, develop according to their own logic, and lose their connection to a particular historical subject.[54] The various realms of such a culture no longer fit together into some meaningful totality, no longer provide a closed world of shared horizons for its members.

It was the independent development of one particular realm of culture—that of technology (*Technik*)—which most concerned Hans Freyer. He had approached the problem of technology and culture in his *Habilitationsschrift* and returned to the theme in *Prometheus* (1923), *Der Staat* (1925), and an important essay of 1929 entitled "Toward a Philosophy of Technology," treating the theme with greater precision and clarity over time.

As Freyer had demonstrated in his *Habilitationsschrift*, it had been common for nineteenth-century European intellectuals to regard the spread of technology as a threat to human values. In Germany this had often been expressed as the antagonism of *Zivilisation* to *Kultur*, and especially during and after the First World War the identification of *Kultur* with Germany and of *Zivilisation* with England or France had become widespread. The Latin etymology of *Zivilisation* was itself a mark of the purported foreignness of technology to the German soul. Freyer's own approach to the problem restated and reformulated this fear of the danger posed by technology to culture. But he believed that many of his intellectual contemporaries had botched the problem and that it was soluble through political action.

Freyer argued that by regarding technology as external and inimical to culture, contemporary philosophers had ignored the most important development in modern cultural history, namely the rise of the technological attitude. The rise of modern technology, Freyer wrote, marked a turning point in the history of the West and perhaps in world history.[55] A belief in the plasticity of matter and the possibility of man's active intervention in the natural world was the cultural basis of modern technology. Its origins lay in a historically unique conception of the relationship of man to the world which had its roots deep in the culture of the West and which had become especially predominant since the eighteenth century. The outlook of the technologist or engineer combined the ethos of science, with its emphasis on objectivity, and the ethos of economics, namely that of resource maximization.[56] To emphasize his contention that technology was not inimical to culture but an inalienable part of modern cul-

---

[54] Ibid., 68, 72.
[55] Hans Freyer, "Zur Philosophie der Technik" (1929–30), 200.   [56] Ibid., 193.

ture—including German culture—Freyer referred to it in *Der Staat* not as *Zivilisation* but by the Germanic equivalent, *Gesittung*, which connoted a connection to inherited practice. While the history of culture might well follow a circular pattern of periods of blossoming and decline, the development of technology was unilinear: in the history of technology, progress was a reality.[57] This left open the question of the cultural significance of the new eminence of technology.

Among the interpretations of technology that Freyer found most important was Simmel's.[58] The development of technology, Freyer's teacher had argued, was an extreme instance of the more general "dialectic of means." The attainment of some meaningful end requires that we develop the means to that end. The means that we develop are intrinsically meaningless and possess value only in relation to their ultimate goal. Yet to reach an ultimate goal, we must focus our concern on the next step in the development of the means to its attainment. The more complex the system of means, the more likely we are to lose sight of the ultimate goal of our action. The system of means thus comes to dominate our lives, while ends fade from view.[59] According to this analysis the growing sophistication and omnipresence of technology had led to a "slave revolt" of means against ends, in which a concern with means came to dominate over the ends to which they were originally subordinated.

Like Simmel, Freyer was apprehensive about the perceived aimlessness of a modern technological society. Yet the source of Freyer's concern differed from that of his teacher. Freyer conceived of culture not in the aestheticist or humanist sense in which Simmel and other cultural critics had used it—as a synonym for high culture or cultivated learning—but in a broader, more anthropological sense, as the sum of the beliefs and institutions of a collectivity. Freyer's concern was that the expanding role of technology would result in the decline of collective purpose and the dissolution of particular cultures. Technology and its associated pursuits of science and economics were no respecters of national bounds. The intrinsic logic of these fields was transnational. Left to flourish according to its intrinsic logic and without political control, technology led to the dissolution of political and cultural barriers.[60] The unguided spread of technology would lead to an artificial "crust" over the face of the earth, a "secondary system" without a historical or organic connection to any particular

---

[57] Freyer, *Der Staat*, 170.

[58] For Simmel's view of technology, see, e.g., his "Krisis der Kultur," in his *Der Krieg und die geistigen Entscheidungen* (1917), 45–46.

[59] Freyer, "Technik," 196–97.

[60] Freyer, *Der Staat*, 174–75.

collective culture. All of humanity would eventually be absorbed into "a rationalized order of objective relations, an economic trading company."[61] Given Freyer's premise that meaning arose only from cultural particularity, this prospect was tantamount to universal meaninglessness.

Yet it was Freyer's contention that his prospect of a dawning age devoid of meaning was not an inexorable consequence of the development of technology. Technology might lack intrinsic meaning and purpose, but general purposelessness and an absence of "totality" threatened modern society not because it was dominated by technology but rather by capitalism. The development of technology in modern Europe had until now gone hand in hand with that of capitalism, a system based upon the maximization of individual profit. It was capitalism, not technology, that was responsible for the loss of common goals in modern society. The challenge facing his contemporaries, Freyer believed, was to dissolve the connection between technology and capitalism. The political task at hand was the reintegration of technology into the "totality of life of the European nations."[62]

The stage of collective history that Freyer termed *Stil* was characterized by the efflorescence of the individual realms of culture, but by a loss of cultural coherence. While Freyer asserted that the succession of *Glaube*, *Stil*, and *Staat* might be a recurrent pattern in history, he intimated that the crisis of coherence in the present was more intense than at any time in the past and that it would be solved by a solution without historical precedent.[63] The linkage of technology with capitalism now threatened to lead to the dissolution of those collective historical cultures which were the source of social integration and the only true source of meaning for the individual.

It was the third stage of history, at the threshold of which Europe now stood, to which Freyer devoted the bulk of *Der Staat*, his most programmatic work of the 1920s. In good Hegelian fashion, this third stage would maintain the cultural and especially technological achievements of *Stil* but would integrate them into a closed totality based upon the reassertion of collective particularity, in a manner that recaptured the community of shared faith. Indeed, the reassertion of the transcendent value of one's particular *Volk* was to be the essence of the faith that would reintegrate society, and the preservation of the *Volk* was to serve as the transcendent goal to which all aspects of culture, the

61 Freyer, *Prometheus*, 55–56.

62 Freyer, "Technik," 201. On the attitudes of thinkers of the Weimar right toward technology, see Herf, *Reactionary Modernism*, passim; pp. 121–129 are devoted to Freyer's writings on technology.

63 Freyer, *Der Staat*, 96.

economy, and technology were to be subordinated. The agency that would guarantee and control this subordination loomed so large that it gave its name to the third stage of history—the state.

Like other radical political theories of the era, Freyer's method for the re-creation of a political totality was highly voluntaristic. Though he did assert that the *Volk* had an objective basis in language, history, and even nature, he considered these as necessary but insufficient conditions for a collective polit-ical revival. It was only through a heightened consciousness of national partic-ularity, through a will to act as a collectivity, that the *Volk* could become a po-liticized collectivity.[64] Like Lenin's criticism of the Russian "economists" in *What Is to Be Done?* (1906) or Georg Lukács's critique of "orthodox Marxism" in *History and Class Consciousness* (1923), Freyer stressed that natural or histor-ical processes, left to themselves, would never create a new totality.[65] Only through a heightened awareness of the need for such a totality could the masses be brought to revolution. In Freyer's political theory—as in that of Lenin and Lukács—the burden of moving history forward therefore fell upon those who, in Lukács's words, embodied "the point of view of totality,"[66] or as Freyer put it, "Only those who know the true direction of *Geist* have a right to historical action."[67] Culture could remain mired at the fragmented stage of *Stil*, or it could move ahead to a new totality through "the political turn of Geist," under the leadership of those willing to abandon petit bourgeois caution and accept the "wager" of revolution.[68]

The words *Tat* and *Wagnis* are among the most recurrent in Freyer's writ-ings of the 1920s and 1930s. Both words expressed the voluntaristic thrust of his thought, the belief that knowledge could never provide the certain basis of action, and indeed that it was only the decision to act that made knowledge possible.[69] Only those who were conscious of the need for action would acquire the knowledge necessary to undertake it; only those sufficiently alienated from contemporary life would accept the risks of the wager of revolution.

Freyer considered himself in the category of those who had "returned to the eternal sources of life," to an assertion of collective particularity, and who sought "to do nothing less than build a temple to our own honor and sacred-ness."[70] His books *Prometheus* and *Der Staat* were explicitly intended to further

[64] Ibid., 112, 145.

[65] Ibid., 112.

[66] Georg Lukács, *History and Class Conscious-ness*, 27.

[67] Freyer, *Der Staat*, 37–38.

[68] Freyer, *Prometheus*, 16.

[69] This became the premise of Freyer's epis-temology of the social sciences in his *Soziologie als Wirklichkeitswissenschaft* (1930); see chapter 4.

[70] Freyer, *Prometheus*, 89.

the self-awareness of those who shared this sensibility, to help forge a legion (*Hundertschaft*) that would await the signal to action.[71] The same aim was less blatant, thought no less apparent, even in Freyer's most abstract and "scholarly" work of those years, his *Theorie des objektiven Geistes*, much of which culminated in the assertion that the decision to maintain culture (and hence meaning) required "a revolution in the cultural-philosophical sense of the word," a conscious reassertion of cultural particularity.[72]

In the early 1920s, however, Freyer regarded the revolution that he sought as a long-range goal. "He who has gone through the desert never enters the promised land," he wrote in 1922, and again in 1924.[73] The actual seizure of power must await the proper hour. In the meantime it was the mission of those who embodied the new cultural consciousness to spread its ideals. It was necessary to begin with men and politics as they were and to discover the forces leading to the new state, forces that were still "interwined with the dross of the present."[74] This task fell especially upon those who taught. If the teacher were successful, his students would reach new shores unimaginable to him, Freyer wrote.[75]

Freyer's works were addressed not primarily to the German academic or pedagogic public but to the generation that had seen active service in the war. He set his hopes upon "the youth that has grown through the war from play to earnestness, from romantic emotion to a yearning for real goals; decimated, all have passed through death, the survivors mysteriously laden with the energies of the fallen."[76] He described this generation as "antibourgeois," a generation for whom the *Volk* had again become a reality.[77]

It was these works of the early 1920s that most dramatically displayed the impact of the war on Freyer's thought. The echoes of the war are audible throughout Freyer's description of the genesis and functioning of the new state whose coming he heralded.[78] Yet it was not the war as the average German had experienced it. Rather it was Freyer's own experience of the war as a release from arbitrariness and as a bestower of purpose, as a provider of collective goals to which the individual could subordinate himself, which was reflected in his social theory of the 1920s. Borrowing from the eschatological

[71] Freyer, *Der Staat*, 40.

[72] Freyer, *Theorie*, 103.

[73] Freyer, *Prometheus*, 125; Freyer, *Der Staat*, 160.

[74] Freyer, *Prometheus*, 125–29.

[75] Freyer, *Der Staat*, 159–60.

[76] Freyer, *Prometheus*, 7.

[77] Freyer, *Der Staat*, 216.

[78] On the war's impact on thinkers of the "conservative revolution," see Herf, *Reactionary Modernism*, and Hans-Ulrich Wehler, "Der Verfall der deutschen Kriegstheorie," in his *Krisenherde des Kaiserreichs*.

tradition he had explored in his prewar essay on utopia, Freyer termed the structure that the *Volk* and the state would create the *Reich*. The *Reich* represented a condition in which the alienation and fragmentation of the present had been overcome. The diversity of pursuits characteristic of the present would continue, but each occupation would now be oriented by the state to the purposes of the *Reich*. Thus each occupation would now become a calling (*Beruf*), its occupant aware that his development of technical means served the ultimate end of the preservation of the *Reich*.[79]

But how was the reassertion of collective ethnic purpose to occur? How could men be made to subordinate the pursuit of their own proximate economic and occupational aims to those of the collectivity? These questions brought Freyer up against the Machiavellian dilemma of how to create virtue out of a corrupt citizenry.

In Freyer's work of the early 1920s—in what one might term his presociological writings—the catalyst of this historical transformation was a particular individual, whom Freyer called the *Führer*. Freyer's own experience as an officer provided him with a heightened awareness of the role of leadership in galvanizing a group for collective struggle. It was the role of the *Führer* to forge the fragmented society of the present into a self-conscious *Volk*.[80] His work was in turn completed by the statesman (*Staatsmann*) who used the instruments of the state to create a virtuous citizenry, one committed to the preservation of the *Reich*. Freyer assumed that the interests of the statesman would be at one with those of the state. It did not even occur to him that the power of the statesman might ever be in need of institutional or constitutional limitation.[81]

Freyer's images of leadership were drawn from the artistic and military realms. Political action was portrayed as a creative act, and the *Führer* or statesman as a creative artist, who gives form to his *Volk* as an artist gives form to his work of art.[82] The *Führer* or statesman bestows continuity on the flux of life.[83] The raw material to be formed is of course made up of living men and women, who, in their present condition, are little inclined to subordinate their perceived interests to those of the *Volk*, *Staat*, and *Reich*. The *Führer* and statesman, in Freyer's description, rely upon a combination of spontaneous authority and coercion (*Zwang, Macht*) to form men and women into a *Volk*. Freyer regarded this combination as the means by which the successful officer formed his men into a unit in order to accomplish some military goal. Throughout these works

---

[79] Freyer, *Der Staat*, 126.
[80] Ibid., 110.
[81] Freyer, *Theorie*, 55; Freyer, *Der Staat*, 203–7.

[82] Freyer, *Theorie*, 54–55.
[83] Freyer, *Der Staat*, 110.

of the early 1920s images of the leader as artist alternate with those of military command as a model of leadership.[84]

The role of the *Führer* was not to impose some foreign objective upon those whom he led but rather to bring to the fore their "better possibilities," to know their "deeper will," to make them into what they ought to be.[85] Yet how could the *Führer* know what men ought to be, what their better possibilities were? Freyer offered no answer other than the self-certainty of the *Führer* that he represented the real historical will of the *Volk* and suggested that the ultimate warrant for his authority was his own historical success.[86] The means that the *Führer* used to transform the mass into a self-conscious group were ultimately unimportant, and, according to Freyer, his sovereignty and authority were to be unlimited.[87]

This attribution of unlimited power to the *Führer* and statesman corresponded to the magnitude of the historical role that they were to play. The *Reich* that he envisaged was to re-create that closed, self-sufficient, self-affirming community which he associated with the stage of *Glaube*.[88] "This self-created world should completely, utterly, and objectively enclose a particular group; should so surround it that no alien influences can penetrate its realm."[89] Thus all human pursuits again acquire a sense of meaning—"nothing is insignificant, and nothing is isolated."[90] This integration of all realms of human endeavor in the *Reich* was to be accomplished by state control. It was the state that was to decide the relative weight that each human endeavor would have in "the whole."[91] Above all, it was the realms of technology and the economy that were to be freed from the system based on the maximization of individual utility and reoriented instead to the purposes of the *Volk*.[92] The specific legal or institutional measures by which this was to be achieved were fundamentally unimportant and uninteresting to him.

Freyer thus considered himself a socialist in that he favored state control of the economy in the interests of the collective *Volk*.[93] Unlike political theorists of the left, however, Freyer did not envision socialism as resulting in a decline of hierarchy or in the end of the division of labor. On the contrary, he advocated harnessing modern technology to the goals of the *Volk* and regarded a high degree of occupational specialization and a vertical stratification of voca-

[84] Ibid., 116 and passim.
[85] Ibid., 109.
[86] Ibid., 113–14.
[87] Ibid., 199–204.
[88] Freyer, *Theorie*, 90–91; Freyer, *Prometheus*, 4–5.

[89] Freyer, *Der Staat*, 99.
[90] Freyer, *Prometheus*, 4.
[91] Freyer, *Der Staat*, 105.
[92] Ibid., 128, 175.
[93] Ibid., 176.

tions as necessary structural elements of a highly technological society. Unlike the primitive communism of *Glaube*, society at the historical level of the state would be characterized by an inequality of property and privilege. This structure of privilege was to be based upon one's achievements and responsibilities in the maintenance of the *Volk* and the state.[94]

In keeping with his neo-Hegelian perspective, Freyer described the state as the ultimate objectification of *Geist*, its most concrete, institutional expression. As with the economy and technology, so too were all other realms of human endeavor to be guided by the state in the interests of the *Volk*. The role of the state, Freyer wrote, was to politicize all elements of culture. The most powerful means of politicization was through the law, which ought to leave no area of life outside its sphere of influence. He scoffed at the liberal, "negative" view of freedom that sought to secure "so-called individual freedom" from the "so-called coercion of the law." True freedom, he wrote, is positive freedom, "freedom not from the state, but through the state; not in contrast to law, but in the law itself."[95] Freedom in this sense meant the freedom to participate in the self-realization of the *Volksgeist*, the freedom to subordinate oneself to the goal of collective self-assertion.[96]

Yet Freyer recognized that not all men would voluntarily submit themselves to such a purpose, and hence coercion by the state plays a large and positive role in his political theory. The world can be changed only through power (*Macht*), he wrote, which remained "one of the integrative and formative forces of the human world."[97] It is *Macht* which creates form out of the flux of life, and which makes the individual into "a necessary link in the exalted whole of the Reich." The powers of the state thus "clutch the individual in such a way that there is no evading it. They summon him; if he doesn't heed they urge him, if he doesn't obey they force him."[98]

While Freyer advocated the omnipresent possibility of state coercion as a tool of collective integration, he did not favor the unremitting deployment of state power. Though power played a redemptive role in his political theory in creating and maintaining the state, he regarded real power as lying not in overt coercion but rather in the voluntary, indeed enthusiastic consent of the governed to the aims of those who exercised power.[99] Hence the crucial role of the *Führer* is galvanizing the general will of the *Volk*. Freyer by no means valued

94 Ibid., 116.

95 Ibid., 165–67.

96 For a classic statement of the negative and positive conceptions of freedom, see Isaiah Berlin, "Two Concepts of Liberty," in his *Four Essays* *on Liberty.*

97 Freyer, *Prometheus*, 14.

98 Freyer, *Der Staat*, 133–34; similarly Freyer, *Prometheus*, 91–94.

99 Freyer, *Der Staat*, 137–38.

the coercive role of government for its own sake, nor did he believe that the more law the better. He often indicated that the *Führer*, the statesman, and the law itself ought to follow an economy of means, that it was not the magnitude of state control that counted, but rather its effectiveness. There were in principle, however, to be no limits on the power of the *Führer* or of the state.[100]

This refusal in principle to limit the power of the state places Freyer's theory at odds with that of classical liberalism. Yet his essentially benevolent view of power also differs from that of traditional or authoritarian conservatives—such as Luther or de Maistre—who viewed the power of the prince or of the hangman as a necessary coercive limitation on man's essentially evil will.[101] The specter that haunted Freyer's view of man was not that of natural evil but of purposelessness in the face of multiple, arbitrary possibilities. Hence power was positive not because it set limits on man's opportunity to do evil but because it promised to free men from the necessity of choosing among multiple possibilities. Freyer's totalitarian political theory was thus based upon a philosophical anthropology that had a good deal in common with modern existentialism. Yet it hoped to create a state that relieved man from the necessity of choosing. Through political power Freyer sought to create a new era of faith, a "positive age" in the Comtean sense.[102] It was such an era of faith that Freyer sought to re-create through political power. Thus in Freyer's radical conservative political theory, as in radical political theories of the left, the path beyond alienation led through the deployment of political power and coercion.

Freyer's belief in the beneficent role of power and force also extended to the realm of international affairs. Unlike theorists of Manchesterian liberalism or of the radical left, Freyer did not regard the elimination of international conflict as possible. Like traditional conservatives he regarded such conflict as inexorable, but unlike them he regarded war as an indispensable element in the creation and preservation of the intense political consciousness that he believed ought to characterize the state.

The inexorability of conflict in international affairs and the consequent necessity of military preparedness had long been a staple of conservative theories of international relations; its quintessence is expressed in the dictum *Si vis pacem, para bellum* (If you desire peace, prepare for war). This perspective is based upon the premise that war is inherently evil, and its avoidance is therefore the task—though not necessarily the prime task—of the statesman.

---

[100] Ibid., 136.

[101] On this view of man as dangerous, see Greiffenhagen, *Dilemma des Konservatismus*, 270–71. Leonard Krieger has called attention to a similar view of man underlying Kant's political philosophy; see his *The German Idea of Freedom*, 90ff.

[102] Freyer, *Prometheus*, 106.

Those thinkers most sensitive to the difficulty of collective integration have tended to stress the integrative function of war. External war as creating the virtue necessary for internal consolidation has been a recurrent theme in modern European social thought since at least the time of Machiavelli.[103] Hegel was among the most emphatic, though hardly the earliest, thinkers in this respect.[104] In Freyer's work, however, the integrative function of war moves to the center of social theory. Two decades earlier William James had sought a moral equivalent of war; contrasting his own experience of the war with the years of cultural emptiness that succeeded it, Freyer concluded that there *was* no moral equivalent of war. His political theory of the 1920s was testimony to his belief that only actual war or the preparation for it could create the degree of consistent political commitment that he expected from the citizens of his state.

"War," he wrote, citing the dictum of Heraclitus, "is the father of all things, . . . if not in the literal sense then certainly for the thing of all things, the work of all works, that structure in which the creativity of *Geist* reaches its earthly goal, for the hardest, most objective and all-encompassing thing that can ever be created—for the state."[105] "The war stands at the beginning of our German present," he wrote, and he went on to provide an evocative description of the entire nation as it had been mobilized during the war. These years had been characterized by "unconditional sacrifice," Freyer wrote, by total government control of national resources, and by the suspension of financial and utilitarian considerations in an effort to avoid national defeat. Though an exceptional event in the life of the state, these years of "highest demands and highest achievements" actually revealed the historical quintessence of the state. The war was not a horror to be forgotten as quickly as possible but rather a foretaste of the new age dawning.[106]

War for Freyer was the essence of politics. "The state as a state is constituted by war and is continuously reconstituted by the preparation for war."[107] This was true in two senses.

Given the legitimate divergence between *Volksgeister* and the impossibility of reconciling their conflicting claims before some higher tribunal, Freyer expected that states would remain in a situation of open or latent war. A state that

---

[103] See Weintraub, "Virtue," chapter 3 and passim.

[104] See, for example, G.W.F. Hegel, *Philosophy of Right*, par. 324; and Shlomo Avineri, *Hegel's Theory of the Modern State*, chapter 10.

[105] Freyer, *Der Staat*, 143.

[106] Ibid., 140–41. The re-creation of "total

mobilization" was later to become the cornerstone of another intellectual of the radical right, Ernst Jünger; see esp. his essay, "Die totale Mobilmachung," in *Krieg und Krieger*, ed. Ernst Jünger (1930).

[107] Freyer, *Der Staat*, 143.

shunned the possibility of war would cease to be a sovereign actor on the stage of history and would only be the object of the action of others. The only alternative was a constant preparedness for war. All foreign policy, in this perspective, was based upon the latent or overt threat to go to war with other states. Foreign policy, Freyer wrote, "was the continuation of war by other means."[108]

Yet war was the essence of the state in a second, more important sense. The constant need to prepare for war provided the intensity of emotional commitment that for Freyer is characteristic of politics, the constant reminder of the primacy of political over particular interests. Thus the state was created and maintained not by social contract but by the struggle against external threats.[109] Lest these threats subside, the struggle slacken, and the degree of political commitment falter, Freyer provided a conception of international relations that ensured that the external struggle of the state would continue in perpetuity. In Freyer's view the state exists not only to assert the interests of the *Volk*; in order to do so more effectively, it must constantly attempt to expand its external range of control, to reorient its surrounding to its own needs. Imperialism, then, is the essence of the state; "It must conquer in order to be." The *Reich* acquires its meaning from the constant need to defend and expand its borders.[110] Imperialism, in Freyer's political theory, stems from the need to maintain external relations of conflict in order to achieve national integration in an all-encompassing polity. Foreign policy above all played a functional role in the internal integration of the total state.

Freyer was by no means an advocate of continuous war, however. The state must constantly be prepared to use force and coercion in foreign affairs as in internal ones, he asserted, and in principle no limits existed in either realm. But just as an economy of means was to be exercised in the internal use of direct coercive intervention by the state, so too were diplomacy and strategy—both based upon the constant threat of the use of force—to replace actual war whenever they were more efficient in securing the interests of the *Reich*. There was a spectrum of techniques through which the *Reich* could exert control over others, Freyer wrote, ranging from spheres of interest and areas of influence to suzerain states, vassal states, and colonies. The "art of conquest" lay in exercising a maximum of control with a minimum of actual occupation.[111] Already Freyer demonstrated an interest in strategy and diplomacy that was to grow after 1933.

Preparation for war was therefore a crucial element of Freyer's political phi-

---

[108] Ibid., 142.
[109] Ibid., 144–45.

[110] Ibid., 144–49.
[111] Ibid., 146–47, 198.

losophy of the 1920s. Only the transformation of consciousness facilitated by collective preparation for war could bring about the all-encompassing politicization of existence that was the ultimate goal of his political program.

A good deal of Freyer's social theory and the philosophical anthropology upon which it was based was a restatement in contemporary terms—in a vocabulary drawn from *Lebensphilosophie* and adapted to German historicism—of older conservative themes about the need for order and external limits on the self and the ineluctability of tradition. Yet it differed from, indeed contradicted, traditional conservatism. His radical conservatism owed more to the quest for the re-creation of imperial virtue in Machiavelli's *Discourses on Livy* than to the conservatism of Burke and his German counterparts. Like many conservative theorists Freyer believed that the source of community lay in the past. But given his cultural critique of the modern age, it had to lie in the distant past. Since the German *Volk* was not united by religion and had never been united in a tightly integrated political unit, the precise content of the shared past was never specified. Freyer did not speak on behalf of an existing institutionalized community of belief that he sought to protect. Freed from such commitments by his education and experience in the youth movement, he sought—together with those who shared his situation and sensibility—to create and institutionalize a community of belief.

Freyer's Neo-Hegelianism and Its Significance

Freyer's writings of the early 1920s exude the influence of Hegel. His books of the period bear the very Hegelian titles *Theorie des objektiven Geistes* and *Der Staat*. Contemporaries recognized these works as a part of a "Hegel Renaissance" which had its origins in the decade before the war and which reached its apogee in the 1920s.[112] Though the influence of Hegel on Freyer's work were real enough, the "neo-" in Freyer's Hegelianism was at least as important.

That the return to Hegel was part of a larger quest within German cultural life for a new *Orientierungswissenschaft* has already been noted. As a keen contemporary commentator remarked, Hegel had developed the most thoroughgoing, all-encompassing system of philosophy ever attempted; the promise of

---

[112] On the Hegel Renaissance, see Lukács, *Die Zerstörung der Vernunft*, 1:7–38; Wilhelm Windelband, *Die Erneuerung des Hegelianismus* (1910); Heinrich Levy, *Die Hegel-Renaissance in der deutschen Philosophie* (1927); Helmut Klages, *Geschichte der Soziologie*, 154–64; and Petra Christian, *Einheit und Zwiespalt*, 18ff. On Freyer's relationship to Hegel and to Dilthey, I have been aided but not persuaded by Ernst Michael Lange, "Rezeption und Revision von Themen Hegel'schen Denkens im frühen Werk Hans Freyers."

re-creating such a system was the major source of the renewed interest in his works.[113] In the opening pages of his *Theorie des objektiven Geistes* Freyer expressed his own admiration for this comprehensive aspect of Hegel's accomplishment. Freyer regarded his own book as a tentative attempt to develop a new philosophy of culture as the basis of a new comprehensive philosophy that would build upon the insights of *Lebensphilosophie*.[114]

Yet Freyer was emphatic as to the gap between his system and Hegel's. Any attempt to revive Hegelian idealism en bloc, he wrote, was alchemy. Its central metaphysic had long been rendered implausible by the criticisms aimed at it by later, more empirically oriented critics, and it was now beyond rehabilitation.[115] Freyer echoed the critique of Hegel leveled by Wilhelm Dilthey, whose historical study *Der junge Hegel* (1905) and subsequent philosophical works had been most responsible for the renewed interest in Hegel. Dilthey and Freyer (and indeed most subsequent advocates of a return to Hegel, down to Charles Taylor in our own time) objected to the rationalist core of Hegel's philosophy, the assumption that all of history represented the self-alienation of a single *Weltgeist* that could ultimately recognize itself in philosophy.[116] Dilthey and Freyer objected to Hegel's attempt to deduce history from ideal constructions such as *Vernunft* and *Weltgeist*. They regarded history as the creation of *Leben*, which was in good part irrational. They sought instead to search for whatever unity lay in history in the connections between the various values and institutions *within* each historical culture.[117]

Hegel's system had been an attempt to reconcile what he regarded as the metaphysical rationalist absolutism of Rousseau, Kant, and the Enlightenment with the emphasis on the historical basis of particular cultures characteristic of Montesquieu, Herder, and the Historical School. He attempted to explain the *Volksgeist* as a particular embodiment of the development of reason in history, as a link in the chain leading to the self-comprehension of the *Weltgeist* in its universality.[118] The abandonment of Hegel's metaphysical rationalism therefore entailed the affirmation of the particularistic, historical elements of his thought and led to what Ernst Troeltsch had characterized as "an unlimited

[113] Levy, *Hegel-Renaissance*, 92. On the attraction of the concept of "totality" see Martin Jay, *Marxism and Totality*, esp. 21ff.

[114] Freyer, *Theorie*, 10–12.

[115] Ibid., 11.

[116] Levy, *Hegel-Renaissance*, 18; Gadamer, *Truth*, 194ff.; Charles Taylor, *Hegel*, 569.

[117] Wilhelm Dilthey, "Der Aufbau der geschichtlichen Welt in den Geisteswissenschaften" (1910), in his *Gesammelte Schriften*, 7:148–52.

[118] See, for example, G.W.F. Hegel, *Reason in History*, 87; and Hegel, *Philosophy of Right*, par. 344.

historicism and relativism."[119] This was precisely the position of Freyer, and indeed of many of the thinkers associated with the Hegel Renaissance. While Hegel played an important role in Freyer's thought, it was a Hegel who tended to be conflated with the Historical School and the German romantics.[120]

Though he differed from Hegel in this fundamental respect, Freyer's philosophical anthropology with its emphasis on the necessity of limits upon the individual and on stable institutions as a source of personal identity owed a great deal to Hegel. The problem of objective *Geist* for Hegel is the problem of how the individual, with his limitless, unfocused subjective will, acquires a sense of limits and of obligations that give him a sense of particularity but also of participation in a larger ethical community.[121] Dilthey too based his view of objective *Geist* upon "the inner need to fix something firm in the restless change of sense impressions, desires and feelings, something that enables one's life to be steady and unified."[122] This stability and continuity, Dilthey believed, was provided by the "shared moral world" of objective *Geist*.[123] Freyer's philosophical anthropology and his social theory as a whole owed a good deal to this Hegelian legacy.

These predilections explain why for Hegel as for Freyer the freedom emphasized by classical political economy was perceived as "negative" freedom, as freedom *from* collective purpose. Hegel sought to *complement* this negative freedom, which he saw as characteristic of the economic realm, with the positive freedom of the state. Freyer, however, had been influenced by the Marxist critique of Hegel, which regarded the modern state as little more than an extension of the unethical interests of the economic realm; by the Simmelian view of modern culture, which held that cultural fragmentation had dissolved the sense of a common ethical world; and by his own view of technology, as tending to destroy the particularity of each historical ethical community. Freyer therefore called for a state far more powerful and all-encompassing than the one envisioned by Hegel, in order to contain and counteract these characteristic trends of modernity.

[119] Quoted in Levy, *Hegel-Renaissance*, 24.

[120] This abandonment of Hegel's metaphysical rationalism was already evident in Dilthey and continued to be characteristic of the Hegel Renaissance, a point particularly stressed by Lukács in *Die Zerstörung*. This is also the upshot of Taylor's analysis, which regards as the most enduring elements of Hegel's thought those which he took from Herder and Hölderlin (Taylor, *Hegel*, esp. 566–71.) Since Freyer, following Dilthey, dropped the notion of the self-comprehension of the *Weltgeist*, he regarded the realms of philosophy, religion, and art as objective *Geist*, not as absolute *Geist*.

[121] See, e.g., Hegel, *Philosophy of Right*, par. 142–49.

[122] Quoted in Gadamer, *Truth*, 210.

[123] Quoted in ibid., 208.

Like Dilthey before him, Freyer was attracted by the prominence of the concept of "totality" in Hegel's thought, by its focus on the interconnection of all
elements of a culture. Yet the concept played a very different role in their philosophies. For Hegel, philosophy was essentially a retrospective venture that
reconciled man to his world by explaining it as an interconnected whole and as
a product of historical necessity. Dilthey revived the Hegelian "objective *Geist*"
and "totality" in order to lay a methodological foundation for the human sciences (*Geisteswissenschaften*). Dilthey's philosophy was oriented toward a scientific comprehension of the past. Hegel's concepts of objective *Geist* and totality,
grounded not in the Hegelian *Weltgeist* but in the irrational, contingent facts of
world history, were to serve this end.[124]

Hans Freyer sought to transform Dilthey's method for the scientific understanding of the past into a philosophy of culture that would provide norms for
the future, to adapt Dilthey's principled historicism from a method of understanding what *had* been to a program prescribing what *ought* to be. The concept of totality thereby became a critical concept, a demand that the parts of a
society and culture *ought* to cohere together into a meaningful whole. The desired totality was to be based upon an affirmation of the particular culture of
one's *Volk*, to which one belonged by virtue of the contingent facts of history
and geography.

Hegel's *Philosophy of Right* had described the morally integrative role of a
state that he believed already existed in his own time, if only in an imperfect
form. The realms of the family and of civil society were thought by Hegel to
play an integrative role alongside the state and hence were moments—albeit
lower ones—of ethics (*Sittlichkeit*). Freyer's *Der Staat*, by contrast, was the description of a state that was yet to be, a state that had to counteract the centrif-
ugal trends of modern culture and of the economy—hence the increased emphasis in Freyer's work on the theme of war as functioning to remind the
citizen of the primacy of his political obligations. The war whose historical
function Hegel had analyzed was the limited war of the Napoleonic era; the
war whose integrative mission Freyer extolled was the "total mobilization" of
the First World War.[125] Thus the central Hegelian concepts of objective *Geist*,

---

[124] Wilhelm Dilthey, "Plan der Fortsetzung
zum Aufbau der Geschichtlichen Welt in den
Geisteswissenschaften," in his *Gesammelte
Schriften*, 7:287–88.

[125] For a comparison of the scope of organization during the Napoleonic era and during
the First World War, see William H. McNeill, *The

Pursuit of Power, 185–214, 317–44.

This difference of emphasis between Hegel
and Freyer is particularly worth noting since
Karl Popper's influential account of Hegel's significance presents an image of Hegel as reflected
in the work of German neo-Hegelians such as
Hans Freyer. Popper's dominant metaphor of

totality, the state, and war recurred in Freyer's work, but with a change of emphasis and with new connotations.

Freyer between Ideology and Social Science

The author of *Prometheus, Theorie des objektiven Geistes*, and *Der Staat* was both an academic social theorist and a political ideologist. His works were addressed to both professional philosophers and social scientists and to a broader audience of politically interested readers beyond the walls of the academy. The conflicting norms encountered by Freyer in his roles as political ideologist and academic social scientist influenced his radical conservative social thought as well as the reception of his work.

As programmatic ideological statements Freyer's works of the early 1920s shared many of the themes prominent in the discourse of the new radical Weimar right. Above all, Freyer shared its emphasis on the *Volk*—defined by common language, history, and in some vague sense by nature (blood or race)—as the basic unit of politics. A possible consequence of this view, and one that Freyer affirmed, was the need for German rearmament in an effort not only to rectify the terms of the Treaty of Versailles but to forcibly integrate all of German-speaking Europe into a new *Reich*. The exalted role of war in Freyer's thought not only complemented these foreign policy aims but appealed to the constituency of front-line war veterans, many of whom had served in the *Freikorps* after the war and who remained alienated from their unheroic—and often impoverished—fate upon their return to civilian life. The centrality of *Führertum* in the creation and maintenance of tightly integrated social groups had been a commonplace of the youth movement before the war. After the war the image of the *Führer* was militarized, and this new image of leadership was prominent in Freyer's *Der Staat*, as in most works of the radical right. Freyer's *Prometheus, Der Staat*, and, to a lesser extent, *Theorie des objektiven Geistes* shared those key words—*Volk, Führer, Blut, Krieg, Macht, Reich*—which bound together the political discourse of the radical right, and which crossed the

---

"open" and "closed" societies is of course Freyer's own, but with the evaluative connotations reversed, and his description of "the closed society" is a good paraphrase of Freyer's goals. Plato and Hegel were among the most important influences on Freyer's political thought, and what most impressed him was precisely their visions of a closed society. Whatever the faults of Popper's work as a historically accurate interpretation of Plato and Hegel, it is of considerable use in understanding the manner in which they were "read" and taught by central European intellectuals in the interwar years; see Karl R. Popper, *The Open Society and Its Enemies*, 2 vols., 64–66, 70.

fleeting borders between "young conservatives," "revolutionary nationalists," and "*völkisch*" and "national-socialist" groups.[126]

References to contemporary events appeared in both *Prometheus* and *Der Staat*. In the latter Freyer contrasted the world-historical certainty of the statesman—who is at one with the metaphysical essence of the state—with contemporary "politicians" (*Politiker*) who follow a policy of muddling through in an attempt to satisfy all interest groups.[127] The stress on power vis-à-vis other states as the sine qua non of state sovereignty, the emphasis on the political significance of the protection and recovery of border areas, the insistence that the state ought to embrace the entire *Volk*, defined as all those who shared a common language—all of these implied not only a revision of the Treaty of Versailles but a return to the political goals of pan-Germanism.[128] The political implications of these works were clear to contemporary readers. A positive review in the (normally liberal) *Vossische Zeitung* noted, "It is hard to conceive of a state more absolute than the state absolutism which Freyer heralds," but praised *Der Staat* for being antipacifist, anti-pan-European, and opposed to the League of Nations.[129]

To the present-day reader Freyer's emphasis in *Der Staat* on the historical role and power of the *Führer*, the centrality of the *Volk* and war in his thought, and his advocacy of a national socialism may call to mind another work written in 1924, Adolf Hitler's *Mein Kampf*. The two books do indeed share many themes, not as a result of mutual influence but because they both emerged from a common realm of discourse on the Weimar radical right, a realm that had its roots in the youth movement, the *völkisch* movement, and the transformative experience of the First World War.

Yet even Freyer's most "ideological" works are distinguished from those of radical conservative ideologists such as Edgar Jung, Ernst Jünger, Moeller van den Bruck, Oswald Spengler, and Adolf Hitler by their strongly social scientific cast. Those values—blood, leadership, hierarchy, war, myth, and so on—affirmed by others as of ultimate *intrinsic value* are usually regarded by Freyer with an eye toward their social *function*.

The emphasis on function over substance in Freyer's work can be attributed to the influence of the norms of academic social thought on his thought. It is

---

[126] On the major characteristics of the political philosophy of the radical right in Weimar, see Kurt Sontheimer, *Antidemokratisches Denken in der Weimarer Republik*. For a somewhat artificial attempt to differentiate the radical right into distinct groups, see Arnim Mohler, *Die konser-* *vative Revolution in Deutschland, 1918–1932*.

[127] Freyer, *Der Staat*, 201–3.

[128] Ibid., 126, 145–49.

[129] Otto Ernst Haase, review of *Der Staat*, by Hans Freyer, in *Die Vossische Zeitung* (Berlin), 31 March 1926.

evident when one compares even Freyer's most overtly ideological works, such as *Der Staat*, to parallel passages in the work of Oswald Spengler, who was perhaps the single most important extra-academic ideological influence on Freyer's work of the early 1920s. Indeed, a good deal of Freyer's writing from his *Habilitationsschrift* through *Der Staat* was an effort to recast central themes in Spengler's thought (including "form," war, the state, and technology) in the terms of academic philosophy and social science. Yet in "translating" Spenglerian themes into a more academic social scientific idiom, Freyer transformed them as well. Both Spengler and Freyer, for example, stressed the inexorability of war in human affairs. But while for Spengler internal policy exists merely for the sake of foreign policy, namely to prepare for war, the emphasis in Freyer's treatment of the subject is on the function that external enmity fulfills in the internal integration of the state.[130]

This social-scientific cast of Freyer's thought, even in his most ideological works of the early 1920s, is also evident in the universal categories of all three works. Freyer's contentions about the particularistic origins of culture, the threat of technology to cultural unity, the integrative role of war, and the exalted role of leadership were stated as general propositions of social theory, relevant in principle at least to other societies outside his own.

Thus Freyer's works of the early 1920s were already marked by the effects of his dual role as radical conservative ideologist and as academic social scientist. With his appointment to an academic chair of sociology in 1925 the reconciliation of these roles became the focus of his theoretical and practical endeavors.

[130] Oswald Spengler, *Der Untergang des Abendlandes* (1923), 2:452, 545–55.

CHAPTER FOUR

Ideology and Social Science in Freyer's Practice of Sociology, 1925–1933

Ideology and Social Science in the History of Sociology: Some Typical Patterns

Hans Freyer's career as a sociologist was shaped by the tensions between political ideology and academic social science. These tensions took very different forms in the liberal democracy of the Weimar Republic and the totalitarian one-party state of the Third Reich. To illuminate the significance of Freyer's career as a sociologist, a brief excursus into the relationships between ideologies and the ethos of social science in liberal and totalitarian regimes is in order. The generalizations that follow are intended as working hypotheses, to be explored and exemplified in the chapters that follow.

Sociology as an academic discipline encompasses two rather disparate pursuits, subject to divergent fortunes by transformations of political regime. While they are often combined in practice, the distinction between the two strands is useful for understanding the political fate of sociology.

One strand within sociology has been concerned with the development of techniques of social reportage, primarily through the progressive refinement of empirical measurement and its statistical analysis. The techniques of sociographic sociology can be utilized for a wide range of purposes and hence by liberal, authoritarian, and totalitarian regimes. Whenever a government perceives the need for sociographic information in order to guide, control, or channel social processes, it will have an interest in the promotion of empirical social research. The practitioners of sociographic sociology and their techniques can be transferred from one political regime to another with relative ease.

The other strand of sociology, that of sociological theory, is more closely connected to normative concerns and is more sensitive to changes of political regime. A descendant of philosophy, sociological theory purports to explain the relationship among man, his beliefs, and his institutions. By design or through its unintended consequences, it touches upon the larger patterns and purposes of human existence. Its concerns therefore overlap with existing ideologies, that is, with comprehensive, ultimate interpretations of reality to which communities of adherents have subscribed. Examples of such "authoritative communities" are religious denominations, cultural movements, and ideologically based political parties.

All modern societies have been characterized by "pluralism"—the existence within them of a plurality of authoritative communities, each with its interpretation of the ultimate purpose of society. It was a major innovation of modern liberalism as a political theory to regard this pluralism of interests and values as the possible basis of a shared political order. Liberal political regimes are distinguished from totalitarian regimes in that some pluralism of ideologies and authoritative communities is regarded as legitimate. To the extent that this is the case, the sphere of government intervention is institutionally limited, and tolerance is regarded as an intrinsic political value.

The institutionalized academic discipline of sociology is a very recent phenomenon, hardly older than the twentieth century. The desirability of such a discipline has not always been self-evident. It appears that sociology owes its institutionalization within the university to the perceived need by those in control of academic institutions for some theory of society that would reconcile or stand above the ideologies of opposing authoritative communities by the demonstration of some superior truth.[1] Yet once this process has begun, the position of the university within a liberal polity tends to promote the development of a particular ethos of social science, one that stamps the style and substance of academic sociological theory. For reasons that we will explore, totalitarian regimes are hostile to the style and substance of sociological theory as it develops within a liberal polity.

The legitimated pluralism of a liberal polity tends to promote a particular set of norms within academic social science. These norms arise less from government intention than from the attempt of academic social science to win recognition both inside and outside the university. Insofar as they seek recognition from the members of multiple authoritative communities, institutions of social science in a liberal polity develop an ethos that refuses to accord *a priori* favored status to the ultimate claims of any particular authoritative community. The dominance of the concept of "function" within sociological theory can be explained in good part by its relationship to this institutional ethos of

---

[1] On the role of such considerations in the institutionalization of sociology in France and England, see Victor Karady, "The Durkheimi-ans in Academe," 73–74; and Philip Abrams, *The Origins of British Sociology, 1834–1914*, 150–53.

academic social science.[2] By "function" we mean the positive or negative role that a social or cultural item plays in the maintenance of some larger social or cultural structure.[3] Academic social science in a liberal polity tends toward a "functionalist" perspective on the world. To conceive of social or cultural phenomena primarily by reference to their *function* is to open the door to the possibility of functional equivalents, functional alternatives, or functional substitutes.[4] The functionalism characteristic of academic sociological theory suggests, if only tacitly, that the belief or institution under discussion is not indispensable. Authoritative communities, by contrast, regard particular beliefs or institutions as valid because they are *uniquely true* and hence indispensable. Since functionalism does not extend prior recognition to the claims of any authoritative community, it is the mode of explanation favored by the institutionalized ethos of the university within a liberal polity. The refusal of functionalists to regard as true and indispensable the ideological claims and revered institutions of existing authoritative communities creates an inevitable tension between the ideologies of authoritative communities and the ethos of academic social science.[5]

Ideology may be distinguished from social science by reference to its style and function, as well as to the stance of its proponents.[6] Ideological activity is a form of social action aimed at ordering or reordering the world through the articulation of an inclusive system of meaning. The stance of ideologists toward the situation they describe is one of commitment to the intrinsic value of the phenomena under examination; social scientists, on the other hand, culti-

---

[2] On functionalism in the sense defined as characteristic of modern social science, see Robert Merton, "Manifest and Latent Functions," in his *Social Theory and Social Structure*, 100–101. See also Kingsley Davis, "The Myth of Functional Analysis as a Special Method in Sociology and Anthropology"; and Wilbert E. Moore, "Functionalism."

[3] This definition is a paraphrase of a definition of functionalism offered by B. Malinowski, quoted in Merton, "Manifest and Latent Functions," 76, and amended in light of Merton's criticisms.

[4] Merton, "Manifest and Latent Functions," 87–90.

[5] Social-scientific institutions favoring functionalist social science are not the only sort that exist in a liberal polity. Alongside them are insti-

tutions of social research and theory that are controlled by or oriented to one particular authoritative community. Such institutions—seminaries, sectarian universities, research organizations tied to parties or economic associations—are intended to embody some ideological orthodoxy. Only when they seek the recognition of those outside their sponsoring authoritative community are they likely to adopt the language of functionalist social science.

[6] This paragraph and the next draw heavily upon the distinctions between ideology and science in Clifford Geertz, "Ideology as a Cultural System," in his *The Interpretation of Cultures*, esp. 230–33, and the discussion of ideology in Keith Michael Baker, "On the Problem of the Ideological Origins of the French Revolution," 203.

vate an attitude of relative disinterestedness toward the intrinsic worth of the same phenomena. The work of ideologists primarily serves a justificatory or apologetic function; it seeks to establish or defend some belief or institution. The work of social scientists, by contrast, is diagnostic and critical. The language of social science seeks to maximize objectivity; hence its style is spare and restrained. The language of ideology, by contrast, seeks to motivate action by appeal to sentiment—hence its resort to a more vivid, emotive, and suggestive prose style.

To conceive of social or cultural phenomena primarily by reference to their function is to cultivate a mode of thought that is "critical" not by virtue of its judgments but by virtue of its very presuppositions.[7] For the concept of function implies the possibility that some *other* social or cultural item might play the same role in the maintenance of the larger structure. It is in this sense, above all, that it is at odds with the stance of the ideologist and the apologetic function of his work.

The terms *ideologist* and *social scientist* are designations of two roles, both of which can be adopted by the same individual. Like the distinction between ideology and social science, the possibility and desirability of separating these two roles have been a matter of continuing debate. Our concern is with the tensions that arise within a person who attempts to play both roles either simultaneously or in succession, and with the patterns that arise within the history of a social-scientific discipline out of the interaction of ideology and social science. These patterns are not unique to sociology and may be found to some degree in all of the social sciences. The history of sociology as a discipline has been marked by the repeated interaction of ideology and social science, in the senses defined above. Those whom the discipline has come to regard as founding fathers or forefathers were overtly ideological: Saint-Simon, Comte, and Marx wrote works of social theory and analysis that they regarded as scientific but whose primary aim was to demonstrate the structural instability of the present social order and suggest the indispensable prerequisites of a more legitimate future order. Yet each ideological system of social thought is transformed by its transplantation into the academy, insofar as the academy embodies the norms associated with the pursuit of free inquiry, which include the consideration of propositions regardless of their ideological origin. To the extent that the advocates of an ideological system of social thought seek to institutionalize it within the academy—a setting that requires the legitimation of

---

[7] See Peter Berger, "Introduction," to his *Facing Up to Modernity*, xii–xiv.

the propositions of the system by those who do not share a commitment to its ideology—the advocates will tend to internalize the norms of academic social science. Not only will the overtly ideological aspects of the system be de-emphasized, but the erstwhile ideological advocates will tend to conform to the norm of the academic setting which holds that all propositions are open to critical scrutiny and hence must be viewed from a functionalist perspective. As the ethos of social science comes to dominate over that of ideology, there is a tendency for those structures once viewed as of inherent value and necessity to come to be regarded as one possibility among others.

The academization of social theory has thus tended to result in a pattern of deideologization in the history of sociology as an academic discipline.[8] As we will see, however, there is also a counterpattern tending toward reideologization. Together these patterns form a discernible (though by no means regular) cycle of de- and reideologization of the discipline, a cycle that Freyer's career exemplifies and helps to elucidate.

In the history of social science, the biography of the individual social theorist often recapitulates the history of the discipline. An individual is likely to be drawn into the systematic study of society only because of some prior interest in the nature of social conflict and consensus, an interest most likely to be engendered by active ideological commitment. Having been led into the discipline of sociology by ideology, he is likely to find himself increasingly assimilated into the functionalist norms of academic social science.

These relationships between ideology and social science help to account for a number of patterns in the history of sociology.

On the level of history, as Giddens has noted, each generation of social theorists has tended to dismiss its predecessors as unscientific.[9] This is true, to the extent—but only to the extent—that successive generations of sociologists are more influenced by the norms of the academy than their predecessors. For as a body of thought is integrated into the academic setting, it will tend to lose its

---

[8] One example of the partial deideologization of a body of thought through its assimilation into the academy is the transformation of French positivism from Saint-Simon to Comte to Durkheim. The successful academic institutionalization of Durkheim's thought ultimately led to even greater deideologization, as the Durkheimians came to value their commitment to specialized social science over their involvement with public affairs. Originally institutionalized within the educational system of the Third Republic as part of a program of laicization, the academization of Durkheimianism led ultimately to its erosion as a coherent system of thought. See Karady, "The Durkheimians," esp. 84; and Roger Geiger, "Durkheimian Sociology under Attack," esp. 130–31.

[9] Anthony Giddens, "Four Myths in the History of Social Thought."

ideological thrust. Later theorists whose expectations of theoretical adequacy are more influenced by the social-scientific, functionalist norms of the academic environment will thus be increasingly censorious of the ideological aspects in the work of their predecessors.

The individual who has traversed the path from ideologist to social scientist is apt to regard his own early work as unduly ideological. The pejorative *Jugendwerk* expresses the embarrassment of the mature social theorist at the relative inadequacy of his own early writings as measured by the scientific norms that he has come to expect of himself. There is thus a structurally induced tendency for the mature theorist to distance himself from his own early works, to confine them to some prescientific stage of his own development that ought to be bracketed out of his authentic *oeuvre*.

A second structural pattern is the tendency of mature social theorists to dismiss the work of youthful colleagues as unscientific, that is, as overly ideological. From the perspective of the mature social scientist the work of his young colleague may not seem to warrant the label *social science* at all.

The relationship between senior practitioners and novices within the discipline thus typically falls into one of two patterns: empathy, or the distaste of unconscious self-recognition. In the former case the senior practitioner recognizes the ideological *engagement* of the novice as the growing pains on the path to scientific maturity. In the second response the senior practitioner, having adopted the scientific norms of his academic environment, regards the ideological tendencies of the novice with principled distaste.

The obverse pattern may be expected from the opposite end of the age spectrum. The budding sociologist, himself only a short distance from the ideological origins that drew him into the discipline of sociology in the first place, is likely to have a critical perspective on the current work of the senior practitioners in his field. To him, the nonideological tone of their work appears as an implicit justification of the social status quo, and "dry" to boot. He is apt to be attracted to those among his senior colleagues who have remained the most ideological in their orientation. These unremittingly ideological seniors are likely to be regarded with suspicion by more scientifically oriented peers and thus to have remained outside the mainstream of the discipline.

Thus sociology as a discipline finds itself in a paradoxical situation. It strives to legitimate itself within the university by conforming to the norms of science and by distancing itself from its ideological roots. Yet it is likely to attract into its ranks those with explicit ideological commitments. Thus its recruitment thrives both qualitatively and quantitatively in periods of general ideological intensity.[10] The result of this influx of ideologically or activistically oriented novices is—at least in the short run—to shift the boundary between central and peripheral figures within the senior practitioners of the discipline, to reverse the position of insiders and outsiders.

The periodic entry of ideologically committed novices into the discipline creates a pattern of return to origins on both the historical and the biographical level. The novice close to his ideological origins is likely to be attracted to the origins of the discipline precisely because they are more overtly ideological. He will then discover and conclude that either (1) the origins of the discipline lie not in a commitment to science but in an ideological commitment not dissimilar to his own (and conclude that the discipline ought to return to its authentic, ideological origins); or (2) the origins of the discipline lie not in a commitment to science but in an ideological commitment opposed to the novice's own (and conclude that the entire discipline is ideological and ought to recognize itself as such and accept the legitimacy of the frankly ideological posture of the novice); or (3) a combination of (1) and (2): there are two ideological roots of the purportedly scientific discipline, the good one (with which the novice identifies) and the evil one (which he opposes). The task at hand is to reassert the former and to weed out the baneful influences of the latter.[11]

On the biographical level, the novice is likely to be most attracted to those works of his seniors which the latter are most likely to regard as embarrassing *Jugendwerke*. And this is because it is precisely the ideological commitment in such works that evokes empathy from the novice and embarrassment from the senior practitioner. In the extreme case we find the republication by the novice of early works by the senior practitioner against the expressed desire of the latter.[12]

Hans Freyer's intellectual career, while marked by some degree of ideological commitment at all points, serves as an illustrative instance of these broader patterns in the history of sociology. The posited relationships between the novice and the senior practitioner are exemplified in the case of Freyer and Fer-

---

[10] For an exemplification of the larger pattern described here in the instance of a generation of American socialists who entered sociology as a result of their political activism of the 1930s, see Seymour Martin Lipset, "From Socialism to Sociology."

[11] Among the many works in this vein are C. Wright Mills, *The Sociological Imagination*; Irving M. Zeitlin, *Ideology and the Development of So-*ciological Theory; A. Dawe, "The Two Sociologies"; J. David Colfax, *Radical Sociology*; and Anthony Giddens, "Classical Sociological Theory and the Origins of Modern Sociology."

[12] A classic instance of this phenomenon was the republication in 1968 due to student demand and against the author's better judgment of Max Horkheimer's essays of the 1930s. See Martin Jay, *The Dialectical Imagination*, 287.

dinand Tönnies. The pattern of an activistically motivated return to the ideological origins of sociology is demonstrated in Freyer's sociological writings of the late 1920s and early 1930s. The attraction of novices in a period of general ideological intensity to the more recalcitrantly ideological senior practitioners of the discipline is illustrated by the public reception of Freyer's work in the early 1930s.

Freyer and Tönnies as Novice and Senior Practitioner

Freyer's interest in sociology was awakened when as a university student he read Ferdinand Tönnies' *Gemeinschaft und Gesellschaft*. The first edition of the book had appeared in 1887, and public interest in it was sufficiently meager to make a second edition unnecessary for some twenty-five years. It was the first edition that inspired the young Freyer. The revised second edition, which appeared in 1912, was sufficiently different in emphasis to warrant a brief comparison of the two editions.[13]

The dichotomy that gave the work its title remained the focus of Tönnies' concern throughout his long career, which spanned the years from the book's publication to his death in 1935. *Gemeinschaft* (community) was a social condition that the individual affirmed as an end in itself and that expressed his *Wesenwille* (essential will). In *Gesellschaft* (society), by contrast, the individual's existence was dominated by structures that were arbitrary in relation to his essential will and that he regarded purely as means. Yet the status of these concepts in Tönnies' work altered considerably in the course of his career. In the first edition of the book—the one that so impressed the young Freyer—*Gemeinschaft* and *Gesellschaft* were portrayed primarily as successive historical stages, the first based upon the medieval European village, the second on modern capitalist society. The direction of historical development was from *Gemeinschaft* to *Gesellschaft*. The inherent instability of *Gesellschaft* was stressed (Tönnies' characterization of *Gesellschaft* having been derived largely from Hobbes and Marx), and its moral deficiency was implicit throughout the book. Thus the first edition was a critical commentary upon the present and suggested that *Gesellschaft* could and should be overcome, though it offered few indications as to how this might occur.

---

[13] The following comparison of the two editions of *Gemeinschaft und Gesellschaft* draws upon René König, "Die Begriffe Gemeinschaft und Gesellschaft bei Ferdinand Tönnies"; and Tönnies' prefaces to the first and second editions, reprinted in *Ferdinand Tönnies: On Sociology*, ed. Werner Cahnman and Rudolf Heberle; as well as Tönnies' book itself.

This first edition of *Gemeinschaft und Gesellschaft*, though the product of a remarkable and mature mind, was very much a *Jugendwerk* in the sense described above. It had emerged from the young Ferdinand Tönnies' attempt to give social-scientific form to his own cultural and political alienation from contemporary Germany.[14] It was precisely this critical, ideological element of the book that so attracted the young Hans Freyer when he read it as a student. As he recalled in a eulogy for Tönnies published in 1936,

In the first two decades after its publication, Tönnies' *Jugendwerk* stood in isolation. . . . But isolated and out of keeping with the spirit of the age as the book was for almost a quarter of a century, it was also relevant and influential; but always in such a way that the individual had to discover it for himself, so to speak. Many personal memories of those who entered into scholarship in the period before the war and who were searching for a scientific interpretation of history confirm that Tönnies' *Gemeinschaft und Gesellschaft* had this extraordinary existence and effect. . . . The book did not so much combine philosophy, history, and systematic sociology as take them all back to the point from which they all originate, namely to the existential question "What are we and where do we stand? Where are we coming from and where are we going, we men of modern, bourgeois society, who still carry community within us not only as a memory or a yearning but as a reality, but who are no longer a community?"[15]

Thus in his third year of university study Freyer and a friend wrote to Tönnies, explaining that they were involved in sociological studies and were writing to Tönnies for advice as "the authority in the field of sociology."[16]

Tönnies was the founder of the German Sociological Association and one of the major lobbyists for the establishment of chairs of sociology within the German universities. As Tönnies became active in the attempt to win academic acceptance for sociology as a discipline, the status that he claimed for his concepts underwent a shift. The second edition of the work carried the subtitle *Grundbegriffe der reinen Soziologie*, which indicated the new status that Tönnies assigned to his concepts. They were now portrayed as basic concepts of "pure" sociology, atemporal, functional forms, applicable to any historical situation. By the 1920s, when Freyer emerged on the sociological scene in Germany, Tönnies had become the Nestor of an academized sociology that prided itself on the formalism of its categories and on its value neutrality.[17]

[14] On the biographical background of the first edition, see Arthur Mitzman, *Sociology and Estrangement*, 63–101.

[15] Hans Freyer, "Ferdinand Tönnies und seine Stellung in der deutschen Soziologie," 3–4.

[16] Hans Freyer to Ferdinand Tönnies, 19 March 1910, NT.

[17] Dirk Käsler, "Der Streit um die Bestimmung der Soziologie," 227; Käsler, "Soziologie zwischen Distanz und Praxis," 21–23.

Though Freyer's work *Der Staat* was eclectic in terms of the theorists and historians from whom it borrowed, the single most important influence on it was undoubtedly Tönnies' *Gemeinschaft und Gesellschaft*. The first two stages of Freyer's three-stage philosophy of history were essentially embroidered versions of *Gemeinschaft* (*Glaube* in Freyer's recension, though he also used the term *Gemeinschaft*) and *Gesellschaft* (Freyer's *Stil*). Even the statist solution advocated by Freyer had been explored but not embraced by Tönnies. Yet the tone and style of *Der Staat* was far less austere, far more emotive, evocative, and *engagé* than any of Tönnies' sociological works, including the first edition of his masterwork.

Against this biographical background as well as the pattern of interaction between novices and senior practitioners posited earlier it is instructive to read Tönnies' review of Freyer's *Der Staat*, which appeared in an academic journal two years after Freyer had assumed the first chair of sociology at a German university.

A curious book—a book about the state that is almost unprecedented, though reminiscent in some spots of ideas present and past: of romanticism old and new, but with a strong admixture of rationalism. . . . A sense of the contents of this small book can't be conveyed through extracts. With so individual, subjective (in the lofty sense) a work the question is whether one can assimilate it and wants to. The answer depends on many factors including the age of the reader and even more on whether and to what degree one has thought about these problems on one's own. I do not regard this "view into the essence of things" [*Wesensschau*] as having furthered authentic scientific knowledge. Nor do I see the utility of the division of historical development into the three stages of faith, style, and the state. It may be a weakness when one cannot follow the high flight of so rich a spirit. I suspect, however, that the great majority of those who legitimately call themselves sociologists will be as little inclined as I am to affirm this mixture of knowledge and the search for truth with prophecy and the cult of the hero. I must reject most sharply the manner of contrasting *Gesellschaft* and *Gemeinschaft* (on pp. 90–91). If this is the philosophy of culture, then between the philosophy of culture and sociology there lies an unbridgeable gap.[18]

The problem of paternity in the history of ideas is always a vexing one. Yet here is a remarkable case indeed. The son—a natural son to be sure, the unanticipated product of his father's wayward ideological youth—pays homage to his aged, academically ensconced forebear. The latter not only fails to acknowledge paternity but disavows any familial resemblance.[19]

[18] Ferdinand Tönnies, Review of *Der Staat*, by Hans Freyer, in *Monatsschrift für Kriminalpsycho-* *logie und der Strafrechtsreform* (1927).

[19] Later judges, however, would not only rec-

Tönnies' biting rejection was a foretaste of the reception that the Weimar sociological establishment was to accord Freyer.

The Ambiguous Position of Sociology in Weimar Germany

Sociology enjoyed considerable support among left-wing and liberal politicians and bureaucrats during the first decade of the Weimar Republic—not least among those who knew little about it. Indeed, their enthusiasm for sociology tended to be inversely proportional to their knowledge of current developments within the discipline. To those who saw the revolution of 1918 as a break with the past, the very novelty of the discipline seemed to recommend it: its institutionalization within the academy, so it was believed, would break with the stale learning of the past. Politicians on both the left and the right often assumed an intrinsic affinity of "sociology" for "socialism." Others, especially "bourgeois" politicians and bureaucrats sympathetic to the new republic but sensitive to its fragility, looked to the new science to assist in the process of national integration.[20]

These hopes for the new discipline were raised early in the history of the new republic. One of the first declarations of the Independent Socialist Adolf Hoffmann, the Prussian minister of education in the immediate postrevolutionary government, included a plea for the creation of chairs of sociology.[21] A major champion of the new discipline was Carl Heinrich Becker, who from 1919 to 1930 occupied the post of *Staatssekretär* (the highest subpolitical post) and then of minister in the Prussian Ministry of Education. A former university professor (of oriental studies), Becker was close to the Deutsche Demokratische Partei, the liberal democratic party that in the early years after its founding in 1918 included several of Germany's foremost academic intellectuals in its ranks. Though Becker's jurisdiction was confined to Prussia, his influence extended beyond its borders.[22] Becker's conception of the proper role of scholarship and of sociology is therefore important for understanding the context in which Freyer arrived at his own formulation of these problems.

---

ognize the resemblance but visit the sins of the son upon the father. See, for example, Ralf Dahrendorf, "Soziologie und Nationalsozialismus," 96.

[20] See Dirk Käsler, *Die frühe deutsche Soziologie 1909 bis 1934 und ihre Entstehungs-Milieus*, 78ff.

[21] Adolf Hoffmann, quoted in Georg von Below, "Soziologie als Lehrfach," 59. On Hoff-

mann, see Karl Dietrich Erdmann, *Die Weimarer Republik*, 263–64.

[22] On Carl H. Becker, see Kurt Düwell, "Staat und Wissenschaft in der Weimarer Epoche"; and the memoir by his son, Hellmut Becker, "Portrait eines Kulturministers." Interview with Hellmut Becker.

Like many other democratic (and socialist) political figures in the young republic, Becker was distressed by Germany's territorial losses and struck above
all by the disunity within his nation. He often referred to the many internal
divisions—provincial separatism, confessional antipathies, and class conflict—
that threatened the unity of the republic.[23] During the *Kaiserreich*, Becker argued, national unity had been created and maintained by military means; in
the republic it was the cultural policy of the government that would have to
make the nation cohere.[24] He sought an educational policy that would foster a
common collective ethos and contribute to national integration.[25]

Becker considered the contemporary German university poorly suited to
this task because of what he regarded as its overspecialization and self-satisfied
isolation from contemporary reality.[26] He saw in sociology a discipline that
would combine the findings of other branches of knowledge and provide the
student with a synthetic orientation toward his society.[27] "The struggle for sociology is basically a struggle for a new concept of scholarship [*Wissenschaft*],"
Becker wrote.[28] His view of sociology was very broad indeed: it was to encompass the scientific study of politics and of contemporary history, and ultimately
to foster political conviction.[29]

Becker's exalted plans for sociology were bitterly attacked by Georg von Below, a respected historian of very conservative political sympathies. If chairs of
sociology were to be established at German universities, he argued, it was only
because of a vogue among politicians—many of whom, in their ignorance, con-
fused sociology with socialism—and not because a consensus of German scholars recognized sociology as a legitimate separate discipline.[30] The synthetic
conception of sociology offered by Becker was nothing but a license for dilet-
tantism, scoffed Below: indeed, this conception of sociology had recently been
rejected by many of those who considered themselves sociologists. Moreover,
a distinct discipline focused upon the study of social relations was superfluous
and methodologically fallacious; such relations could only be understood in
relationship to politics and to culture and in this sense had long been a focus
of German historical scholarship.[31]

[23] Carl H. Becker, *Kulturpolitische Aufgaben des
Reiches* (1919), 3; idem, *Die pädagogische Akademie
im Aufbau unseres nationalen Bildungswesen* (1926),
19ff.

[24] Becker, *Aufgaben*, 3.

[25] Ibid., 2; Becker, *Akademie*, 10ff.

[26] Becker, *Aufgaben*, 11; idem, *Akademie*, 52.

[27] Becker, *Gedanken zur Hochschulreform* (1919),

quoted in M. Rainer Lepsius, "Die Soziologie
der Zwischenkriegszeit," 12.

[28] Becker quoted in Lepsius, "Soziologie," 13.

[29] Becker quoted in Lepsius, "Soziologie," 11.

[30] Below, "Soziologie als Lehrfach," 59–60.

[31] Ibid., passim. On Below's critique of sociology, see Dietrich Fischer, *Die deutsche Geschichtswissenschaft*, 97–115.

These opening volleys in the "struggle for sociology" during the Weimar Republic were echoed in the years that followed, but the pattern remained the same. From outside the university came the demand for a dynamic, synthetic discipline that would help students orient themselves in the world and lead to political conviction. Inside the university sociology was regarded with skepticism by representatives of traditional, more established disciplines. This tension was felt most acutely by the sociologists, who owed the existence of their jobs to the politicians but sought legitimacy in the eyes of their academic colleagues.

The history of sociology in the decades before the First World War had already been marked by the struggle to legitimate the new science within the university. Though the small group of academics who considered themselves sociologists included some of the most powerful minds in the academy—including Max Weber, Georg Simmel, and Ferdinand Tönnies—there were as yet no chairs of sociology within the universities. One of the major aims of the Deutsche Gesellschaft für Soziologie in the years between its founding in 1909 and the First World War had been to lobby for the establishment of sociology within the university system.[32] Max Weber's contention that sociology must eschew value judgments—in Weber's own case a product of deep philosophical conviction—was broadly accepted in the DGS and indeed written into its constitution, because many members, including Weber, felt that this stance of objectivity and political neutrality would contribute to the academic legitimation of the discipline.[33] "As sociologists," Ferdinand Tönnies told the participants of the first conference of the DGS, "we intend to concern ourselves only with what *is* and not with what *ought to be* according to various persuasions and motives."[34]

The desire for academic legitimacy also spurred the attempt to develop a conception of sociology that would clearly distinguish it from history, philosophy, psychology, and economics. Sociology as a separate academic field would be acceptable to the practitioners of these traditional disciplines only if it did not threaten to tread on their toes. Hence Simmel and Weber tried to arrive at a limiting conception of sociology, as a "science of social forms" or a "science concerned with interpretive understanding of social action."

The foremost stalwart of a limited and value-neutral conception of sociology

---

[32] Joachim Matthes, *Einführung in das Studium der Soziologie*, 25–29.

[33] Käsler, "Streit," 199–245, 203–8.

[34] Quoted in Käsler, "Streit," 204.

after the First World War was Leopold von Wiese, who also devoted himself to the institutionalization of the discipline within the academy. An economist by training, Wiese was a lifelong adherent to the theories of classical political economy. When in 1918 the mayor of Cologne, Konrad Adenauer, agreed to create a sociological research institute under municipal sponsorship and sought to appoint representatives of Christian, socialist, and liberal capitalist perspectives to its leadership, Wiese was chosen a representative of the liberal capitalist stream.[35] Wiese devoted himself to the creation of a clearly delimited, distinct science of sociology and to its institutionalization as a separate discipline in the university system.[36] His own system of sociology began with the notion that all social relations could be divided into processes of attraction and separation, and on this foundation he constructed a classification of all existing social relations.[37] He resolutely opposed as "speculative" any attempts to make of sociology an interpretation of history or a normative science that would describe not only what society was but what it ought to be.[38]

Though his own system of sociology was regarded as barren by many contemporaries and by almost all later sociologists,[39] from an institutional perspective Wiese was perhaps the most important figure in Weimar sociology. From the reestablishment of the DGS in 1919 through 1933, Wiese ran the organization, its publications, and its conventions in his capacity as secretary.[40] The *Kölner Vierteljahrshefte für Soziologie*, founded by Wiese in 1921, was the first German journal devoted exclusively to sociology and an important influence within the discipline until it stopped publication in 1934.[41] By the second half of the 1920s Wiese's emphasis on the need for sociology to become a distinct discipline that eschewed political commitment and focused upon a description of the forms of social life set the tone at the conventions of the DGS.[42] This more limited and austere conception of sociology was at odds with the high expectations of Becker and other politicians who had pressed for the institutionalization of the discipline within the university. It was also at odds with the expectations that Hans Freyer brought to the discipline that in 1924 he was called upon to profess.

[35] Heine von Alemann, "Leopold von Wiese und das Forschungsinstitut für Sozialwissenschaften in Köln 1919 bis 1934," 351–52, 377.

[36] Ibid., 359.

[37] Ibid., 362–63.

[38] Ibid., 361.

[39] Ibid., 360ff. See also the evaluations of

Wiese by his contemporaries in Dirk Käsler, *Soziologische Abenteuer: Earle Edward Eubank besucht europäische Soziologen im Sommer 1934*, passim.

[40] Alemann, "Leopold von Wiese," 367.

[41] Ibid., 358.

[42] Käsler, "Streit," 226–40.

The Politics of a Professorship

The process by which Freyer was appointed to a chair of sociology at the University of Leipzig displayed all of the patterns already evident at the national level: the high expectations of sociology by its supporters outside the academy, its disputed status within the university, and the confusion of ideology and social science.

The initiative to found a chair of sociology came originally from the DGS, which in June 1914 sent a proposal to the faculties of the major German universities asking them to establish chairs of sociology.[43] A committee of senior professors including Karl Lamprecht and Karl Bücher was organized to consider the request. When it met, Bücher, who gave occasional courses in sociology, expressed his reservations about the creation of a new chair, arguing that sociology could not be considered a science with its own delimited subject matter and that there was no scholar in Germany worthy of appointing to such a chair. Lamprecht, however, argued that the creation of a chair would help to consolidate the discipline.[44] The emergency situation during the war allowed the split committee to reach a diplomatic compromise: it recommended to the Ministry of Education that the teaching of sociology at the university eventually be expanded but that the problem be deferred until the war's end.[45]

After the war the commission was reconstituted. When it first met in April 1920, its leading members included Freyer's mentor, Felix Krueger; Erich Brandenburg, a conservative historian with whom Freyer had also studied; an economist, Ludwig Pohle; and Theodor Litt, the recently appointed professor of philosophy and pedagogy. Its deliberations were postponed first in 1920 and again in 1921 when the Ministry of Education declared that it lacked the resources to fund a new chair and indeed could not even afford to appoint a full professor to the chair vacated by Bücher's retirement.[46] On Krueger's urging the ministry agreed in May 1922 to provide Hans Freyer with a part-time instructorship (*kleiner Lehrauftrag*) to teach sociology, but Freyer's appointment in Kiel shortly thereafter left the position unfilled.[47]

[43] DGS to Universität Leipzig, 5 June 1914, UAL, B2/20/07. The identical letter is reproduced in Matthes, 215–17.

[44] Protocols of the Kommissionssitzung über Einrichtung ein Prof. f. Soziologie, 24 July 1914, 19 January 1915, UAL, B2/20/07.

[45] Protocol of the Kommissionssitzung über Einrichtung ein Prof. f. Soziologie, 4 February 1915, UAL, B2/20/07.

[46] Letter of the Kultusministerium, 24 November 1920; Dekan to Mitglieder der Kommission für Soziologie, 20 June 1921; both in UAL, PA Freyer, 17–18.

[47] Letter of Krueger, 26 June 1922, UAL, PA Freyer, 19.

The proposed chair of sociology might have remained a dead letter had it not become a weapon in the deepening conflict between the ever more left-wing governments of Saxony and the faculty of the university. From October 1919 through the end of 1920 the provincial government was controlled by the majority socialists with the support of the liberal Democratic party, in whose hands the Ministry of Education lay. The provincial elections of November 1920 showed a slight shift to the right among voters, but the constellation of seats in the *Landtag* led to a minority government of Social Democrats and Independent Socialists that ruled by the parliamentary sufferance of the small Communist faction.[48]

This put the supporters of the government in a situation of latent conflict with the faculty of the university, many of whom (including Felix Krueger) were sympathetic to the German Nationalists and hostile to the republic. On ceremonial occasions this latent antagonism became blatant, as speeches in the Saxon Landtag make clear. In May 1922 a representative of the Social Democratic party reported to the Landtag that in the course of a workers' demonstration in front of the university on 1 May, the flag of the republic had been removed from the university flagpole by conservative fraternity students and replaced by the flag of the university flown at half-mast. Protests by the workers and clashes with police had followed. The university—from the rector on down to the students—was a bastion of counterrevolution, lamented the Socialist spokesman.[49]

A Communist member of the Landtag complained that the *Reichgründungs-feier*—the annual commemoration of the founding of the Bismarckian *Reich*—continued to be celebrated at the university and provided an occasion for the glorification of the old *Reich*, of Bismarck and the Hohenzollerns. Such behavior had made the university an object of hatred for German workers, he asserted. The university was a bastion of political reaction, and the overspecialization of its faculty failed to provide the students with insight into the broad contexts of contemporary life. Only a synthetic science beyond the boundaries of the traditional disciplines, a "theory of society" (*Gesellschaftslehre*), could provide such knowledge, he claimed.[50]

At the same session a representative of the Social Democrats presented a government report on the University of Leipzig that announced the government's intention to increase the influence of the Ministry of Education "as the

[48] Ernst Rudolf Huber, *Deutsche Verfassungs-geschichte seit 1789*, 6:803–4.

[49] Verhandlungen des sächsischen Landtages, 1–6 Wahlperiode (Dresden, 1920–), 3902–3.

[50] Ibid., 3896–97.

representative of the public" in comparison to the faculty, which it termed "a relatively small group." The ministry—under the control of Fleißner, a member of the Social Democrats' left wing, which favored cooperation with the Communists—announced its intention to create several new chairs, including one for *Gesellschaftswissenschaft*, and to fill one of the existing chairs of *Nationalökonomie* with a Marxist.[51]

It was probably financial exigencies that once again delayed government action on the matter, but on 15 March 1923 the Ministry of Education informed the faculty commission that it was ready to appoint a professor of sociology and requested the faculty's recommendations. It was the tradition in Saxony, as elsewhere in Germany, that university appointments were made by the ministry from a list of three candidates submitted by the faculty.

The faculty committee met in May and June of 1923 and had great difficulty in agreeing not only on a list of candidates but on whether a list ought to be submitted at all. Erich Brandenburg favored breaking off the discussion entirely on the grounds that sociology was not a distinct discipline—a criticism leveled by Bücher and Below on earlier occasions. Unable to persuade his colleagues, he finally recommended Oswald Spengler for the post—a suggestion opposed by Theodor Litt, who had inveighed against Spengler on methodological grounds.[52] Finally the committee agreed on a list of names. In order of preference it recommended Alfred Vierkandt, a sociologist who had followed Wundt's traditions of *Völkerpsychologie*; Othmar Spann, a representative of extreme idealism in sociology; and Hans Freyer.[53] The memorandum recommending Freyer (written by Krueger) noted that the committee rated him third only because sociology was not so clearly his major field as in the case of Vierkandt and Spann, not because it considered him inferior to the other two candidates. The committee members regarded Freyer as appropriate for the post because they hoped that sociology in Germany would retain a close connection to Freyer's areas of specialization, namely the philosophy of culture, the history of ideas, the philosophy of history, and ethics[54]—precisely those concerns abjured by Wiese and other advocates of a "delimited" discipline of sociology.

In the meantime the government of Saxony had moved further to the left, as in late March an administration headed by the left-wing Socialist Erich Zeigner came to power.[55] It was his administration that informed the faculty on 5

[51] Ibid., 3884.
[52] Protocols of the Kommissionssitzung über Einrichtung einer Prof. f. Soziologie, 15 May 1923, 6 June 1923, UAL, PA Freyer, 35–39.
[53] Ibid., 39.
[54] UAL, PA Freyer, 46–52.
[55] Huber, *Verfassungsgeschichte*, 805–7.

July 1923 that it had decided to override the recommendations of the faculty commission and appoint Prof. Max Adler of Vienna to the new chair of sociology.[56] Adler was at the time lecturer on *Gesellschaftslehre* at the University of Vienna. A philosopher who devoted much of his work to a neo-Kantian legitimation of Marxism, Adler was one of the foremost ideologists of the Austrian Socialist party and one of the founders of Austro-Marxism.[57] He was perhaps the most distinguished scholarly interpreter of the relevance of Marx for sociological thought, and his essay "Marx als Denker" (1909) had been an important influence on Johann Plenge, and, through him, on Hans Freyer.

The ministry justified this unusual step with the explanation that "a scientific orientation that had been of the greatest influence on contemporary intellectual and social life" ought to be represented within the academy.[58] The faculty objected vociferously to this breach of academic custom. Decisions of this type were to be made on scholarly grounds, it wrote; the role of the professor was to represent "an objective, delimited area of knowledge," not a world view or a political orientation. The faculty committee had considered Adler, it claimed, but rejected him because he was a poor lecturer, was not a creative thinker, and lacked historical knowledge. The behavior of the ministry, the faculty wrote, appeared to confirm press reports that the government's sole concern had been to appoint a representative of Marxism and that it had begun to negotiate with Adler before it had requested the faculty's recommendation. The faculty emphasized that it was willing in principle to appoint Marxists, so long as they were distinguished representatives of their disciplines, and had in fact recommended two Marxists a year earlier to fill a chair of political economy.[59]

The altercation over the chair of sociology was one of several between the Ministry of Education and faculty of the university during the course of 1923. A similar conflict developed over the ministry's intention to appoint Siegmund Hellmann, a liberal historian (and, like Adler, a Jew by birth) to fill a chair of medieval history, again overriding the recommendation of the faculty.[60]

The proximate cause of this new interventionism on the part of the Ministry of Education was Dr. Robert Ulich, who early in 1923 had become the *Hochschulreferent* (the official responsible for university appointments) in the min-

[56] Letter of Kultusminister Fleißner, 5 July 1923, UAL, PA Freyer, 53.

[57] On Max Adler, see Reinhard Knoll et al., "Der österreichische Beitrag zur Soziologie von der Jahrhundertwende bis 1938."

[58] Letter of Kultusminister Fleißner, 5 July 1923.

[59] Philosophische Fakultät to Kultusministerium, 19 July 1923, UAL, PA Freyer, 54–56.

[60] On the controversy, see Hermann Heimpel, "Nekrolog"; and the draft of a letter from Walter Goetz to the Saxon Landtag, apparently written early in 1923, BAK, Nachlaß Goetz, no. 89, fol. 1.

istry. Ulich had attended the same Dresden Gymnasium as Hans Freyer, his senior by three years. Later Ulich, like Freyer, studied philosophy and history in Leipzig, and by the time the war broke out the two were old friends. Unlike Freyer, Ulich had spent part of the war working in a factory in Berlin, an experience that had led him toward socialism. Returning to Leipzig after the war, he had become involved in the workers' education movement and was closely identified with the Social Democratic party.[61] These political credentials were a key factor in his appointment to so responsible a post in the Ministry of Education in 1923.

Ulich refused to abide by the faculty's recommendations because he believed that the existing faculty systematically ignored potential appointees of Jewish origin or of leftist political sympathies. In overriding the faculty's recommendations he saw himself as using the only tool available to break through the ideological and social old-boy network, an instrument favored by his friend Carl Heinrich Becker.[62]

At the end of October, the government of the *Reich* intervened militarily to depose the Zeigner government, which it feared was preparing for civil war.[63] In the new government formed at the beginning of 1924, the Ministry of Education fell into the hands of Fritz Kaiser, the leader of the right-wing German People's party.[64] Relations between the ministry and the Leipzig faculty appear to have improved under his stewardship, though Ulich remained *Hochschulreferent*. Siegmund Hellmann assumed the chair of history despite the objections of his prospective colleagues and was largely ostracized as a result.[65] Max Adler turned down his prospective appointment rather than share Hellmann's fate.[66]

In the atmosphere of mutual suspicion that pervaded the relationship between the faculty and the ministry in 1924 Hans Freyer emerged as the ideal compromise candidate. To the members of the faculty committee at Leipzig he was a known quantity, a student of Krueger and of Brandenburg who, they had reason to expect, would not stray too far from the intellectual and political fold. The reasons for Ulich's approval of the appointment cannot be reconstructed with certainty but are not difficult to infer. Freyer was not only an old friend who shared Ulich's antibourgeois sentiments and desire for social and

[61] Robert Ulich, "An Autobiography," 421–24.

[62] Ibid., 426–27; interview with Hellmut Becker.

[63] Huber, *Verfassungsgeschichte*, 807–8; Werner

Angress, *The Stillborn Revolution*.

[64] Huber, *Verfassungsgeschichte*, 808.

[65] Heimpel, "Nekrolog."

[66] Walter Goetz to Saxon Landtag, early 1923, BAK, Nachlaß Goetz, no. 89, fol. 1.

cultural renewal (as expressed in *Antäus*); in his *Habilitationsschrift* of 1919 he had committed himself to a German socialism, a concept with a good deal of currency within the Social Democratic party in the early postwar years.[67] Freyer's more militantly nationalist, imperialist, and overtly totalitarian works had been published only very recently (*Prometheus*, 1923) or were just being written (*Der Staat*, published late in 1925). So it was that in September 1924 Ulich traveled to Kiel to discuss with his old friend the conditions under which he would assume the new chair of sociology at their alma mater.[68] In October Freyer met with Carl Becker, who in his capacity as Prussian minister of education was Freyer's employer at the University of Kiel. Becker advised him to accept the new chair.[69] Shortly thereafter Freyer sent his letter of acceptance to his former teachers and future colleagues at Leipzig.

The letter conveys a good deal about Freyer's own conception of sociology. In assuming the new chair, he wrote, he would now shift the focus of his interests from philosophy to sociology. But he emphasized his belief that sociology must remain closely tied to cultural philosophy and to the philosophy of history.[70]

Just how seriously Freyer took the link between the philosophy of culture and sociology was revealed in his inaugural lecture at Leipzig and in articles published shortly thereafter. His inaugural lecture, delivered in the autumn of 1925 and entitled "Soziologie als Geisteswissenschaft," not only expressed his own understanding of the discipline he had been appointed to profess but may have been intended to reassure skeptics of the new discipline within the Leipzig faculty that the newcomer would not be a foreign body in their midst. After tracing the origins of sociology to French positivism, with its belief that the social sciences ought to model their methodology on that of the natural sciences, Freyer emphasized that he intended to develop sociology as a legatee of German idealism and romanticism.[71] The philosophical premises of German ide-

[67] On the concept of "German socialism" within the postwar Social Democratic party see Karl Pribram, "Deutscher Nationalismus und deutscher Sozialismus" (1922).

[68] "Abschrift: Dresden, 22.9.24" (signed by Robert Ulich and Hans Freyer), File: "Ministerium für Volksbildung: Institut für Soziologie an der Universität Leipzig," Sächsische Hauptarchiv Dresden.

[69] The request for the appointment is in a letter from Hans Freyer to C. H. Becker, 13 October 1924, Geheimes Staatsarchiv Preußischer

Kulturbesitz, Nachlaß Becker, rep. 92, no. 740; Käthe Freyer reported to Hans Linde that Becker encouraged her husband to accept the new post (interview with Hans Linde). Later letters in the Nachlaß Becker demonstrate Becker's respect for Freyer, whose advice he occasionally sought during the next half decade.

[70] Letter of 24 October 1924, UAL, PA Freyer, 57–61.

[71] Hans Freyer, "Soziologie als Geisteswissenschaft" (1926), 121.

alism and romanticism were far more profound than their positivist counterparts, Freyer asserted (though few members of his audience needed to be
reassured on this point). These premises included an emphasis on the *Volk*, on
individuality (in the sense of historical particularity), and on *Geist*. The upshot
of this methodological legacy for sociology was to regard each historical social
structure as the embodiment of a "meaningful spiritual content" (*geistiger Sin-*
negehalt).[72] Social structure was to be studied as a product not of nature but of
culture, and the role of sociology as *Geisteswissenschaft* was to explain social
structure in light of the particular meaning (*Sinn*) that held the culture as a
whole together.[73]

This focus upon the centrality of cultural norms in the process of social integration was characteristic of German idealist social thought, and Freyer's
conception of sociology as of 1925 can quite rightly be considered "idealistic"
in Parsons' sense.[74] Indeed, Freyer's conception of sociology at this point
showed affinities to the work of Othmar Spann, a neoromantic social theorist
at the University of Vienna who regarded societies as essentially the embodiments of ideas.[75] Freyer cooperated with Spann on a new scholarly series
largely devoted to the rediscovery of German romantic social thought and
planned to devote his next book to Plato's theory of the state.[76] Freyer's philosophy of history—expounded at length in *Der Staat* and in brief in his inaugural
lecture[77]—emphasized the role of cultural ideals in maintaining and transforming social structures and displayed a minimal concern for social structure
as a causal factor in historical change. But as Freyer devoted himself to the
study of sociology thereafter, the study of social groups and their divergent
interests were to become more prominent in his conception of the discipline.

Up to 1925, and indeed through his early years as a professor of sociology
in Leipzig, Freyer seemed to regard the shift from the alienated present to the
total state of the future largely as a matter of will; the role of philosophy—and,
at first, of sociology—was admonitory and exhortatory. But as Freyer threw

[72] Ibid., 122.

[73] Ibid., 123–26. This view is reinforced in
Hans Freyer, "Geschichte und Soziologie"
(1926), 201–11.

[74] Talcott Parsons, *The Structure of Social Ac-*
tion, 82.

[75] See the succinct summary of Spann's
thought in Raymond Aron, *German Sociology*, 32.

[76] See the series *Deutsche Beiträge zur Wirt-*
schafts- und Gesellschaftslehre, "herausgegeben

von Othmar Spann und Georg von Below in
Verbindung mit Hanns Dorn, Hans Freyer,
Friedrich Lenz, Eduard Lukas" (Jena, 1926–).

According to a publisher's announcement on
the back cover of Julius Frankenberger, *Walpur-*
gis: Zur Gestalt von Goethes Faust, volume three of
the series *Staat und Geist*, the projected eighth
volume was to be a work by Freyer entitled
"Politeia, eine Linie durch Platons Werk."

[77] Freyer, "Soziologie als Geisteswissenschaft."

himself into his new role as sociologist, his conception not only of sociology but of his own task was to alter subtly but importantly. The shift in Freyer's conception of sociology and of his own role found expression in a new programmatic designation of sociology as a *Wirklichkeitswissenschaft*—a science of reality. The goal of sociology remained the supersession of "bourgeois society," and the role of will in social science and in politics remained crucial. What was new was a turn toward the empirical study of social reality in an attempt to discover the evidence of social discontent that would make the supersession of bourgeois society possible. This was the essence of the theory of sociology that Freyer formulated in his writings of 1927 to 1931 and of the practice of sociology at his institute in Leipzig.

Freyer's Institute of Sociology: Colleagues, Students, and Disciples

Though Freyer's hopes for the discipline of sociology were large, the Institute of Sociology that he founded in the autumn of 1925 was, physically and organizationally at least, a very modest affair. Accommodated within the building of the Institut für Kultur- und Universalgeschichte, the institute consisted of a seminar room that housed a small library, a director's office, and a small office for the institute's sole *Assistent*.[78] The permanent personnel of the institute consisted of Freyer and Willy Bloßfeldt, an old friend from the youth movement.[79] Others who offered courses under the institute's auspices did so while holding appointments elsewhere in the university.

The institute was run in a very informal fashion; there was no secretary, no office hours, no structure of required courses for a major in sociology.[80] The borders between formal instruction and informal discussion were fleeting: Freyer's fortnightly colloquium met on Friday evenings from 8:00 to 10:00 and then dismissed to a nearby *Weinstube*.[81] The unstructured, *gemeinschaftlich* spirit of the youth movement, of cohesion through a common search for answers to personally important questions, dominated the atmosphere of the institute.

The number of students associated with the institute rose from about sev-

[78] Hans Linde, "Soziologie in Leipzig, 1925–1945," 103.

[79] On Bloßfeldt, see his "Lebenslauf," File: "Ministerium für Volksbildung: Institut für Soziologie an der Universität Leipzig," Sächs. Hauptarchiv Dresden.

[80] Linde, "Soziologie in Leipzig," 103.

[81] Ibid., 105.

enty a year after its founding to almost one hundred in the early 1930s.[82] This
was a surprisingly large number for a new discipline in a university population
of several thousand and a comment upon Freyer's appeal to his students.

About a dozen *Privatdozenten, Habilitanden,* and *Doktoranden* formed the
central core of the institute's activity at any one time. Their background and
concerns provide an insight into the close connection between ideological
commitment and sociological research within Freyer's institute.

Freyer's closest collaborator in Leipzig was Gunther Ipsen. Born in 1899 as
the son of an Austrian professor, Ipsen had volunteered for the Austro-Hungarian army when he came of age in 1917 and had spent over a year as a pris-
oner of war in Italy. In 1920 he came to Leipzig to continue his studies, where
he attended a course on the philosophy of history offered by Hans Freyer,
then a young *Privatdozent.*[83] The friendship between Freyer and Ipsen soon
outgrew its academic origins, and when Freyer's *Antäus* was reprinted in 1922
it bore a dedication to Ipsen. Following in Freyer's footsteps, Ipsen spent the
year following his graduation (1922–23) as a teacher at the Freischulgemeinde
Wickersdorf and was active in the Deutsche Freischar, the largest group within
the youth movement of the 1920s.[84] Birth into the *Bildungsbürgertum,* active
war service as a volunteer, and involvement in the youth movement were characteristics that Freyer shared with Ipsen and indeed with most of his closest
students.

After Freyer's return to Leipzig his relationship with Ipsen turned to one of
scholarly and cultural-political collaboration. Together with André Jolles—a
cultural historian of Flemish origin who had become a German *völkisch* nationalist and had fought in the Kaiser's army as a volunteer[85]—Freyer and Ipsen
launched a series entitled "State and Spirit: Works Devoted to Reflection and
Reconstruction" (*Staat und Geist: Arbeiten im Dienste der Besinnung und des Auf-
baus*). The initial volume of the series was a second printing of Freyer's *Der
Staat,* in 1926.[86] Only three volumes were ultimately published in the series,
owing to the bankruptcy of its publisher; among the volumes projected was an
introduction to Hegel's philosophy of *Geist* by Ipsen and a volume by Freyer
on Plato's political philosophy.[87]

---

[82] The figures are from reports in the file,
"Ministerium für Volksbildung: Institut für So-
ziologie an der Universität Leipzig," Sächs.
Hauptarchiv Dresden.

[83] UAL, PA Gunther Ipsen, 3–4.

[84] Ibid.; see also the many contributions to periodicals of the youth movement listed in "Ver-

zeichnis der wissenschaftlichen Veröffentlichungen von Gunther Ipsen," in *Entzifferung,* ed.
Harold Jürgensen, 168–74.

[85] UAL, PA André Jolles, 4ff.

[86] Wiegandt Verlag (Leipzig, 1926).

[87] Publisher's announcement on the back
cover of Frankenberger, *Walpurgis,* cited in n. 78.

In the years after 1926 both Freyer and Ipsen turned toward more contemporary and empirical concerns in keeping with Freyer's new conception of sociology as a *Wirklichkeitswissenschaft*. After his habilitation by Felix Krueger in 1925, Ipsen lectured as a *Privatdozent* in Freyer's sociological institute, beginning with a course on the philosophy of history in 1926. Although topics in the history of sociological thought and on politics and the state remained prominent in the institute's offerings from 1925 to 1933, there was an increasing emphasis on the empirical study of contemporary social structure. In 1929, for example, Freyer and Ipsen offered a course together called "The Occupational Structure of Germany based on the Census of 1925."[88] Though Freyer was not expert in statistical analysis, Ipsen was, and he attempted to develop mathematical techniques through which census data could be reaggregated to provide a portrait of contemporary social structure and processes.[89] Other courses offered by Freyer reflect this concern with the empirical study of social processes, including courses on the social structure of contemporary Germany, the sociology of occupations, and the sociology of the metropolis.

The distinctiveness of Freyer's particular conception of sociology was reflected not in these courses on sociological theory and contemporary social structure—subjects that would serve as the mainstay of virtually any sociological program of studies—but in the historical and political emphasis of his institute.

The courses offered by Freyer and Ipsen reflected Freyer's belief that social structures must be understood historically and with a view toward the dynamic tensions that led to their stabilization and dissolution. Freyer had studied with two eminent historians—Karl Lamprecht and Karl Bücher—who had stressed the importance of social history, and it was a historical approach to the study of contemporary society that was emphasized in Freyer's institute in courses such as "On Sociological Historiography, Especially Historical Materialism" (offered by Freyer in 1927) and "Sociological Tutorial on the Bismarckian *Reich*" (offered by Ipsen in the same semester).[90] The intimate relationship of sociology to history—a working assumption of many of the founders of German sociology before 1918 (including, above all, Max Weber)—was thus maintained in Leipzig during the Weimar years, at a time when the general drift of the disciplines of sociology and history was away from each other.[91]

---

[88] Cited in Linde, "Soziologie in Leipzig."
[89] Ibid., 108.
[90] Ibid., 107.
[91] The linkage between the two disciplines in

Freyer's institute eventually contributed to the renaissance of social history in Germany. Here the most important personal link was Werner Conze, who studied briefly with Freyer in Leip-

Freyer's emphasis on politics and the state was also reflected in the courses offered in his institute. Indeed, almost one-third of Freyer's own courses from 1925 to 1933 dealt with political topics, including not only political sociology (for example, "State and Society in the Age of Capitalism") but also political theory and political science.[92]

But Freyer's institute was "political" in a second sense as well. Many of its faculty members and students were politically engaged, and this *engagement* not only affected their research choices but was often reflected in their scholarship.

This combination of scholarship and *engagement* is evident in the sociological writings and research of Gunther Ipsen. Ipsen's primary field of research was the history and sociology of the German peasantry. His writings on the subject during the late 1920s and early 1930s reveal that his choice of topic arose from a radical conservative sensibility and a *völkisch* ideology. As we have seen, the *Volk* was embraced as a focus of ideological commitment because it was thought to embody a cultural and biological link with the past at a time when the forces of social and cultural modernization were attenuating such continuity. A frequent corollary of this view was a high valuation of those sections of the population regarded as least affected by the social and cultural transformations of modernity and as a living link with ancient ways of life. It was the German peasantry that the *völkisch* thinkers esteemed above all. The image of the peasant as embodying the living continuity with the ancient, particular past of the *Volk* was most strikingly formulated by W. H. Riehl (1823–97), an acute observer of mid-nineteenth-century German society.[93] In their turn toward greater empirical research, Freyer and Ipsen looked to the work of Riehl, whose *Volkskunde* had established a native German tradition of descriptive empirical research with strong national and ethical elements.[94]

---

zig and later with Ipsen in Königsberg, and whose seminar in Heidelberg became the center of the renewed interest of German social history in the 1950s. See the preface and introduction to Werner Conze, *Hirschenhof: Die Geschichte einer deutschen Sprachinsel in Livland* (1934); and the introduction to his *Agrarverfassung und Bevölkerung in Litauen und Weißrußland* (1940), in which he acknowledges his personal and methodological debt to Ipsen.

Freyer's influence on German historiography after the Second World War is discussed in chapter 9.

[92] Cited in Linde, "Soziologie in Leipzig"; courses offered in the institute from 1928 to 1933 are listed in Üner, "Hans Freyer," 240–46.

[93] "Es ruht eine unüberwindliche konservative Macht in der deutschen Nation, ein fester, trotz allem Wechsel beharrender Kern—und das sind unsere Bauern. . . . In dem Bauernstande allein noch ragt die Geschichte alten deutschen Volkstums leibhaftig in die moderne Welt herüber" (W. H. Riehl, *Die Naturgeschichte des deutschen Volkes*, ed. Gunther Ipsen, 221–22).

[94] In his *Einleitung in die Soziologie* (1931), 80–83, Freyer went so far as to designate Riehl a

It was this set of ideological assumptions that motivated Ipsen's research on the social, economic, and political developments that had weakened the way of life of the peasantry. The contemporary decline of the peasantry, he wrote, "is one of the most threatening phenomena of our age, for it endangers the existence of the nation at its root."[95] His research on the contemporary peasantry led him to conclude that it was alienated from the mainstream of "bourgeois-industrial society" in Germany and that the peasantry formed an important, though ignored, source of resistance to that society.[96]

A brief description of the research activities of his institute submitted by Freyer to a professional journal in 1929 reveals the focus of its research on those social strata which, like the peasantry, were rarely the center of contemporary sociological concern. In addition to the working class, upon which much empirical work centered in the 1920s, the members of the institute devoted particular studies to the "development of the white-collar strata [Angestelltenschaft] and the social structure of the commercial strata [Handelsgewerbes] and of the bureaucracy."[97] Freyer and Ipsen focused their attention on those social groups—the peasantry, the white-collar workers, the commercial Mittelstand, and the bureaucracy—which stood outside or between the Bürgertum on the one hand and the industrial proletariat on the other. It was the increasing alienation of these groups from the social and political structure of the Weimar Republic that formed the sociological basis of Freyer's prediction of an antibourgeois revolution from the right in the spring of 1931.

A second focus of Ipsen's research, the sociology of central and eastern Europe, was also an outgrowth of his radical conservative, völkisch ideological presuppositions. If the state was to represent not the rational assent of independent individuals or groups with legitimately divergent interests but rather the collective self-assertion of an ethnic-linguistic Volk, then it was incumbent upon it to extend its jurisdiction over the entire Volk. From this perspective the kleindeutsch solution to the German problem represented by the Bismarckian state was clearly unsatisfactory, since it left so many ethnic Germans (the so-

---

father of German sociology, along with Lorenz von Stein and Karl Marx.

95 Gunther Ipsen, "Das Dorf als Beispiel einer echten Gruppe," (1928–29), 23; see also his Antrittsvorlesung of 1931, published as Gunther Ipsen, Programm einer Soziologie des deutschen Volkstums (1933), 14–16.

96 Ipsen, "Dorf," 22–24; Ipsen, Programm, 5–6. In his "Soziologie des Dorfes" (1932), 2, he referred to the relationship of the "Landvolk" to "industrieller Gesellschaft" as the central social question of the day.

97 Hans Freyer, "Soziologie als Wirklichkeitswissenschaft" (1929), 265–66. For the contemporary literature on the various components of the Mittelstand, see Herman Lebovics, Social Conservatism and the Middle Classes in Germany, 1914–1933, chapter 1.

called *Auslandsdeutsche* or *Volksdeutsche*) outside the boundaries of the German state. In keeping with his *völkisch* premises Ipsen not only rejected the boundaries of Bismarckian Germany but held that the nation-state itself was an inappropriate political structure for central and eastern Europe, in which German communities were scattered throughout areas in which other ethnic groups predominated. He viewed the nation-state as the political correlate of the rise of bourgeois society in the nineteenth century and as a disaster for central Europe. Ipsen sought not only a social order that would supersede bourgeois society but a political order that would replace the nation-state by a new German *Reich* stretching across eastern Europe, which would bring about the political unity of the German *Volk*.[98] In the meantime he devoted himself to the sociological study of the *Auslandsdeutschen* and was a major contributor to the *Handwörterbuch des Grenz- und Auslandsdeutschtums*, of which he and Freyer (along with many other prominent German professors) were editors.[99]

These ideological concerns for the fate of the peasantry and the *Auslandsdeutschen*—a concern that was dominant in Ipsen's work and shared to a considerable degree by Freyer—were concretized in a program of research that stretched beyond the confines of the university into the youth movement. In the late 1920s and early 1930s Ipsen organized a series of "Dorfwochen," study trips to peasant villages in Germany and to villages of the *Auslandsdeutschen* in Hungary and Romania. A group of students—drawn from Freyer and Ipsen's students at Leipzig and from members of the Schlesische Jungmannschaft, a branch of the Deutsche Freischar—would spend several weeks as participant-observers in a peasant village, living and working with a peasant family. Afternoons were spent obtaining statistical and documentary material in local archives in order to gather contemporary social and economic information relating to the peasantry. Such research projects combined ideological commitment with the collection and scientific analysis of empirical data.[100] It was the practical embodiment of Freyer's conception of sociology.

It was through Ipsen and through many of their students in the youth movement that Freyer came to have a greater interest in east-central European affairs. Though he wrote little on foreign affairs between 1925 and 1933, the implications of Freyer's political emphasis on the *Volk* for German relations

[98] Ipsen, *Programm*, 16–17; idem, "Das Erbe des Reiches" (1932), 64–66.

[99] *Handwörterbuch des Grenz- und Auslandsdeutschtums* (1933).

[100] On the *Dorfwochen*, see Linde, 106–7; Heinz Beutler, "Dorfforschung am Grenzschul-heim Boberhaus," and Helmut Klocke, "Begegnung mit der Dorfforschung in Ungarn und Rumanien," both in Walter Greiff et al., *Gespräch und Aktion in Gruppe und Gesellschaft, 1919–1969*; also Hans Dehmel, "Hans Freyer," 10.

with east-central Europe were bound to be ambivalent. This ambivalence was already experienced by those of Freyer's students in the youth movement who shared his *völkisch* emphasis. Many of them saw it as their mission to strengthen contacts with Germans living as minorities in the east-central European successor states in order to keep these isolated communities within the German cultural orbit.[101] The *Fahrt* (group excursion), which before the war had been intended to bring the members of the movement closer to nature, took on a new significance. During the 1920s and 1930s its purpose became to bring the members closer to the *Auslandsdeutschen*.[102] Yet the Deutsche Freischar also had contacts with comparable groups of young Hungarians, Romanians, and Bulgarians who shared their national-populist orientation.[103] Stimulated by such contacts into a greater interest in the affairs of these nations, some members of the youth movement around Freyer and Ipsen went on to pursue academic careers in eastern European studies. Later, as eastern European specialists, many were to play a role in the implementation of policies that were inimical to the interests of these eastern European nationalities.

The third faculty member closely associated with Freyer's sociological institute was Hugo Fischer. Fischer's background reveals a familiar pattern. Born in 1897 to a *bildungsbürgerlich* family, he had fought in the First World War and had been severely wounded. After the war he had studied philosophy, history, and psychology in Leipzig. In 1926 he had habilitated with Felix Krueger in 1926 with a work on Hegel that, in typical neo-Hegelian fashion, emphasized Hegel's link to German romanticism.[104] His later works explored themes close to Freyer's heart: Nietzsche and Marx as analysts of the decadence of bourgeois society (a pairing typical of the circles around Freyer); the war experience as the beginning of a new cultural era; the need for a new, more all-encompassing conception of the state; and an activist conception of scholarship.[105] As a *Privatdozent*, Fischer eked out a marginal economic existence by offering lectures on social philosophy and political philosophy with provocative

---

[101] Alice Gräfin Hardenberg, "Bündische Jugend und Ausland," 28–32.

[102] Ibid., 26–28.

[103] See the essays in Greiff et al., *Gespräch*.

[104] Hugo Fischer, *Hegels Methode in ihrer ideologiegeschichtlichen Notwendigkeit* (1926).

[105] Hugo Fischer, *Nietzsche Apostata* (1931); idem, *Marx und sein Verhältnis zu Staat und Wirtschaft* (1932); idem, "Der deutsche Infanterist von 1917" (1934); idem, "Politik und Metaphysik" (1932).

In a letter to the dean of the philosophical faculty written in April 1932, Fischer described his conception of scholarship: "Der Philosoph hat überwissenschaftliche Aufgaben. . . . Denn das deutsche Volk bricht zu neuen Zielen auf, und die Theorie kann Praxis nicht vorausgehen. Das deutsche Volk kämpft um einen letzten Sinn seiner Existenz, und die Philosophie ist die geistige Intensivierung dieses Kampfes" (UAL, PA Fischer, 46–47).

titles such as "Truth and Ideology in the Political Theories and Movements of the Present," "Toward a Characterization and Critique of Liberalism," "The *Lebensraum* of Modern Nations," and "On Dictatorship."

Though lower in academic rank than Freyer and Ipsen (who on Freyer's initiative had been named *außerplanmässiger außerordentlicher Professor*, a step up from *Privatdozent*),[106] Fischer played an important role in disseminating Freyer's ideas to a wider and more political audience. He edited the journal of the Deutsche Philosophische Gesellschaft, the *Blätter für deutsche Philosophie*, which became something of a house journal of the Freyer circle, with Ipsen serving as book review editor. Ernst Jünger, one of the leading authors of the radical right, was a close friend of Fischer, whom Jünger considered the most important living philosopher. Jünger's book of 1932, *Der Arbeiter*, was written under Fischer's influence.[107] *Der Arbeiter*, in turn, influenced Martin Heidegger's writings on technology.[108] Fischer also helped edit the political journal *Die Tat*, which from 1928 to 1933 was the most influential political journal of the radical right, and was a frequent contributor to *Widerstand*, the journal of the National Bolshevik movement.[109] Fischer was a link in the chain that bound Freyer to the communicative network of the intellectual right.

Freyer, Ipsen, and Fischer formed the core of the Institute of Sociology. All three were unequivocally men of the right, and just as unmistakably men little attracted to the "right" in the sense of the maintenance of the status quo or (like the major political party of the Weimar right, the Deutschnationale Volkspartei) to the restoration of the monarchical status quo ante. None of the three had a good word to say about capitalism or parliamentary democracy. The scholarship of all three was motivated by broadly political concerns, though none, as of 1930 at least, could be identified with an existing political party.

Among Freyer's colleagues outside of the Institute of Sociology, Theodor Litt, professor of pedagogy, deserves particular attention not only because Litt's intellectual background was so similar to Freyer's, or because his areas of scholarly concern closely bordered on Freyer's own, or even because the two men were personal friends. Rather, Litt will be an object of continuing concern because despite these similarities, at key forks in his philosophical and political development he made choices at odds with Freyer's. From Freyer's perspective, Litt represents the path not taken. He thus provides us with a morally im-

---

[106] UAL, PA Ipsen, 25.

[107] On Fischer's connection to the Tatkreis and the Widerstandskreis, see Mohler, *Konservative Revolution*, 457; and Jean Pierre Faye, *Tota-*

litäre Sprachen, 1:448.

[108] See George Steiner, *Martin Heidegger*, 138.

[109] Ernst Niekisch, *Gewagtes Leben*, 192.

portant control instance. It is unfortunate but inevitable that a historical account of an individual's intellectual and political development that explains later actions by reference to prior experience should make it appear that his development was necessary, indeed inevitable. It tends to make of its human subject not an *actor* but a *reactor* to external events, to portray him as *nothing but* the sum of his roles. It tends, that is, to disguise the fact of moral choice in human life, to bracket out that which makes moral agency possible. Litt's path shows us what Freyer *might* have chosen to do but did not.

Born seven years earlier than Freyer as the son of a Gymnasium professor in Düsseldorf, Litt was too old to have participated in the youth movement. But the catastrophe of the First World War affected him profoundly nonetheless. In his first book, written at about the time of Freyer's *Antäus*, Litt wrote that the war demanded "that man determine his place within the historical world on the basis of the new situation of thought and feeling."[110] In 1920 Litt was called to the new chair of pedagogy in Leipzig. The hopes placed upon pedagogy in the early years of the Weimar Republic were similar to those placed upon sociology: both were greeted as synthesizing disciplines that would bridge the gap between the academy and the outside world. Litt's own conception of the discipline was exceedingly broad. The role of pedagogic theory for him was to provide the teacher with an awareness of the situation of his age, and Litt's works dealt as often with broad problems in the philosophy of culture as with specific problems of the school. Like Freyer, he sought a renewal of Hegelian thought on the basis of Dilthey's concepts of life and experience.[111] His important early work on the philosophy of culture, *Individuum und Gemeinschaft* (which went through three considerably altered editions from 1919 to 1926), influenced Freyer's *Theorie des objektiven Geistes* (1923) and was in turn influenced by it.

With so much in common it is not surprising that Litt encouraged Freyer's call to Leipzig in 1924 or that the two men cooperated with each other thereafter. Freyer was a frequent contributor to *Die Erziehung*, of which Litt was an editor, and Litt served on the editorial board of the *Blätter für deutsche Philosophie*, with which Freyer was closely associated. Their students were recruited from the same circles—primarily those of the youth movement—and they often cosponsored dissertations.[112] A personal friendship developed between

[110] Theodor Litt, *Geschichte und Leben* (1918), quoted in Friedhelm Nicolin, "Pädagogische Theorie als Selbstkritik der Pädagogik," 269.

[111] Theodor Litt, *Individuum und Gemeinschaft,* 3d ed. (1926), 378 and passim.

[112] See the listing of dissertations in Üner, "Hans Freyer," 236–39.

Freyer and Litt, and in an article published in 1930 in honor of Litt's fiftieth birthday Freyer praised him as "a clear mind who acts as an intellectual conscience amid the confusion of opinions and desires."[113]

We will later have occasion to explore the differences that divided the two friends in the years immediately before and after Hitler's accession to power. Though an intellectual portrait of Theodor Litt would be inappropriate in this context, several elements of his social theory and political commitments that distinguished him from Freyer during the 1920s are significant for an understanding of his later actions.

Like Freyer, Litt was concerned with the social origins of identity and with the problem of social cohesion. Yet he criticized the attempt to derive the individual's identity primarily from his role in "society" conceived of as a whole. Litt was also skeptical of theories that explained social cohesion as the result of common purposes held by all members of a society. Indeed, Litt called attention to the multiplicity of small groups that mediated the relationship between the individual on one hand and society as a whole on the other. He focused on the role played by those groups limited enough in size so that each member of the group was in personal contact with all others—which he termed "closed circles of the first degree"—in forming individual identity and creating a sense of transindividual purpose. According to Litt larger, more impersonal social groups—what he termed "closed circles of the second degree"—derived their cohesion and purposes largely from the intricate circle of smaller groups of which these were composed.[114]

This social-theoretical stress on the mediating function of small social groups could have political consequences. By insisting that social and individual identity were not primarily the result of goals shared by the entire society, it made the perceived absence of such collective purposes appear less threatening, and a radical political solution less urgent. Litt's work therefore called both Freyer's theoretical premises and his political solution into question. Moreover, Litt's whole conceptual framework made a totalitarian solution to the problem of collective purpose not only superfluous but counterproductive, since such a solution endangered those "closed circles of the first order" in which personal identity and social cohesion were held to originate.[115]

Whether as a logical consequence of his social theory or on the basis of some independently affirmed decision, Litt was—again, in contradistinction to Freyer—a vocal supporter of Weimar's parliamentary democracy. His support

---

[113] Hans Freyer, "Theodor Litt zum fünfzigsten Geburtstag" (1930).

[114] Litt, *Individuum*, 382.

[115] Ibid., 394.

for the republican constitution began in 1919 and was expressed not only in works explicitly devoted to the teaching of civics but in those devoted to broader problems as well.[116]

Though Litt, like Freyer, used the concept of *Volk* in his writings on the philosophy of culture, he did so in a way that ruled out the mystificatory uses of the term in Freyer's work. He explicitly rejected both the notion of a metaphysical *Volksgeist* that was the historical *cause* of a collective culture and the possibility of casting light on cultural development by reference to race and blood.[117] While Freyer drew upon Spengler's organic concept of the *Volk* in his writings, Litt made Spengler the focus of his attack on all forms of organic thought that mystified the process of cultural creation.[118] In comparing Litt's writing to Freyer's, the former's emphasis on clarity and precision may at first appear merely stylistic, but it in fact revealed a difference of mind. Freyer's activism made him impatient with precision and quick to employ emotive language; even his most academic writings often seemed intended to seduce the reader rather than convince him. Litt's style was drier, more systematic, indeed plodding, befitting an attempt to convince the reader by logical demonstration. It was perhaps this quality of mind to which Freyer referred when he wrote of Litt as an "intellectual conscience" to those around him.

In evaluating Hans Freyer's intellectual influence we must distinguish between his audience, his intellectual collaborators, his students, and his disciples. His largest audience was composed of those whom he reached primarily through his writings and with whom he had only sporadic personal contact, if any. His influence upon the members of such an audience was diffuse; for most of them his was one voice among others that helped determine their intellectual commitments and personal choices. Freyer's intellectual collaborators were those of equal or near-equal intellectual standing with whom he felt a close intellectual and political affinity, those from whom he borrowed ideas and who in turn borrowed from him. As of the early 1930s these included not only Gunther Ipsen and Hugo Fischer at Leipzig but also the political philosopher and jurist Carl Schmitt and his disciples Ernst Forsthoff and Ernst Rudolf Huber. The political writings of Freyer's intellectual collaborators and his influence upon a wider audience are examined in chapter 6. Here we must briefly consider his influence upon his students and disciples. By "students" is meant all of those who studied intensively with Freyer in the course of their

---

[116] Wolfgang Klafki, "Theodor Litts Stellung zur Weimarer Republik und seine Auseinandersetzung mit dem Nationalsozialismus," 204–9.

[117] Litt, *Individuum*, 332ff., 398.
[118] Ibid., passim.

studies and who were influenced by him to some degree. By "disciples" is meant that subgroup of students who regarded their intellectual activity as a direct continuation, development, or expansion of the ideas of their master. It is to several of Freyer's representative students that we now turn.

In the 1920s sociology was a relatively new and unconventional addition to the academy. The more conservative among the student body—the members of student corps and fraternities who looked forward to jobs in business and government through the "old-boy network"—were the least likely recruits to the new discipline, and there were no students of this type closely associated with the institute.[119] It was rather those students who had become critical of their society by virtue of their pre- or extra-academic activities who were attracted to a discipline that promised to reveal the workings of the body social, and those who were actively engaged in attempting to bring about collective change who sought systematic knowledge of "society."

Thus it was the ranks of the youth movement and its associated groups that contributed the lion's share of students of sociology at Leipzig. Most of these students, like Freyer and his comrades two decades earlier, were disaffected from their origins in the educated bourgeoisie. They differed from Freyer's prewar cohort of the movement by their more overtly social and political concerns and by their practical activity in attempting to bring about collective renewal.

Many of Freyer's students from within the youth movement were associated with the Leuchtenburgkreis, including Fritz Borinski, its leader. The Leuchtenburgkreis was a group of fifty to one hundred young people—some of them students, some slightly older—many of whom occupied leadership positions in the Saxon branch of the Deutsche Freischar, the largest wing of the youth movement in the 1920s. They met once or twice per year on a mountaintop near Jena to discuss moral and political themes. At its inception after the war the group had been connected to the youth organization of the German Democratic party, but the independent ethos of the youth movement quickly came into conflict with the more prosaic spirit of party activity, and in 1923 the group cut its ties to the party.[120] The political and intellectual tone of the group was set by its leader, Fritz Borinski, who was increasingly drawn toward the Social Democratic party and to a radical, ethical socialism as propounded in the *Neue Blätter für den Sozialismus*, a journal whose editors in-

---

[119] Linde, "Soziologie," 105–6. On the members of the student corps, see Jarausch, *Students*, chapter 5.

[120] On the Leuchtenburgkreis, see Fritz Borinski et al., *Jugend im politischen Protest: Der Leuchtenburgkreis*.

cluded Paul Tillich, himself an adjunct professor at Freyer's institute during the 1920s.[121] Though the Leuchtenburgkreis regarded itself as above parties its ideological discussions were distinguished by a strong commitment to the German nation as well as to socialism. Capitalism left the working class alienated from national life, it was argued, and hence socialism was a prerequisite for the integration of the working class into the life of the nation.[122] The members of the group regarded themselves as antibourgeois and as critics of the Weimar state.[123]

Many older members of the Leuchtenburgkreis, that is, those born shortly after the turn of the century, were actively involved in worker education. Some taught at the Volkshochschule in Leipzig, an institution for adult education founded after 1918 by academic socialists such as the political philosopher Hermann Heller with the financial support of the Leipzig municipal government. Heller also organized a "Seminar für freies Volksbildungswesen" at the University of Leipzig, which served as a bridge between the university and the Volkshochschule. Most of the teachers at the Volkshochschule were of a Marxist orientation and affiliated with the Social Democratic party or the Communist party. They sought to expose young workers to the world of learning otherwise closed to them but also to strengthen their class consciousness.[124] The Leuchtenburgkreis and the Volkshochschule were the institutional bases of those of Freyer's students who came essentially from the political left.

The cooperation of Freyer and Ipsen with the Schlesische Jungmannschaft has been mentioned with regard to the study of the peasant *Dorf* and of southeastern Europe. The members of this group—also part of the nonparty Deutsche Freischar—had a nationalist peasantist orientation. Yet their social concerns extended beyond the peasantry and their practical activity included the development of the *Arbeitslager*, one of the most novel attempts of the youth movement to create institutions of social renewal. The *Arbeitslager* began in the mid-1920s as an attempt to use common physical labor as a pedagogic tool to strengthen the group experience within the *Bünde* (groups) of the youth

[121] On Tillich's politics during the Weimar era, see Alexander Schwan, "Zeitgenössische Philosophie und Theologie in ihrem Verhältnis zur Weimarer Republik," 278–81.

[122] Borinski, *Jugend*, esp. the essay by Werner Reinhard, "Leuchtenburgkreis und deutsche Nation."

[123] Ibid.; see also Werner Reinhard, "Politische Jugendbewegung in der Weimarer Zeit,"

in *Politische Bildung in der Demokratie: Fritz Borinski zum 65. Geburtstag*, ed. Gerd Doerry (Berlin, 1968).

[124] Fritz Borinski, "Autobiographie"; Kurt Riedel, "Arbeiterbildung und Leuchtenburgkreis," in Borinski, *Jugend*. See the works by Reinhard cited above as well as the documents reprinted in Borinski, *Jugend*.

movement. Beginning in 1928 the Schlesische Jungmannschaft began to organize *Arbeitslager* made up of young urban workers, peasants, and students from the youth movement. Its purpose remained primarily pedagogic: common activity served to create a basis of *Gemeinschaft* among social groups that otherwise remained estranged from one another. The actual physical tasks, such as drainage, were combined with discussions of cultural and political themes, group singing, and theater.[125] The project caught the eye and gained the support of a number of professors, pedagogues, and intellectuals who were concerned with the deep social divisions within the German nation and in search of sources of national and social renewal. As the depression brought massive unemployment to Germany the nature and function of the *Arbeitslager* was transformed to provide work for hundreds of thousands of young men shut out of employment in the private labor market. Work now became the center of the *Arbeitslager*, which were extended in size and duration and initiated at other locations throughout Germany. In the summer of 1931 the government of the *Reich* began to provide funds for the *Arbeitslager* under the rubric of "voluntary labor service" (*freiwilliger Arbeitsdienst*).[126] Hans Freyer and Gunther Ipsen also looked with favor upon the new social experiment.[127]

At the apex of these activities was Hans Dehmel, who after meeting Freyer and Ipsen went to the Institute of Sociology in Leipzig in 1930 to work with the latter on rural sociology. Dehmel had been part of the Wandervogel before the First World War. When war broke out he volunteered for service, and during the war organized former members of the youth movement in uniform into an organization known as the Feldwandervogel. Immediately after the war he became the leader of a group of war veterans of Wandervogel origin who formed the so-called Wandervogel Legion, part of the *Grenzschütz-Ost* of the Freikorps, which sought to protect the German border in disputed Silesia. During the 1920s he founded the Schlesische Jungmannschaft and was instrumental in the establishment of the *Arbeitslager*. In 1930 he became the national *Führer* of the Deutsche Freischar, then the largest independent (i.e., nonparty) body within the youth movement. From 1930 to 1932 he pursued his studies in Leipzig, then broke them off to assume a position as adviser to the *Reichskommissar für den freiwilligen Arbeitsdienst*.[128]

---

[125] On the various stages in the development of the *Arbeitslager*, see Hans Freyer, "Arbeitslager und Arbeitsdienst" (1932), reprinted in Greiff et al., *Gespräch*.

[126] Werner Kindt, ed., *Die deutsche Jugendbewegung 1920 bis 1933*, 1521ff.

[127] Freyer, "Arbeitslager"; see also Gunther Ipsen's introduction to Hans Raupach, *Arbeitsdienst in Bulgarien* (1932).

[128] Rudolf Jentsch, "Hans Dehmel—Wirken und Werk."

Like Borinski and the Leuchtenburgkreis, Dehmel and the Schlesische Jungmannschaft were deeply involved in practical social activities that grew out of their idealistic commitments. In the case of Borinski the ideology was socialist with a strong admixture of nationalism, and the practical activity was mainly oriented to the working class. Dehmel's group was more decidedly nationalist and placed a greater emphasis on the role of the peasantry, but it too was anticapitalist. It was from these circles of idealistic social activists that most of Freyer's students were drawn in the years from 1925 to 1933.

Beginning about 1930, a third group of idealist-activists began to play a greater role in Freyer's student clientele: students who were politically active in the National Socialist movement. A sketch of one of their number will serve to illustrate this type, as Borinski and Dehmel have served to represent their respective circles.

Werner Studentkowski was a member of the National Socialist faction of the Saxon Landtag when he studied with Hans Freyer in the early 1930s. Born in Kiev of German parents in 1903, he had worked for two years in a bank before beginning his university studies, which he pursued intermittently from 1921 to 1927. Soon his studies took second place to the National Socialist party, which he joined in 1925 and which soon became the focus of his life. At the university he was a leader of the National Socialist Student League, then a small minority at Leipzig.[129] In 1926 he became a professional propagandist (*Reichsredner*) for the party, which dispatched him in the following year to work in Berlin with Josef Goebbels. Employing Goebbels' tactic of public brawling to gain attention for his cause, he was arrested and fined seventy marks.[130] A rousing speaker who addressed mass rallies around the country, Studentkowski promised that the coming Nazi revolution would be a true social solution, unlike that of 1918.[131] In 1928 he returned to party work in Leipzig; a well-known political orator on and off campus in Leipzig, he became a member of the Saxon Landtag in 1930. Thus by the time he became Freyer's student in 1931 the twenty-eight-year-old Studentkowski was already a political veteran—an *alter Kämpfer*. His return to the university by no means precluded continuing political activity: records show that he was fined five hundred

[129] Werner Studentkowski, "Personalfragebogen," 22 September 1937, File: "Werner Studentkowski," BDC. In 1927–28 the NSDStB received only 6.6 percent of the vote in the student council (AStA) elections at the University of Leipzig, according to the documents reprinted in Albrecht Tyrell, ed., *Führer Befiehl*, 381.

[130] Studentkowski, "Personalfragebogen." On Goebbels' use of this tactic, see Joachim Fest, *The Face of the Third Reich*, 90ff.

[131] See the reports on him in the files of the Nachrichtensammelstelle of the Reichsministerium des Innern, BAK, R134/90, 23, 163.

marks in 1932 for insulting the president of the Leipzig police force on the occasion of the ban on the Sturmabteilung (SA).[132]

When his initial dissertation topic fell through for lack of source material Freyer suggested to Studentkowski that he write a doctoral thesis on the social and occupational composition of the National Socialist German Workers' party (NSDAP). The project, Freyer emphasized, would be of great scholarly interest given the contemporary significance of the party. Pleased by this prospect Studentkowski wrote to Gregor Strasser, then the head of the party's national organization, asking him to intercede with Hitler if necessary to gain access to the membership files of the party in Munich, which were to provide the raw material for a statistical analysis.[133] Strasser was supportive, as was Hitler, and Studentkowski worked on the project for over a year. Historians may regard as unfortunate Studentkowski's failure to complete his dissertation, but the cause of his failure was more unfortunate still: with Hitler's rise to power in 1933 Studentkowski became too occupied with his new tasks as a government official to complete his thesis.[134]

How were Tillichian socialists, peasant nationalists from the youth movement, and National Socialist agitators able to work with a single professor, especially one as ideologically committed as Hans Freyer? The answer lies partly in Freyer's personality, partly in his conception of sociology.

Freyer's political and social theory was anything but liberal, and his conception of the role of the university, as we will see, was not liberal either. Yet his personality was liberal, if by the term we mean open-minded or tolerant. Thus throughout his career Freyer seems to have had good personal relations with colleagues, students, and others whose politics or view of the world were very different from his own. He appears to have been comfortable with a wide variety of students, and they in turn were comfortable with him.[135]

The mutual attraction of Freyer to socially or politically activist students was of a piece with his conception of sociology, according to which value judgments connected to an activist participation in society were the existential source of sociological theorizing and research. Sociology was the transformation of activist commitment into systematic, scholarly research; the number of research

[132] Studentkowski, "Personalfragebogen."

[133] Werner Studentkowski to Gregor Strasser, 24 July 1931, BAK, NS22/1067, fol. 1.

[134] Letter of "Schu" to Studentkowski, 28 July 1931, BAK, NS22/1067. Studentkowski's failure to complete the dissertation was reported in a letter written by Hans Freyer to Albrecht Tyrell in 1968, cited in Tyrell, 380.

[135] Interview with Ernest Manheim, Martha's Vineyard, 15 August 1983. This aspect of Freyer's personality is described (in a rather exaggerated fashion) in the memoir by Helmut Schelsky, "Die verschiedenen Weisen, wie mann Demokrat sein kann: Erinnerungen an Hans Freyer, Helmuth Plessner und andere," in his *Rückblicke eines "Anti-Soziologen,"* 143–45.

programs was limited only by the number of ideological perspectives in contemporary society. Given this conception of sociology Freyer was likely to attract activists as his students. Yet given his acceptance of a multiplicity of starting points, his belief that each student should follow his own ideological star, he was unlikely to develop around him a "school" with an established program of common research.[136]

This close relationship between extrascholarly activism and academic research, already visible in Freyer's own dissertation and *Habilitationsschrift*, is evident in many of the dissertations that Freyer sponsored before 1933. Hilde Reisig, a member of the Leuchtenburgkreis active in worker education, wrote a dissertation called "The Role of *Bildung* in the Political Thought of the German Labor Movement from the 1840s to the World War," a work modeled on Freyer's *Habilitationsschrift*.[137] Arkadij Gurland, a Russian-born student of Freyer active in the Social Democratic party (and later a member of the "Frankfurt Institute") wrote a thesis entitled "Means of Production, State, Class Dictatorship: An Immanent Interpretation of the Concept of Dictatorship in the Materialistic View of History."[138] Before becoming a lecturer at the Hochschule für Politik in Berlin, Sigmund Neumann completed a dissertation on "The Stages of Prussian Conservatism" with Freyer.[139] Thus the close relationship of ideological commitment and social research at Freyer's institute reflected his theory of sociology.

Freyer's liberal personality and pluralistic conception of sociology were likely to attract many students but few disciples—that is, students who conceived of themselves as "Freyerians" and sought to develop his distinctive approach to sociology. Insofar as Freyer ever had such a disciple it was Karl-Heinz Pfeffer.

It was not until the age of twenty-four, when he had almost completed his doctorate, that Karl-Heinz Pfeffer became a student and disciple of Hans Freyer. The attraction of the younger man to the older was not surprising given their remarkably similar backgrounds. Born into the Protestant *Bildungsbürgertum* in 1906, Pfeffer had studied history and *Anglistik* (English language and history) at a number of German universities and had spent the 1928–29 academic year at Stanford.

During his student years Pfeffer was deeply involved in various segments of

---

[136] Compare Üner, "Hans Freyer," which attempts to apply the notion of "school" to Freyer and his institute.

[137] Hilde Fischer-Reisig, "Zur Entstehung einer Dissertation," in Borinski et al., *Jugend*.

[138] Arkadij Gurland, *Produktionsweise—Staat—Klassendiktatur* (1929).

[139] Sigmund Neumann, *Die Stufen des preußischen Konservatismus* (1928).

the youth movement. In 1924 he joined the Jungnationaler Bund, the largest organization of the overtly right-wing branch of the movement.[140] The Bund was born after the First World War from the same resurgent nationalism that had spawned the Fichte-Gesellschaft, an organization with which it had informal links. Among its mottoes was "Youth is conservative and revolutionary at the same time," a line that could have been written by Hans Freyer.[141] Unlike the Deutsche Freischar, the Jungnationaler Bund excluded Jews from its ranks and participated in the agitational campaign against the Young Plan in 1930.[142] Later that year the Jungnationaler Bund combined with the Großdeutscher Bund led by Admiral von Trotha—another radically nationalist but more decidedly militaristic group—into the Freischar junger Nation, to which Pfeffer also belonged. Despite differences of tone, style, and even substance, the Jungnationaler Bund was in close contact with the Deutsche Freischar; from 1927 on, when he participated in one of the *Arbeitslager* of the Deutsche Freischar and one of its trips to England, Pfeffer had links to this group too.[143] From 1925 through 1930 Pfeffer was also active in the Deutsch-akademische Gildenschaft, a "guild" of like-minded university students and professors. On their minds was a variety of *völkisch* ideology that was explicitly racist and anti-Semitic.[144] Like many of those in the youth movement, Pfeffer belonged to several organizations within its institutional orbit.

It was probably through his contact with the Deutsche Freischar that Pfeffer, then a student in Berlin, learned of Hans Freyer. Perhaps through hearing him lecture, more likely through a reading of the recently published *Soziologie als Wirklichkeitswissenschaft*, Pfeffer became deeply impressed by Freyer. In August 1930 he went to Leipzig, and after spending a month with Freyer he decided to devote himself to the study of sociology.[145] After further studies in Paris, Heidelberg, and London—where, in Pfeffer's words, he "tried in vain to represent the social science of the new Germany in the thoroughly liberal atmosphere of the LSE [London School of Economics]"—Pfeffer set sail in August 1932 for Australia. There he planned to conduct research for a sociological study using the categories of Freyer's sociological theory.

Before leaving Germany he published a long article in the journal of the Freischar junger Nation, entitled "Hans Freyer, an Interpreter of Our Time." The article was intended to acquaint readers who knew Freyer only from his

---

[140] Karl Heinz Pfeffer, "Fragebogen, 1935," UAL, PA Pfeffer, 2.

[141] Quoted in Kindt, *Jugendbewegung*, 489.

[142] Ibid., 495.

[143] Ibid., 493; Pfeffer, "Lebenslauf, 1934," UAL, PA Pfeffer, 4–9.

[144] Kindt, *Jugendbewegung*, 1376.

[145] Pfeffer, "Lebenslauf."

Revolution von rechts with the remainder of his thought. Freyer's work, Pfeffer wrote in acolytic tones, was indispensable to the readers of the journal if they were to achieve their collective goals. His article was clearly a labor of love; in the space of ten pages he attempted to give a précis of all of Freyer's work, from *Antäus* through *Revolution von rechts*.[146] Pfeffer's relationship with Freyer was clearly one of discipleship in both a professional and a spiritual sense. Pfeffer's feelings, as we will see, were reciprocated by the master, who must have seen in the novice a younger reflection of himself. Pfeffer was soon to outdo Freyer in his commitment to ideology over social science. Tönnies, as a deideologized senior practitioner, had rejected Freyer's attempt to rekindle the ideological fire within his *Jugendwerk*. Freyer—by 1930 a senior practitioner in his discipline, but one who had remained ideologically committed and committed to ideology—welcomed the ideological zeal of the novice Pfeffer with open arms.

[146] Karl-Heinz Pfeffer, "Hans Freyer, ein Deuter unserer Zeit," *Jungnationale Stimmen* (1931–32), 343–54.

CHAPTER FIVE

Ideology and Social Science in Freyer's
Theory of Sociology, 1925–1933

In two books and two articles published between 1929 and 1931 Hans Freyer spelled out the theory behind the practice of sociology at his institute at Leipzig.[1] Freyer called his program "*Soziologie als Wirklichkeitswissenschaft*" (sociology as a science of reality). To the contemporary German reader versed in recent social-scientific controversies, this phrase had considerable resonance. It had been coined by Max Weber, in a major methodological essay published in 1904 on the occasion of his assumption of the co-editorship of the *Archiv für Sozialwissenschaften und Sozialpolitik*, the most important German social-scientific periodical of its day. Entitled "The 'Objectivity' of Knowledge in Social Science and Social Policy," the essay set forth Weber's views on the relationship between values and social science.[2] Though Freyer's divergences from Weber's strictures were, as we will see, at least as significant as his borrowings, the title *Soziologie als Wirklichkeitswissenschaft* immediately alerted the knowledgeable reader that the problem of the relationship of the social scientist to the object of his study was to be the focus of discussion. Even the less knowledgeable reader would realize that at a time when even art prided itself on its "new realism" (*neue Sachlichkeit*), here was a sociology that claimed the mastery not of abstract categories but of reality itself. *Soziologie als Wirklichkeitswissenschaft*, then, was as much a promise as a book title.

[1] Hans Freyer, "Rezension von O. Spann, *Gesellschaftsphilosophie*" (1929–30); idem, "Soziologie als Wirklichkeitswissenschaft" (1929); idem, *Soziologie als Wirklichkeitswissenschaft: Logische Grundlegung des Systems der Soziologie* (1930), hereafter cited as *SW*; idem, *Einleitung in die Soziologie* (1931), hereafter cited as *ES*. These two books overlap considerably in substance, though they differ in purpose and organization. *SW* was intended primarily to provide a philosophical basis for the further development of sociology and was aimed at an audience of specialists in philosophy and the social sciences. *ES*, an introduction to sociology, emphasized the history of sociological theory and reiterated many of the central notions of *SW* in a somewhat popularized form. A revised version of the latter work was published in a Japanese translation in 1955 and a Turkish translation in 1957.

[2] Max Weber, "Die 'Objektivität' sozialwissenschaftlicher und sozialpolitischer Erkenntnis" (1904).

Freyer's Interpretation of the Origins of Sociology

Freyer sought to defend an activist brand of sociology. He argued that contemporary German sociology had become academic and methodologically incapable of a radical questioning of the social and political status quo. Freyer's attention to what he termed the "classical" systems of sociology of Saint-Simon, Comte, Marx, and Lorenz von Stein were not intended as merely historical. "At the cradle of sociology," he wrote, "stood the hope that this science could overcome the crisis of the age by getting to the bottom of it, and that politics would one day be applied sociology, as technology is applied physics."[3] The activist tendency of early sociology was for Freyer not a symptom of its youth but part of its very nature.

Sociology, as a discipline with "the social" as its distinct subject matter, Freyer argued, was a product of particular historical circumstances. Its subject matter had traditionally been treated by social philosophy under the broader rubric of political theory, which had centered upon the state. The rise of sociology, Freyer claimed, was made possible by social developments through which society—the realm of private interests —had become autonomous from the state.[4]

Freyer referred to the new reality that had necessitated a distinct science of the social by the Hegelian designation *die bürgerliche Gesellschaft* (bourgeois society or civil society). The rise of the capitalist market economy, which transformed society from one based on hereditary estates into a "bourgeois society" of economic classes, led to the emergence of sociology as a legatee of the philosophy of history in England, France, and Germany, Freyer asserted.[5]

In France, it was Saint-Simon who served as the pivotal figure in the emergence of the new discipline. Freyer emphasized that Saint-Simon's sociology had emerged from his attempt to master the perceived crisis of his age. Freyer focused upon three ideas that he saw as central not only to Saint-Simon's own thought but to sociology as a discipline. The first of these was the notion that history oscillated between "positive" and "critical" epochs, ages of order and of disorder. The second was that the present was a critical age, one of disorder, chaos, and crisis. Third, the role of sociology was to comprehend the causes of the present disorder and help to create a new positive epoch.[6]

---

[3] Freyer, "Soziologie als Wirklichkeitswissenschaft" (1929), 258.

[4] Idem, *SW*, 16 ff.; idem, *ES*, 29–31.

[5] SW, 8; *ES*, 30–32, 40.

[6] *SW*, 165–66; *ES*, 52.

In France, Freyer wrote, the sociology of Saint-Simon and of Comte had emerged from the positivist philosophy of history of Turgot and Condorcet. In Germany, Karl Marx and Lorenz von Stein founded sociology by their transformation of Hegel's idealist philosophy of history in a "realistic" direction. Though what Freyer termed the "classical" sociological systems of Saint-Simon, Comte, Stein, and Marx differed considerably from one another, Freyer professed to discover a common pattern among them. All regarded some previous epoch as having embodied an integrated social order, and all sought to create a positive epoch of order in the future, though they disagreed fundamentally as to the shape of this new order. Most importantly, all adopted a critical stance toward the new bourgeois society created by the spread of capitalism.[7]

In Freyer's interpretation, sociology was in its origin and in its essence "the scientific self-consciousness of bourgeois society, which perceives itself as a critical epoch."[8] Like the traditional philosophy of history from which they sprang, all of these sociological systems sought to orient man in his relationship to the past and the future. But unlike the traditional philosophy of history, all sought to interpret and master the present chaos through the scientific study of social processes.[9]

Evolving out of very different philosophical traditions, French and German sociology sought to fulfill their epochal missions in very different ways. Grounded in the positivist assumption that the social sciences ought to proceed on the model of the natural sciences, Saint-Simon and Comte sought to discover social laws that would provide the basis for a rational social technology. The aim of French sociology, Freyer claimed, had been to free man from the irrational and superstitious traditions of the past through the application of rationally discernible laws.[10]

In Germany, by contrast, sociology emerged out of the intellectual traditions of romanticism and post-Kantian idealism. The legacy of these traditions to later German social thought was organicist and historicist. Organicism held that each historical community should be studied as a whole, with its own internal laws of development, based ultimately upon prerational forces.[11] His-

---

[7] SW, 165–66.

[8] SW, 169.

[9] ES, 86.

[10] ES, 31, 48, 69. Though Freyer did not mention it in the academic sociological works under discussion here, it should be noted that from the perspective of his radical conservative social the-

ory, the positivist attempt to recast society in a rational mold by purging it of its irrational past was tantamount to condemning it to meaninglessness.

[11] ES, 41. Freyer expanded these observations in "Die Romantiker" (1932).

toricism was the related belief that a social unit could be understood only in relation to its past.[12] Though deeply sympathetic to this strain of thought, Freyer assigned it not to the history but to the prehistory of German sociology. Despite their philosophical depth, he explained, the categories of romantic social philosophy were rooted in a social order that preceded bourgeois society and were ill suited for the analysis of the new social reality that was to shape Germany in the nineteenth century.

Freyer regarded Hegel, "the antagonist of romanticism," as the direct forefather of German sociology.[13] It was the dichotomy of the state and bourgeois society as developed in Hegel's *Philosophy of Right* that, according to Freyer, had given German sociology its central problematic.

Bourgeois society as described by Hegel, Freyer wrote, is essentially

economic society, market society, society based on exchange. Hegel extracted the sociological elements from English national economy—especially from Adam Smith—and compressed them into a consistent concept of society. The close connection between society and the economy—the "materialistic" concept of society—which is characteristic of German sociology is therefore already found in Hegel.[14]

Yet Hegel, in Freyer's genealogy, was not the father but the grandfather of German sociology. For Hegel, bourgeois society was a step in the development of *Geist*, the apogee of which was reached in the modern state. It was in the critique of Hegel's premises by Karl Marx and Lorenz von Stein that Freyer saw the true beginning of German sociology. In the late 1840s both Marx and Stein had concluded that historical change was to be explained not as the development of *Geist* but as a result of social processes, and both had come to regard the state and bourgeois society not as moments of ethical development but as real historical forces. German sociology, in Freyer's reading, was born in the "realistic" critique of Hegel first expressed in Marx's critique of the *Philosophy of Right* and in Lorenz von Stein's *Geschichte der sozialen Bewegung in Frankreich* (History of the Social Movement in France).[15]

Stein had depicted the state and bourgeois society not as complementary stages of the ethical will but as real contemporary forces that were in conflict. For him, the *idea* of the state remained the highest stage of freedom, in which all participated as free persons, but the contemporary *reality* of the state was of its domination by the most powerful classes of bourgeois society. The state would remain a shadow of its ideal self unless it was rescued from the control

---

[12] *ES*, 41–43.
[13] Ibid., 44.

[14] Ibid., 64.
[15] Ibid., 91ff.

of the dominant economic interests, by a social monarchy in alliance with the emerging industrial proletariat. In the work of Stein, Freyer reckoned, Hegel's philosophy of *Geist* thus became a realistic science of society, that is, sociology.[16]

Freyer saw a parallel transformation in the work of Karl Marx. Though Freyer regarded Marx as the most important link in the transformation of philosophy into sociology, he tried to separate the wheat from the chaff of Marx's argument. He tried, that is, to distinguish what he regarded as Marx's permanent contribution to sociology from those elements of his work which were time-bound reflections of nineteenth-century thought and social reality. A great deal of Marx's thought was left on the floor of the historical threshing room.

It was Marx's "realistic" transformation of Hegel's philosophy of history that Freyer saw as his essential contribution to sociology. Hegel's conception of history as a dialectical series of spiritual contents (*geistige Gehalte*), embodied in *Volksgeister*, was transformed by Marx into a series of historical societies, each of which contained internal contradictions leading to its eventual supersession. It was this dialectical view of society that Freyer regarded as Marx's contribution to sociology.[17]

The transformation by Marx and Stein of Hegel's philosophy of history into sociology changed the relationship of theory to practice, Freyer explained. For Hegel, world history was the history of the self-comprehension of *Geist*; it was only because this process was essentially complete that philosophy could recognize the contemporary age as one of freedom.[18] For Stein and Marx, by contrast, theory revealed the present to be not the realization of freedom but an era wracked by inner contradictions. By revealing the necessity of change, sociological theory affected human will. Thus sociological theory became political practice.[19]

Thus, although their philosophical origins diverged from those of Saint-Simon and Comte, the "classical" sociological systems of Marx and Stein concurred with their French counterparts in attempting to create a science that would bridge the gap between theory and practice and would contribute to the creation of a new positive epoch.

The differing origins of French and German sociology had, Freyer believed, led to ongoing differences between them as well. In keeping with its positivist heritage, French sociology regarded politics as the technical application of uni-

---

[16] Ibid., 93–95.

[17] *SW*, 99; *ES*, 67.

[18] *SW*, 100.

[19] Ibid., 103; *ES*, 68.

versal, scientific laws. The historicist legacy of the romantics to German sociology was an emphasis on the historical character of all societies; in keeping with its idealist origins, German sociology sought to transform the will of men by making them conscious of the inadequacies of bourgeois society.[20] Freyer regarded his program of "Soziologie als Wirklichkeitswissenschaft" as drawing out the implications of classical German sociology so conceived.[21]

Sociology as a "Science of Reality"

While some conceptions of sociology are easily defined or epitomized, Freyer's conception of sociology as *Wirklichkeitswissenschaft* resists pithy formulation. Freyer compounded four distinct propositions about the nature of sociology into the term *Wirklichkeitswissenschaft*.

By sociology as *Wirklichkeitswissenschaft*, Freyer meant a sociology that was historicist in its perception of the present, holistic in its concepts, voluntaristic in its conception of the relationship between norms and social structure, and—above all—*engagé* and decisionistic in its epistemology.[22] It was Freyer's activist conception of sociology as a science devoted to the supersession of bourgeois society and the creation of a new positive epoch that bound these methodological assumptions together.[23]

The most crucial of Freyer's claims concerned the relationship of the sociologist to the object of his study. Unlike the relationship of the natural scientist to eternal nature, or that of the humanist (*Geisteswissenschaftler*) to the fixed cultural forms of the past, the object of the sociologist—society—was in a constant state of movement, and the direction of that movement depended in part on the will of its members.[24] In attempting to grasp the direction of his own society, the sociologist attempts to know an object to which he himself "existentially belongs."[25] Because of this existential involvement of the sociologist with the society whose developmental patterns he hopes to discover, his relationship to

---

[20] *ES*, 69–70.

[21] In an interview with the visiting American sociologist E. E. Eubank in 1934, Freyer described himself as a modern successor of Stein. See Käsler, *Soziologische Abenteuer*, 106.

[22] On holism, see Karl R. Popper, *The Poverty of Historicism*, 76–83. On "voluntarism" in social theory, see Parsons, *The Structure of Social Action*, 2 vols., regarding the emphasis of voluntaristic systems of social thought on "will" or "effort" as the connecting link between social structure and

"ideals" or "norms" (253n, 396, 440, 719). On "decisionism" as a mood and doctrine, see Krockow, *Die Entscheidung*.

[23] Useful discussions of the debates on historicism and social science in the 1920s are found in Jeffrey Barash, "Martin Heidegger and the Problem of Historical Meaning"; Fischer, *Die deutsche Geschichtswissenschaft*; Iggers, *German Conception of History*.

[24] *SW*, 87–89.

[25] Ibid., 199–200.

the object of his study cannot be neutral or value-free, Freyer argued.[26] The proper attitude of the sociologist is not one of sovereign independence from the object of his study but rather one of moral responsibility toward it and its future. Freyer thus referred to sociology as an *Ethoswissenschaft*, a science in which ethical values were inescapable.[27]

The evaluative attitude of the sociologist toward his society was for Freyer not only a moral necessity but an epistemological one. Social reality could be comprehended only insofar as the sociologist was existentially *concerned* with its further development. At the core of the sociological concepts through which reality is comprehended lies a will to change reality in one or another direction.[28] Sociological perspectives, Freyer wrote, were thus necessarily "utopian" in Karl Mannheim's sense of orientations that attempt to transform the present in the direction of one's own wishes.[29] In *Ideologie und Utopie*, published in 1929, Mannheim had hoped that the sociology of knowledge would provide a tool with which intellectuals, who he believed were "relatively unattached" to any social class, could develop a science of politics that would transcend the partisan perspectives of the present. Freyer did not believe that intellectuals or sociologists could attain such transcendent impartiality. Our perception of what is, he taught, cannot be divorced from our sense of what ought to be.[30]

Sociology as *Wirklichkeitswissenschaft* was the attempt to view the present "dialectically," to discover *which* trends within it were leading to a new form of society. The attainment of sociological knowledge presumed the will to move beyond bourgeois society into a new positive epoch.

Yet, as Freyer realized, there were competing movements in the present, with very different conceptions of how the future ought to look and hence very different perceptions of which contemporary developments were most significant. What was their relationship to the science of sociology, and how was one to judge which of them were correct?

Freyer's answer was that the future would tell which of the contemporary

---

[26] Ibid., 210–11.

[27] Ibid., 91.

[28] Ibid., 298–99. A similar argument had been made by the Marxist sociologist Siegfried Landshut, in his *Kritik der Soziologie* (1929). For other parallels between Freyer and Landshut see René König, "Über das vermeintliche Ende der deutschen Soziologie vor der Machtergreifung des Nationalsozialismus," 20–21.

[29] *SW*, 298.

[30] Ibid., 299. On Mannheim's conception of the sociology of knowledge as the basis of a science of politics see his *Ideologie und Utopie*, chapter 2, as well as the discussion in David Kettler et al., *Karl Mannheim*, chapters 1 and 2. Many of the contemporary contributions to the debate on ideology and social science are reprinted in Volker Meja and Nico Stehr, eds., *Der Streit um die Wissenssoziologie*.

perspectives was valid. Each perspective claimed to know which contemporary trends were most significant in leading to the transformation of society; each claimed, in Hegelian terms, to grasp the "substantial content" of the present. Yet the future direction of society was dependent upon the will of those in the present; it could not be deduced as could a causal chain in the natural sciences. Only one of the perspectives on the present was correct in its claim about which "will" would bridge the gap between present and future. Only in hindsight would the correct sociological analysis of the present become clear.[31]

True knowledge of the present was available only to those who shared the hopes of that movement which would actually prevail over the hopes of competing movements. Thus Freyer concluded with the remarkable sentence that best captures the notion of sociology as *Wirklichkeitswissenschaft: "Wahres Wollen fundiert wahre Erkenntnis"* (True will is the basis of true knowledge).[32]

Freyer shared Karl Mannheim's historicist conception of knowledge as rooted in time and place but not Mannheim's belief that social science could transcend political commitment. Freyer's conception of sociology as *Wirklichkeitswissenschaft* is striking because of the degree to which it carries the claims of political commitment into social science. In opposition to those conceptions of social science which regard nonscientific commitments as baggage to be checked at the door of true science, Freyer emphasized the extent to which such commitments were the key to the house of sociological knowledge. Freyer regarded the nonscientific will, not a set of methodological strictures, as the essential prerequisite of sociological truth.

Freyer realized that he had brought political commitment and sociology into such close proximity that the line between them threatened to vanish entirely. Toward the end of *Soziologie als Wirklichkeitswissenschaft* he devoted five pages (out of three hundred) to an attempt to distinguish between them. He argued that will—the desire to realize some vision of the future—played *a* role, but not the *same* role, in politics and in sociology. In politics the desired vision of the future caused one to see each aspect of current society in terms of its tactical significance for the attainment of the ideal future; social facts were of concern insofar as they helped to realize the ideal future or hinder it.[33] In sociology the will to realize some ideal future was subordinated to the norm of maximizing the theoretical and objective perception of reality. An ideal vision of the future still structures the perception of the present but must be "devalued" into a

[31] Ibid., 307.
[32] Ibid.

[33] Ibid., 300.

working hypothesis about the developmental trends of the present. This hypothesis must then be open to correction through empirical research. As a scientist, the sociologist was commanded to be open-minded, to consider the negative bearing of empirical data on his working hypothesis even when it hindered his political hopes. The search for sociological truth therefore required the "harnessing" or "taming" of the political will. The distinction between politics and sociology was thus one of attitudes, and Freyer acknowledged that the individual often switched from one to the other. It was a thin line, easily crossed, but a line nonetheless.[34]

The other defining characteristics of Freyer's conception of sociology as *Wirklichkeitswissenschaft* were corollaries of this epistemology.

Freyer's notion of sociology as *Wirklichkeitswissenschaft* required a methodological holism. Freyer believed, that is to say, that a particular historical society could and should be conceptualized as a totality, that sociology should provide what Hegel had called a "concrete concept" of the present social order, which grasped it as a whole, pregnant with internal possibilities of transformation.[35] Sociology had to begin not from the bottom up—from the basic eternal forms of interpersonal interaction—but from the top down: all social relationships *within* a society could best be understood by their role in society as a whole. Thus the tendency to neglect the subpolitical levels of social integration evident in Freyer's earlier social theory held true for his new sociology as well.

Freyer's sociology was also marked by its historicism. In keeping with the tenets of *Lebensphilosophie*, he emphasized that society was located within the flow of time, that it was constantly undergoing change.[36] The historicist corollary of this perspective was an emphasis upon the incommensurability of historically separate societies. The major concepts of sociology ought therefore to be historically specific, rather than atemporal or universal, Freyer argued. A particular society could best be understood not statically but historically, with reference to where it had been and where it might be going.[37] In keeping with a long tradition of German historicist criticisms of sociology, Freyer insisted that contemporary society (and indeed any society) must be understood as a particular historical phenomenon (*historische Individualität*).[38]

The last significant corollary of Freyer's conception of sociology as *Wirklichkeitswissenschaft* was a voluntaristic view of social integration. Social structures

---

[34] Ibid., 301–3.
[35] Ibid., 222, 304.
[36] Ibid., 83.
[37] Ibid., 144, 158–59.

[38] Ibid., 221. On the historicist critique of sociology leveled by Heinrich von Treitschke, Georg von Below, and other historians, see Fischer, *Geschichtswissenschaft*.

acquired continuity, he held, when their members shared a common ethos or consensus (*Übereinstimmungswille*) or insofar as their members shared a sense of belonging. Sociology thus had to consider not only the social-structural characteristics of a society but also the "psychic facts of consent, accommodation, consensus, subordination, tensions and contradictions" within each particular society.[39] Here Freyer's functionalism was most explicit: sociology, he wrote, entailed a "functionalizing conception of meaningful cultural entities."[40]

Freyer on Marx and Weber

In *Soziologie als Wirklichkeitswissenschaft* Freyer sought to explicate his own conception of sociology by reference to the thought of other social theorists past and present. It was Karl Marx and Max Weber to whom he devoted the greatest attention, and a brief consideration of Freyer's attitude toward these central figures in the history of sociology is in order, not only because of the quality of his analysis but because of the light it casts upon his own thought.

Freyer admired Karl Marx for his transformation of Hegel's concept of bourgeois society into a dialectical one, one that asserted that bourgeois society contained contradictions that would necessarily lead beyond it to a new stage of history. In so doing, Freyer claimed, Marx had transformed Hegel's contemplative philosophy into a *Wirklichkeitswissenschaft*, oriented toward the transformation of reality.[41] Yet Freyer accepted the ongoing validity of Marx's materialism only in a much qualified sense, as the necessity of looking to social reality as the motive force in history. He rejected the belief that the dialectical contradictions of society *necessarily* lay in its economic structure: this was one possibility to be considered, Freyer wrote, but the contradictions could in principle be in the cultural, political, or legal levels of social reality.[42] Freyer regarded many of the pillars of Marx's thought—including the labor theory of value and the necessarily resulting concentration of capital and immiseration of the proletariat—as reflections of mid-nineteenth-century economic thought and reality that were no longer tenable.[43] Freyer took Marx's image of bourgeois society as a class society, characterized by the struggle of economically

[39] *SW*, 172–75. It is this element of Freyer's conception of sociology that most impressed Talcott Parsons, who adapted some of Freyer's distinctions in formulating his own conception of sociology as a distinct discipline. See Parsons, *The Structure of Social Action* (originally published in 1937), esp. 757–75.

[40] *SW*, 160.

[41] Ibid., 103.

[42] Ibid., 99.

determined classes, to be *a* truth but not the *whole* truth about modern society.[44]

It was above all Marx's theory of culture as ideology to which Freyer objected. The belief that culture was to be interpreted as ideology, that is, as a reflection of the economic structures of society, bestowed upon the latter a metaphysical reality that Freyer regarded as a cul-de-sac for sociological analysis.[45] He saw the idealist approach to the problem—which viewed each society as the "realization" of some idea—as equally one-sided and mistaken. The relationship between culture and society (in the narrow sense) was more complex. Culture was a product of society, but it was also culture that made social cohesion possible.[46] It was up to sociology to consider the role that ideas actually played in the maintenance and transformation of societies, Freyer argued.[47]

Freyer's comments on Max Weber, whom he regarded as the greatest of the postclassical sociologists, are of interest not only for what they reveal about Freyer but because they focused on aspects of Weber's work which were all but ignored in the 1920s, but which later commentators came to regard as central to his *oeuvre*.[48] Weber had not bequeathed a completed sociological system at his death in 1920, and his work found no immediate successors. His writings were much discussed in the German sociological literature of the 1920s, but in a fragmentary manner.[49] Attention was directed above all to Weber's notion of interpretive sociology (*verstehende Soziologie*), of value freedom in social science, to his basic concepts of social action and to his characterizations of bureaucracy, Protestantism, and the forms of domination.[50] Freyer, however, was one of the first to search for thematic unity in the work of a man who had stressed the multiplicity of social phenomena and for the evaluative stance that lay behind the work of the foremost eschewer of value judgments in social science.

Freyer recognized that Weber had advocated the divorce of value judgments from sociology and had rejected the link of sociology to any evaluative philosophy of history. Freyer also acknowledged that Weber had moved away from his predominantly historical concerns and after 1913 had attempted to

---

[43] Ibid., 104.

[44] Ibid., 283; see chapter 5.4.

[45] Ibid., 105–6. Freyer noted that Marx and Engels had modified the one-sided emphasis on the economic *Unterbau* of society vis-à-vis its cultural *Überbau*, especially in their historical accounts and in their correspondence (ibid., 108).

[46] Ibid., 105.

[47] Ibid., 105.

[48] One Weber scholar has recently remarked that Freyer's treatment of Max Weber in *SW* is "uncommonly lucid, empathetic and completely up to today's standards" (Helmut Fogt, "Max Weber und die deutsche Soziologie der Weimarer Republik," 248).

[49] Ibid., 254.

[50] Ibid., 259.

lay the foundations for a formalistic sociology, which would begin with individual action and result in a systematic science of social relations and structures.[51] Freyer's own conception of sociology as a historicist, activist successor to the philosophy of history thus seemed at first sight to be at odds with Weber's theory of sociology.

In fact, Freyer held, Weber's practice of sociology was better than his theory, and if one examined this practice carefully one would find that it was very close to Freyer's own conception of sociology as *Wirklichkeitswissenschaft*.[52]

It was easy for Freyer to prove that Weber had emphasized the historical and individual nature of particular societies. Freyer quoted from Weber's methodological essay of 1904—in which Weber had coined the term *Wirklichkeitswissenschaft*—which maintained:

The starting point of social-scientific interest is doubtless the *real*, that is to say the individual configuration of our own social and cultural life, in its universal—though no less individual—context and in its development out of other, once again, individual social and cultural circumstances.[53]

The sociological ideal types that Weber developed, Freyer noted, were closely tied to actual historical situations, and much of his work was an attempt to cast light on the historical particularity of modern Western society.[54]

Freyer pointed out that like the classical systems of sociology, Weber's sociology was marked by an implicit philosophy of history, namely his understanding of the history of the modern West as one of increasing rationalization.[55] Not only was the spread of rationalization the explicit subject of Weber's sociology of religion, but the typologies of social action, of the forms of domination, and of the principles of legitimation in *Economy and Society* were all constructed with a view to this most central of Weber's concerns.[56]

Unlike most commentators of the time, Freyer drew attention to the fact that while Weber regarded this process of increasing rationalization as inevitable, his own attitude toward it was ambiguous, not to say critical. Freyer offered as an example "one of the great passages" in Weber's sociology of religion, "in which the thought is clearly stated that progressive rationalization may perhaps be creating an ever more arid wasteland, in which perhaps finally the voice of the preacher [i.e., of a no longer rational creation] will allow the au-

[51] *SW*, 146–47, 153–54.

[52] Ibid., 212.

[53] Weber, "Die 'Objektivität,' " p. 172, quoted in Freyer, *SW*, 148.

[54] *SW*, 147–48, 156.

[55] Ibid., 157.

[56] Ibid., 155–57.

thentically human and valuable to break out again."[57] As we have seen in our discussion of Freyer's radical conservatism, he too regarded the process of rationalization—in Weber's sense of the ongoing improvement of technical means that threatened to eclipse all ends based on substantive values—as the dominant trend of modern history. But while Weber warned that such voices in the wilderness might well be a siren's song to which the scientist, at least, should turn a deaf ear, Freyer's conception of sociology made it into a hearing aid for the amplification of just such voices.

Freyer was probably not the first and was certainly not the last to point out that although Weber eschewed value judgments in theory, his substantive work was in fact laced with such judgments.[58] Freyer regarded this too as evidence of the superiority of Weber's practice to his theory.

Aside from crucial differences of generation and of temperament, the difference between Weber and Freyer might be understood as that of a post-Nietzschean Kantian and a post-Nietzschean Hegelian. Both men had been led by Nietzsche to conclude that the individual's allegiance to values was not subject to rational defense, that it necessarily involved nonrational choice.[59] As legatees of the Kantian critique of cognition, both were aware of the degree to which the mind structured the perception of external reality through its own categories. The Nietzschean addendum was that such categories were by no means universal but differed with the subjective, ultimate commitments of the individual.[60]

While both Weber and Freyer spoke of sociology as a science of *Wirklichkeit*, they differed significantly on the degree to which social reality could be comprehended. As an epistemologically radical neo-Kantian, Weber believed that social reality was infinitely complex and had no objective or intrinsic structure. The same social reality could be conceptualized from an infinite number of perspectives, each of which would grasp only a small part of it, and none of which could prove its objective superiority over any other.[61] This implied a

---

[57] Ibid., 157. Freyer was one of the first interpreters of Weber's work to focus attention on its pessimistic cultural implications. This interpretation was expanded in Karl Löwith, "Max Weber und Karl Marx" (1932). For a recent interpretation along similar lines, see Wolfgang J. Mommsen, *The Age of Bureaucracy: Perspectives on the Political Sociology of Max Weber.*

[58] *SW*, 157–212. For similar observations, see Strauss, *Natural Right and History*, 43–44, 52–53; and Eric Voegelin, *The New Science of Politics*, 20–22.

[59] For Nietzsche's influence on Weber in this regard, see the works by Löwith and Mommsen cited above, and most recently, the important discussion in Alasdair MacIntyre, *After Virtue*, 24–26 passim.

[60] For one of Weber's many statements of this position, see Weber, " 'Objektivität,' " 181–82.

[61] The point is made most forcefully by Friedrich H. Tenbruck, "Die Genesis der Methodologie Max Webers." Helpful overviews of recent scholarly literature on Max Weber are Jürgen Kocka, "Kontroversen über Max Weber"; Ste-

modest view of what sociology even at its best could contribute to an understanding of society. Just as the post-Kantian idealists (Fichte, Hegel, Schelling)
had found Kant's stress on the limits of the mind's cognitive ability to comprehend noumenal reality an unbearable limitation, so neo-Hegelians such as
Freyer rejected the modest cognitive claims that neo-Kantians such as Weber
allotted to social science. When Freyer spoke of *Wirklichkeit*, he did so in the
Hegelian sense, as a society that could be grasped in its totality. Freyer asserted
that sociology as *Wirklichkeitswissenschaft* could offer not *an* interpretation of
partial facets of social reality but *the* historically correct conceptualization of
contemporary society, a conceptualization that indicated the prime sources
and direction of social transformation. Ultimately, for Freyer, there was one
correct description of society among the competing perspectives of the present, though it would be proven correct only in retrospect. If Weber's conception of sociology was almost ascetic, Freyer's was almost gnostic.

The Sociology of the Present

Freyer's prime target among contemporary sociologists was Leopold von
Wiese, the dominant organizational figure in German sociology during the
Weimar Republic. Wiese had devoted himself to developing a theory of sociology that would make it an *Einzelwissenschaft*, a separate discipline clearly distinct from history and divorced entirely from the philosophy of history. He
sought to do so by developing a taxonomic, classificatory science of social
forms. Sociology, he claimed, could become an exact and systematic discipline
not by the study of historical societies but by developing a classification of all
the *forms* of interpersonal relations, based upon the fundamental human relations of attraction and repulsion.[62] The system of classificatory concepts developed on this basis was, in principle, timeless.[63] He believed that he could
thus construct a science of the forms of social interaction, which would apply
to all societies rather than to any particular one.

For Freyer, this was close to the opposite of what sociology ought to be.
Wiese's conception of sociology was far too modest, according to Freyer, and
offered no insight into the real social dynamics of the present.[64] Its antihistor-
ical method presented the social forms of individualized, bourgeois society as
if they were eternal, rather than the particular forms of contemporary society.

---

phen Kalberg, "The Search for Thematic Orientations in a Fragmented Oeuvre"; and Steven
Seidman, "The Main Aims and Thematic Structure of Max Weber's Sociology."

[62] *SW*, 59.
[63] Ibid., 63.
[64] Ibid.

In short (though Freyer did not use the term), Freyer accused Wiese's sociology of *reifying* the social forms of bourgeois society, just as classical political economy had reified its economic forms.[65] In so doing, it unintentionally tended to idealize the liberal, bourgeois social order, Freyer argued.[66]

In his own system of sociological concepts and in his analysis of present-day German society Freyer remained faithful to what he termed the "deeply antiliberal" standpoint of the classical systems of sociology.[67]

The concepts that Freyer set forth as central to sociology were supposed to be temporally oriented, to describe a successive historical series of dialectical totalities. The basic historical categories that Freyer suggested in *Soziologie als Wirklichkeitswissenschaft* were essentially those of *Der Staat*, now rephrased in a less emotive and more sociologically descriptive manner. These concepts were community, corporate society, and class society.

Community (*Gemeinschaft*) was once again defined as a closed world of common fate and shared cultural horizons.[68] Again Freyer insisted that such a homogeneous society and culture could be found in its pure form only in prehistory, before the rise of domination (*Herrschaft*).[69] New was his assertion that while community no longer existed in its pristine historical form, it continued to exist in later eras in the "modified" form of the *Volk*. The *Volk* remained an ongoing historical reality, Freyer claimed, upon which later social structures were based.[70]

Even more than in *Der Staat*, Freyer now stressed the inexorability of domination in all societies beyond the stage of prehistoric community. Society (*Gesellschaft*) had historically taken either the form of a corporate society (*Ständegesellschaft*), in which domination was exercised by a closed group united by a common style of life and priding itself on the exercise of domination, or that of a class society (*Klassengesellschaft*), in which inequality of power was based on the functioning of the market.[71] Yet domination remained a reality in class society, even if it was unacknowledged by modern liberal thought.[72] Since, as Freyer made clear, there could be no return to a community free of domination, his descriptions of corporate society and class society reflected his evaluation not only of the present but of possible options for the future.

Freyer described the corporate society of the past as "the model of a *positive* epoch." It was a stable, ongoing structure in which each individual could derive

[65] Ibid., 64–65.
[66] Ibid., 68.
[67] Ibid., 285.
[68] Ibid., 241–45.

[69] Ibid., 238.
[70] Ibid., 229.
[71] Ibid., 268ff., 279.
[72] Ibid., 232ff.

meaning from knowing his place in a social order that gave the appearance of permanence.[73] This social order was created "from above," by a dominating group that prided itself on the exercise of domination, placed duties before rights, and created an ongoing tradition of rule into which its members were educated.[74] Every corporate society eventually developed an ideology of natural right, a system of thought that legitimated its social order as natural, God-given, or decreed by rational necessity. Ideologies, for Freyer, were the self-interpretations and self-legitimations of social orders based upon domination. By identifying a particular social order with universal necessity, they added to the perception that a particular historical order was eternal and thus contributed to its stability.[75]

Freyer's account of the role of ideology within a corporate society was significant in terms of his dual role as radical conservative ideologist and social scientist. Freyer was not backward-looking in the sense of advocating the restoration of some past social order. It was the purported social cohesion, stability, and sense of shared purpose of corporate society that he sought to re-create. Freyer regarded corporate society as the model for any future positive epoch, and the creation of such an epoch was the main purpose of his sociology as *Wirklichkeitswissenschaft*. A key element in the stability of the medieval corporate society, in Freyer's eyes, was the theory of natural right.[76] Yet it was the sociological function of this theory rather than its intrinsic truth that attracted Freyer. In keeping with his historicist premises he assumed that the theory of natural right did not possess the eternal validity that it claimed. Implicit in Freyer's conception of natural right as the ideology of the corporate society was the fact that for him ideologies were of interest not for their truth value but because of their sociological function.

Given these postulates, the proper attitude of the sociologist toward reigning ideologies depended upon his ultimate commitments. It is in this context that Freyer's protest against the claim that the proper role of sociology was to "unmask" every ideology as a product of social interests must be understood.[77] If ideologies functioned to reinforce the stability of a social order, then the role of "unmasker" was appropriate only when the destabilization of the current social order was sought. Should the stabilization of the social order become the goal of the sociologist, then his proper role would be to reinforce the ideology of the social order, to make the central beliefs that reinforced that order seem

[73] Ibid., 272.
[74] Ibid., 262, 268–71.
[75] Ibid., 262.

[76] Ibid.
[77] Ibid., 262–63.

necessary, to make the prevalent ideology appear "natural." From this per-spective, the problem of the actual veracity of a set of beliefs became not only incidental but downright subversive, since it called into question precisely that which ought to remain "self-understood" if the stability of the social order was to be maintained.

Thus the logical consequence of Freyer's comments on ideology and the cor-porate society was that in a positive epoch the role of sociology would change radically, from one that pointed to the dialectical tensions of a critical epoch to one that served to reinforce the new positive social order. This consequence, implicit in *Soziologie als Wirklichkeitswissenschaft*, was made explicit one year later, in his *Einleitung in die Soziologie*. The claim of positivistic and contempo-rary American sociology that a knowledge of social laws would make possible a "social technique" that would help to stabilize the social order, Freyer wrote, could be realized only within an order established on a firm basis.[78] Once the basis of such an order was created, the role of sociology would change.

It was a premise both of Freyer's radical conservatism and of his conception of sociology as *Wirklichkeitswissenschaft* that modern "bourgeois society" was in-herently unstable. He aimed his theoretical guns at those social theorists who, drawing upon the tradition of classical political economy, regarded the market untrammeled by political controls or corporate rights as capable of reconciling the pursuit of self-interest with common benefit.[79] Such a theory was typical of "bourgeois sociology," Freyer claimed, which mistook the legitimating ideol-ogy of bourgeois society for its reality.[80] In reality bourgeois society remained a structure of domination, in which social groups confronted one another in a relationship of antagonism.[81] In corporate societies there was also an ongoing antagonism between social groups, each of whom tried to improve its relative position; only in a class society, however, did the subordinate group aim at transforming the system as a whole.[82] Bourgeois society, according to Freyer, was thus in a permanent state of latent revolution.[83] The recognition of this fact and the concomitant rejection of liberal social theory were the hallmarks of what Freyer considered the authentic tradition of sociology.[84]

At the end of *Soziologie als Wirklichkeitswissenschaft*, Freyer offered several sociological perspectives on the present that were dialectical in their approach

---

[78] *ES*, 147–48. As we will see, Freyer was to suggest just such a role for sociology after 1933.
[79] *SW*, 235, 279.
[80] Ibid., 235.

[81] Ibid., 237.
[82] Ibid., 277–78.
[83] Ibid., 286.
[84] Ibid., 285–86.

to bourgeois society and hence legitimate heirs of the antiliberal founders of sociology.

The first of these solutions for overcoming the permanent crisis of bourgeois society was the Marxist. Its essential premise was that the contemporary social order could be understood purely as a class society, that is, primarily by reference to the class structures and antagonisms created by the workings of the market.[85] For Marx and his followers, it was the *immanent* laws of this social system that led to its polarization into two antagonistic classes: a small minority of exploiting capitalists and a huge majority of exploited workers. The intrinsic dynamics of capitalist class society would result in the dictatorship of the proletariat, an intermediate stage to be followed by the decline of the state, and a vaguely characterized future of "free association" without domination or exploitation.[86]

The Marxist view, Freyer felt, was by virtue of its antipathy to bourgeois society a legitimate sociological perspective upon the present. Ultimately, however, he found that other, non-Marxist perspectives were more open to recognizing sociological evidence that made the Marxist scenario increasingly implausible and offered more plausible solutions to the permanent crisis of bourgeois society.

Among these was a broad range of solutions—from revisionist socialism through conservative organicism based on the *Volk* to a planning-oriented liberalism—that did not believe that the class structure of contemporary society necessarily led to ever-greater polarization but would lead nevertheless to some new social order beyond capitalist class society.[87] Among the phenomena that made these solutions more plausible than the Marxist scenario Freyer noted the growth of new middle strata between the bourgeoisie and the proletariat, the reinforcement of the old *Mittelstände*, the existence of agrarian groups that did not fit comfortably into the model of an industrial class society, and the integration of a large proportion of the proletariat into the democratic welfare state.[88] Freyer's observations—stated in apodictic fashion, without statistical proof—indicated his awareness of those social structural trends of the Weimar Republic which subsequent historians and sociologists have come to consider most significant.[89]

[85] Ibid., 283, 288.
[86] Ibid., 288–89.
[87] Ibid., 289–91.
[88] Ibid., 290, 297,

[89] For a summary of the salient structural trends of German society in the 1920s, see René König, "Zur Soziologie der zwanziger Jahre," in his *Studien zur Soziologie*.

A further advantage of such non-Marxist perspectives, by Freyer's reckoning, was their willingness to recognize the possible significance of factors other than class in overcoming bourgeois society. Among these was the reality of the *Volk* or the nation and international power relations, factors that were recalcitrant to the internationalist premises of Marxism.[90]

Another range of non-Marxist perspectives that Freyer noted were those of the state socialists, whose solutions often overlapped with the non-Marxist solutions cited above. Central to this tradition, stretching from Fichte and Hegel through Lorenz von Stein and Ferdinand Lassalle, was the belief that capitalist society creates contradictions that it is incapable of resolving on its own. The resolution of these tensions could come only through the power of the state—a state that stood above the economics and social interests of class society. This solution sought "the integration and formation of all spheres of civil life through the active power of the state."[91]

The selection of a Marxist or a non-Marxist solution to the transcendence of bourgeois society was, according to Freyer, ultimately a matter of one's political commitment. A careful reader would have noticed Freyer's own commitment to a non-Marxist solution based upon the ongoing reality of the *Völker*, long before he made his stance explicit on the penultimate page of the book.[92]

Ideology and Social Science in the Reception of
Soziologie als Wirklichkeitswissenschaft

In *Soziologie als Wirklichkeitswissenschaft* Freyer tried to bridge the gap between political activism and social science—and between his own roles as ideologist and social scientist. Freyer's argument was a direct challenge to the sociologists who dominated the Deutsche Gesellschaft für Soziologie. They sought to legitimate the discipline of sociology within the university by eschewing political partisanship. Although Freyer had always adhered to an activist conception of scholarship, the book appeared at a time when the economic and political crises of the Weimar Republic were abetting a new wave of political activism among intellectuals. These circumstances are reflected in the reviews that followed the publication of *Soziologie als Wirklichkeitswissenschaft* in the summer of 1930.

The most extensive, critical, and sharp-witted review of the book appeared in the *Kölner Vierteljahreshefte für Soziologie*. Its author, Andreas Walther, was a

[90] *SW*, 297.
[91] Ibid., 292–94.
[92] Ibid., 305–6.

professor of sociology at the University of Hamburg and best known for a book on American sociology, which had helped to awaken German sociologists to the potential importance of empirical social research. Walther found Freyer's book learned and thoughtful but above all *fallstrickreich*—laden with intellectual snares that would prove harmful to the consolidation of German sociology.[93] Freyer's conception of sociology remained speculative and barely differentiated from social philosophy and the philosophy of history, Walther wrote.[94] Like other professional sociologists, Walther perceived Freyer's broad conception of sociology as a threat to sociology as an academic discipline, since it failed to distinguish sociology sufficiently from existing academic fields.[95]

Walther recognized in Freyer's work a prime example of a new wave of what he termed intuitivism in German thought—what another reviewer called the penetration of "existential philosophy into sociology," or what we have referred to as Freyer's "decisionism."[96] While acknowledging the crucial role of intuition and subjective perspectives in the formation of scientific hypotheses, Walther feared that Freyer's argument and style portended the end of scientific objectivity. The essential limit of intuitionism, of all claims at a privileged mode of "seeing," "viewing," or "understanding," was reached when someone else claimed to "see" or "understand" something quite different and the problem arose of how to adjudicate conflicting claims on the basis of proof and discursive thought. When confronted by conflicting opinions, Walther wrote,

radical intuitionists usually choose the only way out, namely to disqualify their opponent's qualifications to "see correctly." Freyer's thought is not so coarse. He does, however, stray away from objective forms of discussion when he refers to his opponents as "academic sociology" (by which he obviously means to imply that they are sunk in routine, since Freyer himself is a duly appointed professor of sociology) or calumniates them as typically "liberal" when they hold a static view of society. The fact that many sections of the book are marked by rhetorical persuasion [*Überredung*] rather than attempts at proof and demonstration points to the internal weakness of all intuitionism, which undervalues the role of discursive argument in establishing truth.[97]

Andreas Walther—whose review was probably written before *Revolution von rechts* was published in mid-1931—was perspicacious in discerning the broader

[93] Andreas Walther, "Das Problem einer 'deutschen' Soziologie," *Kölner Vierteljahreshefte für Soziologie* (1930–31), 513.

[94] Ibid., 514–15.

[95] See especially the comments of Leopold von Wiese in his *System der allgemeinen Soziologie*, 2d ed. (1933), 75ff.

[96] Erich Winter, review of *Soziologie als Wirklichkeitswissenschaft* and *Einleitung in die Soziologie*, by Hans Freyer, in *Zeitschrift für Sozialforschung* (1932), 157–58.

[97] Walther, 517.

ramifications of Freyer's thought. (His review indicated familiarity with Freyer's previous work, including *Der Staat*.) Karl Mannheim, professor of sociology at Frankfurt, shared many of Freyer's methodological predilections, but
not his politics. He appears to have been quite enthusiastic about *Soziologie als
Wirklichkeitswissenschaft* at first.[98] Only after Freyer published *Revolution von
rechts* did he come to rue the consequences that Freyer had drawn from the
notion of the "existentially bound thought" (*Seinsverbundenheit des Denkens*), the
central proposition of Mannheim's *Ideology and Utopia*. In his keynote lecture
to a gathering of German sociologists—including Hans Freyer—in February
1932, Mannheim warned that to draw from his own work the conclusion that
"correct will is the basis of correct knowledge" was to open the door to arbitrariness in sociological theory and to the legitimation of bias and partiality
under the guise of science.[99]

Leopold von Wiese, in an overview of contemporary German sociology
penned not long after Mannheim's talk, was even sharper in rejecting Freyer's
theory of sociology as leading to the subordination of social science to political
ideology. He regarded Freyer as foremost among those who used the cover of
sociology

to purvey interpretations of the past and especially of the present that are dictated by
their own partisan commitments. Some of these pseudosociologists are really politicians;
they explain the present as a culture stage with whatever characteristics correspond
to their personal articles of faith. . . . This type of historicism thus leads to a partisan
sociology of faith and to the decline of science.[100]

Given the mutual methodological and political antagonism between Freyer
and Wiese, it is significant that even *before* Hitler's seizure of power Wiese acknowledged that it was Freyer's brand of sociology which "corresponds to the
wishes of many contemporaries" and was enjoying a wide success among
young people attracted to sociology.[101]

---

[98] The marginal comments in Mannheim's
copy of *SW*—which were almost certainly written shortly after the book appeared in mid-
1930—indicate a careful reading of the methodological portions of the book and Mannheim's
general agreement with much of Freyer's argument there. Among the passages that most impressed him were "Sociology is the philosophy
of an age of transition" (221) and those which
analyzed the role played by ideologies in shaping the perception of social reality (300). Mann-

heim's copy of *SW* is in the library of the faculty
of social sciences of the Hebrew University,
Jerusalem.

[99] Karl Mannheim, *Die Gegenwartsaufgaben der
Soziologie* (1932), 40.

[100] Wiese, *System*, 76. The foreword to the
book is dated 1 January 1933; hence it is reasonable to assume that Wiese penned his criticism of
Freyer during 1932.

[101] Ibid., 81. On events within the DGS in
1933, see chapter 7 below.

Freyer's conception of sociology was viewed with hostility by those sociologists most devoted to the institutionalization of sociology within the academic institutions of the Weimar Republic. Wiese's comments on Freyer's book were scathing; the review by Walther in Wiese's journal, negative though respectful. A lengthy review in the *Archiv für Sozialwissenschaft und Sozialpolitik*, an established journal of academic social science, was somewhat more positive though highly critical.[102] In February of 1932, Freyer attended a convention of German teachers of sociology held in Frankfurt. The meeting had been organized by Wiese and was devoted to standardizing and institutionalizing the teaching of sociology at German universities. A conflict arose between advocates of Wiese's and Freyer's competing conceptions of sociology.[103] Freyer was also confronted by Karl Mannheim, who made the remarks quoted above. The embattled representative of a minority position at this gathering of senior practitioners, Freyer left the conference in a huff, before it officially adjourned.[104]

Outside the established institutional centers of academic sociology, however, Freyer's work was greeted with warmth and even enthusiasm. The *Archiv für angewandte Soziologie*, founded in 1928 and edited by Karl Dunkmann, was the house journal of the Institut für angewandte Soziologie (Institute of Applied Sociology), a small private research facility in Berlin outside the framework of the university.[105] There were close ties between this group and Freyer's Leipzig circle, which published the *Blätter für deutsche Philosophie*. Gunther Ipsen, for example, published important essays in the *Archiv*, while members of the *Archiv* group contributed to the *Blätter*.[106] The reviewer for the *Archiv*, Gerhard Lehmann, regarded Freyer's work as extremely important.[107] He noted that by *Soziologie als Wirklichkeitswissenschaft* Freyer meant much the same as Karl Dunkmann's term *angewandte Soziologie*.[108] The thrust of the review was therefore to advance a common conception of sociology based on shared assumptions.

[102] Josef Pieper, "Wirklichkeitswissenschaftliche Soziologie" (1931).

[103] Leopold von Wiese, "Die Frankfurter Dozententagung."

[104] Freyer's actions and comments at the Frankfurt conference are reported on the basis of personal recollections of Rudolf Heberle contained in a letter to the author of 17 February 1981. See also the report by Wiese cited above.

[105] On the Institut für angewandte Soziologie, see René König, "Soziologie in Berlin um 1930," 44–49.

[106] For example, Gunther Ipsen, "Das Dorf als Beispiel einer echten Gruppe," *Archiv für angewandte Soziologie* (1928–29); Karl Dunkmann, "Die Bedeutung der Zahl in der Soziologie," *Blätter für deutsche Philosophie* (1931–32); Gerhard Lehmann, "Das Problem der Realitätsgebenheit," *Blätter für deutsche Philosophie* (1931–32).

[107] Gerhard Lehmann, "Freyers *Soziologie als Wirklichkeitswissenschaft*," 205.

[108] Ibid., 211.

The immediate reception granted Freyer's book by the *Blätter für deutsche Philosophie* bordered on the ecstatic. Written by Willy Bloßfeldt, an old friend of Freyer's from the *Jugendbewegung* and his sometime *Assistent* at the sociological institute in Leipzig, it called Freyer's work "the first great attempt at a philosophical refounding of sociology since the great fathers of the science."[109]

Lest these be regarded as the words of an acolyte, it should be noted that they were echoed in almost identical terms by a young Heideggerian Marxist writing in the *Philosophische Hefte*, an independent journal of philosophy and social theory. The reviewer, Herbert Marcuse, noted that "the path from Hegel to Marx is sketched by Freyer more insightfully than in any other bourgeois or Marxist interpretation of Marx." He praised Freyer's emphasis on the historicity (*Geschichtlichkeit*) of social structures and the inexorability of decision (*Entscheidung*) in science.[110] In short, it was precisely the historicist and existentialist elements of Freyer's thought which had so distressed Freyer's academic colleagues that attracted Marcuse to Freyer's work. He called it "the first truly philosophical foundation of sociology, and as such a book that cannot be taken seriously enough."[111]

Herbert Marcuse was not the only activist intellectual on the political left to accord a warm reception to *Soziologie als Wirklichkeitswissenschaft*. Writing in the *Neue Blätter für den Sozialismus*, the organ of the Tillich circle of religious socialists, Gerhard Ledig hailed the "activist flavor" of the work, which he felt offered a "logical, scientific foundation of significant depth for the sociological world view of socialism."[112] The reviewer for the official Social Democratic journal, *Die Gesellschaft*, was pleased to find an academic sociologist who rejected formalistic sociology and the possibility of value freedom and who was indebted to Marx for so many of his major insights. The advance of Marx into the midst of "bourgeois sociology," in his view, augured well for the socialist future.[113]

Though these reviewers of the activist intellectual left recognized that Freyer was not on their side of the political divide, they all perceived him—quite correctly—as an intellectual brother under the ideological skin. His *Soziologie als Wirklichkeitswissenschaft* provided ammunition to those who were impatient with the modest claims and dissatisfied by the cautious temper of academic sociology. Hence its appeal to activist intellectuals of the left and right.

---

[109] W. Bloßfeldt, "Der Standort der Soziologie."

[110] Herbert Marcuse, "Zur Auseinandersetzung mit Hans Freyers *Soziologie als Wirklichkeitswissenschaft*" (1931), 84, 86, 91.

[111] Ibid., 91.

[112] Gerhard Ledig, "Hans Freyers Soziologie und der Sozialismus," 293, 291.

[113] Alfred Kleinberg, "Soziologie der goldenen Mitte," 73–74.

Freyer's attraction was by no means limited to younger sociologists or to political intellectuals on the margins of the academy. The most unequivocally positive reception of his work came from a professor of law who shared both his methodological and his political predilections. Otto Koellreuter, professor of law at the University of Jena—already a defender of National Socialism in the legal debates over its status vis-à-vis the Weimar constitution, and later one of the most prominent jurists of the Nazi regime—recommended Freyer's work most highly to the readers of the *Archiv des öffentlichen Rechts.* Freyer's conception of social science as a *Wirklichkeitswissenschaft* premised upon political decision ought to apply to political science (*Staatslehre*) no less than to sociology, Koellreuter claimed.[114] He also subscribed fully to Freyer's own decision that the future lay with the *Volk* and the strengthening of the state, goals that Koellreuter indicated were incompatible with the aims of the Marxist parties or with the present constitution of the republic.[115]

Freyer's attempt at the legitimation of ideological commitment in sociology met with polite rejection on the part of the senior practitioners at the institutional center of the discipline but appealed to young novices and to those on or beyond the margin of academic sociology. Thus, when he left the conference of German sociologists in February 1932 in a fit of pique, he had reason to suspect that he had lost the battle but not the war. As Freyer's political writings of this period demonstrate, he believed that the next battle would be fought on new terrain far more favorable to his radical conservatism and his activist conception of sociology.

[114] Otto Koellreuter, review of *Soziologie als Wirklichkeitswissenschaft,* by Hans Freyer, 159–60, 166.

[115] Ibid., 163–67.

CHAPTER SIX

Revolution from the Right:
Theory, 1925–1933

"A new front is forming on the battlefields of bourgeois society—the revolution from the right." So began Hans Freyer's best-known—and best-selling—work, *Revolution von rechts*, a booklet published in the summer of 1931 and intended to channel the highly fluid currents that raged within German political life. In his *Soziologie als Wirklichkeitswissenschaft*, published the previous summer, Freyer had emphasized the intimate relationship between partisan commitment and social analysis but had tried to draw at least a thin line between ideology and social science. In *Revolution von rechts* he strode unequivocally from the academic lecture hall into the political forum, combining social and political analysis with cultural criticism and clothing both in a rhetorical mantle borrowed from two classics of revolutionary pamphleteering, Abbé Sièyes's *What Is the Third Estate?* and Marx and Engels' *Communist Manifesto.*

Freyer's transformation from professor to pamphleteer was foreshadowed in his radical conservative works of the early 1920s and in his sociological writings of 1925 to 1931. Before turning to *Revolution von rechts* and its impact, we shall have to consider the contexts in which it was written and the motives for Freyer's leap into the political arena in the summer of 1931.

Freyer's Political Writings, 1925–1931

Though Freyer devoted himself primarily to the creation of his sociological institute and to the development of his sociological theory in the years from 1925 to 1931, he continued to lecture to a wide variety of academic and nonacademic groups on the political themes set forth in his earlier work. His call in 1931 for a revolution from the right was a direct continuation of a program which had begun to take shape in his mind before the First World War, which he had formulated in his postwar writings, and on behalf of which he had continued to evangelize thereafter. His early writings, up to and including his *Habilitationsschrift* of 1919, were devoted to the creation of a new "positive epoch," a unified, ethical order that would encompass the individual and save him from the cultural fragmentation and loss of meaning that Freyer saw as characteristic of modernity. His book of 1925, *Der Staat*, provided a blueprint for a future integrated order.[1] In the years thereafter he tried to bring his message to the wider public of the German *Bildungsbürgertum*—to awaken in doctors, engineers, teachers, and students the desire to create the all-encompassing state envisioned in *Der Staat*.

Many of Freyer's students, as we have seen, were recruited from the youth movement. Freyer's influence on this movement reached far beyond his own students: his works were glowingly reviewed in the journal of the Deutsche Freischar, and he was often called upon to address its constituent groups.[2] His message to and influence upon these young men and women are reflected in the protocol of a conference held by one such group, the Leuchtenburgkreis, in 1927.

The topic of its convocation during the weekend of Easter 1927 was "The State." The keynote speech was delivered by Hans Freyer, an invited guest, who spoke on "The Meaning of the Greek Polis." Though the theme may seem "academic," it was clearly intended by Freyer and perceived by his listeners as of immediate contemporary import, and it set the tone for the many discussions that followed.[3]

The flavor and substance of the talk that Freyer delivered to his impressionable student audience is conveyed by its final paragraph:

The power of the Greek polis over its people is founded upon the fact that it has absorbed into itself the Greek spirit in its entirety. Outside the polis there is no life worthy of the name. Only within it is there spiritual existence. Only within it is there freedom (which for the Greeks is never freedom *from* the state, but rather always freedom *to* the state: never bourgeois freedom, but rather always political freedom). The polis is the most unbourgeois type of state conceivable, for it is the state in its purest sense. The omnipotence with which it envelops its inhabitants is boundless. That it may demand any sacrifice in war is taken for granted, since with his death the citizen of the polis merely repays the cost of his nurture. But the polis demands and receives this same degree of

---

[1] See chapters 1–3; also Hans Freyer, *Theorie des objektiven Geistes*, 2d ed. (1929), 128–29, for remarks on revolution as collective cultural self-assertion.

[2] According to Michael H. Kater, *Studentenschaft und Rechtsradikalismus in Deutschland*, 94–95, the membership of the Deutsche Freischar

constituted 1.7 percent of the students enrolled in German universities in 1929.

[3] Hans Muhle, "Rückblick," in *Leuchtenburg Tagungsbericht: 5. Treffen* (1927), 18, copy in Archiv des deutschen Jugendbewegung, Burg Ludwigstein. Partially reprinted in Borinski et al., *Jugend im politischen Protest*, 176–78.

sacrifice in every hour of peace. It is not only a state but also a church. There is no escape from it, including escape into religion. All spiritual activity, all art and science, all ability and all virtue is realized in and for the polis. Works of poetry, of historiography, of art, of music belong not to the realm of individual satisfaction or free inquiry—they are a service to the polis, carried out on its behalf, oriented to its norms. And the boldness with which Athenian democracy is able to elevate the *Volk* . . . to a sovereign position within the state is warranted by this belief: that man is a thoroughly political being, possessed by the state, and that the law of the state powerfully permeates all of its citizens.[4]

The contemporary implications of Freyer's talk did not escape his listeners. The contrast between the idealized polis presented by Freyer and the *Staatsfremdheit* (alienation from the state) of the citizens of the Weimar Republic dominated the discussion for the rest of the weekend.[5] Among the most hotly debated proposals was that of one member of the Leuchtenburgkreis, who— drawing out the implications of Freyer's talk—called for a radical break with Christianity and liberalism and the creation of a new German state on the model of the Greek polis, founded upon a *Staatsmythus* of German soil, history, and the *Volk*.[6] Though this proposal was contested within the Leuchtenburg- kreis, the effect of Freyer's presentation had been to open the minds of his lis- teners to just such a possibility. The function of Freyer's talk had been to offer these young men and women a conceptual foil that served to articulate and intensify their existing alienation from the state and society of the Weimar Republic.

Freyer delivered many such speeches in the late 1920s to groups beyond the walls of the academy, whose members were drawn largely from the *Bildungs- bürgertum*. He addressed branches of the Deutsche Freischar and music teach- ers, doctors, and teachers in the Volkshochschule, as well as academic audi- ences.[7] For the most part these lectures reiterated the major themes of his earlier philosophical works: that the source of meaning for the individual was his participation in a particular historical culture, that the origin of this culture was the *Volk*, rooted in nature and history, that the purpose of the state was to create a realm in which the *Volk* could assert its historical culture.[8] This norm-

[4] Hans Freyer, "Vom Sinn der griechischen Polis," in *Leuchtenburg Tagungsbericht*, 4.

[5] Karl-Ferdinand Druschky, "Der deutsche Staat von 1927: Referat von Fritz Borinski," in *Leuchtenburg Tagungsbericht*, 4–6.

[6] Walter Meyer, "Nachtwächterstaat oder hei- liges Reich: Referat von Hans Muhle," *Leuchten- burg Tagungsbericht*, 10–11; Muhle, "Rückblick,"

17–20.

[7] A dozen or so of these lectures, published mostly in the journals of these professions, are listed in the bibliography of Freyer's works by Dietrich Willers, *Verzeichnis der Schriften von Hans Freyer*.

[8] Hans Freyer, "Ethische Normen und Poli- tik" (1930), 111; Freyer, "Volk und Gemein-

ative portrait of the unified and integrated *Volk* and *Staat* was contrasted with a description of contemporary Germany that stressed its social and political division into mutually antagonistic interest groups and the absence of a cultural consensus as to fundamental values.[9] The antidote was political, and the prime task which Freyer assigned to the state was that of integration, the creation of a "binding collective consciousness" (*bindende Gesamtbewußtsein*) that would make the *Volk* into a collective "political subject" affirming itself on the stage of world history.[10] Yet it was only when contemporary events gave him reason to believe that such a new collective consciousness was developing beyond the narrow confines of the well educated that his message to the *Bildungsbürgertum* changed to one of immediate political relevance.

The Specter of Romantic Impotence

Freyer had championed an all-encompassing *völkisch* state since at least 1925. But there was a gap between portraying such a state as a philosophical ideal and advocating it as an imminent political program. Freyer bridged that gap in the summer of 1931 when he published *Revolution von rechts*, a booklet understood by allies and opponents of National Socialism as an analytic defense of the historical significance and ethical importance of the Nazi movement. He viewed the movement as a vehicle for the realization of his long-standing hopes. Yet this in itself does not explain why a professor well ensconced in the university system of the republic, who stood to gain little personally from a Nazi victory, would become an early voice in what would soon become a chorus of intellectual support for the National Socialist movement. The explanation lies in part in a negative example from the past that haunted Freyer and his circle: the specter of reenacting the impotent fate of the German romantics.

Freyer had always displayed a highly ambivalent attitude toward the German romantics. He was emotionally attracted and intellectually indebted to their emphasis on the value of collective cultural particularity rooted in historical growth and to the holistic tone of their thought—in short, to their normative descriptions of the *Volk* and of the state as a "whole" or "totality."[11] Yet Freyer was critical of the romantics on two counts. He regarded the organic, holistic categories central to romantic thought as singularly inappropriate for

---

schaft" (1929), 15–16; Freyer, "Ethische Normen," 104–13.

[9] Freyer, "Volk und Gemeinschaft," 6, 16–18; Freyer, "Musik und Staat," in his *Über die ethische*

Bedeutung der Musik (1928).

[10] Freyer, "Ethische Normen," 110–13.

[11] Freyer, *Bewertung*, 41–50; idem, *ES*, 41–43; idem, "Die Romantiker," 83–89.

analyzing modern "bourgeois" or "industrial society," which was intrinsically conflict-ridden.[12] It was this weakness that his "dialectical" conception of sociology was intended to obviate.

Freyer's second criticism of the German romantics is essential for understanding his actions in 1931 and in the half decade thereafter. He characterized the romantics as too concerned with the cultivation of their inner experience to act upon and transform the external world.[13] A similar critique of political romanticism was penned by Carl Schmitt, whose writings on this and other matters influenced Freyer even before the two became friends in the late 1920s. In his own study—which focused on Adam Müller, the most influential social and political theorist of German romanticism—Schmitt portrayed the political romantic as a man who remained politically passive, since for him political events were merely an external stimulus to inner experience. To the political romantic Schmitt contrasted the romantic politician, a man motivated by romantic ideals but able to take responsibility for action and make decisions that could transform the external world.[14]

In lectures delivered shortly before and after the publication of *Revolution von rechts*, Freyer returned to the theme of the necessity of personal decision and commitment for the intellectual. Speaking to an audience of professors and graduate students in the spring of 1931, he took issue with Karl Mannheim's notion of a *freischwebende Intelligenz*, an intelligentsia whose supposed lack of ties to the existing class structure allowed it to comprehend the present objectively, without the distortions occasioned by particular social interests.[15] The "free-floating intelligentsia" did not exist as a distinct social group of historical importance, Freyer asserted. On the contrary, *Bildung* could only be based on the decision of the educator to commit himself within the contemporary struggles among competing interest groups.[16] In a lecture delivered shortly thereafter, Freyer criticized the tendency of the romantic—considered now as a type of personality—to remain *standpunktlos*, to refuse to decide between the real options offered by historical fate.[17]

Hans Freyer had spent much of his adult life asserting that he and his contemporaries lived in a critical epoch, an age of social fragmentation and cultural dissolution, which threatened the individual with a life of meaningless-

[12] Freyer, *Bewertung*, 52; idem, *ES*, 44; idem, "Romantiker," 94.

[13] Freyer, *Berwertung*, 38.

[14] Carl Schmitt, *Politische Romantik* (1925), 205–7, 224.

[15] Karl Mannheim, *Ideologie und Utopie* (1929),

chapter 2.

[16] Hans Freyer, "Zur Bildungskrise der Gegenwart," 624. On the debate in the early 1930s regarding the role of the intellectual see Dietz Bering, *Die Intellektuellen*, 290ff.

[17] Freyer, "Romantiker," 91, 94.

ness. He had lectured to a wide variety of audiences in an attempt to heighten their disaffection from the present and prepare them for participation in a movement of collective national self-assertion. He had devoted his sociological studies to discovering signs of such a movement in the body politic. He had stressed time and again the historical responsibility of the intellectual and the ineluctability of his partisan commitment in the struggle to initiate a new positive epoch. When events in Germany gave him reason to believe that a historical turning point was a real possibility, he reacted with alacrity to the opportunity of escaping the politically impotent fate of his romantic predecessors.

The Political and Economic Context of Revolution von rechts

The crisis of political legitimation revealed by the German federal elections of September 1930 formed the backdrop of *Revolution von rechts*. The moral illegitimacy of the current republic had long been the premise of Freyer's political and sociological writings, a premise that he shared with many intellectuals on the right and left.[18] It was the widening delegitimation of the republic in the minds of its nonacademic and nonintellectual citizens that Freyer chronicled and welcomed in *Revolution von rechts*.

Attempts to blame intellectuals (such as Hans Freyer) for the collapse of the Weimar Republic and the rise of Hitler are as ill advised as attempts to exculpate them. No responsible historian would argue with the claim that the crisis of Germany's economy and the resulting failure of parliamentary government were necessary preconditions for Hitler's political success. Necessary preconditions, however, are not sufficient conditions; other nations weathered the effects of economic crisis without the collapse of their political institutions. That so many Germans concluded from the severe economic and parliamentary crises of the late 1920s and early 1930s that liberal democratic government as such was superannuated was due to the dominant interpretation of those crises in the diverse circles of German political culture. It is here, on the dominant interpretations of reality, that intellectuals leave their mark. Intellectuals—those devoted primarily to the systematic interpretation of cultural reality—act on a variety of cultural levels and appeal to a variety of audiences. It was on the higher levels of culture and the most educated level of society that Hans Freyer exerted his influence.

The economic patterns and political events that form the background against which Freyer's booklet was written can only be sketched in brief. Prob-

[18] See especially Sontheimer, *Antidemokratisches Denken*, passim.

lems of parliamentary instability and sluggish economic growth had plagued the Weimar Republic long before the effects of the world depression exacerbated both ills. From 1919 through 1928, the average government cabinet lasted only fifteen months, and even the half decade after 1924, often referred to as the "phase of stabilization," appears more like a "phase of reduced conflict" when examined closely.[19] Unemployment never fell below 1.3 million during the 1920s, real economic growth was laggard, the rate of wages and the demands of the Weimar welfare state made for a lack of domestic capital formation, and a diminution of foreign investment capital had led to a downturn of the German economy well before the stock market crash in New York.[20]

By the summer of 1929, the existence of the depression was unmistakable. Unemployment rose to 1.9 million, inventories increased, and major corporations began to fail.[21] In the Thuringian provincial elections of December 1929 the National Socialist party scored its first political breakthrough, garnering 11.3 percent of the vote and contributing its first cabinet minister to a German provincial government.[22] In March 1930 came the dissolution of the last cabinet based upon a parliamentary majority that the Weimar Republic was to know. The issue on which the government fell, the seemingly unimportant matter of a small alteration of unemployment insurance premiums and benefits, was in fact the tip of a socioeconomic iceberg. In withholding its support from the government, the Social Democratic party acceded to the demands of its unionized constituents, who feared that this was merely the first step of a larger program of the captains of German heavy industry to peel back existing welfare-state provisions. Those who advocated a diminution of benefits held their ground, in the belief that without a cut in public spending and in real wage rates German industry would become uncompetitive in the international marketplace.[23] In a situation in which each side placed its perceived economic interests above those of the preservation of parliamentary democracy, the irreconcilable demands of opposing economic groups led to a governmental stalemate irresolvable by parliamentary means.

---

[19] Gordon Craig, *Germany: 1866–1945*, 509; Andreas Hillgruber and Michael Stürmer, "Diskussion," in Erdmann and Schulze, eds., *Weimar*, 141.

[20] Knut Borchardt, "Wirtschaftliche Ursachen des Scheiterns der Weimarer Republik," in Erdmann and Schulze, *Weimar*, 211–50, esp. 225–38. For subsequent reconsiderations of the "Borchardt thesis" see *Geschichte und Gesellschaft* (1985), 11:273–376.

[21] Charles Kindelberger, *The World in Depression*, 116–17.

[22] Karl Dietrich Bracher, *Die Auflösung der Weimarer Republik*, 298.

[23] Craig, *Germany*, 531–33; Borchardt, "Ursachen," 229–32; Gerald D. Feldman, "Eine Gesamtdarstellung Weimars?"; and especially Henry A. Turner, Jr., *German Big Business and the Rise of Hitler*, 100–103.

The result was a new cabinet headed by Heinrich Brüning, who attempted to govern through emergency powers granted by the *Reichspräsident*. When his deflationary budget was voted down by the Reichstag in July 1930, Brüning promulgated the budget by decree, dissolved the Reichstag, and called new elections for 14 September, the latest date possible under the provisions of the constitution. A month earlier, in June 1930, the National Socialists gained 14.4 percent of the vote in elections in Freyer's province of Saxony.

In September 1930, with almost three million Germans unemployed and welfare benefits cut by the government's deflationary policy, the most pivotal election in the history of the republic was held. Its most dramatic result was a leap in the electoral strength of the National Socialists. From 0.8 million votes and 12 Reichstag seats in 1928, they had jumped to 6.4 million votes and 107 Reichstag seats, becoming the second largest party in Germany, with 18.3 percent of the popular vote. Support for the Communist party—like the National Socialist party a determined enemy of the republic—grew from 3.3 to 4.6 million votes, giving it 77 out of the 577 deputies in the Reichstag. Fear of civil disorder and of the economic implications of the National Socialists' anticapitalist rhetoric led to the collapse of the foreign market for German treasury bills and a flight of domestic capital abroad, thereby exacerbating the country's economic ills.[24]

While the other major parties sought to protect the economic turf of their supporters, the National Socialists invoked collective comradeship and sacrifice. In the midst of economic depression and parliamentary stalemate the National Socialists exuded determination and confidently proclaimed, "The future belongs to us."

It was one thing to win over almost one-fifth of German voters, but quite another to gain the support of a broader electorate and convince Germany's military, economic, and intellectual elites not to stand in the way of a Nazi victory. It was in this context that Freyer penned his most explicitly political work.

Freyer's Revolution von rechts

In the spring of 1931 Freyer wrote *Revolution von rechts*, in an attempt to actively influence the course of contemporary German history. *Revolution von rechts* was distinguished from Freyer's earlier works in its explicit attempt to affect matters on the immediate political agenda. Though never mentioned explicitly, it was the potential transformation of German politics presented by

[24] Erich Eyck, *A History of the Weimar Republic*, 2:284; Turner, *German Big Business*, 124.

the electoral gains of the National Socialists in September 1930 that was the immediate stimulus to the writing of the pamphlet as well as its central point of reference.

Freyer's central proposition, stated in a three-page preamble to the pamphlet, was that National Socialism represented a new political phenomenon—one not amenable to explanation by means of the existing socioeconomic categories that dominated the interpretation of contemporary politics; the first modern movement capable of resisting the temptation to become co-opted into the system of liberal democratic capitalism; and the only existing movement capable of truly transforming that system. Freyer's ostensible purpose was to clarify the historical significance of the movement. Yet the style of the work—emotional, metaphorical, enticing in its rhythms and images—was intended to persuade by both rational argument and literary manipulation. Freyer sought to convince his readers that the time of political choice was at hand—that the choice was support of, or opposition to, the new movement, and that those who had long dwelt upon the ethical shortcomings of bourgeois society ought to choose the path of open support.

Yet so bald and sober a summary of the overture to *Revolution von rechts* cannot capture its tone or style so well as excerpts from its preamble:

A new front is forming on the battlefields of bourgeois society—the revolution from the right. With that magnetic power inherent in the battle cry of the future even before it has been sounded, it draws into its ranks the toughest, the most alert, the most timely men from all camps. It is still lining up, but it will strike. Its movement is still a mere assembly of spirits, lacking awareness, symbols, or direction. But overnight the front will arise. It will reach beyond the old parties with their petrified programs and antiquated ideologies. It will successfully challenge the conceit that the rigidified class antagonisms of contemporary reality—which have led on both sides to a petit bourgeois world—can be politically productive. It will do away with the ossified remnants of the nineteenth century and free the way for the history of the twentieth. . . .

He who thinks in the schema of the day before yesterday, of bourgeoisie and proletariat, of class struggle and economic peace, of progress and reaction, and recognizes nothing in the world but problems of distribution and insurance premiums for those who get the short end of the stick, nothing but opposing interests and a state that mediates between them—he naturally fails to see that since yesterday a regrouping of goals and forces is in process. He confuses the revolution of the right with all sorts of polite and unthreatening troublemakers and cranks of the old world—with national romanticism, with counterrevolutionary activism, with some idealistically trimmed *juste milieu*, or with the much touted state above the parties. He thinks, "Here is an imitation of fascism, Action Française bottled in Germany, or a Soviet Germany made enticing for romantics with the aid of certain reminiscences taken from German legal history." . . . But even those in whom the new will is active are for the most part only half conscious of what is occurring. They speak the frenetic language of a past radicalism when they seek to explain themselves. Or they fail to face up to the fact that things appear different when one looks forward than they have for the last century. Though it is very promising that the revolution from the right has silently formed the elements of a new society in the midst of the old one without having proved or justified itself, the time has come for the new reality to gain a first conception of itself [*die neue Wirklichkeit einen ersten Begriff ihrer selbst gewinnt*].

It is not a matter of convincing doubters, of encouraging waverers, of attracting opponents or dislodging the committed. . . . It is simply a matter of stating some present facts, of making us conscious of some developments shaping the future, and of posing the decisions inherent in those developments to those involved in them.

This matter has long been in process. It needs no stimulus or awakening. But it does require a gradual awareness of what is in question and of how far along we are. Every opportunity can be missed, every force can stray off course. At a particular moment an automatic development must be raised to intentional action, events to decision, the massing of troops to a front. Only the most ruthless clarity about itself will disengage the revolution now in process from the forces of the old right with which it is currently linked in many ways, will save it from the danger of serving as the horse for a monarchist, big-capitalist, or petit bourgeois cart. Only the most ruthless clarity about itself will avert it from confusing itself with itself, that is, from identifying itself definitively with one of the waves that it has created on the superficial surface of the present.

In front of our eyes, under our fingertips, in our very heads, social reality has transformed itself, unnoticed but unmistakably. So let us open our eyes, grasp the matter at hand, set our heads in order and transform our ideas about social reality.[25]

After this highly emotive preamble, *Revolution von rechts* continued in a somewhat more subdued tone and with greater historical specificity. Freyer's reflections on the concept of revolution were followed by a long meditation on the history and nature of "industrial society," the taming of the Marxist revolutionary alternative and its absorption into the Weimar state, a brief accounting of the contemporary sources of alienation from "industrial society," and finally a portrait of a new state that would integrate modern technology into a closed world of meaning.

Freyer used the term *industrial society* (borrowed from Saint-Simon) as a synonym for what he elsewhere called "bourgeois society" (Hegel's term), or (following Tönnies) simply "society."[26] "Industrial society" was the complex cre-

---

[25] Hans Freyer, *Revolution von rechts* (1931), 5–7.

[26] On the history of the concept of *Gesellschaft*, see Manfred Riedel, "Gesellschaft, bürgerliche" and "Gesellschaft, Gemeinschaft."

ated by the spread of the market mechanism and its domination over older economic, social, political, and cultural institutions—what Freyer (following Karl Marx) also called "capitalism."

Freyer's central contentions about industrial society were consistent with his earlier works. It represented the absolutization of the values of production and consumption, values that had previously been subordinated to some larger cultural framework. These values Freyer described as "abstract," by which he meant that they followed an internal rationality, independent of particular historical societies and their cultural traditions.[27] According to its own ideals, he wrote, industrial society was "a perpetual motion of commodity values, units of labor, means of exchange, and mass needs."[28] He also returned to his favorite metaphor to describe the salient features of industrial society:

All previous ages felt themselves anchored somewhere and were so anchored as a result. . . . Industrial society, however, rests upon nothing but the calculation of the materials and forces of which it is constructed. It is not grounded upon natural soil, but rather floats free. [*Sie ist nicht auf gewachsenem Boden gegründet, sondern schwebt frei.*] No sap flows through it other than its own rationality.[29]

"The nineteenth century," in Freyer's usage, was not a chronological designation but referred instead to the mind-set appropriate to industrial society. Individual and collective action in industrial society, according to Freyer, was based on "interest," the pursuit of individual or group self-advantage.[30] The natural social units of industrial society were therefore classes, groups organized for the pursuit of collective interests. Industrial society was thus in a permanent state of revolution from below, of chronic or acute class conflict.[31]

In historical materialism Freyer saw the mode of thought most appropriate to industrial society, and he saw the Marxist movement as the most significant political phenomenon of "the nineteenth century" considered in both its chronological and its cultural sense. With its recognition of the dominant role of economic interests in modern society, Marxism made explicit the real dynamics of industrial society in the nineteenth century.[32] Freyer regarded the socialist movement of the working class as the great revolutionary movement of the nineteenth century, as a movement aimed at transcending industrial society, as the embodiment of a "new historical principle."[33] Freyer acknowl-

[27] Freyer, *Revolution*, 19–20.
[28] Ibid., 21.
[29] Ibid., 20–21.
[30] Ibid., 19, 34, 38.
[31] Ibid., 9, 15.
[32] Ibid., 19.
[33] Ibid., 22, 17.

edged the crucial role played by this pursuit of collective interests in bringing about social progress for the oppressed within industrial society.[34]

The second section of *Revolution von rechts* was entitled "The Self-Liquidation of the Nineteenth Century." Freyer asserted that the socialist movement of the working class—the embodiment of the hope for a revolution of the left that would transcend industrial society—had been definitively and irrevocably absorbed into industrial society. In response to the successful political organization of the proletariat, politics had been transformed into a struggle over material welfare: through the development of *Sozialpolitik* (governmentally enacted social provisions), industrial society had moved from the era of laissez-faire to the new era of industrial society in its socially expanded form. In this new era the material condition of the proletariat was ameliorated sufficiently to lift it above the absolute misery that Marx (quite rightly, in Freyer's estimation) had deemed necessary for socialist revolution to occur. Thus, Freyer wrote, the revisionist socialists of the turn of the century had merely been speaking the truth about what their movement had become, a nonrevolutionary movement that sought an expansion of rights and benefits *within* industrial society.[35] The essential elements of capitalism had remained intact.[36]

Freyer recognized that the communists continued to embody the old revolutionary intentions of the nineteenth century but asserted that they simply refused to come to terms with the de facto decision of the proletariat to seek its welfare *within* industrial society. "Even an army of unemployed," he wrote, referring to contemporary conditions, "falls under the new logic: as soon as they arise they become an object of *Sozialpolitik*." They too could be integrated into the non-revolutionary logic of industrial society, Freyer believed.[37]

Freyer's emphasis, then, was on the unexpectedly successful capacity of welfare-state capitalism to co-opt its opposition and hence diffuse revolutionary challenges. He did not regard the social and legal gains made by the working class as entirely irreversible. On the contrary, he saw class conflicts as an intrinsic feature of industrial society and recognized that these gains would fluctuate as economic cycles continually altered the balance of forces between the competing organized interests of the working and entrepreneurial classes.[38] It was not cultural consensus but the objective strength of these politically organized social interest groups that kept both sides playing by the rules of a game in which the stakes were the distribution of the goods produced by industrial so-

[34] Ibid., 17, 31.
[35] Ibid., 26–28, 33.
[36] Ibid., 30.
[37] Ibid., 31–32.
[38] Ibid., 33–34.

ciety. But their mutual participation assured that it was *this* game and no other which would continue to be played. It was this disappearance of realistic hopes for a revolution from the left that Freyer dubbed "the self-liquidation of the nineteenth century."

Much of *Revolution von rechts* was devoted to a dissection of the role of the state in industrial society. Freyer claimed that the state had become nothing but the broker between organized social interests.[39] In the early stage of industrial society the power and sovereignty of the state had been systematically diminished by political liberalism, which had created the freedom for capitalism to mold society according to its own dynamic. The rise of the socialist movement and its integration into industrial society through *Sozialpolitik* had made the state itself into the battleground of organized social and economic interests. Parliamentary democracy meant nothing more—or less—than the surrender of the state to the umbrella organizations of interest groups.[40] Following the lead of Carl Schmitt, Freyer referred to the welfare state of industrial society as "pluralistic," as the institutionalized reflection of the changing balance of social forces within industrial society. Such a state, Freyer wrote, lacked the essential attributes of a real state, namely sovereign power *over* industrial society, a "binding collective consciousness," and continuity of purpose. "It is the sum of all that is unpolitical," he concluded.[41]

Freyer's portrait of industrial society as a system whose internal rationality led to the degradation of man to the roles of worker and consumer was essentially critical. But he acknowledged that capitalism had led to the development of technology and means of organization that had vastly increased man's power over nature. Under capitalism this new technological and organizational apparatus had come to dominate men and to subordinate them to its logic. The challenge for the future, Freyer wrote, was to subordinate this technical apparatus to human purposes.[42]

Revolution von rechts was addressed to the problem that had motivated Freyer's sociological works, namely the discovery of contemporary developments that could lead beyond bourgeois society.[43] "Revolution," he wrote, "is the birth of a new principle in the history of society. Revolutionaries are those who embody this new principle before it becomes historical reality."[44] Given the

39 Ibid., 23, 58–60.

40 Ibid., 39, 59–60.

41 Ibid., 60; for a similar analysis, see Carl Schmitt, "Staatsethik und pluralistischer Staat"

(1930), 28–42.

42 Freyer, *Revolution*, 29, 40–41, 47–49.

43 Ibid., 16–17.

44 Ibid., 18.

taming of the working-class movement through the social state, where did the social wellsprings of revolution lie?

Freyer's answer was that the true contemporary opponent of industrial society, and hence the real revolutionary subject of the revolution from the right, was the *Volk*.[45] In *Soziologie als Wirklichkeitswissenschaft* Freyer had rejected the belief that the dialectical contradictions within bourgeois society *necessarily* lay in its economic structure rather than on the cultural or political levels. In *Revolution von rechts* he reiterated that the nature of the new revolutionary movement of the *Volk* could not be understood on the basis of class analysis. Such an analysis presupposed that men were driven to revolutionary action by collective economic self-interest; it presupposed that men acted out of the motives characteristic of industrial society. Yet the essence and the hope of the new revolutionary movement of the present, in Freyer's analysis, lay in its rejection of social interest as the primary motive of political action. Since industrial society in the form of the welfare state was capable of absorbing challenges based upon social interests by co-opting its opponents, only a movement that rejected such interests could offer a revolutionary challenge to the welfare state.[46]

Freyer regarded the attempt to create a revolution based upon the collective self-interest of the oppressed classes as the hallmark of the failed revolution of the left. It was the break from this source of motivation for political action that he sought to emphasize by characterizing the revolution of the *Volk* as a "revolution of the right." While he recognized that the term *right* had usually been applied to the politics of those advantaged social groups who sought to protect *their* collective self-interest from the challenge of the left, Freyer stressed that this was not the sort of revolution he had in mind. Indeed, he warned, in the opening passage quoted above, against the possibility that the revolution of the *Volk* might be diverted by what he termed the "old," "capitalist," or "reactionary" right. The revolution of the right was the revolution of those who did not define themselves by their social interest and hence could not be co-opted by the existing system of industrial society.[47] Unlike the left or the old right, it sought not to capture the state for its social benefit but to liberate the state from its degraded condition as a forum for the pursuit of social interests.[48]

Freyer also forswore a sociological analysis of the new revolution of the *Volk*, on the grounds that he sought to offer not an analysis of its chances of success but an account of its essence and of its historical significance:

[45] Ibid., 44 and passim.
[46] Ibid., 43–44, 69.

[47] Ibid., 54.
[48] Ibid., 55, 61.

It is wrong to try to prove the legitimacy of a revolution through a theoretical analysis of the proportion of strength on each side. It would downgrade revolutionary events to the level of tactical maneuvers in which duty lies in the cautious examination of chances of success. . . .

Therefore we leave it to the analysts of industrial society to study the symptoms of torpor, the rhythms of crises, the accumulation of opposing forces, and on this basis to construct a formula for the immanent development of this system. If one seeks to grasp the revolutionary content of the present one must proceed quite differently. Principle must be opposed to principle: the principle of *Volk* against that of industrial society. The question of which side legitimacy and history stand on is no longer a matter of theory, but of history itself.[49]

Freyer claimed, in other words, to offer an ideological and not a social-scientific account of contemporary events. Implicit in his hesitancy to engage in social-scientific analysis was his recognition of the tacit delegitimating effect of a mode of analysis that described the movement at hand in functional terms, thus suggesting that some other ideology might fulfill the same function and calling attention to the arbitrary elements of the movement's stated goals. For the most part, he described the movement in question in terms such as *geschichtliche Kraft, Stoßkraft im Tageslicht des Geschehens, Aufbruch, Prozeß*—images that suggested the inevitability and inexorability of natural forces and hence added to the ideological tone of the pamphlet.[50]

Although he abjured an explicit sociological analysis of the revolution whose cause he championed, Freyer did offer a sketch of the social processes that had made such a revolution possible. While the capitalist and proletarian classes were at the core of modern capitalism, Freyer wrote, the expansion of industrial society had come to envelop the old middle classes and the peasantry. In so doing, it had transformed their status. "Portions of the old middle class," he wrote, "have been transformed into a *declassé Kleinbürgertum*. They now lead an existence that although it remains independent has become insignificant, an existence out of keeping with the times, unhistorical, and lacking in pride." The expansion of the market had made the independent artisan obsolete; his descendants had become office workers, a new stratum of industrial society. The peasant had been absorbed into the market economy, his village transformed by the demands of the city. This process, Freyer made clear, was irreversible and would be continued in any future social order. Yet industrial society ignored and devalued those aspects of the life of the peasant which were not geared toward its own values of production and consumption. The peas-

---

[49] Ibid., 44.

[50] Ibid., 50, 52–53.

ant's fate, according to Freyer, had become one of "stultification, alienation, and a marginal historical position with depraving effects."[51]

Since, in Freyer's view, industrial society treated man as nothing but a producer and consumer, it had failed to provide the individual with a sense of belonging to a larger whole. It was this pent-up discontent with the inability of industrial society to provide a higher meaning or collective purpose to its members that Freyer saw as the real source of the new revolution of the right.[52] Although he insisted that this discontent existed among members of all social classes, his actual description pointed to the old middle classes, the new white-collar strata, and the peasantry as its most important social loci. "Whenever the *Mittelstand* is torn asunder, the peasantry threatened, islands of self-reliance destroyed, enterprise bureaucratized, in short wherever industrial society comes to maturity, . . . new power is added to the new core of the *Volk*."[53]

It was to the *Volk* that Freyer looked for the source of resistance to industrial society. But what did he mean by this most elusive of terms? His answer was twofold.

On the one hand, Freyer used the term *Volk* in the sense in which it had been used by German romanticism and historicism, as a primordial force that was the root cause of the historical development of a collective culture.[54] As we have seen, this concept had appeared frequently in Freyer's earlier radical conservative writings and embodied conceptual confusions of which he himself was aware. It presumed a unity within German culture that was by no means historically evident and verbally transformed the *effects* of historical developments that had led to a sense of collective cultural identity into the *cause* of these historical developments. Hence the inevitable haziness of the term *Volk* when used in the romantic, historicist sense.

Any philosophy of history that stresses the role of automatic or quasi-natural factors in historical development is liable to engender an attitude of passivity within its adherents. For it is foolish to exert oneself on behalf of a process that will occur regardless of one's intentions or actions. It was against such quietistic implications of the Marxism of the Second International that Sorel, Lenin, and Lukács had revolted with a new, more voluntarist Marxism which stressed the role of will in the historical process. Here once again Freyer may be seen as Lukács's counterpart on the right. It was to obviate the quietistic effects of the romantic-historicist concept of *Volk* that Freyer introduced a second definition of the *Volk*.

---

[51] Ibid., 46–47.
[52] Ibid., 47–49.

[53] Ibid., 52.
[54] Ibid., 51; see also 63.

The *Volk* in *Revolution von rechts* consisted of all those who refused to define themselves in terms of their social class and economic self-interest. In a deliberate paraphrase of Sièyes's famous rhetorical contention that the Third Estate was "nothing" in the political order of the present but was actually "everything," Freyer wrote of the *Volk* as "nothing" in industrial society which would become "everything" in the future. By this he meant that in terms of the category of social interest which characterized "bourgeois society," the *Volk* was without substance. In calling attention to the contemporary movement of the *Volk* Freyer was therefore referring primarily to a change in *consciousness* and to the political ramifications of this cultural change:

> History occurs in the will of men. . . . The political movement of the present is nothing other than a transformation in the basic material of a human group. The nineteenth century has been left behind because there are men who are of the twentieth. The principle of industrial society has become invalid because there are men who are no longer defined by their social interest.[55]

Freyer's emphasis on the role of ideas or cultural norms in social cohesion and social change had a long and distinguished pedigree in modern sociological thought. In *Soziologie als Wirklichkeitswissenschaft*, Freyer had criticized Marxism for underestimating the causal role of cultural transformations in the process of historical change. Freyer's analysis in *Revolution von rechts* was therefore sociological in the sense in which he understood the term: it drew attention to the role of psychic discontent within liberal capitalism as a source of impending historical change.[56]

---

[55] Ibid., 71–72.

[56] As an application of Freyer's theory of sociology, *Revolution von rechts* must be judged a qualified success. The purpose of sociology as *Wirklichkeitswissenschaft* was to search out those social, cultural, and political forces most likely to lead to a supersession of liberal capitalism. Freyer called attention to the discontent of the peasantry, the old *Mittelstand* of artisans and small shopkeepers, and the new stratum of white-collar workers as factors in the appeal of National Socialism. Yet he insisted that the party's appeal lay in its rejection of interest-politics-as-usual and suggested the limits of attempts to comprehend National Socialism based on theories of vocational interest. Recent studies of the vocational basis of the Nazi vote indicate that its social basis was far broader than the advocates of the "lower-middle-class" theory of National Socialism had maintained. As James Sheehan has noted in a perspicacious review of these studies, their effect is to call into question the assumption that the vote can be explained principally in terms of occupationally based motivations (Sheehan, "National Socialism and German Society," 857).

Freyer's analysis of the revolution of the right as a revolt against the loss of a sense of larger meaning and purpose due to the dislocating effects of liberal capitalism has been echoed by later historians, including Ernst Nolte's phenomenological analysis of fascism as resistance to "practical transcendence," a term that Nolte regards as equivalent to the concept of "prog-

Yet this analytic, social-scientific perspective was intimately combined in *Revolution von rechts* with an advocatory, ideological stance. The pamphlet not only analyzed and described this wave of anticapitalism; it also idealized it and obfuscated it. The idealization occurred by playing down the element of economic self-interest in the anticapitalism of the old and new middle classes. By using the term *Volk* in *both* the romantic-historicist sense of identification with a particular historical ethnic group *and* in the sense of sheer anticapitalist affect, Freyer sought to channel the latter into the former. Through the frequent use of terms such as *Kraft* or *Stoßkraft* to refer to the movement of the disaffected, Freyer substituted emotive metaphor for sober description, in a manner intended to dramatize the process.

The source of Freyer's enthusiasm for the gathering momentum of National Socialism is not difficult to discover. He saw in it a mass embodiment of that cultural critique of modernity which had been developed by earlier generations of German social theorists and which lay at the heart of his own work.[57] Not surprisingly he devoted the final chapter of *Revolution von rechts* to an invocation of the new order that the revolution would create. Freyer avowed that little could be said about the state to be created by the revolution from the right.[58] He then proceeded to say a good deal about it, all of which revealed his hope that the revolution would bring about the realization of the state envisioned in his own *Der Staat*.

"Man is free," Freyer wrote, "when he is free *in* his *Volk*, and when it is free in its realm [*Raum*]. Man is free when he is part of a concrete collective will, which takes responsibility for its history. Only reality can decide whether such a collective will will exist, a will that binds men and endows their private existence with historical meaning."[59] The real emancipation of man therefore occurred when he lived in a state "emancipated" from the interest politics of industrial society.[60]

The new state was to be "freed" from the egoistical demands of industrial society in order to engage in real history, namely the integration of the *Volk* for the sake of collective self-assertion and the acquisition of temporal power.[61] This was the higher collective purpose to which all were to be subordinated. The capitalist economy with its logic of production for profit was to be re-

---

ress" without the optimistic connotations of the latter (see Nolte, *Der Faschismus in seiner Epoche*, esp. vii, 541–47).

[57] Freyer, *Revolution*, 72.

[58] Ibid., 61.

[59] Ibid., 69.

[60] Ibid., 61.

[61] Ibid., 65.

placed by state socialism (*Staatssozialismus*), in which production would occur for the sake of collective historical self-assertion.[62] As in *Der Staat*, Freyer regarded the rate and manner in which the economy was to be brought under state control to be a secondary, tactical problem.[63] The new state would continue and expand what Freyer regarded as the two greatest accomplishments of industrial society—the development of technology and of governmental social policy (*Sozialpolitik*). Yet the significance of each would be transformed. Technological modes of thought would now be clearly subordinated to those of politics.[64] Government social measures would continue not because of the struggles of social groups acting according to egoistic self-interest but by virtue of a truly collective ethos that would pervade the new state.[65] The role of the state would be one of ongoing intervention in order to shape the *Volksordnung*.[66] The new state brought about by the revolution from the right would thus combine technology and social organization with the "endlessly deep roots" of the *Volk*.[67] It would solve the problem to which Freyer's work had been devoted: the reconciliation of modern technology with a sense of collective identity and individual meaning rooted in the particularist past. Freyer saw in the revolution from the right a real, mass political embodiment of his own cultural criticism and the possibility of realizing the total state that he had long advocated.

Above all, *Revolution von rechts* was an attempt on Freyer's part to broaden the existing support for the National Socialist movement. Behind its central metaphor—of a "new front" forming "on the battlefield of bourgeois society," in which the revolution of the right represented the regenerative forces of the future arrayed against the superannuated forces of the past—lay the demand that each individual commit himself to one side or the other. The pamphlet was intended to influence a select audience; arguments about the formation of a new dialectical subject of history, about the restoration of meaning in a world of technology, or about the re-creation of the primacy of political over economic modes of thought were neither likely nor intended to convince farmers, shopkeepers, or white-collar workers—not to speak of blue-collar workers or entrepreneurs—about the justice of the National Socialist cause. *Revolution von rechts* spoke the language of the German *Bildungsbürgertum*. It was addressed to Freyer's students in the youth movement, for most of whom the question of

---

[62] Ibid., 66–67.

[63] Ibid., 64–65.

[64] Ibid., 66.

[65] Ibid., 67–70.

[66] Ibid., 70.

[67] Ibid., 72.

their relationship to National Socialism was the most burning of the day;[68] to Freyer's peers in the professoriate and the government bureaucracy; to the writers and editorialists of journals and newspapers that helped to form public opinion.[69] In 1931 the *Bildungsbürgertum* to whom Freyer's book was addressed was deeply ambivalent about National Socialism, admiring the idealism and nationalism of many of its adherents but repelled by the violence and vulgarity of the movement as a whole. It was into this delicate balance that Freyer threw his lot, by his interpretation of the Nazi electoral success as evidence of a revolution of the right that offered a tangible historical solution to problems that had lain at the center of German social thought for over a generation.

Though National Socialism was not endorsed by name in *Revolution von rechts*, and though some later maintained that the object of his enthusiasm had not been National Socialism, the booklet was understood at the time of its publication as an endorsement of National Socialism by Freyer's students of all political persuasions—and by Freyer himself.[70] Shortly after the publication of *Revolution von rechts* he told his student Ernst Manheim that he had written the booklet with the Nazis in mind and regarded the text as crystal clear in this regard.[71] Werner Studentkowski, a prominent National Socialist orator and Freyer's doctoral student, described Freyer in a letter written to Gregor Strasser at the time of the publication of *Revolution von rechts* as "the Leipzig sociologist Dr. Freyer, who is sympathetic to us" ("*der uns nahestehende Leipziger Soziologe Dr. Freyer*").[72] Reviewing the book for the *Neue Blätter für den Sozialismus*,

---

[68] On this problem, see the review articles by Peter Stachura, "Deutsche Jugendbewegung und Nationalsozialismus," and Winifred Mogge, " 'Der gespante Bogen': Jugendbewegung und Nationalsozialismus."

[69] The importance of the orientation of the bourgeois press in influencing the electoral choice of Nazi voters is demonstrated in Richard F. Hamilton, *Who Voted for Hitler?*, passim.

[70] In an article on the occasion of Freyer's eightieth birthday, his friend Arnold Gehlen wrote, "Die Schrift 'Revolution von rechts' (1932) stand dem Nationalsozialismus durchaus fern wie der Mann überhaupt. . . . sie stand den Volkskonservativen nahe die das Ausmaß des bevorstehenden Erdrutsches nicht übersahen" (Arnold Gehlen, "Hans Freyer: Zu seinem 80. Geburtstag," *Frankfurter Allgemeine Zeitung*, 29

July 1967). Since a point-by-point refutation of all the erroneous claims made about Freyer in the primary and secondary literature could fill a small book, I have by and large forgone the opportunity. Gehlen's claim in this case appears to have been a careless fabrication. The *Volkskonservativen* were a small group that splintered away from the Nationalist conservatives in January 1930 because of the growing closeness of the main party, under Hugenberg, to the National Socialists. They joined the Brüning cabinet shortly thereafter, where they remained through 1932.

[71] Interview with Ernest Manheim, Martha's Vineyard, 20 August 1981.

[72] Werner Studentkowski to Gregor Strasser, 24 July 1931, BAK, NS22/1067, fol. 1.

another Freyer student, Fritz Borinski, confessed his admiration for his teacher but rejected what he regarded as the clearly "fascist" consequences of the book.[73] The political implications of *Revolution von rechts* were palpable to Freyer's readers of all political stripes.

But one did not have to be a student of Freyer or even a perspicacious reader to conclude that the National Socialist movement was the key subject of *Revolution von rechts*. On the very first page of the pamphlet the revolution from the right was contrasted to "the old parties"; and when Freyer wrote that the phenomenon of the revolution from the right had been misinterpreted as a German imitation of fascism or of the Action Française there was only one contemporary party to whom such interpretations had been frequently applied. The allusion to National Socialism was clear.

Why, in a booklet so clearly about National Socialism, did the words *National Socialism* never appear? The answer lies in part in Freyer's reservations about National Socialism, in part in his personal caution, and in part in the intellectual milieu in which he wrote.

The process of Freyer's attraction to and ultimate disillusionment with National Socialism was far more subtle than a development from uncritical support to unalloyed condemnation. Even during the period of Freyer's greatest enthusiasm toward National Socialism (1931–34) he maintained reservations about the political sagacity of the movement, and the later waning of his support would be slowed and mitigated by his respect for the foreign policy successes of the regime in reasserting national power and reversing the provisions of the Treaty of Versailles.

Some of Freyer's mental reservations about National Socialism are evident when *Revolution von rechts* is read carefully and in light of his previous work. Although *Revolution von rechts* was clearly *about* the National Socialist movement, it was not a blanket endorsement of National Socialism in its current form. In view of the stress on *Führertum* in Freyer's earlier radical conservative writings, his failure to mention not only Adolf Hitler but the importance of *Führertum* in *Revolution von rechts* is a telling indication that as of 1931 he remained skeptical of Hitler's ability to lead the revolution of the right to a successful culmination.

[73] Fritz Borinski, "Revolution des 20. Jahrhunderts—Revolution von rechts?" Borinski used the term *fascist* to refer to National Socialism, in keeping with contemporary usage in socialist circles. In retrospect this confusion of National Socialism with Italian Fascism appears symptomatic of that systematic underestimation of National Socialism by both its allies and opponents which played so important a role in its political victory.

An unequivocal supporter of National Socialism, writing in 1931, would not have described the movement as "without consciousness, without a symbol, without leadership."[74] The revolution, Freyer warned, must be clear about itself, lest it "confuse itself with itself, that is, identify itself definitively with any of the waves it has created on the surface of the present."[75] Freyer, like other radical conservative intellectuals, appears to have believed that National Socialism had by no means taken on its final form as of 1931—that it was itself in a process of flux. The stated purpose of his pamphlet was to provide the movement with historical clarity about what it represented, in order to help guide its future action.[76] Freyer's intention was not to "moderate" the party. On the contrary, what he most feared was the possibility that it might be diverted from its revolutionary path or co-opted by the interest politics characteristic of industrial society and its state. He warned of the need to distance the movement from the "old right" of monarchists, big capitalists, and *Kleinbürger* and from all "banal reaction."[77] *Revolution von rechts* was thus a brief for revolutionary purity.

Freyer's failure to refer explicitly to the party was evidence not only of his reservations about National Socialism but of a gap between Freyer's rhetoric and his character that was to become all the more apparent in the years to follow. For while Freyer's writings had stressed the need for decision (*Entscheidung*), action (*Tat*), and a willingness to act decisively in the face of uncertainty (*Wagnis*), he was in fact by disposition rather cautious, especially where his personal fate was concerned. It was, of course, not his personal caution but his programmatic radicalism that the rhetoric of *Revolution von rechts* conveyed to Freyer's readers.

Freyer's caution was not only a quirk of personality. Even among those of his academic colleagues who went so far as to become members of the Nazi party during the final years of the Weimar Republic, there was a reluctance to become publicly and explicitly identified with the Nazi movement. The German professor was after all a civil servant (*Beamter*), employed by a government still in the hands of non-Nazis; fear of dismissal or of professional disadvantage therefore acted as a motive for political caution among the professoriate before 1933.[78] Concern about governmental reprisal was not entirely unfounded, as

[74] Freyer, *Revolution*, 5.
[75] Ibid., 6–7.
[76] Ibid., 6.
[77] Ibid., 6, 63.
[78] See Anselm Faust, "Professoren für die NSDAP," 40; and Michael H. Kater, "Die nationalsozialistische Machtergreifung an den deutschen Hochschulen: Zum Politischen Verhalten akademischer Lehrer bis 1939," 58.

demonstrated by the case of Ernst Krieck, who in June 1931 was suspended from his post as professor at the Pädagogische Akademie Frankfurt by the Prussian minister of culture (a Social Democratic appointee) for concluding a speech to students with the words *"Heil dem Dritten Reich."*[79] Though there is no evidence that Freyer worried about the possible negative effects of *Revolution von rechts* on his academic career, such considerations may have added to his reluctance to endorse National Socialism by name in his pamphlet.

The Intellectual Context of Revolution von rechts

It was not the political and economic stalemate of the final years of the Weimar Republic that led to Freyer's advocacy of an all-encompassing state in *Revolution von rechts*. As we have seen, Freyer had conceived and developed such an ideal in works stretching back over a decade. The Nazi electoral success of September 1930 appeared to Freyer as an opportunity to realize his long-standing hopes for the creation of a total state. This goal was shared by other intellectuals in Freyer's milieu who influenced his thought and were influenced by it. "The concept of the totalitarian," writes one of the major historians of National Socialism, "as a postulate and program was optimistic and idealistic in its origins; as a supposedly constructive political idea it was enthusiastically welcomed, celebrated, defended, and extolled."[80] The cultural network in which the ideal of the totalitarian state was developed and spread by Freyer's associates and admirers included other academic intellectuals, intellectuals in positions of bureaucratic power, younger intellectuals pursuing journalistic careers, and the aspiring intellectuals in the German youth movement.

Carl Schmitt was among the most prominent academic advocates of a totalitarian state in the years between 1929 and 1933.[81] A professor of law in Bonn

[79] See Gerhard Müller, *Ernst Krieck*, 88ff.

[80] Gerhard Schulz, "Der Begriff des Totalitarismus und des Nationalsozialismus," 453.

[81] The secondary literature on Carl Schmitt is immense and growing. The best study of Schmitt's political career is Joseph Bendersky, *Carl Schmitt: Theorist for the Reich*, which demonstrates that Schmitt was not an active supporter of National Socialism until 1933, but rather an accomplice of General von Schleicher's earlier attempt at a plebiscitarian dictatorship. The book is flawed by its insistence that a man who shared the radical conservative critique of mo-

dernity, who advocated a "total state," who published in revolutionary conservative periodicals, and whose friends included many of the leading advocates of a conservative revolution ought not to be considered a conservative revolutionary, since he attempted to reach his goals through an interpretation of the Weimar constitution that jettisoned all of its liberal and parliamentary features. Among the most useful works on Schmitt's thought before 1933, which set them in their contemporary intellectual context, are Leo Strauss, "Comments on Carl Schmitt's *Der Begriff des Politischen*" (1932); Heinrich Wohlge-

and then in Berlin, Schmitt was a legal theorist with a strong philosophical, sociological, and historical bent. Among his major works of the early Weimar years was *Die geistesgeschichtliche Lage des heutigen Parlamentarismus* (1923), which aimed to demonstrate that parliamentary government had lost its intellectual legitimacy. A complementary series of studies explored the theme of dictatorship.[82] The broad thrust of much of his writing even before 1928 was the demonstration that a plebiscitarian dictatorship was permitted by the Weimar constitution and required by contemporary circumstances.[83] Freyer was much taken with Schmitt's work, invited him to speak at his institute, and befriended him in the late 1920s.[84]

In May 1929 Schmitt presented his analysis of contemporary politics to a gathering of German philosophers. The contemporary state, he argued, had become subordinated to the pluralistic social interests of civil society, thus robbing it of its unity and sovereignty.[85] This reflected what he took to be a false understanding of pluralism: legitimate pluralism existed not in the domination of the state by competing socioeconomic interest groups but in the competition among the cultures of the *Völker*, each embodied in its own state.[86] The foremost obligation of contemporary political philosophers was therefore to foster an awareness of the need for a unified state embodying a collective culture, a "concrete and real order."[87] Such a state would take control of "the economic, pedagogic, and psychotechnical means by which experience shows consensus can be created," rather than leaving them in the hands of individuals and social groupings whose goals might conflict with those of the state.[88] Schmitt insisted that he was a "democrat," opposed to the superannuated "liberalism" of the nineteenth century. But he regarded elections among competing parties chosen by secret ballot as "liberal." Real democracy, as Schmitt

---

muth, "Das Wesen des Politischen in der heutigen deutschen neoromantischen Staatslehre" (1932); Karl Löwith, "Max Weber und seine Nachfolger" (1940); Hans Barth, "Die Krise des Wahrheitsbegriffs in den Staatswissenschaften" (1940), in his *Fluten und Dämme*; Krockow, *Die Entscheidung*; Lutz-Arwed Bentin, *Johannes Popitz und Carl Schmitt*; and Ellen Kennedy, "Introduction: Carl Schmitt's *Parlamentarismus* in Historical Context."

[82] Carl Schmitt, *Die Diktatur* (1921).

[83] Carl Schmitt, "Die Diktatur des Reichspräsidenten nach Art. 48 der Reichsverfassung" (1924); idem, "Die Gegensatz von Parlamenta-

rismus und moderner Massendemokratie" (1926).

[84] Interview with Ernest Manheim; interview with Käthe Freyer.

[85] Carl Schmitt, "Staatsethik und pluralistischer Staat" (1930), 28–31. The lecture was delivered at the *Generalversammlung* of the *Kant-Gesellschaft* in May 1929. Freyer also attended, and he delivered a paper on "Ethische Normen und Politik," cited above.

[86] Ibid., 37–40.

[87] Ibid., 41–42.

[88] Ibid., 35.

understood it, did away with the "disintegrating" pursuit of private interest that such elections encouraged. By Schmitt's reckoning, the Italian Fascist election of 1928 in which the voter could choose for or against a single list of candidates was more democratic, since it allowed the "unity of the *Volk*" to express itself in the electoral process.[89]

In the course of expanding these ideas Carl Schmitt and his students introduced the term *total state* into the political culture of the German right at the end of the Weimar Republic. The concept itself antedated the new term; as we have seen, it had been articulated earlier by Hans Freyer, among others. Schmitt discussed the notion of the total state in two essays that he published in 1931 and 1933 in the *Europäische Revue*, one of the most intellectually demanding journals of German radical conservatism. The first of these essays was entitled "The Turn to the Total State."[90] Here the term *total state* had an opprobrious connotation. In contradistinction to the noninterventionist state demanded by nineteenth-century liberalism, the contemporary state was in the process of becoming a "total state" in the sense that it was required to intervene in all areas of civil life.[91] Yet, Schmitt lamented, the Weimar state was incapable of exercising the legislative authority demanded by this new reality, because parliament now served to divide the state's power among politically organized social interests.[92] In an article published in February 1933, he made the implications of his analysis clearer. The contemporary German state, he wrote, had become total "out of weakness"; it was forced by the demands of the parties to expand into all areas of life and was incapable of setting its own priorities. It was a total state "in a purely quantitative sense," but not in its "intensity and political energy."

To this weak, indecisive total state "in the purely quantitative sense," Schmitt counterposed the ideal of the total state "in the qualitative sense":

> The total state in this sense is an especially strong state. It is total in the sense of its quality and of its energy, of what the fascist state calls the *stato totalitario*, by which it means primarily that the new means of power belong exclusively to the state and serve the purpose of augmenting its power. Such a state allows no forces to arise within it that might be inimical to it, limit it, or fragment it. It does not think of surrendering the new means of power to its enemies and destroyers and allowing its power to be undermined by categories such as liberalism, *Rechtsstaat*, or whatever. Such a state can distinguish friend from foe. In this sense every authentic state is a total state; it has in all ages been

---

[89] Carl Schmitt, "Wesen und Werden des fascistischen Staates," 109.

[90] Carl Schmitt, "Die Wendung zum totalen Staat" (April 1931), 241–47.

[91] Ibid., 242–43.

[92] Ibid., 247.

a *societas perfecta* of the secular world. The political theorists have long known that the political is the total; what is new is only the new technical means about whose political ramifications one must be clear.[93]

Among the first to sympathetically delineate the historical background and political implications of Schmitt's concept of the total state was Ernst Forsthoff, a young legal theorist who stood in a relationship of discipleship to Schmitt comparable to the relationship of Karl-Heinz Pfeffer to Hans Freyer. Born in 1902, Forsthoff, like Pfeffer, was a member of the Deutschnationale Jugendbund during the 1920s.[94] He studied in the mid-1920s with Carl Schmitt in Bonn, earned a degree in 1930, and moved to Berlin, where under various pseudonyms he became a major contributor to *Der Ring*, another journal of the radical right.[95] In an article, "Constitutional Law and the World War," published under his real name in the *Blätter für deutsche Philosophie* in the summer of 1931, Forsthoff claimed that German political life was only now coming to terms with the spiritual legacy of the world war.

The war was no longer conducted by the army alone but by the entire nation through the deployment of all material and personal reserves. Ernst Jünger had termed this "total mobilization." Every military achievement is a political achievement. The mobilization of the entire nation therefore means the elimination of all limits on the political, the first turn toward a total state for which the distinctions between the political and the unpolitical, the public and the private are no longer valid. Today, therefore, the entry of the war experience into the spiritual life of the nation means the transition toward a total state.[96]

[93] Ibid., 67. Schmitt emphasized the need for state control of the economy and of technology time and again in his writings of the early 1930s. Only in two lectures to the Association of Rhineland Industrialists (delivered in 1930 and 1932) did he refrain from doing so. Marxist analysts of Schmitt's career have focused on these two speeches, as evidence that Schmitt was above all an apologist for bourgeois economic interests (see, e.g., Jean Pierre Faye, *Totalitäre Sprachen*, 2:881–89; Ingeborg Maus, *Bürgerliche Rechtstheorie und Faschismus: Zur sozialen Funktion und aktuellen Wirkung der Theorie Carl Schmitts*, esp. 152ff.). In fact, these lectures were by no means representative, and their attempt to link a new "strong state" with a decline in state intervention in the economic realm appears to be a case of playing to the audience, whom Schmitt wanted

to win over to his notion of a plebiscitarian dictatorship of the *Reichspräsident* (see Bentin, *Popitz und Schmitt*, 98–100). More typical was Schmitt's claim that an authentically illiberal state would be more likely to wield its power against the "capitalistic interests of the employers" (Schmitt, "Wesen," 112).

[94] "Ernst Forsthoff," Internationales Biographisches Archiv (Munzinger-Archiv), 2 November 1974; BAK, R21, Wissenschaftler-Kartei: "Ernst Forsthoff."

[95] On Forsthoff's pseudonyms, see the bibliography of his works in Roman Schnur, ed., *Festschrift für Ernst Forsthoff*.

[96] Ernst Forsthoff, "Staatsrechtswissenschaft und Weltkrieg" (1931). Jünger first used the term as the title of his essay "Die totale Mobilmachung," published in *Krieg und Krieger*, ed.

In the summer of 1932 Forsthoff broke from *Der Ring*, which was too influenced by heavy industry for his taste. Over the course of the next year he was closely associated with Wilhelm Stapel and A. E. Günther, the editors of the radical conservative journal *Deutsches Volkstum* and mentors of the Hanseatische Verlagsanstalt, the largest of the radical conservative publishing conglomerates.[97] In the spring of 1932 Forsthoff contributed to a collection of essays by radical conservative intellectuals from this circle entitled "What We Expect of National Socialism."[98] Both the terminology and the substance of his essay reveal the influence of Schmitt and Freyer on the expectations that young intellectuals such as Forsthoff brought to National Socialism:

> As part of the larger process of the liquidation of the nineteenth century a state will arise whose most outstanding characteristic is no longer neutrality vis-à-vis the realms of social life (economy, scholarship, culture) but rather *authority*. The state will be truly political, and its encompassing political substance will suffuse all those areas of life which liberalism had made autonomous, i.e., which it had sealed off from the state.[99]

One year later Forsthoff, like Freyer, was to proclaim that his expectations had been met, in a booklet entitled *The Total State*.

Johannes Popitz was another intellectual tied to Hans Freyer and Carl Schmitt by the bonds of friendship, whose political evolution from 1929 through 1933 is likely to have influenced Freyer and been influenced by him.[100] Popitz was one of the most respected civil servants in Germany, as well as an adjunct professor of law in Berlin. From 1925 through the end of 1929, Popitz was *Staatssekretär* (the highest civil service position) in the *Reich* Ministry of Finance. A man in the Prussian state tradition, who regarded the bureaucracy almost as the Platonic guardian of the nation, Popitz had by 1927 concluded that the "polyarchy" of public and semipublic centers of economic influence threatened the unity of the German state and made an effective government tax policy impossible.[101] By 1931 he had come to share Schmitt's critique of the Weimar parliamentary system as resulting in the domination of organized social interests: he too cast about for a method of re-creating "the

---

Ernst Jünger (1930). Hans Freyer, as we have seen, had already drawn similar conclusions about the political ramifications of the war experience.

[97] On the Hanseatische Verlangsanstalt and Stapel's role in it, see Stark, *Entrepreneurs*, 27 and passim.

[98] "Dr. Friedrich Grüter" (Ernst Forsthoff), "Die Gliederung des Reiches."

[99] Ibid., 82–83.

[100] Freyer's friendship with Popitz was confirmed in the interviews with Ernest Manheim and Käthe Freyer cited above.

[101] Bentin, *Popitz und Schmitt*, 13–19.

spiritual and ethical unity of state and *Volk*."[102] The troubled political pluralism of the Weimar Republic heightened the receptivity of traditional Prussian conservatives like Popitz to radical conservative ideas.

In sketching the intellectual milieu in which Freyer moved and wrote, two lines of influence may be distinguished. One line—what one might call the horizontal one—linked Freyer to intellectuals of approximately equal status and comparable institutional moorings. Freyer was connected through friendship and political affinity to a circle of intellectuals of high institutional and intellectual prestige: to academic intellectuals such as Schmitt, and to Popitz who straddled the border between the university and the upper reaches of the governmental bureaucracy. Another line of influence—the vertical one—linked Freyer to intellectual circles outside the academy whose members occupied positions of lower intellectual prestige, but often of greater influence, through publication in journals aimed at a broader audience that was educated but not necessarily academic. In this category were the extra-academic journals of the political right and the student journals of the youth movement.

The most influential intellectual journal of the political right in the years from 1929 to 1933 was *Die Tat*. When Hans Freyer published his first article in Eugen Diederichs' *Die Tat* in 1919, the journal was fairly esoteric and limited in its appeal. In 1928, the last year of Diederichs' editorship, the circulation of *Die Tat* was a mere one thousand. Under its new editor, Hans Zehrer, the journal kept its "hand on the pulse of history": it offered its growing readership a systematic account of what it regarded as the bankruptcy of capitalism and liberal democracy in Germany. Written in a style that conveyed intellectual self-assurance and ideological zeal, *Die Tat* provided the intellectual guideposts for a large, educated audience as its circulation grew to thirty-thousand in the course of 1930. From 1929 to 1933 no journal was more influential among the nonleftist intelligentsia.[103]

It was written by a handful of journalists who, by writing under a number of pseudonyms, gave the impression of a larger stable of ideologically homogenous authors. The core writers shared a remarkably similar past. Of the four journalists at the center of the Tatkreis—Hans Zehrer, Ernst Wilhelm Esch-

---

[102] Quoted in ibid., 32; see also 13–35, passim.

[103] The most penetrating and balanced interpretive account of the Tatkreis is Kurt Sontheimer, "Der Tatkreis" (1959), now in his *Deutschland zwischen Demokratie und Antidemokratie*. Useful sources of additional information include Faye, *Totalitäre Sprachen*, 443–508 passim; Walter Struve, *Elites against Democracy*, 353–76; Ebbo Demant, *Von Schleicher zu Springer: Hans Zehrer als politischer Publizist*; and Klaus Fritzsche, *Politische Romantik und Gegenrevolution*.

mann, Giselher Wirsing, and Ferdinand Zimmermann—all had studied sociology or related disciplines. Zehrer and Zimmermann had studied with Werner Sombart and Ernst Troeltsch in Berlin; Eschmann had studied with Alfred Weber and Wirsing with Carl Brinkmann, both in Heidelberg in the late 1920s.[104] Most were close to the youth movement: Zehrer, the oldest of the quartet, had belonged to the *Altwandervogel* before the war, while Eschmann (born in 1904) was a leader of the Deutsche Freischar and as of 1928 was active in the Sächsische Jungmannschaft, to which Hans Freyer was a mentor.[105]

Freyer's works were read within the Tatkreis well before he published *Revolution von rechts* in 1931. The journal's enthusiastic review of *Revolution von rechts*, for example, began by noting its continuity with Freyer's earlier work, *Der Staat*.[106] Yet the influence was by no means unidirectional: Freyer was a regular reader of *Die Tat*, and his emphasis on the alienation of the middle strata as the driving force of an anticapitalist, statist, and nationalist revolution had been characteristic of the Tatkreis since 1929.[107] It is not surprising then that *Die Tat* gave its readers a careful and uncritical summary of *Revolution von rechts* and welcomed Freyer as a comrade in arms in the struggle for a statist revolution.[108]

A step below *Die Tat* in terms of intellectual prestige, circulation, and the average age of their readers were the periodicals of the youth movement, in which *Revolution von rechts* was greeted with even greater enthusiasm. The national journal of the Deutsche Freischar published excerpts from Freyer's booklet. Its reviewer praised the work as a confirmation of the ethos of the *Jugendbewegung*: Freyer's revolution of the right was based not upon the forces of reaction but on the "new men" which the youth movement had long endeavored to create.[109] The journal of the radical right-wing Jungnationaler Bund published a glowing review of Freyer's book, then followed it up with a long article by his disciple, Karl-Heinz Pfeffer.[110]

[104] Sontheimer, "Tatkreis," 61; Demant, *Zehrer*, 62–63.

[105] On Zehrer's membership in the Altwandervogel, see Struve, *Elites*, 371n; on Eschmann's role in the Deutsche Freischar, see Kindt, ed., *Die deutsche Jugendbewegung, 1920–1933*, 1541.

[106] Horst Grüneberg, "Revolution von rechts" (1931), 240–41.

[107] Ernest Manheim, Freyer's friend at the time, confirms that Freyer was a careful reader of *Die Tat* and that much of his analysis of contemporary political events was based upon reading a wide range of newspapers and periodicals rather than on firsthand knowledge or empirical studies. Interview with Ernest Manheim.

[108] "Wir begrüßen Freyer als Mitkämpfer bei der Revolution von rechts, d.h. vom Ganzen, vom Staat her" (Grüneberg, "Revolution von rechts," 241).

[109] Review of *Revolution von rechts*, in *Deutsche Freischar* (1931), 86–87.

[110] Pfeffer, "Hans Freyer." On p. 343 Pfeffer cites the earlier review by the journal's editor,

Freyer's intellectual coordinates were set by other academic intellectuals such as Schmitt, Forsthoff, and Popitz on the one hand, and on the other by the authors and readers of a ladder of extra-academic periodicals descending in prestige from *Die Tat* and the *Europäische Revue* down through the "middlebrow" journals of the radical right such as the *Deutsche Rundschau* and finally to the periodicals of the youth movement.[111] Ideas and intellectual influence moved up this ladder as well as down it.

The interest generated among intellectuals in the academy, in the milieu of the youth movement, and on the broader radical intellectual right made *Revolution von rechts* a publishing success by the modest standard of his publisher, Eugen Diederichs. The book's first printing of three thousand copies was sold out before the end of 1931, necessitating a second printing of which another thousand copies were sold by the end of 1932. These figures indicate that *Revolution von rechts* reached a larger audience than any of Freyer's earlier works. Even this best-selling of his works of the Weimar years reached a much more limited audience than more journalistic works such as *Die Ende des Kapitalismus* (1931) by the economic correspondent of *Die Tat*, Ferdinand Zimmermann, which sold almost twenty-five thousand copies from 1931 to 1932. Yet the historical significance of Freyer's *Revolution von rechts* may lie in the fact that it was men like Zimmermann who were most likely to read it and be influenced by it.[112]

In his evaluation of the Tatkreis and its influence, Kurt Sontheimer has offered a number of observations germane to an understanding of Freyer's role in the years from 1931 to 1933. The appeal of *Die Tat* to its readers lay in the fact that it was ideologically close to National Socialism without being National Socialist. Many educated Germans who were attracted to the Nazis out of antiliberal, anticapitalist, and imperialist beliefs nevertheless found the primitive ideology and brutal behavior of the National Socialists repellent. *Die Tat*

Rudolf Craemer, which pointed out Freyer's great significance for the readers of the journal.

[111] Freyer was asked repeatedly by the editor of the *Deutsche Rundschau*, Rudolf Pechel, to contribute to his journal. The first solicitation was made in 1928, and several more were made in the period between the publication of *Revolution von rechts* and February 1933, indicating the high prestige with which Freyer was regarded on the intellectual right. Freyer agreed to contribute but ultimately sent his pieces elsewhere. The

correspondence between Freyer and Pechel is in BAK, NL33, File: "Freyer." On Pechel and his journal, see Volker Mauersberg, *Rudolf Pechel und die "Deutsche Rundschau."*

[112] Of Freyer's earlier works published by Diederichs, *Antäus* had sold only one thousand copies in the first year after its publication in 1918, *Prometheus* less than five hundred in the first year after its publication in 1923 (sales figures from the archives of the Eugen Diederichs Verlag, Cologne).

sprang into the breach, explaining the reasons why the republic ought to be abandoned and a new *Reich* established in terms that were more sophisticated than those which the National Socialists could offer on their own behalf. It allowed those who considered themselves part of a national spiritual elite to welcome the political success of National Socialism while maintaining mental reservations as to the final shape and leadership of the new *Reich*. It thus functioned ultimately to make National Socialism *salonfähig* among educated Germans.[113]

This analysis could be applied *mutatis mutandis* to Hans Freyer's role in these years. If the authors of *Die Tat* could interpret National Socialism in terms that appealed to the typical young, educated reader, Freyer could bring to bear the full weight of German philosophy and social theory to explain the moral desirability and historical necessity of a revolution of the right—a revolution that only one existing political movement was in a position to carry out. If the Tatkreis helped to make support for National Socialism acceptable among educated Germans, then Freyer helped make it acceptable among the most educated of Germans, the professoriate. And just as educated Germans looked to *Die Tat* for guidance in the last troubled years of the Weimar Republic, so did Freyer's academic colleagues and students come increasingly to look to him to interpret contemporary events and their implications for the academy.[114]

The Politicization of the Academy

It was among German university students that National Socialism first triumphed.[115] The National Socialists had been a tiny group within the student body, as within the population at large, as of early 1929. Then, during the

[113] Sontheimer, "Tatkreis," 85–87. For similar observations by a contemporary observer, see Siegfried Marck, "Überfaschismus? Betrachtungen zu H. Freyers *Revolution von rechts*" (1931), 412–19, esp. 415.

[114] On the personal level as well, members of the Tatkreis sought to hedge their bets with regard to the shape of the new *Reich*. While the editorial line of the journal, set by Hans Zehrer, demanded an authoritarian government based on the support of the trade unions and the purported left wing of the NSDAP, and ultimately supported the attempt of Schleicher to head such a government, Ferdinand Zimmermann maintained close contact with Himmler begin-

ning in the summer of 1932. After Hitler's seizure of power he joined the SS and like most members of the Tatkreis pursued a very successful career in the Third Reich (Demant, *Zehrer*, 60–61, 75–77).

[115] On the causes and methods of the National Socialist success within the student body after 1929, see Anselm Faust, *Der Nationalsozialistische Deutsche Studentenbund*; Kater, *Studentenschaft*; Hans-Peter Bleuel and Ernst Klinnert, *Deutsche Studenten auf dem Weg ins Dritte Reich*; and Geoffrey J. Giles, *Students and National Socialism in Germany*, 62–72. There is an excellent summary in Bracher, *Auflösung*, 132–34.

1929–30 semester, came what worried observers termed the *Sturm auf die Hochschulen* (assault on the universities). In the student elections of February 1930 at the University of Leipzig, the National Socialists increased their vote fivefold. One year later, they captured a majority of seats on the Leipzig student council. Similar developments were occurring at other universities and institutions of higher technical education across Germany. The National Convention of Students (Deutsche Studententag), dominated by the National Socialist Student League, elected a Nazi student activist from the University of Leipzig, Gerhard Krüger, as its leader in July 1932 and voted to institute the *Führerprinzip* (leader principle) within all student unions.[116] It was in this context that Freyer entered the growing debate on the role of politics in the university and the relationship of the academy to the state.

Freyer first broached the topic in a lecture, "The Contemporary Crisis of Education," delivered in the spring of 1931, at about the time that he was completing work on *Revolution von rechts*.[117] He traced the social origins and intellectual presuppositions of the humanistic ideal of *Bildung* and concluded that, under present conditions, the attempt to give the individual a sense of participation in a larger "totality" through education was bound to fail, since contemporary industrial society was a critical age without "immanent meaning."[118] Since the present was a critical epoch and hence transitional by definition, *Bildung* meant the acquisition of insight into the factors leading beyond such an epoch. Such insight (as Freyer had argued in *Soziologie als Wirklichkeitswissenschaft*) was possible only on the basis of commitment (*Entscheidung*) to one of the competing positions and competing groups offered by present circumstances. Freyer acknowledged that this position opened the door to the "radicalization" of education—and welcomed this as the necessary response to the existing critical age.[119]

Freyer published this address in the autumn 1931 issue of *Die Erziehung*, a leading pedagogic journal edited by his friend Theodor Litt and others. When Litt was elected by his colleagues at the University of Leipzig to the post of rector, he decided to devote his inaugural address to the topic "The University and Politics."[120] The lecture included an implicit critique of Freyer's recent

---

[116] Faust, *Studentenbund*, 37–38.

[117] Hans Freyer, "Die Bildungskrise der Gegenwart," 597–626. The lecture was delivered at the Internationale Hochschulkurse in Davos between 23 March and 11 April 1931 (see the report on the conference in *Die Erziehung* 6 [1931]: 659–60). Freyer signed the book contract for

Revolution von rechts on 9 April 1931 (Archives of the Eugen Diederichs Verlag, Cologne).

[118] Freyer, "Bildungskrise," 613–15.

[119] Ibid., 618, 624–25.

[120] Theodor Litt, "Hochschule und Politik" (1932).

writings on the proper role of scholarship *(Wissenschaft)* and of the university.

The problem of its relationship to politics had become a burning one for the German university, Litt maintained. Not long ago political authorities had demanded of the university that it help prepare the way for a new social order. The university had been expected to provide confirmation for that which the ruling parties thought they already knew, and when the universities refused to go along they were assailed as embodiments of "reaction."[121] From the other side of the political spectrum, it was now maintained that the real task of the university was to convey a particular intepretation and evaluation of *völkischen Lebens*. While it had previously been fashionable to accuse the university of standing on the wrong side of the political fence, the current trend was to accuse it of not having decided where it stood on the vital questions facing the *Volk* and the state. This accusation of indecision was disingenuous, Litt claimed, for behind the call for *Entscheidung* was the expectation that the decision would follow the political line of the caller.[122]

The relationship of *Wissenschaft* to politics, Litt asserted, was one that only *Wissenschaft* could determine if it were to remain *Wissenschaft*. Were the university to allow the decision about the direction of its work to be determined by some authority outside the university, it would abandon the very idea of scholarship. Those who sought to transform the university according to extrascientific *Entscheidungen* ought to recognize that they were demanding the sacrifice of the basic principles of scientific research.[123] In fact, argued Litt, the university fulfilled its responsibility to the nation most fully when it guided its activity by the search for truth that was intrinsic to *Wissenschaft*, and when it created a zone for calm reflection and critical self-scrutiny in which young people might learn to resist the temptations of "mass thought and mass will." The university, he concluded, was most "actual" when it refused to follow the demands of the moment.[124]

Freyer picked up the gauntlet in an essay in *Die Erziehung* entitled "The University as Elite School of the State."[125] The demand for a separation of *Wissenschaft* from the state, he wrote, was based upon the liberal view of the state as simply an institution of power for the purpose of security. This view required the existence of separate realms free of state intervention, of which scholarship was one, the economy another.[126] Whatever validity this limited view of the state may have possessed in the nineteenth century, it in no way accorded

---

[121] Ibid., 135–38.
[122] Ibid., 137–39.
[123] Ibid., 141.
[124] Ibid., 148.

[125] Hans Freyer, "Die Universität als hohe Schule des Staates" (1932).
[126] Ibid., 520–21.

with the reality of the contemporary state, which was "total" (in Schmitt's sense of a "weak total state") and forced by competing political parties and interest groups to intervene in all areas of life. Nowhere had this process of politicization gone further than among the age cohort from which the university students were drawn.[127] Under these circumstances, Freyer wrote, he did not intend to call into question the necessity of scientific autonomy or freedom of research and teaching, but rather to reexamine certain assumptions about the nature of *Wissenschaft*.[128]

Modern philosophy, Freyer wrote, had called attention to the untenability of the "positivist" notion of science that had predominated during the nineteenth century.[129] Social scientific understanding (*geisteswissenschaftlichen Verstehens*), Freyer claimed, was made possible only by extrascientific assumption that arose from concrete historical circumstances, and the true task of philosophy was to make men conscious of the assumptions that were implicit in the *Geist* of a particular era.[130] Indeed, the proper role of scholarship was to clarify the authentic substance of an age, that which was "valid" and future-oriented within it (*sein gültiger Zukunftswille*). Such knowledge was obtainable—as he had shown in *Soziologie als Wirklichkeitswissenschaft*—only on the basis of commitment (*Entscheidung*).[131] It was this view of scholarship that the university ought to embody.[132]

Freyer concluded his essay with some comments on the relationship of scholarship to the state. According to German idealism, Freyer recalled, the state ought to be the embodiment of the current stage of *Geist*, which it was the task of *Wissenschaft* to conceptualize. It was necessary, Freyer cautioned, to distinguish between the "empirical state" of the present and the historically valid concept of the state, which might exist "only as a movement." It was the task of *Wissenschaft* to identify with this historically valid conception of the state both when it was embodied in a movement and when it became the official state. Scholarship would not receive its presuppositions from such a state; rather it would share its basic assumptions, since both state and science reflected a common historical stage of *Geist*.[133]

By the summer of 1932 Freyer and some of those around him were convinced that the political victory of National Socialism was historically imminent and were already beginning to act in accordance with the new *Geist*. Ernst Manheim, who had followed Freyer from Kiel to Leipzig, was preparing to receive

[127] Ibid., 532–34.
[128] Ibid., 536–37.
[129] Ibid., 669.
[130] Ibid., 671. Freyer alludes to the Hegelian origins of this mode of thought.
[131] Ibid., 675, 677.
[132] Ibid., 679.
[133] Ibid., 688–89.

his habilitation—which would allow him to teach as a *Privatdozent* at a German university—from Freyer, his teacher and friend. On a visit to Hungary in the summer of 1932, Freyer told Manheim's parents that it would be impossible to find their son a position as a *Privatdozent* due to the "anti-intellectualism"—a polite euphemism for anti-Semitism—that would soon dominate the German university system. Soon thereafter Freyer informed Manheim that although his *Habilitationsschrift* was already in print, Freyer could not habilitate him.[134]

In interpreting this incident and similar ones that were to follow, it is worth remembering that Hans Freyer was not an anti-Semite. His voluminous writings had been free of even a hint of anti-Semitism. Indeed, he had remarked to Manheim that he regarded the anti-Semitism of the Nazis as counterproductive in that it prevented the full assimilation of the German Jews into German culture, the course that Freyer favored.[135] Freyer's treatment of Manheim was evidence not of ideological antipathy to Jews but rather of a more pragmatic willingness not to let personal reservations about Nazi anti-Semitism stand in the way of his support of the only movement that seemed to offer the possibility of realizing his long-standing hope of a new, positive order. Moreover, Freyer was in sufficient contact with Nazi students to realize that when the National Socialists came to power to have habilitated a Jew might jeopardize his position in the new order. The distinction between opportunism and a willingness to accede to the cunning of history was probably difficult even for Freyer to discern.

Several incidents in the autumn of 1932 reveal the extent to which the dominant voices among the German professoriate had become reluctant to speak ill of the young National Socialists who sat before them in the lecture halls and seminar rooms. In October 1932, after a number of incidents in which Nazi students had harassed and disrupted the lectures of professors of whom they disapproved, Theodor Litt proposed a resolution at the Conference of German Universities condemning the irresponsible and mendacious nature of the Nazi student groups. The resolution was opposed by Eduard Spranger—a prominent philosopher, co-editor of *Die Erziehung*, and a friend of both Litt and Freyer—on the grounds that the Nazi student movement was "genuine in its core, though undisciplined in its form." The resolution failed to pass.[136]

---

[134] Interview with Ernest Manheim, Martha's Vineyard, 15 August 1983. The proposed *Habilitationsschrift* was first published as Ernst Manheim, *Die Träger der öffentlichen Meinung* (1933) and was republished under the title *Aufklärung und öffentliche Meinung* (1979).

[135] Interview with Ernest Manheim.

[136] Eduard Spranger, "Mein Konflikt mit der nationalsozialistischen Regierung 1933," 457. On disruptions and harassment of professors, see Bracher, *Auflösung*, 134.

Theodor Litt had confronted Nazi students in his capacity as rector of the University of Leipzig and had been the object of their abuse, including death threats.[137] The man chosen by Litt's colleagues to replace him at the end of his tenure as rector in October 1932 was Hans Achelis, professor of church history and archaeology, who had demonstrated his support for the National Socialist students by appearing at the Nazi-dominated Deutsche Studententag in July 1932.[138] The son of this new rector, Johann Daniel Achelis, a young lecturer in the history of medicine who was a member of the circle around Freyer, had himself joined the National Socialist Student League during the previous academic year.[139] The faculty of philosophy elected as its new dean Hans Freyer.

The change at the helm of the university from Litt to Achelis and Freyer quickly made itself felt. On 28 November, Gerhard Kessler, a professor of economics and a leading member of the Deutsche Staatspartei, published an article in the liberal *Neue Leipziger Zeitung* entitled "Deutschland, Erwache!" (Germany Awaken!). The article was a blistering and trenchant attack on the contradictory and demagogic promises made by the National Socialists.[140] When Kessler stood up the next day to deliver his regular lecture he was confronted by threatening students shouting, "Schmierfink raus!" ("Out, you pig!"). The rector, Achelis, appeared in the lecture hall and—to student applause—declared that Kessler would not lecture that day.[141] Informed that more disruptions were planned for Kessler's lecture the next day, Achelis decided that Kessler ought to cancel it as well and dispatched Freyer, in his capacity as dean, to Kessler's home to convince him of the wisdom of this course of action.[142] The action of the university senate was equivocal: it adopted a resolution expressing regret at Kessler's article but condemned the students for expressing their disagreement in a manner that violated the manners of the academy. It also removed Kessler from his position as chairman of the board that administered student financial aid, an action that the students viewed as a vindication of their protest. On 1 December the Nazi chairman of the student union apologized to Kessler in the name of the students, apparently on the advice of the rector. All in all, the affair had gone well enough for the National

---

[137] Friedhelm Nicolin, "Theodor Litt und der Nationalsozialismus," 96.

[138] Faust, *Studentenbund*, 37–38.

[139] BAK, R21, Wissenschaftler-Kartei: "Johann Daniel Achelis."

[140] A copy of the article is in UAL, PA Kessler, 46.

[141] Report in the (NSDAP) *Leipziger Tageszeitung*, 29 November 1932, copy in UAL, PA Kessler.

[142] Report of Johann Daniel Achelis to Volksbildungsministerium, 17 December 1932, in UAL, PA Kessler, 84–90.

Socialists that the party's *Leipziger Tageszeitung* could proclaim: *"Deutscher Geist siegt!"* (A Victory for the German Spirit!).[143]

On 18 January 1933, with the newspapers filled with speculation over the negotiations in Berlin between Schleicher, Papen, Hugenberg, Hindenburg, and Hitler, the faculty and students of the University of Leipzig assembled in annual commemoration of the founding of the Bismarckian *Reich*. They were addressed by Hans Freyer. Germany, he told them, was in an hour of political distress and the collapse of the final illusions about this distress. He intended to offer some "scholarly reflections" on the forces that made it possible "to build men into a state and a *Reich*," to create a structure of domination (*Herrschaftsgebilde*) that could "tear men up from their natural situation into a political existence." The creation of such a structure was dependent upon "the grip of a single man" who could mold a historical situation into a "concrete future." But it also demanded a general willingness to sacrifice: "a readiness to live and die for the *Reich*." "We elders," Freyer continued, "who stand before you as a decimated and more than decimated generation confess to the experience of the war—which tore us out of our bourgeois security—as the decisive experience of our lives, the experience that one can die for the *Reich*."

Freyer advised his student listeners to show some patience and prepare themselves for sacrificial participation in the political future of the German *Volk*. He concluded:

German history is opening up today—despite inner confusion and outer constriction—for him who has faith and can wait a little. We do not yet see, but we do anticipate a rebirth of the *Reich*, beyond that of Bismarck, which will not be handed us on a silver platter, but on whose behalf we will one day be able to struggle.[144]

The wait was not a long one. On 30 January Adolf Hitler was appointed chancellor. In the election of 5 March the National Socialists and their Nationalist allies won 52 percent of the vote. On 23 March the Enabling Act was passed by the Reichstag and Reichsrat, giving the new government dictatorial legal authority for four years.

The lead article in the April 1933 issue of *Die Tat* was entitled "Die Revolution von Rechts."[145]

[143] A copy of the article is in UAL, PA Kessler.

[144] Hans Freyer, "Rede zur Reichsgründungsfeier," *Leipziger Studentenschaft*, 26 January 1933,

49–51.

[145] Hans Zehrer, "Die Revolution von Rechts," *Die Tat* (1933), 1.

CHAPTER SEVEN

Revolution from the Right:
Practice, 1933–1935

It was the promise of creating a community of collective purpose through political power that attracted Hans Freyer and other intellectuals to the total state. On the eve of the Third Reich, Freyer articulated that promise in a vocabulary of virtue borrowed from Machiavelli. Freyer regarded "bourgeois society" as the modern version of what Machiavelli had termed "corruption." Freyer's speeches and writings demonstrate his absorption in the neo-Machiavellian problem of using power to transform the purported egoism of bourgeois existence into a virtuous political community. It was through this neo-Machiavellian lens that Freyer viewed the new government of Adolf Hitler, and he set out to do his part to harness social science for the construction of a new *Reich*.

The new government soon demonstrated its willingness to use power to transform existing institutions in its own image, in a process known as *Gleichschaltung*. In the course of this process Freyer and other prestigious radical conservatives were catapulted into positions of greater influence than they had previously known. Yet their sudden rise was often due less to the explicit choices of the regime than to the attempt of their colleagues to come to terms with the new revolution from the right. In the Weimar era, Freyer's attempt to straddle the line between ideology and social science left him in the wings of the sociological profession. In the early years of the Third Reich, it would move him into the spotlight, where the ideological heat was more intense.

Virtue and Domination: Freyer's Political Philosophy
on the Eve of the Third Reich

In January of 1933, Freyer lectured to a variety of audiences on the relationship of political domination to collective virtue, a theme that remained central to his intellectual endeavors and political activity in the years that followed.[1] In

---

[1] Freyer, "Rede zur Reichsgründungsfeier"; Freyer, *Herrschaft und Planung: Zwei Grundbe-*

his lectures, Freyer distinguished between two modes of collective existence, the natural and the political. Where the members of a *Volk* were devoted to the pursuit of individual self-interest, the *Volk* remained mired in a "natural existence" of reproduction, economic production, and enjoyment of the amenities of "civilization." Such a *Volk*, according to Freyer, was destined to remain the "object" rather than the subject of history, its collective fate at the mercy of others.[2]

To become a collective subject in history—to lead a "historical" existence—meant to become a political *Volk*, the ideal instance of which Freyer called a *Reich*. Within the *Reich*, existence was politicized and characterized by "the renunciation of private egoism, the sacrifice of natural man, and the readiness for action for the sake of long-term goals." This long-term goal was the ability to carve out and defend a geographic area of one's own—what Freyer called a *Raum*, or in the idiom of the day, *Lebensraum*. Only through its willingness to sacrifice the present for the future could the *Volk* preserve the collective legacy of its past.[3]

In his contrast between a "natural" and a "political" *Volk*, Freyer borrowed from the legacy of Niccolò Machiavelli. It was Machiavelli who had first distinguished between those peoples who possessed *virtù* and hence were capable of collective self-defense and those who lacked this quality and were at the mercy of others.[4] At least since the time of Fichte and Hegel, Machiavelli's work in general and the concept of historical versus unhistorical peoples in particular had been a source of fascination for German intellectuals. In 1924 the German historian Friedrich Meinecke (whose work Freyer admired and whom he subsequently befriended) had published *Die Idee der Staatsräson*, much of which was devoted to the interpretation of Machiavelli in modern German thought.[5] Shortly thereafter Freyer himself turned to the study of Machiavelli and the

griffe der politischen Ethik (1933), was delivered as a lecture to the Berlin chapter of the Deutsche Philosophische Gesellschaft in early January 1933, according to the *Leipziger Neueste Nachrichten* of 16 January 1933, 3; Freyer, *Der politische Begriff des Volkes* (1933)—though there is no definite indication of when this lecture was delivered, it appears to have been in late 1932 or early 1933.

[2] Freyer, *Herrschaft*, 33, 35, 39.

[3] Ibid., 35, 33–36.

[4] On the concept of *virtù* in Machiavelli, see,

esp., J.G.A. Pocock, *The Machiavellian Moment*, chapters 6–7; and Jerrold Seigel, "Virtù in and since the Renaissance"; Quentin Skinner, *Machiavelli*, 53ff.; and Weintraub, "Virtue," chapter 3. The concept of liberty as popular control that recent Anglo-American writers have emphasized in their exploration of Machiavelli's thought was virtually absent from Freyer's discussion.

[5] Friedrich Meinecke, *Die Idee der Staatsräson* (1924).

problem of "Machiavellism" as German intellectuals had conceived it, namely the relationship between force, morality, and national regeneration. Though the influence of Freyer's reading of Machiavelli was already felt in his *Der Staat* (published in 1925), it was in 1933 that the Machiavellian problem moved into the foreground of Freyer's work, and in the decade thereafter he devoted no less than four books and articles to it.[6]

In early 1933 Freyer approached the problem of the use of power in the process of collective moral regeneration in a manner that did more to obscure than to illuminate the moral and political dilemmas involved.[7] His key theme was that an integrated, political *Volk* could be created and maintained only through *Herrschaft*.[8] *Herrschaft* therefore emerged as the sine qua non for the creation of the closed *Reich* that Freyer had sought since his earliest writings. In the work of Max Weber, Freyer saw an antidote to the tendency of social theorists to underrate the role of *Herrschaft* in history. It was Weber's "insight," Freyer wrote, that "*Herrschaft* is historically the most important structural element of social reality, all social life is formed by *Herrschaft*, and only through *Herrschaft* is it oriented to a goal of action."[9]

The obscurities of Freyer's discussion of *Herrschaft* reflected the ambiguities of radical conservatism with regard to the problem of political authority. It was this ambiguity that had led radical conservatives to advocate a revolution from the right and led many to see in National Socialism the embodiment of their hopes. The increasingly differentiated usage of the term *Herrschaft* in Freyer's writings during the Third Reich reflected his growing awareness of the limitations of political power in the creation of moral authority, an awareness central to his social theory of the 1950s.

Herrschaft, according to Freyer, was a relationship among unequals that was never free of an element of coercion. For without coercion (*Zwang*) it was impossible "to snatch men, who by their very nature and style of life are quite sat-

---

[6] Hans Freyer, *Politische Begriff des Volkes* (1933); idem, *Pallas Athene: Ethik des politischen Volkes* (1935); idem, *Über Fichtes Machiavelli-Aufsatz* (1936); idem, *Machiavelli* (1938); idem, "Machiavelli und die Lehre vom Handeln" (1938); *Preußentum und Aufklärung: Eine Studie über Friedrich des Großen, Antimachiavel* (1944, never distributed).

[7] The problem is pithily posed by Alasdair MacIntyre in his discussion of Jacobinism: "you cannot hope to re-invent morality on the scale of a whole nation when the very idiom of the morality which you seek to re-invent is alien in one way to the vast mass of ordinary people and in another to the intellectual elite. The attempt to impose morality by terror—the solution of St. Just—is the desperate expedient of those who already glimpse this fact but will not admit it" (MacIntyre, *After Virtue*, 221).

[8] *Herrschaft*, 26, 29, 31, 35–37.

[9] Ibid., 24.

isfied to lead a private existence, into a political existence." Yet, Freyer empha-sized, a structure of *Herrschaft* could achieve stability and continuity only if it rested upon the consent, and indeed the profound consent, of the ruled. Stable rule depended upon the ability of those who exercised domination to achieve legitimacy, to create consent among the *Volk*.[10]

Herein lay the political ambiguity of Freyer's conception of *Herrschaft*: the ultimate stability of a political *Volk* depended upon popular acceptance of the form of domination, but the leadership stratum that was to awaken the collec-tive desire to become a political *Volk* was not required to await the legitimated assent of those it hoped to rule. On the contrary, it had to be prepared to use coercion to integrate those whom it intended to rule, to create a political *Volk* united by a common will out of the mass of men inclined to pursue their pri-vate, egoistic interests.[11] Coercive political power thus became a tool in the cre-ation of a stable, integrated society united in collective purpose. Since legiti-mation could *follow* the imposition of rule, there was no need for an institutional mechanism—such as democratic elections—by which the prefer-ence of the population for its choice of ruler could be tested. Since the degree of politicization required to integrate the *Volk* for its collective preservation could not be limited in theory, no limits could be set on the potential use of coercive force by the government. Freyer's concept of *Herrschaft* drew no sharp distinction between *obedience*, based on the moral authority of the rulers as recognized by the ruled, and *compliance*, which arose as a response to coercion or the threat thereof.[12]

Yet Freyer's message at the dawn of the Third Reich emphasized that the long-term effectiveness of a system of domination depended upon its ability to awaken the assent of the *Volk*. The task of *Herrschaft* was not only to "form" the *Volk* as a whole through a higher, ethical goal but to link each individual to this goal in the innermost core of his being, to "activate" him for collective en-deavor.[13] Returning to Machiavelli's image of *virtù* as a substance possessed to

[10] Ibid., 31–33.

[11] Ibid., 32, 37, 39.

[12] Max Weber, to whose writings on *Herrschaft* Freyer was particularly indebted, was by no means consistent in his use of the term, espe-cially in *Wirtschaft und Gesellschaft*, which was written over a long period of time. In some parts of the book he stressed the element of *legitimacy* as an intrinsic part of the obedience characteris-tic of *Herrschaft* (see, for example, Max Weber, *Wirtschaft und Gesellschaft*, 122–23; English trans-lation, *Economy and Society*, 212–15). In other passages on the concept of *Herrschaft*, however, Weber stressed the element of compliance to an order regardless of the motivation—including fear—upon which compliance is based (Weber, *Wirtschaft*, 28–29, 606–7; idem, *Economy*, 53–54, 946–47). See also the discussion of Weber's usage of *Herrschaft* by Guenther Roth in Weber, *Economy*, 61–62; and Reinhard Bendix, *Max Weber*, 292.

[13] Freyer, *Herrschaft*, 31.

differing degrees by various peoples in the course of history, Freyer wrote of the ability to create a legitimate *Herrschaft* as the evidence of the "political substance" of the *Volk*.[14]

Freyer had always been attracted to the vision of a political collectivity united by its subordination to some common ethical purpose. In another lecture delivered on the eve of the Third Reich, entitled "The Political Concept of the *Volk*," Freyer endorsed the new *völkisch* nationalism now transforming Germany because, in contrast to the democratic nationalism of western Europe, it was both "revolutionary" and "conservative"—"revolutionary" in that it called for a politicization of the *Volk* and the creation of a new positive epoch, "conservative" in that it aimed to preserve the historical heritage (*Erbe*) of the German *Volk*.[15] Yet, as was frequently the case in Freyer's writings, the ethical content that the *Volk* was to preserve remained extraordinarily nebulous. Collective self-assertion remained the "ethical" purpose for the sake of which the *Volk* was to be politicized.[16]

By the time Freyer's lectures reached print in mid-1933, the politicization of the German *Volk* was in full swing.

The Gleichschaltung *of the University of Leipzig,*
1933–1934

The *Gleichschaltung* of the German universities—their "synchronization" with the aims of National Socialism—occurred by virtue of pressures from below, from above, and from inside the faculty. The experience of Freyer, his students and colleagues in the philosophical faculty of the University of Leipzig, and his friends elsewhere provide examples of the various directions from which *Gleichschaltung* came and the forms that it took.

From below came pressure from the student body. As we have seen, the student council had been dominated by the National Socialist Student League (Nationalsozialistischer Deutscher Studentenbund, or NSDStB) for some two years before Hitler's seizure of power. The council was the first institution at the university to be restructured along National Socialist lines. On 22 April 1933 the elective, democratic constitution of the student council was replaced by the *Führersystem*. The change came about by order of a federal law but had been demanded by the Nazi-dominated national council of students (Deutsche

[14] Ibid., 36.
[15] Freyer, *Politische Begriff*, 18. Freyer referred to non-Nazi theorists such as Moeller van den Bruck, Max H. Boehm, and Wilhelm Stapel.
[16] Ibid., 23

Studentenschaft) as its national congress of July 1932.[17] As occurred elsewhere during the first year of the new *Reich*, Nazi students, emboldened by events at the national level and confident that they would no longer be subject to discipline by the faculty or the government, destroyed books by authors considered to be enemies of the *Reich* and disrupted the lectures of professors considered critical of the regime.[18] Yet such actions did not play a major role at Leipzig. More important in terms of its effect on the university was the demand by students that they be consulted on new faculty appointments, to pass upon the ideological fitness of the candidates. Above all it was in their capacity as potential informers, ready to report critical statements by faculty members (and by each other) to party authorities, that the National Socialist students influenced the atmosphere of the academy in Leipzig as elsewhere.

It was the *Gleichschaltung* from above that had the most dramatic and far-reaching effects.[19] Two weeks after the Reichstag's passage of the Enabling Act, which conferred dictatorial power upon the Nazi-dominated government, the Law for the Restoration of the Professional Civil Service was promulgated by the Ministry of the Interior on 7 April 1933.[20] The law provided for dismissal from the civil service on grounds of inadequate training (a euphemism for those appointed by virtue of political affiliation before 1933), lack of political reliability, and "non-Aryan" descent (except when the incumbent had been appointed before the war, had fought in the war, or had lost a father or son in the war). Since privately owned institutes of higher education were

[17] See the April 1933 issues of the *Leipziger Studentenschaft*. On the July 1932 congress of the Deutsche Studentenbund, see Anselm Faust, *Der Nationalsozialistische Deutsche Studentenbund*, 2:39–42.

[18] Giles, *German Students*, 119ff.

[19] Useful general accounts of the *Gleichschaltung* of the universities are found in Karl Dietrich Bracher, *Stufen der Machtergreifung*, 420–40; Gerhard Schulz, *Die Anfänge des totalitären Maßnahmenstaates*, 237–42; Karl Dietrich Bracher, *The German Dictatorship*, 247–71. Two important collections of essays are Hans-Joachim Lieber et al., *Universitätstage, 1966: Nationalsozialismus und die deutsche Universität*; and Manfred Heinemann, ed., *Erziehung und Schulung im Dritten Reich*, vol. 2: *Hochschule und Erwachsenbildung*. Uwe Dietrich Adam, *Hochschule und Nationalsozialismus: Die Universität Tubingen*

im Dritten Reich, is an excellent case study of one university during the Nazi era. Also valuable for comparative purposes, though narrower and legalistic, is Birgit Vezina, *"Die Gleichschaltung" der Universität Heidelberg*. Outstanding disciplinary histories include Helmut Heiber, *Walther Frank und sein Reichsinstitut für die Geschichte des neuen Deutschlands*; Alan D. Beyerchen, *Scientists under Hitler*; and Ulfried Geuter, *Die Professionalisierung der deutschen Psychologie im Nationalsozialismus*. Edward Y. Hartshorne, *The German Universities and National Socialism* (1937), is a contemporary study of enduring value.

[20] The most thorough study of the origins and workings of the law is in Hans Mommsen, *Beamtentum im Dritten Reich*; see also Martin Broszat, *The Hitler State*, 241–61. The most thorough discussion of the law as applied to the universities is in Vezina, 31–48.

unknown in Germany, all German university professors were civil servants and hence subject to the new decrees.

Friends of Hans Freyer were involved in both the drafting of this law and its implementation within the university.

Freyer's friend Johannes Popitz was among those involved in formulating the law. Increasingly critical during the 1920s of the pluralistic party democracy of Weimar, Popitz had been appointed Prussian minister of finance in October 1932 by Franz von Papen. With Hitler's assumption of power at the end of January 1933, he was temporarily demoted to minister without portfolio, but he resumed his former post on 24 April 1933. Two days later he expressed to the Mittwochs-Gesellschaft—a small study circle that included distinguished scholars, bureaucrats, and army officials—his relief at the elimination of the pluralistic state of Weimar, which had been dominated by parties and interest groups lacking an "ideal of the total." Like Carl Schmitt, Popitz had not been a supporter of Hitler before January 1933 but now hoped that National Socialism would provide a vehicle for the reestablishment of a strong German state and for a new "*Herrschaft* based on knowledge and a sense of responsibility, tied to the *Volk* and serving it."[21] He was confident that it was possible for men like himself to "tutor" the more responsible leaders of the party, to raise them to the level of statesmen. In an attempt to retain some influence on events, Popitz put his invaluable experience in the fields of taxation, budgetary planning, and administrative law at the disposal of the regime. Among his first contributions to the new regime was to participate in drafting the Law for the Restoration of the Professional Civil Service.[22]

Others close to Freyer were involved in the law's implementation. Wilhelm Ahlmann, Freyer's former student and his close friend in Leipzig, left for Berlin in the spring of 1933 to serve as adviser to the university division of the Prussian Ministry of Education.[23] Of independent means, he appears to have gone to Berlin as the equivalent of a dollar-a-year man, eager, as he told an old friend, to reverse the *Überfremdung* (foreign infiltration) of German scholarship—a contemporary euphemism for expelling Jews from the academy.[24] Ahlmann did not last in his governmental post, however, and left it in the autumn. More successful was Freyer's friend Johann Daniel Achelis, a junior professor of medicine at the University of Leipzig.[25] In March he too came to

[21] Bentin, *Popitz und Schmitt*, 38–39.

[22] Ibid., 44–45.

[23] Johann Daniel Achelis et al., *Tymbos für Wil-* *helm Ahlmann*, xi.

[24] Interview with Ellen Rhodius.

[25] Interview with Ernest Manheim.

Berlin to serve in the Prussian Education Ministry, where he remained as *Personalreferent* until his departure in September 1934 to assume a chair of physiology at the University of Heidelberg. As *Personalreferent* Achelis was the individual responsible for recommending new appointees to the many academic posts that opened up in 1933 as a result of the enforcement of the new law.[26]

Before March 1933 it was rare for German professors to hold actual membership in the NSDAP or to offer it public support.[27] Of the members of the faculty of philosophy at Leipzig, for example, only four appear to have joined the party before 1933, and of these only one—Arthur Golf, a professor of animal husbandry—was a full professor.[28] A public petition of German professors in favor of Hitler's presidential bid of November 1932 carried only two signatures from Leipzig.[29] The Reichstag election of March 1933 saw the first flurry of open professorial identification with the party. A proclamation of university professors in support of the National Socialist list carried sixteen signatures from Leipzig, most of them from non-*Ordinarien* (i.e., junior or unchaired professors).[30] The victory of the Nazis and the passage of the Enabling Act marked a turning point. In April and May half a dozen members of Leipzig's philosophical faculty joined the party. Among them were three friends of Hans Freyer: Helmut Berve, the chaired professor of ancient history; André Jolles, an unchaired professor of Germanic language and culture; and Arnold Gehlen, a young philosopher. So began the voluntary self-*Gleichschaltung* within the faculty itself.

The first measure of the *Gleichschaltung* from above struck at the faculty member most deeply identified with the opposition to National Socialism. On 20 March the Nazi-controlled Saxon Ministry of Education informed Gerhard Kessler, whose vociferous public attack on Hitler had led during the previous semester to the disruption of his lectures by Nazi students, that in order to avoid such disturbances, he was forbidden to teach during the upcoming semester on grounds of public security.[31] That summer Kessler was first placed under detention and then sent to a concentration camp. Released in the autumn of 1933, he went into hiding under an assumed name before emigrating to Istanbul.[32] Kessler's opposition to National Socialism had occurred beyond

[26] On Achelis, see BDC, File: "Johann Daniel Achelis."

[27] See Faust, "Professoren."

[28] UAL, Philosophische Fakultät, E66, Betr. NSDAP.

[29] "Deutsche Hochschullehrer für Adolf Hitler!" *Völkische Beobachter*, 5 November 1932.

[30] "Die deutsche Geisteswelt für Liste 1," *Völkische Beobachter*, Süddeutsche Ausgabe 62, 3 March 1933, Beiblatt.

[31] Wilhelm Hartnacke to Gerhard Kessler, 20 March 1933, UAL, PA Kessler, 99; also *Leipziger Neueste Nachrichten*, 24 March 1933.

[32] UAL, PA Kessler, 107–8, 121–23.

the boundaries of the academy, and he was the only member of the Leipzig faculty to meet so harsh a fate in 1933. Yet his treatment certainly served to heighten the atmosphere of fear that began to pervade the faculty during the spring and summer of 1933.

This fear was motivated by the more mundane concern of holding onto one's job, a concern no doubt exacerbated by the financial insecurity of most of the Leipzig faculty, including Freyer. Beginning in April and continuing through August, professors opened their newspapers each morning to discover which of their colleagues had been dismissed by the government under the provisions of the Law for the Restoration of the Professional Civil Service. Faculty meetings began with the announcement of the latest colleagues to have been prematurely *emeritiert* and forced into retirement or to have had their *venia legendi* (permission to teach) withdrawn.[33]

By the end of the autumn of 1933 some nineteen faculty members had been removed from their teaching posts. Among these were several prominent members of the faculty of philosophy. Gerhard Kessler was the first. Siegmund Hellmann, a professor of medieval history forced on the faculty by the Saxon Ministry of Education in 1923, was another of those removed from office. As a Jew by birth and a democrat by persuasion, Hellmann was doubly anathema to the regime. Following his dismissal he moved to Munich. There he worked on a history of Germany until deported to Theresienstadt in July 1942, where he died some months later.[34] Hans Driesch, a senior professor of philosophy, was prematurely retired by the regime in September 1933 because of his support during the Weimar Republic for leftist and pacifist professors who had been threatened by their students.[35]

By May and June the *Gleichschaltung* from above, from below, and from inside the faculty was proceeding apace. From above came the decree that any student not of "German ancestry" would be required to submit a "declaration of descent."[36] Shortly thereafter the *Leipziger Neueste Nachrichten*—the town's leading conservative newspaper—carried an item in its regular columns devoted to university affairs, reporting on the relative percentage of "Aryan" and "non-Aryan" students in the various faculties of the university.[37]

[33] See, e.g., "Protokoll der Sitzung der gesamten philosophischen Fakultät, 27 September 1933," UAL.

[34] On the dismissals of 1933, see Herbert Helbig, *Universität Leipzig*, 106; Manfred Unger, "Georg Sacke"; and Gerhard Heitz, "Rudolf Kotzschke (1867–1949)," 262–74. On Hellmann, see Heimpel, "Nekrolog"; and Heiber, *Walther Frank*, 697.

[35] Hans Driesch, *Lebenserinnerungen*, 271.

[36] *Leipziger Studentenschaft*, 23 May 1933.

[37] "Arische und nichtarische Studenten an der Universität Leipzig," *Leipziger Neueste Nachrichten*, 21 July 1933, 2.

From below came the "Campaign of Enlightenment against the Un-German Spirit" (*Aufklärungsfeldzug wider den undeutschen Geist*), in which students gathered and burned works by "un-German" authors from libraries across the country.[38] The University of Leipzig appears to have been spared the worst excesses of this campaign: students merely removed the books from the student library, rather than actually incinerating them.[39]

The most thoughtful proposal for the political transformation of the university from within the Leipzig faculty came from Hans Freyer, in a series of lectures delivered in May and June and entitled "The Political Semester: A Proposal for the Reform of the University."[40] Freyer's booklet was one of a score of works devoted to this problem published in the early months of the National Socialist regime.[41] Yet Freyer's booklet was not primarily a response to the new pressures from above and below but a further concretization of plans for a politicization of the university that he had been developing since 1931.

Between the publication of *Revolution von rechts* and the National Socialist seizure of power Freyer had lectured widely to pedagogues and philosophers of education on the contemporary crisis of education.[42] The transformation of the meaningless cultural order of the present through political action was a prerequisite for a new educational ideal, Freyer had maintained.

Freyer began "The Political Semester" with the proclamation of a new educational ideal that had originated in the youth movement and had by virtue of recent events become "the valid norm" for the entire society.

The educational ideal that is valid for us is the ideal of the *political man*, who is rooted in his *Volkstum*, who regards himself as historically responsible for the fate of his state, and who devotes himself with spiritual sovereignty to the transformation of the future.[43]

The Germans, according to Freyer, were at long last becoming a political *Volk*. As such they required not a "free-floating intelligentsia" but rather "an estate

---

[38] Hans-Wolfgang Stratz, "Die studentische 'Aktion wider den undeutschen Geist' im Frühjahr 1933."

[39] *Leipziger Studentenschaft*, 22 June 1933.

[40] Hans Freyer, *Das politische Semester: Ein Vorschlag zur Universitätsreform* (1933). The contract for the book was signed with Diederichs Verlag on 22 May 1933, at which time the manuscript was complete. The book sold 930 copies in 1933, after which it became passé (Cologne, Eugen Diederichs Verlag Archiv).

[41] Several such plans are discussed in Geoffrey Giles, "Die Idee der politischen Universität: Hochschulreform nach der Machtergreifung"; also the comprehensive review of works on the subject by Hugo Marx in the *Zeitschrift für Sozialforschung* 3 (1934): 137–42.

[42] Hans Freyer, "Zur Bildungskrise der Gegenwart" (1931); idem, "Die Universität als hohe Schule des Staates" (1932); idem, "Zur Ethik des Berufes" (1933).

[43] Freyer, *Semester*, 7–9.

of the politically educated" (*einen Stand politisch Gebildeter*). The moral authority of the university depended upon its ability to fulfill the task of creating such
a group.[44]

The process of political cultivation (*politische Bildung*), Freyer wrote, was
based upon the broader process of political education (*politische Erziehung*),
which created the *will* to devote oneself to *Volk* and *Staat*. It was to universal
military conscription and to obligatory national labor service that Freyer
looked as the institutional basis of political education.[45] The reinstitution of
universal conscription had long been demanded by the right as a first step toward "breaking the chains of Versailles" and the reassertion of German power.
Labor service had been pioneered by Freyer's students in the youth movement
on a voluntary basis, and even before 1933 Freyer had expressed the hope that
it would be absorbed by the state and made a universal obligation.[46] Labor
service on behalf of the state, Freyer maintained, would rescue labor from its
degraded modern condition as a commodity, provided by contract for the sake
of individual gain. It would create a new "ethos of work" beyond "bourgeois
and proletarian materialism" that would form the basis of a new "national
socialism."[47]

The process of political cultivation within the university was to occur within
the context of professional training and through the addition of a "political semester." To the normal course of disciplinary or professional studies would be
added courses devoted to "the political significance of the vocation in question
and its meaning in the collective order."[48]

The centerpiece of Freyer's proposal for university reform was the "political
semester," a sort of political general education curriculum that would be obligatory for all students during their first semester of studies. Freyer conceived of
these lectures as on the borderline between social science and ideology: "neither scientific lectures in the conventional sense of the word nor patriotic ser-
mons in the sense of the patriotic instruction of the war years." Their purpose

44 Ibid., 16.
45 Ibid., 18.
46 Hans Freyer, "Arbeitslager."
47 Freyer, *Semester*, 19–20.
48 Freyer, *Semester*, 32. As an example of the
political aspect of vocational training, Freyer
suggested that doctors be instructed in "the historical laws of the rise and decline of *Völker*; the
social conditions under which contemporary
people fall sick and are healed; the biological basis of historical greatness and decline; and the

preservation and dilution of racial purity" (p.
33). This rare reference to race was not merely a
bow to the spirit of the times; Freyer had used
similar words some years earlier in describing
the vocation of the physician. Like so many of
his contemporaries in the 1920s he appears to
have had a vague belief in the importance of eu-
genics, though this was never a significant element of his social and political thought. See
Hans Freyer, "Der Arzt und die Gesellschaft"
(1929).

was to convey to the student "a sense of the norms of political greatness," insight into the dynamics of political events, and the factual basis for comprehending Germany's contemporary political situation. The curriculum was thus to provide a historical and factual basis for judging contemporary events, but also to awaken the student's "ethical awareness."[49]

The themes suggested by Freyer for such lecture series are worth noting, both because they presage his own subsequent teaching and because of the contrast they present to the public lecture series actually implemented in Leipzig by the National Socialist Student League. Topics that Freyer saw as appropriate for sensitizing the student to the norms of political greatness were "Caesar's Monarchy and the Rule of Pompeii," "Friedrich the Great's Struggle for Silesia," and "Bismarck Founds the Empire." In order to provide insight into the dynamic of political events, Freyer recommended courses entitled "The Struggle for the Rhine," "The Construction of England's Global Empire," "Prussia and Germany," and "The Structure of Armies and the Forms of War." To convey a factual basis for the understanding of Germany's position in the contemporary world, Freyer proposed courses entitled "The System of Versailles," "The Great Powers of Contemporary World Politics," "The Germans of Middle and Eastern Europe," and "The Structure of German Industry."[50]

In this manner Freyer sought to transform the university into the "elite school of the state" (*hohe Schule des Staates*) that he had advocated before 1933. Three elements of his proposal stand out. Despite some of its rhetoric, and in contrast to some other contemporary proposals, Freyer's plans left almost all of the existing institutional structure of the university intact, including disciplinary specialization and faculty control.[51] Despite the emphasis in his political writings on the desirability of a total state, Freyer shrank from applying his strictures to his own institution and demanded instead that the university transform *itself* from within.[52] Lastly, the substance of his "political semester," though ideological, was intended to utilize the disciplines of history, sociology, and political science to convey an ethos of political grandeur that was broadly radical conservative rather than narrowly National Socialist in orientation.[53]

[49] Freyer, *Semester*, 22.

[50] Ibid., 23.

[51] Compare the contemporary proposal of Ernst Krieck, a National Socialist ideologist appointed rector of the University of Frankfurt in May 1933. In his *Die Erneuerung der Universität* (1933), he encouraged the students to play the decisive role in determining the content of their courses.

[52] Freyer, *Semester*, 16.

[53] Again the comparison of Freyer's proposal with that of Krieck is instructive. The latter constantly invoked the *Führer*, the *Bewegung*, and Horst Wessel, as well as the central role of racial science in the new curriculum.

During the months immediately before and after the *Machtergreifung*, Hans Freyer's star rose within his own university and in the broader German academic firmament. From the representative of a young and somewhat peripheral discipline, he moved to the center of public attention in Leipzig. In November 1932 his colleagues in the philosophical faculty elected him as their dean; in January 1933 they chose him to address the *Reichsgründungsfeier* before the assembled faculty and student body. During the early months of the new regime, many National Socialist students looked to him as a mentor; and the public lectures that comprised *Das politische Semester* were delivered to an audience that filled the *Auditorium maximum* of the university to overflowing.[54] During the propaganda campaign preceding the plebiscite of November 1933 affirming Germany's withdrawal from the League of Nations, it was Hans Freyer who addressed the assembled faculty on "The University Campaign for the Twelfth of November."[55]

While for a few of Freyer's friends and students the *Gleichschaltung* brought scholarly careers in Germany to an abrupt end, and while others lived with the fear of having their careers cut short, for Freyer himself and many of those around him the *Gleichschaltung* was a source not only of collective hope but of personal advance.

Those hardest hit by the events of 1933 were of course Freyer's students and colleagues of Jewish origin or of leftist orientation. As we have seen, Ernst Manheim, Freyer's most advanced student, was forced by events to leave Germany for London on the eve of his planned habilitation. Fritz Borinski, the leader of the Leuchtenburgkreis and the assistant director of the Seminar für freies Volksbildungswesen, which connected the Leipzig Volkshochschule to the university, found that by August 1933 the latter institutions had been *gleichgeschaltet*, while the Leuchtenburgkreis had dissolved itself under pressure from the police. The *Neue Blätter für den Sozialismus*, to which he had been a frequent contributor, had been banned. Its editor, Freyer's former colleague Paul Tillich, had been expelled from his chair of philosophy at the University of Frankfurt. Soon Borinski, like Manheim and Tillich, was forced to emigrate.[56]

How did Freyer feel about the hardships created for some of his friends, stu-

---

[54] On Freyer's prestige among students oriented to National Socialism, see Helmut Schelsky, "Zur Entstehungsgeschichte der bundesdeutschen Soziologie," in his *Rückblicke eines 'Anti-Soziologen,'* 23. Freyer's public lecture of June 1933, "Neugestaltung der deutschen Hochschule und die Bedeutung der Wehr-

dienst," is summarized in *Leipziger Studentenschaft*, 21 June 1933, 31.

[55] Hans Freyer, "Der Einsatz der Universität fur den 12. November," *Leipziger Hochschulzeitung*, 10 November 1933 (copy in UAL, PA Freyer, 83).

[56] See Fritz Borinski, "Autobiographie," 29.

dents, and colleagues by the National Socialist revolution he supported? The question cannot be answered with certainty, since Freyer left behind no diaries and few extant letters from these years. Yet given his belief in the redemptive role of political power in the process of cultural integration, it is likely that he sought whatever solace he required in the oft-heard dictum of those years: *Wo gehobelt wird, fallen Späne* (Where there is planing to be done, shavings must fall)—the German equivalent of "You can't make an omelet without breaking eggs."[57]

The process of *Gleichschaltung* had its winners as well as its losers, and many of Freyer's friends and students were among the former. During the summer of 1933 the head of the Office for Political Education of the Leipzig branch of the National Socialist Student League proposed the creation of a "Seminar for Political Education," to be connected with Freyer's sociological institute, through which university professors would provide "political education" to German workers who would otherwise lack such opportunities. Freyer as well as the rector (Achelis) were amenable, as was the Saxon Ministry of the Interior. Shortly thereafter the Seminar für freies Volksbildungswesen, which had been headed by Fritz Borinski under the sponsorship of Theodor Litt's educational institute, was transferred to Freyer's sociological institute, where it was to be headed by Freyer's friend Gunther Ipsen. Control of the seminar therefore moved from Freyer's democratically oriented colleague Litt and his Social Democratic–oriented student Borinski to his radical conservative friend and colleague Ipsen. It would ultimately reopen in a new form under the directorship of Freyer's student Werner Studentkowski, a National Socialist activist.[58]

To some of those around Freyer, the first wave of *Gleichschaltung* in 1933 and 1934 destroyed the possibility of a scholarly career in Germany. But for many of those who had shared his radical conservative orientation, the events of 1933 and 1934 pushed them up the academic ladder, as the posts of those removed were filled with men regarded as intellectual supporters of the new regime. Since the decision-making posts regarding university appointments were filled in the Prussian Ministry of Education by Freyer's friends Achelis and (through September 1933) Ahlmann, and (beginning in February 1934) in the Saxon Ministry of Education by his doctoral student Werner Student-

[57] On the invocation of this dictum in 1933 and the mentality it assumes, see Karl Dietrich Bracher, "Die Gleichschaltung der deutschen Universität," in Lieber et al., *Universitätstage*, 129–30.

[58] UAL, B1/14/53, File: "Seminar für politische Bildung."

kowski, it is not surprising that intellectuals from Freyer's circle filled so many of the academic holes left by the purge.[59] Their climb up the slippery pole was often aided by membership in the party or in one of its associated organizations, such as the SA.

Typical was the case of Freyer's close friend and colleague Gunther Ipsen. Ipsen had received his habilitation from Felix Krueger in 1925. Since that time his career advancement had been slow. During the summer of 1933 the Seminar für freies Volksbildungswesen was put under his control. In October he was called to the University of Königsberg as *außerordentlicher Professor*. In November he joined the SA. In January 1935 he was named to a full professorship. In 1937 he became a member of the NSDAP. Following the *Anschluß* with Austria, Ipsen was called to a chair at the University of Vienna, where he remained until conscripted during the war.[60]

Another striking success story was Arnold Gehlen. Something of a philosophical prodigy, Gehlen was habilitated in 1931 at age twenty-seven by Hans Driesch, the senior professor of philosophy at Leipzig. Active in the Fichte-Gesellschaft and Fichte-Hochschule, he was part of Freyer's social and intellectual circle. On 1 April 1933 he joined the Nazi party and his career took off. On 6 May he was appointed to teach philosophy at the University of Frankfurt as a temporary replacement for Paul Tillich, who had been expelled from his chair because of his leftist political orientation. Gehlen spent the following semester as Freyer's *Assistent* in Leipzig. Shortly thereafter he was appointed as a temporary replacement for his own teacher, Driesch, who had been prematurely retired by the new regime. In November 1934 he was appointed as Driesch's successor. Four years later he accepted the chair of philosophy at Königsberg. In 1940 he joined Ipsen in Vienna, eventually heading the institutes of philosophy and psychology there.[61]

Freyer's Institute of Politics

In the autumn of 1933, Hans Freyer was named to succeed Walter Goetz as head of the Institut für Kultur- und Universalgeschichte of the University of

[59] Studentkowski's appointment as *Oberregierungsrat* in the Saxon Ministerium für Volksbildung as of 1 February 1934 is noted in his "SA-Personalbogen," BDC.

[60] UAL, PA Ipsen, 3–4, 25, 38, 40; BAK, R21, Wissenschaftler Kartei, Gunther Ipsen. See also the (somewhat inaccurate) Internationales Bio-graphisches Archiv (Munzinger Archiv), Gunther Ipsen. For a character sketch, see Schelsky, "Entstehungsgeschichte," 27.

[61] On Gehlen's career, see Werner Rügemer, *Philosophische Anthropologie und Epochenkrise*, 92ff, and the appendix to this book.

Leipzig, one of the largest and best-endowed institutes of historical research in Germany. A study of the process by which he came to hold so prestigious a post demonstrates how the interaction of the *Gleichschaltung* from below, from above, and from within brought ever greater prominence to Hans Freyer during the early stages of the new *Reich*.

Walter Goetz was due to retire in October 1933. In November 1932 a faculty commission was convened to recommend a successor to the Saxon Ministry of Education. On 30 January 1933, the day of Hitler's appointment as chancellor, the commission recommended Hermann Aubin, professor of medieval history at Breslau, to fill the chair that Goetz would vacate. The response of the Ministry of Education, now in Nazi hands, came on 1 April. The ministry refused the faculty's nominee and requested a list of three possible candidates from the faculty.[62]

When the commission reconvened on 8 May, Freyer read aloud the letter from the ministry. He went on to explain the unarticulated reason for the rejection, namely political objections to Aubin. Professor Frings, a friend of Aubin, volunteered to provide materials proving Aubin's political reliability. Goetz, a member of the commission to name his successor, expressed his concern that none of the other candidates possessed sufficient breadth to head the institute, which had a broad, comparativist orientation. Finally Helmut Berve, a senior professor of ancient history who had recently joined the Nazi party and was to become a figure of great influence at Leipzig in the months and years ahead, recommended Oswald Spengler, perhaps the most influential radical conservative author of the 1920s, as Goetz's successor. After mulling over the suggestion for a week, the other members of the committee agreed.[63] In their memorandum to the minister the commission noted that in recommending Spengler they had considered "new facets that have come to the fore in view of the changed cultural-political situation." They praised not only his historical works but his political tracts of the 1920s, which had made him "a great pioneer of our national future," and noted that his selection was favored by the student body.[64]

The ministry accepted the recommendation of the faculty, and Freyer, in his capacity as dean, was dispatched to negotiate with the candidate.[65] Spengler

---

[62] UAL, B2/20/49, 4–23.

[63] "Niederschrift der Sitzung der Kommission für Wiederbesetzung des ordentlichen Professur für Geschichte, 8 May 1933; 15 May 1933," UAL, B2/20/49, 25–26.

[64] Philosophische Fakultät der Universität Leipzig to Ministerium für Volksbildung zu Dresden, 18 May 1933, UAL, B2/20/49, 31–37.

[65] Ibid., 38; interview with Käthe Freyer.

refused the offer, explaining that his style of work demanded near-total seclusion and that his constitution was such that bouts of extended conversation inevitably resulted in headaches.[66] The faculty commission convened once again in July. Faced with a ministry seemingly determined to transform the institute in a more ideological direction, the faculty submitted a letter from its first choice, Hermann Aubin, attesting to his devotion to the cause of the *Volk*, and recommended that the institute be transformed into a center for *Deutschtumsforschung* (Germanic studies). Freyer was delegated to present the commission's case to the ministry.[67] But once again the faculty's nomination of Aubin was rejected from above.

Suddenly a multiplicity of claimants stepped forward with plans for the professorial chair and the institute. One Professor Ueberschaar—a junior professor of Japanese studies and a member of the NSDAP since November 1932—spoke to the ministry in his capacity as *Führer* of the Saxon branch of the university division of the National Socialist Teachers Association, with a plan to devote the institute to the development of a National Socialist historiography. As its prospective head he recommended Hans Neumann of Bonn, who had recently distinguished himself by speaking at the student book burnings there.[68] The Nazi student association had yet another plan. Wolf Friedrich was a student of Freyer's who at the time was both prominent in the Nazi student association and an adviser on university affairs to the leadership of the Nazi party in Saxony. Friedrich discussed with Freyer and with the ministry plans for the creation of a *wissenschaftliche Führerschule* (scientific school of leadership) to be connected to the institute.[69]

Out of this whirlwind of talks, it was ultimately Hans Freyer who emerged as victor in the battle for control of the institute. In September the ministry informed the faculty that it intended to transform the primary purpose of the institute into "political education"; the study of history was to serve as a means

---

[66] Oswald Spengler to Ministerium für Volksbildung, 24 June 1933, UAL, B2/20/49, 39.

[67] "Niederschrift der Sitzung der Kommission für Wiederbesetzung des ordentlichen Professur für Geschichte, 3 July 1933," UAL, B2/20/49, 40–45.

[68] Von Seydowitz (of the Ministerium) to Dekan der philosophischen Fakultät, 14 July 1933, UAL B1/14/19, 2:4–6. On Neumann, see Bollmus, *Amt Rosenberg*, 320–21.

[69] The conversation is mentioned in Hans Freyer to "Herr Kollege" (probably the dean of the faculty) 13 September 1933, UAL B1/14/19, 2:13–17. On Friedrich's position at the time, see National Archives, T81, Roll 239, frame 5024386, 22 September 1933, in which he is listed as *Gaufachberater für Hochschulfragen bei der Gauleitung Sachsen, NSDAP*. When he received his doctorate the following year, he was tested by Hans Freyer in the field of sociology (UAL, Promotionsbuch 6). On Friedrich, see also Faust, *Studentenbund*, passim.

toward "a deepened understanding of contemporary politics." The new institute was to be headed by Hans Freyer, who was to be appointed as Goetz's successor. The ministry added that a program of National Socialist "political education" was to occur in the upcoming semester in connection with the
institute. It was to consist of a lecture series "on the idea of National Socialism
and on racial practice" (*Rassenpflege*), which was to be compulsory for all students. The program would also offer courses on various aspects of National
Socialism, attendance at which would be open to all. The ministry informed
Freyer that it "would be grateful" if Werner Studentkowski could be integrated into the new institute.[70]

In an accompanying letter the minister of education, Hartnacke, informed
the faculty that "the spirit of National Socialism must permeate the various
branches of scholarship . . . scientific thought must be tied to the political will
of the state. . . . It is a matter of transforming and redesigning the contemporary university in the spirit of National Socialism." As proof of his intentions,
he recommended that the faculty consider filling the chair of economics formerly held by Gerhard Kessler with Dr. Walter Schmidt, the economics editor
of the *Völkische Beobachter*. The chair of journalism (*Zeitungswissenschaft*), he
wrote, would henceforth be devoted to the role of propaganda in the new
state.[71]

In response to the ministry's declaration, Freyer wrote a long letter to the
faculty commission explaining his intentions and requesting the commission's
approval of his appointment. He sought to assure his colleagues that under his
leadership the institute would maintain its scientific character even while carrying out the task of political education. "I am convinced," he wrote, "that the
university must play an active role in the political education of its students on
its own and with its specific means, that is to say through scientific teaching"
(*wissenschaftliche Lehre*). It is clear from his letter that he sought to use the institute to realize his plans for political education as spelled out in *Das politische
Semester*. These plans included obligatory lecture courses in the first semester,
as well as an evening lecture series. This political education was to be based on
scholarship and carried out under the control of a faculty member, namely
Freyer himself. Only if the plans for a "*wissenschaftliche Führerschule*" associated
with the institute were realized would there be a post for Studentkowski,
Freyer wrote.

[70] "Abschrift aus der Verordnung d. Min.
f.V., 5 September 1933," UAL, B1/14/19, 2:11–
12.

[71] Wilhelm Hartnacke to Philosophische Fakultät, 5 September 1933, copy in UAL, PA
Freyer, 69–71.

The disciplinary focus of the institute would now shift from history to "political science" (*politische Wissenschaften*). Yet the content of its courses was not to differ radically from those which Freyer had offered under the rubric of sociology. "It has long been my conviction that sociology has assumed the legacy of the old science of politics and that in so doing it must rest heavily on historical studies," Freyer noted in the letter to his colleagues. Indeed, the disciplinary designation of those who majored at the new institute could remain "sociology," and the institute of sociology might live on as a division of the new institute. Freyer suggested that since sociology would be represented at the new institute by himself, it would be advisable to fill his existing chair (of sociology) with a young historian with an interest in political education.[72]

The response of the faculty commission to the nomination of Freyer was by and large one of relief. The tone was set by Freyer's friend Helmut Berve, who emphasized that with this move the faculty would grasp the initiative on the question of political education. He regarded Freyer as brilliantly suited to the post and was pleased that a candidate of scholarly significance had been chosen. His statement reflected a widespread fear among university faculties that control of their institutions was slipping out of their hands and into those of the Nazi students and of the Nazi-dominated Ministry of Education.[73] Other members of the commission who regretted the reorientation of the institute from the purposes of its founder, Karl Lamprecht, nevertheless welcomed the appointment of Freyer "as a way of preserving the institute and its treasures," a reference to the considerable endowment of the institute and its library of some fifty thousand volumes. The members of the commission were of course aware that it was not they who had suggested the appointment of Freyer or the transformation of the institute into a center for "political education"—and that both would occur regardless of their wishes. They seem to have felt that, given their options, the appointment of Freyer was the least of evils.[74]

Yet the ultimate fate of political education at Leipzig was more modest than Freyer had envisioned in his *Das politische Semester* and less controlled by Freyer than he had planned. When the new semester began, there were in fact three levels of "political education." The Nazi-controlled student association (*Studen-*

[72] Hans Freyer to "Herr Kollege," 13 September 1933, copy in UAL, B1/14/19, 2:13–17. The letter was sent from Burgbrohl in western Germany where Freyer was vacationing.

[73] See Adam, *Hochschule*, 49–57; Giles, "Idee," 50–60; and Reece C. Kelly, "German Professoriate under Nazism: A Failure of Totalitarian Aspirations," 262–64.

[74] "Niederschrift der Sitzung der Kommission für Wiederbesetzung des ordentlichen Professur für Geschichte, 21 September 1933," UAL, B1/14/19, 2: 18–19.

tenschaft) successfully asserted its right to conduct all courses for new students through its "Office for Political Education."[75]

All further general political education was placed in the hands of a new "Seminar for Political Education" created at the initiative of the educational office (*Gauschulungsamt*) of the NSDAP and formally connected to Freyer's new institute. It was headed by Freyer's former doctoral student Werner Studentkowski, who by the autumn of 1933 was not only head of the Nazi educational office for Saxony (*Gauschulungsleiter*) but a member of the Reichstag.[76] The seminar sponsored courses by Studentkowski and others on National Socialist themes, as well as an evening lecture series in which faculty members lectured on topics of purported political import (Berve on "The Significance of Race in History," Freyer on "The Peasantry," Gehlen on "German Idealism and the Present").[77]

The seminar was officially opened with great fanfare with a ceremony in the auditorium of the university in November 1933. Among the guests of honor were the minister of education, Dr. Hartnacke, and Martin Mutschmann, the Nazi *Gauleiter* appointed by Hitler as *Reichstatthalter* in Saxony and the de facto ruler of the province at the time. Mutschmann, among the least educated of the Nazi *Gauleiter*, told his audience that in the past age of liberalism a good deal of complicated knowledge had been crammed into the *Volk*, but since it was "false knowledge" it had remained without effect. He urged the students to turn to the new, uncomplicated, German conception of knowledge, which rested on the fundamental principle "You are nothing; your *Volk* is all" (*Du bist nichts; dein Volk ist alles*). After speeches by Hans Freyer and Werner Studentkowski, the ceremony ended with the singing of the "Horst-Wessel-Lied." It was an auspicious beginning.[78]

If this was a long way from the tone and substance of Freyer's *Das politische Semester*, the victory of unabashed National Socialist ideologues over the faculty for control of the political education of the student body was a pyrrhic one. For none of these courses were compulsory (probably a concession to the faculty), which made the entire enterprise rather insignificant, especially as the initial enthusiasm of the student body waned.[79] Finally in 1936, after years of

[75] Ministerium für Volksbildung to Metzdorf (of the NSDStB), 9 November 1933, Sächsisches Hauptarchiv Dresden, Ministerium für Volksbildung, 10230/41.

[76] *Akademische Reden gehalten am 31. Oktober 1934 in der Aula der Universität Leipzig aus Anlass des 525. Jahres ihres Gründung* (1934).

[77] Universität Leipzig, *Verzeichnis der Vorlesungen, 1933–34* (1933).

[78] *Leipziger Neueste Nachrichten*, 25 November 1933, 3.

[79] *Leipziger Hochschulzeitung*, 10 November 1933, copy in UAL, B1/14/53, 16.

petty competition between the National Socialist German Student League, the Nazi-controlled Deutsche Studentenschaft, and the party's *Gauschulungsamt*, it was ruled that exclusive control over political education was to rest with the National Socialist German Student League, and the "Seminar for Political Education" cut its ties with Freyer's institute.[80]

Freyer's hopes for contributing to the development of the new *Reich* through political education did find partial realization in the institute of which he had been appointed director. The institute did not formally change its name from the Institut für Kultur- und Universalgeschichte, and continued to offer a few traditional history courses each year, given mostly by Herbert Schönebaum, who had been *Assistent* at the institute since Karl Lamprecht's time. The bulk of the institute's courses, listed in the course catalogue under the rubric "politics and sociology," fulfilled the intentions outlined by Freyer in *Das politische Semester* and in his letter to the faculty.

The program of studies at Freyer's institute from 1933 through 1938 (when he assumed a post as visiting professor in Budapest) was clearly intended to produce the "estate of the politically cultivated" called for in his programmatic work of 1933. Its aim was to utilize history and sociology to prepare men for the exercise of *Herrschaft*, not in the sense of learning how to gain individual power but rather for the scientific formulation of the internal and foreign policy of the new *Reich*. With the inauguration of a new *Reich*, and hence a new potentially organic epoch, the task of social science was no longer one of criticism but one of aiding in the consolidation of the new totality.

The courses taught by Freyer himself reflected this aim. Some two-fifths of his offerings were devoted to politics. These included courses devoted to the history of political theory (the political thought of Plato, Machiavelli, and Nietzsche, and the history of utopianism), and to the political reflections of great German statesmen of the past who were regarded as models for the future. In this category were Friedrich the Great, Baron von Stein, and Bismarck.

Approximately half of Freyer's offerings fell under the broad rubric of sociology. Among them were courses in the history of sociological thought (especially in Germany) and the social structure of the German *Volk* in the nineteenth and twentieth centuries, as well as sociological topics with a contemporary ideological resonance, such as "Sociology of the Army," "*Aus-*

---

[80] See Sächsisches Hauptarchiv Dresden, Ministerium für Volksbildung, 10230/41, passim. On the ongoing conflict between the various student groups after 1933, see Faust, *Studentenbund*, 2:121–35.

landsdeutschtum," "Volk and Economy," "The Age of Capitalism," and "Problems of National Socialism."

A third broad area covered by the institute's offerings was foreign affairs. While Freyer lectured on "Contemporary World Powers," "The British Empire," and "Political History since Versailles," for the most part he confined himself to sponsoring lectures by others in this area. Each semester he chaired a colloquium at which papers were presented by scholars, politicians, and bureaucrats from inside and outside the University of Leipzig. These colloquia focused most frequently on problems of the *Auslandsdeutschen*, a topic of long-standing interest at the Institut für Kulturgeschichte but now of renewed ideological import. A second focus of the institute was southeastern Europe, to which Freyer increasingly turned his attention during the mid-1930s.

The teaching of contemporary foreign affairs rested primarily with several of Freyer's students, each of whom specialized in a region of particular concern to the foreign policy of the Third Reich. All had been students of Freyer's and Ipsen's before 1933 and had adopted a sociographic approach to their regions of expertise. Dr. Werner Markert was an expert on Soviet affairs and was secretary-general of the Society on Eastern Europe. Dr. Karl Günzel, who had received his doctorate from Freyer in 1934, developed a regional expertise on Yugoslavia. In both cases, their interests in eastern Europe stemmed from the youth movement, with its concern for the fate of the *Auslandsdeutschen* and for intercultural understanding between *Völker*. Both spent the final years of the Third Reich in the agencies of German military intelligence.[81]

Others who offered courses at Freyer's institute in the early years of the Third Reich were Arnold Gehlen, who taught political philosophy, and two holdovers from Freyer's sociological institute: Hugo Fischer, who taught political and general philosophy, and Joachim Wach, who offered courses on the philosophy of history and the sociology of religion.

The key figure at Freyer's institute, in addition to Freyer himself, was Karl-Heinz Pfeffer. He served as Freyer's *Assistent* beginning in late 1933, as a lecturer at the institute after 1934, and finally as acting director from 1938 until 1940, when he left for a more prominent position in Berlin. The case of Pfeffer illustrates how an intellectual disciple of Freyer could shift the activist orientation toward social science in which Freyer had pioneered toward the complete ideologization of social science favored by a totalitarian regime. Pfeffer's career provides an excellent example of how a sincere commitment to Na-

---

[81] Leipzig course catalogues; interview with Helmut Schelsky, Münster; interview with Hans Linde.

tional Socialism—understood in Freyer's terms of a revolution against the capitalistic, liberal "nineteenth century"—could blend with careerism to produce professional success in the Third Reich. While Pfeffer's attempt to reconceptualize sociological theory in totally ideological terms will be explored in the next chapter, his teaching activity and career path are of interest in the present context.

The Nazi seizure of power found Karl-Heinz Pfeffer at the other end of the world. He spent the period from August 1932 to September 1933 in Australia, conducting empirical research for a sociological study that he intended to use as the basis of his habilitation by Hans Freyer. The book, entitled *Die bürgerliche Gesellschaft in Australien*, combined a wealth of statistical evidence and information on trends in public opinion, as well as Pfeffer's own survey research on the self-understanding of Australians, and filtered it all through categories culled from Freyer's *Soziologie als Wirklichkeitswissenschaft*. Pfeffer concluded on the basis of his research that Australia was likely to remain a "bourgeois society" with goals that were *kleinbürgerlich* and unheroic, marked by latent but controlled class conflict.[82]

Yet even in far-off Sydney, Australia, Pfeffer had been active on behalf of the new revolution of the right, working with the German consul there to organize a group called the Bund der Freunde der Hitlerbewegung. By the time he returned home in November 1933, it was too late to join the NSDAP, the party having declared a membership freeze to prevent its dilution by careerists. Pfeffer did the next best thing and joined the SA.

In December 1933 Pfeffer came to Leipzig to act first as Freyer's *Assistent* at the Institut für Kultur- und Universalgeschichte, and after being habilitated by Freyer one year later, assumed the position of lecturer (*Dozent*) in Freyer's institute. In his letter of evaluation in support of Pfeffer's habilitation, Freyer was very positive not only about the candidate's work but about his character. "SA service and military sports [*Wehrsport*] are not externally imposed in his case but internally motivated obligations," wrote Freyer. (Indeed, Pfeffer was so earnest about the paramilitary *Wehrsport* that he lost the use of an eye during one such exercise.) In addition to his scholarly talent, Freyer continued, Pfeffer was always helpful to students. "He is predestined by his entire personality to become a *Dozent* of the desired new type," Freyer predicted.[83]

---

[82] Karl-Heinz Pfeffer, *Die bürgerliche Gesellschaft in Australien* (1936). The book was published in the series *Neue deutsche Forschung: Abteilung Volkslehre und Gesellschaftskunde*, edited by Gunther Ipsen.

[83] UAL, PA Pfeffer, 2–9, 35–36. On Pfeffer, see also *Kommittee zur Untersuchung ... Eine Dokumentation: Die wissenschaftliche und politische Karriere des Dr. phil. habil. Karl Heinz Pfeffer*.

At Freyer's institute Pfeffer taught a broad range of courses, almost all of which were ideologically charged. The largest group concerned rural sociology and the peasantry, themes pioneered in Leipzig by Gunther Ipsen. A second group of courses focused on ethnic Germans abroad and in the ethnically mixed regions of eastern Germany. A number of courses focused upon the sociological thought of German writers who were outside the conventional sociological canon, such as Justus Möser, Ernst Moritz Arndt, and Wilhelm Heinrich Riehl. Pfeffer also offered occasional courses in empirical methods and in the study of *Raumforschung*, a German version of regional planning that was to thrive in the course of the Third Reich as Germany conquered vast areas that it intended to resettle. Finally, Pfeffer, who had begun his university education in the field of English studies and whose spouse was British, offered courses on Britain and the British Empire. It was in this field as well as as a theorist of "German sociology" that Pfeffer was to make his mark in the late 1930s and 1940s.

All in all then, Freyer's institute of political education remained a partial but tangible realization of the plans he had set out in his pamphlet of 1933. Of his many plans and hopes of the year 1933, it was the only one to achieve even moderate success.

Institutional Self-Gleichschaltung: *The German Sociological Association*

The process by which Hans Freyer rose from marginality within the Deutsche Gesellschaft für Soziologie (DGS) to its presidency in the course of 1933 is instructive. It demonstrates how a dual role as academic social scientist and as political ideologist worked to the advantage of Freyer and those like him in the early stages of the new regime. It provides a case study of how a professional organization could be transformed from within, in the absence of the open threat of governmental intervention—a pattern often repeated in the first year of the new regime.[84] And it reveals that the hostility of National Socialist

[84] This account is based largely on the voluminous correspondence in the Nachlaß Tönnies, as well as on documents in the Nachlaß Plenge. The brief account by Leopold von Wiese, "Die Deutsche Gesellschaft für Soziologie, Persönliche Eindrücke in den ersten fünfzig Jahren," 16–17, is not entirely accurate, especially in its implication that the choice of Freyer to head the organization was due to explicit governmental pressure. There is no evidence for this claim in the documents, and indeed there is considerable evidence to the contrary. See also Carsten Klingemann, "Soziologen vor dem Nationalsozialismus: Szenen aus der Selbstgleichschaltung der Deutsche Gesellschaft für Soziologie."

ideologists and activists was directed not at sociology as such but at specific types of social theorizing.

From its refounding in 1919 through 1932, the DGS had been in the hands of Leopold von Wiese, whose liberal politics and formalistic sociology Hans Freyer had long opposed. During the 1920s and early 1930s, Freyer had betrayed little interest in the DGS or in the professionalization of the discipline of sociology. Freyer accepted an invitation to join the governing board (*Rat*) of the association in 1929,[85] but he appears to have kept a very low profile in the DGS through 1931. In February 1932, as we have seen, he played the role of antagonist to Wiese at the congress of German sociologists in Frankfurt, from which he departed in disgust.

The dismissal of many of the leading representatives of German sociology from their university posts during the summer of 1933 provided the background against which the self-*Gleichschaltung* of the DGS unfolded. Among the most prominent chairholders dismissed during this first wave were Theodor Geiger, Eugen Rosenstock-Huessy, Max Horkheimer, Paul Tillich, Karl Mannheim, and Alfred Weber. To many observers, including other sociologists, it may well have seemed as if their discipline as such was slated for extinction by the new National Socialist regime. Yet in fact it was only sociologists identified with the left (Geiger, Tillich, Weber) or those of Jewish origin (Rosenstock-Huessy, Horkheimer, Mannheim) who were ousted in this first wave. Nevertheless, the anxiety created among other practitioners of sociology must be taken into account in considering the events that followed, since many on the right identified the discipline of sociology as "Jewish" and "left."[86]

How inaccurate this characterization had been was soon to be demonstrated by events. Even during the Weimar Republic several of the better-known members of the DGS, such as Werner Sombart, Hans Freyer, and Carl Schmitt, had been associated with the radical conservative right. Yet the two men who had run the DGS since its refounding in 1919—Ferdinand Tönnies as its president, and Leopold von Wiese as its corresponding secretary—were identified with social democracy and Weimar liberalism respectively.

The eighth sociological convention (*Soziologentag*) of the DGS had been scheduled to take place in Kiel in April 1933 and was to honor Ferdinand Tönnies, one of the original founders of the society and its figurehead. Even before Hitler's accession to power, Tönnies had written to Wiese warning him of

---

[85] Wiese to Franz Wilhelm Jerusalem, 1 July 1933, NT.

[86] On the reputation of sociology during the

Weimar Republic, see Erhard Stölting, "Kontinuitäten und Brüche in der deutschen Soziologie 1933/34."

the negative light in which the Nazi-oriented press of Kiel would cast the proceedings and cautioning that Tönnies' very presence might provoke young Nazis to rioting. The uncertain situation created by the Nazi political victories of March led Wiese to postpone the convention.[87]

In late June, Wiese received a letter from Franz Wilhelm Jerusalem, a professor of law and sociology in Jena, bitterly attacking Wiese for running the DGS as a liberal organization. Jerusalem informed the leadership of the DGS that he and others who shared his objections had already arranged a convention of their own. Should the DGS object, the dissidents would found their own sociological association.

Wiese responded that although he was a liberal, he had made every effort to involve sociologists of all political and methodological orientations in the conferences of the DGS and in its governing board. He cited Hans Freyer as a representative of Jerusalem's own orientation who had joined the board of the DGS some years earlier. Since Freyer would probably attend the meeting of the board in August, wrote Wiese, Jerusalem's views were sure to get a hearing.[88] Jerusalem responded with a second letter, more abusive than the first.[89]

It was the threat of a counterorganization of sociologists more in keeping with the spirit of National Socialism that motivated Wiese to call an emergency meeting of the board. The meeting was attended by twelve members of the board; Freyer, however, was not among them. Before the meeting, Bernard Harms, head of the prestigious Institute on the World Economy at the University of Kiel and a senior member of the DGS, took the aging and somewhat disoriented Tönnies aside and explained to him the necessities of the situation as he and other members of the DGS understood them. The DGS must adapt itself to the new political circumstances created by the national revolution, Harms explained. "They" would not tolerate Tönnies as the president of the DGS, Harms continued—without specifying to Tönnies, or perhaps to himself, who "they" were. It was advisable therefore for Tönnies to step down and for the board to appoint Werner Sombart, who would not be objectionable to "them," in his stead. Harms's remarks expressed the consensus of the assembled members of the board, to whose wishes the exhausted and dispirited Tönnies acquiesced.[90]

Wiese opened the session by explaining that although the DGS had hereto-

---

[87] Ferdinand Tönnies to Wiese, 26 January 1933, NT; Wiese to Ferdinand Tönnies, 8 May 1933, NT.

[88] Wiese to Franz Wilhelm Jerusalem, 1 July 1933, NT.

[89] Wiese to Ferdinand Tönnies, 26 July 1933, NT.

[90] Ferdinand Tönnies to Wiese, 22 August 1933, NT.

fore remained entirely free from the taint of partisan politics, it was advisable on practical grounds to establish connections to the National Socialist movement and to the government by restructuring the organization and expanding its membership. He nominated Werner Sombart as the new president of the organization and Hans Freyer as a member of a governing committee to consist of the president, Freyer, and Wiese himself. Both nominations were accepted by a unanimous vote of the board.

Wiese informed the board of a request by Jerusalem that control of an upcoming sociological convention be placed in the hands of Hans Freyer and Jerusalem himself. Yet Freyer had written to him, Wiese reported, disclaiming any connection with Jerusalem's demand. Another board member, Theodor Geiger, reported that Freyer had personally assured him that he would not support any action that might harm the DGS. The assembled members therefore found it unnecessary to vote on Jerusalem's demand.

After considerable discussion about the future composition of the governing board, those assembled adopted a resolution that reelected to their ranks "all existing members, insofar as they are not excluded on the grounds of suspension from their academic posts or emigration abroad"—a resolution with the ring of tolerance but one that excluded almost all Jewish or leftist colleagues, who almost invariably fell into the latter categories. In addition several men considered close to the new regime were added to the board (Erwin von Beckerath, Willy Gierlichs, and Max Rumpf), and membership in the DGS was extended to several more (H.F.K. Günther, Ernst Krieck, Eugen Fischer, and Gunther Ipsen).[91]

Shortly thereafter Tönnies wrote Wiese protesting that he had not been in full control of his faculties during the meeting at Lübeck.[92] The appointment of Sombart to the presidency, the exclusion of Jewish members from the governing board, and the creation of the triumvirate were all contrary to the constitution of the DGS, Tönnies continued, and were an unconscionable and unnecessary attempt to adapt to the new political situation.[93]

In mid-August, Wiese, Freyer, and Sombart met at the latter's home in Berlin to respond to Tönnies' complaint and to consider the appropriate strategy for preserving the organization.[94] Wiese and Sombart clearly felt guilty about their shoddy treatment of Tönnies, and together with Freyer they decided that

[91] "Protokoll der außerordentlichen Rats- und Ausschußsitzung am Donnerstag, den 3. August 1933 in Lübeck," DGS Papers, Mappe "Zu DGS und 3. Reich."
[92] On Tönnies' exhaustion in Lübeck, see also

the letter of his son-in-law, Rudolf Heberle, to Wiese, 13 September 1933, NT.
[93] Ibid.
[94] Wiese to Ferdinand Tönnies, 24 August 1933, NT.

Tönnies would remain the nominal president and would be co-opted into their committee, while Sombart would be termed the "presumptive president" until the next *Soziologentag*. They also annulled the decision to expel the Jewish members of the governing board, and froze the membership of the association for the time being, thus obviating any pressures to expel old members or take on new ones.

Most importantly, however, the triumvirate decided for the time being to maintain as low a profile as possible. They temporarily suspended the activity of the DGS and decided that their committee would be reactivated only if "especially important events make a public statement by the representatives of the association absolutely necessary." In order to keep the organization's public profile as low as possible Wiese, Sombart, and Freyer sent the letter conveying their decision only to the few members of the DGS who had attended the meeting in Lübeck.[95]

The "especially important events" anticipated by the new leadership of the DGS were not long in coming. In November many members of the DGS received in the mail a manifesto entitled "To the German Sociologists." A few excerpts convey its flavor:

> In the epoch of the development of the German state and *Volk* that dawned early this year, few sciences have so immediate, so comprehensive, and so important a task to fulfill as sociology. German sociology must not therefore shirk the call of the *Reichskanzler* for the cooperation of all men of good will. The fate and future of the German *Volk* lie in the hands of sociology as well.
>
> The Deutsche Gesellschaft für Soziologie—which ought to have taken the lead and given direction to this cooperation—has failed. . . .
>
> The leadership of the association has been in the hands of an individual whose world view and conception of science are dominated by a one-sidedly liberal train of thought; it is no wonder that he has demonstrated no understanding for the new age now dawning.
>
> We therefore invite German sociologists to Jena for a conference on 6 and 7 January 1934.

The manifesto was signed by Günther, Höhn, Jerusalem, Krieck, and Walther, who were billed as the featured speakers at the planned conference.[96] Ernst Krieck, who was to speak on "Education through the Orders of the *Volk*,"

---

[95] "Rundschreiben an einige Mitglieder des Rats der Deutschen Gesellschaft für Soziologie, 22 September 1933," NT. A copy was also sent to Carl Brinkmann, a prominent member of the DGS who had not attended the Lübeck gathering.

[96] "An die deutschen Soziologen! November 1933," NP.

was perhaps the best known of this heterogeneous quintet in 1933. We have encountered him earlier, first as part of the circle around Eugen Diederichs and a gushing admirer of Freyer's *Antäus*, later as a *cause célèbre* in 1931 for his advocacy of a "Third Reich." By 1933 he was one of the most touted of National Socialist intellectuals, the official pedagogue of the movement, the rector of the University of Frankfurt, and the editor of his own periodical, *Volk im Werden*.

Hans F. K. Günther was another prominent Nazi academic intellectual. Long a leading theorist of racial pseudoscience, he had been appointed to a chair of social anthropology at the University of Jena in 1930 by Wilhelm Frick, the Nazi minister of the interior in the government of Thuringia.[97] Günther was to address the conference on "Sociology and Racial Research."

Franz Jerusalem, who had sent Wiese the first news of the planned conference, was a professor of law and sociology in Jena. Though he had taught there since 1918, it was only during Frick's term that he had been appointed to a chair. Jerusalem was to address the gathering on "*Gemeinschaft* as a Problem of Our Age." This had long been the central theme of his own voluminous sociological writings, which claimed that history demonstrated an oscillation between "collectivist" epochs in which *Gemeinschaft* was especially strong and "individualistic" epochs in which *Gemeinschaft* was weak. Thus, like Hans Freyer—though in a somewhat more vulgar form—Jerusalem combined the alternation of critical and organic epochs so prominent in the work of Saint-Simon and Comte with Tönnies' revival of the romantic concept of *Gemeinschaft*.[98]

The organizer of the conference was Dr. Reinhard Höhn, who at the time was a mere *Assistent* to Jerusalem but was soon to become the most influential—and feared—social scientist in the Third Reich. Born into the *Bildungsbürgertum* in 1908, Höhn (like Karl-Heinz Pfeffer) had been active during the late 1920s in a radical right-wing branch of the youth movement, the Jungdeutschen Orden. In the early 1930s he broke with this group and in 1932 took up contact with the Schutzstaffel (SS), then in formation. Having completed his doctoral studies in law, Höhn served in the late 1920s and early 1930s as *Assistent* to Jerusalem and wrote works of political philosophy heavily influenced by Carl Schmitt. Like many others, Höhn joined the NSDAP in the spring of 1933. In the autumn of 1933, when he was organizing the confer-

---

[97] On Günther, see Mosse, *Crisis*; and Robert Wistrich, *Who's Who in Nazi Germany*, 114–15.

[98] On Jerusalem, see *Internationales Soziologenlexikon*, 196.

ence of insurgent sociologists, he joined the SS.[99] Höhn was to deliver the closing address to the conference, entitled "The Practical Tasks of Sociology in the Present."[100]

The jarring name on the list of sponsors was Andreas Walther, professor of sociology in Hamburg. While the other signatories were of radical conservative or National Socialist provenance, Walther's reputation had been as a liberal, an expositor of Max Weber, and an advocate of empirical social research along American lines. He was the author of a searching methodological critique of Freyer's *Soziologie als Wirklichkeitswissenschaft*, which had appeared in Wiese's *Kölner Vierteljahresheft für Soziologie*. Yet on 1 May 1933 Andreas Walther too joined the Nazi party. His motives for doing so and for his subsequent actions seem to have been "nonideological": he appears to have sought to protect his seminar and his livelihood and above all was eager for an opportunity to apply the empirical methodology he championed to the task of social engineering.[101] Whatever his motives, Walther was to play a key role in the elevation of Freyer to the leadership of the DGS.

In response to the tangible attack on the DGS and its leadership, Leopold von Wiese sent a notice to all members of the organization, inviting them to an emergency meeting in Berlin on 29 December 1933. In an accompanying explanation he made it clear that many members of the association found its current structure "not in keeping with the times," and that the emergency meeting might decide to dissolve the DGS or refound it in some new form.[102] Wiese and Sombart tinkered with suggestions for a new structure, and Wiese even considered renaming the organization the "NS-Soziologenbund" (National Socialist League of Sociologists). [103]

Writing to Wiese in mid-December, Walther laid out his proposed course of action. Unless the DGS completely transformed itself, he wrote, the "Jena" group would found a counterorganization.

I know from reports which have reached me that in that case a campaign will be

[99] On Höhn's career, see Heiber, *Walther Frank*, 880–88 passim, as well as Höhn's file at the BDC. Höhn's admiration for Schmitt was most succinctly expressed in his essay, "Carl Schmitt als Gegner der liberalen Politik" (1932); see also Bendersky, *Carl Schmitt*, 232ff.

[100] "Treffen der Deutschen Soziologen in Jena am 6. und 7. Januar 1934: Tagesordnung," copy in NP.

[101] Rainer Waßner, "Andreas Walther und das

Seminar für Soziologie in Hamburg zwischen 1926 und 1945."

[102] "Einladung zur außerordentlichen Mitgliedversammlung der Deutschen Gesellschaft für Soziologie," NP; "Einladung zur außerordentlichen Versammlung des Rats und geschäftsführenden Ausschußes, . . ." copies in NP and NT.

[103] Klingemann, "Soziologen."

launched in the press and in the public—one that we moderates will not be able to prevent—which will not only harm the personal repute of respected members of our association, and which could heavily discredit the cause of sociology in Germany for some
time. . . .

Today German sociology needs a leader [*Führer*] whose name is a symbol of the new
Germany. A number of colleagues have therefore enthusiastically agreed to nominate
Herr Freyer as president and *Geschäftsführer*. May we be spared in the Berlin sessions
from having to spell out why other colleagues for whom we have the highest scholarly
regard are today not a symbol of the new Germany. . . .

We will not retreat in Berlin from the demand for Freyer's appointment as *Führer*. If
you campaign for it all will go smoothly. I am convinced that without this, or in the case
of the failure of the Berlin negotiations, the Jena group will found its own organization
which it would be difficult to challenge after the fact. I too would join it *faute de mieux*.[104]

Despite their attempts to reorganize the structure of the DGS so that it
would survive under their leadership, Wiese and Sombart balked at the prospect of giving up control of the organization at the membership meeting in
Berlin. In a letter to Tönnies, whose poor health prevented him from attending the Berlin gathering, Wiese described the meeting as an ugly confrontation. "The opposition"—led by Max Hildebert Boehm, a *völkisch* sociologist
from Jena and a former close associate of Moeller van den Bruck—presented
an ultimatum along the lines of Walther's letter. Its primary demand was that
Freyer be named *Führer* at once, and its prime supporters included Walther,
Max Rumpf, Carl Brinkmann, and apparently Freyer as well. The final vote,
with only fourteen members present, was seven to six in favor of the resolution, with Sombart abstaining. Hans Freyer was declared the sole *Führer* of the
organization, to whom its records were to be transferred. Sombart was so upset
by the decision that he threatened to resign from the association, but he was
prevailed upon to remain at least for the time being.[105]

A letter to Tönnies from a former student who had attended the Berlin
meeting and had voted in favor of the reorganization casts light on the motives
of those present. It was clear, he wrote, that Freyer, Walther, and the rest of
the "opposition" sought to preserve the DGS as an academic, scientific body, in
contradistinction to the plans of the Jena group to turn it into a pedagogic or
political organization. But more important in his decision to vote for Freyer,
he wrote, was his adherence to a conception of sociology that had the *Volk* as
its object and would function as a science "within the political and *völkischen*

[104] Andreas Walther to Wiese, 19 December   [105] Wiese to Ferdinand Tönnies, 3 January
1933, copy in NT.   1934, NT.

realm."[106] Freyer's elevation to the leadership of the DGS was thus motivated by both the tactical considerations and the ideological proclivities of its rump membership.

In the case of the *Gleichschaltung* of the Institut für Kulturgeschichte in Leipzig and of the German Sociological Association, Hans Freyer was propelled by events into positions of prestige far beyond those he had occupied—or could have expected to occupy—before 1933. In both cases Freyer rose to the top through a similar dynamic. Pressure to transform an institution previously headed by those sympathetic to the liberal democratic Weimar regime in a direction thought to be acceptable to the new regime came from within the academy (in both cases) and (in the case of the institute in Leipzig) from the new government. Two motives spurred those within the academy who sought to raise Freyer to a position of leadership within their institutions. Some were unsympathetic or indifferent toward the new regime and looked to Freyer to help preserve the existence of their professional institutions and of their livelihood. Others were in fundamental sympathy with the goals of the regime (as they understood them) and sought a reorientation of social science in the direction of ideological engagement on behalf of the new order. Freyer was perceived by his more social-scientifically oriented colleagues as a man recognized both inside and outside the academy as a representative of the new ideological engagement demanded by the holders of power, yet who retained a residual commitment to the canons of scholarly academic social science. To the devotees of ideologically engaged social science Freyer appeared as a recognized standard-bearer of their demands. Freyer's rise to positions of prominence during the first year of the National Socialist regime was a result of his ongoing straddle of the roles of social scientist and ideologist.

Similar dynamics propelled Freyer into a host of honorific posts in the early years of the Third Reich. He became a member of the governing board of the Deutsche Philosophische Gesellschaft, member of the Deutsche Akademie, co-editor of the *Zeitschrift für deutsche Philosophie* (the *gleichgeschaltet* successor of *Logos*, one of the most distinguished periodicals of German academic philosophy), co-editor of the series *Neue deutsche Forschungen* published by the prestigious academic publishing house of Junker und Dünnhaupt, and a member of the Akademie für deutsches Recht.[107]

---

[106] Hermann Curth to Ferdinand Tönnies, 29 December 1933, NT.

[107] On Freyer's election to the *Vorstand* of the Deutsche Philosophische Gesellschaft, see *Leipziger Neueste Nachrichten*, 6 October 1933, 2. On his membership in the Deutsche Akademie, see the membership list in Hans-Adolf Jacobson, *Karl Haushofer*. On his membership in the Akademie für deutsches Recht see Klingemann, "Soziologen."

Freyer's new salience in the German academic world was based upon the perception of him as a reputable social scientist regarded as ideologically acceptable by representatives of the Nazi regime. The institutional dynamics that led to the self-*Gleichschaltung* of the DGS appear to have been typical of the time and were replicated in many other academic professional associations.[108] In 1933 and 1934 many governmental and even party posts related to the control of the academy and of social science were in the hands of Freyer's friends, students, or admirers.[109] As this constellation changed, so did the opportunities available to Freyer to realize his hopes and plans for the new *Reich*. Yet for Freyer and other radical conservative intellectuals in his circle, the revolution from the right had begun on a promising note.

Freyer's Self-Gleichschaltung

For the two decades before 1933, Hans Freyer had sought a new, stable order based on a shared sense of collective purpose and a firm structure of domination. The accession of the National Socialists to power in 1933 seemed to offer the opportunity he had long awaited. Both his writings and his actions in the year after Hitler's appointment as chancellor on 30 January 1933 indicate that Freyer subordinated whatever doubts he may have had about the new regime to the task of shaping the Third Reich into a new organic epoch.

In his writings of the Weimar period, Freyer had claimed that the stability of positive epochs rested upon a structure of domination (*Herrschaft*) reinforced by a universally accepted ideology that made the current order seem both necessary and timeless. Hence it is no surprise that during the first year of the new regime, when his hopes that the new *Reich* might inaugurate a new positive ep-

[108] See, for example, Ulrich Geuter, "'Gleichschaltung' von oben? Universitätspolitische Strategien und Verhaltensweisen in der Psychologie während der Nationalsozialismus"; M. G. Ash, "Ein Institut und eine Zeitschrift: Zur Geschichte der Berliner Psychologischen Instituts und der Zeitschrift *Psychologische Forschung* vor und nach 1933." Other examples include the case of the academic/ideologist Adolf Rein, an advocate before 1933 of a politicized university, who in early 1934 was elected rector of the University of Hamburg by the university senate (see Giles, *Students*, 152). Martin Heidegger was elected rector of the University of Freiburg in 1933 under analogous circumstances (see Karl A. Moehling, *Martin Heidegger and the Nazi Party*, 21–63).

[109] Yet another admirer of Freyer to occupy a post of influence in the governmental agencies of the new *Reich* was Erich Rothacker, a neoromantic philosopher and sociologist, who in 1933 was appointed *Referent* in Goebbels' new Ministry of Propaganda (see the letter of Max H. Boehm to Staatssekretär Lammers of the Reichskanzlei, 11 April 1933, BAK, R43II/948, 3). Rothacker's political trajectory resembled Freyer's, though, less cautious than Freyer, he identified himself explicitly with National Socialism in 1932 (see Faust, "Professoren," 44).

och were at their height, Freyer threw himself into the articulation of an ideology based on the concept of the *Volk*.

During that year Freyer delivered more lectures and published more essays than ever before. It was not only the volume and salience of his public activity that now changed. His numerous essays and articles became overtly ideological in tone and substance. The ideology was no longer critical but orthodox; it sought not to undermine the political order but to bolster it at home and abroad. Freyer did not abandon his role as social scientist. But in keeping with his earlier strictures regarding the role of social science in a positive epoch, he now sought to create a social science that would serve to reinforce the new political order.

Typical of these outpourings of ideological affirmation was a lecture entitled "Das Volk als werdende Ganzheit," published in the *Festschrift* in honor of his mentor, Felix Krueger.

Here the *Volk* was described in a manner that was vague and evocative, a manner that served not to clarify the concept but to mystify it:

> . . . the *Volk* is a developing whole. The *Volk* can be ground down by class conflict; and we were in danger of this occurring. Today this danger is recognized as such, and the new process of becoming a *Volk* [*Volkwerdung*] has begun. The new order of the *Volk* rises piece by piece from the ruins of industrial society, like a building that strives upwards and reveals its structure. . . . A *Volk* with sparse space for settlement [*Siedlungsraum*], industrialized to a dangerous degree, in a politically threatening location in the center of Europe: this is the point of departure for the development of the German *Volk*.[110]

Nowhere is the conflict between the intrinsically critical nature of social science and the apologetic function of ideology more clearly demonstrated than in Freyer's description of "the real historical forces that create a *Volksgemeinschaft*." Such forces, wrote Freyer, were not accessible to a sociology that focused upon "the social" in a narrow sense; indeed, they were perhaps not fully explicable by scientific analysis but could only be conjured up by the poet or the great historian. Foremost among these "mysterious powers" was that of *Führertum* (leadership):

> The *Volk* is integrated above all when there exists a *Führer* to whose person every *Volk* comrade [*Volksgenossen*] is mysteriously oriented, whose will radiates over all, whose model stamps the young.

Another such "mysterious force" was the presence of goals for which the *Volk*

---

[110] Hans Freyer, "Das Volk als werdende Ganzheit" (1934), 6.

was willing to live and die. A third was the peasantry, which had remained a strongly "volk-laden" (*volkhaft*) stratum despite the ravages of industrial class society.[111]

Such passages were characteristic of Freyer's lectures and speeches of 1933 to 1934. They affirmed certain cornerstones of National Socialist ideology with a minimum of critical distance. They served to woo the assent of the governed to their new rulers. In short, Freyer helped provide the legitimating ideology that he saw as a necessary part of a positive epoch, of a new *Reich*.

Did Freyer believe the words that he spoke? In terms of his influence the question is irrelevant: most of his young or unsophisticated listeners certainly assumed that he said what he meant. Yet the problem is worth considering, not only because it concerns Freyer's intellectual and political development but because it will be suggested that, at a later stage of the Third Reich, Freyer "wrote between the lines," in an attempt to publicly convey his criticism of the regime.

The probable answer is that Freyer was ingenuous in these early affirmations of the Third Reich. The vigor of his intellectual and institutional efforts on behalf of the regime bespeak sincerity. Had Freyer been at odds with what he perceived as the thrust of Nazi policy, he could simply have stilled his pen and his tongue without suffering negative professional consequences. Freyer was not among those whom the more influential elements of the new regime regarded with suspicion. On the contrary, in its early years the regime made efforts to bolster its legitimacy by wooing prestigious nonparty intellectuals of the right.[112] Nor was professional opportunism—a rampant phenomenon in these years—a likely motivation of Freyer's behavior, for he was well established in the academy, and there is little evidence that he harbored higher political or academic ambitions. If so, he would have joined the party as had ambitious friends such as Helmut Berve and Carl Schmitt.

Rather, Freyer appears to have been genuinely inspired by the success of *a* revolution of the right, and hopeful that it might be or might become *the* revolution from the right for which he had long campaigned.

Freyer's public statements and actions went through two stages in the course of 1933. In public lectures delivered and published in the first half of 1933, when Hitler ruled as the head of a Nazi-conservative coalition, Freyer affirmed recent events as a turning point in German history. Yet he spoke of the transformation as if it were the product of a broad revolutionary conservative

---

[111] Ibid., 7–8.

[112] A rough parallel may be found in the Soviet treatment of Russian fellow travelers such as Maxim Gorky after the Bolshevik Revolution. See David Caute, *The Fellow-Travellers*, 32–42.

movement, rather than of the National Socialist party. The words *National So-cialism* or *Adolf Hitler* appear in none of these lectures. The intellectuals cited by Freyer as the spiritual fathers and guides of this transformation were Os-wald Spengler, Moeller van den Bruck, Wilhelm Stapel, and more distantly, Friedrich Nietzsche.[113] In the many lectures and articles that he published in the first half of 1933, Freyer noted that it was not biology or race but identifi-cation with the collective past and a readiness to subordinate the individual to a state organized to preserve this collectivity that constituted a "political *Volk*."[114] This emphasis upon the primacy of the political in the preservation of the *Volk* and the inadequacy of biological modes of thought distinguished Freyer's statements from those of orthodox National Socialists.

To many of his readers—and perhaps to Freyer himself—this might have appeared to be a distinction without a difference, or at least a difference not worth quarreling over. Before 1933, National Socialists had welcomed and in-deed wooed the support of conservative and radical conservative intellectuals who were sympathetic toward National Socialism without subscribing to its ra-cial ideology. After the Nazi rise to power the situation became more compli-cated. Given the vagueness of Nazi ideology, it was often difficult to specify what was ideologically orthodox, even by those elements within the party dis-posed to do so. Many party members in policymaking positions did not feel compelled to exclude the support of those who were close but not wedded to National Socialism. For just as the regime tolerated the existence and avidly sought the support of the non-Nazi leadership of the army, of private indus-try, and of the bureaucracy in order to attain its own goals, so too were "prag-matists" within the party prepared to utilize intellectuals such as Freyer for their own purposes. Among these purposes were the legitimation of the re-gime to the German *Bildungsbürgertum* and to the educated classes abroad in countries whose support or at least toleration was required by the Third Reich. As we will see, Freyer was effectively utilized by the regime for just these functions.

Side by side with this pragmatic willingness to forgo complete ideological or-thodoxy in the interests of garnering broad intellectual support for the regime went a countervailing trend toward the imposition of ideological orthodoxy

---

[113] Freyer, *Semester*. The book's contents indi-cate that it originated as a series of lectures deliv-ered in Leipzig. Freyer published excerpts from it as "Bildungsreform," *Leipziger Studentenschaft* 18 (23 May 1933): 23–24. *Der politische Begriff des Volkes* originated as a lecture in Kiel in the first

half of 1933. There Freyer cites Moeller and Stapel on pages 16–18.

[114] See, for example, Freyer, *Begriff*, 18; also idem, *Herrschaft*; idem, *Semester*; idem, "Einlei-tung," to J. G. Fichte, *Reden an die deutsche Nation* (1933), 9–10.

regardless of cost. This conflict between ideological activism and the pragmatic shoring up of power existed in various forms in each realm of governmental policy and throughout the course of the Third Reich. Among the best-known examples are the conflict between Hitler and Ernst Roehm, which resulted in the physical elimination of the latter in the name of the former's pragmatism during the intraparty purge of June 1934, and the triumph of the ideologically motivated murder of European Jewry despite its economic and military costs to the *Reich*.[115] Perhaps the most important such struggle in the realm of culture took place between ideological advocates of a "German physics" on the one hand and those Nazi leaders who desired an atomic bomb and were eager to promote the appropriate scientific theories regardless of their "non-Aryan" origins.[116] A similar struggle occurred in other cultural realms, not least in those of social science and political ideology.

As early as mid-1933, Freyer's contemporary writings were criticized by some National Socialist organizations for their lack of ideological orthodoxy. Within the Amt Rosenberg, an office headed by the official Nazi ideologist, Alfred Rosenberg, and devoted to the propagation of National Socialist ideologist orthodoxy,[117] Freyer's lecture "The Political Concept of the *Volk*" met a hostile response. An anonymous reviewer in its "Office for the Supervision of Scholarship" (*Hauptamt Wissenschaft/Amt Wissenschaftsbeobachtung und -wertung*) found that Freyer had dealt with the concept of the *Volk* and race in a manner that stressed the role of cultural continuity at the expense of "vital racial substance" and had called into question the importance of the "biologically based National Socialist philosophy of history." Freyer's concept of race was thus "sociological" rather than "substantial," and the reviewer recommended that the book be "sharply rejected as Marxist." This appears to have been the first of many negative reports on Freyer's writings and activities within the cultural apparatus of the Nazi party.[118] At about the same time, doubts about the ideological reliability of Freyer's *Das politische Semester* were raised within the local branch of the National Socialist student organization, though this was clearly a minority opinion within the organization.[119]

---

[115] On the elimination of Roehm, see Wolfgang Sauer, *Die Mobilmachung der Gewalt*, 324–64. On the extermination of the Jews as an instance of the primacy of ideology, see, among other sources, T. W. Mason, "The Primacy of Politics: Politics and Economics in National Socialist Germany."

[116] See Bayerchen, *Scientists*.

[117] Rosenberg's official title was Der Beauftragte des Führers für Überwachung der gesamten geistigen und weltanschaulichen Schulung und Erziehung der NSDAP.

[118] The review is unsigned and undated (BAK, NS15, 171–72, which is the same as National Archives, T81, frames 034313–4).

[119] The incident is referred to in Thiel (Gau-

Freyer was unlikely to be aware of these particular attacks upon him within the various Nazi organizations of cultural control. But the general atmosphere of fear within the philosophical faculty as the process of *Gleichschaltung* picked up steam in the late spring and summer of 1933 made him aware of the extreme standards of ideological orthodoxy in such organizations.[120] Freyer adjusted his rhetoric accordingly. After the summer of 1933, he began to include explicit and often effusive praise of National Socialism and of Adolf Hitler in his public addresses and published essays.[121]

Though Freyer's explicit affirmation of Hitler and National Socialism was "opportune," it was not necessarily insincere. By the autumn of 1933, Hitler had consolidated his power internally—with help from Freyer's friends such as Johannes Popitz, Wilhelm Ahlmann, and Carl Schmitt—thus inaugurating the stable *Herrschaft* that Freyer had long regarded as a prerequisite of collective integration. At least as important to Freyer were Hitler's foreign policy initiatives, especially his withdrawal of Germany from the League of Nations in October 1933. Revision of the postwar treaties had long been a major goal of Freyer and his circle, who regarded the new states of central and eastern Europe as tools of the Anglo-French attempt to constrain the German *Volk*, and as the inappropriate imposition of the western European model of the democratic nation-state on central and eastern Europe.[122] After Germany's withdrawal from the League of Nations, the regime called for a plebiscite to be held on 12 November and organized a broad propaganda campaign to ensure a favorable outcome. As part of the campaign Freyer addressed a rally of the Leipzig faculty on "The Engagement of the University for November 12" (*"Die Einsatz der Universität für den 12. November"*). In his speech Freyer praised Hitler's

---

studentenführer of Saxony) to Münster (Dekan der philosophischen Fakultät), 13 April 1937, UAL, PA Freyer, 108.

[120] In May 1933, for example, Felix Krueger, long renowned as standing on the far right of the faculty and a veteran member of the Nazi-dominated Kampfbund für deutsche Kultur, was accused by some students of having condemned anti-Semitism during a public lecture. Krueger felt compelled to defend himself in an open letter in which he defended his long and open record of anti-Semitism. What he had actually said, Krueger explained, was that anti-Semitism and anti- Bolshevism *taken alone* were purely negative and an inadequate basis for German national rebirth. This explanation was ac-

cepted by the students (see "Zur Maifest der Universität," *Leipziger Neueste Nachrichten*, 13 May 1933, and 18 May 1933).

[121] See, for example, Hans Freyer, "Von der Volksbildung zur politischen Schulung," 9. This article was originally an address to the Reichstagung der deutschen Volkshochschulen, held in Hamburg in September 1933 (see Hans Wenke, "Die pädagogische Lage in Deutschland," 578n). See Hans Freyer, "Tradition und Revolution im gegenwärtigen Europa" (1934), 88–90; idem, "Tradition und Revolution im Weltbild" (1934), 758; idem, "Das Politische als Problem der Philosophie" (1935), 361.

[122] Freyer, *Begriff*, 5, 6, 12; see also Ipsen, "Das Erbe des Reichs."

decision to withdraw from the League of Nations as "the first and perhaps decisive step toward a true liquidation of the Versailles system." The postwar era had finally been ended by "the bold but prudent, swift and clear action of a statesman who can depend upon his *Volk*." "With this step," Freyer told his audience, "an awakened *Volk*, united under a *Führer* in whom it has faith, begins a new epoch in its history."[123]

These were not mere ephemeral outpourings but themes to which Freyer was to return time and again during the early years of the Third Reich in works addressed to fellow academics and to a broader public. These themes were fused with biographical reflections in a speech which Freyer delivered for the first time in January 1934 and which, in modified form, he was to deliver to audiences throughout Germany and Europe in the years to follow. Both the content and the initial context of this address deserve closer inspection.

From 3 to 6 January 1934, Freyer attended the ninth congress of the League for Cultural Cooperation (*Verband für kulturelle Zusammenarbeit*), held in Budapest. The founder and general secretary of the league was Karl Anton Prinz Rohan, a radical conservative intellectual resident in Berlin. Rohan was also editor of the *Europäische Revue*, the most highbrow and cosmopolitan of the radical conservative magazines, in which Hans Freyer, Carl Schmitt, Arnold Gehlen, and other radical conservative intellectuals often published.[124] In attendance at the congress were politically interested intellectuals and intellectually inclined politicians from some fourteen nations.[125] The topic of the conference, chosen with a view to recent events in Germany, was "Tradition and Revolution in Contemporary Europe." Present as "representatives of the new Germany" were Hans Freyer; A. E. Günther, a radical conservative journalist and editor of the collection *What We Expect from National Socialism* (1932); and Privy Councilor Leisler Kiep, a politician from Hamburg. According to Freyer's subsequent report, the conference demonstrated the gap between the representatives of those countries—especially France—who maintained the nineteenth-century tradition of liberalism, democracy, and the nation-state, on the one hand, and the representatives of the "new Europe" of the twentieth century on the other. In this latter category Freyer placed the representatives of Nazi Germany, Fascist Italy, revisionist Hungary, and "the fascist youth of Spain and Bulgaria."

[123] The speech was published as Hans Freyer, "Der Einsatz der Universität für den 12. November," *Leipziger Hochschulzeitung*, 10 November 1933, copy in UAL, PA Freyer, 83.

[124] On Rohan, see Mohler, *Konservative Revolution*, 437–38.

[125] This description of the congress is based upon Freyer's account in "Tradition und Revolution im gegenwärtigen Europa," 86–90.

The congress marks Freyer's first visit abroad as a semiofficial representative of the Third Reich. His success as a cultural ambassador of the new Germany in 1934 was rewarded with further missions, culminating in his years in Budapest from 1938 to 1945.

Freyer began his address to the congress on an autobiographical—indeed, almost confessional—note. He spoke of his origins in the youth movement and of the sense he had shared with his comrades that they represented a breakthrough to a "new humanity." Their revolutionary claims, Freyer observed in retrospect, had been somewhat naive, romanticized, and exaggerated. Yet the movement had been significant as a herald of disillusionment with the social and cultural order of nineteenth-century "bourgeois society." As Vico and Herder, Comte and Hegel had recognized, all great historical transformations had been the products of a change of collective consciousness, in which existing values ceased to be regarded as valid. It was such a change of consciousness that the youth movement had embodied.

Such a consciousness could become an effective historical force, Freyer continued, only when it became a mass phenomenon. This had occurred in the new nationalism that began to spread over the globe in the 1920s. In contrast to the nationalism of the nineteenth century, which was closely tied to the bourgeoisie and the triumph of liberalism, the new nationalism of the twentieth century was antibourgeois, illiberal, and combined with elements of socialism. Most importantly, the new nationalism recognized the primacy of politics in human history. In contrast to liberalism, it viewed the state as "the reality that draws upon and extends over all realms of culture." Politics was not a particular realm of cultural life but the site of "total historical decisions." The modish terms of the past decade in Germany, such as *Entscheidung* and *Wirklichkeit*, had had political connotations, Freyer told his audience. With a clear allusion to his own writings of the early 1930s, as well as to intellectuals such as Martin Heidegger and Carl Schmitt, Freyer claimed that "Decision [*Entscheidung*] meant a concrete decision for or against a particular political movement, or the even more concrete decision for or against a particular leader [*Führer*]: in our case for or against Adolf Hitler."[126]

In its emphasis on the role of politics, of decision, and of will in history, Freyer explained, the new nationalism was at odds with the deterministic thrust of bourgeois liberalism and of Marxism. It disputed the primacy of automatic, self-developing processes in history characteristic of nineteenth-

[126] Freyer, "Tradition und Revolution im Weltbild," 69–71.

century views of progress. It stressed the possibility of "new beginnings" in history, brought about by human will and decision.[127]

Yet the new nationalism, which Freyer also referred to as the revolution from the right, was profoundly conservative as well. Freyer was, as usual, vague as to the content of this conservatism. He defined it in opposition to *"Bodenlosigkeit"* (groundlessness):

A life is *bodenlos* when it is cut off from its place [*Standort*] and from its roots, especially from the most primeval strata of one's people [*urwüchsigen Schichten des Volkstums*]. A will is *bodenlos* when it lacks a concrete standpoint within a historical existence. Knowledge is *bodenlos* when it pursues the abstract ideal of putting all presuppositions aside and therefore arrives at pallid bits of evidence, never at conclusions that are tied to reality and valid for real life.

The opposite of *Bodenlosigkeit*, and hence the central characteristic of the new nationalism, was *Bodenständigkeit*, best translated as "groundedness" or "rootedness in the soil." It meant "the recognition and affirmation of one's essential fundaments" (*seinsmäßige Grundlagen*). He added an obfuscatory explanation of Nazi racism that was bound to mollify a skeptical foreign audience:

The deepest and most important of these fundaments is the *Volkstum*. It is here that all the talk of race originates and has its truth. When one objects that this is pure biology, that after all spiritual matters cannot be derived from their natural basis, or when one objects that there are no pure races—these objections fail to grasp the concept of race that is a component of the new world view. Race is understood not in the sense of "mere" biology but rather as the organic involvement of contemporary man in the concrete reality of his *Volk*, which reaches back through millennia but which is present in its millennial depth; which has deposited itself in man's bodily and psychic existence, and which confers an intrinsic norm upon all the expressions of a culture, even the highest, most individual creations.[128]

Freyer concluded his talk by asserting that the epochal transformation underway in Germany was occurring in each European nation, "each in its own way." It would ultimately result in "a new form and a new harmony of Europe."[129]

With minor modifications Freyer continued to deliver this speech for the next several years. The key elements remained constant: National Socialism as a revolution from the right, a culmination of the cultural criticism of the nine-

[127] Ibid., 72–73.
[128] Ibid., 74–75.
[129] Ibid., 76.

teenth century and of the youth movement; a new recognition of the centrality of political leadership and decision in history; the need to repoliticize existence; and the radical conservative commitment to cultural and ethnic particularity.[130]

Three aspects of this speech are particularly striking. First, the tradition or cultural past evoked as the normative basis of the new culture remained entirely without substance. No concrete elements of the purported tradition were ever defined; it was the mere fact of continuity, of traditionality, that was evoked. In place of specified links with the past, it is the necessity of such links that was emphasized. The place of real traditions was usurped by metaphors of stability and continuity—*Boden, Grund, Tiefe*. Freyer's radical conservatism has long stressed the function of tradition rather than its substance. His gingerly approach to the significance of biological racism in his Budapest speech betokened an unwillingness to recognize that those with a less functionalist view of reality might regard terms such as *blood* and *race* as more than emotive metaphors of continuity, useful in the process of social integration. Indeed, given the lack of a homogeneous German cultural past, those who sought "rootedness" in history were left with little more than continuity of common biological ancestry as the source of collective identity. In this sense, Nazism represented the attempt to take radical conservatism to its logical conclusion—to conclusions more radical than most radical conservatives were willing to draw.[131]

A second feature of the speech was the link that it established between National Socialism and the cultural movements of which Freyer had been a part. By tracing the spiritual genealogy of National Socialism back through the new nationalism of the 1920s, the youth movement, and the nineteenth-century cultural critics of liberal society, Freyer attempted not only to legitimate National Socialism in the eyes of the educated bourgeoisie but to legitimate himself in the eyes of orthodox National Socialists. The speech may have been intended to function—and probably did function—as a lubricant in Freyer's contacts with the wheels of power in Nazi Germany. Yet the presentation of National Socialism as the potential legatee of the capital of discontent amassed by radical conservatism was in keeping with those of Freyer's writings which

[130] Hans Freyer, "Vom geschichtlichen Selbstbewußtsein des 20. Jahrhunderts" (1936).

[131] In the first year of the Nazi regime at least two social theorists of radical conservative sympathies pointed in print to the functional utility of the new myth of racism in the process of collective integration, while alluding to its scientific untenability. See W. E. Mühlmann, "Die Hitler-Bewegung" (1933), 135–36; and Arnold Gehlen, "Rasse und Staat" (1933–34), 204.

antedated the *Gleichschaltung* of intellectual life. On the basis of Freyer's previous writings and actions, there is no reason to suppose that his words were fundamentally insincere when they were penned at the beginning of 1934.

The Budapest speech was also important as Freyer's first foray into the field of cultural diplomacy. It was formulated to reassure his audience of foreign intellectuals and diplomats of the benign and beneficent nature of National Socialism. Those aspects of Nazi ideology likely to cause the greatest consternation among foreigners, namely the movement's bellicosity and its principled racism, were diffused. While militant preparedness for war formed a central tenet of Freyer's political philosophy, and while he waxed enthusiastically in favor of the reinstitution of military conscription in lectures delivered to German audiences during 1933, he assured his foreign listeners of the ultimate compatibility of National Socialism with a peaceful European order.[132] While he told German audiences that the concept of *Volk* so central to his radical conservatism was "virtually untranslatable" and incompatible with the western European concept of "nation,"[133] in his Budapest speech and its variants for external consumption he spoke of National Socialism as a German version of a broader nationalist revolution from the right sweeping across contemporary Europe.[134]

In his public activity during the early years of the new regime Hans Freyer combined ideological affirmation of the new regime with the ability to modulate his message for a diversity of audiences. Add to this his international reputation and his ability to formulate the provincial crudities of National Socialist thought and action into learned, cosmopolitan terms, and it is clear why Hans Freyer and other fellow-traveling academic intellectuals like him, rather than more orthodox National Socialist ideologues, were often chosen by the regime as its cultural ambassadors.[135]

In terms of the trajectory of Freyer's hopes for National Socialism, the fate of his Budapest speech is more important than its content. Since the First World War and through the early years of the Third Reich, Freyer had been eager to convey his reflections on the social and political trends of the day. The Budapest speech fit into this engaged pattern: whatever its concessions to its

---

[132] Freyer, "Tradition und Revolution im Weltbild," 75–76.

[133] Freyer, *Begriff*.

[134] Freyer, "Das geschichtliche Selbstbewußtsein," delivered in Rome in May 1935; idem, "Vom geschichtlichen Selbstbewußtsein," published in Bucharest in 1936.

[135] The mission of Alfred Rosenberg, the chief Nazi ideologist, to London in May 1933 ended as a foreign policy disaster for the new government. See John P. Fox, "Alfred Rosenberg in London."

CHAPTER EIGHT

The Dynamics of Disillusionment,
1935–1945

In a torrent of lectures and articles in the years immediately after 1933 Hans Freyer had welcomed the new regime, which he hoped would inaugurate a new, positive epoch. By 1936 Freyer began a retreat to more distanced scholarship and to writings that expressed a veiled critique of National Socialism. By 1937 he had decided to leave Germany for a teaching post abroad, albeit under the auspices of the German government.

What had occurred to make Freyer change his mind about the promise of Hitler's regime and its ability to fulfill his hopes of superseding bourgeois society? The answer requires a reconstruction of the professional and academic spheres in which the Third Reich impinged most directly on Freyer.

The onset of Freyer's disillusionment with National Socialism, the dawning of the realization that it was inherently incapable of bringing about a new, positive epoch of common subordination to a collective purpose, cannot be dated with precision. In all probability there was no moment of truth or sudden flash of insight in which he was struck by the enormity of his error. Disillusionment came not suddenly but by degrees. Freyer shared this process of disillusionment with many other German intellectuals who went from identification with the regime through stages of doubt, skepticism, concern, and antipathy before the German defeat in 1945. Intellectuals shared this disillusionment with many of their nonintellectual countrymen.[1] But just as intellectuals once had their distinct reasons for welcoming the rise of National Socialism, so their ultimate disillusion had its own dynamics. Very few Germans were willing to cross the dangerous divide separating disillusioned antipathy to the Nazi regime from active resistance to it. Yet the July 1944 conspirators were probably correct in believing that among prominent Germans who remained outwardly loyal to the Nazi regime they had many passive sympathizers on whom they could call if their coup succeeded. Among these was Hans Freyer.

---

[1] On the growing disaffection from the regime during the war see Martin Broszat, "Zur Struktur der NS-Massenbewegung," 75.

Like most Germans, Freyer remained at his post to the end, fulfilling the functions that the National Socialist regime required long after he had come to reject its legitimacy. His belated disillusionment did not slow down the National Socialist behemoth as it tore up Europe and finally Germany itself. Only after 1945 would political consequences flow from the principled rejection of totalitarianism to which Freyer and other intellectuals on the right were led under the impact of National Socialism.

Freyer and the Fortunes of Sociology in the Third Reich

After his election as *Führer* of the German Sociological Association, Freyer returned to Leipzig and began to take steps to carry out the *Selbst-Gleichschaltung* of the organization that the majority of its voting members had desired.

He dispatched a letter to all members informing them of the decision of the emergency meeting to reorganize the DGS "according to the *Führerprinzip.*" Since those assembled had resolved to apply for membership in the Akademie für deutsches Recht, Freyer wrote, he had taken it upon himself to create an advisory board that would "scrutinize the membership rolls accordingly"— another euphemism for eliminating the Jewish members, who would not be eligible for the Nazi Akademie. New offers of membership were to be made, especially to scholars from other disciplines who were oriented to sociology or "*Volkswissenschaft.*"[2] Those invited to join were professors of sociology, law, philosophy, and pedagogy who were known as supporters of the new regime. They included party ideologues in the academy, such as Bäumler, Koellreuter, and Krieck; Carl Schmitt's disciples Ernst Forsthoff and Ernst Rudolf Huber; and Freyer's friend Gunther Ipsen.[3]

In another letter Freyer urged his colleagues—in keeping with the decision of the recent DGS meeting—to attend the upcoming congress of sociologists in Jena, especially since it might offer an occasion to discuss the future shape of the DGS.[4]

It is impossible to know how many of Freyer's colleagues complied with his request to attend the conference in Jena organized by the dissidents from the DGS. Freyer himself could not have attended even had he wanted to, since he

[2] "Rundschreiben an die Mitglieder" (signed Hans Freyer), 30 December 1933, NP. On the Akademie für deutsches Recht, see Hermann Weinkauff, *Die deutsche Justiz und der Nationalsozialismus.*

[3] Hans Freyer, der Vorsitzende, Deutsche Gesellschaft für Soziologie to "Herr Kollege," 2 January 1934, copy in Amt Rosenberg, File: "Hans Freyer," T81, roll 194, frame 034531, National Archives, Washington, D.C.

[4] "Rundschreiben an die Mitglieder," 30 December 1933.

was in Budapest at an international conference of the League for Cultural Co-operation. It is clear from published reports that none of the members of the DGS instrumental in its self-*Gleichschaltung* played a public role at the Jena congress.

Though the role of race and inheritance was not new to mainstream sociology in Germany, it was to achieve a new salience during the Third Reich. A harbinger of the new prominence of racial pseudoscience in Germany was the address in Jena by Prof. H.F.K. Günther, "Sociology and Race Research." He stressed the importance of race, inheritance, and "selection" in the development of the *Volk* and urged greater attention to the racial determinants of German culture.[5]

Günther's conception of sociology was far from Freyer's. But another address to the congress, by Ernst Krieck, bore signs of Freyer's influence. Krieck cautioned against the notion of science as grounded in some universal reason. It was time to recognize, Krieck asserted, that sociology was a *Wirklichkeitswissenschaft*, tied to personal, time-bound presuppositions.[6] Though Freyer's name was never mentioned, the very terminology betrayed his influence.

While Freyer's conception of sociology had stressed the role of ideological commitment within social science, the addresses at Jena suggested the complete replacement of critical, distanced, functionalist social science by apologetic ideology. Speaker after speaker intoned the importance of *Gemeinschaft* and *Volk* as the appropriate categories around which sociology in the new *Reich* ought to be built. They stressed that all scholarship was to be regarded primarily as service to the *Volk*. In keeping with its new apologetic function, sociology was to be closely related to pedagogy, to serve in the inculcation of the concepts of *Volk* and *Gemeinschaft* among the population at large.[7] These categories were proffered not as ideal-typical hypotheses or heuristic conceptualizations for purposes of research but rather as real entities whose primacy was to remain unquestioned. Sociology was portrayed as the science of the *Volk*, and some sociologists took to calling their discipline by the Germanic *Volkswissenschaft* rather than by the latinate *Soziologie*.

The demand for the utter ideologization of sociology was articulated most forcefully by Reinhard Höhn, the most junior of the speakers at Jena, who was soon to emerge as the most influential. Höhn began his address with a polemical attack on the sociology of Leopold von Wiese, which Höhn denounced as

---

[5] Quoted in Justus Beyer, "Die Tagung der deutschen Soziologen in Jena und die Aufgabe der Wissenschaft im neuen Staate," 196.

[6] Ernst Krieck quoted in Beyer, "Tagung."

[7] See Beyer, "Tagung"; as well as H. Lorenz Stoltenberg, "Das Treffen Deutscher Soziologen in Jena vom 5. bis 7. Januar 1934," 200.

"individualistic" because it conceived of the relations between individuals as the ultimate stuff of sociology. This conception of sociology, Höhn claimed, was shared by Johann Plenge and to some degree by most sociologists of the Weimar years. Such theorizing was part of a degenerate individualistic age now passing. The new sociology of the Third Reich, by contrast, began with the knowledge that the individual existed only as a member of *Gemeinschaften*, such as the family, the village, the SA troop, and the *Volk*. "Individualistic" sociology was to be eschewed because it asserted the possibility of tension between the person and the *Gemeinschaften* in which he lived.[8] Höhn thus advocated a conception of sociology that would make literally inconceivable the possibility of conflict between the individual and the ideologically prescribed groups in which he lived.

If one of Höhn's causes was the enforcement of ideological orthodoxy within sociology, a second was the adaptation of sociology to the practical purposes of the regime. By early 1934 he had already been appointed to a post with the *Arbeitsdienst* (Labor Service), which seemed to offer an opportunity for the application of social science.[9]

Höhn's appearance at Jena demonstrated the traits that were to place him among the most successful social scientists of the Third Reich: zeal in the use of ideological orthodoxy to discredit potential competitors, an awareness of the regime's need for applied social science, and a thinly veiled will to self-advancement. Unfortunately for Hans Freyer and those within the DGS who sought to put their services at the disposal of the Nazi regime, Höhn had staked out the field of sociology as his own turf.

Freyer responded in two essays on the contemporary tasks of German sociology.[10] He defended the existing tradition of German sociology—at least as delineated in his earlier works—as having long been devoted to the supersession of bourgeois society.[11] While in his earlier writings Freyer had traced antibourgeois themes in French sociology (in the works of Saint-Simon and Comte), these were no longer mentioned in the articles of 1934. Instead Freyer noted that both English natural law theory and the French Enlightenment had produced doctrines that viewed the capitalist social order as natural.[12] A fundamental antipathy toward "bourgeois society" was thus made to seem the ex-

---

[8] A revised version of his talk at Jena was published as Reinhard Höhn, "Die Wandlung in der Soziologie," 642–45.

[9] Beyer, "Tagung," 196.

[10] Hans Freyer, "Volkwerdung: Gedanken

über den Standort und über die Aufgaben der Soziologie" (1934); idem, "Gegenwartsaufgaben der deutschen Soziologie" (1935).

[11] Freyer, "Gegenwartsaufgaben," 117–30.

[12] Ibid., 122–23.

clusive prerogative of *German* sociology, now presented in contrast to western European thought. Freyer thus attempted to legitimate his brand of sociology in terms of the regnant antiwestern ideology of the regime.

The National Socialist revolution, Freyer wrote, marked the beginning of the supersession of the era of liberal, industrial society, the creation of a political *Volk*, and the reintegration of society into the state. Since sociology had its origin in the separation of civil society from the state, the end of this separation would eventually result in the absorption of sociology by political science (*Staatswissenschaften*). Yet that time had not yet come, since many of the structures and problems of bourgeois, industrial society remained, including those of class antagonisms and continuing special interests. These after-effects of bourgeois society required empirical study. The task of sociology was now to assist the state in determining which aspects of industrial society were necessary prerequisites for a modern *Volk*, and which *gemeinschaftliche* elements of the past the regime could call upon in the process of national regeneration.[13] Freyer warned against replacing empirical research into the real social conditions of the present with idyllic, romantic evocations of *Gemeinschaft*.[14]

Early in 1934 Freyer was involved in launching a new sociological periodical, entitled *Volksspiegel: Zeitschrift für deutsche Soziologie und Volkswissenschaft*. The guiding hand behind the journal was that of Max Rumpf, professor of sociology and *Volkstumsforschung* at the Handelshochschule in Nuremberg and among those responsible for Freyer's elevation to the presidency of the DGS.[15] The masthead listed Rumpf, Freyer, and Max Hildebert Boehm as editors. Rumpf was responsible for editing the substantive articles while Boehm edited the book reviews. Freyer contributed an article to the first issue but was largely a figurehead. It was by virtue of his connection with the journal that its title page could announce that the *Volksspiegel* was published "in association with the Deutsche Gesellschaft für Soziologie."

Alongside nostalgic evocations of the peasantry (Rumpf's specialty) and the *Grenzdeutschen* (Boehm's major concern), and attempts to define the term *Volk*, the first two years of the journal included a number of articles that met Freyer's criterion of empirical investigations into the effects of industrial capitalism on German society and into the factors making for national regeneration. Among the best of these was an article by Rudolf Heberle, summarizing his study of the sociological origins of National Socialist electoral support in

---

[13] Ibid., 134–38; Freyer, "Volkwerdung," 8.
[14] Freyer, "Gegenwartsaufgaben," 138, 143; idem, "Volkswerdung," 6.

[15] Rumpf acknowledged his role as initiator of the periodical in vol. 6, p. 122. On the *Volksspiegel*, see Rainer Wiebe, "Der Volksspiegel."

rural Schleswig-Holstein—a study widely regarded as a classic of electoral sociology.[16]

It soon became clear, however, that the *Volksspiegel* and the sociologists who were its editors did not enjoy the favor of important elements in the Nazi regime. Early in 1935, the National Socialist Reichsstelle zur Förderung des deutschen Schrifttums, which evaluated the ideological reliability of all periodicals, declared that the *Volksspiegel* was "not above suspicion and not recommended," a decision that limited its market among party and public institutions. In February, Rumpf wrote to Andreas Walther informing him of the journal's troubles and of the friendly advice of an official in the Ministry of Education that it obtain written recommendations from "a few unobjectionable old party members attesting to the journal's value and loyalty."[17] To bolster the journal's standing with the party, the racial sociologist H.F.K. Günther and Adolf Helbok, a professor in Innsbruck and longtime member of the Austrian Nazi party, were added to its editorial board. In 1936 Freyer and Boehm were dropped as titular editors of the journal, its subtitle was changed to *Zeitschrift für deutsche Volkswissenschaft* (thus eliminating any mention of sociology), and mention of the DGS was removed from its masthead. Its articles became even less scholarly, and it was eventually absorbed by the National Socialist Teachers Union.[18]

At the same time that the *Volksspiegel* was coming under attack, Freyer discovered (and informed Boehm) that his letters were being opened. Outraged, Freyer visited his former student Studentkowski and demanded an immediate end to interference with his mail.[19] Freyer assumed that the man responsible was Reinhard Höhn.[20]

His assumption was almost certainly correct, for by 1935 Höhn had become the cultural adviser (*Kulturreferent*) of the Security Service of the SS, the Sicherheitsdienst (SD). As head of the *Zentralabteilung* II/2 in the SD headquarters in Berlin, Höhn was responsible for "*Gegnerforschung*" (research on enemies) and for reporting on opinion within broad areas of German life. Among his primary concerns was ensuring the ideological orthodoxy of the German pro-

[16] Rudolf Heberle, "Die politische Haltung des Landvolks in Schleswig-Holstein, 1918–1932: Ergebnisse einer politisch-soziographischen Untersuchung" (1934). Heberle's study was eventually published as *Landbevölkerung und Nationalsozialismus* (1963); an English summary appeared as *From Democracy to Nazism: A Regional Case Study on Political Parties in Germany*.

[17] Max Rumpf to Andreas Walther, 11 February 1935, extract in SD-Hauptamt, Betr. Carl Schmitt, BAK, R58/854, 202.

[18] Wiebe, "Volksspiegel," 27ff.

[19] Interview with Käthe Freyer.

[20] M. H. Boehm to K. H. Pfeffer, 15 December 1949, Nachlaß Boehm, vol. 5, BAK.

fessoriate. As a man who enjoyed Himmler's personal confidence, and with the power of the SS to back up his recommendations, Höhn became one of the most feared figures in the cultural apparatus of the Third Reich.[21]

Freyer thus found himself and the DGS confronted by a man who had initiated an attack on the DGS and who was willing and able to use his position in the secret police to pursue his quest for control over sociology in Germany.

Early in 1936 Leopold von Wiese, in his capacity as German correspondent of the *Fédération Internationale des Sociétés et Instituts de Sociologie*, wrote to Freyer inquiring as to the current status of the DGS. Freyer explained the inactivity of the DGS since his assumption of its presidency:

As regards the association: up till now it was to be feared and expected that certain persons to whom I cannot bring myself to grant a decisive influence on the association would use any public appearance of the association to win such influence. Unfortunately I cannot go into greater detail in a letter. I hope that this danger can be eliminated in the near future and will once again pursue negotiations in Berlin to this end at the end of March.

Recent experiences, Freyer explained to Wiese, had convinced him that any attempt to activate the organization would have brought it into "very bad hands."[22]

There is no indication that Freyer achieved any success in the upcoming negotiations reported in this letter to Wiese, probably because the Ministry of Education, with whom he was presumably to negotiate, also stood in fear of Höhn.[23]

The attempt by Freyer and some other members of the DGS to put their conceptions of sociology at the service of the National Socialist regime was thus stymied by influential Nazis who sought their own hegemony over the field. Rather than allow his leadership of the DGS to mark him as a target, Freyer allowed the organization to lapse into inactivity. He virtually ceased to publish on sociological topics after 1935, rather than provide opportunities for attacks upon him by Höhn. Freyer had hoped to adapt his conception of sociology to the consolidation of the new German *Reich*. By 1935 it was clear that he would not be allowed to do so.

Other sociologists, including some of Freyer's students, were far more will-

---

[21] Helmut Heiber, *Walther Frank und sein Reichsinstitut für Geschichte des neuen Deutschlands*, 124, 581n, 881, 886 passim; also Heinz Höhne, *The Order of the Death's Head*, 215. Höhn was also a key figure in a campaign of 1936 against Carl Schmitt on grounds of ideological unreliability.

See Bendersky, *Carl Schmitt*, 232–33, 246–48.

[22] Leopold von Wiese to Hans Freyer, 21 January 1936; Freyer to Wiese, 19 February 1936, both in the Deutsche Gesellschaft für Soziologie Papers, Mappe "Zu DGS und 3. Reich."

[23] Heiber, *Walther Frank*, 124.

ing and able to adapt themselves to the forms of sociology most welcomed by the holders of power in the Third Reich. On the one hand, statements of complete ideological orthodoxy were favored, especially those which eliminated any suggestion of possible functional equivalents for conceptual categories such as the *Volk*. On the other hand, empirical research on topics related to the internal or foreign policy goals of the *Reich* were encouraged. Recent studies of the history of sociology indicate that compared to the Weimar era the sociographic strand of sociology grew in extent and importance during the Third Reich. There seems to be growing evidence that those social scientists who thrived under the Nazi regime did so not primarily because of the affinity of their theories to Nazi ideology but because those who wielded power believed in the utility of their empirical research.[24] Two men habilitated by Freyer during the Third Reich demonstrate this general pattern.

In 1937, under Freyer's sponsorship, Dr. Karl Valentin Müller was granted the right to teach sociology at German universities. Müller had not been a student of Freyer's, and his habilitation was based on books and articles that he had published since receiving his doctoral degree. Once drawn to the Social Democratic party by his concern for "the social question," Müller had been led by the theories of H.F.K. Günther and other scientific racists to conclude that social achievement was largely a matter of inherited racial characteristics and the "the social question" required a eugenic answer. Though a nominal member of the Social Democratic party until 1933, he had long been active in racist associations, had been a frequent contributor to the leading journals of racial science, and had maintained good relations with National Socialists.[25] In his book *The Rise of the Worker through Race and Mastery*, on the basis of which he received his habilitation, Müller maintained that the degree of "Nordic blood" varied directly with social status and that upward social mobility within the working class was due to the inherited superiority of those workers whose

[24] On the panoply of organizations under which empirical sociological research was conducted in Nazi Germany, see Carsten Klingemann, "Heimatsoziologie oder Ordnunginstrument? Fachgeschichtliche Aspekte der Soziologie in Deutschland zwischen 1933 und 1945"; idem, "Vergangenheitsbewältigung oder Geschichtsschreibung? Unerwünschte Traditionsbestände deutscher Soziologie zwischen 1933 and 1945"; idem, "Soziologie an Hochschulen im NS-Staat"; Thomas Hahn, "Industriesoziologie als Wirklichkeitswissenschaft? Zwischen Empire und Kult"; and "Schwerpunkt: Soziologie im Nationalsozialismus?," a special issue of *Soziale Welt*, vol. 35, nos. 1/2 (1984), devoted to sociology under National Socialism. Less reliable, but also worth consulting, is Waltraut Bergmann et al., *Soziologie im Faschismus*. For additional evidence on the utilization of applied social science in the Third Reich see Geoffrey Cocks, *Psychotherapy in the Third Reich*; and Geuter, *Professionalisierung*.

[25] UAL, PA Müller, "Lebenslauf," 1936, 19–30.

origins lay in the peasantry or the artisanry.[26] Another of Müller's major concerns, the role of race in areas of mixed ethnic settlement, was expressed in the title of his trial lecture, "The Significance of German Blood in Southeast Europe."[27] Despite the reservations of some of Freyer's colleagues—a professor of statistics noted that Müller's statistical evidence did not warrant the conclusions he had drawn from it; a professor of medicine doubted that Müller fully understood the biological concepts that he employed—Freyer gave a positive evaluation of Müller and of the significance of his research and recommended his habilitation.[28]

Given his ideological convictions and eagerness to adapt statistical and empirical methods to the goals of National Socialism, the rapidity with which Müller was promoted is unsurprising. In 1938 he became a *Privatdozent* at Freyer's institute and shortly thereafter was named to a junior professorship in Dresden, before being called in 1941 to the chair of "social anthropology" at the German university of Prague, where he headed an "Institute for Social Anthropology and *Volksbiologie*."[29]

Though habilitation by Freyer was a necessary prerequisite for Müller's academic career, his brand of sociology owed nothing to Freyer. The case of Karl-Heinz Pfeffer, who was habilitated by Freyer in 1934, was quite different. Time and again Pfeffer took Freyer's writings and adapted them to the ideology of the Third Reich.

Freyer had sought to establish a historicist, anticapitalist sociology focused upon the dichotomy of state and bourgeois society, with its lineage in German writers such as Hegel, Lorenz von Stein, Karl Marx, and (to a lesser extent) W. H. Riehl and Heinrich von Treitschke.[30] In 1939 Pfeffer produced a work entitled *Die deutsche Schule der Soziologie*. The book was published by Quelle und Meyer, the same firm that had published Freyer's *Einleitung in die Soziologie*. But how different were the tone and the content of the two works! Pfeffer began by regretting the disrepute attached to the term *sociology* in the Third Reich but acknowledged that sociology had in the recent past all too often

---

[26] Karl Valentin Müller, *Die Aufsteig des Arbeiters durch Rasse und Meisterschaft* (1935), 74, 154–55.

[27] PA Müller, 87.

[28] UAL, PA Müller, "Gutachten, 10.12.1936," 40–43; UAL, "Protokoll der Sitzung der philosophische-historische Abteilung der Philosophischen Fakultät, 3.6.1937."

[29] BAK, R21, Wissenschaftlerkartei, Karl Valentin Müller. See the uniformly positive evaluations of Müller's ideological reliability in BAK, R21, PA Müller. For a bibliography of Müller's writings and a euphemistic description of their contents see H. G. Rasch, "Müller, Karl Valentin."

[30] See Freyer, *SW*; idem, *ES*, esp. 62–87; idem, "Gegenwartsaufgaben."

served as a vehicle for Western thought, or for Jewish thought, which was equally dangerous. Pfeffer stressed that contemporary German sociology, as he interpreted it, had nothing to do with this discredited Western-Jewish tradition.[31] Pfeffer's lineage of "classical" German sociologists was intended to highlight past theorists of the *Volk*. It consisted of an odd agglomeration of Fichte, Adam Müller, Herder, Hegel, Möser, Arndt, List, Rodbertus, Constantin Frantz, Paul de Lagarde, W. H. Riehl, and Nietzsche. Many of these thinkers had to be adjusted rather radically to fit Pfeffer's procrustean, *völkisch* bed. Nietzsche, for example, was hailed for recognizing "the biological determination of the *Volk*'s existence."[32] Recent sociologists who had focused their work on the *Volk*—such as Freyer's former co-editors of the *Volksspiegel*, Rumpf and Boehm—were chastised for employing too "formal" a concept of the *Volk*.[33] Pfeffer ended his work with a description of sociology which eliminated the possibility of functional equivalents for the role of the *Volk* in the process of social cohesion, which was entirely apologetic in terms drawn from the regime's racial ideology, and which demanded empirical research for the regime's ends.[34]

Shortly thereafter Pfeffer published a book on the peasantry that combined the romantic view of the peasantry that Nazi ideology favored with a good deal of empirical information on matters such as regional variations in the structure of the peasant household. The book was replete with anti-Semitic asides and ended with a call for national expansion to provide space for peasant settlement.[35]

In the summer of 1940, Pfeffer left Freyer's institute to serve as the acting incumbent of the chair in British studies at the newly created faculty of foreign studies (*Auslandswissenschaftliche Fakultät*) at the University of Berlin, and in 1943 he was appointed full professor there. The new institute was headed by Dr. Alfred Six, an SS officer active in the Reichssicherheitshauptamt and a colleague of Reinhard Höhn's.[36]

[31] Karl-Heinz Pfeffer, *Die deutsche Schule der Soziologie* (1939), 3.

[32] Ibid., 124.

[33] Ibid., 128.

[34] "Die völkische Gesellschaftslehre begreift die Arbeitsordnung nur von der Wirklichkeit des politischen Volkes her. . . . Sie überwindet . . . die in der bürgerlichen Gesellschaft erreichte Vormacht der Arbeitswelt durch die Vormacht der Rasse. Nicht die Stellung in der Arbeitsordnung, sondern die Art gibt den Platz im Volk. . . .

"Gerade indem die deutsche Volks- und Gesellschaftslehre sich zu ihrer eigenen Geschichte bekennt, sieht sie vor sich nicht die spinnende Aufgabe der Methodologie, sondern den Dienst exakter Einzelforschung in politischer Ausrichtung" (ibid., 132, 134).

[35] Karl-Heinz Pfeffer, *Der Bauer* (1939).

[36] See Kommittee zur Untersuchung . . . , *Eine Dokumentation: Die wissenschaftliche und politische Karriere des Dr. phil. habil. Karl-Heinz Pfeffer*, 13. On Six, see also Heiber, 478.

Pfeffer's service to the Nazi regime during the war years, in addition to frequent lectures throughout occupied Europe, included at least two works noteworthy for their seamless blend of Nazi propaganda with empirical research and Freyerian categories of analysis. *England, Vormacht der bürgerlichen Welt*, published in 1940 under the sponsorship of Walther Frank's Reichsinstitut für Geschichte des neuen Deutschlands, portrayed the conflict between England and Germany in terms taken from Freyer's writings. England was depicted as the land of "bourgeois society," its peasantry destroyed, its nobility and working classes decayed as a result of the domination of capitalism. Germany, by contrast, had overcome "bourgeois society" and hence offered a new beginning to the peoples of Europe. The war was thus a struggle between England, the embodiment of "the nineteenth century," and Germany, the champion of the twentieth. Pfeffer's book went through five editions from 1940 to 1943; 125,000 copies were eventually printed, including an edition of 41,000 for the education of troops in the field.[37] Unlike his teacher Freyer, Pfeffer was enthusiastically endorsed by the Amt Rosenberg.[38]

In 1943 Pfeffer outdid his own high standard of propagandistic zeal with a booklet entitled *Der englische Krieg auch ein jüdischer Krieg*. The booklet was published by the educational arm of the Amt Rosenberg (Amt Parteiamtlich Lehrmittel) in its *Schriftenreihe der weltanschaulichen Schulungsarbeit der NSDAP*. Its cover bore the warning "For internal distribution only!" (*Nur für den Dienstgebrauch!*). Pfeffer explained that although the majority of the plutocratic elite that led England into war with Germany was *not* Jewish in the literal sense, the Jews of England were sufficiently powerful to exert tremendous influence nevertheless. Since their influence was a result of their power in the capitalist economy, the more capitalist England had become the more it had come under Jewish domination. Jewish influence was coordinated by the Jewish Board of Deputies, Pfeffer wrote, and functioned out of the public eye in organizations such as Political and Economic Planning (PEP), which was itself under the influence of the Jewish capitalist Israel Sieff. Pfeffer stressed that since England was the home of liberalism and capitalism, which provided the necessary conditions for Jewish social mobility, the interests of England were identical to those of the Jews. "Thus," Pfeffer concluded, "the war against the plutocracy is a war against the Jews."[39]

Pfeffer continued both his academic rise and his interest in sociology to the

---

[37] Karl-Heinz Pfeffer, *England, Vormacht der bürgerlichen Welt* (1940); Heiber, *Walther Frank*, 558–59, 670.

[38] See YIVO Institute Archives, Amt Rosenberg Collection, File: "Karl-Heinz Pfeffer."

[39] Karl-Heinz Pfeffer, *Der englische Krieg auch ein jüdischer Krieg* (1943), 3–16. (A copy is in the Deutsche Bücherei, Leipzig.)

very end of the war. In January 1944 he was appointed acting president of the Deutsche Auslandswissenschaftliche Institut in Berlin and in June 1944 became dean of the Auslandswissenschaftliche Fakultät in Berlin.[40] As late as 1944 he participated in a sociological study group convened by Otto Ohlendorf, one of the most influential social scientists in the SD, in the "Gästehaus Wannsee."[41]

How did Hans Freyer react to the ever more propagandistic activities of his disciple? In departing for Budapest in 1938, he left Pfeffer in charge of his institute in Leipzig and, according to Pfeffer at least, saw the manuscript of his *Deutsche Schule der Soziologie* before it went to the publisher.[42] It is impossible to know quite what Freyer thought of Pfeffer's writings and activities after 1939. For by then Freyer found himself unable to follow his disciple into the promised land of National Socialism.[43]

The University of Leipzig, 1935–1938

The reality of the Third Reich impinged most directly on Hans Freyer at his own university. Events there provided the immediate context for his disillusionment. By 1937 Freyer had seen several of his closest colleagues dismissed from their teaching duties and found himself under personal attack.

While the University of Leipzig was not totally transformed by National Socialism, the impact of the Nazi regime affected both the structure of power within the university and some of the teaching and research carried out within its confines.

On 1 January 1934 the *Führerprinzip*, already implemented within the student government, was extended to the faculty as well. The rector was now to be named by the Ministry of Education, and he in turn was to choose the deans, the academic senate, and incumbents of other posts formerly elected by the

[40] BAK, R21, PA Pfeffer.

[41] Karl-Heinz Pfeffer to M. H. Boehm, 14 December 1949, BAK, Nachlaß Boehm, vol. 5. No armchair social engineer, Ohlendorf had by then done his part to create *Lebensraum* in the east by commanding an *Einsatzkommando* that murdered tens of thousands of Jews in the Ukraine in 1941 and 1942. On Ohlendorf, see Lawrence D. Stokes, "Otto Ohlendorf, the Sicherheitsdienst and Public Opinion in Nazi Germany."

[42] Karl-Heinz Pfeffer to M. H. Boehm, 21 December 1949, BAK, Nachlaß Boehm, vol. 5.

[43] Cf. Hans Freyer, "Gesellschaft und Geschichte" (1937), 16–17. Here Freyer suggested that the object of sociology was not *Gesellschaft* but the *Volk* in its historical transformations. Taken out of context (as, for example, in Ronald Gielke, "Faschistische Ideologie im Werk Hans Freyers," 52–53) this may seem to resemble Pfeffer's attempt at creating an orthodox National Socialist sociology. In context, it is clear that Freyer's objection is not to the concept of *Gesellschaft* as such but to an unhistorical use of the concept and to sociology that ignores the role of culture and politics.

faculty.[44] In 1934 the government named Prof. Arthur Golf, a member of the NSDAP since 1932 and a man already elected to the post of rector by the faculty in the autumn of 1933, as its choice of rector.

Competing with the rector and with the traditional structure of faculty governance in the university was another *Führer*: the head of the Dozentenschaft, an organization created by the Nazi party for faculty members. Among his major tasks was to pass judgment upon the political reliability of all candidates for faculty posts, a judgment based most often on reports and rumors gathered from among Nazi informants within the faculty.[45] The distrust that many Nazi leaders as well as the more ardent young Nazis active in the Dozentenschaft bore toward the faculty of the university is captured by the remarks of the Leipzig *Dozentenführer*, Koeppen, at a commemorative ceremony late in 1934. With the exception of a small group of students and their faculty supporters, he claimed, the university had played no role in the NSDAP's "fourteen-year-long struggle for the German soul." The renewal of the German university had therefore to come from the Nazi movement.[46]

Though many within the leadership of the Nazi party hoped to transform the university in the image of National Socialism, they could by no means agree just what that image was. Moreover, ideological conflicts in the realm of culture, as in most realms within Nazi Germany, were often intertwined with battles for institutional power and personal influence.[47] A confidential report of the Reichssicherheitshauptamt at the end of 1938 concluded that "despite the far-reaching extension of cultural organizations, there is no united cultural plan." In the absence of a coordinated cultural policy, each of a dozen party and state organizations followed a cultural policy of its own.[48] Among the panoply of organizations attempting to influence university appointments through assessments of the political reliability of candidates were the Amt Rosenberg, the Amt Hess, the NS-Studentenbund, the NS-Dozentenbund, the SA, the SS, the SD, and the Reichssicherheitshauptamt, not to speak of the party's *Gauleiter* and *Kreisleiter*.[49]

---

44 See Hellmut Seier, "Der Rektor als Führer."

45 In 1935 the Dozentenschaft was succeeded by the NS-Dozentenbund, which played a similar role in appointments. See Reece Kelly, "Die gescheiterte nationalsozialistischen Personalpolitik"; and idem, "German Professoriate under Nazism: A Failure of Totalitarian Aspirations."

46 "Ansprache des Leiters der Dozentenschaft, Dr. Koeppen," in *Akademische Reden gehalten am 31. Oktober 1934 in der Aula der Univer-*

sität Leipzig aus Anlaß des 525. Jahrestages ihrer Gründung (1934), 24.

47 On the ubiquity of institutional conflict in the Third Reich, see the works by Arendt, Heiber, Bollmus, and Adam cited in the Introduction.

48 Reichssicherheitshauptamt, *Jahreslagebericht 1938 des Sicherheitshauptamtes*, vol. 2: *Kulturelles Leben*, 1–2, BAK, R58.

What did this profusion of rival organizations of cultural control mean to the individual professor living under the National Socialist regime? Several examples from Freyer's immediate milieu help to provide a sense of the regime's effects on the quality of academic life in the years from 1934 through 1938.

Theodor Litt, whom Freyer had characterized in 1930 as "a clear mind who acts as an intellectual conscience amid the confusion of opinions and desires," was among those subject to harassment under the new regime. As a vocal opponent during the final years of the Weimar Republic of attempts by National Socialist students to disrupt and politicize the university, Litt had earned the ire of Nazi student groups. As early as May 1933, the Nazi-controlled student association (Studentenschaft) of Leipzig began a campaign against Litt, demanding that he resign as *Prorektor* of the university, a step that he refused to take.[50]

Litt's actions in the years thereafter reveal a publicly enunciated and privately reiterated unwillingness to compromise the scholarly pursuit of truth in the interests of political expediency—even when, as in Litt's case, it eventually led the regime to silence him completely. In the early months of the regime, for example, a pedagogic institute in Munich invited him to address a conference on "Education in the National Socialist State." Litt accepted the invitation and announced he would speak on "The Place of the *Geisteswissenschaften* in the National Socialist State." The National Socialist Teachers Union of Saxony wrote to the Bavarian minister of culture, warning him that Litt was considered "politically incriminated" because of his conflict with National Socialist student groups. Shortly thereafter the organizers of the conference wrote to Litt requesting that he voluntarily withdraw from participation. Litt refused to go quietly; instead he published the address he had planned to deliver in Munich in his journal, *Die Erziehung*, along with a note explaining that it was the unaltered text of a lecture that had not been delivered because the organizers of the conference had found themselves compelled to remove him from the program. The published lecture included an exposition of the impossibility of reconciling scientific inquiry with externally imposed theories and an elucidation of the irreconcilability of scientific historical research with the racial view of history.[51] Litt's seminars and lecture courses at Leipzig were well known for their systematic analytical criticisms of the ideological claims of National Socialism.[52]

[49] Aharon Kleinberger, "Gab es eine nationalsozialistische Hochschulpolitik?," 14.

[50] Friedhelm Nicolin, "Theodor Litt und der Nationalsozialismus," 99–100.

[51] Ibid., 100, 104–8.

[52] See the transcript of his remarks to his sem-

Late in 1934 an article attacking Litt appeared in the *Völkischer Beobachter*, which was in turn reprinted in the *Leipziger Hochschulzeitung* of 17 December. Student disruptions of Litt's lectures led the rector to cancel Litt's classes temporarily.[53] When he resumed lecturing in the new year, his first lecture was attended by the rector and by a swarm of uniformed Nazi functionaries. Litt began his lecture with the sentence, "Ladies and Gentlemen, after this somewhat involuntary interruption of our course, and out of consideration to our guests, rather than continue where I left off—I'd like to speak on 'biological materialism'!" Litt then proceeded to offer a critique of Alfred Rosenberg's racial theory.[54]

A year later, yet another published attack on Litt called attention once again to his distance from National Socialism, this time in the pedagogic journal *Vergangenheit und Gegenwart*. Its author was Freyer's former student Werner Studentkowski. The article was republished in the newspaper of the Leipzig branch of the Nazi student league, thereby maintaining pressure on Litt.[55]

Another form of pressure on Litt was government interference with his ability to travel abroad. A philosopher of international renown, Litt was often invited to speak outside Germany. During 1935 and 1936 the Ministry of Education denied him permission to speak in Holland and Switzerland. In the fall of 1936 he was allowed to travel to Austria to deliver a series of lectures, but while he was there he received word from the German embassy forbidding him to deliver a planned radio address.

In late 1936, disgusted by this ongoing harassment, Litt applied for early retirement (*Emeritierung*), a form of resignation that would allow him to receive a pension. In a letter explaining his request, he lamented that the treatment to which he was subjected would make it impossible for him to fulfill his professional responsibilities. "I would never be able to know whether something I would say or write in good faith would be condemned by some official as injurious to the national interest," he wrote. "I would continually feel persecuted by the mistrust of the authorities, always prone to the possibility of humiliating experiences such as the ones I have just gone through."[56]

---

inar on 12 May 1933, reprinted in ibid., 98–99. This was also confirmed in numerous conversations with those who studied at Leipzig during the 1930s.

[53] *Leipziger Tageszeitung*, 9 January 1935 (copy in UAL, PA Litt, 72); Albert Reble, "Albert Reble," 268.

[54] Nicolin, "Theodor Litt," 101–2.

[55] The original article appeared in *Vergangenheit und Gegenwart*, no. 9 (1935). It was reprinted in the *Offene Visier* (Leipzig), 20 February 1936. (A copy of the latter is in UAL, PA Litt, 76.)

[56] Nicolin, "Theodor Litt," 103.

Litt's application was accepted in July 1937. Thus Freyer saw one of his most respected colleagues and a friend who shared many of his intellectual interests removed from the university.

Another colleague close to Freyer who was dismissed, one whose treatment seems to have exercised the faculty even more than Litt's was Joachim Wach.

Like Freyer, Wach had deep roots at the University of Leipzig. He had studied at Leipzig, received his doctorate there in 1922, and had taught there ever since. Though he was best known as historian and sociologist of religion, Wach shared many of Freyer's philosophical interests. In addition to his courses on religion, Wach taught courses in the Institut für Kulturgeschichte (before and after 1933) and in Freyer's Institut für Soziologie on the philosophy of history in nineteenth-century German thought and on Nietzsche, Max Weber, and Ernst Troeltsch. Wach, like Freyer, was a senior mentor to the Deutsche Freischar of the youth movement. Last but not least, both were veterans of the Great War.

Like Hans Freyer, Joachim Wach was a Christian, the son of Christian parents. But unlike Freyer, Wach had four Jewish grandparents.[57]

Despite his Jewish lineage, Wach had been exempted from the wave of expulsions in 1933 because of his veteran status. In deference to Hindenburg, the Law for the Restoration of the Professional Civil Service of April 1933 had excluded "non-Aryan" combat veterans (*Frontkämpfer*) from its provisions. Wach was one of four members of the Leipzig faculty who continued to teach under this provision.

In May 1935, two years after the first purge of the faculty, the exemption for non-Aryan *Frontkämpfer* was repealed by the central government in Berlin. The news that Wach and his three similarly situated colleagues were to be dismissed led to the first—and only—open protest by members of the university faculty. At a combined faculty meeting of May 1935 several senior professors rose and expressed their distress or outrage at the new measures. They protested that the dismissals were unfair, that they were causing discontent among the students, and that those professors who had not been *Frontkämpfer* would now be ashamed to face their dismissed colleagues who were. Werner Heisenberg, professor of physics at Leipzig, expressed doubt that the measures were in keeping with the law of 1933, which had stated that *Frontkämpfer* were part of the *Volksgemeinschaft*. He regarded it as a comradely duty to aid those in-

---

[57] For Wach's courses up to 1933, see Üner, "Hans Freyer," 243–45. On his lineage and connection to the Freischar, see the informant's re- port on Freyer and his institute (discussed below), in BAK, NS15, no. 202, 172–90.

volved in any way possible, he said. The dean, Freyer's friend Berve, promised to convey the faculty's sentiments to the Ministry of Education.[58]

Though Hans Freyer does not appear to have spoken at the meeting, he too must have shared the pent-up discontent with ongoing government and party interference in the university, which had finally exploded into the open, if only for a brief moment.

Perhaps the most disconcerting event at Leipzig, from Freyer's perspective, concerned his former teacher and mentor Felix Krueger. During the Weimar Republic, Krueger had a well-deserved reputation as a right-wing activist on the faculty. He had helped found the Fichte-Gesellschaft, was a member of the Nazi-dominated Kampfbund für deutsche Kultur and the Committee against the Young Plan, and was a frequent speaker at anti-Versailles rallies on campus.

The coming of the Third Reich catapulted Felix Krueger upward within the academic world, as it did so many of Freyer's associates. In April 1933 he became president of the German Psychological Association. In March 1935 he was appointed rector of the University of Leipzig by the Ministry of Education in Berlin.

The official ceremony inaugurating Krueger's rectorship took place in September. His first act as rector was to offer the *"Heilruf"* to the *Volk* and its *Führer*. In his rectoral address he reminded his listeners that "the struggle for truth always has racial and *völkisch* roots."[59]

Exactly what happened next remains obscure. Felix Krueger's racial lineage had been under investigation by the Ministry of the Interior since mid-1933, when he had failed to supply adequate documentary proof of his Aryan ancestry.[60] Several months after assuming the rectorship, Krueger appears to have used the phrase "noble, Jewish heart" during a lecture on Spinoza. During subsequent lectures uniformed Nazis stood outside his lecture hall to warn students away.[61] At the beginning of January 1936 the Ministry of Education demanded that he give up the rectorship temporarily, "on grounds of health."[62] On 2 February an article entitled "Abstrakte Geistigkeit" appeared

[58] "Protokoll der Sitzungen der gesamten philosophischen Fakultäten, 8 May 1935," UAL.

[59] Reports of the ceremony in the *Leipziger Tageszeitung* and the *Leipziger Neueste Nachrichten* of 7 September 1935 (copies in UAL, PA Krueger, 69–70).

[60] Letter (titled A:XVII 347) to Sachverständigen für Rassenforschung beim Reichsministerium des Innern, 24 August 1933, Ministerium für Volksbildung, File: "Felix Krueger" 10281/199, Sächsisches Landeshauptarchiv Dresden.

[61] Interview with Gerhard Liebers. Liebers was a student at the University of Leipzig from 1933 to 1939.

[62] Arthur Golf to "Dekane," 11 January 1936, UAL, PA Krueger, 77.

in the Nazi-owned *Leipziger Tageszeitung*, attacking an unnamed professor for singing a hymn of praise to a Jew, Spinoza, during the course of a lecture. The article—so clearly aimed at Krueger that it found its way into his personnel file—went on to attack the notion that there were "decent Jews" who ought not to fall under the anti-Semitic laws of the *Reich*.[63]

Krueger's supporters in the student body responded to this attack by attending his lecture of 13 February en masse and applauding him vigorously, thus violating an order of the Nazi *Reichsstaathalter*, who had forbidden any demonstrative actions. The next day a letter arrived from the Saxon Ministry of Education, informing Krueger that his lectures had been canceled for the remainder of the semester. The letter was signed by Werner Studentkowski.[64]

The year that followed was an anxious one for Felix Krueger, a man in his sixties. Continuing attacks upon him—including, apparently, those of his own *Assistenten*—led him to resign as chairman of the German Psychological Association.[65] He devoted a good deal of energy to attempting to prove to the Reichstelle für Sippenforschung that there were no Jews in his family and to the provincial authorities that there had never been many in his institute.[66] In September 1937 Krueger suffered a heart attack and applied for emeritus status.[67] Shortly thereafter the ultimate cause of Krueger's anxiety became clear. He received a letter from Studentkowski of the Saxon Ministry of Education informing him that the Reichstelle für Sippenforschung had determined that Krueger's grandfather had been "a full-blooded Jew." Felix Krueger was therefore considered a "*Mischling*."[68] Three months later Krueger too was *emeritiert*.

Thus by mid-1937 Hans Freyer had seen not only his friends and close colleagues Theodor Litt and Joachim Wach expelled from the university; even Felix Krueger, who appeared to have been beyond reproach by the standards of the regime, had been brought down. If a man like Krueger could be named

---

[63] "Abstrakte Geistigkeit," *Leipziger Tageszeitung*, 9 February 1936, copy in UAL, PA Krueger, 78.

[64] Sächs. Volksbildungsministerium to Felix Krueger, 14 February 1936, UAL, PA Krueger, 79.

[65] Felix Krueger to Reichserziehungsministerium, 28 September 1936, copy in Sächs. Landeshauptarchiv Dresden, Ministerium für Volksbildung, "Felix Krueger" 10281/199.

[66] Sächs. Landeshauptarchiv Dresden, Ministerium für Volksbildung, File: "Felix Krueger."

This file contains references to his ongoing correspondence with the Reichstelle für Sippenforschung. On his attempt to prove the paucity of Jews at his institute, see "Niederschrift" (signed Rosenberg), 12 December 1936, UAL, PA Krueger, 85.

[67] Felix Krueger to Volksbildungsministerium, 28 September 1937, UAL, PA Krueger, 88.

[68] Werner Studentkowski to Felix Krueger, 28 December 1937, UAL, PA Krueger, 92.

rector of the university one day and prohibited from teaching the next owing to ideologically unorthodox statements in the course of his lectures, then, Freyer may have reasoned, no one could feel secure.

Freyer was aware that he and his institute were not above suspicion. As we have seen, he knew that his mail had been opened. Through his participation in hiring committees he could see that the leaders of the National Socialist Professors Organization gathered information and compiled reports on faculty members from informants among the students and faculty. These reports— often based upon little more than rumor—concerned past political allegiances, purported philo-Semitism (of which past or present Jewish students were taken to be a sign), and remarks that could be interpreted as inimical to the regime or its ideology. Freyer also knew from his own experience that such information could be used to block an appointment, as well as bring down a chaired professor such as Krueger.[69]

Though the individual files of the Gestapo and the SD were largely destroyed by those organizations in the closing days of the war, at least one extensive informant's report on Freyer has survived. Some nineteen typed pages in length, it offers numerous indications of its sources of information, of the manner in which Freyer operated his institute, and the grounds on which he was subject to attack by zealous National Socialists.[70]

From internal evidence it is clear that the author of the report held a doctorate in history and was a committed National Socialist with a Prussianist bent. Though the motives for his extensive attack are unclear, such denunciations were frequently written by younger, professionally ambitious Nazi scholars who sought to displace the objects of their attack.[71]

As was often the case with such denunciations, the document was based upon a mixture of fact, rumor, and distortion. Freyer was depicted as an opportunist (*Konjunkturritter*) who had been on the left during the 1920s (his friendship with the former *Kulturminister*, Carl Heinrich Becker, was offered

---

[69] The appointment of Freyer's favored candidate for a chair in southeast European studies, Prof. Gesemann, was blocked by such reports in 1936 and 1937. UAL, B2/20/45, Südosteuropa-Institut, 100ff.

[70] A surviving copy of the report, entitled "Bericht über Herrn Professor Dr. Hans Freyer," and dated 6 June 1935, exists in the files of the Amt Rosenberg. BAK, NS15, no. 202, pp. 172–90; also in National Archives T81, roll 194, frames 0345315–0345333.

[71] A well-documented instance is the public attack on the senior Berlin historian Hermann Oncken by Walther Frank, a young Nazi historian in search of a senior academic post for himself. Frank's attack, which appeared several months before the secret denunciation of Freyer, was written while he was working for Alfred Rosenberg as surveillant of the discipline of history (Heiber, *Walther Frank*, 114–15). Whether he played a role in commissioning the denunciation of Freyer is unclear.

as evidence) and had written *Revolution von rechts* only when it was clear that the star of the right was on the rise. His close association with the Freischar was highlighted, an organization described as crypto-Bolshevist in its goals and similar to the Masonic lodges in its mode of operation. Freyer was accused—here with greater justice—of having had Jews and leftists among his friends and students at least as late as January 1933. Among those cited were Ernst Manheim ("*der ungarische kommunistische Jude Manheim*"), Fritz Borinski, Joachim Wach, and Willy Bloßfeldt. The author noted that Heinrich Drucker, the son of a well-known Jewish lawyer in Leipzig, continued to study at Freyer's institute. Another member of Freyer's institute, Hugo Fischer, had through 1932 ordered materials for the institute from the international communist propaganda organization run by Willi Münzenberg. Confronted recently by these materials, the report went on, Fischer had claimed they were ordered for "bibliographic" purposes, and Freyer had claimed he was unaware of their presence.

The author of the report was also distressed by the variety of political opinion represented by the speakers in Freyer's colloquia (though most were in fact of the non-Nazi political right) and by Freyer's willingness to tolerate the open expression by a foreign student of criticism of the policy of the Nazi regime toward ethnic Germans abroad. The portrait of Freyer's institute which emerges from the report is of a realm of relatively free scholarly discussion.[72]

Perhaps the most interesting accusation made against Freyer in the report was that he conveyed to his close students the impression that the leadership of the *Reich* was by no means unified but composed of several groups with shifting degrees of influence.[73] What appeared as heresy to the writer of the report may appear as perspicacious in retrospect.

Where did the author of this report get his information? Much of it came from low-ranking faculty members, especially from Dr. Herbert Schönebaum, of Freyer's Institut für Kultur- und Universalgeschichte. Though almost Freyer's age, Schönebaum was only an *Oberassistent*. He was among those who had joined the Nazi party in the spring of 1933, probably to advance his career.[74] Schönebaum had studied with Karl Lamprecht and regarded himself as the keeper of Lamprecht's legacy.[75] Judging from internal evidence in the 1935

---

[72] See Hans Linde, "Soziologie in Leipzig," 112; Helmut Schelsky, "Die verschiedenen Weisen, wie man Demokrat sein kann: Erinnerungen an Hans Freyer, Helmuth Plessner und andere," 143.

[73] "Bericht."

[74] UAL, Philosophische Fakultät, "Betr. NSDAP 1934–1942," E66.

[75] See *Karl Lamprecht: Ausgewählte Schriften*; Herbert Schönebaum, "Karl Lamprecht, Leben

report, his role of informant against Freyer appears to have been motivated above all by resentment against him as a sociological usurper of Lamprecht's historical institute.[76] Among the others who provided information against Freyer and his circle were two additional *Assistenten* at other institutes, the *Führer* of the Dozentenschaft, Koeppen, and his deputy, Mathias, as well as a professor from Königsberg. In addition, the writer of the report had access to files at Gestapo headquarters in Dresden, which contained copies of correspondence between Freyer's friends. It is clear from the report that the writer himself had attended Freyer's colloquia in an effort to gather information.

Given his awareness of the ubiquity of denunciations at the university, Freyer almost certainly realized that he too was an object of surveillance.

Other extant documents reveal the suspicion with which Freyer had come to be regarded by various National Socialist groups. An SS report on the Büro Ribbentrop—a National Socialist foreign policy organization that worked parallel to the foreign office until Ribbentrop's appointment as foreign minister in 1938—named Freyer as among those who exerted the greatest influence on Professor Oberlander, the man responsible for eastern European problems in Ribbentrop's organization. Freyer, Max Hildebert Boehm, and Erich Rothacker were regarded by the SS as harmful because they used Nazi terms such as *Volk* while interpreting them in a cultural rather than racial sense.[77] By 1937, Heinrich Harmjanz, a candidate for an important post in the Ministry of Education, had to defend himself from the accusation of association with the "*bündisch-reactionary circle*" around Freyer.[78]

In 1936 Hans Freyer published *Die politische Insel*, which was both a scholarly history of utopian thought and a subtly conveyed Aesopian critique of the pretensions of the Third Reich.[79] Short excerpts from the book, though by no means its most critical portions, were published in several newspapers, including the 1937 New Year's edition of the *Stuttgarter Neues Tageblatt*.[80]

und Werk eines Kämpfers um die Geschichtswissenschaft, 1856–1913."

[76] This impression was confirmed in an interview with Gerhard Liebers, who knew Schönebaum well during the period in question.

[77] Die Dienstelle des Außerordentlichen und Bevollmächtigen Botschafters des Deutschen Reiches, ihre Mitarbeiter und politischen Auswirkungen," ca. 1936, in the file of SS officer Dr. Lothar Kuehne, BDC.

[78] "Betr.: Dozent Dr. Heinrich Harmjanz" (unsigned), 16 March 1937, File: "Heinrich Harmjanz," BDC.

[79] The book itself is discussed below.

[80] I have been unable to locate the original of this article but assume it is similar to or identical with Freyer's article, "Das Land Utopia, ein ewiger Traum der Menschheit," in *Aus Zeit und Leben: Wochenbeilage des Hannoverschen Anzeigers*, 17 January 1937, copy in UAL, PA Freyer, 105ff.

In March 1937 Freyer received a worried letter from an editor of the news-paper informing him that his article had aroused the suspicion of the local National Socialist student association, which had written to its counterpart in Saxony in search of information on Freyer and his attitude toward the regime. The Saxons had provided a negative evaluation of Freyer's loyalty to National Socialism. This had led to problems for the newspaper. "The whole business has been going on since January," wrote the editor. "It is not only the local student association that has expressed concern about the essay and its author," he added ominously.[81]

One week later the editor in chief of the paper wrote to the dean of Freyer's faculty in a tone of greater distress. There was considerable concern with Freyer's article among "party circles" who regarded the article as incompatible with National Socialism. "In their statements to me there was mention time and again of discussions on the matter within party organizations." A *Gau* meeting was cited in which local political leaders had denounced Freyer for his "critical attitude" toward the regime.[82]

The dean defused the incident. He obtained a letter from the local *Studentenführer* stating that while there had been some doubts about Freyer at the time of the publication of his *Das politische Semester*, cooperation between Freyer and the student leadership was now problem-free.[83] The letter was for-warded to Stuttgart and seems to have brought the incident to an end.[84]

Despite his rhetoric about the importance of risk and wager in life, Hans Freyer was a cautious man by nature.[85] From 1935 to 1937 he had seen Wach forced into emigration, Litt compelled by harassment into "voluntary" retirement, and Krueger first removed from his rectorship, then hectored to the point of a heart attack. His friend Carl Schmitt, who had gone to great lengths to accommodate himself to National Socialism, had fallen from grace, brought down by Reinhard Höhn.[86] Another longtime member of Freyer's institute of sociology, Hugo Fischer, had been dogged by suspicion because of his ties to

---

[81] Emil Belzner to Hans Freyer, 18 March 1937, UAL, PA Freyer, 104.

[82] Hauptschriftenleiter, *Stuttgarter Neues Tageblatt* to Dekan der philosophischen Fakultät, 24 March 1937, UAL, PA Freyer, 107.

[83] Thiel, Gaustudentenführer Sachsen to De-kan (Münster), 13 April 1937, UAL, PA Freyer, 108.

[84] Dekan to Hans Freyer, 16 April 1937, UAL, PA Freyer, 109.

[85] Freyer's friend Gehlen gave him the nick-name "vorsichtiges Hänschen." Interview with Helmut Schelsky. See also Schelsky, *Rückblicke*, 149.

[86] Bendersky, *Carl Schmitt*, 195–242.

[87] See "Niederschrift, Sitzung der Kommis-sion betr. Ernennung Fischer zum nichtpl. ao. Professor, 15 January 1936," UAL, PA Fischer, 63–64.

Ernst Jünger and the National Bolshevist Widerstandskreis.[87] In 1936 Fischer took a leave of absence on grounds of poor health. Early in 1938 he managed to find a minor position in Norway, and he remained in exile through the balance of the Nazi years.[88]

By 1937 Freyer had witnessed the departure from the University of Leipzig of many of his closest colleagues under varying degrees of duress. The attack upon him by the Stuttgart students and the degree of suspicion toward him within Nazi circles that it brought to light may have been the straw that broke the camel's back. Tired of the constant possibility of denunciation or criticism from one or another of the many organizations of cultural control, Freyer in mid-1937 set in motion a process that allowed him and his family to spend the second half of the Third Reich beyond the borders of Nazi Germany.[89]

What effect did Freyer's gradual disillusion have on his public behavior, on the political image he conveyed to his students?

The testimony of Freyer's former students and colleagues at Leipzig in the years prior to his departure for Budapest in 1938—including those who were fundamentally hostile to National Socialism—confirms the image of a man deliberately ambiguous in his relationship to the Hitler regime. In lectures and public appearances Freyer would give no hint that he was anything but a supporter of the regime, though he appeared less enthusiastic than colleagues and disciples such as Ipsen or Pfeffer. Colleagues opposed to National Socialism knew—by means of the sixth sense attuned to verbal codes which it is almost impossible for the historian to reconstruct—that Freyer could be "trusted," and to them he confided his own critical attitude toward the regime.[90] Intelligent students who themselves harbored anti-Nazi sympathies and who participated in Freyer's seminars also perceived his critical attitude, expressed in Aesopian form.[91] Whether Freyer's behavior is seen as deceptive (*täuschend*) or as

[88] "Niederschrift," 89, 97; Linde, "Soziologie in Leipzig," 109.

[89] Cf. Schelsky, "Verschiedene," 148. The insidious effect of informants and denunciations on the quality of academic life in the Third Reich is noted by Karl Dietrich Bracher, "Die Gleichschaltung der deutschen Universität," 135–36; Kleinberger, "Gab es?," 17. For an outstanding firsthand account, see Gerhard Ritter, "The German Professor in the Third Reich."

[90] Interview with Gerhard Liebers; interviews with Hans-Georg Gadamer. See especially the public comments by Gadamer at the *Arbeitsta-*

gung of the Fritz-Thyssen Stiftung, seconded by Alfred Heuß (Karl-Siegbert Rehberg, ed., Protokoll. Arbeitstagung der Fritz-Thyssen-Stiftung, "Gab es eine 'Leipziger Schule' der Soziologie und Sozialphilosophie?" am 29. und 30. April 1982, 25–26).

[91] Interview with Hellmut Becker, West Berlin, 27 May 1982. Becker, the son of Carl Heinrich Becker, the liberal Prussian minister of culture during the Weimar Republic, studied law at Leipzig beginning in 1937 and participated as a student in Freyer's seminar.

clever (*geschickt*) depends upon the retrospective eye of the observer.[92] Freyer apparently deflected no student from confirmed National Socialist beliefs, while more skeptical students could find validation in Freyer's behavior and utterances.

Documents of Disillusion: Freyer's Writings, 1935–1944

In the decade after 1934, Freyer's relationship to the National Socialist regime developed from personal disaffection to principled dissent. The development of his critique of National Socialism can be traced in the books that he published in the Third Reich and in other works written "for the desk drawer," to be published under more favorable conditions.

Some methodological strictures for the interpretation of such texts were sketched by Leo Strauss in his essay "Persecution and the Art of Writing," first published in 1941.[93] The contemporary experience of intellectuals under totalitarian regimes was the explicit starting point of Strauss's reflections. In an ideologically based regime in which heterodox intellectuals are subject to persecution, he wrote, "a man of independent thought can utter his views in public and remain unharmed, provided he moves with circumspection. He can even utter them in print without incurring any danger, provided he is capable of writing between the lines." Works written under these circumstances contain an exoteric message—"a popular teaching of an edifying character which is in the foreground"—and an esoteric message addressed to particularly intelligent or trustworthy readers, which appears "between the lines."[94]

The techniques of writing "between the lines" during the Third Reich have been studied mainly by historians of literature. Among dissenting novelists in the Third Reich there developed a style characterized by "a tendency toward the veiled remark, the significant pause, the double or triple meaning. It also involved reliance on the sensitivity of the reader to pick up a literary allusion, a biblical reference or a historical parallel with relevance to National Socialism." Indeed, the only literary development of the Nazi era was "progressive refinements in techniques of making oblique statements."[95] The use of these allusive or Aesopian techniques was not confined to fiction or *belles lettres*. They

---

[92] The first adjective was applied by Gadamer, the second by Liebers.

[93] Leo Strauss, "Persecution and the Art of Writing," reprinted in his *Persecution and the Art of Writing*, to which page references refer.

[94] Strauss, "Persecution," 24–30.

[95] J. M. Ritchie, *German Literature under National Socialism*, 119. See also the useful discussion of the character and limits of this mode of writing in R. Schnell, "Innere Emigration und kulturelle Dissidenz," esp. 218–20.

were used by journalists and by academic intellectuals such as Hans Freyer as well.

The ability of the like-minded to interpret the heterodox meaning beneath seemingly orthodox or unpolitical statements is a skill well developed under totalitarian regimes. Such statements were necessarily ambiguous: had they not been they would not have fulfilled their function of expressing dissent while avoiding censorship or punishment. When the critical contemporary allusions were too obvious the works in question were not allowed to reach the public. Those concerned with recapturing the intellectual dynamics of life in a totalitarian regime must try to read as the author's intended reader would have read.[96] Though the possibility of recapturing this original meaning is fraught with hazards, the historian must "adapt the rules of certainty which guide his research to the nature of his subject."[97] This requires a subtle form of reading, with rules other than those appropriate to works written in open societies. The citation of sources in such works, for example, is often not an indication of influence but an attempt to demonstrate to the censor—who is presumed to be a none-too-subtle reader—the ideological acceptability of the work. Conversely, the most important intellectual influences may, for political reasons, not be mentioned at all. If the *argument* of the work is at odds with the orthodox sources cited, or with the orthodox terminology employed, then such citations and terminology should be understood as genuflections or as camouflage, not as indicative of the work's political meaning.

These difficulties in recapturing the meaning and significance of texts written in the Third Reich are compounded in the case of intellectuals like Freyer, whose disenchantment with the regime was gradual, so that the texts sometimes reflect a genuine *ambivalence* toward the regime. Yet it is possible to reconstruct his trajectory of disillusion by tracing his changing position toward key issues as reflected in successive texts.

The first evidence of Freyer's alarm at the direction taken by the National Socialist regime appeared in his writings of 1935. It was in the midst of a text that was in good part an apology for the regime. *Pallas Athene* was a work of political reflection, cast in the philosophic-poetic style of Freyer's works of the early 1920s, *Antäus* and *Prometheus*. Once again Freyer used a figure from Greek mythology as an embodiment of his contemporary concerns. The choice of Athena, the protectress of the polis, reflected the book's theme: the

---

[96] For a more extended discussion of the use of Aesopian writing in the Third Reich and the appropriate rules of interpretation see Muller, "Enttäuschung."

[97] Strauss, "Persecution," 30.

creation and preservation of an integrated cultural and political order. The book's subtitle *Ethik des politischen Volkes* announced this goal. The ancient polis was clearly intended as a model for contemporary Germany.

The subtitle was conceived only after the book had been written and partially obscures Freyer's original purpose. He had intended to subtitle the work "Theory of the Conservative Revolution" but changed it in the spring of 1935 at the suggestion of his publisher, Niels Diederichs of the Eugen Diederichs Verlag.[98] The book was thus written in late 1934 and early 1935. Before turning to the book's contents it is necessary to glance at its political context in order to understand the significance of the original subtitle.

The timing of the composition of *Pallas Athene*, as well as its contents, indicate that the book was in part Freyer's response to the events of 30 June 1934. On this so-called Night of the Long Knives, Ernst Roehm and other leaders of the SA were systematically murdered by the SS. The murders occurred with the collusion of the army and were intended to put to rest Roehm's challenge to it. This cooperation has led many retrospective analysts of the Third Reich to regard 30 June 1934 as the end of the "revolution from below," as an attempt by Hitler to consolidate his control at the expense of the more radical forces in his party.

Yet it was not this facet of events of 30 June which was most likely to strike contemporary radical conservatives such as Freyer. They were more concerned with the other series of murders that occurred on 30 June, those of intellectuals and politicians who were radical conservatives or leading figures in Nazi splinter groups. These included Kurt von Schleicher and his assistant Kurt von Bredow, who had tried in vain to bring about their own revolution from the right in late 1932, and Herbert von Bose and Edgar Jung, two radical conservatives closely associated with Franz von Papen, Hitler's vice-chancellor at the time. Shortly before the night of 30 June, Papen had delivered an address in Marburg, written by Jung and critical of the Nazi claim to exclusive leadership of the "German revolution."[99] Another victim of the blood purge was Gregor Strasser, who until his fall from Hitler's grace at the end of 1932 had been the Nazi leader most respected by non-Nazi radical conservatives.[100] Contemporary observers were likely to be struck above all by the fact that the

[98] Hans Freyer to Niels Diederichs, 1 February 1935; Diederichs to Freyer, 12 March 1935, Universitätsarchiv Jena, Sammlung Diederichs.

[99] On Jung, see Walter Struve, *Elites against Democracy*, chapter 10, esp. 250–52.

[100] On Gregor Strasser's role and reputation in 1932, see Peter Stachura, " 'Der Fall Strasser': Gregor Strasser, Hitler and National Socialism, 1930–32."

use of political murder—which had been carried out by the SA and other Nazi organizations in a spasmodic manner without direction from above—was now obviously an accepted tool of government policy, carried out by the SS, tolerated by the army, and legalized by a post facto law of 3 July 1934.[101]

The alarm that Freyer displayed in his writings of 1935 was not due to his identification with Schleicher, Papen, Strasser, or their followers. Rather, the events of June 30 and the legislation that followed destroyed any non-Nazi counterweight to Hitler's power in the cabinet and provided further evidence of the suspicion with which many Nazis viewed the conservatives and radical conservatives who had helped them to power. Those who had been necessary to the National Socialist attainment of power now seemed to some as obstacles to the totalitarian claims of the Nazi movement.

On the rhetorical or ideological level, the friction between radical conservatives and some National Socialists took the form of conflicting claims regarding the relationship of the state to the Nazi party. Freyer and other radical conservatives had long sought to create a closed, integrated culture through an all-encompassing state. In National Socialism they saw a mass, popular movement that would pave the way for such a state, and in 1933 they believed that the hour of "the total state" had dawned. The theme of the "total" or "totalitarian" state long favored by Freyer and his circle was echoed in the course of 1933 by Goebbels and by Hitler himself.[102]

After the summer of 1934, however, the Nazis changed their tune. As Hitler, with the SS as his major instrument, consolidated his power vis-à-vis the claims of the SA on the one hand, and those of his nonparty allies on the other, a change of emphasis occurred in official rhetoric. In his concluding address to the Nazi party congress of September 1934, Hitler launched an attack on the theory of the total state. It was not the claim to total power that he disputed. But the site of this power was to be the party, not the state. "The state is not our master; we are the masters of the state," he concluded.[103] In retrospect it appears that this change of rhetoric was not immediately accompanied by an actual strengthening of the power of the party at the expense of the state bureaucracy.[104] Yet this could not have been clear to Freyer at the time. The

[101] On the events and significance of 30 June, see Wolfgang Sauer, *Die Mobilmachung der Gewalt*, 324–64; Broszat, *The Hitler State*, 204–15; Bracher, *The German Dictatorship*, 236–44.

Among those involved in the retrospective legitimation of "the blood purge" was Carl Schmitt. See Bendersky, *Carl Schmitt*, 214–18.

[102] See the quotes in Franz Neumann, *Behemoth*, 48–49.

[103] Quoted in ibid., 65.

[104] Broszat, *The Hitler State*, 213.

murder of non-Nazi fellow travelers of the regime and the rhetorical emphasis from the top on the *Führer* and the party as the only locus of authority probably confirmed for Freyer what his own experience in the DGS and at the University of Leipzig was already indicating: in place of a new unity created by the state, or the subordination of individual interests to those of the collectivity, Nazi Germany was shaped by ongoing internal struggles for power, accompanied by the demand for ideological purity and party orthodoxy. None of this boded well for the future of non-Nazi fellow travelers of the revolution from the right.

In the introduction to *Pallas Athene*, Freyer insisted that in the present historic moment an attempt by scholars to turn away from events in the name of freedom of the spirit was morally irresponsible. The present moment was one of renewal, when history was pregnant with meaning. The role of the intellect was to grasp the meaning inherent in contemporary events.[105]

Much of the book was a restatement of Freyer's favorite theme: the contrast between "bourgeois" and "political" existence. The former was governed by the mundane quest for comfort and security, the latter by the pursuit of virtue, in Machiavelli's sense.[106] Only through *Herrschaft*, wrote Freyer, could the *Bürger* be torn out of his desire for comfort, for economic betterment, and for security. The creation of the ancient polis as of the modern *Reich* demanded the "violation of human nature" (*Vergewältigung der menschlichen Natur*), without which men would remain mired in their private concerns, never creating "temples, fortresses, or palaces."[107] This process of forcefully tearing the individual out of his private realm and preparing him to sacrifice for collective goals Freyer referred to as "the alchemy of politics."[108] The alchemy of politics, he wrote, required leaders capable of arousing the enthusiasm and faith of the masses of the *Volk*.[109]

The new theme of *Pallas Athene* was announced in its original subtitle, "Theory of the Conservative Revolution." "No matter how revolutionary it is in its origins," wrote Freyer, "the ultimate meaning of all politics is conservative." The true test of political leadership was to create a stable, durable political structure after the flames of initial enthusiasm had abated. The key to this second stage of the revolution was the ability to turn revolutionary passion and excitement into a more sober, stable order.[110] An authentically creative politics,

[105] Hans Freyer, *Pallas Athene: Ethik des politischen Volkes* (1935), 7–10.
   [106] Ibid., 38, 45.
   [107] Ibid., 49–51, 71–79.

[108] Ibid., 51.
[109] Ibid., 56–58.
[110] Ibid., 59–61.

wrote Freyer in obvious reference to recent events, must be able to "control the forces it has unleashed," to transform "the fanatics of attack into fanatics of defense."[111]

As always, Freyer insisted that real stability depended upon continuity with the legacy of the past, on a connection with the "unvanquished sources of the *Volk*." But once again he provided little inkling as to the content of this legacy.[112] He concluded the book with an image that conjured up this purported continuity of German history in the most bathetic of terms:

> In pictures of our grandfathers we recognize our face. Are a hundred generations really so many more than three? To the eternal will of the blood the difference is small. The present-day peasant behind his plow and the soldier beneath his modern helmet are of the same stock as the Vikings, the barbarian invaders and the Teutoburg forest. . . .
>
> Only those ages are great whose thought and action are linked to this timeless essence. A knowledge of the power of roots arises in them, independent of research. Above all, the roots themselves reawake to a new spring. History in its immediacy arises out of them once more. The anonymous *Volk* rises up and pronounces a political "yes." Out of the old sap there arises once again an epoch that has meaning.[113]

Pallas Athene marked Freyer's last and most explicit attempt at ideological writing during the Third Reich. Its tone was not only engaged but rhapsodic, its style not merely belletristic but poetic. Its thoughts on history, leadership, and the state were conveyed through a cataract of images and often paradoxical assertions. Most contemporary reviewers remarked upon the poetic style and ideological substance of the book. Their assessment of Freyer's style depended upon their evaluation of the ideology it conveyed.

Arnold Gehlen, a professor of philosophy at Leipzig who was Freyer's former assistant and current colleague, reviewed *Pallas Athene* for the radical conservative journal *Europäische Revue*. He found the book a font of wisdom, its poetic style a fruitful use of analogy to convey the contradictions and paradoxes of political life.[114]

The most biting critique of the style and substance of Freyer's book was published in the *Berliner Tageblatt*. This newspaper, once the flagship daily of the liberal Mosse publishing empire, had been *gleichgeschaltet* in 1933 and kept open by Goebbels as a showpiece of the "free press" in the Third Reich. Among its reporters, however, was Hans Gerth, a left-wing sociologist, who

[111] Ibid., 64, 120.
[112] Ibid., 120, passim.
[113] Ibid., 122.

[114] Arnold Gehlen, review of *Pallas Athene*, by Hans Freyer (1936), 147–49.

was able to convey to the (largely liberal and Jewish) readership of the paper a critique of the regime and its cultural life. Gerth did so by means of an ironic style, as demonstrated in his review of Freyer's book. Gerth began by parodying Freyer's purple prose:

> Erected high on the acropolis, the citadel on top of the city, stood the image of the goddess. Head high, shield to the side. Lance pointed heavenward so that its tip in the gleam of the sun sinking into the sea could show the goal and the way even to the distant ships. Under this sign, under the image of the virgin, the goddess of the pugnacious spirit and of laborious creation, stand the essays of this cleverest of the young German sociologists.

Gerth then ridiculed the contradictory assertions of Freyer's book, which Gehlen perceived as wise paradox:

> It is devoted to elaborating the historical existence of the *Volk*, which is eternal, in that it is continually rejuvenated . . . which gains a shape through breaking forms whose countenance radiates when its face darkens. . . .
>
> One can compile many such paradoxes. What can one do with it? Not much. Freyer's book does not stand in the ranks of works of political enlightenment which since Machiavelli's work have accompanied political practice in the hope of making a science of politics. Freyer's work does not belong in this stream of theory. It is a political theory of redemption, which like all real faith ends in paradox. . . . Under the sign of the images of the gods the essays form a political tract. . . . Words full of wise beauty, and cleverly stated, but they are oriented not primarily to the intellect—despite their spiritedness—but to the feelings.[115]

The book was reviewed with enthusiasm in the *Nationalsozialistische Partei-Korrespondenz*, the party's press service. Uncritical acclaim for Freyer's work in a party journal during the Third Reich was unusual. The reviewer was the journal's editor, Gerhard Krüger, a former Nazi student activist whom Freyer had awarded a doctorate some months earlier for a very insubstantial dissertation entitled *Student und Revolution*.[116] Krüger repaid the favor in his enthusiastic review.

[115] Hans Gerth, review of *Pallas Athene, Berliner Tageblatt*, 26 May 1935. On Gerth's journalistic activity for the *Tageblatt*, see the interview with him in Mathias Greffrath, ed., *Die Zerstörung einer Zukunft*, 68–78.

[116] Gerhard Krueger, *Student und Revolution: Ein Beitrag zur Soziologie der revolutionären Bewe-*

gung (1934). The dissertation was accepted by the faculty in September 1934, with Freyer as first reader. It received a grade of "hinreichend," the lowest possible passing grade. Since the work was little more than a propaganda tract, this was a generous assessment on Freyer's part.

More typical of the response to Freyer's work in party circles was the review by Wolfgang Erxleben of the Amt Rosenberg, that kennel of ideological watchdogs. Though he regarded the book as "an intelligent and honorable path to the spirit of our *Führer*," his review was quite critical. He found disturbing Freyer's description of the political action of the *Führer* as a wager that could come to nought unless met by a readiness of the *Volk* to be formed, since it cast doubt upon the "necessary relationship" between the *Führer*'s acts and the "inner, vital laws of the German *Volk*." Moreover, only at the end of the book did Freyer refer to "the eternal law of our blood and race." In short, from the perspective of this ideologue, even Freyer's most ideological work carried far too many traces of relativizing social-scientific analysis and threatened to undermine belief in the inexorable necessity of the pillars of Nazi ideology. Erxleben found Freyer insufficiently committed and concluded that the equivocation in his book made it unable to speak to the heart.[117]

Yet Erxleben was quite correct in noting that Freyer's book contained passages that suggested the possible inadequacy of the current leader and his movement.

In *Pallas Athene* Freyer introduced a distinction between authentic and inauthentic states. Enduring states, he wrote, were not simply structures of power. Coercion, terror, mass organizations, and mass suggestion might be used to create a state but could not preserve one. The ultimate criterion distinguishing authentic from inauthentic states was their degree of popular legitimacy: it was the ongoing faith of the populace in the government and the regime's historical depth that distinguished the authentic state from a tyranny.[118]

Freyer reiterated these reflections in stronger terms in an article entitled "Wille zum Staat," which was published shortly after *Pallas Athene* as a précis of the larger work. After noting the role of power (*Macht*), political action, and the political will of the *Führer* in the creation of the state, Freyer continued:

States, however, are not simply structures of power or artificial creations of violence: where they are only this, they lack the power of rootedness and are without essential significance, indeed without support and duration. One can succeed temporarily in bringing order to mass existence through all sorts of external means of coercion, of terror, and of organization. But the ideal of the political is not thereby fulfilled. The first serious challenge—and, if none occurs, the normal march of time will inevitably raise the ques-

[117] Wolfgang Erxleben, review of *Pallas Athene*, by Hans Freyer, in *Der deutsche Volkserzieher*, 1 March 1936, 225, copy in BAK, NS15, no. 202, 191–92.
[118] Freyer, *Pallas Athene*, 90–91.

tion of whether the state has won the spirit of the people. If this question is not answered with the affirmation of the multitude, it will not fade away but become louder and ever more urgent.[119]

Though *Pallas Athene* and "Willie zum Staat" read for the most part like a defense of National Socialism to its cultured despisers, their warnings against dependence on terror and organized coercion in the creation of a stable polity marked a significant turn in Freyer's thought. Up to 1934 it was the constructive, formative role of political power in the creation of a new community of collective purpose that had fascinated him. In his previous writing, the distinction between *Herrschaft* as legitimate authority and as the use of force had never been central. Only now, under the press of his actual experience of a movement seeking total *Herrschaft* and willing to use unlimited force to do so, did the limits and dangers of uncontrolled political power begin to concern him as a political theorist and publicist.

In his public lectures during and after 1935, Freyer continued to affirm his allegiance to the regime; he continued to deliver his Budapest speech of January 1934 with slight variations. Yet these variations hinted at his growing skepticism about the ideological claims of National Socialism and alarm at its actual practice. In his speeches of 1933 and in his Budapest address of 1934, Freyer tacitly acknowledged that he regarded the National Socialist conception of biological racism as the basis of collective identity and of cultural cohesion as implausible. By 1935 he began subtly to call attention to the problematic nature of any attempt to found a state upon biological, racist premises. In an essay of 1935, "The Political as a Problem for Philosophy," published in the journal of the Deutsche Philosophische Gesellschaft, Freyer alluded to the Hegelian notion of the role of philosophy as "its age grasped in thought." Among the most "immediate philosophical problems connected to the contemporary renewal of the German *Volk*" was that posed by the ideal of the *völkisch* state, he wrote. The problem was the relationship of the *Volk* as a political entity "to its existence as a natural type, to the continuity of blood [*Blutstrom*], and the imprint of prehistoric millennia." What sorts of political norms, Freyer asked, could be derived from these "deep levels of the *Volk*"?[120]

Freyer posed the question but gave no explicit answer, for to do so would have meant tackling Nazi ideology head on. He came close to this in a version of his standard propaganda talk published in Bucharest, Romania, in 1936. At

---

[119] Freyer, "Der Wille zum Staat" (1935), 192.
[120] Hans Freyer, "Das Politische als Problem der Philosophie" (1935–36), 66–67.

the end of an article in which he repeated his standard observations on the importance of political action and on the *Volk* as a source of identity and continuity, Freyer diverged from earlier versions of the talk, adding that

the two typical dangers of this modern historical consciousness are on the one hand an extreme activism, and on the other hand a plunge into the prehistoric night of determination by nature: and the possibilities of a short circuit between these two extremes are many.[121]

But Freyer's gradual disengagement from the cause of the Third Reich was reflected less by subtle shifts in his ideological writings than by his retreat from the role of ideologist. During the Weimar years Freyer had straddled the roles of ideologist and social scientist. In his *Habilitationsschrift* and works such as *Soziologie als Wirklichkeitswissenschaft*, he had made use of the methods of social-scientific research and argument for the ultimately ideological goal of undermining the legitimacy of "bourgeois society" and preparing the spiritual ground for a new positive epoch, a new *Reich*. His explicitly ideological works of those years, such as *Revolution von rechts*, had contained a large dose of sociological analysis. Yet even while he plunged into a flurry of ideological activity in the last years of the Weimar Republic, Freyer had continued to produce works that measured up to the highest standards of social-scientific research and critical distance, such as his essay "Systems of Universal Historical Reflection," which inaugurated a distinguished historical series edited by the historian Walter Goetz.[122]

Beginning with Hitler's assumption of the chancellorship in January 1933, Freyer's writing began a phase of near-total ideological involvement that lasted through 1935. Then, beginning in 1936, he embraced scholarship with a vengeance, producing works that conformed to his role as distanced, analytic social scientist in tone and overt content.

In an afterword to a new edition of one of Nietzsche's *Untimely Meditations*, published in 1937, Freyer called attention to the ongoing importance of "untimely reflection." The role of *Geist* (spirit or intellect), he wrote, was to shun the overly immediate and to provide criteria for evaluating contemporary

[121] Freyer, "Vom geschichtlichen Selbstbewußtsein des 20. Jahrhunderts," *Mélanges D. Gusti (Archiv pour la Science et la Reform Sociales)* 13 (1936): 7.

[122] Hans Freyer, "Systeme der weltgeschichtlichen Betrachtung," in *Propyläen-Weltgeschichte*, ed. Walter Goetz, vol. 1: *Das Erwachen der Mensch-*

heit (1931), 3–28. The essay appeared in Spanish in Ortega y Gasset's journal, *Revista de occidente* (Madrid) 33 (1931): 249–93. For another work of critical scholarship from 1931, see Freyer, "Typen und Stufen der Kultur," in *Handwörterbuch der Soziologie*.

reality by preserving norms that acted as a counterexample to the present. Ironically in view of his own recent *engagement*, Freyer contrasted the true *Geistigen* (men of the spirit) to "intellectuals" who were inextricably tied to their age either by kowtowing to it or by constant criticism of it.[123] These remarks were at odds with the emphasis on *engagement* so prominent in Freyer's writing up to 1935. It was this abandonment of the ideological mode of writing more than the Aesopian criticisms of the Third Reich that signaled his disillusion with the National Socialist revolution of the right.

Objective, accurate scholarship could in itself serve to deflate National Socialist claims. At a time when Alfred Bäumler and other Nazi stalwarts were reinterpreting Nietzsche as a forerunner of National Socialist ideology, Freyer contributed an article on Nietzsche to a volume entitled *Die großen Deutschen.* Freyer's tone was scholarly, his portrait of Nietzsche's life and thought judicious. In the biographical portion he noted Nietzsche's partial descent from the Polish nobility and his pride in his non-German origins. Freyer also conveyed Nietzsche's self-proclaimed struggle against all things German and against the German in himself. Though Freyer interpreted this struggle as based upon Nietzsche's high hopes for Germany, his article was critical of Nietzsche and far from the regime's ideologically preferred portrait.[124]

The Political Island: A History of Utopias from Plato to the Present, published in 1936, marked a further milestone on his road away from the affirmation of a total, political solution to the cultural problems of modernity. Not only was it a significant work of scholarly research, clear and sober in tone; it also suggested the folly of the attempt to realize a closed world of collective purpose through political action.

Yet this was the program to which Freyer had long been devoted. His first work on the problem of utopia, written on the eve of the First World War and published in 1920, had closed with a criticism of previous utopians for having ignored the problem of transforming the closed states of their imagining into reality. Freyer's enumeration of the characteristic features of utopian schemes in his work of 1936—the creation of an encapsulated, politicized order, based on a shared faith, with institutions that created citizens totally devoted to its preservation—was not appreciably different from his early essay on utopia. What had changed were his views on the wisdom of attempting to transform utopian ideals into reality.

[123] Hans Freyer, "Nachtwort," to Friedrich Nietzsche, *Vom Nutzen und Nachteil der Historie für das Leben* (1937), 89–91. On the history of the use of the designation *intellectuals* as a term of abuse, see Dietz Bering, *Die Intellektuellen: Geschichte eines Schimpfwortes.*

[124] Hans Freyer, "Friedrich Nietzsche, 1844–1900" (1936).

Freyer's description and analysis of various utopian and chiliastic works, though of interest to scholars of utopianism, are less significant for our purposes than his analysis of the historical attempts to establish such utopias. Attempts to realize the ideal of the best state, Freyer wrote, had always failed to create a significant historical structure or had resulted in a "frightening monster." As examples of the latter, he cited the attempt of the Anabaptists to create a chiliastic utopia in Münster in the mid-sixteenth century.[125] The experiment, Freyer wrote, began with the elimination of the magistracy and the rule of law, developed into a rule of terror, and ended with the execution of its leader and the collapse of this "heaven on earth." The idea of a thousand-year *Reich* and of a new Zion—realized by very impure hands, to be sure—became a horrible intermezzo of unleashed lust and bloodthirstiness."[126] It must surely have occurred to some of Freyer's readers that he had penned this description with more than the sixteenth century in mind.

As a second example of the monstrous result of attempts to realize utopian plans, Freyer cited the closed settlements of Amerindians established by the Jesuit order in Paraguay during the seventeenth century. On the surface, wrote Freyer, these settlements appeared to have translated Campanella's *City of the Sun* into reality. Economic activity, marriage, and religious instruction were closely integrated and controlled by the ruling Jesuits. It gave the appearance of a rationally planned, self-enclosed, and self-perpetuating community.

In fact, Freyer wrote, this appearance was deceptive; and the reality of the Jesuit experiment in Paraguay was important for developing a critique of utopia. The actions of its inhabitants were not governed by their internalization of the demands of a rational order but by the ongoing intervention of the Jesuits, backed by the whip of the Corregidors, natives chosen by the Jesuits as their accessories. A communal state in appearance, it had in reality functioned as a system of coerced labor that served the power interests of its Jesuit rulers.

All utopian conceptions, Freyer continued, even those which were purportedly democratic, would lead to the creation of far more unified and concentrated positions of power than had existed in previous states. Modern utopias regularly called for the concentration of social power in the hands of banks that were to control all credit, offices of foreign trade that were to control the economic surplus of the entire economy, or similar centralized institutions. Yet they proceeded on the assumption that the incumbents of these new agglom-

[125] Compare Hans Freyer, "Das Problem der Utopie" (1920), 328–33, to his *Die politische Insel: Eine Geschichte der Utopien von Platon bis zur Ge-* *genwart* (1936), 22–38.
[126] Freyer, *Insel*, 160.

erations of power would act as if they were entirely lacking in self-interest. It was at this point, Freyer wrote, that most utopian visions broke off. The Jesuit experiment allowed for empirical observation of what actually occurred when such a scheme was put into operation. It thus permitted a realistic answer to the question of "*cui bono?*" In fact it was a new ruling caste that benefited and exercised its control for the sake of goals far removed from the common welfare.[127]

Together with Freyer's reassessment of the utopian project went a reevaluation of the significance of Plato's major works. In Freyer's essay of 1914 and throughout the two decades that followed, it was Plato's *Republic*, with its vision of a fully integrated polity in which control was vested in the hands of the wise, that had most attracted him.[128] In his book of 1936, by contrast, Freyer stressed that it was *only* in the unlikely circumstance of rule by philosopher kings that the concentration of government power envisioned in the *Republic might* make political sense.[129] In his evaluation of Plato's political philosophy, Freyer placed a new emphasis on Plato's late work the *Laws*. It was Plato's call in the *Laws* for a state based upon law, institutions, and a formal system of administration rather than the unbounded rule of the wise advocated in the *Republic* that Freyer now emphasized.[130] In his 1914 essay Freyer had devoted only one sentence to the *Laws*, Plato's portrait of the "second-best state," describing it as a product of "the wisdom of age but also of a good deal of compromise and the abandonment of a good part of Plato's collapsed hopes for Sicily."[131] In 1936, as his own hopes were collapsing, Freyer returned to the riddle of the relationship between the *Republic* and the *Laws*.

The term *second-best state* is often taken as the solution to this riddle; the state of the *Laws* is interpreted as a conscious reconciliation with the conditions of reality, as a return to earth and a turning away from the divine goal, as a concession or compromise. These notions, especially the latter, i.e., the *Laws* as a work of concession and compromise, lead to serious misconceptions. Far more accurate is the oft-drawn comparison of this work of Plato's old age with the second part of [Goethe's] *Faust* and with *Wilhelm Meisters Wanderjahre*, works . . . of wise resignation.[132]

The proper role of utopia, Freyer concluded, was to remain "nowhere," be-

[127] Ibid., 160–64.
[128] Freyer, "Das Problem der Utopie," 340–42. In the late 1920s Freyer had intended to write a book on Plato focused on the *Republic*. Freyer had taught the *Republic* in his seminars and, as one of his students recalls, was much attracted by the notion of an integrated society founded and controlled by intellectuals. Interview with Ernest Manheim.
[129] Freyer, *Insel*, 163.
[130] Ibid., 60–63.
[131] Freyer, "Das Problem der Utopie," 341.
[132] Idem, *Insel*, 62.

yond politics, to serve at best as an ideal.[133] The publication of *The Political Island* marked Freyer's own transition from utopianism to a wiser resignation.

In 1938, shortly before his departure for Budapest, Freyer published *Machiavelli*, his last work of scholarship to be published and distributed in the Third Reich. Freyer had long been attracted to Machiavelli as an analyst of power and its role in the re-creation of collective virtue. Even before 1933 Freyer had taught Machiavelli in his courses on politics, and after 1933, when he assumed a chair of political science, it was to Machiavelli that he turned as the founder of a science of *Herrschaft*.

Freyer's renewed fascination with Machiavelli had thus grown out of his ideological commitment to the creation of a leadership stratum for the new *Reich*. As he became increasingly disillusioned with the prospects for the new *Reich*, the scholarly fruits of his research remained even while its ideological motive faded. Ironically, *Machiavelli* was perhaps the closest Freyer ever came to publishing a work of "pure," distanced social science.

The book was a study of Machiavelli's political thought, which drew upon the political and biographical context of Machiavelli's major works in order to explicate their meaning. Freyer distinguished three levels of Machiavelli's thought. The first, the amoral, technical science of how to gain and maintain political power, corresponded to what was usually termed "Machiavellism."[134] Deeper than this level was Machiavelli's ongoing concern for the creation of political virtue, those collective qualities which made possible the creation of an empire (*Reich*), best exemplified by imperial Rome and reflected in his *Discourses*.[135] The third level, which Freyer saw reflected in *The Prince* and in its dedication to Lorenzo de' Medici, Freyer termed the "ethic of the historical moment." For Freyer, as for Machiavelli, the contemplation of politics from the perspective of universal ethical norms was "typically unpolitical." The problem of the re-creation of virtue at a particular historical moment demanded that the truly political man adapt the available means to this end.[136] Fourteenth-century Venice was not first-century Rome; the Roman people were a "young people" with their virtue intact, while the Venice of Machiavelli's time was marked by corruption.[137] *The Prince* was a book about the struggle against the corrupt condition. Corrupt peoples, wrote Freyer in his summary of Machiavelli's thought, produced not rulers marked by virtue but political adventurers who could, temporarily at least, master fate (*fortuna*).[138]

[133] Ibid., 165–66.
[134] Hans Freyer, *Machiavelli* (1938), 92–96 passim.
[135] Ibid., 98–124.
[136] Ibid., 79, 149.
[137] Ibid., 107.
[138] Ibid., 135.

Here Freyer's interpretation of Machiavelli reflected his own recent experience. Freyer portrayed Machiavelli's dedication of *The Prince* to Lorenzo de' Medici, a man of *fortuna* rather than of *virtù*, as the prime example of Machiavelli's "ethic of the political moment." The demand of the hour was the unification of Italy and its liberation from foreign domination. The question facing Machiavelli was "who was in a position to do so." "One cannot invent the men capable of fulfilling the demands of the hour," Freyer wrote; "one must take them as they are."[139] It may well be that Freyer had resorted to this logic to still his own doubts about Adolf Hitler.

Toward the end of his book Freyer cast doubt on Machiavelli's claim that a corrupt ruler could bring about a renewal of virtue through corrupt means, in terms that had considerable contemporary resonance:

> Virtue cannot be coerced; it comes and goes, is present or not. It is extremely doubtful that by means of a rule of terror [*Schreckenherrschaft*] one can form a political *Volk*, rather than simply a Cesare Borgia state, . . . It is similarly doubtful that when one fights corruption with corrupt means one can create real *virtù*, rather than simply successfully deterred criminals. Here is where the critique of the second and more authentic Machiavellism ought to begin, which pushes the alchemy of politics so far that it seeks to make corruption plus corruption equal to gold.[140]

Later Freyer used the figure of Machiavelli to pen a still sharper critique of the reality of National Socialism. This most Aesopian of Freyer's books arose in conjunction with seminars that he gave at Leipzig in 1936 and 1937, and if the memory of one of his students is correct, Freyer had completed the manuscript before 1940 but declined to publish it out of caution.[141] Printed in Leipzig in 1944 as *Prussiandom and Enlightenment: A Study of Friedrich the Great's "Antimachiavel,"* the book never reached its public. The entire edition, together with other books by the same publisher, was destroyed before the book could be distributed, under circumstances that remain obscure.[142]

In the book Freyer used Friedrich's critique of *The Prince* to present an extended, veiled attack on the tendency of National Socialism to substitute force

---

[139] Ibid., 141–42.

[140] Ibid., 150.

[141] Interview with Helmut Schelsky. Freyer offered a seminar entitled "Preußentum als politisches und ethisches Prinzip," during the summer semester of 1936, and another one year later entitled "Preußen (Idee und geschichtliche Wirklichkeit)."

[142] Hans Freyer, *Preußentum und Aufklärung:*

Eine Studie über Friedrich des Großen, Antimachiavel (1944). The sole extant copy was in the possession of Freyer's widow, Frau Käthe Freyer, who kindly allowed me to make a photocopy of it. After the manuscript of this book went to press, Freyer's book was finally published as Hans Freyer, *Preußentum und Aufklärung*, ed. Elfriede Üner (Weinheim, 1986).

for legitimacy. Freyer's repeated theme was the distinction between legitimate and illegitimate *Herrschaft*, with Cesare Borgia now conceived as the quintessence of the latter.

The attempt to serve a moral order by use of criminal means is a self-contradiction. . . . Whoever usurps power over men merely on the basis of some constellation of power, without inner legitimacy, finds himself in need of constantly expanding the means to support his power. . . . Finally matters reach the stage of that "cascade of crime" [described by Friedrich]: the methods become ever more harsh, ever more cruel, ever more tyrannical. Ultimately the whole structure collapses and buries its founder, proof that the ethical order of the world has not disappeared and that authentic *Herrschaft* cannot be founded upon forces that destroy it.[143]

Read carefully, with a sensitivity to their Aesopian allusions, Freyer's historical works written during the Third Reich conveyed his increasing disillusionment with the regime. Despite its warnings, Freyer's book on Machiavelli was dedicated "to those who love the fatherland more than the soul," a quotation drawn from Machiavelli's letters. Freyer's subsequent actions demonstrate the corrupting effects of serving the fatherland under a fundamentally corrupt regime.

Cultural Ambassador of the Reich, 1938–1945

In the summer of 1938, Hans Freyer moved with his family to Hungary, where he became the first (and, as it turned out, sole) incumbent of a visiting professorship in German cultural history at the University of Budapest. From 1941 through 1944 he was also head of the German Scientific Institute there. Both the chair and the institute were creations of the German Foreign Office, aimed at winning the sympathy of the Hungarian intellectual elite to the German cause.

Freyer's decision to serve as a cultural representative of the *Reich* abroad was a variant of a common career choice among conservative and radical conservative members of the *Bildungsbürgertum* who were disillusioned with Hitler's regime. They often gravitated to the army or the foreign service. Within these institutions, which were perceived as less tainted by National Socialist influence, they believed it was possible to serve the nation in the broad sense without serving the interests of National Socialism.[144] Whether this common choice

---

[143] Freyer, *Preußentum*, 69.
[144] After his disillusionment with the Nazi

regime, the poet Gottfried Benn joined the Reichswehr, which he described as "the aristo-

ultimately served to put a brake on the regime's more radical goals or whether it allowed the regime to use these members of the *Bildungsbürgertum* more effectively for its own ends remains an open question. The evidence in regard to Hans Freyer seems to support the latter verdict.

But how did a professor of sociology who spoke not a word of Hungarian come to hold such a post in the first place?

The sociology of southeastern Europe had been a topic of research at Freyer's institute before 1933. A scholarly concern with the area had been inspired by the efforts of the youth movement to establish contact with ethnic German minorities, as well as with the sovereign nationalities of the region. Up to 1933 the sociological study of southeastern Europe had been the purview of Gunther Ipsen.

The coming of the Third Reich brought a new salience to the problems of the ethnic Germans of eastern Europe (the so-called *Auslandsdeutschen* or *Volksdeutschen*) and renewed interest in the creation of a sphere of German hegemony in eastern and southeastern Europe. As early as 1933 there were attempts to harness these political currents to an expansion of southeastern European scholarship at Leipzig. The new rector of the university recalled that the city of Leipzig had long been a center of economic and political contact with southeastern Europe. In the irredentist idiom of the day he referred to Leipzig as a *Grenz-Universität* (a university on the border of the *Reich*) and staked its claim to dominance in the area of southeastern European studies, a claim strongly backed by the provincial Ministry of Education.[145]

Neither southeastern Europe in general nor Hungary in particular had been an area of Freyer's expertise before 1933. With Ipsen's departure for Königsberg in 1933, and with the upsurge in interest in southeastern European studies at the University of Leipzig, Hans Freyer assumed a greater role as a sponsor of research and teaching on the region.[146] Freyer's interest in Hungary seemed to wax as his hopes for the revolution from the right waned. During 1935 he accompanied a group of students from his institute to a summer program in Hungarian studies near Lake Balaton and in Budapest. He returned there again the next summer, lectured briefly, and began to form contacts among Hungarian academic intellectuals.[147]

---

cratic form of emigration." See Glenn R. Cuomo, "Purging an 'Art-Bolshevist': The Persecution of Gottfried Benn in the Years 1933–1938," 90.

[145] "Akademische Reden," 16–17. The rector refers here to his speech of November 1933.

[146] Interview with Walter Hildebrandt.

[147] Hans Freyer to Reichswissenschaftsministerium, 14 June 1936, UAL, PA Freyer, 95, 99.

At the same time Freyer became active in the expansion of southeast European studies at Leipzig. Early in 1936 it was decided to transform the unoccupied chair of sociology (vacated by Freyer in 1933) into a chair for the study of southeastern Europe, the centerpiece of a new institute to be housed within Freyer's Institut für Kulturgeschichte.[148] As was frequently the case during the Third Reich, political obstacles drew out the process of appointing a director. The candidate favored by Freyer, a Slavicist named Gesemann, was under consideration for over a year. A series of secret reports gathered by his *Dozentenführer* commenting on Gesemann's political associations, his purported philo-Semitism, and his divorce led to the rejection of his candidacy early in March 1937.[149] When the new institute opened its doors in September 1936, Freyer was the acting director of its division on the history and culture of southeastern Europe and the sponsor of its colloquium. Early in 1937 he delivered a public lecture, "German Cultural Influence in Southeastern Europe," stressing the historical and contemporary links between Germans and the peoples of southeastern Europe.[150] Shortly thereafter he opened the inaugural issue of the institute's journal with an article on mutual "understanding" (*Verstehen*) between peoples as the basis of scholarly dialogue.[151] Hans Freyer appeared to be remaking himself as a cultural diplomat with an expertise in southeastern Europe. In 1937 Freyer took advantage of an opportunity to leave Germany for one of the most desirable cities of central Europe, while remaining a well-remunerated public servant of the Third Reich.

Freyer was able to create such opportunities for himself because he continued to have admirers in the upper reaches of the cultural bureaucracies of the Third Reich. His sponsor in this case was Heinrich Harmjanz, a young *Volkskundler* (folklorist) and committed National Socialist from the University of Königsberg. Harmjanz had worked closely there with Freyer's old friend Gunther Ipsen. Harmjanz and Ipsen were co-editors of the *Zeitschrift für Volkskunde*, and Harmjanz had published a monograph in a series edited by Ipsen, Freyer, and Erich Rothacker.[152] In March 1937 Harmjanz joined the Ministry of Education as the official responsible for university appointments in the *Geisteswissenschaften*.[153]

In the second half of 1937 Hans Freyer was in contact with Harmjanz about

[148] "Memorandum" (signed Zinßner), 12 January 1936, UAL, B2/20/45.

[149] Ibid., passim.

[150] Hans A. Münster, "Das neue Leipziger Südosteuropa Institut" (April 1937), 80, 85.

[151] Hans Freyer, "Grundsätzliches über Verstehen, Verständigung und wissenschaftliches Gespräch zwischen Völkern" (April 1937).

[152] Heiber, *Walther Frank*, 649–50; Linde, "Soziologie in Leipzig," 121, 129.

[153] Heinrich Harmjanz, "Lebenslauf," in File: "Heinrich Harmjanz," BDC.

a post as first incumbent of a new visiting professorship of German cultural history at the University of Budapest.[154] In May 1938 he was officially nominated for the post by the philosophical faculty of the University of Budapest.[155]

The visiting professorship in German cultural history to which Freyer had been appointed was no ordinary academic chair. It had come into being as the product of extended negotiations on cultural cooperation between the governments of Horthy's Hungary and Hitler's Germany.[156] As early as 1935 the German ambassador in Budapest regarded the creation of such a chair as very much in the interests of the *Reich*.[157] Provisions for the chair were included in a comprehensive cultural agreement of 1936, and in October 1937 a committee composed of representatives of the Hungarian Ministry of Education met with representatives of the German Ministry of Education and the German Foreign Office to discuss details of the appointment. Potential occupants of the chair were to be nominated by the Ministry of Education and formally invited by the faculty of the University of Budapest.[158] Freyer's name was not among those originally suggested by the Hungarians, but when he was nominated by the German Ministry of Education, the suggestion was well received by both the Hungarian Ministry of Education and the philosophical faculty in Budapest.[159]

The German Foreign Office was pleased to obtain so prestigious an occupant for its chair in Budapest and hoped to appoint Freyer for three years beginning in September 1938. But the Saxon Ministry of Education insisted that the University of Leipzig could not spare him for that long. The ministry agreed to a leave of two years, without the possibility of extension.[160] Yet when Freyer moved with his family to Budapest, he took with him all his furniture and his library, suggesting an intention to remain abroad for more than two years.[161]

[154] Hans Freyer to Sächs. Ministerium für Volksbildung, 18 January 1938, UAL, PA Freyer, 113–14. In the letter Freyer refers to recent negotiations with Harmjanz.

[155] Hans Freyer to Dekan, 12 May 1938, UAL, PA Freyer, 116.

[156] The possibility of such a chair was first raised in 1934 in discussions between the Hungarian and German ministers of education. "Niederschrift," meeting of 13 October 1934, PA-AA, Gesandschaft Budapest, Kult. 2, no. 1, "Kulturabkommen," Bonn.

[157] Von Mackensen of Gesandschaft Budapest to Auswärtiges Amt Berlin, 25 May 1936, PA-AA, Gesandschaft Budapest, Kult. 2, no. 1,

"Kulturabkommen."

[158] "Abschrift zu Kult. Gen. 681," PA-AA, Gesandschaft Budapest, Kult. 2, no. 1, "Kulturpolitischen Beziehungen Ungarns zu Deutschland."

[159] Von Szily, Hungarian Ministry of Education, to Zschintsch, Reichserziehungsministerium, 27 April 1938, BAK, 21/208.

[160] Hans Freyer to Sächs. Ministerium für Volksbildung, 18 January 1938, UAL, PA Freyer, 113–14; Sächs. Ministerium für Volksbildung to Reichserziehungsministerium, 3 February 1938, UAL, PA Freyer, 115.

[161] Interview with Käthe Freyer.

Freyer and his family ultimately remained in Budapest until almost the end of the Second World War. The German Foreign Office repeatedly requested and received an extension of Freyer's stay in Budapest on the grounds that he was indispensable there.[162] With much of the teaching staff of the University of Leipzig drafted during the war, Freyer offered courses there during the summers of 1942 and 1943 but returned to Budapest for the bulk of the year.[163]

It is not difficult to understand why Freyer and his family should have preferred their life in Budapest to that in Leipzig. Budapest was a charming city for those who could afford to live well, and Freyer—who drew salaries from the University of Budapest, the German Ministry of Education, and the German Foreign Office—could. He lived with his family in a home in the heart of Budapest, where for some time conditions were less affected by the shortages of the war years than within the German *Reich*.[164]

But how did a professor of cultural history make himself "indispensable" in the eyes of the German Foreign Office?

As a visiting professor Freyer lectured in German to his Hungarian students. His duties at the University of Budapest were not onerous. Freyer taught a series of survey courses on German cultural history from the Middle Ages through the twentieth century and offered seminars on his favorite authors and topics: Hegel's philosophy of history, Nietzsche's philosophy of culture, Ranke's historiography, and the political testaments of Friedrich the Great and Bismarck, as well as German sociological thought. Yet it was not Freyer's teaching at the university that made him "indispensable" to the German embassy in Budapest.

Beginning in 1941 Freyer assumed a second official role, as head of the Deutsches Wissenschaftliches Institut (DWI) in Budapest. The DWI was one of a dozen such institutes founded by the German Foreign Office in European capitals between 1940 and 1943.[165] Each institute was made up of a language-study section, operated by the Deutsche Akademie in Munich; a student exchange bureau, operated by the Deutsche Akademische Austauschdienst; a library; and a "scholarly section," which formed the core of the institute.

---

[162] Reichserziehungsministerium to Sächs. Ministerium für Volksbildung, 9 February 1940; 2 March 1942; 18 January 1943; 22 April 1944, UAL, PA Freyer, 125, 133, 137, 147.

[163] Hans Freyer to Dekan, 7 April 1943, UAL, PA Freyer, 142.

[164] Interview with Käthe Freyer; interview with Ruth Buchenhorst. Ruth Buchenhorst was the librarian at the DWI in Budapest and a friend of the Freyer family.

[165] Volkhard Laitenberger, *Akademischer Austausch und auswärtige Kulturpolitik*, 150–51; Erich Siebert, "Die Rolle der Kultur- und Wissenschaftspolitik bei der Expansion des deutschen Imperialismus," 199–205.

The DWIs sought to function as a very sophisticated form of propaganda, whose effectiveness lay in their distance from normal propagandistic activity. As the chief of the cultural-political division of the German Foreign Office explained, "The propaganda of the scientific institutes ought to be in their scholarly accomplishments. The circles to which we are oriented are for the most part sophisticated, extremely critical, and not always our friends in advance."[166]

To this end prominent German scholars were chosen to head the various DWIs.[167] They were encouraged to gain the support of local scholars and intellectuals through scholarly lectures and projects sponsored by the institute, as well as to transmit information about such circles back to the Foreign Office.[168]

The image that Freyer's DWI in Budapest—like its counterparts elsewhere on the continent—sought to project was of German science, scholarship, and culture at their best. Freyer compiled a library for the institute that included the collected works of Goethe, Schiller, Hegel, Dilthey, and Weber.[169] The institute planned to translate and publish in German a series of works by Hungarian historians.[170] Among the German lecturers who visited the DWI Budapest were Ferdinand Sauerbruch, a distinguished surgeon and former rector of the University of Berlin, as well as the physicists Werner Heisenberg and Kurt Hahn. Others were old friends of Freyer's such as Carl Schmitt and Ernst Rudolf Huber, as well as Andreas Predöhl, a former colleague from Kiel, head of the Institute on the World Economy there and a leading advocate of the necessity of closed economic blocs.[171]

In addition to the positive image of German culture conveyed by Freyer's person, his institute, and its distinguished guests, his home was a meeting place for German and Hungarian scholars. In a report to the Foreign Office on his trip to Budapest, Predöhl praised Freyer as "the center of German *Kulturpolitik*" there.[172]

The best evidence of Freyer's success as a cultural ambassador to the Hungarian intellectual elite was his relationship to Gyula Szekfü. In the Horthy era

[166] "Bericht über die Tagung der Präsidenten der Kulturinstitute des auswärtigen Amtes vom 28. und 29. September 1942," BAK, R51, vol. 62.

[167] Laitenberger, *Austausch*, 150.

[168] "Bericht über die Tagung."

[169] Hans Freyer, ed., *Katalog der wissenschaftlichen Bibliothek—DWI Budapest*, 2 vols. (Budapest, 1941–42), copy in the Deutsche Bücherei Leipzig.

[170] Hans Freyer, "Das DWI in Budapest" (1941), 101.

[171] Interview with Ruth Buchenhorst, as well as PA-AA Gesandschaft Budapest, Kult. 2, nos. 1a–1d, passim.

[172] "Bericht des o. Prof. Andreas Predöhl über seine Vortragsreise nach Ungarn von 26. Februar bis 1. März 1940," PA-AA, Gesandschaft Budapest, Kult. 2, no. 1d: "Predöhl."

Szekfü was not only the most distinguished historian of Hungary; he was also the most noted ideologist of Hungarian nationalism.[173] On the intellectual level the affinity of Szekfü to Freyer is not difficult to explain. Like Freyer, Szekfü had been deeply influenced by the traditions of German historicism. He conceived of Hungarian history as the successive development of a unique *Volksgeist* or *Volksseele* and adopted Dilthey's method of retrospective empathetic reconstruction as the basis of his own historiography.[174] Moreover, like Freyer, Szekfü conceived of nineteenth-century liberalism as a threat to the uniqueness and integrity of Hungarian culture.[175]

While Szekfü was predisposed to a philo-German course for Hungary by virtue of his intellectual training and conception of Hungarian culture, he was cautious in his relationship toward the National Socialist *Reich*. Like many Hungarian elite intellectuals, he welcomed the benefits of territorial expansion that Hungary secured through its alliance with Hitler's Germany, while remaining suspicious of German hegemonic intentions toward Hungary. As an advocate of consevative reform who conceived of Hungary as part of a broader Germanic, Christian culture, Szekfü was not the sort to seek the company of National Socialist ideologues.[176]

In view of Szekfü's central role among the Hungarian intellectual elite, his cooperation with Freyer was a stunning success for the German propaganda effort—hence the enthusiasm with which an attaché in Budapest reported to the Foreign Office that Freyer had been approached by Szekfü to create a seminar for German cultural history at the University of Budapest and had offered his full cooperation.[177] Szekfü was among those frequently invited to lectures that distinguished German professors delivered at Freyer's Deutsches Wissenschaftliches Institut, and his attendance there served to boost its prestige.[178]

Freyer's reputation and behavior in Budapest won him the favor of the

---

[173] Steven Bela Vardy, *Modern Hungarian Historiography*, 62.

[174] Ibid., 47, 63–71.

[175] Ibid., 68–71.

[176] Ibid., 80, 88–89. On the distinction between the Horthyite right and the National Socialist right in interwar Hungary, see Istvan Deak, "Hungary," 364–65. On the ambivalent attitude of the Hungarian elite toward Nazi Germany from 1938 to 1944, see the report of the German consul, von Jagow, entitled "Propagandalage in Ungarn," 23 November 1942, PA-AA, Kult.-Pol., Geheim-Generalia, vol. 6; Siebert,

"Rolle," 192, 356; Joseph Rothschild, *East Central Europe between the Two World Wars*, 177–88; Andrew Janos, *The Politics of Backwardness in Hungary, 1825–1945*, 285–312.

[177] Graf. Strachwitz, Budapest, to Auswärtiges Amt, Berlin, 8 April 1940. See also Hans Freyer to Deutsche Gesandschaft Budapest, 19 March 1940; and Schäfer-Rumelin, Auswärtiges Amt, to Deutsche Gesandschaft Budapest, 18 April 1940. All in PA-AA, Budapest 112, Kult. 10, no. 1, "Hochschulwesen in Ungarn, 1939–41."

[178] Interview with Ruth Buchenhorst.

Hungarian Ministry of Culture. The ministry was headed by another conservative intellectual, Bálint Hóman, a historian of medieval Hungary who together with Szekfü had edited the major synthetic work on Hungarian history
published in the interwar years.[179] Freyer was on excellent personal terms with
Koloman von Szily, the deputy minister of culture.[180] It is no surprise that
when Freyer's appointment neared expiration in 1940, the Hungarian Ministry of Culture joined in requesting its extension.[181]

Yet in addition to his success in his overt public roles in the intellectual life
of Budapest, Hans Freyer fulfilled several functions behind the scenes that
contributed to his "indispensability" in Budapest. He worked closely with the
staff of the German consulate in Budapest, serving as the German ambassador's adviser on cultural affairs.[182] The ambassador at the time of Freyer's arrival was Otto von Erdmannsdorf, a member of the Saxon nobility who had
graduated from Freyer's Gymnasium in Dresden. Freyer developed a close relationship with Erdmannsdorf and also befriended Erdmannsdorf's successor, Dietrich von Jagow, an old SA officer who became ambassador in 1941.[183]
In addition, Freyer—who maintained contacts with a variety of Hungarian
political factions—served as an unofficial adviser to the representatives of
the German army in Budapest, mediated through the latter's adjutant, the
Göttingen historian Percy Ernst Schramm.[184]

Another of Freyer's covert functions in Budapest was to provide a constant
stream of information on Hungarian intellectuals to the German government.
The Foreign Office encouraged German scholarly associations to invite Hungarian colleagues to conferences and guest lectureships in the *Reich*. Such invitations were not be extended to all Hungarian scholars, however: those who
were of "non-Aryan" origin or hostile in their attitude toward the Third Reich
were not to be invited to Germany. Even before Freyer's arrival in Budapest
the Foreign Office had been at pains to avoid the extension of invitations to
men of Jewish "racial" origin, who were prominently represented among
Hungarian academic intellectuals.[185]

Among Freyer's regular activities in Budapest (and among those which

[179] On Homan, see Vardy, *Historiography*, passim.
[180] Interview with Käthe Freyer.
[181] "Niederschrift," signed Zschintzsch, 12
March 1940, BAK, 21/208.
[182] Schelsky, "Die verschiedenen Weisen,"
149–50. Freyer's role as cultural adviser is borne
out by files of the German consulate in Budapest, now in the PA-AA, which unfortunately

are not extant beyond 1941.
[183] Schelsky, "Die verschiedenen Weisen,"
151; interview with Käthe Freyer.
[184] Schelsky, "Die verschiedenen Weisen,"
150.
[185] See the report on cultural relations with
Hungary in 1937, marked "Zu W U 2733," PA-
AA, Kult. Zw, "Deutsch-ungarische Gesellschaft," 5.

made him indispensable to the German consulate there) was the compilation of reports on the scholarly accomplishments, ethnic origins, and political attitudes toward Germany of scores of Hungarian scholars. Freyer reported which scholars were Jews, half-Jews, baptized Jews, married to Jews, or known as philo-Semitic. It was up to the Foreign Office to decide whether or not to proffer invitations, but any negative information in Freyer's reports led almost inevitably to the cancellation of plans to invite the scholars in question. The Budapest consulate also offered reports, based on Freyer's advice, on the political and racial "reliability" of Hungarian scholars to German periodicals and publishers who requested such information. These reports appear to have been based in part on rumors supplied by anti-Semitic and enthusiastically pro-German faculty members. Compiling them no doubt took a good deal of Freyer's time. Helmut Schelsky, a student of Freyer's from Leipzig who served as his assistant at the DWI Budapest in 1940 and 1941, aided his teacher in gathering such information.[186]

Yet even as Freyer transmitted the reports of informers, he was also—as he suspected—being informed upon.[187] Among the attachés of the Budapest consulate where Freyer spent much of his time was a full-time employee of the SD, sent there to report on his colleagues.[188] Abroad, Freyer did not fully elude the Third Reich's apparatus of cultural control. Ironically, he escaped the full weight of the apparatus only by becoming part of its periphery.

Freyer's success as a link to the Hungarian intelligentsia came to an end in March 1944, when Hitler—dissatisfied by what he perceived as the minimal war effort of his ally and by its relative laxity in dealing with "the Jewish question"—ordered the occupation of Hungary by German troops and placed the country under the control of Edmund Veesenmayer of the SS. Hungarian opposition leaders were rounded up wholesale by the Gestapo, and Adolf Eichmann arrived in Budapest with his *Sondereinsatzkommando* to organize the efficient murder of Greater Hungary's 725,000 Jews, as well as over 100,000 "racially Jewish" converts to Christianity.[189] These subjects of Freyer's frequent reports now became the victims of his compatriots. Even those conservative Hungarian intellectuals formerly well disposed toward the DWI turned

---

[186] For examples of such reports, see PA-AA, Gesandschaft Budapest, Kult. 2, no. 1, "Gastvorlesungen—Ungarische Wissenschaftler nach Deutschland," passim; Kult. 10, no. 2, "Professoren und Lehrer."

[187] In an interview with the author, Ruth Buchenhorst mentioned that Freyer believed he

was under surveillance in Budapest.

[188] Richard Henschel, "Erklärung unter Eid," in *Das Dritte Reich und seine Diener*, ed. Leon Poliakov and Josef Wulf, 149. The file of the SD agent in question, Ernst Kienast, at the BDC, confirms this account.

[189] Rothschild, *East Central Europe*, 199.

their backs on him after March 1944, when the face of the SS began to replace that of Hans Freyer as the image of German culture in Budapest.

Freyer and his family left Hungary for Dresden in the summer of 1944, and he planned to resume his teaching duties in Leipzig shortly thereafter.[190] In October 1944, after an attempt by Horthy to arrange an armistice with the Allied powers, the Germans replaced him with Ferenc Szálasi, the leader of the Arrow Cross. Veesenmayer now requested that Freyer return to Budapest to resume the activity of the DWI "for the sake of appearances."[191] Freyer stalled but returned to Hungary in December to aid in the evacuation of pro-German scholars by the retreating German army.[192]

Freyer's disillusionment with Hitler's foreign policy had begun a good deal earlier, though how early cannot be determined with precision. It did not require a great deal of historical insight to conclude that Germany would lose the war; a sense of *Realpolitik* free of illusions sufficed in Freyer's case. Upon hearing the news of Germany's attack on the Soviet Union in June 1941, Freyer turned to the librarian of his institute, a close friend of the Freyer family, and remarked that the war was now lost.[193] By this date at the latest, Freyer had become disillusioned with the foreign policy of the Nazi regime as he had earlier become disillusioned with its internal policy.

Indeed, while serving as an official representative of the Third Reich, Freyer worked from 1939 through 1945 on a massive history of Europe, whose central theme—the cultural unity and continuity of the civilization of Christian Europe—made its ultimate publication dependent upon the defeat of the Third Reich. The book, entitled *Weltgeschichte Europas*, was first published in 1948. It marked the abandonment of his belief in the salvational role of the state and of German nationalism, and a turn from radical conservatism to the more traditionalist conservatism of his later work.

Although Freyer appears to have concluded some years earlier that the war was lost, he served the German *Reich*—and, whatever his reservations, the ends of its rulers—through its final months.

Freyer's process of disillusionment with National Socialism was shared by those involved in the attempted assassination of Hitler and coup d'état of 20 July 1944, many of whom were themselves former supporters of the Nazi regime.[194] Among Freyer's friends who participated directly in the revolt—and

[190] Interview with Käthe Freyer; Hans Freyer to Rektor (signed Dresden) 2 June 1944, UAL, PA Freyer, 152.

[191] Reichserziehungsministerium to Dekan Leipzig, 31 October 1944, UAL, PA Freyer, 176.

[192] Reichserziehungsministerium to Rektor, 5 December 1944; Dekan to Freyer, 11 January 1945, UAL, PA Freyer, 180, 157c.

[193] Interview with Ruth Buchenhorst.

[194] On the erstwhile support of the Nazi re-

who paid for its failure with their lives—were Johannes Popitz and Albrecht Haushofer.[195] Wilhelm Ahlmann, a close friend who visited with Freyer in Budapest as late as 1944, was a confidant of Graf von Stauffenberg. Though he had disagreed with Stauffenberg's plans on ethical and tactical grounds, Ahlmann committed suicide in December 1944 to escape divulging the names of Stauffenberg's associates to the Gestapo.[196] Carl Goerdeler, who would have become head of the provisional government had the coup succeeded, had been acquainted as mayor of Leipzig with Freyer. The reports of Goerdeler's interrogation by the Gestapo indicate that he intended Hans Freyer to be responsible for the planning of university affairs in his government.[197] The man whose plans for university reform in the Third Reich had come to nought in 1933 might thus have achieved greater influence in its successor. There is no evidence that Freyer knew of the plot against Hitler or that he was aware of Goerdeler's plans for him. Freyer did not actively resist the regime, but he was part of the cultural environment of dissidence from which the active resistance emerged.[198]

Unlike his friends Popitz, Haushofer, Ahlmann, and Goerdeler—not to speak of countless former students who fell in the Second World War—Hans Freyer survived the National Socialist *Reich*. Yet the experiment in revolution from the right had cost him heavily. His institute in Leipzig was destroyed by an Allied bomb attack in December 1943.[199] He lost his library in the German evacuation from Budapest. His mother and sister were killed in the fire bombing of Dresden in February 1945.[200] Freyer had wagered on the re-creation of collective virtue through political power—and lost. It was not a risk he would encourage again.

---

gime by many of those subsequently involved in the conspiracy against Hitler, see Richard Löwenthal, "Cultural Change and Generation Change in Postwar Western Germany," 35, 39; Hans Mommsen, "Die Widerstand gegen Hitler und die deutsche Gesellschaft," 81–104, esp. 95; Fritz Stern, "Der Nationalsozialismus als Versuchung"; and Klemens von Klemperer, "Widerstand—Résistance: The Place of the German Resistance in the European Resistance against National Socialism."

[195] On their role, see Peter Hoffmann, *The History of the German Resistance*. On the development of Popitz's opposition to the regime see Bentin, *Schmitt und Popitz*, 53ff.; and Klaus Scholder's introduction to *Die Mittwochs-*

Gesellschaft.

[196] Or so at least it is claimed in the biographical sketch written by his friends in Johann Daniel Achelis et al., *Tymbos für Wilhelm Ahlmann: Ein Gedenkbuch*, xii.

[197] BAK, NS6, Sammlung 20. Juli 1944, no. 14, p. 17, published in Archiv Peter für historische und zeitgeschichtliche Dokumentation, ed., *Spiegelbild einer Verschwörung*, 433.

[198] On resistance and *"weltanschaulicher Dissidenz"* see Richard Löwenthal, "Widerstand im totalen Staat," 11–24.

[199] Dekan to Reichserziehungsministerium, 19 June 1944, UAL, PA Freyer, 1–5.

[200] Interview with Barbara Stowasser (Freyer's daughter).

CHAPTER NINE

New Conservatism and a New Respectability, 1945–1961

The disillusioned radical conservatives for whom National Socialism had been the god that failed played almost no role in the initial creation of a new liberal democratic state in West Germany. In the years of occupation between the end of the war and the founding of the Federal Republic in 1949, they were kept off the public stage and on the defensive by a combination of Allied pressure, anti-Nazi Germans, and the legal process of denazification. Despite the indubitable failings of denazification, it did put those who had supported or cooperated closely with the Nazi regime on ice at the very time when the major decisions about the future shape of the West German polity were being made.[1] Those decisions were made largely by opponents of the former regime, above all by political democrats and economic liberals with a rather conservative world view, especially Konrad Adenauer, who dominated the politics of the new Federal Republic for the first decade and a half after its founding. The ideological premises of Adenauer and those closest to him were articulated by intellectuals such as Wilhelm Röpke, who had long opposed the statism and cultural particularism of German radical conservatism. Freyer and those who shared his past were forced toward the margins of academic and intellectual life.

In the course of the 1950s, Freyer and other former radical conservatives whose careers had been in eclipse in the immediate postwar years returned to positions of prominence in German intellectual life. The process by which Freyer regained respectability was typical of many others of his political stripe. It included a period of work in the private sector and an association with church institutions that helped pave the road to renewed public respectability. Finally came reinstatement within the university, aided by government legislation.

[1] On denazification see Lutz Niethammer, *Die Mitläuferfabrik: Die Entnazifizierung am Beispiel Bayerns*, esp. 652–53.

The Freyer who returned to respectability within the public institutions of the new Federal Republic was not the radical conservative of 1933. Disillusioned by the experience of National Socialism, reinforced in his distrust of the totalitarianism of the left by his experience in postwar East Germany, Freyer emerged as a spokesman for a brand of conservatism reconciled with liberal democracy. In this too his development was typical of many other erstwhile radical conservative intellectuals: past disillusionment with National Socialism, the present threat of communism, and the unanticipated economic and political success of liberal democratic capitalism in the Federal Republic led to a revision of their conservatism. Their more liberal conservatism overlapped considerably with the conservative liberalism of Röpke and the German neoliberals. Indeed, the new ideology of conservatism articulated by Freyer and other erstwhile radical conservatives now served to legitimate liberal democracy and the capitalist welfare state in the social thought and political culture of the German right.[2] As a result of disenchantment with the other god that failed, for the first time in German history the political culture of the right was dominated by a conservatism reconciled in principle with liberal democracy.[3]

The University of Leipzig: From Denazification to Sovietization

With the collapse of the Third Reich, Germany underwent its third transformation of political forms in three decades. Each regime had made attempts to maintain or transform the university in its own image. The famed autonomy of the German university in the monarchical era was far from complete, and the appointment of professors lay ultimately in the hands of the provincial minister of education.[4] In Saxony, ties between the university faculty and the monarch remained close up to 1918 and even beyond.[5] During the Weimar Republic the new left-wing socialist government of Saxony had been explicit about its hopes of transforming the university through its appointments and the creation of new chairs and institutes of learning. For the most part, its attempts foundered on the rock of faculty resistance. The attempt at the *Gleichschaltung* of the university by the National Socialist regime was far more suc-

---

[2] See Bracher, *Zeit der Ideologien*, 288.

[3] Richard Löwenthal, "Cultural Change and Generation Change in Postwar Western Germany," 35–39.

[4] See Ringer, *German Mandarins*, 37, 51, as well as Jarausch, *Students*.

[5] On the close relationship between the university and the last Saxon monarch, see Kittel, *Universität*, 112–15.

cessful, but a combination of faculty resistance and the sporadic triumphs of pragmatism and respect for academic competence had left a good deal of the previous faculty and structure of learning intact. In the years between the collapse of the Third Reich and the death of Stalin, the University of Leipzig was to undergo an externally imposed political transformation far more thorough than any it had known before. In 1953 it was rechristened the Karl-Marx-Universität as an external symbol of its metamorphosis.

The fate of the University of Leipzig was determined in good part by military events elsewhere in Germany and by diplomatic negotiations abroad. Had military circumstances alone prevailed, the denazification of the university would have occurred under American auspices, for on 18 April 1945 the city of Leipzig was occupied by the American army. General Eisenhower's decision of April 1945 not to press on to Berlin allowed the Russians to capture the capital of the *Reich* in its entirety in May. In mid-June, Truman and Churchill decided to withdraw their armies from Saxony and Thuringia—which were within the Soviet zone of control as specified in Allied protocols—in return for Russian agreement to allow American and British troops to occupy West Berlin, in keeping with the earlier agreements.[6] Thus American forces moved out of Leipzig on 1 July 1945, and the Red Army moved in.

The process of denazifying and rebuilding the University of Leipzig began under the short-lived American occupation. The behavior of the faculty of the university presents a curious parallel to its conduct in 1933. Now as then there were faculty members who sympathized with the new holders of power; and many were, by 1945 at least, in favor of some type of denazification of the university. But above all, as in 1933, the faculty appears to have been concerned to protect itself from the ideologically motivated actions of those who held military and political power. Its strategy, in 1945 as in 1933, was to choose university officials from among those faculty members perceived as having the most credit with the new regime by virtue of their past record. For it was only through such credit that the university could be spared the worst excesses of what the professors believed to be arbitrary interference in their realm of competence. Thus those who were known to their colleagues as professionally competent, untainted by association with the Nazi past, and vaguely democratic in their orientation emerged with a certain spontaneous authority in the summer of 1945.[7]

---

[6] For the military and diplomatic background see William Franklin, "Zonal Boundaries and Access to Berlin," 1–32, esp. 26–28.

[7] A similar pattern appeared elsewhere. At the University of Freiburg, for example, two members of the liberal Freiburg school of econ-

Foremost among these was Hans-Georg Gadamer. Both a classical philologist and a philosopher by training and since 1938 occupant of the chair of philosophy at Leipzig, Gadamer's career bore testimony to the effectiveness and limits of the nazification of the German universities. One of Martin Heidegger's earliest and most distinguished students, Gadamer was so shocked at Heidegger's enthusiastic endorsement of the new regime that he broke off contact with his teacher in 1933.[8] Though Gadamer was a promising young scholar, his path to a professorship at the University of Marburg was blocked after 1933 by the National Socialist Dozentenbund, which held against him his continued contact with Jewish friends and his obvious lack of enthusiasm for the new regime. As a result he remained a *Privatdozent* for almost a decade.[9]

Gadamer's call to the chair of philosophy at Leipzig in 1938 was probably due to the influence of Heinrich Harmjanz, the new official at the German Ministry of Education responsible for university appointments in the *Geisteswissenschaften*: a devoted Nazi since his student years and a man of modest academic achievement, Harmjanz was nevertheless capable of putting professional excellence above ideological orthodoxy in making his appointments.[10] Gadamer, a man with no connections to the party or its associated organs, was chosen by Harmjanz over two other candidates recommended by the philosophical faculty of Leipzig, one of whom was a candidate for party membership, the other a member of the SS.[11]

Though not a politically active opponent of the National Socialist regime, Gadamer was known at Leipzig as a non-Nazi and to his more trusted students and colleagues as an anti-Nazi. Among his friends in Leipzig was Carl Goerdeler. His book of 1938, *Plato und die Dichter*, began with a quotation from Goethe that served as an Aesopian wink to the like-minded: "He who philos-

---

omists played a leading role in the process of denazification. One of them, Franz Böhm, was elected prorector of the university in the first postwar election. See Hugh Ott, "Martin Heidegger und die Universität Freiburg nach 1945," 95–128, esp. 98–99.

[8] Interview with Hans-Georg Gadamer, Aachen, 29 April 1982.

[9] Hans-Georg Gadamer, *Philosophische Lebensjahre*, 55.

[10] For more on Harmjanz, see chapter 8. Gadamer was originally sent by Harmjanz to Leipzig as a temporary replacement for Arnold Gehlen, without any request by the Leipzig

faculty (Heinrich Harmjanz, Reichserziehungsministerium to Hans-Georg Gadamer, 28 March 1938, UAL, PA Gadamer, 26). The probable role of Harmjanz in the appointment was confirmed by Gadamer in a conversation with the author.

[11] The faculty's first choice was Theodor Haering, a noted Hegel scholar who had been a *Parteianwärter* (a candidate for party membership) since November 1937. Gadamer was their second choice. Hans Lipps, the third choice, had been a physician in the SS since 1934 (Dekan to Reichserziehungsministerium, 28 June 1938, UAL, PA Gadamer, 35–44).

ophizes is not at one with the ideas of his age" (*Wer philosophiert, ist mit den Vor-stellungen seiner Zeit nicht einig*). Most of Gadamer's students at Leipzig were op-posed to Nazism, and some were a part of the extended Goerdeler circle. After the abortive attempt on Hitler's life in July 1944, some of these students were arrested. One was shot; another, who later became Gadamer's wife, was released from prison only when the Americans approached Leipzig.[12]

It is not surprising, then, that with the end of the war and the collapse of the existing structure of authority within the university, Gadamer should have emerged as the de facto kingmaker in the events that followed. At first he turned to Theodor Litt as the most appropriate choice to assume the rector-ship of the university. Litt not only had held academic offices in Leipzig before 1933 but had been forced by harassment to resign from his chair of pedagogy in 1937. Litt turned down the offer, however, reasoning that the new rector ought to be someone who had continued to be part of the faculty throughout the Nazi years. Since it was clear that the dismissal of professors tainted by their association with the defeated regime was to be the leading item on the agenda of the university, Litt sought to indicate to the new occupying forces that those who had retained their posts were not ipso facto guilty of National Socialist sympathies and hence to be excluded from the academy. Gadamer then proposed an archaeologist, Bernhard Schweitzer, who on 16 May 1945 was elected rector by his colleagues in the first free elections for administrative posts since 1933. Gadamer was elected dean of the philosophical faculty, to which Freyer belonged.[13]

Under the Potsdam accords each of the occupiers of Germany was commit-ted to removing active National Socialists from official positions and replacing them with those who had not supported the regime. In attempting to do so, all four powers faced a common dilemma: should denazification be conducted primarily by the occupying forces or by the Germans themselves?[14] The for-mer course risked proceeding on the basis of formal criteria (such as party membership) and might result in arbitrary dismissals. The latter course was dependent upon one's evaluation of the political past of the members of the institution in question. It was imprudent, for example, to depend upon a uni-versity faculty, many of whose members owed their chairs to Nazi sympathies,

---

[12] Hans-Georg Gadamer, "Lebenslauf, 26 July 1946," UAL, PA Gadamer, 95; idem, *Philo-sophische Lebensjahre*, 111–22; interview with Renate Drucker; interview with Hans-Georg Gadamer.

[13] Gadamer, *Philosophische Lebensjahre*, 122–24.

[14] For a discussion of these dilemmas, espe-cially in the American zone, see Otto Bachof, "Die 'Entnazifizierung.' "

to denazify itself. The dilemma was real enough, and the Americans came down to some degree on both sides of it. They arrested and imprisoned ten professors for their National Socialist activity, including the head of the institute of anthropology and racial science, the head of the university dermatological clinic, who held a leading position in the SS, and the director of the hygiene institute, who had belonged to the SD. On the whole, however, the Americans complied with the wish of the faculty of the university that denazification be carried out by the faculty itself on a case-by-case basis.[15]

When the American occupation forces withdrew from Leipzig on 1 July—taking with them those natural scientists who might be of military value, as part of "Operation Paperclip"[16]—this policy lost its validity. The new Soviet Military Administration was committed to carrying out the process of denazification through extrauniversity commissions composed according to political considerations and rarely comprising more than one academic member.[17] Yet the administration of the university remained in the hands of its elected officials, for, as in other areas of life, the Soviet authorities in the first year of occupation were more concerned with the creation of a functioning administration than with the dictates of political orthodoxy.[18] Schweitzer, Gadamer, and the other officials elected during the American occupation remained in office. In his inaugural address, Schweitzer warned that the university was not an agent of the politics of the day and that the attempt to utilize the university for political goals, as had so recently occurred, meant the strangulation of the life of the mind.[19] The seeds of conflict over control of the university between the faculty, none of whom were communist in their orientation, and the new Soviet administration were planted.[20] The fate of Hans Freyer became part of the struggle between the faculty and the Soviet occupation authorities for governance of the university.

How was one to evaluate Freyer? The first step in the process of denazification, to which all employees of the university were subject, was the completion of a questionnaire regarding one's past. Freyer filled out the first of many post-

[15] Horst Borusiak, "Die Universität Leipzig nach der Zerschlagung des faschistischen Staates und ihre Neueröffnung am 5. Februar 1946," 365; Bernhard Schweitzer, *Die Universität Leipzig, 1409–1959*, 20.

[16] See the account in Borusiak, "Universität," 366ff.; and Clarence Lasby, *Project Paperclip*, 44–50.

[17] Borusiak, "Universität," 375; Interview with Hans-Georg Gadamer.

[18] J. P. Nettl, *The Eastern Zone and Soviet Policy in Germany 1945–1950*, 16.

[19] Quoted in Herbert Helbig, "Leipzig," 32.

[20] On the Schweitzer period as rector see Helga A. Walsh, "Entnazifizierung und Wiederöffnung der Universität Leipzig, 1945–1946: Ein Bericht des damaligen Rektors Professor Bernhard Schweitzer," 339–72.

war *Fragebogen* for the American Military Government of Germany in May 1945.[21] Asked if he had been a member of the Nazi party, its separate organs, or its associated organizations, he answered "no," which was perfectly true. Required to list his travels abroad, he mentioned only holiday visits to Italy in 1934 and 1936 and his years as visiting professor at the University of Budapest, which, he noted, was "based upon a call [*Berufung*] from the philosophical faculty of Budapest." Both of these statements told the truth, but not the whole truth, and the impression they conveyed was false. In addition to his trips to Italy, Freyer had made a third visit there in 1935 to deliver what was in effect his standard propaganda speech of those years, an earlier version of which he delivered in Budapest in January 1934 on a trip that also remained unmentioned. The invitation of the University of Budapest of 1938 was indeed the efficient cause of his call to Budapest, but hardly, as we have seen, its final cause. Thus, Freyer's *Fragebogen*—to use the language of the day—was "white as snow" (*schneeweiß*), owing in part to deception, but mainly to the fact that Freyer had carefully eschewed membership in any political organization.

When the first rounds of denazification began in the summer and autumn of 1945, Freyer was not among the victims. At this stage it was formal membership that counted above all. At first party members were automatically dismissed from their teaching positions, though some were reinstated when it was demonstrated that their activity had not gone beyond formal affiliation. Reporting on the state of denazification at the University of Leipzig to his friend Eduard Spranger, Theodor Litt noted that while men who had been purely formal members of the Nazi party were being expelled from the university, "people like Freyer—who were clever enough not to join the party—seem to be coming through unscathed."[22]

The university reopened in February 1946, now under Gadamer, who assumed the rectorship after Schweitzer resigned in frustration. Hans Freyer resumed his lecturing, continued as head of the Institut für Kulturgeschichte, and quietly changed his title back to "professor of sociology" from "professor of political science." He not only continued to participate in the habilitation of new candidates but, in the absence of many former faculty members, became acting head of several smaller institutes.[23] His *Assistent* of the 1930s, Heinz Ronte, set about rebuilding the library of the institute, which had been destroyed during Anglo-American bombing raids.

[21] UAL, PA Freyer, 194ff.

[22] Borusiak, "Universität," 381. Theodor Litt to Eduard Spranger, 23 October 1945, BAK, Nachlaß Spranger.

[23] UAL, PA Freyer, 163, 200.

Freyer's position was preserved not only by his formal record but by the support given him by the leading figures of the faculty and administration, including Hans-Georg Gadamer, Friedrich Klingner (a classicist who became dean of the philosophical faculty in 1946), and Theodor Litt. These men had known Freyer for some time: Litt and Freyer had been close intellectually and socially since the 1920s, Klingner had been his colleague since 1930, and Gadamer since 1938. Their evaluations of Freyer in the immediate postwar years were based on personal knowledge of his changing political views. But they were also influenced by another important consideration. The university was desperately short of competent faculty; many younger scholars had been killed during the war years, and some senior scholars had fled to the western zones. It is in this dual light that the evaluations of Freyer by his colleagues must be read.

As dean of the philosophical faculty, Gadamer prepared a denazification report on Freyer in June 1945 based on Freyer's personal dossier and on Gadamer's own knowledge.[24] It was Freyer's prominent assignment in Budapest that made him a candidate for the faculty's denazification proceedings. This activity abroad, wrote Gadamer, "can certainly not be evaluated as political in the narrow, party sense." Freyer had never been a member of the NSDAP, he wrote, and was an acknowledged scholar. Gadamer's report therefore favored Freyer's exoneration. Klingner, Gadamer's successor as dean, reached a similar conclusion. At the beginning of the Nazi years, he noted in a report prepared early in 1946, Freyer's political visions had led him to certain illusions about the regime. But he had soon become disillusioned and condemned National Socialism. Moreover, he was one of the brightest members of the faculty, and a brilliant, stimulating teacher to boot.[25] Theodor Litt's defense of Freyer at a meeting of the faculty senate is even more revealing, for he did not deny that Freyer's political inclinations had been reprehensible but insisted that he had since changed his views profoundly. A decade later Litt offered the same opinion in a confidential letter, in which he wrote that Freyer had "adequately repented and atoned for his National Socialist transgressions."[26] Thus all three men, none of whom was ignorant of Freyer's past activity or of the man himself, fought for his retention. As events were to show, this support was not enough as the authority of the existing faculty was undermined and the university transformed in accordance with the ideology of the new Soviet occu-

[24] Ibid., 159.
[25] Ibid., 161–62.
[26] Litt's remarks to the faculty senate are quoted in Borusiak, "Universität," 356. Litt to Spranger, 20 March 1956, BAK, Nachlaß Spranger.

piers. Within three years not only Freyer but Gadamer, Klingner, and Litt were to leave Leipzig permanently.

The inexorability of the sovietization of the university was hardly evident in 1945, however, either to the faculty or to the students. Schweitzer busied himself with preparing a new constitution for the university, and Gadamer encouraged some colleagues not to move westward.[27] Not only members of the faculty were filled with hope; for the first time in over a decade free political activity was possible, and to many students the future shape of their society and country seemed an open question. The end of Nazi prohibitions against free speech and the threat to such freedom presented by the Soviet presence seemed to many students to make political involvement not only a possibility but a necessity.[28] Though no open elections were held among the students until the end of 1946, it was clear that the majority of the student body—most of which was of lower-middle- or upper-middle-class origin—was unsympathetic to the sovietization of the university.[29] The Soviet military authorities and their German communist supporters were thus confronted by a faculty and student body suspicious of, if not hostile to, their aims.

In the course of 1946, after the initial consolidation of economic, administrative, and educational institutions, the Soviet authorities began to rule with a heavier political hand; and partisan political considerations came to play a greater role in filling positions of authority.[30] The transformation of the political composition of the student body was set in motion, by a governmentally imposed quota system that required that 35 percent of all *Abiturienten* (high school graduates entitled to university admission) be of working-class or peasant origin, and by the admission of so-called *Arbeiterstudenten*, who had graduated from a new preparatory institute. It soon became clear that membership in the SED (Sozialistische Einheitspartei Deutschlands, the name adopted by the communists of the soviet zone after their absorption of the Social Democrats) was an important criterion for the successful completion of the preparatory degree and for admission into the university.[31] In the first student elections—held in December 1946, with 84 percent of those eligible voting—the

[27] Gadamer, *Philosophische Lebensjahre*, 123; interview with Helmut Schelsky.

[28] Interview with Martin Broszat. Broszat was a student at the University of Leipzig at the time.

[29] Borusiak, "Universität," 374; interview with Hans-Georg Gadamer.

[30] Nettl, *Eastern Zone*, 125. Nettl dates the change to October 1946.

[31] Gottfried Berger, *In tyrannos: Die Sowjetisierung der Hochschulen, Dargestellt am Beispiel der Universität Leipzig*, 6–7. Berger was a leader of the CDU student organization at Leipzig in the postwar years. See also Borusiak, "Universität," 380–83; Gadamer, *Philosophische Lebensjahre*, 130.

SED elected eight representatives to the student council, as compared with thirteen representatives of other, "bourgeois" parties.[32] The composition of the faculty was similarly transformed by the creation of new faculties of social science and of education, whose members were largely appointed from among party cadres.[33]

In 1947 and 1948 there was a perceptible tightening of the screws against students and professors who were considered too outspoken in their criticisms of the communist regime. Theodor Litt, whose lectures had been suspended by the National Socialist regime and who resigned out of frustration in 1937, found his lectures suspended again in 1947 by order of the Russians. In his lectures, which were very well attended, Litt had criticized Marxist ideas.[34] Shortly after a senate meeting in June 1948, during which he compared the preference granted to communist students to the methods used by National Socialism,[35] Litt resigned his chair for the second time in a decade. He left for the western zone and a new chair at Bonn. Gadamer and Klingner soon followed. In November 1948 Wolfgang Natonek, since 1946 the popular leader of the student council and a member of the Liberal party (LDP), was arrested together with twenty other members of his party. Accused of espionage, he was sentenced to twenty-five years at hard labor. The liberal student group was banned. This demonstration of naked terror, combined with a government-decreed change in the student electoral system, led to the first communist electoral victory on the student council in December 1948.[36]

Freyer's fate differed from that of some of his "bourgeois" (i.e., noncommunist) colleagues. Much of the sovietization of the institutions of the eastern zone during the years 1946–48 was carried out under the rhetorical guise of antifascism.[37] Freyer was susceptible to such charges by virtue of his past; Gadamer and Litt were not. Men such as Gadamer and Litt were welcomed at universities in the western zone with open arms; Freyer's reception was far more equivocal. Litt and Gadamer could resign their posts in Leipzig and depart for the West at the time of their choosing. Freyer left only after his salary was suspended.

Under these circumstances it was perhaps only a matter of time until Freyer's past began to catch up with him. Political deeds could be hidden or lie buried in archives. But Freyer's past intellectual commitments were preserved in print. As early as November 1945, there were some in Leipzig who began to

32 Berger, *Sowejetisierung*, 5.

33 Gadamer, *Philosophische Lebensjahre*, 126.

34 Ibid., 129.

35 Borusiak, "Universität," 355.

36 Berger, *Sowejetisierung*, 15.

37 Nettl, *Eastern Zone*, 77–78.

notice the more flagrant passages in his past writings,[38] but few had the time, the knowledge, or the inclination to undertake a systematic study of Freyer's previous work.

A decade earlier, however, as a result of the revolution from the right that Freyer had welcomed, two intellectuals of differing ideological persuasions had found themselves in exile and devoted a part of their time to the study of Freyer's work. Both were to affect Freyer's fate after 1945 by calling attention to his earlier work. The first was Georg Lukács. Like Freyer, the young Lukács had been a cultural critic, deeply influenced by Georg Simmel. Lukács, like Freyer, had turned to radical political solutions to the spiritual problems facing modern bourgeois man. But while Freyer had been led to the totalitarian right on his search for the re-creation of a community of collective purpose, the search led Lukács toward the totalitarian left.[39] In the mid-1930s Lukács, by now a leading communist intellectual and erstwhile politician, found himself in exile in the Soviet Union. There he began the manuscript of his critical synopsis of German intellectual history after Marx, *Die Zerstörung der Vernunft* (The Destruction of Reason), the sixth chapter of which, under the heading "Prefascist and Fascist Sociology," was devoted to Othmar Spann, Carl Schmitt—and Hans Freyer.[40] Freyer's second critic, René König, sat writing his *Habilitationsschrift* in Zurich at about the same time as Lukács drafted his critique of Freyer. The title of his work was *Kritik der historisch-existentialistischen Soziologie*; its principal target was Hans Freyer.[41] Though Lukács and König shared neither political nor intellectual allegiances—Lukács was by this time a devoted communist and an orthodox Marxist-Leninist, König a liberal champion of Durkheimian sociology—their perspectives on Freyer were remarkably similar. Both viewed Freyer as a significant link between the romantic, subjectivist trend of previous German sociology and National Socialism. In the long run it was König, soon to become the most influential sociologist in the Federal Republic, who played the more significant role in limiting Freyer's

[38] Theodor Litt to Eduard Spranger, 1 October 1945, BAK, Nachlaß Spranger.

[39] On Lukács's early intellectual and political development, see the works cited in the Introduction.

[40] The work as a whole was first published in Hungary and East Germany in 1954. For the circumstances under which the book was written and the qualities of mind exhibited by Lukács, see David Pike, *Lukács and Brecht*.

[41] The work was first published in 1974, thirty years after it was completed as a *Habilitationsschrift* in Zurich. For the circumstances under which it was composed, see the new foreword of 1974, "Warum ich dieses Buch schrieb," in René König, *Kritik der historisch-existentialistischen Soziologie*. For more on König's role as the leading antagonist of Freyer and his circle among German sociologists in the 1950s and 1960s, see chapter 10.

postwar influence. But it was the publication of Lukács's critique of Freyer in the June 1946 issue of the German communist cultural journal *Aufbau* that set off the train of events that resulted in Freyer's expulsion from the University of Leipzig.[42]

Lukács wrote of Freyer that "whether or not conscious of it from the beginning, he became an ally of those tendencies which helped prepare the victory of fascism." As an explanation for the rise of Freyer's sociology, Lukács offered an orthodox Stalinist and rather abstract account: "Corresponding to the nature and results of the class struggles in Germany during the Weimar Republic, the plainly reactionary tendency in sociology also had to become dominant."[43] As befitted a philosopher and intellectual historian who had matured in the same intellectual milieu as the object of his attack, Lukács was keen in his appraisal of Freyer's intellectual roots. He pointed out not only the affinity of Freyer's work to German existentialism but also his intellectual debts to Dilthey, Weber, and Spengler; there was even a grudging recognition of Freyer's borrowings from Marx. In the course of his summaries of Freyer's *Der Staat* (1925), *Soziologie als Wirklichkeitswissenschaft* (1930), and *Revolution von rechts* (1931), Lukács quoted those passages of Freyer's work in which he most explicitly and forcefully endorsed the role of domination, of war, of race, and of the leader (*Führer*) in history.[44] The quotations were accurate, though not representative of the works from which they were extracted. The net effect was to underline and indeed exaggerate Freyer's intellectual affinities to National Socialism.

The practical results of Lukács's theoretical exposé were not long in coming. Freyer had resumed his teaching duties when the university reopened in February 1946. His courses included a seminar on Hegel and a lecture course on industrial development. It was the appearance of Lukács's article that alerted the broad public at the university to Freyer's previous writings.[45] Shortly thereafter, in November 1946, the head of the Division of Science and Research of the Saxon Ministry of Education informed the rector, Gadamer, that Freyer's presence at the university could no longer be tolerated.[46] His case was again to

[42] Georg Lukács, "Die deutsche Soziologie zwischen dem ersten und dem zweiten Weltkrieg," *Aufbau: Kulturpolitische Monatsschrift* (1946). The essay appeared in a slightly altered and expanded form as part of chapter 6, entitled "Die deutsche Soziologie der imperialistischen Periode," of *Die Zerstörung der Vernunft* (1954).

[43] Lukács, "Die deutsche Soziologie," 591.

[44] Ibid., 593–96.

[45] Interview with Martin Broszat.

[46] A. Simon, Landesverwaltung Sachsen, Volksbildung, Abteilung Wissenschaft und Forschung to Hans-Georg Gadamer, 25 November 1946, confirming their discussion of 20 Novem-

be reconsidered by the municipal (i.e., extrauniversity) denazification commission of Leipzig.

The prospect of Freyer's permanent dismissal by virtue of the decision of such a commission was deeply offensive to Gadamer, not only because of his high estimate of Freyer but because he objected in principle to the evaluation of Freyer's work by a denazification commission composed of men lacking the scholarly competence to do so.[47] The rector thus initiated a series of maneuvers to obviate or delay such a prospect. He asked Freyer to submit his resignation but did not act upon it; instead he granted Freyer an immediate leave of absence (*Urlaub*) and requested that he suspend his lecturing. During the hours when Freyer's lectures would have taken place, a committee of his former students, initiated by Gadamer with the consent of the provincial government, met to discuss Freyer's works and decide whether they were indeed "fascistic." The atmosphere was sufficiently cordial that the discussions were sometimes continued with Freyer himself after the formal meeting! An official confrontation between Freyer and this commission (perhaps conceived by Gadamer as the alternative to an extramural resolution of the problem) never occurred. Gadamer also requisitioned a copy of the manuscript of Freyer's *Weltgeschichte Europas* and convened a session at which the manuscript was discussed by the mayor of Leipzig together with occupation officials and found to be politically unobjectionable.[48]

This activity succeeded in delaying the ultimate disposition of Freyer's case. In the meantime he continued to head and work at the Institut für Kulturgeschichte and to draw his salary.

By late 1947 Gadamer, Litt, and Klingner had all made their way to the western zone. Early in 1948 there were renewed pressures for a final disposition of Freyer's case. The new rector, Erwin Jacobi, suggested to the Ministry of Education that perhaps Freyer could be offered a position at another university in the Soviet zone, in order to preserve his intellectual talents for the cause of scholarship—a proposition to which Freyer was apparently amenable.[49] But this was not to be. On 13 February 1948 the Ministry of Education sent a re-

ber 1946; Hans Freyer to Hans-Georg Gadamer, 2 January 1947, both in UAL, PA Freyer, 219–22.

47 Hans-Georg Gadamer to Landesregierung Sachsen, 2 July 1947, UAL, PA Freyer, 235; interview with Gadamer.

48 UAL, PA Freyer, 221, 224–29; interviews

with Broszat and Gadamer. Broszat had attended Freyer's seminar and lecture course and was a member of the committee.

49 Rektor to Landesregierung Sachsen, Ministerium für Volksbildung, 3 February 1948, UAL, PA Freyer, 237.

quest to the Deutsche Bücherei (the library of record up to 1945) for copies of Freyer's *Das geschichtliche Selbstbewußtsein des 20. Jahrhunderts* (1937), his standard propaganda talk during the Third Reich.[50] Three days later Freyer received a letter dismissing him from his position at the University of Leipzig, "in consideration of the ideology conveyed by your writings."[51]

The purge of the University of Leipzig did not stop at "bourgeois" intellectuals. Walter Markov, Freyer's successor as head of the Institut für Kulturgeschichte—a dedicated communist who had spent most of the Nazi years in prison and was a member of the provincial council of the Saxon SED—was later jailed and expelled from the party for "Titoistic tendencies" but was eventually rehabilitated. Several prominent communist intellectuals who returned from exile after the Second World War to assume chairs at Leipzig, including the philosopher Ernst Bloch and the literary critic Hans Mayer, subsequently emigrated to the Federal Republic.

It may seem puzzling that Freyer remained so long in the eastern zone and even contemplated assuming another university post there after his forced dismissal from the University of Leipzig. But no university post awaited him in the West, even though Freyer had crossed into the western zone several times each year in search of one. His prospects seemed brightest at Göttingen, where he had a number of friends and supporters on the faculty, who pushed for his appointment several times between 1945 and 1948. In December 1945, the dean of the Philosophical Faculty, Herbert Schöffler, offered Freyer a position at Göttingen, to which he responded with alacrity, going so far as to make arrangements for the shipment of his household belongings. The appointment did not win the approval of the Ministry of Education, however.[52] In October of 1947 a committee of the Philosophical Faculty, following the recommendation of the philosopher Nicolai Hartmann, unanimously nominated Freyer as the first occupant of the chair of sociology. Freyer sent his assistant, Hans Ronte, to Göttingen to negotiate on his behalf and completed the various ques-

[50] Ibid., 242.

[51] Hartsch, Landesregierung Sachsen, Ministerium für Volksbildung to Hans Freyer, 16 March 1948, UAL, PA Freyer, 245.

[52] Letter from Hermann Heimpel to the author, 24 February 1986. University of Göttingen, *Sitzungsprotokolle der Philosophischen Fakultät*, 17 December 1945, *Universitätsarchiv Göttingen*. Material from this archive is cited on the basis of excerpts contained in letters from the president and archivist of the University of Göttingen to the author, 9 June 1986 and 16 September 1986. The information is drawn from the files "Ersatzvorschläge für neue Professuren der Rechts- und Staatswissenschaftlichen Fakultät, 1947–1955," from the Personalakte Helmuth Plessner, and from protocols. Freyer to Schöffler, 30 October 1945; Schöffler to Oberpräsident of Hannover, 6 December 1945, *Universitätsarchiv Göttingen*.

tionnaires required for appointment. The recommendation was rejected by the Ministry of Culture of Lower Saxony, which was headed by Adolf Grimme, a Social Democrat who had served as Prussian minister of culture until ousted by Papen in 1932. The Faculty of Law and Political Science wanted the new chair within its purview. In May 1948 its committee put forward a list of three candidates, with Freyer in the middle, sandwiched between Georg Weippert and Carl Brinkmann—all men of the right, who had greeted the events of 1933 warmly.[53] By the end of the year the Ministry of Culture still had made no decision. Then in 1949, Helmuth Plessner, a distinguished philosopher and social theorist who had been forced into emigration in 1933, was invited to Göttingen as visiting professor of sociology. In June 1949 the ministry was asked by both faculties to add Plessner to the list of recommended candidates; the ministry complied and promptly appointed Plessner to the new chair.[54]

In the immediate postwar years, then, Freyer continued to enjoy the respect of many of his peers and colleagues within the German academic world. But his past appears to have been an impediment to obtaining a new academic appointment. His inquiries at other universities in the western zone proved equally fruitless.[55]

It was only outside the academy that Freyer managed to find a source of livelihood in the western zone. On one of his clandestine trips, he arranged with the editor in chief of the Brockhaus publishing firm in Wiesbaden to come to work for the firm if all else failed. In July 1948 Freyer, together with his family and a local guide, escaped over the Harz Mountains into the western zone. He left behind him the city of his birth, the university with which he had been associated for over four decades, and the only vocation he had ever followed. The possibility that the sixty-year-old professor would ever teach again must have seemed rather slim.

The Reorientation of Freyer's Conservatism

Hans Freyer's break with radical conservatism occurred during the Third Reich. As we have seen, his published writings from 1935 to 1944 reveal an

[53] Interview with Heinz Ronte, Bochum, 30 March 1982. "Kommissionssitzung für einen neu zu errichtenden soziologischen Lehrstuhl, Oct. 22, 1947; Dekan Rosemann to Freyer Oct. 24, 1947; "Berufenvorschlag," Dec. 15, 1947; "Berufenvorschlag der Berufunskommission der Rechts- und Staatswissenschaftliche Fakul-

tät," 29 May 1948, *Universitätsarchiv Göttingen*.

[54] Letter of Rechtswissenschaftliche Fakultät to Kultusminister, 7 July 1949, *Universitätsarchiv Göttingen*.

[55] In a letter of 13 August 1948 to Ruth Buchenhorst, Freyer mentions unsuccessful efforts at "Würzburg, Heidelberg, etc."

ever-growing doubt and ever-harsher critique of National Socialism. This failure led Freyer to reevaluate some of his premises and many of his prescriptions. It would be an exaggeration to claim that the experience of the Third Reich led Freyer and other former radical conservatives to an acceptance of liberal, capitalist democracy. That would come later. But it was during the Third Reich itself that he turned his back definitively on the radical conservative project of a total state that politicized society for the militant preservation of the particularity of the *Volk*. Until the Third Reich he had conceived of himself as a radical, at odds with bourgeois culture and bourgeois society, with what he disparagingly called "the nineteenth century." It was the reality of totalitarianism that led Freyer to an appreciation of bourgeois society absent in his earlier work. It was his experience of National Socialism that made Freyer into a conservative.

The typical themes of the new German conservatism that predominated after 1945 were articulated in a massive volume written by Freyer *before* the collapse of the Third Reich, in the years from 1939 to 1945. He retained his belief in the failure of universalistic rationalism and of modern technology to create meaning and purpose. He still looked to the collective past to provide that meaning and identity. But now the past that was to be conserved was not that of Germany but of "Europe"; it was not the values of the *Volk* that were to be preserved but those of classical humanism and Christianity. Written largely during the war years, Freyer's book *Weltgeschichte Europas* was the product of complex and shifting motives. In 1939, when he was unsure what the future would hold, Freyer thought it prudent to embark on a major work sufficiently removed from immediate questions of the day to be publishable, regardless of the military outcome.[56] At some point, probably early in its composition, the book was transformed into a subtle reckoning with radical conservatism and National Socialism and a groundwork for a postwar conservatism. Begun in Budapest while Germany was under National Socialist rule, completed under Soviet occupation, and published in the western zone with the permission of the American occupying authorities in 1948, much of the book's "message" was conveyed by Aesopian allusion.[57]

On the overt level the book's thesis was captured in its oxymoronic title, "Europe's World History." The book was a venture in what Freyer called "contemplative historiography," an attempt to reflect upon the past without subordi-

[56] Schelsky, "Verschiedene," 153, where Schelsky mentions Freyer's similar advice to him after the German attack on the USSR.

[57] Freyer acknowledged as much in the foreword to a later edition of the book. Hans Freyer, *Weltgeschichte Europas*, 2d ed. (1954), 10–11.

nating facts to some preconceived philosophy of history. The history of Europe as a civilization, Freyer contended, could not be understood in isolation from the rest of the world. In contrast to most traditional historiography, his account dealt at length with Europe's encounters with the non-European world. He focused on the formative influence of non-European cultures on the civilization of Europe and on the modern transformation of the non-European world by European thought and technology, which imperialism had transferred beyond Europe's shores.

The conception of the book can be traced to recommendations that Ernst Troeltsch had made some two decades earlier.[58] The First World War and the end of the *Kaiserreich*, Troeltsch believed, had disrupted the sense of continuity between past and present on which national identity and personal identity depended.[59] In order to heal the breach and re-create a sense of commitment to the European past, Troeltsch recommended the writing of a history of Europe that would differ in purpose and method from professional, academic historiography. It would be intended to provide a view of the European past that would be personally significant and attractive to the reader and thus provide a historical basis for his world view. The emphasis of such a history, according to Troeltsch, was to be on those periods of European history in which "the decisive elements of our contemporary life" had come into being.[60] What was portrayed as significant in the European past, Troeltsch recognized, would depend on the needs of the present. Troeltsch sought a critical reconstruction of the history of Europe that would revitalize the past by reconceiving it from the perspective of the present.[61]

After the First World War, Freyer had shared Troeltsch's historicism, but not his liberal brand of conservatism. After his experience of National Socialism, Freyer came to share Troeltsch's more liberal brand of conservatism as well. It was from this perspective that he wrote *Weltgeschichte Europas*.

It is the nature of conservatism to stress the value of the cultural and institutional continuity between the past and the present. *Weltgeschichte Europas* was a conservative credo, which urged upon its readers the need for an active decision in favor of appropriating the legacy of the past.[62] As Freyer acknowledged, it was by no means clear which "past" one ought to try to appropriate. In times of crisis, when the question of collective identity became problematic,

[58] See Ernst Schulin, *Traditionskritik und Rekonstruktionsversuch*, 185–86.
[59] Ernst Troeltsch, *Der Historismus und seine Probleme* (1922), 6.
[60] Ibid., 757.
[61] Ibid., 723–24.
[62] *WE*, 153.

the role of history was to answer the questions "To which past are we obligated?" and "What is worth preserving from the past?"[63] Conceived as an answer to these questions, Freyer's book was intended to suggest to his readers what "their" history was and what they ought to learn from it. Freyer's description and analysis of the history of European civilization was studded with contemporary allusions and parallels. It conveyed a number of "messages" for the present.

Among the repeated themes between the lines of Freyer's book was a message of consolation to his fellow Germans and fellow Europeans whose continent was now occupied by American and Soviet troops. Freyer showed that throughout history the conquerors had adopted the values and the culture of those whom they had conquered.[64] The best-known example, of course, was the relationship of the Romans to the conquered Greeks. This was a parallel frequently cited in the immediate postwar years by German intellectuals, who depicted Europe as Greece and America as Rome.[65] Freyer pointed in addition to the role of the Germanic tribes in preserving the cultural legacy of ancient Greece and of Christianity after their conquest of the older, more developed peoples of the Mediterranean.[66] At the end of his tome, in the pages devoted to recent history, Freyer made it clear that the era of European world hegemony was over and that the future belonged to the great non-European powers, one of which—the United States—was far more likely to preserve the legacy of the European past than its rival, the Soviet Union.[67]

The hallmark of modern European history, in Freyer's account, was the transformation of Europe by the processes of industrialization and political emancipation from legal dependency. These social and political transformations had reordered the nations of Europe into "industrial societies," a theme to which Freyer would devote his subsequent works.[68]

In *Weltgeschichte Europas* and in the works that followed, Freyer continued to adhere to the historicist critique of the Enlightenment that lay behind the works of his radical conservative phase. Universalistic reason (*Vernunft*) in and of itself, Freyer contended, was incapable of sustaining a culture and society. While reason could provide the basis of a critique of historically developed cultures and polities, it could not create a viable substitute out of its own resources. Freyer took aim at what he called "the dogmatism of reason," by which he meant reason that lost an awareness of its own limits and proposed to re-

[63] *WE*, 145–47.
[64] *WE*, 16–17, 86–90, 581–82, 654.
[65] Bracher, *Zeit*, 289n.

[66] *WE*, 654.
[67] *WE*, 771–86.
[68] *WE*, 929–30.

create society and culture according to rationalist slogans such as the goodness of man, the sovereignty of the people, or nature as the sole source of right. He portrayed the descent of the French Revolution into terror as resulting in part from the attempt to build a society according to such simplified rationalist dogmas.[69] What Freyer called "the dialectics of reason" was the tendency of rationalist thought to overstep its own bounds, to delegitimate existing historical institutions by subjecting them to ever-greater rational critique. Unrestrained reason could thus undermine historical cultures and institutions but could not provide adequate substitutes for them. "Unlike the dogmas of religion," he wrote, "the dogmas of reason are not binding and conserving forces" (*bindenden und haltenden Mächte*). Rationalism, in other words, was incapable of fulfilling the functions of collective integration and continuity provided by traditional religion.[70] The attempt to construct a social, political, or religious order purely on a rational basis was thus doomed to failure or disaster.[71]

Social integration and cultural purpose, Freyer believed, could not be provided by reason itself. The task of conservatism, he now maintained, was to preserve the nonrational, historically derived sources of meaning and purpose. He called these "the forces of conservation" (*die haltende Mächte*), which he defined as "all that which preserves form and guards the legacy" of the past.[72] He regretted the inability of most modern European conservatives outside of England to adapt to the social and political changes of industrial society, which had led them toward sterile reaction, irrationalism, or political romanticism.[73] In *Weltgeschichte Europas* Freyer began to develop the lineaments of a new conservatism. Aside from a diffuse antitotalitarianism, the political and social facets of his new conservatism were barely visible in the book. It was the cultural dimension of his new conservatism that found its expression in his wartime book. It described "the forces of conservation" largely in cultural terms.

What were these forces? The answer that Freyer gave to this question marked a departure from his radical conservatism.

The very framework of Freyer's inquiry denied the radical conservative premise that the world was made up of *Völker* or nations each of which expressed itself in a unique and homogeneous culture. With an explicit reference to Spengler but with a broader target in mind, Freyer criticized the notion

[69] *WE*, 884ff.
[70] *WE*, 883.
[71] *WE*, 885ff.
[72] *WE*, 911. The term *haltende Mächte* was adopted by Freyer from W. H. Riehl. Freyer first used it in *WE* to refer to the Byzantine empire and the medieval church.
[73] *WE*, 914, 921, 948–49.

of discrete, incommensurable cultures as "nihilistic," since it negated the possibility of transnational values. By contrast, his history regarded modern Europe as composed of "layers" of culture from the past, and Freyer was at pains to show that major historical cultures had grown by drawing upon the legacy of past cultures.[74] He attacked the notion that each *Volk* embodied some cultural potential that "realized" itself over time and stressed instead the transformation of each *Volk* by historical events and by external influences.[75] The book placed far more emphasis on what the major nations of contemporary Europe *shared* with one another rather than on what separated them. In short, the book abandoned the nation or *Volk* as the prime framework of collective identity and of continuity over time.

The legacy that was now to be appropriated was no longer German but European. Its major points of reference were classical Greece and Christianity.

Freyer's presentation of classical culture and of Christianity struck notes at odds with his former radical conservatism. While classical Greece and Rome had long been regarded as models by radical conservatives, the image of classical Greece that they had adopted was that of the politicized citizenry of the all-encompassing polis. Now the emphases were changed. Freyer contrasted Greek civilization with that of ancient Egypt. The high culture of the Nile basin, Freyer wrote, was a *"totalen Führungssystem"* in which an enforced system of belief did not allow the freedom to pursue truth for its own sake.[76] Greek civilization, by contrast, left room for subjectivity, for personal responsibility in determining how the individual should conduct his life.[77] It made "man the measure of all things." It was the "spiritual freedom" of the Greeks that Freyer now presented as their greatest legacy to European culture.[78] Any attempt to re-create civilization along the Egyptian model, Freyer warned, was bound to be "grotesque."[79]

Like many radical conservatives, Freyer had since his student days turned his back on the active Christianity of his parental home. Christianity had been relegated to a backdrop against which Western culture since the Renaissance and the politics of the modern state had developed. In *Weltgeschichte Europas* it moved back onto center stage.

This rediscovery of the continuing relevance of Christianity was typical of former radical conservatives, and indeed of a large part of the German *Bild-*

---

[74] *WE*, 90.
[75] *WE*, 80–81, 127–30.
[76] *WE*, 226–27, 231–32.

[77] *WE*, 385–87.
[78] *WE*, 333.
[79] *WE*, 390.

ungsbürgertum. The return to religion was among the most striking aspects of German culture in the decade after the war, and like most of the cultural developments of that era, it too had its roots in the Third Reich. Shocked by the nihilism and the destructiveness of the movement in which they had placed their hopes, unsure of their own judgment, and longing for some anchor of spiritual certainty, many educated Germans who had long spurned traditional religion turned to Christianity. In the final pages of *Weltgeschichte Europas,* written shortly after the end of the war, Freyer claimed that the traditional Christian view of history as a past of "unending guilt" had become a living reality for himself and his fellow Germans. They were going through a process of quiet stocktaking in which each individual was obligated to search for his "personal complicity in the general calamity, the roots of the disaster in his own being, and the ways and means of purification."[80] For many erstwhile radicals such as Freyer, the turn from radical conservatism involved a return to the Christian sources that many had abandoned in their youth. Hans Zehrer, the former editor of *Die Tat,* driven from the political stage by the National Socialist regime, discovered the message of the Gospels in 1934. The disaster of National Socialism sent even Ernst Jünger back to the Bible and into a Christian phase during the Second World War.[81]

The Christian revival had other, less elevated sources as well. After the war, when the terms *conservative* and *national* were discredited by virtue of their association with National Socialism, *Christian* provided a banner under which a broad portion of the center-right could organize politically. As we will see, organizations and publications under the aegis of the Evangelical church played a key role in the return to respectability of former radical conservative intellectuals like Freyer. And at a time when the rest of Europe held all things German in disrepute, Christianity served as a cultural bridge to Western Europe.

Freyer's presentation of Christianity in *Weltgeschichte Europas* could appeal to believer and nonbeliever alike. While far from orthodox in tone, Freyer's account emphasized the direct experience of faith in Christ, rather than the institutional body of the church, as the ultimate source of the ongoing influence of Christianity.[82] He regarded Christianity as "the effective origin of the Western essence, and its basic support through the centuries."[83] Yet he went on to define the role of Christianity so vaguely and broadly as to make even those

[80] *WE,* 1005, 1003.

[81] See Hans-Peter Schwarz, *Der konservative Anarchist: Politik und Zeitkritik Ernst Jüngers,* 169ff.; and Schwarz, *Ära, 1949–1957,* 436.

[82] *WE,* 562–66.

[83] *WE,* 279–80, also 564, 700.

phenomena seemingly removed from Christianity part of the Christian legacy. He portrayed the process of secularization not as antithetical to Christianity but as inherent in Christianity itself, and claimed that no matter how secularized elements of Western culture with their origin in Christianity had become, they remained Christian.[84] This bestowal of a Christian veneer upon much of modern culture since the Renaissance was applied with a certain verbal legerdemain. Thus he wrote of philosophical theism as "a Christianity without dogmas and church coercion, a Christianity of reason and of ethical conscience."[85]

The appeal of this interpretation of the link between Christianity and the culture of the West was twofold. It offered a source of cultural continuity that was not nationalist or *völkisch* and was therefore clearly dissociated from National Socialism. By interpreting the legacy of Christianity so liberally, it allowed those Germans far removed from the theological tenets of Christian faith to identify as Christians, yet without challenging them intellectually to rethink their theological premises. Freyer's book conveyed the notion that Christianity continued as a source of meaning to the individual, while saying little about the theological postulates of such an identity or its consequences for conduct. Those steeped in modern European culture could by that very fact comfortably continue to regard themselves as Christians. Freyer's *Weltgeschichte Europas* thus served up a new version of "cultural Protestantism" (*Kulturprotestantismus*), that venerable but fragile faith in which the adjective so overshadowed the noun.

The vision that Freyer offered in *Weltgeschichte Europas* of the European cultural past as a legacy of humanism and Christianity to be reappropriated may have been useful in providing that sense of continuity with the past which conservatives valued. The difficulty lay in its plausibility. Among the first to point this out was Freyer's friend Arnold Gehlen, to whom he sent a copy of the book shortly after it was published in the western zone at the end of 1948. "Is there really an authentic synthesis of the Christian and the Greek" in the culture of Europe? Gehlen asked rhetorically. Or was its "eternal theme the tension between belief and unbelief?" From Gehlen's letter it is clear he believed that such a synthesis was impossible, which had resulted in what he termed "the fundamental mendacity of European culture . . . which makes its appearance from time to time." In perhaps the most lucid analysis of the resurgence of religious identity detached from its basis in faith, Gehlen wrote that the process

---

[84] *WE*, 761–62.   [85] *WE*, 813.

of secularization had led "not only to substitute religions, but even to the phenomenon of a religion becoming a substitute version of itself." Yet this was a truth, Gehlen hastened to add, that it was imprudent to proclaim explicitly.[86]

Freyer's murky presentation of Christianity in *Weltgeschichte Europas* as one of the "forces of conservation" and his subsequent correspondence with Gehlen display a recurrent flaw in the attempt to harness Christianity to the interests of conservatism. Many conservative intellectuals, like Gehlen, were too steeped in the culture of secular rationalism to embrace of the substance of traditional Christian theology. Yet they were rationally convinced that secular rationalism was incapable of providing a firm basis for cultural creativity or social cohesion. If reason was capable of undermining the necessary prerequisites of a culture and society without providing adequate substitutes of its own, then the "rational" solution was to voluntarily refrain from subjecting the "forces of conservation" to full rational scrutiny. Prudence therefore required leaving some questions unanswered, and preferably unasked.[87] Such a strategy could and did appeal to those convinced of the social utility of a set of beliefs that they could not fully share, but it was a fragile basis upon which to build a new conservatism.

The emphasis on the role of Christianity in the legacy that Europeans ought to conserve was new to Freyer's work. The quest for a usable past, the search for a focus of cultural cohesion, the need for a resolution to the anguish of personal guilt—all of these motives came into play in Freyer's depiction of Christianity in *Weltgeschichte Europas*. It was timely and very much a part of the *Zeitgeist*, a response to a felt need that Freyer shared with many other conservative and newly conservative Germans.[88]

The question of religion and faith virtually dropped out of Freyer's writings and lectures after *Weltgeschichte Europas* only to reappear in his last major work, published in 1965. In the case of Freyer—and in this instance, his development was by no means typical or paradigmatic—it was *not* the social utility of religion that he came to value. Indeed, he wrote of the "moralization" of religion, the replacement of its transcendent content with secular morality, as a threat to religion itself.[89] Freyer did not become a churchgoing Christian, and the qual-

---

[86] Gehlen to Freyer, 30 April 1949, in NF.

[87] Valuable recent discussions of these old dilemmas include Philip Rahv, "Religion and the Intellectuals" (1950); Werner Dannhauser, "Religion and the Conservatives"; and Leszek Kolakowski, "Modernity on Endless Trial," 8–12,

esp. 11.

[88] On the spate of such books in the immediate postwar era, see Ernst Nolte, *Deutschland und der kalte Krieg*, 194.

[89] Hans Freyer, *SdZ*, 151–53.

ity of his faith is impossible for the historian to judge. Yet his writings indicate that Freyer not only maintained a lively interest in scholarship on the history and sociology of religion but had come to believe in the reality of God, and in monotheism as a turning point in history. The treatment of monotheism in his late work lacked the typical conservative emphasis on the socially cohesive function of religion. Indeed, he wrote of monotheistic faith as an isolating and individualizing experience, in contrast to the binding institutions of previous religions. It was the God not of de Maistre but of Kierkegaard that Freyer came to acknowledge. Freyer denied that the essential core of monotheistic belief could be recaptured by comparative studies of religion; nor could it be adequately explained by its social function.[90] Such contentions could only be made by a man for whom the sufficient explanation of the continuity of monotheism lay in its *truth*.

Freyer did not forge a conceptual link between his new evaluation of man's relationship to God and his new social and political theory of the postwar decades. God and man's relationship to him went unmentioned in his major postwar book, *Theorie des gegenwärtigen Zeitalters* (Theory of the Present Age). Yet the very terms in which religion was discussed reflect the essential change in Freyer's conservatism. As a radical conservative he had called for a new faith that would inspire a community of common purpose. After the failure of his political hopes and his experience of the Third Reich, it was no longer the problem of collective integration but the preservation of individual autonomy which lay at the center of Freyer's analysis of modernity.

Freyer's New Conservatism

In an essay entitled "Cultural Criticism in the Industrial Age," published in 1960, Freyer described the proper role of cultural criticism as making man aware of the *costs* of technical and economic progress.[91] It was cultural criticism in this sense that lay at the heart of Freyer's writings both before 1933 and after 1945. The dominant theme of his writings in the years between his move to West Germany and his death in 1969—above all in his most important work of the postwar years, published in 1955 as *Theorie des gegenwärtigen Zeitalters*—was that the characteristic processes of modernity tended to destroy those institutions of particularity and historical continuity which fostered identity and

[90] Ibid., 127–37, 147–56.

[91] Hans Freyer, "Das industrielle Zeitalter und die Kulturkritik" (1960), 201–2.

some higher sense of meaning. In this sense his social thought of the 1950s and 1960s exhibited remarkable continuity with the themes of his earlier radical conservatism. It was no longer the threat to the particularity of *collectivities* that now concerned Freyer, however, but the threat to the particularity of the *individual*. His new conservatism, like his former radical conservatism, was descended from the historicist strand of the Counter-Enlightenment. But his shift of focus from the *Volk* to the individual marked the transformation of his radical conservatism into a new, more liberal conservatism.

Not only Freyer's substantive theory but his evaluation of the relationship of ideology to sociology had changed by the 1950s. In his works *Soziologie als Wirklichkeitswissenschaft* (1930) and *Einleitung in die Soziologie* (1931) Freyer had claimed that the existential involvement of the sociologist with the object of his study precluded a stance of value neutrality and that the sociologist's perspective arose from his will to change society in one or another direction. In his *Theorie des gegenwärtigen Zeitalters* of 1955, by contrast, he wrote of the duty of the sociologist to methodically refrain from *engagement* in order to convey the structural characteristics of the social structures he sought to describe. The sociologist, Freyer now claimed, must strive to maintain an "inner distance" from the object of his study in order to think *sine ira et studio*.[92] In the manuscript of a revised edition of his *Einleitung in die Soziologie*, which Freyer appears to have written shortly after *Theorie des gegenwärtigen Zeitalters*, he explicitly embraced the Weberian postulate of value neutrality that he had earlier rejected. "Max Weber's concept of *Wertfreiheit*," Freyer wrote, "is a useful characterization of the spiritual attitude [*Haltung*] to which sociology must discipline itself. An essential aspect of sociological training is educating to develop this attitude." The independence and effectiveness of sociology, Freyer now asserted, depended upon an asceticism that replaced the "natural" attitude of existential involvement with social reality with the "artificial" attitude of *Wertfreiheit*.[93]

The rather one-sided, bleak picture of industrial society in Freyer's works of the 1950s casts doubt upon his success in adhering to the criterion of *Wertfreiheit*. Yet his very embrace of the criterion was significant. Together with Freyer's abandonment of the hope of creating a new organic epoch through political action went a less politicized conception of the role of sociology.

Like his works of the Weimar era, Freyer's major postwar books were intended to provide his fellow citizens with a conceptual compass by which to

92 Freyer, *TGZ*, 12–13.   (manuscript of a revised edition), NF, 23–27.
93 Hans Freyer, *Einleitung in die Soziologie*

orient themselves in the present. All three were very broad in scope and attempted to place the contemporary era in world-historical perspective. The very titles of the works reflected their ambitious aims: *Europe's World History* (1948), *Theory of the Present Age* (1955), *On the Threshold of the Epochs* (1965). These works were intended not for a primarily professional audience but for the larger *Bildungsbürgertum*. Freyer's conception of his own vocation left him impatient with theories of the middle range; for him, it still seemed that no theory was worth anything that did not explain everything.

Freyer's work continued to draw upon the more pessimistic strains of the analyses of modernity proffered by Marx, Tönnies, Simmel, and Weber, now bolstered by Durkheim and updated with references to the writings of Norbert Elias, Jacques Ellul, and Norbert Wiener. Entirely new was Freyer's debt to Alexis de Tocqueville, a liberal conservative resigned to the inevitability of processes he regarded dangerous to individual autonomy.

Yet in place of the politically radical conclusions that Freyer had drawn from his conservative social analysis during the 1920s, there emerged in his post–World War II works an attitude of resignation toward the characteristic processes of modernity and a program that was meliorative rather than revolutionary. Freyer still regarded the domination of technological and economic modes of thought as characteristic of industrial society and as tending toward an eclipse of meaning. But he no longer believed that such alienation could be overcome through the state or through collective political action. Instead he believed that the task of conservatism was to preserve those subpolitical and noneconomic institutions and traditions that might provide meaning within a larger context of alienation. In Freyer's writings of the 1950s and 1960s, liberal democracy and the capitalist welfare state were not extolled but were accepted as preferable to any realistic alternative. The amelioration of alienation and the preservation of meaning was sought not *beyond* such a society but *within* it.

Freyer conceived of the process of modernization (or the development of what he called "*das industrielle Zeitalter*") as the transition to a social order dominated by what he termed "secondary systems." This designation was highly connotative, implying an alienation from a more primary and organic social order. Indeed, Freyer described the social orders of the premodern past as based "*auf gewachsenem Grunde*"—a metaphor of continuity with nature and with the past that had been central to his earlier radical conservatism.[94] The very terminology of Freyer's work therefore betrayed a propensity toward

94 Hans Freyer, *TGZ*, 85, 94, 122.

nostalgia and the unfavorable comparison of the present with the past. Yet Freyer's description of the transition from a social order based *"auf gewachse-nem Grunde"* to one dominated by "secondary systems" served to synthesize the perspectives of a number of the "classical" theorists of modern sociological thought. Hegel's description of bourgeois society, Marx's theory of alienation, Tocqueville's writings on the passing of the *Ancien Régime* and its replacement by the centralized state, Maine's conception of the movement from status to contract, Tönnies' vision of the inexorable replacement of *Gemeinschaft* by *Gesellschaft*, and Weber's writings on the substitution of bureaucratic for traditional domination—all found their echoes in Freyer's dichotomy.

Freyer's portrait of the social structures of the premodern past stressed the firm sense of delimitation and purpose that they provided. The individual in such a social order, according to Freyer, occupied a single, ascriptive status that enveloped his whole person. Educated to occupy this position, the individual was integrated into a complex system of inherited rights and obligations that were continually reinforced by social codes. These social orders were based *"auf gewachsenem Grunde"* or *"auf gewachsenem Boden,"* by which Freyer meant that they were relatively close to the rhythms of nature and the products of particular historical experience. Life in such a social order, in Freyer's description, was characterized by *"Verwurzelung,"* a multiplicity of "roots" within a reliable, ongoing community.[95] The peasant living in his village community (*Dorfgemeinschaft*), the hero of the romantic conservatism of W. H. Riehl, served as Freyer's model for this sort of "rooted" existence.

With the coming of the industrial age at the end of the eighteenth century, these structures *"auf gewachsenem Grunde"* increasingly gave way to what Freyer termed "secondary systems." His description of secondary systems, Freyer acknowledged, did not offer a balanced and complete account of contemporary society. Instead it was a model, an attempt to think through the intrinsic logic of select elements of contemporary reality. The concept was an ideal type, an artificial isolation and overstatement of some aspect of social life for purposes of analysis.[96] In contrast to the relatively small, all-encompassing institutional orders of the past within which the individual found a firm sense of his place and purpose, Freyer described contemporary man in industrial society as confronted by a series of secondary systems, each of which regarded him as a function rather than as a full person.[97]

The major secondary systems, according to Freyer, were those of produc-

---

[95] Ibid., 84–88, 96, 122–23, 159.   [97] Freyer, *TGZ*, 79–106.
[96] Ibid., 80.

tion, consumption, and administration. They grew out of much older trends in the history of Western culture that had accelerated in the industrial age. Foremost among these was an attitude toward the natural world that regarded it primarily as the raw material for human purposes.[98] Modern man related to the world primarily as *homo faber*; his attitude toward it was primarily technical.[99] The industrial age was increasingly driven by the internal dynamic of technique, of the search for productive efficiency. Technique, Freyer wrote, was the "truth" of the contemporary era, as religion had been for the past. Technique was no longer subordinated to some natural human standard; increasingly it was the very availability of new technical possibilities that seemed to set the direction of industrial society.[100]

The emphasis on productive efficiency, Freyer claimed, extended to attitudes toward the human world as well. The attempt to organize labor for maximal productive efficiency had led to an ever-increasing division of labor and the subordination of the worker to the rhythms of the machine. In an effort to maximize output, attempts were now made to "rationalize" all factors of production including human labor. The purpose of much of social science, and especially industrial psychology, was to "rationalize" human labor in the interests of production.[101]

A necessary complement to the new emphasis on the development of technique in the interests of productive efficiency was a novel, open-ended concept of consumption. Consumption habits previously regulated by tradition and social status were necessarily eroded in the industrial age. "It is in the interest of the industrial system that all goods are offered to all men," Freyer wrote. "The notion of a proper level of wants has today become as reactionary as the notion that one might be satisfied with one's lot. . . . The standard of living is the god of the age, and production is his prophet."[102]

Together with the expansion of production and consumption, according to Freyer, had come an expansion of the apparatus of management and administration. The more complex the systems of production and distribution needed to provide for a growing population ever more removed from the rhythms of nature, the greater the degree of planning, administration, and hence bureaucracy required. Max Weber had done the most to clarify the logic

[98] Ibid., 28–29.
[99] Ibid., 30–31.
[100] Ibid., 166–68. This theme was of course neither originated by nor exclusive to Hans Freyer. In *Theorie des gegenwärtigen Zeitalters*, he traced it back to Hegel and Marx. We have seen its influence on the young Freyer in Simmel's formulation of "the tragedy of culture" and in Freyer's Weimar writings on the problem of technique.

[101] Freyer, *TGZ*, 31–43; Freyer, *SdZ*, 276–77.
[102] Freyer, *TGZ*, 91; Freyer, *SdZ*, 226–40.

of legal, bureaucratic domination that increasingly replaced older forms of domination in industrial society.[103]

In the secondary systems of production and administration, authority was functional, based on one's role in the vast division of labor; and domination (*Herrschaft*) was increasingly legalistic, deriving from one's role in the bureaucracy. Older forms of domination and alternate forms of authority seemed out of place within these secondary systems.[104]

Freyer's key contention was that the secondary systems of industrial society were incapable of providing the individual with a sense of meaning. Each of the vast organizations of production, consumption, distribution, and administration related to the individual merely as the bearer of a single function. They tended to "reduce" men to a common minimum required to fulfill their functions as producers, consumers, and objects of administration, Freyer claimed. In this sense the process of "proletarianization" that Marx described in his "Economic and Philosophic Manuscripts of 1844" had, according to Freyer, been extended beyond the working class to much of contemporary society:

> The secondary system is in fact aimed at the creation of the proletarian. It creates him by defining man in terms of his function in the system, by reducing him to this function. All that he himself is is trivialized or allowed to atrophy: personal character into a personal equation, homeland [*Heimat*] to a place of residence with a tinge of dialect, inclinations into hobbies, vocation into job.[105]

This tendency toward universal "proletarianization"—in the sense of standardization at the expense of particularity and individuality—occurred even as the working class was losing its distinct collective identity and was increasingly absorbed into middle-class patterns of consumption and leisure.

Rather than occupying a single status that "rooted" him in an all-encompassing social order, the individual now found himself confronted by a "network" of rules and demands made by the panoply of secondary systems in which he lived, each of which addressed him in only one of his roles: as consumer, worker, taxpayer, voter, and so on.[106] Durkheim, Freyer believed, had captured the essence of life in secondary systems in his description of modern

---

[103] Ibid., 100–106; see also Hans Freyer, "Die soziale Ganze und die Freiheit des Einzelnen unter den Bedingungen des industriellen Zeitalters" (1957), 95–115, esp. 108–9.

[104] Freyer, *TGZ*, 45, 104. For an expansion of these themes, see the (undated and untitled) lecture on hierarchy and authority, which Freyer delivered to the officers of the Bundeswehr in the mid-1950s. NF.

[105] Freyer, *TGZ*, 88–90.

[106] Ibid., 95.

man as "désencadré," as lacking a stable, inclusive framework that provided him with "a reliable world," a delimited circle of others who conveyed an ongoing sense of purpose and meaning.[107] Instead of membership in a single community of collective purpose, the individual was associated with others who occupied a similar role in one of the secondary systems. But these associations were partial, shifting, and "one-dimensional," lacking in deeper purpose or commitment. The domination of secondary systems thus left the individual lonely and insecure.[108]

The social orders of the past, based "*auf gewachsenem Boden*," were the product of a particular, collective history and thus not easily transferable to other landscapes and peoples—hence their multiplicity and specificity.[109] The characteristic systems of industrial society, by contrast, while originally a product of European civilization, were not intrinsically bound to a particular collective history. They were transferable and had been exported beyond Europe by the process of imperialism. Their ongoing transformation of the non-European world was the great theme of contemporary history, Freyer maintained.[110]

The noneconomic and nontechnical forms of status and authority that characterized traditional social orders, Freyer wrote, appeared to act as barriers to the smooth functioning of the modern systems of production, consumption, and distribution. Thus it appeared to be "in the interest" of these systems to destroy traditional, particular, historical social orders. The historical precursor of modern secondary systems, the absolutist state, had striven to eliminate the legal bases of the social orders "*auf gewachsenem Boden*." The characteristic systems of industrial society tended to erode traditional cultures with their noneconomic and nontechnical forms of status and authority. Secondary systems thus strove toward "*Bodenlosigkeit*," to create men without traditional values and commitments that might interfere with their smooth adaptation to the demands of production, consumption, and administration.[111]

Freyer's critical portrait of man in industrial society, while ingenious in

---

[107] Ibid., 97, 137.

[108] Ibid., 136–38. The resemblances between Freyer's critique of modernity and that propounded by his former admirer Herbert Marcuse in his *One-Dimensional Man* (1964) are the result not of the direct influence of the former on the latter but of common intellectual antecedents.

A comparison of Freyer's theory of secondary systems with the work of Niklas Luhmann would indicate cognitive agreement together with evaluative divergence. For Luhmann it is precisely the multiplicity of roles in modern society that provides the basis of human freedom and individuality. See the lucid introduction to Luhmann's work by Stephen Holmes in Niklas Luhmann, *The Differentiation of Society*.

[109] Freyer, *TGZ*, 87.

[110] Ibid., 87, 251ff.; see also Hans Freyer, *WE*, 2:962–72.

[111] Freyer, *TGZ*, 140–41, 180–81.

weaving together divergent strands of modern European social thought with recent works of American social psychologists, was neither original nor unique. It was, on the contrary, a restatement and updating of themes that had been central to sociological thought and to German cultural criticism since the end of the eighteenth century. Freyer himself had chronicled these traditions in his *Habilitationsschrift* on nineteenth-century thought and had reformulated them in his own writings of the Weimar years.[112]

New were the implications that Freyer drew from his analysis of modern industrial society.

Freyer now regarded as "chiliastic" the belief that the intensity of alienation in the present would lead dialectically to a historical stage beyond alienation. Chiliasm, he wrote, served to delegitimate the present through its promise of salvation within history, through its transformation of *Heilsgeschichte* (salvational history) into *Weltgeschichte* (secular history). The devaluation of every given stage of history in the name of some ultimate stage of perfection Freyer denounced as an inauthentic secularization of the religious concept of transcendence, with results that had been historically tragic.[113]

Once Freyer had regarded industrial society as a stage of alienation to be overcome through political action. Now he described the domination of contemporary life by secondary systems and the alienation they represented as inevitable.[114] Whatever the failings of industrial society, Freyer wrote, the collapse of its systems of production, administration, and planning would be disastrous under modern conditions. The moral role of social science, as Freyer now conceived it, was to analyze the characteristic dangers presented by industrial society and to suggest means of avoiding them.[115]

In describing what he regarded as the characteristic dangers of life in secondary systems, Freyer set forth a theory of ideology that departed from his earlier writings on the subject. In his *Soziologie als Wirklichkeitswissenschaft* of 1930, Freyer had written of ideology in terms of the inevitable link between

---

[112] The image of technological and economic progress forming a "thick net" that threatens to "strangle" all indigenous cultures could already be found in Freyer's *Der Staat* (1925), 173–74.

[113] Freyer, *TGZ*, 208–11, 216–18. Freyer drew explicitly on Karl Löwith's *Weltgeschichte und Heilsgeschichte*.

[114] Freyer, *TGZ*, 229.

[115] Ibid., 164; see also Hans Freyer, "Alexis de Tocqueville zum 100. Todestag," Rundfunksendung, 12 April 1959, Süddeutscher Rundfunk (copy in NF), 12, in which Freyer asked rhetorically, "Is he who points out the dangers of his age a pessimist? Even if he does so (like Tocqueville) with the intention of awakening men to these dangers, and of arousing in their will counter-forces against such dangers?"

ideas and social reality. Borrowing from Mannheim's "total theory of ideology," Freyer had insisted that since all knowledge was tied to social reality, social-scientific truth depended ultimately on the fit between the political stance of the observer to the social reality of his time and had concluded that "correct will is the basis of correct knowledge." In *Theorie des gegenwärtigen Zeitalters*, the term *ideology* took on an invidious connotation. Ideologies, in Freyer's new usage, were based on dogmas that purported to explain all and were not open to correction by experience. The way in which ideas were held transformed them into ideologies. A partial truth was exaggerated into an all-encompassing system of belief, was made accessible through easily grasped theses and slogans, and was maintained despite all contradictory evidence.[116] Science, by contrast, operated with tentative hypotheses open to correction by experience.

The spread of ideologies, Freyer wrote, was functionally related to the rise of secondary systems as the dominant institutions of modern life. Previous social orders, he claimed, integrated men from the bottom up, through an interlocking series of obligations and freedoms related to work and to inherited status. Secondary systems, Freyer claimed, destroyed such ties, creating a "vacuum of experience." Ideologies moved in to provide the individual with a sense of meaning and purpose that the characteristic processes of industrial society could not.[117]

It was the rise of the modern systems of production and administration that made possible the emergence of liberalism, Marxism, and legitimist conservatism as ideologies during the nineteenth century.[118] The perils of ideology, Freyer wrote, were intensified in the totalitarian ideologies of the twentieth century, by which he meant fascism, National Socialism, and the Leninist-Stalinist variant of Marxism.[119] Totalitarianism, he now maintained, was the characteristic danger of industrial society because it responded to needs left unfulfilled by secondary systems and represented a deliberate intensification of trends intrinsic to industrial society.[120] Secondary systems left the individual at the mercy of large-scale processes—above all, the fluctuations of the world market—that were difficult for most men to comprehend. Ideologies offered easily assimilable answers to the difficult problem of explaining the real workings of these processes. They pointed to a concrete enemy—the Jew, the capitalist, the kulak—who could be held responsible for the ills of the world.[121] Ide-

---

[116] *TGZ*, 118–26.
[117] Ibid., 123–24.
[118] Ibid., 118.

[119] Ibid., 119.
[120] Ibid., 123, 168–70.
[121] Ibid., 110–11, 125.

ologies filled the spiritual and psychological vacuum created by secondary systems with forms of thought, myth, and ritual that constituted a deformed version of traditional religion.[122]

The spread of the administrative apparatus of the state in industrial society, Freyer maintained, tended toward a concentration of power that increased the threat of totalitarianism.[123] The new possibilities of controlling not only information but the very means of subsistence from some center, he argued, made the strategy of a totalitarian seizure of power more tempting and effective.[124] The historically unprecedented concentration of power within the secondary systems of industrial society made plausible the temptation of total control.

Another characteristic danger of industrial society, the tendency to reduce the individual to the functions required of him by secondary systems, was systematically pursued as a matter of conscious policy under totalitarian regimes, Freyer wrote. Such a regime *aimed* at the reduction of the individual to his function in the system. It set about deliberately depriving the individual of his sense of autonomy and eliminating his ability to resist. Through the process of *Gleichschaltung*, it sought to abolish any possible source of resistance (*Widerstand*) to its total control.[125]

Before 1933 Freyer had sought to supersede the alienation of industrial society through a total state. After his experience of totalitarian rule in both its National Socialist and Stalinist forms, he came to regard state power as part of the problem posed by industrial society rather than part of its solution. In Freyer's new, more liberal conservatism of the 1950s and 1960s, the state was primarily an administrative apparatus, no better and no worse than the other secondary systems that tended to drain modern life of purpose but that were indispensable nonetheless. Though he never doubted that the state in industrial society was bound to play a considerable role in economic redistribution and social planning, he now favored welfare-state capitalism on the grounds that it was less likely to create the degree of concentration of power characteristic of a socialist economy.[126] He regarded the major challenge facing contemporary democracies as the reconciliation of the necessarily large role of the state in social and economic planning with the maintenance of freedom.[127]

In his writings and lectures of the 1950s and 1960s, Freyer also demonstrated an acceptance of pluralistic, democratic government that was at odds with his earlier political thought. Freyer and his circle tended to regard con-

---

[122] Ibid., 127–31.
[123] Ibid., 112.
[124] Ibid., 168–70.

[125] Ibid., 171–74.
[126] Ibid., 115.
[127] Ibid., 101. See Hans Freyer, *SdZ*, 221–22.

temporary politics primarily as a struggle between organized economic interests. Once they had abhorred such a struggle as unworthy of politics and as a
threat to national unity. The experience of the Third Reich had lowered their
expectations of what "politics" ought to provide. The development of the Federal Republic showed that this politicized competition for shares of the economic pie was compatible with a stable polity. Freyer now regarded the balance
of power between organized social groups as a welcome check on the potential
concentration of power within the modern state. The articulation of political
will in modern democracy was possible only through political parties and a
multiplicity of organized interests, he maintained.[128] As with his newfound
reconciliation to welfare-state capitalism, Freyer's approval of pluralistic democracy was evidence not of enthusiasm for its intrinsic merits but of a conviction that the plausible contemporary alternatives were worse. The choice, as he
saw it, was between two political forms of industrial society: the Eastern form
of "totalitarian communism" and the Western form of the "democratic
welfare-state" (*Sozialstaat*).[129] Such a political order was worthy of support, he
told a conference of German historians in 1956, because it made possible the
pursuit of individual autonomy.

We are committed to the welfare state in its Western form because it allows for this possibility, rather than falling victim to the next purge. Whether this commitment will be
strong enough for us . . . to defend this system of life intellectually—this we cannot
know, but only hope for and urge on.[130]

While Freyer had come to accept the inevitability of industrial society and
the relative superiority of its welfare-capitalist, pluralist-democratic form, his
emphasis lay elsewhere, on traditions that predated the modern age and on
institutions that lay outside the realms of politics and production.

Freyer referred to the institutions and traditions that he sought to bolster as
"*Widerstände*" (resistances) or as "*haltende Mächte*" (forces of conservation or
support). He chose these metaphors because of their multiple connotations.
The institutions and traditions that Freyer now favored "resisted" the domination of modern life by secondary systems, by offering the individual a sense
of purpose that the secondary systems could not supply. At the same time
Freyer used these metaphors to convey his contention that industrial society

---

[128] Freyer, "Soziale Ganze," 109–10.
[129] Hans Freyer, "Industrielle Gesellschaft,"
(1959), 293.
[130] Freyer, "Soziale Ganze," 114. For one of

many reiterations of this theme in Freyer's later
writings, see his "Ordnung und Freiheit: Über
die geistigen Grundlagen der westlichen Indus-
trielkultur," 408–14, esp. 411.

depended for its stability on institutions and traditions that were *not* created by secondary systems and that continued to exist in their interstices.[131]

In contrast to his earlier, radical conservatism, Freyer no longer sought "to create institutions worth conserving." Instead he stressed the need to preserve and affirm the multiplicity of historical cultures in the face of the universalizing thrust of secondary systems. Only the conscious reappropriation of one's own historical tradition, he asserted, could provide contemporary culture with "weight," and the individual with a sense of identity beyond the one-dimensionality of his roles amid the secondary systems. Freyer thus continued to affirm the functional necessity of tradition, of the cultivation of connections with a particular cultural past. Yet the concept of the tradition or *"Erbe"* available for reappropriation was broader and looser than in his earlier usage. Indeed, it was so loose as to amount to an advocacy of the role of tradition in general rather than any specific tradition. His emphasis on the function of tradition rather than the preservation of one tradition in particular thus amounted to a sociological defense of traditionalism.[132]

Most importantly in terms of the transformation of his conservatism, Freyer no longer sought to make the preservation of collective particularity a goal of political action. While secondary systems inclined men to believe in the power of organization and intentional action, he wrote, the deliberate attempt to organize the reappropriation of tradition most often led to its distortion. The appropriation of the legacy of the past, Freyer now insisted, could not be organized; it depended upon the will of the individual.[133] Though never made explicit, the implication of Freyer's argument was that the desire to appropriate one's cultural past could only be encouraged through persuasion and exhortation. Much of Freyer's writing and lecturing, from his book *Weltgeschichte*

---

[131] Freyer, *TGZ*, 147ff., 177, 188–89, 334–36 and passim; see also Hans Freyer, "Der Fortschritt und die haltenden Mächte" (1952–53), 287–97. Freyer's contention was yet another variant of the thesis that the functioning of the market tends to erode the social institutions and cultural values on which a market society depends. For the history of this theme and its variations see Albert O. Hirschman, "Rival Interpretations of Market Society: Civilizing, Destructive, or Feeble?" esp. 1466–70. This was one of the major themes of Joseph Schumpeter's *Capitalism, Socialism, and Democracy*, 121–64, a work that Freyer admired.

[132] Freyer, *TGZ*, 159, 179–80, 250ff. There is a close resemblance between Freyer's traditionalism and the very influential interpretation of Hegel put forward by Joachim Ritter one year later. See Joachim Ritter, *Hegel and the French Revolution*, esp. 75–82. The similarity between Freyer's analysis and that of Ritter is noted in Jürgen Habermas, "Drei Perspektiven: Linkshegelianer, Rechtshegelianer und Nietzsche," 89–94, which includes a brief exposition of what Habermas terms Ritter's *"historistisch aufgeklärten Traditionalismus."* See also Hermann Lübbe, "Laudatio," in *Gedenkschrift Joachim Ritter*, 14–21.

[133] Freyer, *TGZ*, 202–5.

Europas (written during the war and published in 1948) through his works of the 1960s must be understood in these terms.

In contrast to his earlier stress on the state and on political action as the solution to the cultural problems of modernity, Freyer now looked to institutions within the subpolitical and subeconomic "private sphere" as the major source of "resistance" to the domination of secondary systems. The family—an institution ignored in his earlier work—took on a new, central role in his social thought, both as a mediator between past and present and as the locus of relationships not formed or limited by calculations of personal gain.[134] In addition to the family, Freyer now stressed the importance of those social contexts in which the individual was more than the bearer of a single function or in which his relationship with others was based on other than functional authority. These included, potentially at least, the neighborhood, fellowship, and the relationship between teacher and student, pastor and congregation, doctor and patient, officer and troop.[135] He expressed a hope that work could be structured so as to expand the role of individual responsibility. But his stress lay on the importance of institutions *outside* the secondary systems that might provide the individual with an ongoing sense of identity and purpose, to offset the alienation that he viewed as intrinsic to industrial society.[136]

The tendency of life in industrial society, as Freyer described it, was to subordinate the individual to the purposes of the secondary systems.[137] The stress on "adjustment" to the norms of the secondary systems, taken to its extreme, led to "hollow men," conformist individuals without an autonomous will.[138] Yet modern industrial society, at least in its Western, democratic form, required men capable of initiative and autonomous decision. This was possible only if the individual was able to maintain some inner distance from the demands of the secondary systems, if he offered some resistance to them.[139] Secondary systems, according to Freyer, thus depended upon human qualities that they themselves endangered.[140]

For Freyer the preservation of the autonomous individual as a full "person"

[134] Ibid., 185–86; idem, "Die Familie als Sicherheit in unserer Zeit" (1960), esp. 1038–41. Freyer was part of a broad rediscovery of the social role of the family among German sociologists, exemplified by Helmut Schelsky's *Wandlungen der deutschen Familie in der Gegenwart* of 1953.

[135] Freyer, "Soziale Ganze," 113; Freyer, untitled lecture to Bundeswehr officers on authority and hierarchy, NF, 29–30.

[136] Freyer, "Industrielle Gesellschaft," 291–92.

[137] *SdZ*, 266–74.

[138] *TGZ*, 47, 58–59.

[139] *TGZ*, 133–34.

[140] For related reflections see Arnold Gehlen, *Sozialpsychologische Probleme in der industriellen Gesellschaft* (1949), 42–45.

rather than as a mere bearer of the functions demanded of him by the secondary systems depended on a sense of "historicity," of one's active embrace of the legacy of the past.[141] By identifying individual autonomy with a commitment to tradition, Freyer reconciled his traditionalism and historicism with his newfound concern for individual freedom.

Together with Freyer's new concern for the preservation of individual autonomy and the protection of the private sphere went a changed evaluation of the bourgeoisie. In Freyer's radical conservative phase, he had used the word *bourgeois* as a term of opprobrium and had trumpeted his disaffection from the recent past by scoffing at the bourgeois spirit of the nineteenth century. In his liberal conservative phase, he recognized the cultural importance of the "private sphere" that the bourgeoisie had carved out and described the bourgeoisie as responsible for many of the cultural values of the modern West. Among the challenges of the present, he wrote in 1950, was to preserve the best characteristics of the *Bürgertum*, despite its decline as a distinct class whose independence was guaranteed by the ownership of wealth.[142] He regarded with favor the development of what he called the "postbourgeoisie" (*Nachbürgertum*), a large middle class capable of preserving much of the heritage of the bourgeoisie, though its security derived from its social entitlements guaranteed by the state, rather than from the ownership of substantial personal property.[143] The bourgeois liberalism that the young (and not-so-young) Freyer had once regarded with scorn was now part of the heritage of the past that Freyer sought to preserve.[144] It was a mark of the distance he had traversed, from radical to liberal conservatism.

Freyer's major postwar work, *Theorie des gegenwärtigen Zeitalters*, received considerable attention in the German press when it appeared in 1955. The German edition sold some sixteen thousand copies, a substantial audience for a work of social analysis, even one aimed at nonspecialists. During the next decade the book appeared in Dutch, Spanish, and French translations. Excerpts or related articles were published in many of the journals aimed at the *Bildungsbürgertum*, including *Wort und Wahrheit*, *Merkur*, *Christ und Welt*, and *Universitas*, as well as academically oriented journals such as the *Zeitschrift für die gesamte Staatswissenschaft* and the *Historische Zeitschrift*. Two of Freyer's coin-

---

[141] *TGZ*, 235–38; *SdZ*, 328–29.

[142] Freyer, "Mittelstand ist nicht Bürgertum" (1950), 10.

[143] Freyer, "Stein's Bürgerideal und die mo-derne Wirklichkeit" (1957); Freyer, "Bürgertum" (1959); *SdZ*, 210–11, 262–64.

[144] Freyer, "Soziale Ganze," passim.

ages, the concepts of "secondary systems" and of "*haltende Mächte*," made their way into the intellectual discourse of the period.

The broad thrust of Freyer's book was remarkably similar to a work of social analysis that had met with a wide audience in the United States, David Riesman's *The Lonely Crowd*, first published in 1950. There is no evidence that Freyer knew of Riesman's book while he was writing his own. The German translation of *The Lonely Crowd*, which appeared in 1956 with an introduction by Freyer's former student Helmut Schelsky, was probably the work of American social science most warmly greeted by Freyer and others in his circle, such as Schelsky and Arnold Gehlen.[145] It was the contention of Riesman and his co-authors, Nathan Glazer and Reuel Denney, that the dominant structures of American society tended to transform character from an orientation toward tradition and firmly held principles (inner direction) toward a more pliable personality type oriented toward adaptation, a type described as shallow and anxious. Though apparently a prototypical work of "American" social science in both its method and its style, the book resonated with the themes of the European tradition of cultural criticism of mass society.[146] Modernity was seen as a process of alienation in which men were reduced by the new institutions they had created. Freyer and his circle could thus look into "the American mirror" and see a reflection of their own predilections.[147]

The implicit cultural criticism of *The Lonely Crowd*—made more explicit in a long preface to the abridged edition of 1961—shared a common intellectual root with Freyer's own. The Hegelian vision of "bourgeois society" (the realms of economic production and consumption) as a human creation that dehumanized its creator lay behind the work of Freyer and the Hegelians of the right as well as the work of Erich Fromm and Hegelians of the left, many of whom had also gone through the trajectory of disillusionment with totalitarian solutions to the purported problems of modernity. Riesman knew Fromm and had been deeply influenced by him; the central construct of *The Lonely Crowd*, that of "other-directed man," was based on Fromm's notion of "market direction."[148] Riesman's work of the 1950s conveyed a sense of the inexorability of

---

[145] For the impact of *The Lonely Crowd* on Gehlen, see his frequent references to the book and its key concepts in the volume of his collected essays, entitled *Einblicke*. Riesman's book was repeatedly cited by Freyer, especially in *SdZ* which restates much of the argument of *TGZ* in terminology explicitly borrowed from Riesman.

[146] Daniel Bell's essay "America as a Mass Society: A Critique," remains one of the best summaries and analyses of the perennial themes of this tradition.

[147] See Schelsky's review of Riesman's work, "Im Spiegel des Amerikaners" (1956).

[148] Riesman, *The Lonely Crowd*, xiv, xxxiii, 22n.

the processes described as leading to the reduction of the individual, with little hope of a political cure for the malaise he described.[149] This too conformed to the sensibility of Freyer and many members of his circle in the decades after 1945.

During the Weimar Republic and into the Third Reich, Freyer and the radical conservatives lay on the opposite side of the ideological divide from market-oriented German neoliberals such as Wilhelm Röpke and the members of the "Freiburg School."[150] Far less burdened than the erstwhile radical conservatives by close association with National Socialism, the neoliberals played a formative role in the political and economic development of the Federal Republic.[151] Röpke, among the most conservative of this circle, was particularly influential in providing ideological orientation to the Adenauer wing of the Christian Democratic party. It was Röpke's brand of conservative liberalism that stamped the first decade of the new republic.[152]

In the postwar years, as Freyer was moving in the direction of greater liberalism, he met Röpke moving the other way. Röpke's *Jenseits von Angebot und Nachfrage* (1958) not only referred positively to Freyer's *Theorie des gegenwärtigen Zeitalters* but shared much of Freyer's belief in the purported "depersonalization" wrought by modern "mass society."[153] The greater emphasis on the protection of individual automony in Freyer's new conservatism, as well as its reconciliation with the market economy and with Christianity, led to a growing consensus between Freyer's brand of liberal conservatism and the conservative liberalism of German neoliberals such as Röpke. This theoretical reconciliation was paralleled by the return of Freyer and his circle to greater public respectability.

[149] Ibid., xxxiii. The parallels between Freyer's intellectual and political development and that of Max Horkheimer, a deradicalized erstwhile Hegelian of the left, merit greater investigation. Both arrived at a resigned acceptance of technological society and liberal democracy that emphasized the preservation of noneconomic institutions and cultural traditions as means of preserving individual autonomy. See, for example, Max Horkheimer, "Kritische Theorie gestern und heute" (1970). For an attempt to trace some parallels between the work of Freyer and of Horkheimer and Adorno, see Michael T. Greven, "Konservative Kultur- und Zivilisationskritik."

[150] See Röpke's attack on the anticapitalism of the Weimar intellectual right, written under the pseudonym Ulrich Unfried, "Die Intellektuellen und der Kapitalismus," *Frankfurter Zeitung*, 5, 11, and 13 September 1931, cited in Sontheimer, *Antidemokratisches*, 276n.

[151] For a useful overview of the intellectual and political development of the neoliberals see Anthony Nicholls, "The Other Germany—The 'Neo-Liberals.' "

[152] On Röpke and his intellectual influence in this period see Hans-Peter Schwarz, *Vom Reich zur Bundesrepublik*, 393ff., 425ff.

[153] See esp. the chapter on "modern mass society" in *Jenseits*. On the overlap of German liberalism and conservatism in this period see Greiffenhagen, *Dilemma*, 306–7.

A New Respectability

The half decade following his move from Leipzig to the western zone in 1948 was a period of economic deprivation and vocational frustration for Hans Freyer. Like other Germans in the western zone who had formerly held positions in the civil service but were now suspect by virtue of their activities in the Third Reich, Freyer went to work in the private sector. As an editor at the venerable publishing house of Brockhaus, now seeking to reestablish itself after its move from Leipzig in the eastern zone to Wiesbaden in the western, Freyer was set to work producing a two-volume version of the famed *Brockhauslexikon*.[154] His work for Brockhaus took up all of his time, leaving him little opportunity for scholarly endeavors.[155] The first edition of his reflective history of Europe, *Weltgeschichte Europas*, published in 1948, was a *succès d'estime* but a commercial flop.[156] The only financial gain from this edition came in 1951 when Freyer was awarded the *Kulturpreis* of the city of Wiesbaden; he used the emolument to purchase furniture for his apartment.[157]

Like many former radical conservative intellectuals who had been compromised by their support of the National Socialist regime, Hans Freyer's road to renewed public respectability led through the institutions of organized religion, in his case of the Evangelical (Lutheran) church. He lectured on the need to preserve cultural ties to the past at conferences sponsored by the Evangelical church and published for the first time in religious journals, such as *Christ und Welt, Evangelische Welt*, and *Wort und Wahrheit: Monatsschrift für Religion und Kultur*.[158] Freyer thus participated in the short-lived return of much of the German *Bildungsbürgertum* to Christianity that marked the immediate postwar years.[159] Freyer's reconciliation with Christianity was not opportunistic; it was heralded in his book *Weltgeschichte Europas*, written during the war. But it was opportune. It was through the cultural organs of the Evangelical church that he reached his nonacademic audience. *Weltgeschichte Europas* received one of

---

[154] On the Brockhaus Verlag, see A. Hübscher, *Hundertfünfzig Jahre F. A. Brockhaus.* Freyer was the major contributor to *Der Kleine Brockhaus*, 2 vols. (1949–50).

[155] Interview with Käthe Freyer; interview with Barbara Stowasser; Hans Freyer to Leopold von Wiese, 16 September 1951, DGS Papers, Ordner: "Ordentliche Mitglieder, A-F, 1945–55."

[156] Among the most enthusiastic reviews were those in the *Westdeutsche Zeitung*, 7 November

1949, 5; and the *Deutsche Universitäts-Zeitung*, 2 December 1949, 16, by Werner Conze.

[157] Interview with Käthe Freyer.

[158] See Hans Freyer, "Die soziale Umschichtung," *Christ und Welt* (1949); idem, "Zwischen Fortschritt und Erbe," *Evangelische Welt* (1951); idem, "Der Fortschritt und die haltenden Mächte," *Zeitwende* (1952–53); idem, "Der Geist im Zeitalter der Technik," *Wort und Wahrheit* (1952).

[159] Interview with Joseph Pieper.

its earliest and most enthusiastic reviews in *Christ und Welt*, then the flagship of the Protestant press and perhaps the most influential conservative weekly journal of politics and culture.[160] The journal was edited by Giselher Wirsing, a former editor of the radical conservative *Die Tat*, and included many other former radical conservatives among its contributors. Unlike *Die Tat, Christ und Welt* was a platform for democratic conservatism, close to the Christian Democrats in its sympathies. The journal continued to publish Freyer's work thereafter.[161] Thus for Freyer as for many other former radical conservatives who had once served the Nazi regime, the road to respectability led through the organizational structures of the church.

Freyer's path to renewed repute was smoothed by the hospitality of some of his colleagues known for their distance from National Socialism. In 1949 he took part in a conference on social science convened by Leopold von Wiese, and the next year in a conference of philosophers organized by Helmuth Plessner, who had recently returned from exile in Holland.[162]

It was in the discipline of history, however, that Hans Freyer was most warmly received in the 1950s. The field of history was dominated in the postwar years by men of conservative temperament who had stayed in Germany during the Nazi years. While most had considered themselves "nationally minded" before 1933 and had been impressed by Hitler's foreign policy successes up to and including the *Anschluss* in 1938, the experience of the Third Reich led most of them from German nationalism toward a "Europeanist" orientation and from statism toward a greater emphasis on the rights of the individual. Their writings and lectures in the postwar years emphasized many of the themes prominent in Freyer's *Weltgeschichte Europas*.[163]

[160] The review appeared in *Christ und Welt*, 20 October 1949, and was signed "W," probably for Wirsing. On the status of the journal at the time see Frederic Spotts, *The Churches and Politics in Germany*, 21.

[161] Hans Freyer, "Die soziale Umschichtung"; Freyer, "Leben auf eigene Faust: Die Idee der Freiheit im technischen Zeitalter" (1958); "Werden wir mit unserer Umwelt fertig?" (1960).

[162] See Hans Freyer, "Die sozialen und kulturellen Folgen der großen Bevölkerungsvermehrung des 19. Jahrhunderts in soziologisch-politischer Beziehung," in *Synthetische Anthropologie: Vorträge . . . der "Konferenz zur Förderung der verbundenen Wissenschaften vom Menschen" am 27.–*

28. Sept. 1949 in Mainz, ed. Leopold von Wiese and K. G. Specht, 151–56; and "Gestaltungskräfte der Geschichte: Symposium. Vorsitz Prof. Dr. Hans Freyer," in *Symphilosophein: Bericht über den dritten deutschen Kongreß für Philosophie Bremen 1950*, 211–35. On Plessner, see Hans Paul Bahrdt, "Belehrungen durch Helmuth Plessner," 533–37.

[163] The salience of these themes in the postwar years is noted by Hans-Gunther Zmarzlik, *Wieviel Zukunft hat unsere Vergangenheit*, 26–30; Gustav Strübel, "1945—Neuanfang oder versäumte Gelegenheit," 168–79, 176; Ernst Schulin, *Traditionskritik*, 133–37.

Typical of this pattern of intellectual and political development was Gerhard Ritter, who emerged as the most powerful figure among German historians in the decade and a half after the Second World War.[164] Ritter invited Freyer to address the convention of German historians (*Historikertag*) in 1951.[165] In his talk on "Sociology and Historiography," Freyer returned to his emphasis in *Soziologie als Wirklichkeitswissenschaft* on the close relationship between sociology and history. He recommended to the assembled historians that they pay greater attention to the development of the broad structural processes of modern industrial society, such as the social effects of economic cycles, demographic patterns related to industrialization, and changing patterns of social mobility.[166] The talk was well received, and five years later Freyer was invited once again to address the *Historikertag*. This time he delivered a stylistically austere summary of his thoughts on "secondary systems" that many of those present regarded as "a masterpiece of German historiography."[167]

Freyer's greatest influence within the academy may have been in the turn toward social history in Germany. This change of direction is sometimes dated to the rise of the student movement in the 1960s. But its institutional foundation was laid in the 1950s, largely by men who had begun their academic careers some two decades before. The most direct link between Freyer and the new social history was Werner Conze, a historian who had studied briefly with Freyer in Leipzig and who later became an assistant to Ipsen in Königsberg during the 1930s. It was Conze who in 1956 founded the Working Group for Modern Social History at his Institute for Social and Economic History at the University of Heidelberg, which became the institutional focal point of the new German social history. Conze's formulation of his plans for the institute were studded with concepts derived from Freyer. Many of those to whom he looked for advice in developing the program of his institute were men who either had studied with Freyer or Ipsen (such as Carl Jantke) or were erstwhile radical conservatives (such as Otto Brunner or Georg Weippert). Conze and the historians and sociologists with whom he felt an affinity perceived themselves as the heirs of a weakly developed tradition of historically oriented social

[164] On Ritter see Klaus Schwabe and Rolf Reichardt, eds., *Gerhard Ritter*.

[165] Hans Freyer to Leopold von Wiese, 16 September 1951, DGS Papers, Ordner: "Ordentliche Mitglieder, A-F, 1945–55."

[166] Hans Freyer, "Soziologie und Geschichtswissenschaften (Referat auf dem Deutschen Historikertag in Marburg am 14. September 1951)."

[167] Freyer, "Das soziale Ganze"; see the review of it in *Das Parlament*, 12 February 1958.

science and sociologically enriched historiography. They were disaffected from the nonhistorical orientation of the dominant German sociology of the 1950s.[168] Theodor Schieder, who along with Conze promoted a rapprochement between history and sociology in the 1950s, also held Freyer in high esteem.[169] Freyer played no direct institutional role in the renaissance of social history in the Federal Republic, but references to the heuristic fecundity of his ideas are to be found in the work of these historians as well as in programmatic statements by younger champions of social history.[170]

The return of Freyer to academic teaching was made possible by a federal law that proved to be a turning point for those tainted by their previous association with the National Socialist regime. It provided the vehicle by which many of Freyer's former radical conservative colleagues returned to the German universities.

The law in question, article 131 of the Basic Law of the Federal Republic, was passed by the Bundestag in 1949. It provided for the restitution in office of all those who were civil servants of the German *Reich* as of 8 May 1945. As originally passed in 1949, the law was intended to aid refugees from the eastern zone and ethnic Germans from regions no longer under German jurisdiction.[171] But two years of intensive lobbying from a wide range of groups—not least academics who had been removed from office because of their close collaboration with the former regime—had an effect. Under the implementing legislation passed by the Bundestag in 1951 the law was extended to include all former civil servants removed from office by the western occupying powers, provided they did not fall into the two most severe categories of legal guilt on the denazification scale. Moreover, since the denazification process in the Soviet zone had no legal standing in the Federal Republic, all of those who had been removed from office in the East fell under the provisions of article 131.[172]

---

[168] Werner Conze, "Die Gründung des Arbeitskreises für moderne Sozialgeschichte," 23–32.

[169] Letter of Conze to author, 16 April 1986.

[170] Werner Conze, Review of *Weltgeschichte Europas*, by Hans Freyer (1949); Otto Brunner, *Neue Wege der Sozialgeschichte* (1956) passim; Hans-Ulrich Wehler, "Einleitung" to *Moderne deutsche Sozialgeschichte*, ed. Hans-Ulrich Wehler, 12; Hans Mommsen, "Sozialgeschichte," 30–34; Wolfgang J. Mommsen, "Die Geschichtswissenschaft in der modernen Industriegesellschaft," 150–54.

For estimates of Freyer's influence on German historiography, see Georg G. Iggers, *Deutsche Geschichtswissenschaft*, 353–54; Eckart Pankoke, "Technischer Fortschritt und kulturelles Erbe: Hans Freyers Gegenwartsdiagnosen in historischer Perspektive," 148–49.

[171] Georg Anders, *Gesetz zur Regelung der Rechtsverhältnisse der unter Artikel 131 des Grundgesetz fallenden Personen*, 3d ed., 396.

[172] Ibid., 15–18, 47–48. For an example of the lobbying effort on behalf of academics, see the collection of articles from *Christ und Welt*, pub-

In order to reabsorb all those entitled to restitution in office under the law, public agencies were required to fill all available personnel openings with "131ers" until they comprised at least one-fifth of total personnel slots (*Beamtenplanstellen*).[173]

Under a supplementary law enacted in July 1953, the federal government was required to provide funds to the states (*Länder*) to create temporary professorships or emeritus professorships for all university teachers who fell under article 131.[174] There was thus a great incentive for universities to hire these "131ers." The law led to the readmission into academic life of a great many of those who had been excluded during the denazification era.[175]

It was under these circumstances that Freyer returned to the academy. Late in 1953 came the offer of a visiting professorship at the University of Münster in Westphalia. The initiative behind the offer came from Prof. Andreas Predöhl, professor of economics at Münster and an old friend dating back to Freyer's years at Kiel. In his petition to the dean on behalf of Freyer, Predöhl praised Freyer's scholarly breadth and stressed the need to "redeem this leading German scholar from the drudgery of anonymous work on the *Brockhaus-lexikon*."[176] Freyer was ultimately appointed emeritus professor of sociology at Münster, where he taught (with the exception of several semesters as a visiting professor in Ankara, Turkey) from 1953 to 1963.[177]

Freyer's respectability continued to grow through the course of the 1950s. In the middle of the decade he was invited by General Hans Speidel—Rommel's former chief of staff and a participant in the coup attempt of July 1944, who had since become Adenauer's chief military adviser—to lecture to officers of the new Bundeswehr as part of its program of education for moral responsibility ("*innere Führung*").[178] His portrait appeared in a coffee-table book enti-

---

lished as "Stifterverband für die deutsche Wissenschaft," in *Forschung heißt Arbeit und Brot* (1950).

[173] Anders, *Gesetz*, 21–22.

[174] Ibid., 328–29.

[175] For the effect of the law on the University of Münster, see Lothar Kurz and Klaus Witte, "Die Entnazifizierung an der Universität Münster," 125. For a more general overview of the effects of the law on the universities, see Otto Bachof," 'Entnazifizierung,' " 205–11.

[176] Andreas Predöhl et al., to Dekan der Rechts- und Staatswissenschaftlichen Fakultät,

24 July 1953, Universitätsarchiv Münster, Kurator, Personalakten no. 5609, Bd. 1.

[177] Kultusminister, Nordrhein-Westfalen to Rektor, Universität Münster, 15 November 1956, titled: "Betr: zu Erkennung der Rechtstellung eines entpflichteten Hochschullehrers gemäß Paragraph 78a, Absatz 2, Grundgesetz 131," Universitätsarchiv Münster, Kurator, Personalakten no. 5609, Bd. 1.

[178] Interview with Käthe Freyer; see also "Spezialisten gegen Marx und Lenin," *Der Spiegel*, 24 September 1958, 18. On Speidel and his conception of officer education, see Hans Speidel, *Aus*

tled *The Spiritual Face of Germany*, along with those of Konrad Adenauer and Martin Heidegger.[179] He was awarded an honorary degree by the University of Münster in 1957 and the Service Cross (*Verdienstkreuz*) of the German Federal Republic in 1958. He was invited to lecture on the radio and to a wide variety of academic and extra-academic audiences. In 1961 it was Hans Freyer who wrote the chapter on contemporary society and culture for the prestigious *Propyläen-Weltgeschichte*, alongside such luminaries as Raymond Aron, Gabriel Marcel, Golo Mann, and Carlo Schmid.[180] On the surface of German intellectual life, Freyer appeared to have achieved the status of a grand old man.

---

unserer Zeit. Erinnerungen, 348–51; Gordon A. Craig, *The Germans*, 244ff.

Freyer's lectures to the officers on the topic of hierarchy and authority are in NF.

[179] Erich Retzlaff et al., *Das geistige Gesicht Deutschlands* (1952).

[180] Hans Freyer, "Gesellschaft und Kultur," in *Propyläen-Weltgeschichte. Eine Universalgeschichte*, ed. Golo Mann, vol. 10: *Die Welt von heute* (1961), 499–591.

CHAPTER TEN

Hans Freyer and the Fate of German Intellectual Conservatism, 1945–1985

The public respectability that Freyer and other erstwhile radical conservatives regained in the 1950s proved fragile and superficial. Though they were accepted and even honored by the public institutions of the new liberal and democratic republic, they were, after all, the same men who had once aided in the destruction of liberal democracy while lauding and serving its totalitarian successor. The immediate past became a problem for Hans Freyer, one that he shared with many of his countrymen. Public individuals were faced with the dilemma of how to present their personal histories. Rather than exorcise their past errors by confronting them publicly, Freyer and others like him sought to excise them from the collective memory. Despite their efforts, the past of Freyer and his circle remained fresh in the minds of those who recalled their role as heralds of the total state. The unexorcised past of the radical conservatives came to haunt them and to discredit conservative social thought among the generation of intellectuals who came of age in the postwar era. Among this younger generation of intellectuals, the renewal of historicist and conservative themes in West German social thought ultimately came about not so much because of the former radical conservatives as in spite of them.

German Conservatives and the Dilemmas of the Past

Perhaps the most perdurable of conservative themes is the necessity of continuity with the past. Whether it is argued that only the particular past of one's group can form the basis of a meaningful culture, or that the continuous existence of institutions is evidence of their worth, or that continuity with the past provides institutions with an emotional weight that adds to their stability—in any case the importance of identification with an ongoing past has always been among the most important arrows in the conservative quiver. The claim that the characteristic processes of modernity tend to cut the link between the present and the past has been a recurrent refrain of conservative thought and was a *Leitmotiv* of Freyer's work.

If the problem of collective identification with the national past had seemed necessary but difficult to German conservatives before 1933, after 1945 the problem took on far larger dimensions. Before 1933 the past may have seemed irrelevant or old-fashioned: after 1945 it appeared to many sensitive Germans as downright sinister. The enormity of the German defeat, followed by the revelation of the scope of Nazi crimes, led to a general discrediting of National Socialism. Contrary to Allied expectations—and to reports in the American press thereafter—National Socialism exercised remarkably little appeal in the years after the defeat; indeed, the decline of its popularity had begun well before the defeat itself. In the decades after 1945 Germans tended to identify as Europeans, as Christians, or as members of humanity—in short, as anything but Germans. Now the immediate past meant Hitler and Auschwitz; who wanted to identify with *that*?[1] As we have seen, Freyer too turned away from the *Volk* or nation as the main source of identification with the past.

Yet the need for *some* relationship to the collective national past remained. How were Germans to conceive of the relationship between their pre-Nazi history and the Third Reich? And what was the relationship of the present to the immediate past of National Socialism? The need for a "usable past" was especially acute for German conservatives after 1945. It was *they* after all who put the most emphasis on the virtues of historical continuity.

The notion that the National Socialist era was "repressed" in postwar Germany, that it went unmentioned or was systematically ignored, will not bear serious scrutiny.[2] The intellectual life of the years between the defeat and the *Wirtschaftswunder* (economic miracle) remains underilluminated by historical research, but it is remembered by many participants as an era of intense self-examination and high intellectual seriousness.[3] Though the struggle for phys-

---

[1] On the surprisingly limited appeal of National Socialism in the postwar era and the dilemmas of German identity in the face of the Nazi past see Schwarz, *Ära Adenauer, 1957–1963*, 344ff.; Richard Löwenthal, "Cultural Change," 34–55, esp. 37–38; Friedrich Tenbruck, "Alltagsnormen und Lebensgefühle in der Bundesrepublik," 292; Hermann Lübbe, "Der Nationalsozialismus im deutschen Nachkriegsbewußtsein"; and Walter Laqueur, *Germany Today: A Personal Report*, 147ff. On the declining appeal of National Socialism before 1945

see Ian Kershaw, *Political Opinion and Political Dissent in the Third Reich: Bavaria 1933–1945*; and Martin Broszat, "Zur Struktur der NS-Massenbewegung."

[2] As noted by Lübbe, "Nationalsozialismus," and Ernst Nolte, *Deutschland und der Kalte Krieg*, 190ff.

[3] Löwenthal, "Cultural Change," 37, writes that in this period "Germans read more serious books and periodicals and conducted more serious discussions in small, private circles than for many years before or after." See also Schelsky,

ical survival was the order of the day—this was the era in which many Germans, including Freyer, depended on packages of clothing and food from relatives or organizations abroad—the causes of Germany's descent into barbarism was the subject of sustained reflection among German intellectuals.

A spate of books and articles dealt with the causes of National Socialism. Most of the answers offered confirmed the prior predilections of the author. National Socialism became not a mirror in which the competing ideologies within German political culture saw themselves but a prism through which they refracted their ideological convictions. Marxist writers attributed the rise of National Socialism to capitalism, neoliberals to socialism, Catholics to the Reformation, Protestants to secularization.[4] Spokesmen for each ideological orientation tended to interpret the experience of National Socialism in a way that reinforced their respective ideological claims.

How did Freyer and other former radical conservative supporters of the National Socialist regime treat National Socialism in their writings of the postwar decades? What did they make of their own role in the creation and consolidation of the Third Reich?

In his postwar writings, Freyer first dealt with National Socialism in the concluding chapter of *Weltgeschichte Europas*, written at the close of the Second World War. Freyer claimed that while it was too soon to understand the events of the war historically, it was not too early for moral judgment.[5] He wrote of German guilt and the need for each German to reflect on his "complicity in the general disaster." But he recommended that this be done in silence, within the individual heart. There was also a need, he wrote, for "theoretical self-reflection on the negativity of the present."[6] The question of guilt was thus mooted, but without being specific about what individual Germans were guilty of or whether some Germans were more guilty than others.

In some of his public lectures and essays of the 1950s Freyer commented on the difficulty of maintaining a positive relationship to the German past. In a lecture entitled "The Idea of the Fatherland" (probably delivered to Bundeswehr officers in the mid-1950s), he asked rhetorically whether in the interests

---

Rückblicke, 76–77; James D. Wilkinson, *The Intellectual Resistance in Europe*, chapter 5. This view was repeatedly voiced in the author's interviews with those who had been professors (Joseph Pieper) or university students (Martin Broszat) during the period.

[4] For the neoliberal analysis see Friedrich A. Hayek, *The Road to Serfdom*, chapter 12. On German interpretations of Nazism in the immediate postwar era see Barbro Eberan, *Luther? . . . Die Debatte um die Schuldfrage 1945–1949*; and more generally Ernst Nolte, *Theorien über den Faschismus*.

[5] *WE*, 998.

[6] *WE*, 1003.

of continuity it was possible simply to excise a guilt-laden chapter of the past. He answered in the negative. In such a case, Freyer told his audience, coming to terms with the past meant "overcoming" it in the sense in which a wound was "overcome"—by continuing to live with it in the future.[7] In an essay of 1957 Freyer touched again upon the theme of German guilt. "We can say it and ought to say it," he wrote. "But we don't like to concede to others the right to reproach us with it, since that makes it seem as if they didn't have any of their own."[8] Guilt was acknowledged but diffused.

Freyer's theoretical reflections on National Socialism appeared in his book *Theorie des gegenwärtigen Zeitalters*, published in 1955. There National Socialism was mentioned by name, but it was dealt with entirely under the rubric of the relationship of "totalitarianism" to secondary systems. Though National Socialism and communism were described as two versions of totalitarianism, Freyer devoted far greater attention to communism. The entire discussion of totalitarianism, in turn, was subordinated to the description of secondary systems and their characteristic dangers. The stain of the Third Reich was not whitewashed, but it was diluted and dissolved into much larger phenomena. This dilution of the guilt of the immediate past was one way in which former radical conservatives sought to come to terms with it. It was as if the burden of the past would be easier to bear if it were spread more broadly.[9]

In Freyer's last major work of the postwar years, *Schwelle der Zeiten*, the Third Reich was given even less attention. Seen in world-historical perspective, it was part of the "era of the world wars," which were most notable for speeding up the characteristic processes of the secondary systems and bringing an end to European world hegemony.[10] National Socialism was not even mentioned by name.

Within the context of Cold War Germany theoretical constructs such as "totalitarianism" or "secondary systems" could therefore function to shift responsibility from groups, intellectual traditions, and individuals who were responsible for the victory of National Socialism. This is not to deny the heuristic value of these constructs, only to recall that the theory of totalitarianism served a different set of functions in the Federal Republic when espoused by those

---

[7] Freyer, Lecture on "Vaterlandsidee," 21–22, in NF.

[8] Hans Freyer, "Ein Zeitalter sucht sich selbst" (1957), 4.

[9] On the ways in which German institutions attempted to come to terms with the National Socialist past see Nolte, *Deutschland*, 190ff., and David Clay Large, " 'A Gift to the German Future?' The Anti-Nazi Resistance Movement and West German Rearmament."

[10] *SdZ*, 311.

who had themselves once advocated totalitarian solutions to the problems of modernity.

The fact that Freyer himself had once been an advocate of such solutions, that his theoretical analysis had led him to support National Socialism, or that he had served the regime abroad—none of this could be gleaned from Freyer's writings after 1945.

Freyer's colleague Theodor Litt did not share this inclination to keep the question of responsibility for the Third Reich at arm's length. Following his departure from Leipzig, Litt became professor of pedagogy in Bonn and a leading theorist of education for liberal democracy in West Germany. Once again the contrast between Freyer and Theodor Litt is instructive. In 1947 Litt warned against an incipient tendency "in certain parties to regard it as a duty to overlook our recent past entirely," to look to the future by looking away from the past. Such an attempt to unburden the Germans by averting their eyes from the historical sources of National Socialism would ultimately serve to confirm those who saw the *entire* German past as a prelude to Hitler, Litt warned.[11] In an essay published in the mid-1950s, Litt called attention to the role of the universities and of the *Bildungsbürgertum* in the success of National Socialism. "The representatives of so-called culture ought to have been the first to show up the emptiness of the National-Socialist ideology," he wrote, and he tried to explain the intellectual climate that had led to their failure to do so. Among those who had created the climate of ideas that had helped legitimate National Socialism, Litt noted, there were those—such as Spengler or Ernst Jünger—who had distanced themselves from National Socialism after it came to power. "It was not the first time that an idea that caused no scruples either in its author or in its readers as long as it existed only on paper aroused terror of itself as soon as it took tangible shape in practice," he wrote.[12]

Such reflections were not to be found in the work of Hans Freyer or of other former radical conservatives. In this he was typical of other erstwhile radical conservatives for whom National Socialism had been "the god that failed."

A comparison of Freyer and his circle with those intellectuals for whom communism was "the god that failed" reveals at least one suggestive divergence. Put simply, there is no document on the German intellectual postwar right that corresponds to *The God That Failed,* no autobiographical account by

---

[11] Theodor Litt, *Wege und Irrwege geschichtlichen Denkens* (1948), 134–39. The foreword is dated Leipzig, Autumn 1947.

[12] Theodor Litt, "The National-Socialist Use of Moral Tendencies in Germany," 439, 451.

a German intellectual in which the attraction to National Socialism is acknowledged, the role of the author in legitimating the regime is confessed, and the
reasons for one's change of heart are spelled out.[13] The rare exceptions were
more on the order of apologias than confessions or warnings to others who
might be similarly tempted.[14]

It is always difficult to acknowledge guilt, even to oneself. To do so publicly
is more difficult still. To do so when the guilt involves support of perhaps the
most morally reprehensible regime in history is all the more painful. The
temptation to remain silent about one's own complicity was therefore great. It
was a temptation to which Freyer and most other former radical conservatives
succumbed. When millions of one's countrymen were faced by the same dilemma and chose the same solution, one could always count on being in good
company. Another factor worth considering is that by 1945 Freyer and many
like him had considered themselves opponents of the regime for some time.
Given the tendency of human memory to confuse what was with what ought to
have been, it was easy to overestimate the intensity and the longevity of one's
opposition. The bureaucratic process of denazification, carried out in the western zone according to formal criteria that were unreliable in determining responsibility, and subordinated in the eastern zone to the goals of sovietization,
exacerbated resistance to the public fixing of personal responsibility.[15]

The external circumstances confronting Arthur Koestler and the other authors of *The God That Failed* differed considerably from those of Freyer and the
erstwhile intellectual supporters of National Socialism. Koestler and his co-authors published their famed and influential collection in 1949, at a time when
many Western intellectuals, especially in France and Italy, leaned toward support of the Soviet Union or of electorally powerful indigenous communist parties. Their autobiographical reflections on the lure of communism were therefore addressed to immediate political controversies. These authors knew that
some of their former comrades might label them traitors to the cause of prog-

[13] The author of an afterword to a collection
of biographical essays by disillusioned German
communists published in 1963 noted the relative lack of comparable writings by former National Socialists. Carola Stern, "Bilanz."

[14] See, for example, Gottfried Benn, "Doppelleben" (1950); and Carl Schmitt, *Ex Captivitate
Salus* (1950). An idiosyncratic exception is Kurt
Zeisel, *Das verlorene Gewissen*, 8th ed. (1962), 19–
66, in which the author dealt at some length with

his support of National Socialism, but did so in
order to expose the former National Socialist
sympathies of conservative intellectuals such as
Rudolf Pechel who after 1945 had condemned
other intellectuals for their collaboration with
the National Socialist regime. The book was first
published in 1957.

[15] See Sontheimer, *Antidemokratisches Denken*
(Studienausgabe), 330–31.

ress, but they also knew they could count on a positive reception of their confessions from the broader public.

Freyer and other erstwhile supporters of National Socialism faced a quite different situation. By the time they began to publish again, several years after the war, there was no prospect of the political recrudescence of National Socialism. Nor was there a large potential readership on the right eager to sift through the errors of the recent past. On the contrary, most Germans on the political right regarded themselves as more sinned against than sinning.[16] The political need to reflect publicly upon past mistakes may have seemed less urgent to former supporters of National Socialism than to former communists, and the anticipated response of their audience less favorable. In any case, there appeared no counterpart on the right to the collection *The God That Failed*.

As we have seen, Freyer's political and social thought had been reshaped by his experience of National Socialism. Yet nowhere in print did he ever discuss his own response to what had occurred. Unwilling to publicly acknowledge his former hopes for National Socialism, he could not publicly explain the causes and extent of his disillusionment.

Rather than confessing past errors, Freyer—like most intellectuals who had once been prominent public supporters of the National Socialist regime—tried to cover his tracks. Biographical entries in reference works were rewritten to omit his more compromising works, such as *Revolution von rechts, Das politische Semester*, or *Pallas Athene*.[17] Friends who were in a position to know better used the columns of major newspapers to burnish one another's image through misrepresentation of past writings and actions. Carl Schmitt published a salute to Freyer in *Christ und Welt* in which he discussed only Freyer's postwar works and called attention to Freyer's friendship with Wilhelm Ahlmann, described by Schmitt as "a friend who in December 1944, chose death at his own hands to save himself and his friends from further political persecution."[18] Arnold Gehlen's article about Freyer in the *Frankfurter Allgemeine Zeitung*, written on

---

[16] See Gerhard Ritter's analysis of a letter from his publisher at the conservative publishing house of Quelle und Meyer, who had informed Ritter that the prospective readers of his book were inclined to forget Hitler's destructiveness, or evaluate it more moderately in light of the behavior of other powers. Parts of the publisher's letter and Ritter's disapproving response are published in Klaus Schwabe and Rolf Rei-

chardt, eds., *Gerhard Ritter: Ein politischer Historiker in seinen Briefen*, 502–3.

[17] See, for example, "Hans Freyer," Internationales Biographisches Archiv (Munzinger-Archiv). These biographical entries were often written in part by the subjects themselves.

[18] Carl Schmitt, "Die andere Hegel-Linie: Hans Freyer zum 70. Geburtstag," *Christ und Welt* (1967), copy in NF.

the occasion of Freyer's eightieth birthday, suggested that *Revolution von rechts* was "thoroughly distanced from National Socialism, as was the man himself," and that Freyer had voluntarily left his professorship in Leipzig in 1948 in order to come to the western zone.[19] In such ways the past was tendentiously reconstrued.

Freyer and others like him may have felt that their past actions were matters appropriate for personal moral reflection but not for public scrutiny. Or they may simply have hoped that with a lack of candor and the passage of time their actions would pass from public awareness. In fact the absence of any explicit confession of personal error comparable to *The God That Failed* had quite the opposite effect. The absence of such an admission fed the suspicion that Freyer had emerged from the collapse of the Third Reich defeated but not transformed.

The Limits of Respectability

Freyer's past set limits on his acceptance and respectability within German intellectual life in the postwar era. Among the postwar generations of German intellectuals, conservative social thought was often suspect by virtue of the past of its bearers. At a time when the mentors of the younger generation of American liberal intellectuals were focusing upon the limits of the liberal imagination and the need to temper progressivist expectations of the beneficent direction of history, their German counterparts were unreceptive to conservative analyses of the limits of liberal democracy. In the eyes of these intellectuals, who defined themselves above all by their antipathy to National Socialism, a cloud of suspicion hung over the social theory of Freyer and other conservatives who shared his checkered past. Many of the most promising of the postwar generation of German intellectuals defined themselves primarily as "antifascist" and saw their task as consolidating a liberal democratic republic in Germany.[20] Among the reviews of Freyer's major postwar work, *Theorie des gegenwärtigen Zeitalters*, were those of a young political philosopher, Hermann Lübbe, and a young political scientist, Kurt Sontheimer, who were to emerge as prominent political intellectuals in the decades to follow. These young in-

---

[19] Arnold Gehlen, "Hans Freyer: Zu seinem 80. Geburtstag," *Frankfurter Allgemeine Zeitung*, 29 July 1967.

[20] Helmut Schelsky, "Die Generationen der Bundesrepublik," 186; Friedrich H. Tenbruck,

"Deutsche Soziologie im internationalen Kontext: Ihre Ideengeschichte und ihr Gesellschaftsbezug," 79–80; Schwarz, *Ära Adenauer, 1949–1957*, 431ff.

tellectuals, who identified primarily as liberal democrats, found Freyer's *Theorie des gegenwärtigen Zeitalters* lacking in commitment toward political democracy. While they recognized that his politics were no longer those of his *Revolution von rechts*, they regarded his emphasis on the shortcomings of modernity as intrinsically threatening to the development of a liberal and democratic culture in the Federal Republic.[21]

Freyer's influence on the younger generation of intellectuals was also inhibited by the speculative character of his thought and the metaphorical style of his writing. Many who had spent their youth under the constant assault of National Socialist ideology and had awakened to its profound mendacity developed a hunger for empirical experience and a distaste for somewhat vague profundities.[22] Both the style and the content of Freyer's thought were poorly suited to the mood of the postwar generation of academically trained intellectuals. While he was publicly honored, and while his *Theorie des gegenwärtigen Zeitalters* sold better than his earlier works, his message of dashed hopes and modest expectations probably appealed primarily to those *Bildungsbürger* who had shared his ardor in 1933 and experienced his disillusion by 1945. The role of this generation after 1945 should not be slighted—it was members of this generation, after all, who established the first successful liberal democratic republic in Germany. But among those intellectuals who came of age in the years after the war and who began to publish in the 1950s, Freyer's work had limited appeal.[23]

Yet it was not only the content of Freyer's message but the biography of its bearer that constrained its appeal.

In university faculties and other cultural institutions, former supporters of National Socialism and former opponents (who had stayed in Germany or been forced into emigration) worked alongside one another. Those who returned from emigration or from National Socialist prisons and those known for their antipathy to the previous regime were granted priority in filling positions of high visibility, first by the Allied authorities, then by the German political authorities and by their own colleagues.[24] But divergent pasts left a res-

---

[21] See the reviews of *Theorie des gegenwärtigen Zeitalters* by Kurt Sontheimer, "Soziologische Spekulationen" (1955); and Hermann Lübbe, "Die resignierte konservative Revolution" (1959).

[22] M. Rainer Lepsius, "Die Entwicklung der Soziologie nach dem zweiten Weltkrieg," 38.

[23] Tenbruck, "Deutsche Soziologie," 79; inter-

view with Helmut Schelsky.

[24] See, for example, the case of Julius Ebbinghaus, a professor of philosophy at Marburg known for his anti-Nazi orientation, who became the first rector of the university after the war; and of Hans-Georg Gadamer, whose postwar rectorship at Leipzig is discussed above. Note also the honors heaped upon Max Hork-

idue of mutual suspicion, bridged in various degrees by a tact and discretion grown out of mutual necessity. On the public level these differences were rarely mooted.[25] But they lay just beneath the surface of public life, emerging through the facade of comity when it suited the purposes of one party or another to have them do so.

Though Freyer and most of his students of the 1930s eventually found work as sociologists in the 1950s, a rather successful attempt to keep them out of positions of influence and prestige within academic sociology and its representative institutions was conducted by those who regarded Freyer and his circle as morally disqualified by their former support of National Socialism. The moral, political, and psychological quandaries raised by the coexistence within German sociology of those who had once identified themselves with the National Socialist cause and those who, either within Germany or from exile, had opposed it remained a latent source of tension within the discipline. From time to time it burst out into overt contention. This antagonism eventually took an organizational form in the rivalry between the Deutsche Gesellschaft für Soziologie and the associates of the Institut International de Sociologie, which erupted into public conflict in 1958.[26]

The problem of how those sociologists who had once identified themselves with the cause of National Socialism ought to be treated by those colleagues who had not reached back to the immediate postwar era. In a circular letter of 1946 in which he announced his intention of reestablishing the DGS, Leopold von Wiese suggested that those individuals who had actively participated in the destruction of the DGS at its last meeting of December 1933 not be allowed to participate in the organization.[27] The question was debated by the handful of sociologists in the western zones who convened in order to reestablish the as-

---

heimer upon his return to Frankfurt from the United States in 1949. See Martin Jay, *The Dialectical Imagination*, 280–87.

[25] Schwarz, *Ära Adenauer, 1957–1963*, 20; Lübbe, "Nationalsozialismus," 587.

[26] For references to these tensions and conflicts—which, though overlain by other issues, remained a source of mistrust among German sociologists into the 1980s—see Tenbruck, "Deutsche Soziologie," 80; Lepsius, "Entwicklung," 43; Linde, "Soziologie in Leipzig," 111; Helmut Schelsky, "Zur Entstehungsgeschichte der bundesdeutschen Soziologie," 11–69, and "Die verschiedenen Weisen, wie man Demokrat

sein kann," both in his *Rückblicke*; René König, *Leben im Widerspruch*, 189–90; idem, "Die alten Geister kehren wieder . . . ," 538–48.

For a useful—though, as the conflict among sociologists described below reveals, slightly rosy—description of the relationship within the academy between former supporters and opponents of National Socialism, see Lübbe, "Nationalsozialismus," 586–90.

[27] Leopold von Wiese, "Rundschreiben in Sachen der Forschung und des Studiums der Soziologie," early 1946, DGS Papers, Ordner: "Rundschreiben."

sociation. Their discussion focused on the readmission of Carl Brinkmann, the most academically distinguished of those who had pressed for Freyer's elevation to *Führer* of the DGS.

Wiese maintained that Brinkmann's actions in 1933 represented a betrayal of science and that he ought to be excluded. Other colleagues, however, argued that it was better to be generous than vengeful in such matters and that the future atmosphere would be "burdened" by the exclusion of distinguished sociologists on the basis of their actions in 1933. This was the dominant sentiment among those assembled, who voted eight to four in favor of Brinkmann's admission.[28]

Wiese resumed personal relations with Hans Freyer in mid-1947, during one of Freyer's visits to the western zone. He appears to have offered Freyer membership in the reestablished DGS, but Freyer requested that the offer be postponed.[29]

By 1950 the DGS had co-opted as members many of those who had taught sociology or related fields during the Third Reich. These included not only Brinkmann but some of those more directly associated with Freyer, including Arnold Gehlen, who held a post at the Staatliche Akademie für Verwaltungs-wissenschaften in Speyer; Helmut Schelsky, then at the Akademie für Gemeinwirtschaft in Hamburg; and Karl Valentin Müller, now head of an Institut für Begabtenforschung (Institute for the Study of the Gifted) in Hannover.[30] Conspicuous by their absence from the membership roster of the DGS, however, were Freyer, Gunther Ipsen, and Max Hildebert Boehm, all of whom had been prominent in the self-*Gleichschaltung* of the DGS in 1933.

Meanwhile, on the international level, tensions regarding the proper role of former fascist sympathizers in postwar sociology were also being felt. In 1948 the International Sociological Association (ISA) was founded in Oslo under the auspices of UNESCO as an umbrella group of national sociological organizations. Active in its founding were Wiese and René König, a German émigré teaching in Zurich. Among those who attended the founding meeting in Oslo—apparently uninvited—was Corrado Gini, a renowned Italian demographer and statistician who had cooperated closely with the Fascist regime. He had also been vice-president of the Institut International de Sociologie (IIS),

[28] The fullest report of these proceedings is the handwritten "Protokoll der Sitzung der Deutschen Gesellschaft für Soziologie, Sonnabend, 21 September 1946, Frankfurt a.M.," DGS Papers, Ordner: "Wiedergründung."

[29] Hans Freyer to Leopold von Wiese, 31 July 1947, DGS Papers, Ordner: "Ordentliche Mitglieder, A-F, 1945–55"; Wiese to Freyer, 24 April 1951, DGS Papers, Ordner: "Confédération internationale de Sociologie."

[30] On Müller's activity in the 1950s, see Rasch, "Karl Valentin Müller."

the sole international organization of sociologists prior to the Second World War. Rebuffed in the councils of the new ISA on account of his Fascist past, Gini attempted to reactivate the IIS as a competitor to the new ISA. After plans were announced to hold the first world congress of the ISA in Zurich in September 1950 (to be organized by René König), Gini declared that the IIS would hold its own congress in Rome during the same month.[31]

Interest in Gini's group was greatest among those German sociologists who had known him during the 1930s and 1940s and had shared his political orientation. They now found themselves overtly excluded or tacitly marginalized within the DGS and academic sociology.[32] Late in 1950 Max Hildebert Boehm wrote to Gini, informing him that he and some of his colleagues were interested in creating an organization of *"Soziologen und Volksforscher"* outside the framework of the DGS. Boehm suggested that this group might form a German section of the IIS.[33] Shortly thereafter a group of sociologists that included Boehm, Brinkmann, Ipsen, Müller, Freyer, and Schelsky met in Wiesbaden as the German section of Gini's IIS. They elected Freyer as their spokesman.

It is clear from letters of Freyer to Wiese and from other reports reaching the latter that there was little internal agreement within this group as to its role vis-à-vis the DGS. Freyer was among those who sought to maintain a very loose organizational framework for the German section of the IIS, so as to prevent the appearance of rivalry with the DGS. Immediately after the founding meeting, Freyer wrote to Wiese inviting him to join the new section and assuring him that the organization was not a competitor of the DGS.[34] Wiese declined, citing his prominent position in the ISA. He invited Freyer once again to rejoin the DGS, an offer that Freyer accepted.[35] The cooperation between Wiese and

---

[31] "Entwicklung des Verhältnisses IIS-ISA, 1949–1951," n.d., DGS Papers, Ordner: "IIS ab 1958–59"; König, *Leben*, 160–61; interview with René König.

[32] See, for example, the letter of 29 May 1951 by Freyer's friend Ipsen, to his colleague Bulow, quoted in Johannes Weyer, "Der 'Bürgerkrieg in der Soziologie': Die westdeutsche Soziologie zwischen Amerikanisierung und Restauration," in Papcke, ed., *Ordnung*, 280–304. On the exclusion from academic sociology of those applied sociologists who had collaborated with the National Socialist regime see Helmut Schelsky, "Lage und Aufgaben der angewandten Soziolo-

gie in Deutschland."

[33] Max Hildebert Boehm to Corrado Gini, 15 November 1950, BAK, Nachlaß Boehm, vol. 3.

[34] Wilhelm Mühlmann to Wiese, 22 April 1951; Kurt Stegmann to Wiese, 16 March 1951; Hans Freyer to Wiese, 22 April 1951; Kurt Nassauer to Wiese, 22 April 1951, all in DGS Papers, Ordner: "Confédération"; Wiese, "Redekonzept zum 19. September 1951," DGS Papers, Ordner: "Mitgliederversammlungen."

[35] Leopold von Wiese to Hans Freyer, 24 April 1951 and 5 June 1951; Freyer to Wiese, 8 June 1951, all in DGS Papers, Ordner: "Confédération."

Freyer appears to have prevented the German branch of the IIS from consolidating into a schismatic competitor of the DGS. It remained, for the time being, a group of individuals associated with Gini's organization.[36] A public polarization within German sociology based on past politics had been avoided.

The choice of Hans Freyer as the spokeman of the rump of sociologists most active in the German section of the IIS was based, ironically, on the same criterion that had led them to choose Freyer as their official spokesman in 1933, namely that he was the most academically respected and respectable among them. The avoidance of explicit conflict between this group and the more liberal leadership of the DGS stemmed partly from Wiese's respect for Freyer because of Freyer's actions in preventing the DGS from falling into the hands of National Socialist ideologues. In his opening address to the first postwar convention of the DGS, Wiese, without naming Freyer explicitly, spoke positively of his role in the DGS during the Third Reich:

> In December 1933 the existing steering committee was deposed and the leadership of the association transferred to a party member [sic] with full control. . . . The newly elected "Führer" suspended the association's activities. Those of us who at the time regarded this deathly silence as wrong and unfortunate must realize today that he cannot be reproached for this action. The suspension of the association was the only worthy course of action, for it had become impossible to work publicly in the spirit of open research.[37]

In the same address, by contrast, Wiese explicitly attacked Gunther Ipsen for attempting to organize the German delegation to a planned international sociological congress in Bucharest in the autumn of 1939 (which was canceled because of the outbreak of the war) in a "completely grotesque, politically partisan fashion."[38]

Yet Freyer and Ipsen, who had been friends since the early 1920s, remained friends after 1945. Ipsen, who had lost his chair at the University of Vienna with the collapse of the Third Reich, had been unable to find an academic post thereafter and had been excluded from the DGS. In 1951 he began to work at the Forschungsstelle Dortmund, an institute of empirical social research where many politically tainted, empirically oriented sociologists found em-

[36] See Freyer and Wiese's remarks in the "Entwurf zum Protokoll der Mitgliedversammlung des DGS am 29. September 1951," DGS Papers, Ordner: "Mitgliedversammlungen"; Leopold von Wiese to Erik Rinde, 22 October 1951, DGS Papers, Ordner: "Confédération."

[37] Leopold von Wiese, "Erstes Vorwort," *Verhandlungen des Achten Deutschen Soziologentages vom 19. bis 21. September 1946 in Frankfurt a.M.*, 4.

[38] Ibid., 3.

ployment. Conscious of his exclusion from academic sociology because of his record during the Third Reich, Ipsen vented his spleen in private denunciations of König, Wiese, and Max Horkheimer as tools of the United States.[39] Long after the fall of the Nazi regime, common friendship and common experience continued to bind together those of Freyer's circle who had chosen varying degrees of complicity with the regime and who had gone in diverse political directions after 1945.

The next round in the tensions between the former opponents and former supporters of National Socialism among German sociologists came in 1958. The DGS was now headed by Helmuth Plessner, who had returned to Germany from his exile in Holland and assumed the newly created chair of sociology at Göttingen. Another leading figure in the DGS was René König, who had returned from exile in Zurich to assume Wiese's chair in Cologne and the editorship of the *Kölner Zeitschrift für Soziologie und Sozialpsychologie*, the leading journal of German sociology. In his capacity as vice-president of the DGS, König played the key role in this second stage of the conflict.

König returned to Germany as a man with a mission, to develop German sociology in a direction that would aid in the creation of a liberal democratic society. Yet he assigned to sociology a more modest role than had Freyer: in a much-quoted credo, König set out to create a discipline that would be "nothing but sociology." In his concern for the institutional consolidation and professionalization of the discipline, König picked up where Wiese had left off. An avowed spiritual child of Durkheimian positivism, König stressed the need for empirical research and for a conception of sociology clearly distinguished from speculative social philosophy and political ideology.[40] He had devoted his *Habilitationsschrift*, written in Swiss exile in 1937, to a critique of the historicist tradition of German social thought, which he regarded as prejudiced against modern society and prey to a moral nihilism that had paved the way for National Socialism. He used Hans Freyer's works and his political career as the clearest evidence for this contention.[41] In a book published shortly before his return to Germany, König described Freyer as a *Wegbereiter*, one who had prepared the path for National Socialism, a charge that he was to repeat time and again over the course of the next two decades.[42] Part of König's mission,

[39] See his letter of 26 May 1951, quoted in Weyer, "Bürgerkrieg," 287.

[40] König, *Leben*, passim; idem, *Vom Wesen der deutschen Universität*, 3; Tenbruck, "Deutsche Soziologie," 84–85.

[41] König's *Habilitationsschrift* was published as René König, *Kritik der historisch-existenzialistischen Soziologie: Ein Beitrag zur Begründung einer objektiven Soziologie* (1975), passim.

[42] René König, *Soziologie heute* (1949), 125;

then, was to excise the influence of Freyer from organized German sociology. König maintained that while there was room in the German academic life for former National Socialists, especially if they had demonstrated a change of heart, it would set a poor example to the younger generation to allow such men into teaching roles.[43]

A third major figure in German sociology in the late 1950s was Helmut Schelsky. As a student at the University of Leipzig, Schelsky had joined the SA in 1932 and was an enthusiastic supporter of the new regime that came to power in 1933. Schelsky studied philosophy and sociology with Gehlen and Freyer and earned his degrees with two highly theoretical works on Fichte and Hobbes. His disillusionment with National Socialism came during the Second World War and led him to a suspicion of theoretical abstractions and a hunger for empirical research much in keeping with the predilections of the postwar German generation of students of sociology. In the immediate postwar years his work turned to the role of law and of constitutions in providing stability amidst social dynamism. During the 1950s he turned increasingly to empirical and applied social research and published widely read works on the sociology of the family and on the younger "skeptical" generation of Germans. As a professor at the Akademie für Gemeinwirtschaft in Hamburg from 1948 to 1953, Schelsky developed close ties to the German unions and to the Social Democratic party before moving on to a professorship at the University of Hamburg.[44] In the late 1950s, he was perhaps the best-known sociologist in West Germany.

The intellectual relationship between Schelsky, Gehlen, and Freyer in the 1950s was complex and shifting. They frequently borrowed concepts and perspectives from one another, without reaching common conclusions. Schelsky, for example, was impressed by Freyer's criticism of the emphasis on "adjustment" in the social psychology of the 1950s. He agreed with Freyer that noneconomic institutions such as the family had to offer "resistance" to the demands of the market rather than merely adjusting to it. Freyer's critique was the basis of Schelsky's work on educational policy, published in 1961 as *Anpassung oder Widerstand?*[45] Yet on the whole, Schelsky in the 1950s emphasized the

idem, "Zur Soziologie der zwanziger Jahre"; idem, "Nekrologe: Hans Freyer."

[43] König, *Leben*, 189.

[44] This sketch of Schelsky's political and intellectual development draws upon BAK, R21 Wissenschaftler-Kartei; Peter Jochen Winters, "Helmut Schelsky," 21; Schelsky's introduction to *Auf der Suche nach Wirklichkeit*; and Schelsky, "Soziologie—wie ich sie verstand und verstehe," in his *Rückblicke*.

[45] Walter Hildebrandt, "Helmut Schelsky im Zenit," 35; and Schelsky, *Suche*, 270ff.

benefits of industrial society, while Freyer stressed its costs. While Gehlen and Schelsky agreed that the institutional structure of modern society led to an increase in individual subjectivity, Schelsky was inclined to welcome this development, while Gehlen was inclined to deplore it. The past that Schelsky, Freyer, and Gehlen shared predisposed them to take one another's work seriously, despite their substantive divergence.[46] They remained part of a common circle, but not of a common school.

The personal relationship between Schelsky and Freyer waxed and waned. During the mid- and late-1950s, when the conflict between the DGS and the IIS reached its height, Schelsky appears to have kept a personal as well as methodological distance from Freyer, seeing him rarely and citing him infrequently.[47] He appears to have felt it imprudent to be too closely identified with his former teacher.

Shortly after assuming his chair in Cologne, König met with Helmut Schelsky to discuss their future cooperation. König and Schelsky were divided by divergent pasts rather than by political commitments or methodological inclinations. They had more in common than either did with the third major force in German sociology, namely the Frankfurt School. In his discussion with König, Schelsky acknowledged both his youthful enthusiasm for National Socialism and his subsequent change of heart. König insisted that only attempts by Schelsky to reinstate former National Socialist sociologists, especially the notorious Karl-Heinz Pfeffer, would stand in the way of their cooperation. Schelsky assured König that he bore no such intention.[48] In the mid-1950s both men played leading roles in the DGS.

In 1957 the IIS, still under the leadership of Gini, announced that it planned to hold its next international congress in Nuremberg in the autumn of 1958. The congress was to be organized by Karl Valentin Müller; its president was to be Hans Freyer. News of the congress came as a surprise to the president of the DGS, Helmuth Plessner, who at first set about trying to prevent a thematic overlap between the congress and the Soziologentag of the DGS, scheduled for the spring of 1959.[49]

Word of the planned congress roused König into a flurry of activity. He in-

---

[46] A systematic and chronologically nuanced comparison of the writings of Schelsky, Gehlen, and Freyer in the postwar era would be a worthy task, but it is one that cannot be undertaken here. For brief and respectfully critical surveys of Schelsky's postwar work see the two essays by Walter Hildebrandt, "Auf der Suche nach Wirk- lichkeit," and "Helmut Schelsky in Zenit."

[47] Interviews with Barbara Stowasser, Käthe Freyer, and Helmut Schelsky.

[48] Interview with René König; König, *Leben*, 189; René König to Helmuth Plessner, 25 November 1957, DGS Papers, Ordner: "Confédé- ration."

sisted to Plessner that it was morally irresponsible to deal with an old fascist such as Gini. Worse, König wrote Plessner, the German section of the IIS was made up of old National Socialist sympathizers seeking legitimacy. He feared that the congress might lead to a return of their influence within German sociology or a secession from the DGS. König therefore recommended that everything possible be done to discredit the IIS congress. He thought it inopportune to focus explicitly upon the Nazi past of many of the IIS members and suggested it might be more advisable to call public attention on the disputed status of the IIS within international sociological circles.[50] After some hesitation, Plessner agreed.

König and Plessner used their contacts and those of other leading members of the DGS to discredit the upcoming congress. They contacted Theodor Heuss, the president of the Federal Republic and a leading liberal intellectual, and convinced him to withdraw his titular sponsorship of the IIS congress. Attempts were made to convince the Interior Ministry to cancel its financial support. Dossiers were compiled of Gini's many profascist and pro-Nazi statements, as well as of Müller's eugenicist writings during the Third Reich. These were sent not only to government agencies but to leading journalists. The *Frankfurter Allgemeine Zeitung* used the documents supplied by König and Plessner to inform its readers of the ignominious political past of Gini and Müller.[51]

Under these circumstances some of the German sociologists who had at first agreed to attend the IIS congress withdrew. Müller and Freyer sought to rally support for what König and Plessner had turned into a struggle for allegiance.[52] Of the Germans who attended the congress, most were former students or associates of Freyer and Ipsen from their days in Leipzig or Königsberg. The foreign participants were more varied. They included social scientists dissatisfied with the ISA on a number of grounds. Some conservative sociologists regarded the ISA as too liberal; Catholic sociologists saw it as too Protestant; some national groups objected to the dominant American influence in the ISA. A handful of American sociologists antipathetic to empiricist

---

[49] "DGS, Der Präsident" to "Mitglieder des Vorstands und die Vorsitzenden der Fachausschüsse," 20 December 1957, DGS Papers, Ordner: "Confédération."

[50] René König to Helmuth Plessner, 25 November 1957, DGS Papers, Ordner: "Confédération." Helmuth Plessner to René König, 1 February 1958; König to Plessner, 3 February 1958, both in DGS Papers, Ordner: "Alter Vorstand, 1955–59."

[51] "Soziologen distanzieren sich," *Frankfurter Allgemeine Zeitung*, 5 August 1958, 8; Helmuth Plessner to Geeb, Bundesministerium des Innern, 12 May 1958, DGS Papers, Ordner: "Confédération"; René König to Helmuth Plessner, 31 July 1958, DGS Papers, Ordner: "Alter Vorstand, 1955–59."

[52] Karl Valentin Müller to Hans Freyer, 3 June 1958, NF.

trends within American sociology also attended—most notably, Pitirim Soro-kin.[53] Forced by König and Plessner to choose between attending a congress portrayed in the press as a meeting of old fascists and staying away, most German sociologists chose the latter course.

For Helmut Schelsky these events were particularly painful. The conflict between the DGS and the IIS placed him between a rock and a hard place. On the one hand, he was a member of the steering committee (*Vorstand*) of the DGS and entirely out of sympathy with Müller's attempt to organize a congress of the IIS in Germany.[54] On the other hand, he was approached repeatedly by Müller and Freyer, both old associates from Leipzig, to mediate their dispute with the leadership of the DGS.[55] Most of all, Schelsky sought to avoid the open conflict within German sociology over the divergent past political commitments that König felt it important to air publicly.[56] The conflict deepened the mutual suspicion between the two leading German sociologists of the day.[57] Schelsky felt that König and Plessner had been heavy-handed in their campaign against the IIS.

Müller was angered by the campaign of Plessner and König against the Nuremberg Congress, and at the next meeting of the DGS steering committee he moved a vote of no confidence in their leadership. The motion was overwhelmingly defeated, but in the discussion that ensued the tensions created within German sociology by the repressed past were openly articulated for the first time.[58] An attempt by the newly elected president of the DGS, Otto Stammer, to reconcile the parties in the conflict by a "summit meeting" that would include leading representatives from all camps (including König, Plessner, Adorno, Schelsky, Freyer, and Gehlen) met with little success; König refused to attend if Freyer and Gehlen did. Freyer cited other commitments as

[53] See König, *Leben*, 161; Pitirim A. Sorokin, *A Long Journey*, 300–302. The last-minute entreaties to Sorokin to attend the congress and the attention lavished upon him reveal the desperation of the organizers to obtain figures of some prestige. See also Dietrich Ruschemeyer, "XVIII. Kongress des Institut International de Sociologie."

[54] Helmut Schelsky to Helmuth Plessner, 26 December 1957; Helmut Schelsky to René König, 27 March 1958, DGS Papers, Ordner: "Alter Vorstand, 1955–59."

[55] Helmut Schelsky to Helmuth Plessner, 16 May 1958, DGS Papers, Ordner: "Alter Vor-stand, 1955–59"; Karl Valentin Müller to Hans Freyer, 3 June 1958, NF.

[56] Helmut Schelsky to Helmuth Plessner, 26 December 1957, DGS Papers, Ordner: "Alter Vorstand, 1955–59."

[57] René König to Helmuth Plessner, 25 November 1957, DGS Papers, Ordner: "Confédé-ration"; Helmut Schelsky to René König, 27 March 1958, Ordner: "Alter Vorstand, 1955–59."

[58] See "DGS Protokoll der Mitgliedver-sammlung am 24. Mai 1959 in Berlin," *KZfSS* (1959), 567–71.

grounds for turning down the invitation. At the meeting that finally did take place, the question of the tensions created by divergent pasts was not openly confronted.[59]

As in the early 1930s, Freyer had once more become a symbol of the bitter divergences within German sociology. Despite his political deradicalization, the influence within the academic world of those who thought it wrong to forgive or forget the role played by the erstwhile supporters of National Socialism led Freyer to be identified once again with the most discreditable elements of his past.

Shortly thereafter König intensified his attacks on Freyer and his circle. Upon learning that Arnold Gehlen was being considered for a chair in sociology at the University of Heidelberg, König wrote to the Heidelberg faculty seeking to block Gehlen's appointment by recalling the positive references to National Socialism and to Alfred Rosenberg in the 1940 version of Gehlen's book *Der Mensch*.[60] In a widely reprinted lecture delivered shortly thereafter, König characterized the writings of Freyer and the conservative revolutionaries of the 1920s as lacking in intellectual substance and pointed to their affinity with National Socialism. In light of Freyer's failed prognoses in *Revolution von rechts*, König wrote, it was hard to understand why the German reading public continued to gobble up his "empty literary outpourings."[61]

Schelsky perceived König's attacks as the use of the past in the service of current interests, as an attempt to discredit competitors for influence within German sociology.[62] At about the same time, an advisory board headed by Plessner turned down a major grant application from Schelsky. Schelsky believed that Plessner's objections lay in Schelsky's relationship to Gehlen and Leipzig.[63] His attitude changed from one of reconciliation to one of open defiance. In 1961 Schelsky, now professor of sociology in Münster, appointed the most notorious of the sociologists who had studied with Freyer in Leipzig, Karl-Heinz Pfeffer, to a research professorship under the provisions of article 131. He not only confirmed König's worst suspicions but brought renewed public attention to the odious past of Freyer's Leipzig circle.[64]

[59] See W. E. Mühlmann to Otto Stammer, 23 December 1959 and 18 May 1960, and 6 July 1960; Stammer to Theodor Adorno, 5 May 1960; Aktennotiz, 24 February 1960; all in DGS Papers, Ornder "Niederwald Tagung 1960"; Stammer to König 2 November 1960 in DGS Papers, Ordner "IIS ab 1958/59."

[60] König, *Leben*, 189–90; interview with

König.

[61] René König, "Zur Soziologie der zwanziger Jahren" (1960).

[62] Interview with Schelsky.

[63] Schelsky, "Verschiedene Weisen," 140–41.

[64] For the official protest of the DGS over the appointment, see "Protokoll der Vorstandssitzungen der DGS am 4.1.62," DGS Papers. For

Hans Freyer would be recalled by younger sociologists, such as Ralf Dahrendorf, as the man "who did more than any other German sociologist to betray sociology to National Socialism and thereby lead astray a generation of students and young scholars."[65] Freyer, who had long proclaimed the importance of identification with the past, found himself identified by others with a past he had sought to jettison. This identification would color the reception of the work of Freyer and other conservative thinkers by the postwar generation of German intellectuals. That unwelcome identification would determine the fortunes of German intellectual conservatism until well after Freyer's death in 1969.

Epilogue: The Other God That Failed and the Fate of Intellectual Conservatism in West Germany

For the first decade and a half after the Second World War, West German political culture was dominated by an "antitotalitarian consensus." The division between the political left and the political right did not disappear, but both the left and the right had come to accept the rules of the game of liberal democracy. Conservatives considered the experience of National Socialism to have discredited right-wing totalitarian solutions to the problems of a pluralist society, while totalitarianism of the left appeared a tangible reality in the Russian zone of occupation and then in East Germany. Opposition to left-wing totalitarianism was by no means a preserve of the German right; the social democratic left was no less convinced of the evil of communism and the divide that separated imperfect democracies from imperfect totalitarian regimes. Among West German intellectuals sympathy with communism was minuscule during the 1950s, as it was within the larger public. Despite their antipathy toward capitalism, few labor leaders, social democratic politicians, or intellectuals on the left were inclined to regard the political and social system of the Federal Republic as differing from the Third Reich merely in degree. The movement of disillusioned intellectuals toward the political center occurred in most West-

---

the official protest of the Verband Deutscher Studentenschaften, see *Der Kurier* (West Berlin), 6 December 1962. The East Germans, grasping yet another opportunity to embarrass the FRG, published a sixty-five-page exposé based on archival sources in the GDR, Kommittee zur Untersuchung der Verhältnisse an west-deutschen

Universitäten an der Karl-Marx-Universität Leipzig, *Eine Dokumentation: Die wissenschaftliche und politische Karriere des Dr. phil. habil Karl-Heinz Pfeffer*.

[65] Ralf Dahrendorf, "Soziologie und Nationalsozialismus" (1964).

ern societies in the postwar years, but nowhere more than in West Germany. There the collective experiences of the totalitarianisms of the right and left created a basic liberal democratic consensus for the first time in German history.[66] Hans Freyer's political evolution was shared by many of the intellectuals who set the tone of political discourse in the 1950s.

During the 1950s, the National Socialist past was not ignored in German intellectual and political life. But it was often treated as part of much larger, global phenomena or conflated with communism under the rubric of totalitarianism. In either case the effect was to play down the particular horror of National Socialist policies such as euthanasia and genocide and to deflect specific responsibility for what had occurred. Adenauer studiously avoided an atmosphere of public contrition for the horrors of the Nazi era. At the top levels of politics, of the army, of education, and of culture, care was taken to see that those marked by their salience in the National Socialist era were now kept out of the limelight. But few institutions could have excluded all former supporters of the regime, even had their leaders been so inclined; too many Germans had at one time or another backed the Hitler regime to make such an exclusionary policy possible. None of the major parties could afford to alienate a large proportion of potential voters by making too public an issue of the past. In the bureaucracy and the judiciary, in journalism, in economic associations, and in the universities, the general tendency was to avoid inquiries into the personal histories of those who did not overtly oppose the new Germany. The interests of social harmony and political integration seemed best served by not digging too deeply into the past.[67]

Behind this facade of harmony and of forgiving and forgetting, the past continued to play a role in forming allegiances among intellectuals. The struggles within the German Sociological Association provide a case study of such conflicts among intellectuals who had had very different reactions to the rise of National Socialism.

Within this atmosphere those who had once been drawn to National Socialism and who had helped legitimate it were not inclined to offer public explanations of their actions or of the sources of their disillusionment. Yet the effect of this strategy of silence was that while former supporters of the Nazi regime were not openly discredited, a certain odium was attached to them in the minds of the next generation.[68] In the eyes of the rising young intellectuals of

[66] Löwenthal, "Cultural Change," 36–39; Bracher, *Zeit der Ideologien*, 271ff.

[67] Schwarz, *Ära Adenauer, 1957–1963*, 205–7.

[68] See, for example, the relative disrespect

the 1950s, such as Ralf Dahrendorf, Hermann Lübbe, and Kurt Sontheimer, who defined themselves above all by their antipathy to National Socialism, a cloud of suspicion hung over the social theory of Freyer and other conservatives who were known to have contributed to the rise of National Socialism. Among the immediate postwar generations of German intellectuals, conservatism was already suspect by virtue of the past of its bearers.

At the end of the 1950s and the beginning of the 1960s, several factors converged to put German conservatism in an even worse light among intellectuals. Detailed scholarly studies dealing with the rise of the National Socialist regime by the generation of postwar scholars began to appear: Karl Dietrich Bracher's *Die Auflösung der Weimarer Republik* in 1957; Christian Graf von Krockow's *Die Entscheidung: Eine Untersuchung über Ernst Jünger, Carl Schmitt und Martin Heidegger* in 1958; *Die nationalsozialistische Machtergreifung* by Bracher, Schulz, and Sauer in 1960; and Kurt Sontheimer's essay on the Tatkreis in 1959 followed by his *Antidemokratisches Denken in der Weimarer Republik* in 1962. These studies called attention not only to the role of traditional German elites but to that of German intellectuals—many still living and active—in preparing the way and assisting in the rise to power of National Socialism. In a different vein, a series of widely read novels by Günter Grass (*The Tin Drum*, 1959) and Heinrich Böll (*Billiards at Half Past Nine*, 1959, and *The Clown*, 1963) painted a portrait of the culture, society, and politics of West Germany as poisoned by hypocrisy and mendacity resulting from the unwillingness to face up to responsibility for moral failures during the Nazi era. In 1959 a wave of swastika daubings, beginning with a synagogue in Cologne, led to public concern about anti-Semitism and a widespread information campaign by the government and the mass media to counter it. A series of trials of war criminals in West Germany and above all the Eichmann trial in Jerusalem increased public awareness of the horrors committed during the National Socialist regime. At about the same time, information provided by East German authorities revealed the complicity of a good part of the West German judiciary in the systematized injustice of the Nazi era. As a result nearly 150 West German judges and government prosecutors chose "voluntary" retirement in the summer of 1962.[69]

---

shown to Arnold Gehlen compared to Theodor Adorno by two of the most prominent younger sociologists, Heinrich Popitz and Ralf Dahrendorf, at the Jagdschloß Niederwald discussions of 1960, described in Ralf Dahrendorf, "Nachruf auf Theodor Adorno."

[69] Cf. Schwarz, *Ära Adenauer, 1957–1963*, 205–14; Theo Sommer, "The Nazis in the Judiciary," 240–48.

These factors combined to bring about a very different attitude toward the National Socialist past and its relationship to postwar German institutions in the minds of the generation of Germans then coming of age, who were too young to remember the Third Reich themselves. Especially among the upcoming generation of intellectuals, there was a tendency to view the conservative establishment of their country as a shadowy conspiracy of men and institutions who combined a dubious past with a cynical morality and a questionable attachment to democratic institutions.[70]

It was against this background that the "*Spiegel* affair" was played out. In October 1962 the weekly magazine *Der Spiegel*, a journal long critical of the Adenauer government and its minister of defense, Franz Josef Strauss, published a long article based on classified studies and claiming that recent war exercises had shown NATO forces inadequate to fend off an attack by the Warsaw Pact. The government ordered a police search of *Der Spiegel*'s offices and the arrest of the magazine's editor and the article's author on suspicion of treason. These actions were met with a wave of protest in the more influential organs of public opinion and within the universities, where they were seen as evidence of the authoritarianism of the government. This outcry of liberal opinion contributed to the fall of Strauss and then of Adenauer.[71] Changes in political culture cannot be measured with precision, but the reaction to the *Spiegel* affair marked a decided shift in the political culture of the Federal Republic toward a more liberal sensibility.

In the years that followed, as the Social Democrats moved into the federal government (in 1966) and as the Brandt-Scheel government inaugurated a new era of reform in 1969, not a few of the young liberal intellectuals of the 1950s moved into the halls of government, as representatives of the Free Democrats or the Social Democrats. Among those who had greeted Freyer's postwar work with skepticism, Hermann Lübbe became the official responsible for university affairs in the Social Democratic controlled Ministry of Culture of North Rhein-Westphalia in 1966. Ralf Dahrendorf published his influential book *Gesellschaft und Demokratie in Deutschland*, in which he urged his fellow citizens to cast off the suspicions of modernity so characteristic of German social thought. Politically active in the Free Democrats, Dahrendorf in 1969 was elected to the Bundestag and became a deputy minister (*Staatssekretär*) in the Foreign Office.

Intellectuals such as Dahrendorf, Lübbe, or Kurt Sontheimer were by no

---

[70] Schwarz, *Ära Adenauer, 1957–1963*, 216.   [71] Schwarz, *Ära Adenauer, 1957–1963*, 261ff.

means radicals. All three were—and remained—fervent advocates of the virtues of liberal democracy. All three were suspicious of German conservatism.[72] For them the years following the resignation of Adenauer seemed to offer an opportunity to move the liberal democratic society that had grown up under Adenauer in the direction of greater openness and equality of opportunity. The long-awaited liberal hour in politics and culture appeared to have arrived. When Hans Freyer published his last book, *Schwelle der Zeiten*, in 1965, it went unreviewed. Freyer died in 1969 "virtually forgotten," in the words of the conservative journal *Christ und Welt*.[73] The fortunes of German intellectual conservatism seemed at a low ebb.

Within German intellectual life, however, it was not the liberal democratic critics of the Christian Democratic era such as Sontheimer and Dahrendorf who were to set the tone in the decade after the *Spiegel* affair; it was the new student left. Unlike the liberals who had criticized the government and society of West Germany for failure to live up to the ideals of liberal democracy, it was the ideal of liberal democracy itself that the New Left called into question. The institutional beginnings of the German New Left were in the Sozialistischer Deutscher Studentenbund, the student wing of the Social Democratic party, which was expelled by its parent body because of its rejection of the welfare state and the antitotalitarian consensus. The German New Left first became a salient presence at the Free University in Berlin in the summer of 1965, where it began to hold protest actions modeled on those at Berkeley. It reached its high point in the half decade after June 1967, as protest spread beyond Berlin to most university towns.[74]

The era of the student left is too recent a phenomenon to be entirely amenable to historical analysis. It was of course by no means a purely German phenomenon, but seen in comparative perspective the German New Left had its own characteristic emphases and peculiarities. Suspicion of established authority was the hallmark of the New Left in all Western democracies, but in Germany this antiauthoritarianism was coupled with the assertion of a direct link between National Socialism and the political system of the Federal Repub-

---

[72] See, for example, Sontheimer's essay of 1968, "Antidemokratisches Denken in der Bundesrepublik," and his essay of 1969 entitled "Gefahr von rechts—Gefahr von links," both reprinted in his *Deutschland zwischen Demokratie und Antidemokratie*. In both essays he saw the major danger to political democracy as arising from the radical right, which he saw as pursuing themes increasingly influential within the established, parliamentary right.

[73] Waldemar Besson, review of *Gedanken zur Industriegesellschaft*, by Hans Freyer, 14.

[74] On the history of the German New Left see Gerd Langguth, *Die Protestbewegung in der Bundesrepublik Deutschland, 1968–1972*. On its early phases see 39–43.

lic, both of which were pictured as mere variants of "bourgeois domination" (*bürgerliche Herrschaft*). Attempts by the New Left to emphasize the continuity of the Federal Republic with National Socialism reached from the publication of a series entitled "Brown University," in which active professors were confronted with morally incriminating quotations from their books written during the Third Reich, to the selection by the terrorist Red Army Faction of Hans-Martin Schleyer, a former SS officer who had risen to the presidency of the Federation of German Employers, as a victim of kidnapping and murder.[75] Like its New Left counterparts in the United States and France, the German student left regarded the university as a "staging ground" for its conquest of the larger society, but the organized disruption of university life was more widespread and lasted longer in Germany than elsewhere. The willingness of German governments to accede to student demands for a more "democratic" restructuring of decision making within the university fed the politicization of academic life. After the manifest failure of the New Left to foment a successful revolution, many New Leftists adopted a strategy of "the long march through the institutions," which sought to transform society by radicalizing the institutions of culture and politics. Although no precise comparison has yet been undertaken, the German New Left appears to have been more successful than its counterparts elsewhere in institutionalizing its influence within the academy and in other cultural institutions, through the creation of institutes founded upon the ideological assumptions of the New Left (such as "critical peace research"), through filling academic positions with incumbents committed to the ideals of the New Left, and through the institutionalization of New Left ideals in high school curricula.[76]

The appearance of a mass movement that called the very principles of liberal democracy into question, its violent disruption of the academy, and its subsequent institutionalization came as a series of shocks to the postwar generation of liberal intellectuals. It was *their* liberal institutions and ideas that were under attack and seemed to some in danger of giving way to the onslaught of the New Left. The result was a realignment within German intellectual life that pitched prominent reformist socialists, liberals, and conservatives

---

[75] R. Seelinger, ed., *Braune Universität*, 6 vols., 1964ff.; on Schleyer see Tom Bower, *The Pledge Betrayed*, 381–85.

[76] See *Report on German Universities* by the German Universities Commission of the International Council on the Future of the University; Walter Ruegg, "The Intellectual Situation in German Higher Education"; and Guenter Lewy, "The Persisting Heritage of the 1960s in West German Higher Education." On the intellectual assumptions and institutionalization of "critical peace research" see Jeffrey Herf, "War, Peace and the Intellectuals: The West German Peace Movement."

into one camp, allied against intellectual supporters of the New Left. Perhaps the most prominent organizational embodiment of this realignment was the Bund Freiheit der Wissenschaft (League for Freedom in Scholarship), founded in 1970.[77] It was the challenge of the New Left and the "counterculture" to which it was linked that first led prominent representatives of the postwar generation of intellectuals toward a reconsideration of conservatism.

The "counterculture" of the 1960s and 1970s was regarded by its liberal opponents as evidence of the difficulty of modern industrial society in providing a meaning and purpose to its members. It led liberal intellectuals to a concern with the *cost* of the typical processes of modernity, with the limits of rationality, and with the role of tradition—themes which German liberal intellectuals had formerly eschewed. The challenge to liberal democracy posed by the extraparliamentary politics of the New Left and its degeneration into terrorism led some liberals to a renewed awareness of the fragility of liberal political institutions and their dependence upon cultural norms of restraint. By the 1970s, some of the most prominent German liberal intellectuals of the postwar decades had begun a more favorable reassessment of themes traditionally associated with historicist conservatism.

Kurt Sontheimer (born in 1928), an influential political scientist and political commentator long identified with political liberalism, may serve as an example. When Freyer's *Theorie des gegenwärtigen Zeitalters* was published in 1955, Sontheimer reviewed it for the *Frankfurter Hefte*, a leading organ of intellectual opinion at the time. His review, entitled "Sociological Speculation," was dismissive. In the late 1950s and early 1960s his scholarly work called attention to the disastrous consequences of the antidemocratic thought of radical conservative intellectuals on the Weimar Republic. In the late 1960s he remained suspicious of the democratic convictions of German political conservatism.

By the mid-1970s, however, Sontheimer had shifted his focus and become a leading critic of the German intellectual left, which he criticized for what he saw as its irresponsible utopianism.[78] His subsequent work echoed themes long prominent in the work of Freyer and Gehlen.

Today young and old alike, despite their diverse backgrounds, are exposed to the conditions of industrial and consumer society, with its rapid social and technological change

---

[77] See Hans Maier and Michael Zöller, eds., *Bund Freiheit der Wissenschaft: Der Gründungskongreß in Bad Godesberg am 18. November 1970.* On the realignment of intellectuals see Bracher, *Zeit*, 308–9, and Kurt Sontheimer, "Zwei deutsche Republiken und ihre Intellektuellen," esp. 1068–70.

[78] Kurt Sontheimer, *Das Elend unserer Intellektuellen* (1976).

which tends to make social integration more difficult, and is more often detrimental than conducive to the human need for the development of both individual and collective identity.

The industrial society of our age—secularized, characterized by rapid social and technological change—unremittingly relativizes the binding force of social and moral norms. It weakens the integrative ability of social institutions, in which the individual participates—and cares to participate—only as the incumbent of various social roles, rather than as a whole person.[79]

When Freyer's *Theorie des gegenwärtigen Zeitalters* appeared in the 1950s, it had met a cool reception from Hermann Lübbe, a young political philosopher born in 1926. Lübbe took exception to Freyer's one-sided emphasis on the costs of technological progress and regarded Freyer's book as an embodiment of the romantic view of history of the German right that had in the past led Germany to disaster and tended to undermine liberal democracy.[80] After a period of office in the Social Democratic government of Germany's largest state, Lübbe returned to the university in 1970. He attacked governmental concessions to the student movement and became one of the founders of the Bund Freiheit der Wissenschaft and a leading critic of the New Left and its academic supporters.[81] In the 1970s and 1980s Lübbe emerged as a leading proponent of a more conservative liberalism. Lübbe insisted that there came a point at which the costs of social and cultural "emancipation" outweighed its benefits. He now wrote apprehensively of "the ever-accelerating process of the expansion of *Zivilisation*, with its technically homogeneous structures indifferent to particular origin," and sought to counter its negative effects through a conscious affirmation of the legacy of the past (*Mut zur Vergangenheit*). The contemporary demand for full social emancipation, Lübbe wrote, implied the elimination of all contingent, historical characteristics that might limit the individual's success in the marketplace, while the demand for full cultural emancipation meant the elimination of all inherited cultural particularity that might in any way inhibit the individual's willingness and ability to consider new ideas. Taken to its logical conclusion, Lübbe argued, the demand for full emancipation meant the self-destruction of a liberal culture, leaving only culturally homogeneous individuals. To obviate such a possibility, Lübbe recommended the principle "As much commonality based on the recognition of inalienable,

---

[79] Kurt Sontheimer, *Zeitenwende? Die Bundesrepublik Deutschland zwischen alter und alternativer Politik* (1983), 24, 27.

[80] Lübbe, "Resignierte," passim, esp. 137.

[81] See the collections of his essays, Lübbe, *Hochschulreform und Gegenaufklärung* (1972), and *Endstation Terror: Rückblick auf lange Marsche* (1978).

universally valid claims as necessary; as much diversity based on the effective influence of contingent origins as possible." He considered this maxim the appropriate response of conservatives and liberals to the demand for the open-ended emancipation of all.[82]

Ralf Dahrendorf provides another variation on the pattern of a newfound interest in conservative themes among liberal German intellectuals of the postwar generation. Born in 1929 as the scion of a social democratic family, Dahrendorf had been imprisoned as a high school student during the closing months of the Third Reich for his resistance activity. In the 1950s he emerged as a leading young sociologist and liberal social theorist. Dahrendorf sought to push West Germany more rapidly along the road to modernity, to a more "open" society, one that offered its members greater equality of opportunity. In a widely read work published in 1965, Dahrendorf deplored the traditionalism of his countrymen—their "complete lack of motive toward the new possibilities of life, such as upward mobility, geographic mobility, changes of political orientation, or social membership."[83] Active in the Free Democratic party, he was elected first to the provincial diet of Baden-Württemberg, then to the Bundestag, and served briefly in the Ministry of Foreign Affairs. In the 1970s and 1980s Dahrendorf remained a widely read commentator on German affairs, while occupying administrative posts as a commissioner of the European Economic Community in Brussels and then the directorship of the London School of Economics.

While in no sense renouncing his commitment to liberalism, Dahrendorf shifted his priorities markedly in the 1970s. He announced that he was at work on a book to be entitled *Modernity in Eclipse*.[84] After two decades of advocating social reforms that would expand the *choices* open to individuals, Dahrendorf turned his focus in the 1970s to the importance of what he called "ligatures," by which he meant social bonds that "give meaning to the place that the individual occupies."[85] "For almost two centuries," he wrote, "liberalism was the politics of options, that is, the struggle for the expansion of human life chances through the increase of options." Without abjuring this quest, Dahrendorf now sought to "find a path from the anomie of countless options without ties to a world in which options are filled with meaning by virtue of ligatures, . . .

[82] Hermann Lübbe, *Zwischen Trend und Tradition* (1981), 9, 17; idem, "Politische Gleichheitspostulate und ihre sozialen Folgen," 61–78, esp. 74–78.

[83] Ralf Dahrendorf, *Society and Democracy in Germany*, 414. The German original appeared in 1965.

[84] Ralf Dahrendorf, *Life Chances* (1979), 164.

[85] Ibid., 30–31 passim.

strong social ties that are not based on contract and in that sense prerational, which outlast the individual and in that sense have a long time horizon." Dahrendorf did not believe that a return to old ligatures was either possible or desirable, and he noted that "for the time being, the *search* for lasting ties that provide meaning is more evident than their formation."[86] Yet Dahrendorf's writings articulated a newfound awareness among his generation of German liberals of the limits of liberalism as traditionally understood.

Sontheimer, Lübbe, and Dahrendorf were not alone in the new direction of their thought; their cases are intended as illustrative, not exhaustive. As in the United States, the tag *neoconservative* was applied to such intellectuals, who had long prided themselves on their liberalism. The label was first used by opponents as a term of opprobrium, calculated to infuriate by virtue of its connotations. The label was eventually accepted by some liberal intellectuals, such as Lübbe, who had appropriated conservative themes and now resigned themselves to being on the wrong side of "progress" as it had come to be defined.[87] Others, including Dahrendorf, refused to embrace the new designation and tried to distance themselves from those who did.[88] To group Dahrendorf, Sontheimer, and Lübbe under a common heading does not imply that they arrived at a common position, much less a common front. There were major differences between them regarding both theory and contemporary political practice. Of the three, Dahrendorf appeared to have been least shaken by the rise of the New Left and the least inclined to reject it wholeheartedly. Yet all three—among the best-known liberal intellectuals of the immediate postwar generation—came in the 1970s to appropriate themes once regarded as the preserve of intellectual conservatism.

Was the recrudescence of conservative and historicist themes in the writings of major German liberal intellectuals a posthumous vindication of thinkers such as Hans Freyer? It is characteristic of the fate of conservatism in West Germany that those who adopted the label *neoconservative* sought to distance themselves from the imputation of kinship to Freyer and his circle, while it was the opponents of the German neoconservatives who portrayed them as Frey-

---

[86] Ralf Dahrendorf, "Individuelle Leistung, kollektive Verpflichtung und soziale Solidarität," 38–40. See also Ralf Dahrendorf, "Kulturpessimismus vs. Fortschrittshoffnung: Eine notwendige Abgrenzung," in Habermas, *Stichworte*, 1:213–28. For a capsule summary of Dahrendorf's development see the somewhat critical portrait of him in Sontheimer, *Zeitwende*, 111–20.

[87] Lübbe, " 'Neo-Konservative' in der Kritik," (1983), 613–21.

[88] See, for example, Dahrendorf's criticism of the *"Tendenzwendler"* in Dahrendorf, "Kulturpessimismus."

er's heirs.[89] While they lived, Freyer and other former radical conservatives were walking reminders of the fatal attraction of the darker side of German historicism and conservatism. Perhaps it was necessary for them to pass from the scene before those traditions could be appropriated by younger men who had grown up in the shadow of the other god that failed. As the erstwhile intellectual supporters of the revolution of the right passed from reality into memory and finally into history, the generation of intellectuals for whom the value of liberal democracy was self-understood felt freer to turn to perennial conservative concerns. By the 1980s, they could be confident that an awareness of the limits of liberalism would no longer lead their countrymen into the temptation of radical conservatism.

[89] In the first catagory see Hermann Lübbe, "Konservatismus in Deutschland" (1981); in the second see Jürgen Habermas, "Die Kulturkritik der Neokonservativen in der USA und in der Bundesrepublik" (1982), and Habermas's introduction to Habermas, *Stichworte*.

Variations on the Theme of "The Other God That Failed": Ernst Forsthoff, Arnold Gehlen, and Hans Zehrer

We have examined the intellectual and political trajectory of Hans Freyer's career as representative of those for whom National Socialism was "the other god that failed." We have tried to demonstrate the paradigmatic nature of Freyer's intellectual and political biography by focusing on those contexts, events, and patterns which he shared with other intellectuals. To what extent was Freyer's evolution typical? How does it compare with the experience of other prominent radical conservative intellectuals in Germany?

The question cannot yet be answered definitively, for a conclusive answer would require comparable studies, based upon a careful sifting of published writings and unpublished evidence. Such studies remain few and far between. As we have seen, such intellectuals were little inclined to publicly explore or explain their past and sometimes took pains to cover up the trail of their own histories. Biographical essays by their admirers followed suit. Most secondary studies of radical conservative intellectuals have been written without a careful gathering and weighing of evidence; where evidence has been gathered, it has often been used as if by a prosecuting attorney intent on proving that the intellectual in question was and remained "fascist" at heart. Given the paucity of reliable comparative studies, an attempt to demonstrate the typicality of Freyer's trajectory must remain tentative.

To put Freyer's development in perspective, however, it is worth considering the careers of several other erstwhile radical conservative intellectuals in a variety of fields who maintained some degree of influence in the Federal Republic: Ernst Forsthoff (1902–74), a jurist and political theorist; Arnold Gehlen (1904–76), a philosopher and social theorist; and Hans Zehrer (1899–1966), a prominent journalist.

For comparative purposes, the stages of Freyer's trajectory can be schematized. The first stage was one of principled alienation from the liberal, demo-

cratic, capitalist welfare state of the Weimar Republic and the articulate advocacy of an all-encompassing state that would mobilize society and culture for
the militant defense of collective particularity. Next came a period of ingenuous support for National Socialism, based on the hope that the movement
would provide the vehicle through which this ideal state might be realized.
The early years of the Nazi regime were marked by a rise to positions of high
prestige and influence; at the same time the possibility of being attacked for
unorthodoxy by Nazi students and colleagues led to "*Selbst-Gleichschaltung*," an
explicit affirmation of the particular leader and policies of National Socialism.
The stage of disillusionment followed. Though its rate and intensity varied, its
basic sources included personal and professional tribulations at the hands of
the National Socialist apparatus, a recognition that the movement functioned
not to create virtue but as a vehicle for the pursuit of individual and group interests, dismay at the imprudence of Hitler's foreign policy, and revulsion
from the regime's use of terror.[1] Disenchantment led to a disengagement from
immediate questions and a perceptible though tacit distancing from the regime in published works. Yet service within the institutions of the Third Reich
continued until its downfall.

The foreign occupation of Germany and the process of denazification
brought a loss of status and exclusion from jobs in the public sector. Work in
the private sector and participation in religious journals and institutions
helped pave the way to a new respectability, resulting finally in a return to positions of prestige. On the intellectual level the experience of disillusionment
with totalitarianism led to an acceptance of liberal, welfare-state, capitalist democracy, though doubts about the ability of such a society to provide its members with an adequate sense of purpose remained.

Born as the son of a Lutheran pastor in 1902, Ernst Forsthoff participated
in the youth movement, studied law, and became a pupil of Carl Schmitt. From
1930 to 1932 he was a frequent contributor to radical conservative journals. In
an essay published in 1931, he took the wartime experience of "total mobilization" as a model for civil life and advocated a "total state," in which the distinctions between the political and the unpolitical, the public and the private,

---

[1] All of these factors came into play in the
gradual disillusionment of the majority of the
Mittwochs-Gesellschaft, a circle of intellectuals
and politicians in Berlin, a number of whom
Freyer counted as friends. The disaffection of
many members from the regime began in 1935,
when the first of the non-Jewish members of the
Gesellschaft, Hermann Oncken, came under
public attack. See the introduction by Klaus
Scholder to *Die Mittwochs-Gesellschaft*, 25.

would no longer be valid.[2] He contributed, under a pseudonym, to a well-known collection of essays published in 1932 under the title *What We Expect from National Socialism*.[3]

In 1933 Forsthoff published *Der totale Staat*, in which he bade an unfond farewell to the liberal state that had allowed for autonomous spheres of society and proclaimed its supersession by the new "total state" based upon the *Volk*, which would influence all areas of life.[4] He chastised the Weimar state for allowing particular interests to play a political role and welcomed the end of pluralism.[5] While mentioning Hitler and the role of the Nazi party only in passing, he applauded the actions of the new government, including measures taken to eliminate the Jews from cultural and political life.[6] Forsthoff's booklet portrayed the regime in colors borrowed from the works of Carl Schmitt, Ernst Jünger, and Hans Freyer. Despite its unequivocal support for the new government, Forsthoff's book was criticized by Alfred Rosenberg. His response—typical of the process of *Selbst-Gleichschaltung*—was to publish a second edition of his book, in which he placed far greater stress on the *Führer* and the role of the Nazi *Weltanschauung* for the new state.[7]

In the course of 1933 Forsthoff joined the SA; in 1937 he applied for party membership and was accepted. In November 1933, at the age of thirty-one, Forsthoff was named professor of law at Frankfurt—a university with many spaces to fill in 1933, owing to the large number of Jews on its faculty during the Weimar years.[8] In the years that followed he quickly ascended the ladder of prestige within the German university system: in 1935 he was called to Hamburg, in 1936 to Königsberg, and in 1941 to Vienna.

Yet relations between Forsthoff and the National Socialist regime were not entirely smooth. He was called to Vienna in opposition to the recommendations of the NS-Dozentenbund and other party officials.[9] When he arrived there his lectures were disrupted by Nazi students on orders of the *Gauleiter*, Baldur von Schirach. Among the sticking points in his relationship with the regime was its antipathy to Christianity: Forsthoff had provided a legal brief

---

[2] See chapter 6.

[3] Ernst Forsthoff ("Dr. Friedrich Grüter"), "Die Gliederung des Reiches," in *Was wir vom Nationalsozialismus erwarten* (1932).

[4] Ernst Forsthoff, *Der totale Staat* (1933), 7, 38, 42, and passim.

[5] Ibid., 44 and passim.

[6] Ibid., 38–39.

[7] Forsthoff, *Der totale Staat*, 2d ed. (1934), 36, quoted in Ulrich Storost, *Staat und Verfassung bei Ernst Forsthoff*, 79.

[8] BAK, R21, Anhang Wissenschaftlerkartei, Forsthoff; BDC File Forsthoff.

[9] Reichdozentenführer to Amt Rosenberg, Hauptamt Wissenschaft, 30 June 1942, NA-T81 Roll 52, no. 54763–4.

opposing the government's plan to transform the Magdeburg cathedral into a party museum.[10] In 1943 Forsthoff left Vienna for a professorship of public law at the University of Heidelberg.

Forsthoff's disillusionment with the "total state" was expressed in at least two works published during the Third Reich, *Die Verwaltung als Leistungstrager* (1938) and *Die Grenzen des Rechts* (1941). In the latter he attacked the notion of a state that tried to make itself the source of all truth and values. In the former he argued that the major role of the state derived from the bureaucracy, which performed tasks of planning and coordination indispensable in a technologically advanced society. These were to become the themes of his postwar works as well.[11]

The American occupation of Heidelberg led to Forsthoff's dismissal from his university chair. During the years that followed he served in an administrative post in the provincial government of Schleswig-Holstein, while writing a comprehensive work on German administrative law. The book, *Lehrbuch des Verwaltungsrecht* (1950), soon became the standard text in German administrative law, went through edition after edition, and made its author into a man of means. With the end of American administrative control he returned to his professorship at Heidelberg in 1949, where he taught until his retirement. His past resurfaced publicly in 1965. When the University of Vienna announced plans to award him an honorary degree, a socialist member of parliament protested, referring to Forsthoff's writings of the 1930s. Forsthoff chose to decline the award rather than seeking to explain or apologize for his past writings.[12] This strategy of silence was typical of Forsthoff's attitude toward his National Socialist past.[13]

In addition to his technical legal works, Forsthoff produced a steady stream of essays devoted to social and political analysis. The Hegelian distinction between state and society remained a central category in his postwar thought, but its implications were very different from what they had been in his radical conservative phase. The *Rechtsstaat* that protected the rights of the individual and that recognized the distinction between the state and society, which he had once decried as the product of the liberal nineteenth century, now became the

[10] Hans Schneider, "Ernst Forsthoff: 70 Jahre," 1654; Wolfgang Kunkel, "Der Professor im Dritten Reich," 128–29.

[11] Storost, *Staat*, 82–92.

[12] Schneider, "Ernst Forsthoff"; Munzinger-Archiv/Internat. Biograph. Archiv, 2 November

1974.

[13] See his cynical essay on the subject, written under a pseudonym, "Silvio," "Erste Hilfe gegen bittere Wahrheiten," *Christ und Welt*, 1963; see also his response in Rolf Seeliger, ed., *Braune Universität* (1968) 6: 26.

object of his allegiance.[14] He recognized—with some regret—that the concept of the state as the representative of the general interest, above and beyond the forces of civil society, no longer reflected the reality of the West German state. In fact, the economic role of the state and the close working relationship between the representatives of economic interest groups had grown considerably. Yet this economic role of the state Forsthoff now viewed as the source of its legitimacy. With the decline in the prestige of the state (a decline that Forsthoff recognized was hastened by the postwar reaction against National Socialism), the legitimacy of the state increasingly came from its indispensable role in guaranteeing the well-being of its citizens through law and the provisioning of basic administrative, technological, and social services.[15] Once he had decried the political role of particular economic interests as destabilizing. Now he disavowed this view and insisted that the interlocking of the state with the economy was a source of legitimacy and stability for the state itself. The stability of the state, he argued, was now "borrowed" from the stability of industrial society. Forsthoff voiced doubts about the ability of the existing state to protect the general interest in periods of economic crisis, but he regarded such crises as increasingly unlikely.[16] He also drew attention to the inability of a weak state to protect the individual from the possible depredations of technology controlled by particular economic interests.[17] But the thrust of his postwar thought was to recognize the ability of the democratic capitalist welfare state to provide the institutional stability he so valued.

The intellectual and political development of Arnold Gehlen reveals other variations on the theme of attraction to and disillusionment with totalitarian solutions to the problems of modernity.

Gehlen was born into the *Bildungsbürgertum* of Leipzig in 1904; his father was a publisher and book dealer, his mother the daughter of a prominent jurist. Gehlen studied philosophy and completed his habilitation in 1931.[18] The problem of the inability of existing institutions to provide the individual with a reliable, commonly accepted sense of purpose appears early in his work.[19]

---

[14] Ernst Forsthoff, "Begriff und Wesen des sozialen Rechtsstaates" (1953), reprinted in Forsthoff, *Rechtsstaat im Wandel*, 27–56, esp. 53–54; idem, *Der Staat der Industriegesellschaft*, 21–22.

[15] Forsthoff, "Haben wir zuviel oder zuwenig Staat" (1955), in *Rechtsstaat im Wandel*, 63–77, esp. 67–72; idem, *Staat der Industriegesellschaft*, 75–79, 158.

[16] Forsthoff, *Staat*, 164, 167.

[17] Forsthoff, *Staat*, 36–47.

[18] Werner Rügemer, *Philosophische Anthropologie und Epochenkrise*, 35.

[19] See, for example, his *Habilitationsschrift* of 1931, *Wirklicher und unwirklicher Geist*, reprinted in Lothar Samson, ed., *Arnold Gehlen: Philosophische Schriften I*.

For Gehlen the National Socialist ascension to power represented both a political and a personal opportunity. Unlike the more cautious Freyer, he joined the party in 1933 and was active within it through 1936 as a "cell leader" and official of the party's organization for university professors.[20] His professional rise was meteoric. When the new National Socialist government forced Paul Tillich to resign, Gehlen was named as his temporary replacement at the University of Frankfurt in the summer of 1933. After a short period as Freyer's assistant in Leipzig, Gehlen was named to the chair of philosophy at Leipzig previously held by his teacher, Driesch, who had been forced out because of his liberal political views. In 1938 Gehlen moved on to a chair in Königsberg, and in 1940 to another, this time in Vienna. During the war he maintained his academic chair while serving simultaneously in an army psychology unit.[21]

From 1933 to 1935 Gehlen had high hopes for the new regime. Conscious of the primitiveness of National Socialist ideology, but enthused at the prospect of a new institutional order that might overcome what he regarded as the decadent subjectivism and individualism of the modern age, Gehlen set out to develop a proper philosophy of National Socialism. The role of contemporary philosophy, Gehlen asserted in his inaugural lecture at Leipzig in November 1934, was to provide a systematic formulation of the new existential reality of the German *Volk* ushered in by the coming of National Socialism.[22] His writings on the topic came under attack from the Nazi ideologist Ernst Krieck. Gehlen's works after 1935 showed a greater reserve and distance from immediate questions.[23]

In 1940 Gehlen published the first edition of his most important work, entitled *Der Mensch, seine Natur und seine Stellung in der Welt*. In it he put forward a theory of the biological foundations of the human need for institutions, perhaps the most sophisticated attempt in the twentieth century to restate the conservative argument for the necessity of institutions on an entirely naturalistic basis. Though Gehlen drew upon biological research as a foundation for his work, it was not racist, but applied to the human animal as such. Yet in the first edition Gehlen cited with favor the work of the Nazi ideologist Alfred Rosenberg and included several passages favorable to the regime. Gehlen later claimed that he had included these passages in order to ensure permission to

[20] Rügemer, *Philosophische Anthropologie*, 92.
[21] Rügemer, *Philosophische Anthropologie*, 92–96.
[22] Arnold Gehlen, "Der Staat und die Philosophie," reprinted in Arnold Gehlen, *Philoso-*phische Schriften II, ed. Lothar Samson, 295–310, esp. 302–10.
[23] Lothar Samson, "Nachwort," *Arnold Gehlen: Philosophische Schriften II*, 414–15.

publish his book. When official reaction to his book was less negative than he had feared, he removed the most explicitly National Socialist passages from the second edition, published in 1944.[24] Gehlen's book of 1940 was not compatible with National Socialist racism, since it assumed the unity of the human species. But because it set forth a detailed argument regarding the *function* of institutions and the world views that sustained them without offering criteria for preferring one world view to another, it was not intrinsically antipathetic to the National Socialist regime and could be read as a work that affirmed the function of Nazi ideology while casting doubt upon its truth.[25] In Gehlen's book it was the ability of institutions to provide their members with a firm and all-encompassing set of orientations that counted. It was the stabilizing *function*, not the truth or falsity of the beliefs that legitimated institutions, that concerned him.[26]

In the two decades after 1945, Gehlen continued to develop the theory of institutions formulated in his earlier work.[27] Yet he also devoted attention to broad, critical analyses of contemporary society, as did Freyer and Forsthoff. Gehlen argued that the democratic, capitalist welfare state was a "mature" form of modern, technological society. Its stability derived primarily from the demands of technological adaptation, which limited the real choices open to such a society. The age of all-encompassing world views and ideologies that provided for a unified program of collective action was therefore over, he argued. Democracy (by which Gehlen meant its parliamentary and market-based form) and communism were both stable forms of industrial society, but there was no good reason to believe that one would necessarily supersede the other or that either was likely to undergo radical, qualitative change. The shape of modern democracy, Gehlen argued, was already set, and further changes would take place within its parameters. In this sense modern society had entered into what Gehlen called a period of "posthistory."[28]

Gehlen believed that technology, science, and the division of labor were the

[24] Samson, "Nachwort," 415.

[25] See the chapter entitled "Oberste Führungssysteme." Gehlen had made a similar suggestion as early as 1934; see his "Rasse und Staat," *Die Erziehung* (1934), 9:201–04.

[26] For a succinct and informed evaluation of Gehlen's relationship to National Socialism see Karl-Siegbert Rehberg, "Metaphern des Standhaltens: In Memoriam Arnold Gehlen," 394–95.

[27] See his *Urmensch und Spätkultur* (1956); An-

thropologische Forschung* (1961); and *Studien zur Anthropologie und Soziologie* (1963).

[28] Arnold Gehlen, *Über kulturelle Kristallisation* (1961), passim. A similar analysis and resigned sensibility in regard to postwar European capitalist democracy can be found in the work of the French post-Hegelian Alexandre Kojève; see Michael S. Roth, "A Problem of Recognition: Alexandre Kojève and the End of History."

basis of the stability and limits of contemporary society. Yet his attitude toward the phenomena he described was one of ironic resignation. The organizations of a society whose stability and legitimacy derived from technology, science, and the division of labor could *not* provide that sense of noneudaemonistic purpose and duty which characterized traditional and especially archaic "institutions."[29] By failing to provide the individual with an encompassing set of norms based upon his status, the organizational framework of modern society (roughly equivalent to what Freyer called "secondary systems") opened the door to subjectivism, which became the prevailing mood in modern culture.[30] During the last decade of his life, in which the political culture of the West German intelligentsia was transformed by the rise of the New Left, Gehlen regarded the stability of Western democracies as threatened by the combination of subjectivism and utopianism within the intellectual classes.[31]

Gehlen's past seriously impeded his professional standing after the collapse of the National Socialist regime. The summer of 1945 found Gehlen in an American prisoner-of-war camp in Austria.[32] The Americans removed him from his professorship in Vienna, and his easily documented organizational links to the regime probably made it impossible for Gehlen to find another position in the American zone of occupation. Only in 1947 did he find an academic position, not at a university but at the Hochschule für Verwaltungswissenschaften in Speyer, an institution created by the French for the training of bureaucrats. The French were less stringent in their criteria for denazification than the Americans, and many civil servants who could not find work in the American zone moved to the areas of French occupation.[33] Not until 1961 did Gehlen find employment at a university, and even then only at the Technische Hochschule in Aachen, an institution far from the center of social-scientific activity. An attempt by Helmut Schelsky to have the University of Münster award Gehlen an honorary doctorate foundered on the rock of student protest.

Typically, Gehlen wrote very little about his own past and tended to skip over the National Socialist period in his writings.[34] He made a point of repub-

---

[29] This was the theme of *Urmensch und Spätkultur* (1956).

[30] See especially Gehlen, *Der Seele im technischen Zeitalter* (1957).

[31] See Gehlen, *Moral und Hypermoral* (1969); and the essays collected in Arnold Gehlen, *Einblicke*, ed. Karl-Siegbert Rehberg, esp. 253–350. In addition to the works already cited, among the most useful introductions to Gehlen's thought are Friedrich Jonas, *Die Institutionslehre Arnold Gehlens*; Peter L. Berger and Hansfried Kellner, "Arnold Gehlen and the Theory of Institutions"; Berger's foreword to Arnold Gehlen, *Man in the Age of Technology*; Wolf Lepenies, *Melancholie und Gesellschaft*, chapter 9; and Martin Greiffenhagen, *Das Dilemma des Konservatismus in Deutschland*, 316ff.

[32] Rügemer, *Philosophische Anthropologie*, 96.

[33] See Theodor Eschenburg, *Jahre der Besatzung: 1945–1949*, 112, 118.

[34] Rehberg, "Metaphern," 394.

lishing his works of the Nazi era but altered the texts to eliminate those passages which betrayed his affinity to National Socialism.[35]

No Gehlenite "school" arose in West German sociology, not least due to Gehlen's marginal position within the academy after 1945. But the influence of his thought was considerable: not only conservatives but independent leftists such as Jürgen Habermas and the reformist communist Wolfgang Harich recognized the importance of his work and drew upon it. The number of secondary works devoted to his thought was already considerable at the time of his death. Since then interest in his work seems to have increased. In the case of Arnold Gehlen, his erstwhile support of National Socialism served as a brake upon his prestige in the Federal Republic, though not entirely on his intellectual influence.

The case of Hans Zehrer presents a more dramatic variation on the theme of "the other god that failed."

Zehrer's origins betray a now familiar pattern: born in 1899 into the lower reaches of the educated middle class, active in the youth movement, and stamped by the war experience, he studied with the radical conservative sociologist Werner Sombart in Berlin before embarking on a journalistic career. In 1929 he succeeded Eugen Diederichs as editor of *Die Tat*, which he and a small group of like-minded young collaborators transformed into a widely read journal of political opinion, helping to disseminate the critique of capitalism and democracy developed by radical conservatives such as Hans Freyer. The journal did more than any other to articulate and spread the critique of liberal democracy within the *Bildungsbürgertum*.[36] While encouraged by the rise of National Socialism, Zehrer in 1932 became a supporter of General Schleicher's attempt to form a socially minded dictatorship with the support of the army, organized labor, and the purported "left wing" of the Nazi party. When Schleicher was succeeded by Hitler, Zehrer wrote editorials favoring the new government but cautioned against the dictatorship of a single party.[37] After the passage of the Enabling Law, Zehrer published a rhapsodic editorial in praise of Hitler and then an anti-Semitic article demanding the exclusion of the Jews from all major positions in German life.[38]

Most members of the Tatkreis had already established contact with the Nazi

---

[35] For some examples see Rügemer, *Philosophische Anthropologie*, 109–10.

[36] On the Tatkreis see chapter 6 and the works cited therein. For biographical material on Zehrer I have relied on Ebbo Demant, *Von Schleicher zu Springer: Hans Zehrer als politischer Publizist*.

[37] Zehrer in *Die Tat*, April 1933, 15–16, and May 1933, 103–4, quoted in Walter Struve, *Elites against Democracy*, 375.

[38] Zehrer in *Tägliche Rundschau* of 26 March 1933, 2 April 1933, quoted in Demant, *Hans Zehrer*, 115–17.

party in 1932 and went on to successful careers in the Third Reich. Despite his attempt at self-*Gleichschaltung*, the door to influence in the Third Reich was shut in Zehrer's face. In May 1933 a daily newspaper that he had edited was banned by the government, and in June he was dropped from *Die Tat* under Nazi pressure. Because of close association with Schleicher and his marriage to a woman of Jewish origin, Zehrer was forbidden to work as a journalist.[39] From 1934 to 1939 he lived on an island in northern Germany, where he wrote light novels and filmscripts for a living. In 1939 he divorced his wife (who had emigrated to England) and moved to Berlin, where he headed a publishing firm.

Zehrer's utter disillusionment with National Socialism, speeded no doubt by the regime's antipathy to him, was early and thorough. Struck by his own guilt in bringing Hitler to power, Zehrer went into a period of contemplation in late 1933 and 1934 and emerged as a religious believer. His new religious and political views were expounded in a long manuscript written during the Third Reich and published in 1948.

If Zehrer's reservations about Hitler harmed his career after 1933, he was suspect after 1945 by those who remembered his role in the destruction of Weimar democracy. In 1946 plans to name Zehrer editor of the new newspaper of the British occupation zone, *Die Welt*, foundered on the opposition of local Social Democrats, who regarded him as having paved the way for Hitler.[40] As was so often the case among former radical conservative intellectuals, Zehrer's road to respectability ran through the institutions of the church. He resumed his journalistic career in 1948 as editor of the *Sontagsblatt*, a weekly published by the Protestant bishop of Hannover. When Axel Springer bought *Die Welt* from the British in 1953, he hired Zehrer as its editor. Under Zehrer's editorship *Die Welt* became the flagship publication of the Springer press and one of the leading national dailies of the moderate right. He also wrote a column in the Springer's mass-circulation picture-newspaper, the *Bildzeitung*. By 1957 Zehrer was perhaps the best-known political commentator in the Federal Republic, a position he maintained until he was forced out of the editorship of *Die Welt* in 1963.

Zehrer was a journalist and popularizer rather than a systematic thinker, and his postwar views on society and politics are less easily distilled than those of Freyer, Gehlen, or Forsthoff. But like the other former radical conservatives who had been disillusioned by the experience of National Socialism, Zehrer's postwar conservatism demonstrated a continuity of concerns and a discontinuity of solutions compared to his earlier, radical phase. The decline

[39] Demant, *Hans Zehrer*, 117–24.   [40] Ibid., 152–53.

of authority and the purported eclipse of meaning in modern life remained among his foremost themes.[41] His primary political concern, however, was the threat of totalitarianism, which he saw as latent in the social and cultural processes of modern life. The ultimate cause of totalitarianism, according to Zehrer, was secularization: he wrote of fascism and communism as the latest of a series of attempts since the end of the Middle Ages to substitute the human collectivity in place of God as the ultimate source of authority.[42] The bankruptcy of these experiments, he believed, was leading to a recognition of man's inability to provide the answer to the question of his own meaning and purpose, and hence to a greater openness toward divine revelation.[43] As with some other German conservatives, Zehrer's retreat from the god that failed led back to God. His conclusion that personal meaning and salvation were not to be found in the political realm was the premise of a more moderate politics.[44]

Compared to other erstwhile radical conservatives, Zehrer dealt openly and frequently with the Nazi era and the question of responsibility for it. Shut out by the Nazis, after 1945 Zehrer was spared the temptation to conceal his activities during the Third Reich. In a moving piece entitled "The Shadow of the Past," he wrote in 1948 of the inability of the individual to start afresh until he had come to terms with his past and repented for it.[45] But, quite typically of German conservative writers after 1945, he lumped the victims of National Socialism together with other "victims": of unemployment, of forced migration, and of denazification.[46] Zehrer's readers who felt a sense of guilt were urged to repent but simultaneously assured that their guilt was shared by almost everyone else; former victimizers were thus granted an equality of moral status with their former victims. Zehrer summed up the working criterion of Adenauer and those around him to the question of past complicity with National Socialism when he wrote in 1954 that it was not important "what someone *was*, but . . . what he is today, how much energy he has, and what he wants."[47] In 1958 he maintained that the failure to confront their own guilt had led the Germans to turn away from their own history out of bad conscience. Only by facing the "taboo of German guilt" would the Germans be able to establish a link with their own history, he wrote.[48] Yet in the early 1960s he articulated a common complaint among publicists of the German right when he decried the

[41] Hans Zehrer, *Der Mensch in dieser Welt* (1948), 57, 142, and passim.

[42] Ibid., 139–40, 404–6, and passim.

[43] Ibid., 142, 212, and passim.

[44] Hans Zehrer, *Stille vor dem Sturm: Aufsätze zur Zeit* (1948), 61.

[45] "Der Schatten der Vergangenheit, in ibid., 78–82.

[46] "Eingefrorene Menschen," ibid., 82–86.

[47] Zehrer, "In der Asche stöbern," *Die Welt*, 27 May 1954, quoted in Demant, *Hans Zehrer*, 215.

[48] Zehrer, "Rückkehr zur Wirklichkeit," *Die Welt*, 27 December 1958.

REFERENCES

I. PUBLISHED SOURCES

Abrams, M. H. *Natural Supernaturalism*. New York, 1971.

Abrams, Philip. *The Origins of British Sociology, 1834–1914*.

Achelis, Johann Daniel, et al. *Tymbos für Wilhelm Ahlmann: Ein Gedenkbuch*. Berlin, 1951.

Adam, Uwe Dietrich. *Hochschule und Nationalsozialismus: Die Universität Tübingen im Dritten Reich*. Tübingen, 1977.

—— *Judenpolitik im Dritten Reich*. Düsseldorf, 1972.

Akademische Reden gehalten am 31. Oktober 1934 in der Aula der Universität Leipzig aus Anlaß des 525. Jahres ihres Gründung. Leipzig, 1934.

Alemann, Heine von. "Leopold von Wiese und das Forschungsinstitut für Sozialwissenschaften in Köln 1919 bis 1934." In *Geschichte der Soziologie*, ed. Wolf Lepenies, 4 vols., 2: 349–89. Frankfurt, 1981.

Anders, Georg. *Gesetz zur Regelung der Rechtsverhältnisse der Unter Artikel 131 des Grundgesetz fallenden Personen*. 3d ed. Stuttgart, 1954.

Angress, Werner. *The Stillborn Revolution*. Princeton, N.J., 1963.

Arato, Andrew, and Breines, Paul. *The Young Lukács and the Origins of Western Marxism*. New York, 1979.

Archiv Peter für historische und zeitgeschichtliche Dokumentation. *Spiegelbild einer Verschwörung*. Stuttgart, 1961.

Arendt, Hannah. *Origins of Totalitarianism*. New York, 1951.

Aron, Raymond. *German Sociology*. New York, 1964.

—— *Main Currents in Sociological Thought*. 2 vols. New York, 1967.

—— *The Opium of the Intellectuals*. New York, 1957.

Ash, M. G. "Ein Institut und eine Zeitschrift: Zur Geschichte der Berliner Psychologischen Instituts und der Zeitschrift *Psychologische Forschung* vor und nach 1933." In *Psychologie im Nationalsozialismus*, ed. C. F. Graumann, 113–38. Berlin, 1985.

Avineri, Shlomo. *Hegel's Theory of the Modern State*. Cambridge, England, 1972.

Bachof, Otto. "Die 'Entnazifizierung.' " In *Deutsches Geistesleben und Nationalsozialismus*, ed. Andreas Flitner, 195–216. Tübingen, 1965.

Bahrdt, Hans Paul. "Belehrungen durch Helmuth Plessner." *KZfSS* 34 (1982): 533–37.

Baker, Keith Michael. "On the Problem of the Ideological Origins of the French Revolution." In *Intellectual History*, ed. Dominick LaCapra, 197–219. Ithaca, N.Y. 1982.

Barash, Jeffrey. "Martin Heidegger and the Problem of Historical Meaning." Ph.D. diss., University of Chicago, 1982.

Barnes, Harry Elmer, ed. *An Introduction to the History of Sociology*. Chicago, 1948.

Barnes, Harry Elmer. "The Social Philosophy of Ludwig Gumplowicz." In *An Introduction to the History of Sociology*, ed. Harry Elmer Barnes. Chicago, 1948.

Barth, Hans. *Fluten und Dämme: Der philosophische Gedanke in der Politik*. Zurich, 1943.

Baumgarten, Otto, et al., ed. *Geistige und sittliche Wirkungen des Krieges*. Stuttgart, 1927.

Becker, Carl H. *Kulturpolitische Aufgaben des Reiches*. Leipzig, 1919.

—— *Die pädagogische Akademie im Aufbau unseres nationalen Bildungswesen*. Leipzig, 1926.

Becker, Hellmut. "Portrait eines Kulturministers." *Merkur* 30, no. 4 (1976): 365–76.

Bell, Daniel. "America as a Mass Society: A Critique." In his *The End of Ideology*. New York, 1965.

—— *The Winding Passage*. Cambridge, Mass., 1980.

Below, Georg von. "Soziologie als Lehrfach." *Schmollers Jahrbuch* 43 (1919): 59–110.

Bendersky, Joseph. *Carl Schmitt: Theorist for the Reich*. Princeton, N.J., 1983.

Bendix, Reinhard. *Max Weber: An Intellectual Portrait*. New York, 1960.

Benjamin, Walter. "Die religiöse Stellung der neuen Jugend." *Die Tat: Sozial-religiöse Monatsschrift für deutsche Kultur* 6 (1914–15): 210–12.

Benn, Gottfried. "Doppelleben" (1950). Reprinted in *Gottfried Benn: Gesammelte Werke in vier Bänden*, ed. Dieter Wellershoff, 4: 69–172. Weisbaden, 1966.

Bentin, Lutz-Arwed. *Johannes Popitz und Carl Schmitt*. Munich, 1972.

Berger, Gottfried. *In tyrannos: Die Sowejetisierung der Hochschulen, Dargestellt am Beispiel der Universität Leipzig*. N.p., 1951.

Berger, Peter. *Facing Up to Modernity*. New York, 1977.

—— Berger, Brigitte; and Kellner, Hansfried. *The Homeless Mind: Modernization and Consciousness*. New York, 1973.

—— and Kellner, Hansfried. "Arnold Gehlen and the Theory of Institutions." *Social Research* 2, no. 1 (1965): 110–15.

Bergmann, Waltraut, et al. *Soziologie im Faschismus: Darstellung und Texte*. Cologne, 1981.

Bering, Dietz. *Die Intellektuellen: Geschichte eines Schimpfwortes*. Frankfurt, 1982.

Berlin, Isaiah. "The Counter-Enlightenment." In his *Against the Current: Essays in the History of Ideas*. New York, 1980.

—— *Four Essays on Liberty*. London, 1969.

—— *Vico and Herder: Two Studies in the History of Ideas*. New York, 1976.

Besson, Waldemar. Review of *Gedanken zur Industriegesellschaft*, by Hans Freyer (ed. Arnold Gehlen), in *Deutsche Zeitung/Christ und Welt*, 28 August 1970, 14.

Beyer, Justus. "Die Tagung der deutschen Soziologen in Jena und die Aufgabe der Wissenschaft im neuen Staate." *Volk im Werden* 2 (1934): 193–97.

Beyerchen, Alan D. *Scientists under Hitler*. New Haven, Conn., 1977.

Bleuel, Hans-Peter, and Klinnert, Ernst. *Deutsche Studenten auf dem Weg ins Dritte Reich*. Gütersloh, 1967.

Bloom, Alexander. *Prodigal Sons: The New York Intellectuals and Their World*. New York, 1986.

Bloßfeldt, W. "Der Standort der Soziologie." *Blätter für deutsche Philosophie* 5 (1931–32): 116–31.

Blumenberg, Hans. *Säkularisierung und Selbstbehauptung.* Frankfurt, 1974.

Bollmus, Reinhard. *Das Amt Rosenberg und seine Gegner: Zum Machtkampf im national-sozialistischen Herrschaftssystem.* Stuttgart, 1970.

Borinski, Fritz. "Autobiographie." In *Pädagogik in Selbstdarstellung,* ed. Ludwig Pongratz, vol. 2. Hamburg, 1976.

—— "Revolution des 20. Jahrhunderts—Revolution von rechts?" *Neue Blätter für den Sozialismus* 2 (1931): 387–92.

—— et al., ed. *Jugend im politischen Protest: Der Leuchtenburgkreis.* Frankfurt, 1977.

Börner, Wilhelm. Review of *Antäus,* by Hans Freyer. *Archiv für Geschichte der Philosophie* 37: 132.

Borusiak, Horst. "Die Universität Leipzig nach der Zerschlagung des faschistischen Staates und ihre Neueröffnung am 5. Februar 1946." In *Karl-Marx-Universität Leipzig, 1409–1959: Beiträge zur Universitätsgeschichte,* ed. Ernst Engelberg. Leipzig, 1959.

Bower, Tom. *The Pledge Betrayed: America and Britain and the Denazification of Post-War Germany.* Garden City, N.Y. 1982.

Bracher, Karl Dietrich. *Die Auflösung der Weimarer Republik.* Düsseldorf, 1978.

—— *The German Dictatorship.* New York, 1970.

—— "Die Gleichschaltung der deutschen Universität." In *Nationalsozialismus und die deutsche Universität,* by Hans-Joachim Liebers et al., Berlin, 1966.

—— *Stufen der Machtergreifung.* Frankfurt, 1979.

—— *Zeit der Ideologien.* Stuttgart, 1982.

—— *Zeitgeschichtliche Kontroversen.* Munich, 1976.

Broszat, Martin. *The Hitler State.* New York, 1981.

—— "Zur Struktur der NS-Massenbewegung." *Vierteljahresheft für Zeitgeschichte* 31 (1983): 52–76.

Bruch, Rüdiger vom. *Wissenschaft, Politik und öffentliche Meinung: Gelehrtenpolitik im Wilhelmischen Deutschland (1890–1914).* Husum, 1980.

Bruford, W. H. *The German Tradition of Self-Cultivation.* New York, 1975.

Brunner, Otto. *Neue Wege der Sozialgeschichte.* Göttingen, 1956.

—— et al., ed. *Geschichtliche Grundbegriffe.* Vol. 2.

Buruma, Ian. "Japanese Lib." *New York Review of Books,* 13 March 1986, 3–6.

Cassirer, Ernst. *The Problem of Knowledge.* New Haven, Conn., 1950.

Caute, David. *The Fellow-Travellers.* London, 1973.

Chadwick, Owen. *The Secularization of the European Mind in the Nineteenth Century.* Cambridge, England, 1975.

Childers, Thomas. "The Social Basis of the National Socialist Vote." *Journal of Contemporary History* 11 (1975): 17–42.

Christian, Petra. *Einheit und Zwiespalt: Zum hegelianisierenden Denken in der Philosophie und Soziologie Georg Simmels.* Berlin, 1976.

Cocks, Geoffrey. *Psychotherapy in the Third Reich: The Göring Institute.* New York, 1985.

Colfax, J. David. *Radical Sociology.* New York, 1971.

Congdon, Lee. *The Young Lukács.* Chapel Hill, N.C. 1983.

Conze, Werner. *Agrarverfassung und Bevölkerung in Litauen und Weißrußland.* Leipzig. 1940.

—— "Die Gründung des Arbeitskreises für moderne Sozialgeschichte." *Hamburger Jahrbuch für Wirtschafts- und Gesellschaftspolitik* 24 (1979): 23–32.

—— *Hirschenhof: Die Geschichte einer deutschen Sprachinsel in Livland.* Berlin, 1934.

—— Review of *Weltgeschichte Europas,* by Hans Freyer. *Deutsche Universitäts-Zeitung,* 2 December 1949, 16.

Corino, Karl, ed. *Intellektuelle im Bann des Nationalsozialismus.* Hamburg, 1980.

Coser, Lewis; Kadushin, Charles; and Powell, Walter. *Books: The Culture and Commerce of Publishing.* New York, 1982.

Craig, Gordon A. *The Germans.* New York, 1982.

—— *Germany: 1866–1945.* New York, 1978.

Crews, Frederick. "In the Big House of Theory." *New York Review of Books,* 29 May 1986, 36–42.

Crossman. Richard, ed. *The God That Failed.* London, 1949.

Cuomo, Glenn R. "Purging an 'Art-Bolshevist': The Persecution of Gottfried Benn in the Years 1933–1938." *German Studies Review* 9, no. 1 (February 1986): 85–106.

Czok, Karl, and Thieme, Horst, eds. *Leipzig: Geschichte der Stadt in Wort und Bild.* Berlin, 1978.

Dahrendorf, Ralf. "Homo Sociologicus: On the History, Significance, and Limits of the Category of Social Role." In his *Essays in the Theory of Society.* Stanford, 1968.

—— "Individuelle Leistung, kollektive Verpflichtung und soziale Solidarität." In *Solidarität in der Welt der 8oer Jahre: Leistungsgesellschaft und Sozialstaat,* ed. Robert Kopp, 25–43. Basel, 1984.

—— "Kulturpessimismus vs. Fortschrittshoffnung: Eine notwendige Abgrenzung." In *Stichworte zur "Geistigen Situation der Zeit,"* ed. Jürgen Habermas, 2 vols., 1: 213–28. Frankfurt, 1979.

—— *Life Chances.* London, 1979.

—— "Nachruf auf Theodor Adorno." *KZfSS,* 1969.

—— "Soziologie und Nationalsozialismus" (1964). In his *Pfade aud Utopia.* Munich, 1974.

Dannhauser, Werner. "Religion and the Conservatives." *Commentary,* December 1985, 51–55.

Davis, Kingsley. "The Myth of Functional Analysis as a Special Method in Sociology and Anthropology." *American Sociological Review* 24 (December 1959): 757–52.

Dawe, A. "The Two Sociologies." *British Journal of Sociology* 21 (1970): 207–18.

Deak, Istvan. "Hungary." In *The European Right: A Historical Portrait*, ed. Han Rogger and Eugen Weber. Berkeley, Calif., 1966.

Dehmel, Hans. "Hans Freyer." *Der Boberhaus Rundbrief*, no.14 (1970), 10. Copy in Burg Ludwigstein.

Demant, Ebbo. *Von Schleicher zu Springer: Hans Zehrer als politischer Publizist*. Mainz, 1971.

"Die deutsche Geisteswelt für Liste 1." *Völkische Beobachter*, Süddeutsche Ausgabe 62 (3 March 1933), Beiblatt.

"Deutsche Gesellschaft für Soziologie Protokoll der Mitgliedversammlung am 24. Mai 1959 in Berlin." *KZfSS* 11 (1959): 567–71.

"Deutsche Hochschullehrer für Adolf Hitler." *Völkische Beobachter*, 5 November 1932.

Deutscher, Isaac. "The Ex-Communist's Conscience." In his *Heretics and Renegades*. New York, 1969.

Diederichs, Eugen. *Aus meinem Leben*. Jena, 1938.

Diggins, John P. *Up from Communism: Conservative Odysseys in American Intellectual History*. New York, 1975.

Dilthey, Wilhelm. *Gesammelte Schriften*. 12 vols. Leipzig, 1914–1965.

Dittberner, Job. *The End of Ideology and American Social Thought*. Ann Arbor, Mich., 1979.

Driesch, Hans. *Lebenserinnerungen*. Basel, 1951.

Dunkmann, Karl. "Die Bedeutung der Zahl in der Soziologie." *Blätter für deutsche Philosophie* 5 (1931–32): 1–31.

Düwell, Kurt. "Staat und Wissenschaft in der Weimarer Epoche: Zur Kulturpolitik des Ministers C. H. Becker." *Historische Zeitschrift*, Beiheft 1 (1971): 31–65.

Eberan, Barbro. *Luther? Friedrich "der Große"? Wagner? Nietzsche? Wer war an Hitler Schuld? Die Debatte um die Schuldfrage 1945–1949*. Munich, 1983.

Edmundson, Nelson. "The Fichte Society: A Chapter in Germany's Conservative Revolution." Ph.D. diss., Harvard University, 1964.

"Ein Gespräch mit Hans Freyer." *Deutsche Zeitung*, 3 November 1951, 2.

Eisenstadt, S. N. "Intellectuals and Tradition." *Daedalus* 101 (Spring 1972): 1–20.

Eley, Geoff. *Reshaping the German Right*. New Haven, Conn., 1980.

Engelberg, Ernst, ed. *Karl-Marx-Universität Leipzig, 1409–1959: Beiträge zur Universitätsgeschichte*. 2 vols. Leipzig, 1959.

Erdmann, Karl Dietrich. *Die Weimarer Republik*. Munich, 1980.

——— and Schulze, Hagen, eds. *Weimar: Selbstpreisgabe einer Demokratie. Eine Bilanz heute*. Düsseldorf, 1980.

Ermarth, Michael. *Wilhelm Dilthey: The Critique of Historical Reason*. Chicago, 1978.

Eschenburg, Theodor. *Jahre der Besatzung: 1945–1949*. Stuttgart, 1983.

Eyck, Erich. *A History of the Weimar Republic*. 2 vols. New York, 1970.

Falkenfeld, Hellmuth. Review of *Antäus*, by Hans Freyer. *Kantstudien* 25 (1920): 440–14.

Faulenbach, Bernd. "Deutsche Geschichtswissenschaft zwischen Kaiserreich und NS-Diktatur." In *Geschichtswissenschaft in Deutschland*, ed. Bernd Faulenbach, Munich, 1974.

Faust, Anselm. *Der Nationalsozialistische Deutsche Studentenbund.* 2 vols. Düsseldorf, 1973.

—— "Professoren für die NSDAP: Zum politischen Verhalten der Hochschullehrer 1932/3." In *Erziehung und Schulung im Dritten Reich, Teil 2: Hochschule, Erwachsenbildung*, ed. Manfred Heinemann, 31–49. Stuttgart, 1980.

Faye, Jean Pierre. *Totalitäre Sprachen.* 2 vols. Frankfurt, 1977.

Feldman, Gerald D. "Eine Gesamtdarstellung Weimars? Zu Hagen Schulzes Weimar-Buch." *Geschichte und Gesellschaft* 9 (1983): 462–70.

Felice, Renzo de. *Fascism: An Informal Introduction to Its Theory and Practice.* New Brunswick, N.J., 1976.

Fest, Joachim. *The Face of the Third Reich.* New York, 1970.

Fetscher, Iring. "Hans Freyer: Von der Soziologie als Kulturwissenschaft zum Angebot an den Faschismus." In *Intellektuelle im Bann des Nationalsozialismus*, ed. Karl Corino. Hamburg, 1980.

Feuer, Lewis S. *Ideology and the Ideologists.* New York, 1975.

Fischer, Dietrich. *Die deutsche Geschichtswissenschaft von J. G. Droysen bis O. Hintze in ihrem Verhältnis zur Soziologie: Grundzüge eines Methodenproblems.* Cologne, 1966.

Fischer, Hugo. "Der deutsche Infanterist von 1917." *Widerstand* (January 1934), 6–11.

—— *Hegels Methode in ihrer ideologiegeschichtlichen Notwendigkeit.* Leipzig, 1926.

—— *Nietzsche Apostata.* Erfurt, 1931.

—— "Politik und Metaphysik." *Blätter für deutsche Philosophie* 5 (1931–32): 270–91.

Fletcher, Miles. *The Search for a New Order: Intellectuals and Fascism in Prewer Japan.* Chapel Hill, N.C., 1982.

Flitner, Andreas. *Deutsches Geistesleben und Nationalsozialismus: Eine Vortragsreihe der Universität Tübingen.* Tübingen, 1965.

Flitner, Wilhelm. "Erinnerung an Karl Brügmann (1889–1914)." *Jahrbuch des Archivs der deutschen Jugendbewegung* 5 (1973): 95–101.

Fogt, Helmut. "Max Weber und die deutsche Soziologie der Weimarer Republik: Außenseiter oder Gründervater?" *KZfSS Sonderheft* 23 (1981): 245–72.

Forsthoff, Ernst. "Begriff und Wesen des sozialen Rechtsstaates" (1953). Reprinted in his *Rechtsstaat im Wandel*, 27–56. Stuttgart, 1964.

—— ["Silvio"]. "Erste Hilfe gegen bittere Wahrheiten." *Christ und Welt*, no. 34 (1963), 14.

—— ["Dr. Friedrich Grüter"]. "Die Gliederung des Reiches." In *Was wir vom Nationalsozialismus erwarten*, ed. Albrecht Erich Günther. Heilbronn, 1932.

—— "Haben wir zuviel oder zuwenig Staat" (1955). In *Rechtsstaat im Wandel*.

—— *Der Staat der Industriegesellschaft.* Munich, 1971.

—— "Staatsrechts, Wissenschaft und Weltkrieg." *Blätter für deutsche Philosophie* 5 (1931): 292–301.

Fox, John P. "Alfred Rosenberg in London," *Contemporary Review* 213 (July 1968): 6–11.

Fraenkel, Ernst. *The Dual State*. New York, 1941.

Franklin, William. "Zonal Boundaries and Access to Berlin." *World Politics* 16 (October 1963): 1–32

Freyer, Hans. "Alexis de Tocqueville zum 100. Todestag." Rundfunk-Sendung, 12 April 1959, Süddeutscher Rundfunk. Copy in Nachlaß Freyer, Universitätsbibliothek Münster.

—— *Antäus: Grundlegung einer Ethik des bewußten Lebens*. Jena, 1918.

—— "Arbeitslager und Arbeitsdienst." *Studentenwerk* 6 (1932): 1926–33. Reprinted in *Gespräch und Aktion in Gruppe und Gesellschaft 1919–1969: Freundesgabe für Hans Dehmel*, ed. Walter Grieff et al. Frankfurt, 1970.

—— "Der Arzt und die Gesellschaft." In *Der Arzt und der Staat*, ed. L. Ebermayer et al., 9–18. Leipzig, 1929.

—— *Die Bewertung der Wirtschaft im philosophischen Denken des 19. Jahrhunderts*. Leipzig, 1921; 2d ed., Leipzig, 1939.

—— "Bildungsreform." *Leipziger Studentenschaft* 18 (23 May 1933): 23–24.

—— "Bürgertum." *Handwörterbuch der Sozialwissenschaften* 2 (1959): 456.

—— "Das DWI in Budapest." In *Tagung deutscher wissenschaftlicher Ost- und Südostinstitute. Breslau 25. bis 27. September 1941*. Breslau, 1941. Copy in Institut für Zeitgeschichte, Munich.

—— "Einleitung" to *Reden an die deutsche Nation*, by J. G. Fichte. Leipzig, 1933.

—— *Einleitung in die Soziologie*. Leipzig, 1931.

—— "Der Einsatz der Universität für den 12. November." *Leipziger Hochschulzeitung*, 10 November 1933, 83.

—— "Ethische Normen und Politik." *Kantstudien* 35 (1930): 99–114.

—— "Die Familie als Sicherheit in unserer Zeit." *Universitas* 15 (October 1960): 1033–41.

—— "Ferdinand Tönnies und seine Stellung in der deutschen Soziologie." *Weltwirtschaftliches Archiv* 44 (1936): 1–9.

—— "Der Fortschritt und die haltenden Mächte." *Zeitwende* 24 (1952–53): 287–97.

—— "Friedrich der Große—Ein historisches Portrait." *Donaueuropa* (Budapest) 3 (1943): 247–58.

—— "Friedrich Nietzsche 1844–1900." In *Die großen Deutschen: Neue deutsche Biographie*, 4: 39–60. Berlin, 1936.

—— "Gegenwartsaufgaben der deutschen Soziologie." *Zeitschrift für die gesamte Staatswissenschaft* 95 (1935): 116–44.

—— "Der Geist im Zeitalter der Technik." *Wort und Wahrheit* 7 (1952): 183–94.

—— "Gemeinschaft und Volk." In *Philosophie der Gemeinschaft: Sieben Vorträge, gehalten auf der Tagung der deutschen philosophischen Gesellschaft vom. 1.–4. Okt. 1928 in Leipzig*, ed. Felix Krueger, 7–22. Berlin, 1929.

—— "Geschichte und Soziologie (Anläßlich des 10. Todestages vom Karl Lamprecht)." *Vergangenheit und Gegenwart* 16 (1926): 201–11.

Freyer, Hans. *Gesellschaft und Geschichte: Stoffe und Gestalten der deutschen Geschichte*, vol. 2, no. 6. Leipzig and Berlin, 1937.

—— "Gesellschaft und Kultur." In *Propyläen-Weltgeschichte: Eine Universalgeschichte*, ed. Golo Mann, vol. 10: *Die Welt von heute*, 499–591. Berlin, Frankfurt, and Vienna, 1961.

—— "Gestaltungskräfte der Geschichte: Symposium. Vorsitz Prof. Dr. Hans Freyer." In *Symphilosophein: Bericht über den dritten deutschen Kongreß für Philosophie Bremen 1950*, 211–35. Munich, 1952.

—— "Grundsätzliches über Verstehen, Verständigung und Wissenschaftliches Gespräch zwischen Völkern." *Leipziger Vierteljahresschrift für Südosteuropa* 1 (April 1937): 5–13.

—— *Herrschaft und Planung: Zwei Grundbegriffe der politischen Ethik.* Hamburg, 1933.

—— "Industrielle Gesellschaft." In *Staatslexikon: Recht, Wirtschaft, Gesellschaft*, 6th ed., 4: 286–97. Freiburg, 1959.

—— "Das industrielle Zeitalter und die Kulturkritik." In *Wo stehen wir heute?* ed. H. Walter Bähr, 197–206. Gütersloh, 1960.

—— "Das Land Utopia, ein ewiger Traum der Menschheit." *Aus Zeit und Leben: Wochenbeilage des Hannoverschen Anzeigers*, 17 January 1937.

—— *Machiavelli*. Leipzig, 1938.

—— "Machiavelli und die Lehre vom Handeln." *Zeitschrift für deutsche Kulturphilosophie* 4 (1938): 108–37.

—— "Das Material der Pflicht: Eine Studie über Fichtes spätere Sittenlehre." *Kantstudien* 25 (1920): 113–55.

—— "Mittelstand ist nicht Bürgertum." *Frankfurter Allgemeine Zeitung*, 13 December 1950, 10.

—— "Nachwort" to *Vom Nützen und Nachteil der Historie für das Leben*, by Friedrich Nietzsche, 89–95. Leipzig, 1937.

—— "Ordnung und Freiheit: Über die geistigen Grundlagen der westlichen Industriekultur." *Bundesarbeitsblatt* 13 (1962): 408–14.

—— *Pallas Athene: Ethik des politischen Volkes*. Jena, 1935.

—— "Das Politische als Problem der Philosophie." *Blätter für deutsche Philosophie* 9 (1935–36): 347–67.

—— *Der politische Begriff des Volkes: Kieler Vorträge über Volkstums- und Grenzlandfragen und den nordisch-baltischen Raum*. No. 4. Neumünster, 1933.

—— *Die politische Insel: Eine Geschichte der Utopien von Platon bis zur Gegenwart*. Leipzig, 1936.

—— *Das politische Semester: Ein Vorschlag zur Universitätsreform*. Jena, 1933.

—— *Preußentum und Aufklärung: Eine Studie über Friedrich des Großen, Antimachiavel*. Leipzig, 1944 (never distributed).

—— "Das Problem der Utopie." *Deutsche Rundschau* 183 (1920): 321–45.

—— *Prometheus: Ideen zur Philosophie der Kultur*. Jena, 1923.

—— "Rede zur Reichsgründungsfeier." *Leipziger Studentenschaft* 17 (26 January 1933): 49–51.

—— Review of *Erziehung und Vererbung*, by Jean Marie Guyau. *Zeitschrift für pädagogische Psychologie* 14 (1913): 492–93.

—— Review of *Hauptprobleme der Ethik*, by Paul Hensel. *Zeitschrift für pädagogische Psychologie* 15 (1914): 78–80.

—— Review of *Der Untergang des Abendlandes*, vol. 1. by Oswald Spengler. *Die Tat* 2, pt. 1 (1919–20): 304–8.

—— *Revolution von rechts*. Jena, 1931.

—— "Rezension von O. Spann, *Gesellschaftsphilosophie*." *Kölner Vierteljahreshefte für Soziologie* 8 (1929–30): 233–38.

—— "Die Romantiker." In *Gründer der Soziologie: Eine Vortragsreihe. Sozialwissenschaftliche Bausteine*, ed. F. K. Mann, 79–95. Jena, 1932.

—— *Schwelle der Zeiten: Beiträge zur Soziologie der Kultur*. Stuttgart, 1965.

—— "Die soziale Ganze und die Freiheit des Einzelnen unter die Bedingungen des industriellen Zeitalters." *Historische Zeitschrift* 183 (1957): 95–115.

—— "Die soziale Umschichtung." *Christ und Welt*, 29 December 1949, 4.

—— "Die Sozialen und Kulturellen Folgen der großen Bevölkerungsvermehrung des 19. Jahrhunderts in soziologisch-politischer Beziehung." In *Synthetische Anthropologie: Vorträge . . . der "Konferenz zur Förderung der verbundenen Wissenschaften vom Menschen" am 27.–28. Sept. 1949 in Mainz*, ed. Leopold von Wiese and K. G. Specht, 151–56. Bonn, 1950.

—— "Soziologie als Geiteswissenschaft." *Archiv für Kulturgeschichte* 16 (1926): 113–26.

—— "Soziologie als Wirklichkeitswissenschaft." *Zeitschrift für Volkerpsychologie und Soziologie* 5 (1929): 257–66.

—— *Soziologie als Wirklichkeitswissenschaft: Logische Grundlegung des Systems der Soziologie*. Leipzig, 1930.

—— "Soziologie und Geschichtswissenschaften." In *Geschichte in Wissenschaft und Unterricht* 3 (1952): 14–20, reprinted in *Geschichte und Soziologie*, ed. Hans-Ulrich Wehler. Cologne, 1973.

—— *Der Staat*. Leipzig, 1925.

—— "Stein's Bürgerideal und die moderne Wirklichkeit." *Das Parlament*, 11 September 1957, 6–7.

—— "Systeme der weltgeschichtlichen Betrachtung." In *Propyläen-Weltgeschichte*, ed. Walter Goetz, 10 vols.: vol. 1, *Das Erwachen der Menschheit*, 3–28. Berlin, 1931.

—— "Theodor Litt zum fünfzigsten Geburtstag." *Leipziger Neueste Nachrichten*, 27 December 1930.

—— *Theorie des gegenwärtigen Zeitalters*. Stuttgart, 1955.

—— *Theorie des objektiven Geistes: Eine Einleitung in die Kulturphilosophie*. Leipzig, 1923; 2d ed., Leipzig, 1928.

—— "Tradition und Revolution im gegenwärtigen Europa." *Erwachendes Europa* 1 (January 1934): 86–90.

—— "Tradition und Revolution im Weltbild." *Europäische Revue* 10 (1934): 65–76.

Freyer, Hans. "Typen und Stufen der Kultur." In *Handwörterbuch der Soziologie*, 294–308. Stuttgart, 1931.

—— *Über die ethische Bedeutung der Musik: Zwei Vorträge. Werkschriften der Musikantengilde*, no. 5. Wolffenbüttel, 1928.

—— *Über Fichtes Machiavelli-Aufsatz: Berichte über die Verhandlungen der sächsischen Akademie der Wissenschaften*. Leipzig, 1936.

—— "Die Universität als hohe Schule des Staates." *Die Erziehung* 7 (1932): 520–37, 669–89.

—— "Das Volk als werdende Ganzheit." In *Ganzheit und Struktur: Festschrift zum 60. Geburtstag von Felix Krueger*, vol. 3: *Geistige Strukturen: Neue psychologische Studien* 12 (1934): 1–8.

—— "Volkwerdung: Gedanken über den Standort und über die Aufgaben der Soziologie." *Volksspiegel: Zeitschrift für deutsche Soziologie und Volkswissenschaft* 1 (1934): 3–9.

—— "Vom geschichtlichen Selbstbewußtsein des 20. Jahrhunderts." *Mélanges D. Gusti (Archiv pour la Science et la Reform Sociales)*, (Bucharest) 13 (1936): 1–7.

—— "Vom Sinn der griechischen Polis." In *Leuchtenburg Tagungsbericht: 5. Treffen* (n.p., 1927), 3–4. Copy in Burg Ludwigstein.

—— "Von der Volksbildung zur politischen Schulung." *Die Erziehung* 9 (1933–34): 1–12.

—— *Weltgeschichte Europas*. 1st ed., 2 vols. Weisbaden, 1948.

—— "Der Wille zum Staat." *Rheinische Blätter* 12 (1935): 190–94.

—— "Ein Zeitalter sucht sich selbst: Zu der Buchausstellung 'Im Brennpunkt: Zeitgeschichte.' " *Bücherei und Bildung* 9 (1957): 1–5.

—— "Zur Bildungskrise der Gegenwart." *Die Erziehung* 6 (1931): 597–626.

—— "Zur Ethik des Berufes." *Blätter für deutsche Philosophie* 7 (1933–34): 1–21.

—— "Zur Philosophie der Technik." *Blätter für deutsche Philosophie* 3 (1929–30): 192–201.

—— "Zwischen Fortschritt und Erbe." *Evangelische Welt* 5 (1951): 401–4.

—— ed. *Katalog der Wissenschaftlichen Bibliothek—DWI Budapest*. 2 vols. Budapest, 1941–42.

Freyer, Johannes. *Geschichte der Geschichte der Philosophie im achtzehnten Jahrhundert*. In *Beiträge zur Kultur- und Universalgeschichte*, Karl Lamprecht, gen. ed. Vol. 16. Leipzig, 1912.

Friedrich, Carl J.; Curtis, Michael; and Barber, Benjamin R. *Totalitarianism in Perspective: Three Views*. London, 1969.

Frischeisen-Köhler, Max. *Georg Simmel*. Berlin, 1919.

Fritzsche, Klaus. *Politische Romantik und Gegenrevolution*. Frankfurt, 1976.

Gadamer, Hans-Georg. *Philosophical Hermeneutics*. Translated and edited by David E. Linge. Berkeley, Calif., 1977.

—— *Philosophische Lebensjahre*. Frankfurt, 1977.

—— *Truth and Method*. New York, 1982.

Gassen, Kurt, and Landmann, Michael, eds. *Buch des Dankes an Georg Simmel*. Berlin, 1958.

Gay, Peter. *The Party of Humanity: Essays in the French Enlightenment*. New York, 1971.

—— *Weimar Culture: The Outsider as Insider*. New York and Evanston, Ill., 1968.

Gedächtnisfeier zur Friedenssonnenwende. Jena, 1919. Copy in Burg Ludwigstein.

Geertz, Clifford. *The Interpretation of Cultures*. New York, 1973.

Gehlen, Arnold. *Anthropologische Forschung*. Hamburg, 1961.

—— *Einblicke*. Edited by Karl-Siegbert Rehberg. Frankfurt, 1978.

—— "Hans Freyer: Zu seinem 80. Geburtstag." *Frankfurter Allgemeine Zeitung*, 29 July 1967.

—— *Man in the Age of Technology*. New York, 1980.

—— *Der Mensch*. Berlin, 1940.

—— *Moral und Hypermoral*. Frankfurt, 1969.

—— *Philosophische Schriften I*. Edited by Lothar Samson. Frankfurt, 1978.

—— *Philosophische Schriften II*. Edited by Lothar Samson. Frankfurt, 1980.

—— "Rasse und Staat." *Die Erziehung* 9 (1933–34): 201–4.

—— Review of *Pallas Athene* by Hans Freyer. *Europäische Revue*, 12 February 1936, 147–49.

—— *Der Seele im technischen Zeitalter*. Hamburg, 1957.

—— *Sozialpsychologische Probleme in der industriellen Gesellschaft*. Tübingen, 1949.

—— *Studien zur Anthropologie und Soziologie*. Neuwied, 1963.

—— *Über kulturelle Kristallisation*. Bremen, 1961.

—— *Urmensch und Spätkultur*. Frankfurt, 1956.

Geiger, Roger. "Durkheimian Sociology under Attack: The Controversy over Sociology in the École Normales Primaires." In *The Sociological Domain*, ed. Philippe Besnard, 120–36. Cambridge, England, 1983.

Gerth, Hans. Review of *Pallas Athene*, by Hans Freyer. *Berliner Tageblatt*, 26 May 1935.

Geuter, Ulfried. " 'Gleichschaltung' von oben? Universitätspolitische Strategien und Verhaltensweisen in der Psychologie während des Nationalsozialismus." *Psychologische Rundschau* 35, no. 4: 198–213.

—— *Die Professionalisierung der deutschen Psychologie im Nationalsozialismus*. Frankfurt, 1984.

Giddens, Anthony. "Classical Sociological Theory and the Origins of Modern Sociology." *American Journal of Sociology* 81 (1976): 703–29.

—— "Four Myths in the History of Social Thought." *Economy and Society* 1 (1972): 358–85.

Gielke, Ronald. "Faschistische Ideologie im Werk Hans Freyers." *Jahrbuch für Geschichte* 27 (1983): 40–61.

—— "Hans Freyer als Geschichtsphilosoph: Eine kritische Studie zum bürgerlichen Geschichtsdenken in der allgemeinen Krise des Kapitalismus." Ph.D. diss., East Berlin, 1982.

Gielke, Ronald. "Hans Freyer—Vom präfaschistischen Soziologen zum Theoretiker der 'Industriegesellschaft.' " *Zeitschrift für Geschichtswissenschaft* 29 (1981): 597–603.

Giles, Geoffrey J. "Die Idee der politischen Universität: Hochschulreform nach der Machtergreifung." In *Erziehung und Schulung im Dritten Reich*, ed. Manfred Heinemann, 2: 50–60. Stuttgart, 1980.

—— *Students and National Socialism in Germany*. Princeton, N.J., 1985.

Goetz, Walter. *Historiker in meiner Zeit*. Edited by Herbert Grundmann. Cologne, 1957.

—— *Das Wesen der deutschen Kultur*. Darmstadt, 1919.

Greffrath, Mathias. "Der analytische Geist der deutschen Wissenschaft, nicht der spekulative, hat mich beeindrukt: Ein Gespräch mit Ernst Manheim." *KZfSS Sonderheft* 23 (1981): 308–23.

—— ed. *Die Zerstörung einer Zukunft*. Reinbek bei Hamburg, 1979.

Greiff, Walter, et al., eds. *Gespräch und Aktion in Gruppe und Gesellschaft, 1919–1969: Freundesgabe für Hans Dehmel*. Frankfurt, 1970.

Greiffenhagen, Martin. *Das Dilemma des Konservatismus in Deutschland*. 2d ed. Munich, 1977.

Greven, Michael T. "Konservative Kultur- und Zivilisationskritik in der 'Dialektik der Aufklärung' und 'Schwelle der Zeiten.' " Typescript, 1982.

Grüneberg, Horst. "Revolution von rechts." *Die Tat* 23 (1931): 240–41.

Gumplowicz, Ludwig. *Der Rassenkampf: Soziologische Untersuchungen*. 2d ed. Innsbruck, 1909.

Günther, Albrecht Erich, ed. *Was wir vom Nationalsozialismus erwarten*. Heilbronn, 1932.

Gurland, Arkadij. *Produktionsweise—Staat—Klassendiktatur: Versuch einer immanenten Interpretation des Diktaturbegriffs der materialistischen Geschichtsauffassung*. Leipzig, 1929.

Haase, Otto Ernst. Review of *Der Staat*, by Hans Freyer. *Die Vossische Zeitung* (Berlin), 31 March 1926.

Habermas, Jürgen. "Drei Perspektiven: Linkshegelianer, Rechtshegelianer und Nietzsche." In his *Der philosophischen Diskurs der Moderne*, 65–94. Frankfurt, 1985.

—— "Die Kulturkritik der Neokonservativen in der USA and in der Bundesrepublik." *Merkur* 36, no. 11 (November 1982): 1047–61.

—— *Kultur und Kritik*. Frankfurt, 1973.

—— "Modernity versus Postmodernity." *New German Critique* (Winter 1981), 3–14.

—— ed. *Stichworte zur "Geistigen Situation der Zeit."* 2 vols. Frankfurt, 1979.

Hahn, Thomas. "Industriesoziologie als Wirklichkeitswissenschaft? Zwischen Empirie und Kult." In *Geist und Katastrophe: Studien zur Soziologie im Nationalsozialismus*, ed. Urs Jaeggi et al., 174–311. Berlin, 1983.

Hamilton, Alastair. *The Appeal of Fascism: A Study of Intellectuals and Fascism, 1919–1945*. New York, 1971.

Hamilton, Richard F. *Who Voted for Hitler?* Princeton, N.J., 1982.

Hampshire, Stuart. *Morality and Conflict*. Oxford, 1983.

Handwörterbuch des Grenz- und Auslandsdeutschtums. Breslau, 1933.

Hardenberg, Alice Gräfin. "Bündische Jugend und Ausland." Ph.D. diss., Universität München, 1966.

Hartshorne, Edward Y. *The German Universities and National Socialism.* London, 1937.

Hayek, Friedrich. *The Constitution of Liberty.* Chicago, 1960.

—— *The Road to Serfdom.* Chicago, 1944.

Heberle, Rudolf. *From Democracy to Nazism: A Regional Case Study on Political Parties in Germany.* Baton Rouge, La., 1945; reprinted New York, 1970.

—— *Landbevölkerung und Nationalsozialismus.* Munich, 1963.

—— "Die politische Haltung des Landvolks in Schleswig-Holstein, 1918-1932: Ergebnisse einer politisch-soziographischen Untersuchung." *Volksspiegel* 1 (1934): 166–72.

—— "Soziologische Lehr- und Wanderjahre." *KZfSS* (1976): 197–211.

Hegel, G.W.F. *Philosophy of Right.* Translated by T. M. Knox. London, 1967.

—— *Reason in History.* Translated by Robert S. Hartman. Indianapolis, 1953.

Heiber, Helmut. *Walther Frank und sein Reichsinstitut für die Geschichte des neuen Deutschlands.* Stuttgart, 1966.

Heidegger, Martin. *Sein und Zeit.* Tübingen, 1927.

Heimpel, Hermann. "Nekrolog." *Historische Zeitschrift* 174 (1952): 737–39,

Heinemann, Manfred, ed. *Erziehung und Schulung im Dritten Reich.* Vol. 2. Stuttgart, 1980.

Heitz, Gerhard. "Rudolf Kotzschke (1867–1949)." In *Karl-Marx-Universität Leipzig, 1409–1959: Beiträge zur Universitätsgeschichte,* ed. Ernst Engelberg, 2: 262–74. Leipzig, 1959.

Helbig, Herbert. "Leipzig." In *Die Universitäten in Mittel- und Ostdeutschland* (Radio Bremen). Bremen, 1961.

—— *Universität Leipzig.* Frankfurt, 1961.

Hellpach, Willy. "Geschichte als Sozialpsychologie, zugleich eine Epikrise über Karl Lamprecht." In *Kultur und Universalgeschichte. Walter Goetz zu seinem 60. Geburtstage,* 505–11. Leipzig, 1927.

Herf, Jeffrey. *Reactionary Modernism: Technology, Culture, and Politics in Weimar and the Third Reich.* Cambridge, 1984.

—— "War, Peace and the Intellectuals: The West German Peace Movement." *International Security* (Spring 1986), 172–200.

Hermann, Rudolf. *Kulturkritik und konservative Revolution: Zum kulturell-politischen Denken Hoffmannsthals und seinem problemgeschichtlichen Kontext.* Tübingen, 1971.

Hermet, Guy; Hassner, Pierre; and Rupnik, Jacques, eds. *Totalitarismes.* Paris, 1984.

Heuss, Theodor. *Erinnerungen.* Tübingen, 1963.

Hildebrandt, Walter. "Auf der Suche nach Wirklichkeit: Bemerkungen zum Werk Helmut Schelskys." *Moderne Welt* 7, no. 3 (1966): 325–43.

—— "Helmut Schelsky im Zenit." In *Helmut Schelsky—Ein Soziologe in der Bundesrepublik,* ed. Horst Baier. Stuttgart, 1986.

Hintze, Otto, et al., eds. *Deutschland und der Weltkrieg*. Leipzig, 1915.

Hirschman, Albert O. "Rival Interpretations of Market Society: Civilizing, Destructive, or Feeble?" *Journal of Economic Literature* 20 (December 1982): 1463–84.

Höhn, Reinhard. "Carl Schmitt als Gegner der liberalen Politik." *Gegner* 9 (5 May 1932): 6–7.

—— "Die Wandlung in der Soziologie." *Süddeutsche Monatshefte* 31 (August 1934): 642–45.

Höhne, Heinz. *The Order of the Death's Head: The Story of Hitler's SS*. London, 1972.

Hoffmann, Peter. *The History of the German Resistance*. Cambridge, Mass., 1977.

Hofmannsthal, Hugo von. *Das Schriftum als geistiger Raum der Nation*. Munich, 1927.

Hofstadter, Richard. *Anti-Intellectualism in American Life*. New York, 1963.

Hollander, Paul. *Political Pilgrims: Travels of Western Intellectuals to the Soviet Union, China, and Cuba*. New York, 1981.

Hook, Sidney. "The Literature of Political Disillusionment" (1949), reprinted under the title "Communism and the Intellectual" in *The Intellectuals: A Controversial Portrait*, ed. George B. de Huszar, 354–64. Glencoe, Ill., 1960.

Horkheimer, Max. "Kritische Theorie gestern und heute." In his *Gesellschaft im Übergang*, ed. Werner Brede. Frankfurt, 1972.

Horowitz, Irving Louis, ed. *Sociological Self-Images*. Beverly Hills, Calif., 1969.

Howe, Irving, ed. *1984 Revisited: Totalitarianism in Our Century*. New York, 1983.

Huber, Ernst Rudolf. *Deutsche Verfassungsgeschichte seit 1789*. 7 vols. Stuttgart, 1981.

Hübscher, A. *Hundertfünfzig Jahre F. A. Brockhaus*. Wiesbaden, 1955.

Hughes, H. Stuart. *Consciousness and Society: The Reorientation of European Social Thought, 1890–1930*. New York, 1958.

Huntington, Samuel. "Conservatism as an Ideology." In *Political Thought since World War II*, ed. W. J. Stankiewicz. New York, 1964.

Iggers, Georg G. *Deutsche Geschichtswissenschaft*. Munich, 1971.

—— *The German Conception of History*. Middletown, Conn., 1968.

Institut für Zeitgeschichte. *Totalitarismus und Faschismus*. Munich, 1980.

International Council on the Future of the University. *Report on German Universities*. New York, 1977.

International Encyclopedia of the Social Sciences, 1968. S.v. "Bücher, Karl," by Karl Polanyi.

Internationales Biographisches Archiv (Munzinger-Archiv). S.v. "Forsthoff, Ernst"; "Freyer, Hans"; "Ipsen, Gunther."

Internationales Soziologenlexikon. 2d ed. Stuttgart, 1980. S.v. "Jerusalem, Franz Wilhelm"; "Müller, Karl Valentin."

Ipsen, Gunther. "Das Dorf als Beispiel einer echten Gruppe." *Archiv für angewandte Soziologie* 1 (1928–29): 22–41.

—— "Das Erbe des Reiches." In *Was ist das Reich?* ed. Fritz Büchner, 58–66. Oldenberg, 1932.

—— Introduction to *Arbeitsdienst in Bulgarien*, by Hans Raupach. Berlin, 1932.

—— *Programm einer Soziologie des deutschen Volkstums*. Berlin, 1933.

—— "Soziologie des Dorfes." *Leipziger Neueste Nachrichten*, 30 June 1932, 2.

Izenberg, Gerald. *The Existentialist Critique of Freud: The Crisis of Autonomy*. Princeton, N.J., 1976.

—— "Psychohistory and Intellectual History." *History and Theory* 14 (1975): 139–55.

Jacobson, Hans-Adolf. *Karl Haushofer: Leben und Werk*. 2 vols. Boppard, 1979.

Jaeggi, Urs, et al. *Geist und Katastrophe: Studien zur Soziologie im Nationalsozialismus*. Berlin, 1983.

Jahn, Georg. "Die historische Schule der Nationalökonomie und ihr Ausklang." In *Geschichte der Volkswirtschaftslehre*, ed. Antonio Montaner. Cologne, 1967.

Janos, Andrew. *The Politics of Backwardness in Hungary, 1825–1945*. Princeton, N.J., 1982.

Janzen, Walther. "Die soziologische Herkunft der Führungsschicht der deutschen Jugendbewegung, 1900–1933." In *Namen und Werke: Biographien und Beiträge zur Soziologie der Jugendbewegung*, ed. Hinrich Jantzen. Frankfurt, 1976.

Jarausch, Konrad. *Students, Society and Politics in Imperial Germany*. Princeton, N.J., 1982.

Jay, Martin. *The Dialectical Imagination*. Boston, 1973.

—— *Marxism and Totality: The Adventures of a Concept from Lukács to Habermas*. Berkeley, Calif., 1984.

Jentsch, Rudolf. "Hans Dehmel—Wirken und Werk." In *Gespräch und Aktion in Gruppe und Gesellschaft, 1919–1969: Freundesgabe für Hans Dehmel*, ed. Walter Greiff et al., 13–50. Frankfurt, 1970.

Jesse, Eckard. "Renaissance der Totalitarismuskonzeption? Zur Kontroverse um einen strittigen Begriff." *Neue politische Literatur* 28, no. 4 (1983): 459–92.

Jonas, Friedrich. *Die Institutionslehre Arnold Gehlens*. Tübingen, 1966.

Jünger, Ernst, ed. *Krieg und Krieger*. Berlin, 1930.

Jurgensen, Harold, ed. *Entzifferung: Bevölkerung als Gesellschaft in Raum und Zeit. Gunther Ipsen gewidmet*. Göttingen, 1967.

Kadushin, Charles. *The American Intellectual Elite*. Boston, 1974.

Kalberg, Stephen. "The Search for Thematic Orientations in a Fragmented Oeuvre: The Discussion of Max Weber in Recent German Sociological Literature." *Sociology* 13 (1979): 127–39.

Karady, Victor. "The Durkheimians in Academe: A Reconsideration." In *The Sociological Domain: The Durkheimians and the Founding of French Sociology*, ed. Philippe Besnard, 71–89. Cambridge, England, 1983.

Käsler, Dirk. *Die frühe deutsche Soziologie 1909 bis 1934 und ihre Entstehungs-Milieus*. Opladen, 1984.

Käsler, Dirk. "Soziologie zwischen Distanz und Praxis: Zur Wissenschaftssoziologie der frühen deutschen Soziologie." *Soziale Welt* 35, no. 1/2 (1984): 5–47.

—— *Soziologische Abenteuer: Earle Edward Eubank besucht europäische Soziologen im Sommer 1934*. Opladen, 1985.

—— "Die Streit um die Bestimmung der Soziologie auf den deutschen Soziologentagen, 1910–1930." In *KZfSS Sonderheft* 23: *Soziologie in Deutschland und Osterreich 1918–1945*, ed. M. Rainer Lepsius. Opladen, 1981.

Kater, Michael H. "Die nationalsozialistische Machtergreifung an den deutschen Hochschulen: Zum Politischen Verhalten akademischer Lehrer bis 1939." In *Die Freiheit des Anderen*, ed. Hans Jochen Vogel et al., 49–75. Baden-Baden, 1981.

—— *Studentenschaft und Rechtsradikalismus in Deutschland, 1918–1933*. Hamburg, 1975.

Kelly, Reece C. "German Professoriate under Nazism: A Failure of Totalitarian Aspirations." *History of Education Quarterly* 25, no. 3 (1985): 261–80.

—— "Die gescheiterte nationalsozialistischen Personalpolitik." In Heinemann, ed., *Erziehung*, 61–76.

Kennedy, Ellen. "Introduction: Carl Schmitt's *Parliamentarismus* in Historical Context." In *The Crisis of Parliamentary Democracy*, by Carl Schmitt, xiii–1. Cambridge, Mass., 1985.

Kershaw, Ian. *Political Opinion and Political Dissent in the Third Reich: Bavaria 1933–1945*. New York, 1983.

Kettler, David; Meja, Volker; and Stehr, Nico. *Karl Mannheim*. New York, 1984.

Kindelberger, Charles. *The World in Depression, 1929–1939*. Berkeley, Calif., 1973.

Kindt, Werner, ed. *Die deutsche Jugendbewegung 1920 bis 1933: Die bündische Zeit*. Düsseldorf, 1974.

—— ed. *Die Wandervogelzeit*. Düsseldorf, 1968.

Kittel, Rudolf. *Die Universität Leipzig im Jahr der Revolution 1918–19: Rektoratserinnerungen*. Stuttgart, 1930.

Klafki, Wolfgang. "Theodor Litts Stellung zur Weimarer Republik und seine Auseinandersetzung mit dem Nationalsozialismus." In *Pädagogische Analysen und Reflexionen*, ed. Peter-Martin Roeder, 199–241. Weinheim, 1967.

Klages, Helmut. *Geschichte der Soziologie*. Munich, 1972.

Kleinberg, Alfred. "Soziologie der goldenen Mitte." *Die Gesellschaft* 9 (1932): 68–74.

Kleinberger, Aharon. "Gab es eine nationalsozialistische Hochschulpolitik?" In *Erziehung und Schulung im Dritten Reich*, ed. Manfred Heinemann, 9–30. Stuttgart, 1980.

Der kleine Brockhaus. 2 vols. Wiesbaden, 1949–50.

Klemperer, Klemens von. *Germany's New Conservatism: Its History and Dilemma in the Twentieth Century*. Princeton, N.J., 1968.

—— "Widerstand—Résistance: The Place of the German Resistance in the European Resistance against National Socialism." Typescript, 1983.

Klingemann, Carsten. "Heimatsoziologie oder Ordnungsinstrument? Fachgeschichtliche Aspekte der Soziologie in Deutschland zwischen 1933 und 1945." *KZfSS Sonderheft* 23 (1981): 273–307.

—— "Soziologen vor dem Nationalsozialismus: Szenen aus der Selbstgleichschaltung der Deutsche Gesellschaft für Soziologie." In *Soziologiegeschichte: Identität und Krisen einer "engagierten" Diziplin*, ed. J. Hülsdünker and R. Schellhase. Berlin, 1986.

—— "Soziologie an Hochschulen im NS-Staat." *Zeitschrift für Hochschuldidaktik*, 1985.

—— "Vergangenheitsbewältigung oder Geschichtsschreibung? Unerwünschte Traditionsbestände deutscher Soziologie zwischen 1933 and 1945." In *Ordnung und Theorie. Beiträge zur Geschichte der Soziologie in Deutschland*, ed. Sven Papcke, 223–79. Darmstadt, 1986.

—— "Zum gegenwärtigen Stand der Forschung über die Geschichte der Soziologie in Deutschland zwischen 1933 und 1945." Typescript, 1984.

Knoll, Reinhard, et al. "Der österreichische Beitrag zur Soziologie von der Jahrhundertwende bis 1938." *KZfSS Sonderheft* 23 (1981): 73–81.

Kocka, Jürgen. *Facing Total War: German Society, 1914–1918*. Cambridge, Mass., 1984.

—— "Kontroversen über Max Weber." *Neue politische Literatur* 26 (1976): 281–301.

Koellreuter, Otto. Review of *Soziologie als Wirklichkeitswissenschaft*, by Hans Freyer. *Archiv des öffentlichen Rechts* 60 (1932): 159–67.

Kolakowski, Leszek. "Modernity on Endless Trial." *Encounter* (March 1986), 8–12.

Kommittee zur Untersuchung der Verhältnisse an west-deutschen Universitäten an der Karl-Marx-Universität Leipzig. *Eine Dokumentation: Die wissenschaftliche und politische Karriere des Dr. phil. habil. Karl Heinz Pfeffer*. Leipzig, n.d. [1963].

König, René. "Die alten Geister kehren wieder . . ." *KZfSS* 84 (1982): 538–48.

—— "Die Begriffe Gemeinschaft und Gesellschaft bei Ferdinand Tönnies." *KZfSS* 7 (1955): 348–420.

—— *Kritik der historisch-existenzialistischen Soziologie: Ein Beitrag zur Begründung einer objektiven Soziologie*. Munich, 1975.

—— *Leben im Widerspruch: Versuch einer intellektuellen Autobiographie*. Munich, 1980.

—— "Nekrologe: Hans Freyer." *KZfSS* 21 (1969): 438–41.

—— ["Paul Kern"]. Review of *Machiavelli*, by Hans Freyer. *Mass und Wert* 2 (1938–39): 848–54.

—— *Soziologie Heute*. Zurich, 1949.

—— "Soziologie in Berlin um 1930." *KZfSS Sonderheft* 23 (1981): 44–49.

—— *Studien zur Soziologie*. Frankfurt, 1972.

—— "Über das vermeintliche Ende der deutschen Soziologie vor der Machtergreifung des Nationalsozialismus." *KZfSS* 36, no. 1 (1984): 1–42.

—— *Vom Wesen der deutschen Universität*. Darmstadt, 1970.

—— "Zur Soziologie der zwanziger Jahre." In *Die Zeit ohne Eigenschaften*, ed. L. Reinisch, 82–118. Stuttgart, 1961.

Krieck, Ernst. *Die Erneuerung der Universität*. Frankfurt, 1933.

Krieck, Ernst. Review of *Antäus*, by Hans Freyer. *Deutsche Bücherzeitung*, no. 1 (1919).

Krieger, Leonard. *The German Idea of Freedom*. Chicago, 1957.

—— *The Politics of Discretion*. Chicago, 1965.

Krockow, Christian Graf von. *Die Entscheidung: Eine Untersuchung über Ernst Jünger, Carl Schmitt, Martin Heidegger*. Stuttgart, 1958.

Krueger, Felix. "Otto Klemm und das Psychologische Institut der Universität Leipzig." *Zeitschrift für angewändete Psychologie und Charakterkunde* 56 (1939).

—— *Selbstbesinnung in deutscher Not: Rede an die aus dem Felde Zurückgekehrten der Universität Leipzig*. Stuttgart, 1919.

—— gen. ed. *Arbeiten zur Entwicklungspsychologie*. Vol. 1: *Über Entwicklungspsychologie*, by Felix Krueger. Leipzig, 1915.

—— gen. ed. *Deutscher Geist*. Vol. 1: *Deutsche Kultur*, by Bruno Golz. Leipzig, 1921.

Krüger, Gerhard. *Student und Revolution: Ein Beitrag zur Soziologie der revolutionären Bewegung*. Berlin, 1934.

Kultur und Universalgeschichte: Walter Goetz zu seinem 60. Geburtstage. Leipzig, 1927.

Kunkel, Wolfgang. "Der Professor im Dritten Reich." In *Die deutsche Universität im Dritten Reich*, by Helmut Kuhn et al. Munich, 1966.

Kurella, Alfred. "Zur Ethik der neuen Jugend." *Die Tat* 10, pt. 2 (1918–19): 634–37.

Kurz, Lothar, and Witte, Klaus. "Die Entnazifizierung an der Universität Münster." In *200 Jahre zwischen Dom und Schloß. Eine Lesebuch zu Vergangenheit und Gegenwart der Westfälischen Wilhelms-Universität Münster*, ed. Lothar Kurz, 117–26. Münster, 1980.

LaCapra, Dominick, and Kaplan, Steven L., eds. *Modern European Intellectual History*. Ithaca, N.Y., 1982.

Laitenberger, Volkhard. *Akademischer Austausch und auswärtige Kulturpolitik*. Göttingen, 1976.

Lamprecht, Karl. *Karl Lamprecht: Ausgewählte Schriften*. Edited by Herbert Schönebaum. Aalen, 1974.

—— *Krieg und Kultur: Drei vaterländische Vorträge*. Leipzig, 1914.

Landmann, Michael. "Georg Simmel: Konturen seines Denkens." In *Ästhetik und Soziologie um die Jahrhundertwende: Georg Simmel*, ed. Hannes Böhringer and Karlfried Grunder. Frankfurt, 1976.

Landshut, Siegfried. *Kritik der Soziologie*. Munich, 1929.

Lange, Ernst Michael. "Rezeption und Revision von Themen Hegel'schen Denkens im frühen Werk Hans Freyers." Ph.D. diss., Freie Universität Berlin, 1971.

Langguth, Gerd. *Die Protestbewegung in der Bundesrepublik Deutschland, 1968–1972*. Cologne, 1976.

Laqueur, Walter Z., ed. *Fascism: A Reader's Guide*. Berkeley, Calif., 1976.

—— "Fascism: The Second Coming." In his *The Political Psychology of Appeasement: Finlandization and Other Unpopular Essays*. New Brunswick, N.J., 1980.

—— *Germany Today: A Personal Report*. London, 1985.

—— *Young Germany: A History of the German Youth Movement.* New York, 1962.

Large, David Clay. " 'A Gift to the German Future?' The Anti-Nazi Resistance Movement and West German Rearmament." *German Studies Review* 7, no. 3 (October 1984): 499–529.

Lasby, Clarence. *Project Paperclip.* New York, 1971.

Lebovics, Herman. *Social Conservatism and the Middle Classes in Germany, 1914–1933.* Princeton, N.J., 1969.

Lederer, Emil. "Zur Soziologie des Weltkriegs." *Archiv für Sozialwissenschaft und Sozialpolitik* 39 (May 1915): 347–84.

Ledig, Gerhard. "Hans Freyers Soziologie und der Sozialismus." *Neue Blätter für den Sozialismus* 2 (January 1931): 291–94.

Lehmann, Gerhard. "Freyers *Soziologie als Wirklichkeitswissenschaft.*" *Archiv für angewandte Soziologie* 3 (1931): 205–11.

—— "Das Problem der Realitätsgegebenheit." *Blätter für deutsche Philosophie* 5 (1931–32): 424–30.

Lenk, Kurt. *Marx in der Wissenssoziologie.* Neuwied, 1972.

Lepenies, Wolf, ed. *Geschichte der Soziologie.* 4 vols. Frankfurt, 1981.

—— *Melancholie und Gesellschaft.* Frankfurt, 1969.

Lepsius, M. Rainer. "Die Entwicklung der Soziologie nach dem Zweiten Weltkrieg." *KZfSS Sonderheft* 21 (1979): 25–69.

—— "Die Soziologie der Zwischenkriegszeit." *KZfSS Sonderheft* 23 (1981): 7–23.

—— ed. *KZfSS Sonderheft* 23: *Soziologie in Deutschland und Österreich, 1918–1945.* Opladen, 1981.

Leuchtenburg Tagungsbericht: 5. Treffen. N.p., 1927. Copy in Burg Ludwigstein.

Levy, Heinrich. *Die Hegel-Rensaissance in der deutschen Philosophie.* Charlottenberg, 1927.

Lewy, Guenter. "The Persisting Heritage of the 1960s in West German Higher Education." *Minerva* 18, no. 1 (Spring 1980): 1–28.

Lieber, Hans-Joachim. *Kulturkritik und Lebensphilosophie.* Darmstadt, 1974.

—— et al. *Universitätstage, 1966: Nationalsozialismus und die deutsche Universität.* Berlin, 1966.

Liebeschutz, Hans. *Von Georg Simmel zu Franz Rosenzweig.* Tübingen, 1970.

Linde, Hans. "Soziologie in Leipzig, 1925–1945." *KZfSS Sonderheft* 23 (1981): 102–30.

Lipset, Seymour Martin. "From Socialism to Sociology." In *Sociological Self-Images,* ed. Irving Louis Horowitz. Beverly Hills, Calif., 1969.

Litt, Theodor. *Geschichte und Leben.* Leipzig, 1918.

—— "Hochschule und Politik," *Die Erziehung* 7 (1932): 134–48.

—— *Individuum und Gemeinschaft.* 3d ed. Leipzig, 1926.

—— "The National-Socialist Use of Moral Tendencies in Germany." In *The Third Reich,* by UNESCO. London, 1955.

—— *Wege und Irrwege geschichtlichen Denkens.* Munich, 1948.

Löwenthal, Richard. "Cultural Change and Generation Change in Postwar Western

Germany." In *The Federal Republic of Germany and the United States: Changing Political, Social and Economic Relations*, by J. Cooney et al., 34–55. Boulder, Colo., 1984.

—— *Der Romantische Rückfall*. Stuttgart, 1970.

—— "Widerstand im totalen Staat." In *Widerstand und Verweigerung in Deutschland 1933–1945*, ed. Richard Löwenthal and Patrik von zur Mühlen, 11–24. Bonn, 1982.

Löwith, Karl. "Max Weber und Karl Marx." *Archiv für Sozialwissenschaft und Sozialpolitik* 66 (1932): 53–99, 175–214.

—— "Max Weber und seine Nachfolger." *Mass und Wert* 3 (1940): 166–76.

—— *Meaning in History*. Chicago, 1949.

—— *Weltgeschichte und Heilsgeschichte*. Stuttgart, 1953.

Löwy, Michael. *Georg Lukács—From Romanticism to Bolshevism*. New York, 1979.

Lübbe, Hermann. *Endstation Terror: Rückblick auf lange Marsche*. Stuttgart, 1978.

—— *Hochschulreform und Gegenaufklärung*. Freiburg, 1972.

—— "Konservatismus in Deutschland." *Schweizer Monatshefte* 61, no. 12 (December 1981): 977–90.

—— "Laudatio." In *Gedenkschrift Joachim Ritter* (Schriften der Gesellschaft zur Förderung der westfälischen Wilhelms-Universität zu Münster, no. 65), 14–21. Münster, 1978.

—— "Der Nationalsozialismus im deutschen Nachkriegsbewußtsein. *"Historische Zeitschrift* 236 (1983): 586–90.

—— " 'Neo-Konservative' in der Kritik." *Merkur* 37, no. 6 (September 1983): 613–21.

—— "Politische Gleichheitspostulate und ihre sozialen Folgen." In *Solidarität in der Welt der 8oer Jahre: Leistungsgesellschaft und Sozialstaat*, ed. Robert Kopp, 61–78. Basel, 1984.

—— *Politische Philosophie in Deutschland*. Munich, 1974.

—— "Die resignierte konservative Revolution." *Zeitschrift für die gesamte Staatswissenschaft* 115 (1959): 131–38.

—— *Zwischen Trend und Tradition*. Zurich, 1981.

Luhmann, Niklas. *The Differentiation of Society*. New York, 1982.

Lúkacs, Georg. "Die deutsche Soziologie zwischen dem ersten und dem zweiten Weltkrieg." *Aufbau: Kulturpolitische Monatsschrift* 6 (1946): 585–600.

—— *History and Class Consciousness*. Translated by Rodney Livingstone. Cambridge, Mass., 1971.

—— *Die Zerstörung der Vernunft*. 3 vols. Darmstadt, 1974.

Luserke, Martin. *Die Freie Schulgemeinde Wickersdorf*. N.p., n.d. Copy in Burg Ludwigstein.

—— *Vierter Jahresbericht der Freien Schulgemeinde Wickersdorf*. Jena, 1912. Copy in Burg Ludwigstein.

MacIntyre, Alasdair. *After Virtue*. Notre Dame, Ind., 1981.

Mack Smith, Dennis. "The Great Benito?" *New York Review of Books*, 1 May 1980, 30–31.

McNeill, William H. *The Pursuit of Power*. Chicago, 1982.

Maier, Charles S. "The Two Postwar Eras and the Conditions for Stability in Twentieth-Century Western Europe." *American Historical Review* 86 (April 1981): 327–67.

Maier, Hans, and Zöller, Michael, eds. *Bund Freiheit der Wissenschaft: Der Gründungskongreß in Bad Godesberg am 18. November 1970*. Cologne, 1970.

Mandelbaum, Maurice. *History, Man, and Reason: A Study in Nineteenth-Century Thought*. Baltimore, 1971.

Manheim, Ernst. *Aufklärung und öffentliche Meinung*. Edited by Norbert Schindler. Munich, 1979.

—— "The Sociology of Hans Freyer: Sociology as a Nationalistic Program of Social Action." In *An Introduction to the History of Sociology*, ed. Harry Elmer Barnes. Chicago, 1948.

Mann, Golo. *The History of Germany since 1789*. London, 1974.

Mann, Thomas. *Betrachtungen eines Unpolitischen*. Berlin, 1918.

Mannheim, Karl. *Die Gegenwartsaufgaben der Soziologie*. Tübingen, 1932.

—— *Ideologie und Utopie*, Bonn, 1929.

—— "The Problem of Generations." In *Essays in the Sociology of Knowledge*, ed. Paul Kecskemeti, 276–332. New York, 1952.

Marck, Siegfried. "Überfaschismus? Betrachtungen zu H. Freyers *Revolution von rechts*." *Die Gesellschaft* 2 (1931): 412–19.

Marcuse, Herbert. *One-Dimensional Man*. Boston, 1964.

—— "Zur Auseinandersetzung mit Hans Freyers *Soziologie als Wirklichkeitswissenschaft*." *Philosophische Hefte* 3 (1931): 83–91.

Marx, Hugo. Review of *Das politische Semester*, by Hans Freyer. *Zeitschrift für Sozialforschung* 3 (1932): 137–42.

Mason, T. W. "The Primacy of Politics: Politics and Economics in National Socialist Germany." In *The Nature of Fascism*, ed. S. J. Woolf, 165–95. London, 1968.

Matthes, Joachim. *Einführung in das Studium der Soziologie*. 3d ed. Opladen, 1981.

Mau, Hermann. "Die deutschen Jugendbewegung: Rückblick und Ausblick." *Zeitschrift fur Religions- und Geistesgeschichte* 1 (1948): 135–49.

Mauersberg, Volker. *Rudolf Pechel und die "Deutsche Rundschau": Eine Studie zur konservativ-revolutionaren Publizistik in der Weimar Republik*. Bremen, 1971.

Maus, Ingeborg. *Bürgerliche Rechtstheorie und Faschismus: Zur sozialen Funktion und aktuellen Wirkung der Theorie Carl Schmitts*. 2d ed. Munich, 1980.

Meinecke, Friedrich. *Die Idee der Staatsräson*. Munich, 1924. Translated by Douglas Scott as *Machiavellism: The Doctrine of Raison d'État and Its Place in Modern History*. London, 1957.

Meja, Volker, and Stehr, Nico, eds. *Der Streit um die Wissenssoziologie*. 2 vols. Frankfurt, 1982.

Merton, Robert. *Social Theory and Social Structure*. Enlarged ed. New York, 1968.

—— *Sociological Ambivalence and Other Essays*. New York, 1976.

Mills, C. Wright. *The Sociological Imagination*. New York, 1959.

Mitzman, Arthur. *Sociology and Estrangement*. New York, 1973.

Mock, Wolfgang. " 'Manipulation von oben' oder Selbstorganisation an der Basis?" *Historische Zeitschrift* (1981): 358–75.

Moehling, Karl A. "Martin Heidegger and the Nazi Party: An Examination," Ph.D. diss., Dekalb, Ill., 1972.

Mogge, Winifred. " 'Der gespante Bogen': Jugendbewegung and Nationalsozialismus." *Jahrbuch des Archivs der deutschen Jugendbewegung* 13 (1981): 11–34.

Mohler, Arnim. *Die konservative Revolution in Deutschland, 1918–1932*. 2d ed. Darmstadt, 1972.

Mommsen, Hans. *Beamtentum im Dritten Reich*. Stuttgart, 1966.

—— "Sozialgeschichte." In *Moderne deutsche Sozialgeschichte*, ed. Hans-Ulrich Wehler, 27–36. Königstein, 1981.

—— "Die Widerstand gegen Hitler und die deutsche Gesellschaft." *Historische Zeitschrift* 241 (1985): 81–104.

Mommsen, Wolfgang J. *The Age of Bureaucracy: Perspectives on the Political Sociology of Max Weber*. New York, 1974.

—— "Die Geschichtswissenschaft in der modernen Industriegesellschaft." In *Geschichtswissenschaft in Deutschland*, ed. Bernd Faulenbach, 147–68. Munich, 1974.

Moore, Wilbert E. "Functionalism." In *A History of Sociological Analysis*, ed. Tom Bottomore and Robert Nisbet, 321–61. New York, 1978.

Mosse, George L. *The Crisis of German Ideology*. New York, 1964.

—— "Fascism and the Intellectuals." In his *Germans and Jews*. New York, 1970.

—— "National Cemeteries and National Revival: The Cult of the Fallen Soldiers in Germany." *Journal of Contemporary History* 14 (1979): 1–20.

—— *Toward the Final Solution*. New York, 1981.

—— ed. *Police Forces in History*. Beverly Hills, Calif., 1975.

Mozetic, Gerald. "Ein unzeitgemässer Soziologe: Ludwig Gumplowicz." *KZfSS* 37, no. 4 (1985): 621–47.

Mühlmann, W. E. "Die Hitler-Bewegung." *Sociologicus* 9 (June 1933): 129–40.

Müller, Gerhard. *Ernst Krieck und die nationalsozialistische Wissenschaftsreform*. Weinheim, 1978.

Müller, Jakob. *Die Jugendbewegung als deutsche Hauptrichtung neukonservativer Reform*. Zurich, 1971.

Muller, Jerry Z. "Enttäuschung und Zweideutigkeit: Zur Geschichte rechter Sozialwissenschaftler im Dritten Reich." *Geschichte und Gesellschaft*, no. 3 (1986): 289–316.

Müller, Karl Valentin. *Die Aufsteig des Arbeiters durch Rasse und Meisterschaft*. Munich, 1935.

Münster, Hans A. "Das neue Leipziger Südosteuropa-Institut." *Leipziger Vierteljahresschrift für Südosteuropa* 1 (April 1937): 76–87.

Naipaul, V. S. *Among the Believers: An Islamic Journey*. New York, 1981.

Nettl, J. P. *The Eastern Zone and Soviet Policy in Germany, 1945–1950.* London, 1951.

Neumann, Franz. *Behemoth.* 2d ed. New York, 1944.

Neumann, Sigmund. *Die Stufen des preußischen Konservatismus.* Berlin, 1928.

Nicholls, Anthony. "The Other Germany—The 'Neo-Liberals.' " In *Ideas into Politics,* ed. R. J. Bullen et al., 164–78. London, 1984.

Nicolin, Friedhelm. "Pädagogische Theorie als Selbstkritik der Pädagogik: Theodor Litt und die Reformpädagogik." In *Sinn und Geschichtlichkeit: Werk und Wirkung Theodor Litts,* by Josef Derbolav et al., 267–90. Stuttgart, 1980.

—— "Theodor Litt und der Nationalsozialismus." *Pädagogische Rundschau* 36 (1982): 95–122.

Niekisch, Ernst. *Gewagtes Leben.* Cologne, 1958.

Nietzsche, Friedrich. *Unzeitgemässe Betrachtungen.* Frankfurt, 1981.

Nipperdey, Thomas. *Gesellschaft, Kultur, Theorie.* Göttingen, 1976.

Nisbet, Robert. *The Sociological Tradition.* New York, 1966.

Nohl, Hermann. "Vom deutschen Ideal der Geselligkeit: Zum Andenken Karl Brügmanns gewidmet." *Die Tat* 7 (November 1915): 617–41.

Nolte, Ernst. *Deutschland und der Kalte Krieg.* Munich, 1974.

—— *Der Faschismus in seiner Epoche.* 5th ed. Munich, 1979.

—— *Theorien über den Faschismus.* Cologne, 1967.

Oakes, Guy. "Methodological Ambivalence: The Case of Max Weber." *Social Research* 49 (Autumn 1982): 589–615.

Oestreich, Gerhard. "Die Fachhistorie und die Anfänge der sozialgeschichtlichen Forschung in Deutschland." *Historische Zeitschrift* 208 (1969): 320–63.

Ott, Hugh. "Martin Heidegger und die Universität Freiburg nach 1945." *Historisches Jahrbuch* 105, pt. 1 (1985): 95–128.

Pankoke, Eckart. "Technischer Fortschritt und Kulturelles Erbe: Hans Freyers Gegenwartsdiagnosen in historischer Perspektive." *Geschichte in Wissenschaft und Unterricht* 21 (1970): 143–51.

Papcke, Sven, ed. *Ordnung und Theorie: Beiträge zur Geschichte der Soziologie in Deutschland.* Darmstadt, 1986.

Parsons, Talcott. "The Intellectual: A Social Role Category." In *On Intellectuals,* ed. Philip Rieff, 3–24. Garden City, N.Y., 1969.

—— *The Structure of Social Action.* 2 vols. New York, 1968.

Paxton, Robert O. *Vichy France: Old Guard and New Order, 1940–1944.* New York, 1972.

Pells, Richard H. *The Liberal Mind in a Conservative Age.* New York, 1985.

Pfeffer, Karl-Heinz. *Der Bauer.* Leipzig, 1939.

—— *Die bürgerliche Gesellschaft in Australien.* Berlin, 1936.

—— *Die deutsche Schule der Soziologie.* Leipzig, 1939.

—— *England, Vormacht der bürgerlichen Welt.* Hamburg, 1940.

Pfeffer, Karl-Heinz. *Der englische Krieg auch ein jüdischer Krieg.* Munich, 1943.

—— "Hans Freyer, ein Deuter unserer Zeit." *Jungnationale Stimmen* 6 (1931–32): 343–54.

Pieper, Josef. "Wirklichkeitswissenschaftliche Soziologie." *Archiv für Sozialwissenschaften und Sozialpolitik* 66 (1931): 394–407.

Pike, David. *Lukács and Brecht.* Chapel Hill, N.C., 1985.

Plenge, Johann. *Der Krieg und die Volkswirtschaft.* Münster, 1915.

—— *Marx und Hegel.* Tübingen, 1911.

—— *1789 und 1914: Die symbolischen Jahre in der Geschichte des politischen Geistes.* Berlin, 1916.

Plessner, Helmuth. *Gesammelte Schriften.* Vol. 5: *Grenzen der Gemeinschaft.* Frankfurt, 1981.

—— *Die verspätete Nation.* Frankfurt, 1974.

Pocock, J.G.A. *The Machiavellian Moment.* Princeton, N.J., 1975.

Poliakov, Leon, and Wulf, Josef, eds. *Das Dritte Reich und seine Diener.* Berlin, 1956.

Pongratz, Ludwig, ed. *Pädagogik in Selbstdarstellungen.* 2 vols. Hamburg, 1976.

Popper, Karl R. *The Open Society and Its Enemies.* 2 vols. Princeton, N.J., 1966.

—— *The Poverty of Historicism.* New York, 1957.

Pribram, Karl. "Deutscher Nationalismus und deutscher Sozialismus." *Archiv für Sozialwissenschaft und Sozialpolitik* 49 (1922): 298–376.

Putnam, Hilary. *Reason, Truth and History.* Cambridge, Mass., 1981.

Radio Bremen. *Die Universitäten in Mittel- und Ostdeutschland.* Bremen, 1961.

Rahv, Philip. "Religion and the Intellectuals" (1950). In his *Essays on Literature and Politics 1932–1972,* 310–16. Boston, 1978.

Raoul Richter zum Gedächtnis (1871–1912). Leipzig, 1914.

Rasch, H. G. "Müller, Karl Valentin." In *Internationale Soziologenlexikon,* ed. Wilhelm Bernsdorf, 302–3. Stuttgart, 1980.

Reble, Albert. "Albert Reble," in *Pädagogik in Selbstdarstellung,* ed. Ludwig Pongratz, vol. 3. Hamburg, 1978.

Rehberg, Karl-Siegbert. "Metaphern des Standhaltens: In Memoriam Arnold Gehlen." *KZfSS,* no. 2 (1976): 389–98.

—— "Philosophische Anthropologie und die 'Soziologisierung' des Wissens vom Menschen." *KZfSS Sonderheft* 23 (1981): 160–98.

—— ed. "Protokoll: Arbeitstagung der Fritz-Thyssen-Stiftung, 'Gab es eine "Leipziger Schule" der Soziologie und Sozialphilosophie?' am 29. und 30. April 1982." Aachen, 1982. Typescript.

Reichssicherheitshauptamt. *Jahreslagebericht 1938 des Sicherheitshauptamtes,* vol. 2: *Kulturelles Leben.* Copy in BAK.

Reill, Peter. *The German Enlightenment and the Rise of Historicism.* Berkeley, Calif., 1975.

Reinhard, Werner. "Politische Jugendbewegung in der Weimarer Zeit." In *Politische Bildung in der Demokratie: Fritz Borinski zum 65. Geburtstag*, ed. Gerd Doerry. Berlin, 1968.

Reinisch, L., ed. *Die Zeit ohne Eigenschaften*. Stuttgart, 1961.

Revel, Jean-François. *The Totalitarian Temptation*. New York, 1977.

Review of *Revolution von rechts*, by Hans Freyer. *Deutsche Freischar* 4 (1931): 86–87.

Richter, Georg, ed. *Der Königlich Sächsische Militär–St. Heinrichs Orden*. Frankfurt, 1964.

Richter, Raoul. *Friedrich Nietzsche*. 3d ed. Leipzig, 1917.

Riedel, Manfred. "Gesellschaft, bürgerliche" and "Gesellschaft, Gemeinschaft." In *Geschichtliche Grundbegriffe*, ed. Otto Brunner et al., vol. 2. Stuttgart, 1975.

Rieff, Philip. *Fellow Teachers*. New York, 1973.

—— ed. *On Intellectuals*. Garden City, N.Y., 1969.

Riehl, W. H. *Die Naturgeschichte des deutschen Volkes*. Edited by Gunther Ipsen. Leipzig, 1935.

Riesman, David; Glazer, Nathan; and Denney, Reuel. *The Lonely Crowd*. Abridged edition with a new foreword. New Haven, Conn., 1961.

Ringer, Fritz K. *The Decline of the German Mandarins*. Cambridge, Mass., 1969.

Ritchie, J. M. *German Literature under National Socialism*. London, 1983.

Ritter, Gerhard. "The German Professor in the Third Reich." *Review of Politics* 8 (April 1946): 242–54.

—— *Lebendige Vergangenheit*. Munich, 1958.

Ritter, Joachim. *Hegel and the French Revolution*. Cambridge, Mass., 1982.

Robbins, Lionel. "Hayek on Liberty." *Economica* 28 (1961): 66–81.

Rogger, Hans, and Weber, Eugen. *The European Right: A Historical Portrait*. Berkeley, Calif., 1966.

Roll, Eric. *History of Economic Thought*. New York, 1963.

Roth, Michael S. "A Problem of Recognition: Alexandre Kojève and the End of History." *History and Theory* 24, no. 3 (1985): 293–306.

Rothacker, Erich. "Die Geisteswissenschaften." In *Zehn Jahre Deutsche Geschichte, 1918–1928*, 401–8. Berlin, 1928.

—— Review of *Die Bewertung der Wirtschaft im philosophischen Denken des 19. Jahrhunderts*, by Hans Freyer. *Vierteljahreshefte für Sozial- und Wirtschaftsgeschichte* 17 (1924): 232–33.

Rothschild, Joseph. *East Central Europe between the Two World Wars*. Seattle, 1974.

Ruegg, Walter. "The Intellectual Situation in German Higher Education." *Minerva* 13, no. 1 (Spring 1975): 103–20.

Rügemer, Werner. *Philosophische Anthropologie und Epochenkrise*. Cologne, 1979.

Ruschmeyer, Dietrich. "XVIII. Kongress des Institut International de Sociologie." *KZfSS* 10 (1958): 711–13.

Sandel, Michael. *Liberalism and the Limits of Justice*. Cambridge, England, 1985.

Sauer, Wolfgang. *Die Mobilmachung der Gewalt*. Frankfurt, 1979.

Schäfers, Bernhard, ed. *Soziologie und Sozialismus, Organisation und Propaganda: Abhandlungen zum Lebenswerk von Johann Plenge*. Stuttgart, 1967.

Schapiro, Leonard. *Totalitarianism*. London, 1972.

Schelsky, Helmut. *Auf der Suche nach Wirklichkeit: Gesammelte Aufsätze zur Soziologie der Bundesrepublik*. Munich, 1979.

—— "Die Generationen der Bundesrepublik." In *Die andere deutsche Frage: Kultur und Gesellschaft der Bundesrepublik Deutschland nach dreißig Jahren*, ed. Walter Scheel, 178–98. Stuttgart, 1981.

—— "Lage und Aufgaben der angewandten Soziologie in Deutschland." *Soziale Welt* 2 (1950–51): 3–13.

—— "Im Spiegel des Amerikaners." *Wort und Wahrheit* 11 (1956): 362–74.

—— "Die verschiedenen Weisen, wie man Demokrat sein kann: Erinnerungen an Hans Freyer, Helmuth Plessner und andere." In his *Rückblicke eines Anti-Soziologen*. Opladen, 1981.

Schieder, Theodor. "Friedrich der Große und Machiavelli: Das Dilemma von Machtpolitik und Aufklärung." *Historische Zeitschrift* 234 (1981).

Schmitt, Carl. "Die andere Hegel-Linie: Hans Freyer zum 70. Geburtstag." *Christ und Welt* (1967): 265–94.

—— *The Concept of the Political*. Edited by George Schwab. New Brunswick, N.J., 1976.

—— *Die Diktatur*. Munich, 1921.

—— "Die Diktatur des Reichspräsidenten nach Art. 48 der Reichsverfassung." *Veröffentlichungen der Vereinigung der deutschen Staatsrechtlehrer*, no. 1 (1924).

—— *Ex Captivitate Salus*. Cologne, 1950.

—— "Die Gegensatz von Parlamentarismus und moderner Massendemokratie." *Hochland* 23 (1926): 257–70.

—— *Politische Romantik*. 2d ed. Berlin, 1925.

—— "Staatsethik und pluralistischer Staat." *Kantstudien* 35 (1930): 28–42.

—— "Die Wendung zum totalen Staat." *Europäische Revue* 7 (April 1931): 241–50.

—— "Wesen und Werden des fascistischen Staates." *Schmollers Jahrbuch* 53, no. 1 (1929): 107–13.

Schnabel, Franz. *Deutsche Geschichte im neunzehnten Jahrhundert*. 4 vols. Freiburg, 1951.

Schneider, Hans. "Ernst Forsthoff: 70 Jahre." *Neue Juristische Wochenschrift*, no. 37 (1972), 1654.

Schnell, R. "Innere Emigration und kulturelle Dissidenz." In *Widerstand und Verweigerung in Deutschland 1933 bis 1945*, ed. R. Löwenthal and P. von zur Mühlen, 211–25. Bonn, 1982.

Schnur, Roman, ed. *Festschrift für Ernst Forsthoff*. Munich, 1972.

Scholder, Klaus, ed. *Die Mittwochs-Gesellschaft*. Berlin, 1982.

Schönebaum, Herbert. "Karl Lamprecht: Leben und Werk eines Kämpfers um die

Geschichtswissenschaft, 1856–1913." Typescript. Copy in Historisches Archiv der Stadt Köln.

Schorske, Carl. "Generational Tension and Cultural Change: Reflections on the Case of Vienna." *Daedalus* 107, no. 4 (Fall 1978): 111–22.

Schrader, Einhard. "Theorie und Praxis: Johann Plenges Programm eines organisatorischen Sozialismus." In *Soziologie und Sozialismus, Organisation und Propaganda: Abhandlungen zum Lebenswerk von Johann Plenge*, ed. Bernhard Schäfers. Stuttgart, 1967.

Schulin, Ernst. *Traditionskritik und Rekonstruktionsversuch: Studien zur Entwicklung von Geschichtswissenschaft und historischen Denken.* Göttingen, 1979.

Schultz, Susan D. "History as a Moral Force against Individualism: Karl Lamprecht and Methodological Controversies in the German Historical Sciences, 1880–1914." Ph.D. diss., University of Chicago, 1985.

Schulz, Gerhard. *Die Anfänge des totalitären Maßnahmenstaates.* Frankfurt, 1979.

—— "Der Begriff des Totalitarismus und des Nationalsozialismus." In *Wege der Totalitarismusforschung*, ed. Bruno Seidel and Siegfried Jenker. Darmstadt, 1968.

Schumpeter, Joseph. *Capitalism, Socialism, and Democracy.* 3d ed. New York, 1950.

Schwabe, Klaus. *Wissenschaft und Kriegsmoral.* Göttingen, 1969.

—— and Reichardt, Rolf, eds. *Gerhard Ritter: Ein politischer Historiker in seinen Briefen.* Boppard, 1984.

Schwan, Alexander. "Zeitgenössische Philosophie und Theologie in ihrem Verhältnis zur Weimarer Republik." In *Weimar: Selbstpreisgabe einer Demokratie*, ed. K. D. Erdmann and Hagen Schulze, 259–86. Düsseldorf, 1979.

Schwarz, Hans-Peter. *Die Ära Adenauer: Gründerjahre der Republik, 1949–1957.* Stuttgart, 1981.

—— *Die Ära Adenauer: Epochenwechsel, 1957–1963.* Stuttgart, 1983.

—— *Vom Reich zur Bundesrepublik*, 2d ed. Stuttgart, 1980.

—— *Der konservative Anarchist: Politik und Zeitkritik Ernst Jüngers.* Freiburg, 1962.

Schweitzer, Bernhard. *Die Universität Leipzig, 1409–1959.* Tübingen, 1960.

"Schwerpunkt: Soziologie im Nationalsozialismus?" *Soziale Welt* 35, nos. 1/2 (1984).

Seelinger, R., ed. *Braune Universität.* 6 vols. Munich, 1964.

Seidman, Steven. "The Main Aims and Thematic Structure of Max Weber's Sociology." *Canadian Journal of Sociology* 9, no. 4 (Fall 1984): 381–405.

Seier, Hellmut. "Der Rektor als Führer: Zur Hochschulpolitik des Reichserziehungsministeriums, 1934–1945." *Vierteljahreshefte für Zeitgeschichte* 12 (1964): 105–46.

Seigel, Jerrold. "Virtù in and since the Renaissance." In *Dictionary of the History of Ideas.* New York, 1974.

Sheehan, James J. "National Socialism and German Society: Reflections on Recent Research." *Theory and Society* 13 (1984): 851–67.

Shils, Edward. "Intellectuals, Tradition, and the Traditions of Intellectuals: Some Preliminary Considerations." *Daedalus* 101 (Spring 1972): 21–34.

Shklar, Judith. *Freedom and Independence: A Study of the Political Ideas of Hegel's "Phenomenology of Mind."* Cambridge, Mass., 1976.

Siebert, Erich. "Die Rolle der Kultur- und Wissenschaftspolitik bei der Expansion des deutschen Imperialismus nach Bulgarien, Jugoslawien, Rumanien und Ungarn in den Jahren 1938–1944." Ph.D. diss., Humboldt Universität, East Berlin, 1971.

Simmel, Georg. "An Herrn Professor Karl Lamprecht." *Die Zukunft* 10 (May 1913): 233.

—— *Das individuelle Gesetz: Philosophische Exkurse.* Edited by Michael Landmann. Frankfurt, 1968.

—— *Der Krieg und die geistigen Entscheidungen.* Munich, 1917.

—— *Philosophische Kultur.* 3d ed. Leipzig, 1923.

—— *The Philosophy of Money.* Translated by Tom Bottomore and David Frisby. London, 1978.

Sokel, Walter. *The Writer in Extremis.* Stanford, Calif., 1959.

Sommer, Theo. "The Nazis in the Judiciary." In *The Politics of Postwar Germany*, ed. Walter Stahl, 240–48. New York, 1963.

Sontheimer, Kurt. *Antidemokratisches Denken in der Weimarer Republik.* Munich, 1962; and Studienausgabe, Munich, 1968.

—— *Deutschland zwischen Demokratie und Antidemokratie.* Munich, 1971.

—— *Das Elend unserer Intellektuellen.* Hamburg, 1976.

—— "Intellectuals and Politics in Western Germany." *West European Politics* 1 (Fall 1978): 30–41.

—— Review of *Theorie des gegenwärtigen Zeitalters*, by Hans Freyer. *Frankfurter Hefte* 10 (1955): 826–28.

—— *Zeitenwende? Die Bundesrepublik Deutschland zwischen alter und alternativer Politik.* Hamburg, 1983.

—— "Zwei deutsche Republiken und ihre Intellektuellen," *Merkur* 36, #11 (November 1982): 1062–71.

Sorel, Georges. *Reflections on Violence.* Translated by T. E. Hulme and J. Roth. New York, 1961.

Sorokin, Pitirim A. *A Long Journey.* New Haven, 1963.

"Soziologen distanzieren sich." *Frankfurter Allgemeine Zeitung* (5 August 1958), 8.

Spaemann, Robert. *Der Ursprung der Soziologie aus dem Geist der Restauration: Studien über L.G.A. de Bonald.* Munich, 1959.

Spann, Othmar, and Below, George von, eds. *Deutsche Beiträge zur Wirtschafts- und Gesellschaftslehre.* Jena, 1926.

Speidel, Hans. *Aus unserer Zeit: Erinnerungen.* Berlin, 1977.

Spengler, Oswald. *Der Untergang des Abendlandes.* 2 vols. Munich, 1923.

Spotts, Frederic. *The Churches and Politics in Germany.* Middletown, Conn., 1973.

Spranger, Eduard. "Mein Konflikt mit der nationalsozialistischen Regierung 1933." *Universitas* 10 (1955): 457–75.

Stachura, Peter D., "Deutsche Jugendbewegung und Nationalsozialismus," *Jahrbuch des Archivs der deutschen Jugendbewegung* 12 (1980): 35–52.

—— " 'Der Fall Strasser': Gregor Strasser, Hitler and National Socialism, 1930–32." In his *The Shaping of the Nazi State*. London, 1978.

Stankiewicz, W. J., ed. *Political Thought since World War II*. New York, 1964.

Stark, Gary. *Entrepreneurs of Ideology: Neoconservative Publishers in Germany, 1890–1933*. Chapel Hill, N.C., 1981.

Stern, Carola. "Bilanz." In *Das Ende einer Utopie: Hingabe und Selbstbefreiung früherer Kommunisten*, ed. H. Krüger. Olten, 1963.

Stern, Fritz. *The Failure of Illiberalism*. New York, 1972.

—— "Der Nationalsozialismus als Versuchung." In *Reflexionen finsterer Zeit*, ed. O. Hofius, 215–34. Tübingen, 1985.

—— *The Politics of Cultural Despair*. Berkeley, Calif., 1974.

"Stifterverband für die deutsche Wissenschaft." In *Forschung heißt Arbeit und Brot*. Stuttgart, 1950.

Stinchcombe, Arthur. "Merton's Theory of Social Structure." In *The Idea of Social Structure*, ed. Lewis Coser, 11–53. New York, 1975.

Stoltenberg, H. Lorenz. "Das Treffen Deutschen Soziologen in Jena vom 5. bis 7. Januar 1934." *Kölner Vierteljahreshefte für Soziologie* 12 (1933–34): 200.

Stölting, Erhard. "Kontinuitäten und Brüche in der deutschen Soziologie 1933/34." *Soziale Welt* 35, nos. 1/2 (1984): 48–59.

Storost, Ulrich. *Staat und Verfassung bei Ernst Forsthoff*. Frankfurt, 1979.

Strätz, Hans-Wolfgang. "Die studentische 'Aktion wider den undeutschen Geist' im früjahr 1933." *Vierteljahreshefte für Zeitgeschichte* 16 (1968): 346–72.

Strauss, Leo. "Comments on Carl Schmitt's *Der Begriff des Politischen*" (1932). In Carl Schmitt, *The Concept of the Political*, ed. George Schwab. New Brunswick, N.J., 1976.

—— *Natural Right and History*. Chicago, 1953.

—— *Persecution and the Art of Writing*. Glencoe, Ill., 1952.

Stromberg, Roland. *Redemption by War*. Lawrence, Kans., 1982.

Strübel, Gustav. "1945—Neuanfang oder versäumte Gelegenheit." In *Hochschule und Wissenschaft im Dritten Reich*, ed. Jörg Tröger, 168–79. Frankfurt, 1984.

Struve, Walter. *Elites against Democracy*. Princeton, N.J., 1973.

Talmon, Jacob L. *The Origins of Totalitarian Democracy*. London, 1952.

Taylor, Charles. *Hegel*. Cambridge, England, 1975.

Tenbruck, Friedrich H. "Alltagsnormen und Lebensgefühle in der Bundesrepublik." In *Die zweite Republik: 25 Jahre Bundesrepublik Deutschland—Eine Bilanz*, ed. Richard Löwenthal and Hans-Peter Schwarz, 289–310. Stuttgart, 1974.

—— "Deutsche Soziologie im internationalen Kontext: Ihre Ideengeschichte und ihr Gesellschaftsbezug." *KZfSS Sonderheft* 21 (1979): 70–107.

Tenbruck, Friedrich H. "Die Genesis der Methodologie Max Webers." *KZfSS* 11 (1959): 573–630.

—— *Die unbewältigten Sozialwissenschaften.* Graz, 1984.

Tillich, Paul. *Die Sozialistische Entscheidung.* Potsdam, 1933.

Tobler, Douglas Fred. "German Historians and the Weimar Republic." Ph.D. diss., University of Kansas, 1967.

Tönnies, Ferdinand. *Ferdinand Tönnies: On Sociology.* Edited by Werner Cahnman and Rudolf Heberle. Chicago, 1971.

—— Review of *Der Staat,* by Hans Freyer. *Monatsschrift für Kriminalpsychologie und Strafrechtsreform* 18 (1927): 218–19.

Toews, John Edward. *Hegelianism: The Path toward Dialectical Humanism.* New York, 1980.

Troeltsch, Ernst. *Der Historismus und seine Probleme.* Tübingen, 1922.

Tyrell, Albricht, ed. *Führer Befiehl . . . Selbstzeugnisse aus der "Kampfzeit" der NSDAP.* Düsseldorf, 1969.

Ulich, Robert. "An Autobiography." In *Leaders in American Education,* ed. Robert J. Havinghurst. Chicago, 1971.

Üner, Elfriede. "Hans Freyer in der deutschen Soziologie bis 1933: Ein Beitrag zur wissenschaftssoziologischen Einordnung seines Werkes und seiner Wissenschaftsgemeinschaft." Diplomarbeit, Ludwig-Maximilians Universität zu München, 1980.

—— "Jugendbewegung und Soziologie. Wissenschaftssoziologische Skizzen zu Hans Freyers Werk und Wissenschaftsgemeinschaft bis 1933," *KZfSS Sonderheft* 23 (1981): 131–59.

Unger, Manfred. "Georg Sacke—Ein Kämpfer gegen den Faschismus." In *Karl-Marx-Universität Leipzig, 1409–1959: Beiträge zur Universitätsgeschichte,* ed. Ernst Engelberg, 2 vols., 2: 307–30. Leipzig, 1959.

Universität Kiel. *Verzeichnis der Vorlesungen.* 1922–1925.

Universität Leipzig. *Verzeichnis der Vorlesungen.* 1906–1948.

Vardy, Steven Bela. *Modern Hungarian Historiography.* Boulder, Colo., 1976.

Verhandlungen des sächsischen Landtages, 106 Wahlperiode. Dresden, 1920.

Vezina, Birgit. *"Die Gleichschaltung" der Universität Heidelberg.* Heidelberg, 1982.

Vierhaus, Rudolf. "Umrisse einer Sozialgeschichte der Gebildeten in Deutschland." *Quellen und Forschungen aus italienischen Archiven und Bibliotheken,* 60 (1980): 395–415.

Voegelin, Eric. *The New Science of Politics.* Chicago, 1952.

Volkov, Shulamit. *The Rise of Popular Antimodernism in Germany: The Urban Master Artisans, 1873–1896.* Princeton, N.J., 1978.

Vondung, Klaus, ed. *Das wilhelminische Bildungsbürgertum.* Göttingen, 1976.

Walsh, Helga A. "Entnazifizierung und Wiedereröffnung der Universität Leipzig, 1945–

1946: Ein Bericht des damaligen Rektors Professor Bernhard Schweitzer." *Viertel-jahreshefte für Zeitgeschicht* 33, no. 2 (April 1985): 339–72.

Walther, Andreas. "Der Problem einer 'deutschen' Soziologie." *Kölner Vierteljahreshefte für Soziologie* 9 (1930–31): 513–30.

Walzer, Michael. *Spheres of Justice: A Defense of Pluralism and Equality.* New York, 1983.

Waßner, Rainer. "Andreas Walther und das Seminar für Soziologie in Hamburg zwischen 1926 und 1945." In *Ordnung und Theorie,* ed. Sven Papcke, 386–422. Darmstadt, 1986.

Waxman, Chaim I., ed. *The End of Ideology Debate.* New York, 1968.

Weber, Eugen. "Revolution? Counterrevolution? What Revolution?" In *Fascism: A Reader's Guide,* ed. Walter Laqueur, 435–67. Berkeley, Calif., 1976.

Weber, Max. "Die 'Objektivität' sozialwissenschaftlicher und sozialpolitischer Erkenntnis" (1904). In his *Gesammelte Aufsätze zur Wissenschaftslehre,* 146–214. Tübingen, 1922.

—— *Roscher and Knies: The Logical Problem of Historical Economics.* Translated by Guy Oakes. New York, 1975.

—— *Wirtschaft und Gesellschaft.* Tübingen, 1922. Translated as *Economy and Society,* ed. Guenther Roth and Claus Wittich, 2 vols. Berkeley, Calif., 1978.

Wehler, Hans-Ulrich. *Krisenherde des Kaiserreichs, 1871–1918.* Göttingen, 1970.

—— *Moderne deutsche Sozialgeschichte.* Königstein, 1981.

Weinkauff, Hermann. *Die deutsche Justiz und der Nationalsozialismus.* Stuttgart, 1981.

Weingartner, Rudolph H. *Experience and Culture: The Philosophy of Georg Simmel.* Middletown, Conn., 1962.

Weintraub, Jeff A. "Virtue, Community and the Sociology of Liberty: The Notion of Republican Virtue and Its Impact on Modern Western Social Thought." Ph.D. diss., Berkeley, Calif., 1979.

Weintraub, Karl. *Visions of Culture.* Chicago, 1966.

Wenke, Hans. "Die pädagogische Lage in Deutschland." *Die Erziehung* 9 (1933–34): 577ff.

White, Hayden. "Method and Ideology in Intellectual History." In *Modern European Intellectual History,* ed. Dominick LaCapra and Steven L. Kaplan, 280–310. Ithaca, N.Y., 1982.

Whitfield, Stephen J. *Into the Dark: Hannah Arendt and Totalitarianism.* Philadelphia, 1980.

Wiebe, Rainer. "*Der Volksspiegel*: Eine soziologische Zeitschrift im Dritten Reich." Magisterarbeit, Universität Münster, 1981.

Wiese, Leopold von. "Die Deutsche Gesellschaft für Soziologie, Persönliche Eindrücke in der ersten fünfzig Jahren (1909 zu 1959)." *KZfSS* 11 (1959): 16–17.

—— "Erstes Vorwort" to *Verhandlungen des Achten Deutschen Soziologentages vom 19. bis 21. September 1946 in Frankfurt a.M.* Tübingen, 1948.

—— "Die Frankfurter Dozententagung." *Kölner Vierteljahreshefte für Soziologie* 10 (1931–32): 446–48.

—— *System der allgemeinen Soziologie*. 2d ed. Munich, 1933.

Wiese-Schorn, Luise. "Karl Lamprecht: Kulturgeschichtsschreibung zwischen Wissenschaft und Politik." Ph.D. diss., Universität Münster, 1981.

Wilkinson, James. *The Intellectual Resistance in Europe*. Cambridge, Mass., 1981.

Willers, Dietrich. *Verzeichnis der Schriften von Hans Freyer*. Darmstadt, 1966.

Windelband, Wilhelm. *Die Erneuerung des Hegelianismus*. Heidelberg, 1910.

Winter, Erich. Review of *Soziologie als Wirklichkeitswissenschaft* and *Einleitung in die Soziologie*, by Hans Freyer. *Zeitschrift für Sozialforschung* 1 (1932): 157–58.

Winters, Peter Jochen. "Helmut Schelsky." *Christ und Welt* 31 (December 1965).

Wistrich, Robert. *Who's Who in Nazi Germany*. New York, 1982.

Wohl, Robert. *The Generation of 1914*. Cambridge, Mass., 1979.

Wohlgemuth, Heinrich. "Das Wesen des Politischen in der heutigen deutschen neoromantischen Staatslehre." Ph.D. diss., Universität Erlangen, 1932.

Woolf, S. J., ed. *The Nature of Fascism*. London, 1968.

Wundt, Wilhelm. *Elements of Folk Psychology*. New York, 1916.

—— *Die Nationen und ihre Philosophie*. Leipzig, 1915.

—— *Über den wahrhaften Krieg*. Leipzig, 1914.

—— *Völkerpsychologie*. 10 vols. Leipzig, 1911–20.

—— *Die Weltkatastrophe und die deutsche Philosophie*. Erfurt, 1920.

Young, Crawford. *Ideology and Development in Africa*. New Haven, Conn., 1982.

Zehn Jahre Deutsche Geschichte, 1918–1928. Berlin, 1928.

Zehrer, Hans. "Eingeholt und umstellt." *Die Welt*, 29 August 1964.

—— "Kann es wieder geschehen?" *Die Welt*, 26 January 1963.

—— *Der Mensch in dieser Welt*. Hamburg, 1948.

—— "Die Revolution von Rechts." *Die Tat* 25 (1933).

—— "Rückkehr zur Wirklichkeit." *Die Welt*, 27 December 1958.

—— *Stille vor dem Sturm: Aufsätze zur Zeit*. Hamburg, 1948.

—— "Das Volk und die Intelligenz." *Die Welt*, 25 September 1965.

Zeisel, Kurt. *Das verlorene Gewissen*. 8th ed. Munich, 1962.

Zeitlin, Irving M. *Ideology and the Development of Sociological Theory*. Engelwood Cliffs, N.J., 1968.

Zmarzlik, Hans-Gunther. *Wieviel Zukunft hat unsere Vergangenheit: Aufsätze und Überlegungen eines Historikers vom Jahrgang 1922*. Munich, 1970.

"Zur Maierfest der Universität." *Leipziger Neueste Nachrichten*, 13 May 1933; 18 May 1933.

26. *Bericht an die auswärtigen Mitglieder und Freunde der F.S.G. Wickersdorf, Dez. 1912*. N.d., n.p. Copy in Burg Ludwigstein.

II. ARCHIVAL COLLECTIONS

BERLIN. Berlin Document Center.

Achelis, Johann Daniel
Dürckheim-Montmartin, Graf Karlfried von
Forsthoff, Ernst
Harmjanz, Heinrich
Höhn, Reinhard
Kienast, Ernst
Kuehne, Lothar
Studentkowski, Werner

BERLIN. Geheimes Staatsarchiv Preußischer Kulturbesitz.
Nachlaß Carl Becker

BERLIN. Staatsbibliothek Preußischer Kulturbesitz.
Nachlaß Michael Landmann

BIELEFELD. Universitätsbibliothek.
Nachlaß Johann Plenge

BONN. Politisches Archiv, Auswärtiges Amtes.
Gesandschaft Budapest
Kult.-Pol., Geheim-Generalia
Kult. Zw.

BONN. Universitätsbibliothek.
Nachlaß Lamprecht

BURG LUDWIGSTEIN. Archiv der deutschen Jugendbewegung.
Printed works listed under published sources.

COLOGNE. Eugen Diederichs Verlag Archiv.
Eugen Diederichs manuscript
Publication records of Freyer's books
Correspondence with Freyer

DRESDEN. Sächsisches Hauptarchiv.
Ministerium für Volksbildung

GÖTTINGEN. Universitätsarchiv.
Ersatzvorschläge für neue Professuren der Rechts- und Staatswissenschaftlichen
Fakultät, 1947–55
Personalakte Plessner
Sitzungsprotokolle der Philosophischen Fakultät

JENA. Universitätsarchiv.
Sammlung Diederichs

KIEL. Schleswig-Holsteinischen Landesbibliothek.
Nachlaß Ferdinand Tönnies

KOBLENZ. Bundesarchiv.
Nachlaß Max Hildebert Boehm
Nachlaß Walter Goetz
Nachlaß Rudolf Pechel
Nachlaß Eduard Spranger
NS6 Partei-Kanzlei
NS15 Amt Rosenberg
NS22 Reichsorganisationsleiter der NSDAP
R21 Reichministerium für Wissenschaft, Erziehung und Volksbildung
R51 Deutsche Akademie
R58 Reichssicherheitshauptamt
R134 Reichskommissar für die Überwachung der öffentlichen Ordnung und
Nachrichtensammelstelle im Reichsminsterium des Innern

LEIPZIG. Universitätsarchiv.
Personalakten Hans Freyer
Personalakten Hans-Georg Gadamer
Personalakten Gunther Ipsen
Personalakten Gerhard Kessler
Personalakten Felix Krueger
Personalakten Karl Valentin Müller
Personalakten Karl-Heinz Pfeffer
Promotionsakte Hans Freyer
Promotionsbuch 6
Philosophische Fakultät E66, Betr. NSDAP 1934–1942
Sitzungen des gesamte philosophische Fakultät
Zeugnisprotokoll
B1/14/19 Institut für Kultur- und Universalgeschichte
B1/14/53 Seminar für Politische Bildung
B2/20/07 Institut für Soziologie
B2/20/45 Südosteuropa-Institut
B2/20/49 Professur für Geschichte

MANNHEIM. Universität Mannheim.
Lehrstuhl für Soziologie
Papers of the Deutsche Gesellschaft für Soziologie. These papers, temporarily
located at the University of Mannheim when the author used them in 1982, were
to be transferred to the Bundesarchiv Koblenz.
Ordner:
Rundschreiben

Wiedergründung
Ordentliche Mitglieder
Confédération internationale de Sociologie
IIS ab 1958–59
Mitgliederversammlungen
Alter Vorstand, 1955–59

MÜNSTER. Universitätsarchiv.
Personalakten no. 5609 (Hans Freyer)

MÜNSTER. Universitätsbibliothek.
Nachlaß Hans Freyer

NEW YORK. YIVO Institute Archives.
Amt Rosenberg Papers

WASHINGTON, D.C. National Archives.
T81: Records of the National Socialist German Labor Party. Rolls 194, 239.

III. INTERVIEWS

Becker, Hellmut. West Berlin.
27 May 1982.

Broszat, Martin. Munich.
1 June 1982.

Buchenhorst, Ruth. Fritzlar.
14 February 1982.

Drucker, Renate. Leipzig.
April 1982.

Freyer, Käthe. Münster.
23 February 1982.

Gadamer, Hans-Georg. Aachen.
29 April 1982; and Boston,
12 December 1982.

Hildebrandt, Walther. Aachen.
29 April 1982.

König, René. Cologne.
1 February 1982.

Liebers, Gerhard. Münster.
19 February 1982.

Linde, Hans. Karlsruhe.
9 June 1982.

Manheim, Ernest. Martha's Vineyard.
20 August 1981 and
15 August 1983.

Rhodius, Ellen. Burgbrohl bei Koblenz.
May 1982.

Ronte, Heinz. Bochum.
30 March 1982.

Schelsky, Helmut. Münster.
25 February 1982.

Stowasser, Barbara. Washington, D.C.
30 April 1981.

INDEX

Library of Congress Cataloging-in-Publication Data

MULLER, JERRY Z., 1954–
THE OTHER GOD THAT FAILED: HANS FREYER AND THE DERADICALIZATION
OF GERMAN CONSERVATISM / JERRY Z. MULLER.
P.   CM.   BIBLIOGRAPHY: P.
INCLUDES INDEX.
ISBN 0–691–05508–4 (ALK. PAPER)
1. FREYER, HANS, 1887–1969. 2. SOCIOLOGISTS—GERMANY—BIOGRAPHY.
3. SOCIOLOGY—GERMANY—HISTORY—20TH CENTURY. 4. INTELLECTUALS—
GERMANY—HISTORY—20TH CENTURY. 5. NATIONAL SOCIALISM.
6. CONSERVATISM—GERMANY—HISTORY—20TH CENTURY. 7. GERMANY—
INTELLECTUAL LIFE—20TH CENTURY. 8. RADICALISM—GERMANY—
HISTORY—20TH CENTURY. I. TITLE.
HM22.G3F458 1987   301'.0943—dc19   87–18781 CIP

Jerry Z. Muller
is Assistant Professor of History at the
Catholic University of America.